# Contents

# 2

# Health and Illness in the United States   44

**PART TWO**

# Psychosocial Aspects of Health

# 3

Stress and Health   74

# 6

# Lifestyle Risk Factors: Smoking and Health   156

**PART THREE**

# Psychosocial Aspects of Illness

# 7

# Becoming and Being Ill   181

# 8

## Psychosocial Aspects of Specific Disorders: Introduction   208

# 9

## Psychosocial Aspects of Chronic Pain   229

# 10

## Psychosocial Aspects of Cardiovascular Disease   255

# 11

## Psychosocial Aspects of Cancer and Asthma   282

**PART FOUR**

# Psychosocial Aspects of the Medical Care System

## 12
### Adherence to Medical Treatment Programs   308

## 13
### A Psychological Portrait of Health Care Providers   331

# Preface

As its subtitle suggests, this book looks at the newly developing field of health psychology from a psychosocial point of view. I have come to health psychology from the fields of clinical psychology and community mental health—which traditionally have examined human behavior from the psychosocial point of view—and I believe that the future will see a growing partnership of these three fields in considering issues of physical health and illness.

The research of the past two decades has made a compelling case that there is a biology of health, a psychology of health, and a sociology of health and that—whether we are thinking about treatment or about prevention of illness—these three domains must be studied in their natural interactions. Culture invades physiology, and we are seeing a dramatic trend toward an ecumenical view of health and illness. I am hopeful that this book will encourage readers to think about their own health and the health of others from this broader perspective, and that reading it will provide a sense of excitement about how psychological principles and methods can be used to improve our health and increase the effectiveness of our treatments when people become ill.

No field of psychology is more important in the development of public social policy than is health psychology. One of the great tragedies of our rich country is our failure to value the health of all of our citizens. Millions of Americans are without any form of health insurance and cannot afford adequate health care. Hundreds of thousands of elderly Americans must spend themselves into poverty in order to become eligible for an adequate level of medical care. Many countries, where less is spent per capita for health care than in the United States, have lower maternal mortality rates, lower death rates (particularly during the years of childhood), and longer life expectancies.

I hope this book will have an impact not only on what you know about the psychology of health and illness, but also on how you think about health and its importance in any society. There is far more material in the field of health psychology than can be covered in a single book, and I have provided supplementary references throughout to help you obtain additional information on topics that might be of special interest to you.

I want to express special thanks to Ruth Brown and to John and Jaye Zola, who read and commented on the first draft of this book, and to Professor Janet Lapp, California State University at Fresno; Professor Edward Krupat, Massachusetts College; and Professor Charles Kaiser, College of Charleston, whose careful and expert criticisms of the penultimate draft have earned my admiration and gratitude.

# The Conceptual History of Health Psychology

# 1

## INTRODUCTION

This chapter sets the stage for the study of health psychology by discussing five introductory topics. First, the field of health psychology is defined and is placed within the conceptual and methodological context of the larger fields of psychology and epidemiology. Second, the development of the current interest in health psychology is put in a historical context. We briefly explore three historically sequential orientations to the understanding of health and illness—miasma theory, germ theory, and biopsychosocial theory. Third, a number of important concepts related to health and illness are introduced and examined. Included among these concepts are (1) psychosomatic disorders, (2) the health field, and (3) health as a status versus health as a process. Fourth, basic issues that need to be considered in the measurement of health are identified. And finally, a brief overview of human anatomy and physiology is provided as a useful background for the remainder of the volume.

If we start with the commonly accepted definition of psychology as the scientific study of behavior (see, for example, Bourne & Ekstrand, 1985), then we may consider the field of health psychology as the scientific study of health- and illness-related behavior. The concept of behavior is a broad one in this definition and includes thoughts, attitudes, and beliefs as well as observable actions. Thus, *the field of health psychology concerns itself with the scientific study of behavior, thoughts, attitudes, and beliefs related to health and illness.*

### The Methods of Science

In no specialized field of psychology is the word *scientific* more important than in the field of health psychology. The importance of good health and the avoidance of illness in our society can hardly be overemphasized. After all, when we discuss health and illness, we are talking about life and death. Accordingly, it is no surprise that we all search for ways to stay healthy, and that in that search we can easily follow remedies that have little or no demonstrated validity (see, for example, Cassileth, Lusk, Strouse, & Bodenheimer, 1984). Health-related matters have become front-page news, and the national wire services have recently begun the routine monitoring of such professional publications as the *Journal of the American Medical Association* and the *New England Journal of Medicine.*

There is hardly an area of human behavior that is more influenced by mythology, anecdote, and unverified claims than behavior related to health and illness. Thus, it is especially important in a health psychology textbook to describe that field from a scientifically defensible point of view.

Employing a scientific approach to the study of health-related behavior will ultimately permit (1) the measurement and description of behavior, (2) the explanation of behavior, (3) the prediction of behavior, and (4) the control and modification of behavior.

The scientific method has general principles for the definition of constructs and variables, for the development of theory and concepts, and for the evaluation of evidence. These principles provide rules for answering the two general questions implied in any process of inquiry: (1) What do you mean? and (2) How do you know? Answering the first question requires the development of measurement procedures that are reliable and valid. Answering the second requires the use of research methods that lead to trustworthy conclusions.

The rules that govern the use of the scientific method are important not only for establishing the validity of hypotheses but also for refuting them. Indeed, scientific discourse deals only with propositions that can be refuted, even if only theoretically. If we hold health-related beliefs or engage in health-related behaviors that we believe are irrefutable, that is, that we would retain regardless of any evidence to the contrary, we may have interesting and important conversations about them, but these conversations are not science. The scientific method, as a strategy for establishing knowledge, has, however, had enormous impact in certain domains of inquiry, certainly including the field of psychology, and this book will concern itself with the contributions of these methods to health- and illness-related behavior and thought processes.

EVALUATING HEALTH-RELATED RESEARCH.    The foregoing comments about the methods of science are not to suggest, however, that the research that has been conducted in the field of health psychology is invariably methodologically sound. Indeed, reviews of research in the field of health psychology are critical of many of the studies that have been reported in the literature (see, for example, Bradley, 1983; Ziesat, 1981). As with other fields of inquiry in the social sciences, newer research is often sounder than older research (Miller, 1983). The importance of sound research methodology can be seen in a recent survey of twenty-two health psychologists, in which Taylor (1984) found that this group assigned top priority in the training of health psychologists, to the development of methodological expertise, both regarding research design and data analysis.

### Epidemiologic Methods in the Study of Disease Prevalence

Scientists who seek to determine what factors play a role in the distribution and determinants of any disease process are called *epidemiologists*. As a preface to the discussions of the links between psychosocial factors, on the one hand, and health and illness, on the other hand, it is important to provide a brief overview of how such connections are made by epidemiologists in the scientific literature.

Scientists are accustomed to taking two general approaches to the study of the relationship between some suspected casual agent and some disease or disorder. One approach is called *retrospective,* and such studies are often referred to as *case-control* studies. This approach consists of comparing a group of people with the disease under study with a matched control group of people without the disease, in terms of suspected factors in their history. In the case of smoking and lung cancer, for example, a retrospective study would obtain a sample of persons with lung cancer (the cases) and a matched sample of people without lung cancer, either a healthy group or a group of persons with some other disorder (the controls), and determine whether there is a significantly more frequent prior history of smoking in the group with lung cancer than in the group without the disease. Such retrospective studies are relatively inexpensive to carry out and a large number of past-history variables can be explored in a single study. Accordingly, retrospective studies are generally conducted first in the implementation of a research program attempting to identify causal factors in a disease.

The second approach is called *prospective,* and such studies are usually referred to as *cohort* studies. To continue using the example of smoking and lung cancer, in this type of study a group, or cohort, of smokers is identified along with a matched control group of nonsmokers. The two groups are followed for an appropriate period of time in order to determine what the risk of lung cancer is in both groups. Prospective cohort studies ordinarily take a good deal longer than retrospective case-control studies and thus are substantially more expensive to conduct. It is only from prospective studies, however, that the actual risk of becoming ill can be calculated as a function of whether or not the suspected causal circumstance is present (MacMahon & Pugh, 1970). In a retrospective study, many potential causal factors can be evaluated in their relationship to one particular disorder. In a prospective study, many pathological consequences of one suspected causal factor can be evaluated.

In the case of the suspected relationship between smoking and lung cancer, about fifteen retrospective studies were reported before the first prospective study was undertaken (MacMahon & Pugh, 1970).

CRITERIA FOR ESTABLISHING CAUSE.   One of the principal tasks of the field of epidemiology is to understand causative factors in illness. Accordingly, it is important to understand the criteria that are generally used by epidemiologists to establish a causative relationship. Six criteria are generally used, although it should be stressed at the outset that discovering one factor is implicated as the cause of some particular disease does not mean no other factor is involved.

The criteria typically used in epidemiological research for establishing cause (Koop and Luoto, 1982) include:

(1) *Consistency of the association.* This criterion requires that diverse methods of approach provide similar conclusions. The association must be observed repeatedly by multiple investigators, in different locations and situations, at different times, using different methods of study. The more consistently the finding is observed, the more confident one can be about its validity.

(2) *Strength of the association.* The most direct measure of the strength of the association of some psychosocial factor and the risk of some disease is the comparison of death or mobidity rates from the disease among persons with that psychosocial factor present and without that psychosocial factor present. The greater the difference in those rates, the more likely is it that the suspected causative factor is implicated.

(3) *Specificity of the association.* Specificity is judged by the extent to which the presence of a presumed causative factor is associated with one and only one disease. Although the demonstration of specificity makes a causal hypothesis more acceptable, lack of specificity does not mean that the suspected agent is causally unrelated to any of the disorders with which it is associated.

(4) *Temporal relationship of the association.* This criterion requires that exposure to the suspected causative factor must precede the disease. Prospective cohort studies appear to meet this criterion since, by design, they identify study samples in terms of the presence or absence of the presumed prior causative factor.

(5) *Coherence of the association.* This criterion for evaluating the causal significance of an association is based upon its degree of agreement with known facts in the natural history of the disease. Coherence requires, among other criteria, that descriptive epidemiologic results on disease occurrence correlate with measures of exposure to the suspected agent. Perhaps the most important consideration is the observation of a dose-response relationship between agent

and disease, that is, evidence that a progressively increasing occurrence of disease is found among increasingly heavily exposed groups.

(6) *Preventive trial results.* The final criterion for the establishment of a causal connection between a suspected agent and a subsequent disease is to demonstrate that if there is a reduction in the frequency or intensity of the suspected agent, a subsequent reduction in the incidence or severity of the disease will be found.

## THE FIELD OF HEALTH PSYCHOLOGY

In the past two decades, psychologists have become increasingly interested in general health. Psychologists have had a long-standing interest in mental health, of course, but the interest in general health and illness is relatively new, serving to set health psychology apart from all other subspecialties of psychology.

A number of different terms have been developed in recent years to identify particular domains. In addition to identifying areas of subject-matter concentration, these terms also express a sense of "turf" control.

### Behavioral Medicine

One of the most commonly identified domains is *behavioral medicine*—a phrase that suggests a special interest in behavior and behavior change but, at the same time, connotes that the activity functions as part of medical practice. Thus, it should not be surprising that psychologists who identify themselves with the field of behavioral medicine are frequently found employed in medical schools.

Behavioral medicine is an interdisciplinary field that integrates behavioral and biomedical knowledge relevant to health and disease (Miller, 1983; West, 1982). Schwartz and Weiss (1978b) describe the field of behavioral medicine broadly as the interdisciplinary field "concerned with the development and integration of behavioral and biomedical science knowledge and techniques relevant to health and illness and the application of this knowledge and these techniques to prevention, diagnosis, treatment, and rehabilitation" (p. 250; see also Pomerleau & Brady, 1979).

In tracing the history of behavioral medicine, Blanchard (1982) has suggested that three separate events occurred in the early 1970s to create the field. First, a set of well-established treatment techniques designed to change behavior that had long been successfully employed with the mentally ill began to be used with patients with medically related problems such as obesity and the inability to stop smoking. Second, the development of the field of biofeedback was making it possible to effect reliable physiological changes in body functioning. Third, attention began to be directed toward the two chief sources of mortality for adults—cancer and cardiovascular diseases—and toward the ways in which changes in behavior could play a useful role in the treatment and prevention of these conditions. It is important to notice that these events all involved the modification of behavior—a hallmark of the field of behavioral medicine.

According to Agras (1982), four factors help understand why the field of behavioral medicine is now undergoing such rapid development. First, the field of psychosomatic medicine has generated a body of research linking psychological factors to a number of illnesses. Second, the field of behavior therapy and applied behavior analysis has generated a number of apparently effective psychological- and behavioral-oriented treatment procedures for a variety of physical disorders. Third, epidemiological studies—that is, studies that examine the distribution and determinants of disease—have identified a number of psychological and sociological factors that increase the risk associated with a number of different illnesses. Fourth, mainly as a consequence of the rapidly increasing costs of treating the sick, there is a growing interest in the prevention of illness, and in psychological and sociological factors in disease prevention.

In summary, the special emphasis in the field of behavioral medicine appears to be on intervention, that is, on the identification and application of effective and enduring psychological treatment procedures (Agras, 1982; Pomerleau, 1979, 1982; Pomerleau & Brady, 1979). The term *behavioral medicine*, then, focuses on how psychological principles of behavior change can assist in the control of disorders ordinarily thought of within the province of medicine.

### Medical Psychology

A second term that is frequently used to describe an area of specialization within the field of health psychology is *medical psychology*. This term suggests that the principal areas of interest are medical problems, but that domain control is in the hands of psychology, that is, that the field is a specialized area within the larger field of psychology (Asken, 1979).

Bradley and Prokop (1981) have distinguished between the terms *behavioral medicine* and *medical psychology*. They suggest that the special contributions of medical psychology to the field of behavioral medicine can be found in its emphasis on assessment and in its ability to conduct evaluations of diagnostic, preventive, and treatment methods that can lead to major improvements in the quality of medical care. Both of these contributions, empirical in nature, illustrate the common observation that the science of psychology is distinguished by its commitment to an empirical approach to the establishment of its factual base. The term *medical psychology*, then, focuses on how psychologists, working within their own domain, can play a role in the study and control of medical disorders, particularly in terms of the application of empirical and scientific methods to the task.

### Health Care Psychology

A third term, *health care psychology*, has been proposed to identify another important domain. This area of specialization is concerned with health care delivery, that is, on how health services are organized, provided, and financed.

The concept of health care delivery has, on occasion, been extended to very broad dimensions. According to the Task Force Report on Health Research of the American Psychological Association (1976), health care delivery involves more than the treatment of illness. It includes programs of health maintenance, the prevention of infectious disease, the early detection and correction of health defects, reduction in the severity of chronic disease processes through early diagnoses and treatment, and education in positive health practices that reduce the need for subsequent treatment.

Wright (1979) has emphasized the potential contributions of health care psychology to the well-being of children, and has suggested that a special set of disorders—different from adult disorders—comprises the subject matter. In the case of adult health care, major energies are focused on disorders such as cancer, cardiovascular anomalies, and sexual dysfunction, disorders that are not of paramount importance for children. Conversely, in the case of childhood health-care psychology, disorders of principal concern are such commonly encountered ones as bed wetting, learning disability, and hyperactivity, which have relatively little importance to adults.

### Other Related Terms

A number of less common terms describing important subspecialties within the field of health psychology have also been coined, and these terms should be mentioned, if only briefly. The term *behavioral health* has been proposed by Matarazzo (1980) to define "a new interdisciplinary subspecialty within behavioral medicine specifically concerned with maintenance of health and the prevention of illness and dysfunction in currently healthy persons" (p. 807). Its primary emphasis, then, is on health maintenance and disease prevention.

Millon (1982) has proposed the term *clinical health psychology* to refer to "the application of knowledge and methods from all substantive fields of psychology to the promotion and maintenance of mental *and* physical health of the individual and to the prevention, assessment, and treatment of all forms of mental *and* physical disorder to which psychological influences either contribute to or can be used to relieve an individual's distress or dysfunction" (p. 8). This subspecialty, then, emphasizes the contributions that psychologists identified with the field of the mental disorders can make to the understanding of the physical disorders. Other terms that have been advanced for describing activities of psychologists pertinent to health include *public health psychology* (with an emphasis on the application of public health concepts to the field of general health) (Miller, Fowler, & Bridgers, 1982); *clinical neuropsychology* (with an emphasis on how neurological and clinical factors interact in health and illness) (Costa, 1983); and *rehabilitation psychology* (with an emphasis on rehabilitation) (Grzesiak, 1981). All these terms, including the ones already discussed in greater detail, subscribe to one salient fact—psychologists see special contributions that they can make to the general field of health maintenance and health service delivery, and believe that these potential contributions should be actively reflected in how psychologists and physicians are educated (Matarazzo, 1982; Stachnik, 1980).

Four general questions underlie the thinking of people associated with one or more of these approaches to health psychology: (1) Shall the field be thought of as interdisciplinary, or shall a new field be defined from the point of view of the special contributions of the psychologist? (2) What should be the defined domain of the field of health psychology? Should it be thought of as including physical and mental health, or should issues related to mental health remain in their own domain? Should the field be as concerned with health as with illness? (3) Should the domain be primarily concerned with research and theory building, or should it be as concerned with applied issues, such as treatment techniques, prevention of illness, and health service delivery? (4) What levels of analysis are legitimized? That is, should the field be as concerned with group or system issues as it is with individual issues in relation to health maintenance?

A number of writers have suggested that perhaps the best term around which to unify psychologists interested in general health issues is the term that will be used in this volume—*health psychology*. The Division of Health Psychology of the American Psychological Association has proposed that health psychology be defined in the following way:

> *Health psychology* is the aggregate of the specific educational, scientific, and professional contributions of the discipline of psychology to the promotion and maintenance of health, the prevention and treatment of illness, and the identification of etiologic and diagnostic correlates of health, illness, and related dysfunction . . . and to the analysis and improvement of the health care system and health policy formation. (Matarazzo, 1980, p. 815; Albino, 1983, p. 222)

By this definition, then, the four issues identified above have been explicitly or implicitly resolved as follows:

1.  The field of health psychology is concerned with the special contributions that psychologists can make to health.
2.  The term *health* shall be thought of as broadly as possible—to include health as well as illness, physical as well as mental health, and specific disorders and diagnoses as well as the general sense of malaise, robustness, or well-being.
3.  The field shall not be limited to research and theory building, but shall be concerned as well with the application of research and theory to prevention, treatment, and service delivery.
4.  Whatever may impact on health—be it at the level of the individual, the group, or the larger social system, is of legitimate concern to the health psychologist.

The acceptance of the term *health psychology* as the focus for this volume should not be viewed as undervaluing the importance of a multidisciplinary approach to the study of health and illness. Multidisciplinary approaches are becoming increasingly important in the health field—one need only think of such newly developing fields of study as biophysics, neurochemistry, behavior genetics, and sociobiology, to name but a few. While fields of study are departmentalized and often compartmentalized in the university, in the world of research and practice the importance of interdisciplinary collaboration is repeatedly recognized.

## CONCEPTUAL APPROACHES TO HEALTH AND ILLNESS BEHAVIOR

Health behavior and illness behavior are developed and maintained by three interacting regulatory processes—stimulus perception, reinforcement patterns, and cognitive mediation (Bandura, 1977). These three regulatory domains overlap to some extent, so that many of the psychological concepts used to understand behavior and the psychological techniques used to modify behavior can be linked to more than one domain.

In general terms, however, thinking about health and illness behavior in terms of responses to perceived properties of a stimulus encourages the consideration of a variety of intervention strategies designed to modify those perceptions. Thus, for example, teaching a person to relax can reduce the straining associated with some stressful life events.

Health and illness behaviors can also be viewed as learned—by a pattern of reinforcement contingencies—and therefore they can, at least theoretically, be modified by deliberate changes in reinforcement patterns. Using this approach, one can consider a specific health or illness behavior as a habit and can invoke interventions based on what is known about modifying habits. Thus, for example, by a system of specially designed reinforcements it is possible to get people to brush their teeth regularly, or to adhere more faithfully to a recommended course of action prescribed by a physician, or to try to stop smoking.

The final approach to understanding health and illness behaviors is to view them in terms of cognitive mediating variables, a somewhat awkward phrase for the complex set of intellectual and emotional processes that are triggered by a particular situation. Thus, a young woman can be thought to have an eating disorder because of her inability to face her growing physical and sexual maturity with equanimity. A young man can abuse tobacco or alcohol out of a feeling of low self-esteem and inferiority and a need to be accepted by his companions. A seriously ill person can fail to follow a prescribed medical regimen because of the lack of a network of supportive and encouraging friends or because of an unconscious wish to die. From this point of view, changes in health or illness behaviors can only take place if the underlying emotional issues are first successfully resolved. Another approach to changing the nature of cognitive processes is through education. Providing information via consumer health-education programs can result in reductions in certain self-destructive behavior patterns, such as lack of exercise, faulty nutrition, or alcohol abuse.

We will return to these three approaches to health and illness behavior at several points in the book. From this initial overview, however, we see that such behaviors can be thought of as the result of three theoretical causes: as reactions to ascribed stimulus characteristics which can be understood once one has an appreciation of the world through the eyes of the patient; as habitual behavior in its own right; or finally, as a result of cognitive mediating processes that represent a set of emotional realities that motivate behavior.

## MIASMA THEORY

The history of medical thought can be divided into three phases—pregerm theory, germ theory, and postgerm theory. Prior to the middle of the nineteenth century, physicians had relatively little knowledge that could play a useful role in the treatment of disease, although they did have important ideas about disease prevention. Medical care included little more than the creation of settings in which a patient's own restitutive potential could play out to the fullest. At worst, the treatments available were as debilitating as they were restorative. Among the most commonly used "treatments" of the day were bleeding, blistering, or the administration of drugs that would cause purging or vomiting.

Physicians were virtually powerless against the great infectious and nutritional diseases of the day, either in terms of treatment or prevention. Summing up his evaluation of medical practice, Jean Molière (1622–1673), in his play *Le Malade Imaginaire* (The Hypochondriac), was moved to write, "Nearly all men die of their remedies, and not of their illnesses" (Beck, 1968, p. 362).

The earliest systematically developed theory for explaining disease was called *miasma theory*. This theory held that soil polluted with waste products of any kind gave off a poisonous gaseous miasma into the air, and that these miasmas caused disease. This theory, dating from the writings of Hippocrates, suggested that these poisonous substances rose up from the earth and were spread through the winds. People living near swamps, and thus particularly vulnerable to marsh gases, were thought to develop fever from these gases—a fever that came to be known as malaria (bad air).

While miasma theory led to the development of a number of general treatment procedures, its more important contribution to health was its enormously effective role in preventing disease. Florence Nightingale (1820–1910), who is reputed to have founded the nursing profession as a protest against germ theory, and who was a confirmed miasmatist throughout her lifetime, believed that as people became sicker, their disease changed from one disease to another (Cope, 1958).

The early miasmatists declared war on all refuse quite indiscriminately. Accumulated manure was considered just as dangerous as a cesspool contaminating a supply of drinking water. The public health movement had its beginnings with the early environmental and sanitary engineers who sought to prevent disease by removing and preventing the accumulation of filth. Secondary to modification of the environment, miasmatists sought, by public education, to alert the potential victims of disease to the dangers of the environment in which they lived.

From the point of view of social policy, one aspect of miasma theory that bears special recognition is that it approached the task of disease prevention by accepting the necessity of social and environmental change. That is, miasma theory assumed that diseases could be prevented only by improving the quality of life of people who were at risk.

## GERM THEORY: THE BIOLOGIZING OF MEDICINE

The doctrine of miasma dominated medical thinking until the middle of the nineteenth century, when, with the advent of germ theory, the *biologizing* of medicine began. Germ theory gradually replaced miasma theory as the prevailing explanation of infectious disease, in part because its explanations were disease-specific, and thus far more elegant.

In the mid-nineteenth century, the great killers and disablers were the infectious and nutritional diseases. The 100-year period that began around 1850 saw one victory after another, as biological understanding made it possible to control, mainly by prevention, the major infectious diseases (smallpox, typhus, cholera, typhoid fever, plague, malaria, diphtheria, tuberculosis, tetanus) and more recently many sexually transmitted diseases, as well as rubella, polio, and diseases now known to be nutritional in nature (scurvy, beriberi, pellagra, rickets, kwashiorkor, and endemic goiter).

Most medical historians identify Louis Pasteur (1822–1895) and Robert Koch (1834–1910) as preeminent in the development of germ theory, through their founding of the modern science of bacteriology (see Clendening, 1942; Evans, 1978). Pasteur identified bacteria as responsible for the process of fermentation, and developed the procedure of immunization as a way of preventing a number of virulent diseases of the nineteenth century, including anthrax, rabies, and certain forms of cholera (Dubos, 1950).

Koch, who discovered the tuberculosis bacillus in 1882, developed a set of postulates that have been used in almost unchanged form ever since for establishing the infectious nature of a particular disease. According to Koch, in order to establish that a disease had an infectious origin, one had to establish:

1.   That a specific bacillus must be present whenever the disease is present
2.   That the specific bacillus must not occur in other diseases
3.   That it should be possible to isolate the bacillus, and grow it in a hospitable culture

4. That the disease could then be produced in an otherwise healthy organism by injecting it with the bacillus produced in the laboratory.

These dramatic victories against infectious and nutritional diseases came about through the successful invoking of the *disease prevention* paradigm, or theoretical model. This set of assumptions about disease begins with the belief that (1) there is a specific biological precondition or cause required for any disease to manifest itself, and that (2) the process between that cause and its consequences can be interrupted by making a significant change either in the agent (as by inducing sterility in the disease-carrying organism), in the environment (as by spraying the mosquito-bearing swamps to prevent malaria), or in the person at risk (as by immunizing against smallpox or polio).

The thinking that characterized the biological era was *formistic* and *mechanistic* (see Schwartz, 1982). Formistic thinking is either-or thinking—people are either sick or well, a disease is either present or not present, a disease is either caused by a certain germ or not caused by that certain germ. Mechanistic thinking is single-cause single-effect thinking—events (such as illnesses) occur as a result of specific individual causes or chains of individual causes; such causes must be unique and specific. The disciplined invocation of formistic and mechanistic thinking led to the great triumphs over many infectious and nutritional diseases during the period roughly from 1850 to 1950.

In spite of the obvious importance of germ theory, there is reason to believe that miasma theory and the practical programs it generated may have done even more to raise the general level of health in the world. We have already commented on the social policy implications of miasma theory. Germ theory had far different social policy implications. Since specific diseases could now be prevented by appropriate immunizations or diet, there was no compelling reason to improve the quality of life in any general sense. Thus, one of the by-products of the ascendancy of germ theory as the principal explanation of infectious disease was a significant reduction in the sense of urgency regarding the general problem of quality of life, and such specific problems as poverty or urban crowding.

## THE BIOPSYCHOLOGICAL APPROACH TO HEALTH AND ILLNESS

The biological era, in turn, began to diminish in importance as the understanding of the control of infectious and nutritional disease grew. With the reduction in the number of new cases of infectious and nutritional diseases (see Chapter 2), the extent of illness and number of deaths due to chronic disease became more visible. Along with their increased visibility came the realization that a single-minded formistic and mechanistic biological approach to their prevention and treatment was no longer successful. With this realization came an increased interest in how psychosocial factors interacted with biomedical factors in the development of illness—an approach that has been termed *contextual* and *organistic* (Schwartz, 1982).

Contextual thinking assumes that all phenomena (including illness) have multiple causes and can be understood only in the context in which they exist. Organistic thinking is interactive and assumes that everything is connected to everything else. In the case of illness, for example, it is assumed that specific diseases represent the complex interaction of specific environmental stresses and the specific characteristics of the organism—in other words, that psychological stresses increase the susceptibility to biological stresses and vice versa. Organistic thinking is *and* thinking, rather than *either-or* thinking.

The current era, one that might be called the *psychologizing* of medicine, began with the growing realization of the limitations of the biological approach to the understanding of most prevalent current sources of morbidity and mortality (Ahmed, Kolker, & Coehlo, 1979). The biomedical view of disease is giving way to a more complex model, one that, in the words of Jemmott and Locke (1984) "directs attention to interactions among social and psychological as well as biological factors in the etiology, course, and treatment of disease" (p. 78). Furthermore, this emerging view represents a general model, that is, it applies to all diseases, not just to a special subset of diseases (see Friedman & DeMatteo, 1979).

As you will learn, many of the most serious medical problems that concern patients and health care providers alike—such as why patients fail to adhere to medical treatment programs, or why people engage in lifestyles that add measurably to the risk of illness and death- are hardly biological at all. Rather, they are behavioral in origin and their solution lies in changing human behavior (Stachnik, Stoffelmayr, & Hoppe, 1983). The biopsychosocial orientation to health and illness is one that fully recognizes the role of behavior in the maintenance of health and in the development of illness. The subtitle of this text—"a psychosocial perspective"—is meant to indicate that its emphasis is on psychological and sociological factors that play a role in health- and illness-related behavior.

A particularly noteworthy advocate of this broader view of health and illness in the United States is George Engel. Engel, working in the Departments of Psychiatry and Medicine at the University of Rochester, began his career as a physician working in settings where there was considerable interdisciplinary collaboration.

With this history and his consequent multifaceted orientation to the general problem of health and illness, Engel came to see health and illness in a very broad context. He has coined the term *biopsychosocial* to describe the orientation that he believes is required for a physician to understand a patient.

Engel distinguishes this more complex model of health and illness from the *biomedical* model, the model that may today still be dominant in most thinking about illness. Engel (1980) suggests that this more common biomedical model "assumes disease to be fully accounted for by deviations from the norm of measurable biological (somatic) variables. It leaves no room within its framework for the social, psychological, and behavioral dimensions of illness" (p. 130).

Thus, Engel believes that a complete view of health and illness must take into account not only the biology of the person but the psychology and sociology of the person as well, or to put it another way, that there is a biology of health, a psychology of health, and a sociology of health and that these three domains must be studied in their natural interactions (see also McKeown, 1976; Panel on the General Professional Education of the Physician and College Preparation for Medicine, 1984).

The biopsychosocial model for studying health and illness is, thus, a systems approach. The model hypothesizes, first, that in order to understand a particular person's illness and how to treat it, it is imperative to consider the interaction of biological, psychological, and social factors. In addition, the biopsychosocial model hypothesizes that treatments will interact with each other as well as with the person in the environment. With these interactions in mind, it is possible to develop a multidimensional treatment regimen for a particular person-in-the-environment that can be more effective than any unidimensional treatment program.

Second, today's systems approach to the understanding of health and illness distinguishes among three domains of inquiry—factors related to (1) the predisposition to becoming ill, (2) the precipitation of illness in persons already predisposed, and (3) the perpetuation of a disorder in persons already ill.

Thus, with the emergence of the biopsychosocial model of disease, interest is once again turning to how psychological, sociological, and cultural factors play a role—along with biological factors, to be sure—in predisposing people to become ill, in precipitating illness in people who are vulnerable but healthy, and in perpetuating illness once it occurs. The sociocultural level of analysis merges into the fields of sociology and anthropology; the biological level of analysis merges into the study of medicine. Yet, these levels of analysis are all interrelated—culture invades physiology.

## PSYCHOSOMATIC DISORDERS AND HEALTH PSYCHOLOGY

Later in this volume (Chapters 8, 9, 10, and 11), psychological aspects of specific disorders will be examined. Among these disorders are those whose psychological antecedents have long been recognized—the so-called psychosomatic disorders. It should be noted in this introductory chapter, however, that the term *psychosomatic* is itself something of a misnomer, since, in fact, all diseases are psychosomatic (Weiner, 1979). The report on psychosomatic disorders issued by the World Health Organization (1964) puts the same conclusion a little differently. The report suggests that "when we speak of psychological processes and physiological processes, we are speaking of different ways of approaching one phenomenon. The phenomenon itself is not so divided. In this sense, then, there is neither psychogenic nor somatogenic disease but only disease" (p. 6).

One aspect of the undue influence of early psychosomatic concepts on the field of psychology can be noted in the traditional reluctance of psychologists to work with medical specialists other than psychiatrists. This reluctance is clearly coming to an end. Today, there is a growing interest among health psychologists in the assessment, prevention, and treatment of the complete array of medical disorders, and in working with the full spectrum of medical specialists.

### Interactions of Physical and Mental Health

The link between mind and body, between psyche and soma, has long been the subject of philosophical debate. Plato and Aristotle, the two great Greek philosophers, appeared to differ on their views about mind and body. Plato saw them as separable, in part, apparently, because that view allowed for survival of the mind after the death of the body. Aristotle, on the other hand, felt that the soul was inseparable from the body but that the intellect could be thought of as independent of the body. These arguments—as well as those advanced much later in the seventeenth century by Descartes, who also held that mind and body were separable—need to be understood as part of the effort to bring harmony between the newly emerging field of biology and the powerful teachings of the church, for whom concepts like soul and immortality were central.

What is important about the mind-body debate in the context of the historical background of health psychology is that while miasma theory saw the environmental context as crucial for understanding the workings of the body, germ theory tended to emphasize the independence of the body from the mind as well as from the social setting. Contemporary biopsychosocial theory once again links mind and body together, along with the social and cultural context within which the person as a whole functions.

Modern studies of disorders of the mind and the body show them to be highly related. Today, there is a growing collection of evidence that persons in poor *physical* health tend to make high use of mental health facilities and that persons in poor *mental* health tend to make high use of medical care facilities (Aronowitz & Bromberg, 1984; Burns & Burke, 1985; Eastwood, 1975; Kessler, et al., 1987; Regier, Shapiro, Kessler, & Taube, 1984; Vaillant, 1979; Ware, et al., 1984).

The findings linking mental illness and physical illness have been instrumental in suggesting that treatment of mental illness may have, as one of its by-products, a subsequent significant reduction in the use of general health services. In addition, and perhaps even more important, there is considerable evidence that the provision of some form of brief psychotherapy, even in the absence of a diagnosable psychiatric disorder, can have the sometimes dramatic consequence of significantly reducing the use of general medical care (see, for example, Follette & Cummings, 1967; Jones & Vischi, 1979; Mumford, Schlesinger, & Glass, 1982; Schlesinger, Mumford & Glass, 1980).

## THE CONCEPT OF THE HEALTH FIELD

Professional consideration of the field of health and illness was considerably broadened by the work of Marc Lalonde, who served for some years as the Minister of Health and Welfare for the Government of Canada. During this period, and under his direction, his staff published a small volume entitled *A New Perspective on the Health of Canadians* (1974), a report that has become enormously influential in providing a way of thinking comprehensively about health and illness (Robbins, 1984; Terris, 1984).

Lalonde introduced the concept of the *health field* and identified its four components—human biology, the environment, lifestyle, and health care organization. In essence, Lalonde indicated that in order to understand and influence patterns of health and illness it was necessary to understand far more than biology. In his analysis, Lalonde was particularly interested in premature deaths, that is, in deaths that occur prior to age 70.

The concept of premature death has important implications for health planning (Perloff et al., 1984). In the conventional calculation of death rates, in which the total number of deaths in a given population is contrasted with the size of that population, emphasis is necessarily given to deaths in older age groups, since the number of deaths increases with age. If one bases public policy on these death rates, resources will be allocated to reducing the number of deaths that occur late in life. Deaths at younger ages are, however, particularly important, because of the tremendous number of years of life that are lost. Public policy that is based on the analysis of premature deaths tends to focus on prevention rather than treatment, and is thus consistent with one of the important general concepts of central interest to health psychologists.

As death rates are conventionally calculated (see Chapter 2), diseases of the heart are the leading cause of death, with cancer, cerebrovascular diseases, and accidents ranked second, third, and fourth. In contrast, the premature death rate—which takes into account the average number of years of life lost—ranks accidents (mainly involving motor vehicles) first, followed by cancer, and then diseases of the heart. Cerebrovascular diseases, ranked third in cause of death, rank eighth in cause of premature death, and homicide, a cause of death that does not appear among the ten leading causes of death, ranks fifth among the causes of premature death.

In addition to understanding human biology and genetics in the control of premature deaths, it is necessary, according to Lalonde, to understand the environment, that is, those matters outside the body that can affect health, such as food and water purity, air pollution, sewage disposal practices, noise control, and road and vehicular safety, over which the individual has little if any control. Many of these environmental factors are associated with social class, of course, and it is important to include poverty as an environmental variable over which many people have little if any control. In addition, it is important to understand lifestyle, that is, those decisions people make about their own behavior that can affect their health, such as overeating, smoking, abuse of alcohol and other drugs, insufficient exercise, or careless driving, over which they have considerable control. Finally, it is necessary to understand the health care organization, that is, the quality, quantity, and distribution of health-related services in any community.

What is particularly interesting about this schema for viewing health and illness is that it provides a framework for gathering and interpreting health-related information in a very innovative manner. If a random sample of people is asked what would be the most important thing that could be done to reduce the incidence of premature deaths in a community, the largest proportion tend to point to needed improvements in the medical care system, that is, the health care organization—more physicians, more nurses, more hospital beds, and so forth.

Contrary to this prevailing opinion, Lalonde has found that in the case of automobile fatalities, for example, 75 percent of these deaths can be accounted for by pathological lifestyles, 20 percent by the environment, and only 5 percent by defects in the health service delivery system. Similarly, it has been estimated that self-destructive lifestyles account for about half of all premature deaths and that 20 percent of these premature deaths can be attributed to just two behaviors—cigarette smoking and excessive use of alcohol (see also Breslow, Fielding, & Lave, 1980).

Illnesses attributable to self-destructive lifestyles appear in unsuspected settings. Roueché (1984) has, for example, recently described a midwestern outbreak of salmonella, a serious and potentially life-threatening form of food poisoning, that was discovered to be caused by the smoking of contaminated marijuana.

The implications of the health field concept and the analyses that emerge from it are clear: The strategy with the greatest potential for reducing premature deaths may be to develop intervention programs that focus on the psychology and sociology of illness, rather than on the biology of illness.

## TWO VIEWS OF HEALTH: STATUS OR PROCESS

Rene Dubos (1959) has distinguished between two views of health, represented metaphorically by the Greek goddess Hygeia who watched over the health of Athens, on the one hand, and the Greek healer Aesculapius. To Hygeia, from whose name comes the modern word *hygiene,* is attributed the belief that people can remain healthy if they live according to reason. In contrast, Aesculapius, who is reputed to have lived in the twelfth century B.C., and who became famous as a surgeon and expert on the healing powers of plants, represented the view that health was a condition that could be lost and could, on occasion, be retrieved by the physician.

Medical historians would generally concede that the followers of

Aesculapius have had the upper hand in the battle with the followers of Hygiea, particularly with the advent of germ theory a little over a century ago, and the doctrine that for each specific disease there is a specific etiology and specific treatment. Indeed, the advances in medical and surgical treatment in the past century have been extraordinary. With the growing interest in health as thriving wellness and not only as the absence of disease, however, and with the increasing realization of the inherent limitations of the curative approach to well-being, there is a reemerging interest in the teachings of Hygiea, and in the achievement of an optimal balance between these two metaphorical figures from the ancient past. Health is, it is increasingly acknowledged, not a static utopian state but a process that cannot be fully understood except in its ever-changing sociocultural context.

## THE MEASUREMENT OF HEALTH

Defining *health* is complex because the concept of health has a number of different dimensions. Thus, one view of health has identified two dimensions—objective disability and subjective distress. Another view has identified three dimensions—physical function, social health, and emotional health. Still another view of health defines four components—physical health, mental health, social health, and general health perceptions (Lipscomb, 1982; Ware et al., 1980). Each of these ways of thinking about health has associated with it a strategy for assessing health.

Physical health is defined by Ware and associates in terms of functional status—"the capacity to perform a variety of activities that are normal for an individual in good health" (Ware et al., 1980, p. 11). Six categories of activities have been identified: (1) self-care activities, (2) mobility, (3) physical activities, (4) role activities, (5) household activities, and (6) leisure activities. Mental health is assessed by Ware and associates in terms of the presence of symptoms of depression and other mood disorders, and of anxiety disorders. In addition, the assessment includes positive aspects such as the feeling of well-being, self-control, and the positive components of mood, thoughts, and feelings.

Social health has been defined in terms of interpersonal interactions and activities, such as visits with friends, or membership in clubs, and in terms of subjective ratings of such factors as how well one is getting along with others. In general, the measure of social health seems very similar to the assessment of social support systems that might serve to moderate the effects of stress on health (see Chapter 3). Finally, the concept of general health perception deals with how people view their own health and is assessed in terms of perceptions of past, current, and future health, judgments of resistance to illness, worries about health, and the extent to which people perceive illness to be a part of their lives.

Centuries ago, when the mortality rate was far higher than it is today, and when most deaths were a consequence of infectious disease or battle injuries, all that may have mattered was being alive. With the dramatic decreases in mortality rate from infectious and nutritional diseases over the past century (see Chapter 2), and with the ensuing increased incidence of chronic disease, interest in health status has turned to the examination of morbidity and disability, that is, to the assessment of health status among the living.

Finally, within the last two or three decades, it has become clear that being healthy and being without illness are not synoymous—that, in the words of the constitution of the World Health Organization, "health is a state of complete physical, mental and social well-being and not merely the absence of disease and illness" (cited in Sullivan, 1974, p. 2). Sigerist has proposed a similar positive definition of health—"Health is . . . not simply the absence of disease: it is something positive, a joyful attitude toward life, and a cheerful acceptance of the responsibilities that life puts on the individual (cited in Jette, 1980). Experience with people who are ill reveals very quickly that there are widely different ways of coping with illness, that is, that there are sick ways of being well and healthy ways of being ill (Farber, 1976; Williamson & Pearse, 1966).

These concepts of health have a political quality about them, equating health, in part, with the ability to manage one's life without undue interference from the outside, that is, with the sense of self-efficacy (Illich, 1976). As these various approaches to the conceptualization of health and illness suggest, the assessment of health status must also include identifying differing degrees of health among people who are apparently free of illness.

At the level of the individual, the most common and simplest—although not necessarily the most valid—way of assessing health status is by self-report. "Healthy" means no significant symptoms. Health status is also assessed by physicians, based upon clinical examination and laboratory findings. On occasion, self-report and physical examinations may yield dramatically different conclusions. For example, there are certain forms of tumors that are more ominous if they are not painful than if they are. In these cases, the absence of pain is treated as a significant deviation from normally expected behavior.

Far more common are the reports of pain and discomfort from patients when no objective signs of illness can be found. Furthermore, as Sullivan (1974) has noted, physicians may differ among each other, depending not only on the reliability and validity of their judgments but also on their point of view in conducting the examination. To a typical primary care physician, a person is judged to be healthy if there are no signs of a diagnosable illness. To an industrial physician, healthy means "able to work"; to a military physician, healthy means "able to fight." To the health statistician, interested in predicting health status at some time in the future, healthy means "unlikely to become ill" (Sanders, 1964).

Sullivan (1971) has proposed an interesting strategy for subdividing estimated total life expectancy into two components—that portion of life expectancy that would be free of disability, and that portion that would include disability. As calculated by Sullivan, for males in the mid-1960s, for example, life expectancy free of disability was 62.5 years, and life expectancy with disability was 5.3 years, resulting in a total life expectancy of 67.8 years.

The necessity to disentangle the concepts of quality of life and of life expectancy is becoming increasingly important as medical science is developing techniques and medications for extending life span in persons who formerly would have succumbed to their illnesses. Thus, as antibiotics have been developed that prevent persons with chronic diseases from dying from once-fatal secondary infections, a by-product is an increase in the duration of the chronic disease (Gruenberg, 1977).

## AN OVERVIEW OF HUMAN ANATOMY AND PHYSIOLOGY

Since the subject matter of this book is the human body, it is appropriate to provide a brief introductory perspective regarding its structure and functioning, that is, its anatomy and physiology. In such presentations, the human organism is commonly divided into organ systems (such as the cardiovascular system), which in turn comprise individual organs (such as the heart or the lungs), which in turn are built from a variety of tissues, which are in turn constructed from various cells. The human body is a completely interdependent system, that is, everything is connected to everything else. Thus, dividing the body into organ systems is somewhat arbitrary, but it is necessary to make easier some understanding of the most important ways in which organs work together. The major organ systems include the cardiovascular system, the respiratory system, the digestive system, the urinary system, the endocrine system, the reproductive system, and the nervous system.

Under normal conditions, the human organism maintains an internal balance through a series of complex biochemical processes that together are called *homeostasis,* a term coined by Walter Cannon in 1932, in his book *The Wisdom of the Body.* Indeed, most physiologists view illness as the result of a failure of homeostatic balance (see, for example, Guyton, 1982; Strand, 1983; Tortora & Evans, 1986). Homeostasis is disturbed by stresses that can originate outside the body (such as injury, poisoning, loud noise, surgical procedures, or exercise) as well as inside the body (such as pain, high blood pressure, tumors, or unpleasant thoughts). The study of physiology is, in part, the study of how the body's regulatory processes keep the internal environment stable and keep it functioning within tolerable limits, and how, at times of illness, the body fails to maintain that satisfactory balance.

### The Cardiovascular System

The cardiovascular system carries blood throughout the body. The blood brings nutrients, oxygen, and warmth to all living cells in the body and, at the same time, collects excess water, heat, carbon dioxide, and other waste products. The cardiovascular system includes two major components—the heart, and the network of blood vessels, also called the vascular system.

The heart, roughly the size of a closed fist, lies between the lungs and is held in place by a pericardial sac that is firm enough to keep it in its proper anatomical position while still allowing it enough freedom of movement to be able to contract and expand as it beats. The interior of the heart is divided into four chambers—the right and left atria located in the upper portion, and the right and left ventricles, located in the lower portion of the heart (see Figure 1–1). Blood enters the heart through veins into the right atrium, from which it flows into the right ventricle and then through the pulmonary arteries, leading to lungs where it releases its carbon dioxide and takes on oxygen. From the lungs, the blood returns to the heart via pulmonary veins that empty into the left atrium. The blood travels from the left atrium into the left ventricle and then via the ascending aorta to the rest of the vascular system. Separating the four chambers are a set of delicate valves that permit the blood to flow in only one direction.

The vascular system consists of literally thousands of miles of branching

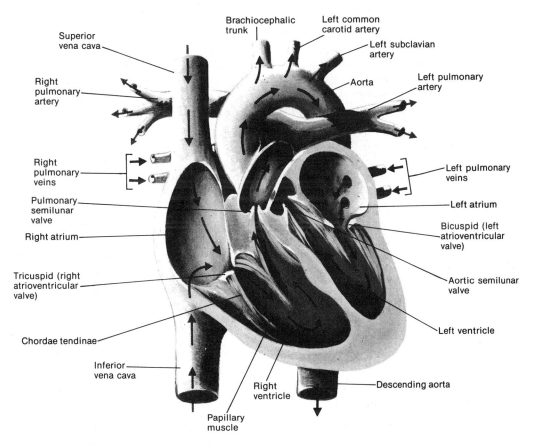

**Figure 1–1**   The Human Heart
From *Anatomy and Physiology* by William F. Evans. © 1983 by Prentice-Hall, Inc. Used by permission.

hollow blood vessels that deliver blood to all parts of the body. Blood vessels are usually divided into four types: the arteries that distribute blood under high pressure to tissues in various parts of the body, the smaller arterioles that reduce the pressure under which the blood is flowing through the arteries and help in distributing the blood, the tiny capillaries that have permeable walls and are embedded throughout the tissues of the body, and the veins that collect the blood from the capillaries and return it to the heart. At any given moment, about 7 percent of the blood is within the heart, about 9 percent is in the lungs, and the remaining 84 percent is circulating throughout the rest of the body.

The blood is made up of (1) hemoglobin, a complex protein that is carried by red blood cells also called erythrocytes; (2) white blood cells, also called leukocytes, that fight infections whenever they occur in the body; (3) platelets, also called thrombocytes, that assist in the process of clotting; and (4) plasma, the liquid in which the blood cells are suspended.

DISORDERS OF THE CARDIOVASCULAR SYSTEM.    The heart, like all pumps that are in constant use, can wear out, and in about 20 percent of people over the age of 60, it does wear out. In addition, the heart can fail to function properly because of congenital anatomical defects. Such defects occur in about 1 percent of births and result in a significant malformation and malfunctioning of the heart. Coronary artery disease can develop, usually because the muscles in the heart do not receive enough blood. Blood pressure can become too high, a condition termed hypertension. The heart can develop arrhythmia (or as it is sometimes called, dysrhythmia) that is, an irregularity in its beat. Congestive heart failure can develop when the heart is no longer strong enough to pump a sufficient amount of blood to supply the oxygen demands of the body.

In the vascular system, an aneurysm, or thinning and bulging of a vein or artery can develop. Atherosclerosis can develop as a consequence of the buildup of fatty substances, especially triglicerides and cholesterol, that block the walls of arteries near the heart. Other blockages, called thromboses, can occur in veins usually in the lower extremities that can be life-threatening because they can become dislodged and move into the lungs where they can stop blood circulation. Constriction or narrowing of the arteries near the heart can cause considerable pain, usually called angina pectoris, that is associated with the reduction in the coronary blood flow.

The blood itself can develop abnormalities, including deficiencies in red blood cells or proteins and other forms of anemia; and disorders of the white blood cells including infectious mononucleosis, and leukemia (an uncontrolled, speeded-up production of white cells that can result in severe infections and internal hemorrhaging).

### The Respiratory System

The respiratory system includes the nose and mouth, the pharynx or throat, the larynx or voice box, the trachea or windpipe, and the lungs with their complex system of passageways or bronchi through which air passes (see Figure

1–2). A ventilating system of respiratory muscles expands the chest cavity that surrounds the lungs during inhalation and contracts the chest cavity during exhalation. The task of the respiratory system is twofold—first, raising the oxygen content of the blood, while second, removing excess carbon dioxide from it. The respiratory and cardiovascular systems work together in oxygenating and purifying the blood.

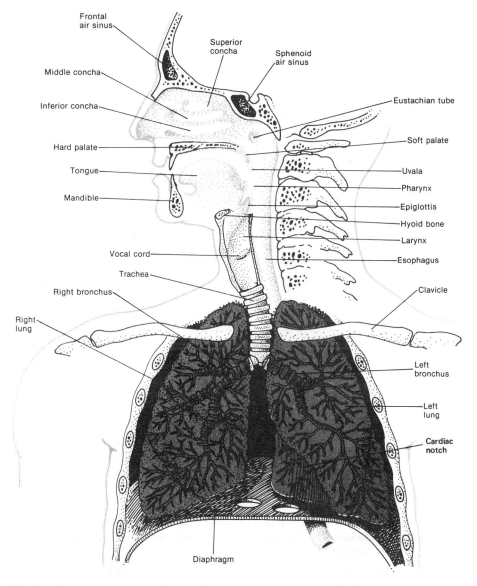

**Figure 1–2**  Organs of the Respiratory System
From *Anatomy and Physiology* by William F. Evans. © 1983 by Prentice-Hall, Inc. Used by permission.

Air entering through the nose is warmed, filtered, and moistened. The pharynx serves as a passageway for air (and for food), and while food empties into the esophagus, air moves into the larynx where it is filtered of dust or other impurities before moving into the trachea, where it is again filtered, and then into the bronchi of the lungs. Thus, by the time that air reaches the lungs, it has been thoroughly cleansed, moistened and warmed.

The bronchi and their supportive tissue structures constitute the lungs. The beginning sections of the bronchi are composed primarily of cartilage, but as they branch they become finer and finer and the cartilage is replaced by smooth muscle tissue. By the time the bronchi have completely divided, they are microscopic in size, and it is in these tiny bronchi and their associated capillaries that the exchange of oxygen and carbon dioxide between the lungs and the vascular system takes place.

DISORDERS OF THE RESPIRATORY SYSTEM.    Abnormalities of the respiratory system vary tremendously in their severity, from relatively mild conditions, such as hay fever or other allergies, to severe and sometimes fatal conditions, such as lung cancer. Among the milder conditions, in addition to most allergies, should be included bronchitis—(inflammation of the bronchi), usually the result of excessive smoking, air pollution, or respiratory infection—and so-called common colds or influenza, ordinarily the result of a viral infection.

More severe respiratory disorders include bronchial asthma, a severe allergic reaction characterized by wheezing and difficulty in breathing, that is thought to be the result of spasmodic contractions of the smooth muscle tissues in the walls of the smaller bronchi; emphysema, in which the walls of the bronchi lose their elasticity with the result that it becomes increasingly difficult for efficient gas exchange to take place and for the person to exhale; and pneumonia, an acute infection or inflammation of the lungs in which fluids enter the areas where gas exchange takes place, reducing the amount of needed air space in the lungs.

The severe respiratory disorders, in addition to lung cancer, include tuberculosis—a chronic bacterial infection far less common than was the case half a century ago, but still the most fatal communicable disease; sudden infant death syndrome (SIDS)—a poorly understood respiratory disease that results in the death of some 10,000 babies every year in the United States alone; pulmonary embolisms—or blood clots that can be fatal by obstructing circulation to lung tissues; and carbon monoxide poisoning.

### The Digestive System

The ultimate source of energy that fuels the body is food. In the form that it is eaten, however, food is not usable as an energy source. It must be mechanically and chemically digested, that is, transformed into molecular-sized pieces that can penetrate the walls of the digestive organs into the blood and then into cell membranes that then provide needed energy to keep the body functioning.

   Digestion begins in the mouth. The cheeks and lips help keep food in a position so that the teeth can reduce the size of food particles. The salivary glands add saliva to food for the purposes of softening, dissolving, and lubricating food prior to its being swallowed, and the tongue maneuvers food for chewing and swallowing (see Figure 1–3).

   Food then enters the gastrointestinal tract (also called the alimentary canal), a 30-foot long tube that runs from the throat to the anus and that includes the esophagus, stomach, small intestine, and large intestine. Muscular

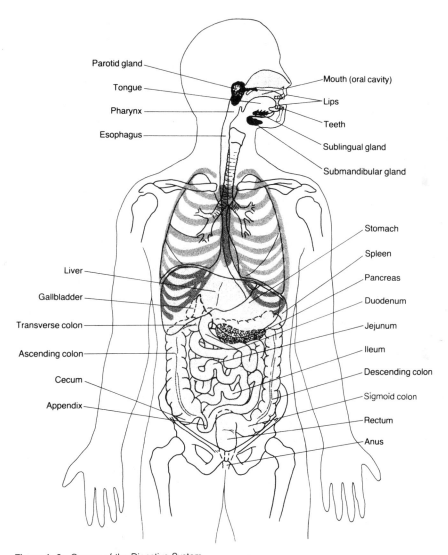

**Figure 1–3**   Organs of the Digestive System

From *Principles of Human Physiology* by Gerard J. Tortora, Ronald L. Evans, and Nicholas P. Anagnostakos. © 1982. Reprinted by permission of Harper & Row, Publishers, Inc.

contractions churn the food as it passes through the gastrointestinal tract, and various secretions along the tract help decompose food by chemical means. At periodic intervals throughout the gastrointestinal tract, a number of valves exist that help prevent food from moving back up toward the mouth.

The stomach secretes large amounts of a number of different gastric juices. These kill many bacteria that are present in food, further decompose food that is swallowed, and digest proteins in the food. Other secretions produced in the pancreas, gallbladder, and liver are added to the digestive process as food passes into the small intestine, where the process of food absorption continues. About 90 percent of all food absorption occurs in the small intestine. Undigested materials proceed into the large intestine where they become semisolid as much of the remaining water is absorbed, and where mucus is secreted and added to help in their evacuation through the rectum and anal canal.

DISORDERS OF THE DIGESTIVE SYSTEM. The most common abnormalities of the digestive system include tooth decay (technically called dental caries) and gum disease, as well as a variety of other conditions, including peritonitis (a bacterial inflammation of the lining of the abdominal cavity); peptic and gastric ulcers (lesions in the alimentary canal thought to be due to excess secretion of acidic gastric juices); appendicitis; diverticulitis (a weakening of the musculature of the walls of the large intestine usually thought to be due to a lack of sufficient bulk in the diet); hepatitis (various forms of inflammation of the liver); and gallstones (due to the fusion of crystallized cholesterol in the gallbladder).

More severe diseases of the digestive system include cirrhosis of the liver (a chronic and dangerous inflammation of the liver, often associated with excess alcohol intake); benign and malignant tumors (most commonly found in the large intestine, and the cause of about 30 percent of all deaths due to cancer); anorexia nervosa (a severe eating disorder found predominantly in young, single females, that can result in depression, absence of menstruation, and, in most severe cases, death through starvation); and bulimia (another eating disorder characterized by alternate binging and purging. Both anorexia and bulimia are thought to have significant psychological components and to require some form of psychotherapy as part of the treatment program.

### The Urinary System

The urinary system is made up of the kidneys, the ureters, the bladder, and the urethra (see Figure 1–4). Digestion of nutrients by body cells results in the production of wastes and excess water, and in the concentration of excess amounts of sodium, chlorides, phosphates, and other chemicals that can be toxic if they are not regulated. The primary function of the urinary system is to maintain homeostasis by controlling the concentration and volume of blood by removing or restoring water and a variety of chemicals, and by assisting in the excretion of wastes.

The kidneys regulate the concentration and volume of the blood and

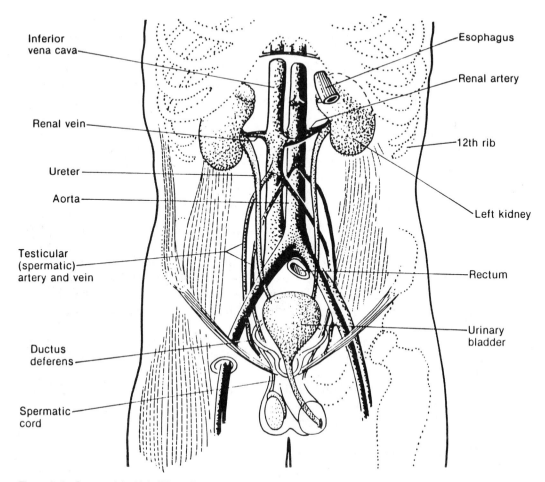

Inferior vena cava

Renal vein

Ureter

Aorta

Testicular (spermatic) artery and vein

Ductus deferens

Spermatic cord

Esophagus

Renal artery

12th rib

Left kidney

Rectum

Urinary bladder

**Figure 1–4**  Organs of the Male Urinary System
From *Anatomy and Physiology* by William F. Evans. © 1983 by Prentice-Hall, Inc. Used by permission.

remove wastes from the blood in the form of urine. Urine is excreted from each kidney through its ureter, and it is then stored in the urinary bladder until it is expelled from the body through the urethra. The kidneys are very active organs. While weighing less than 1 percent of the body, they use about 8 percent of the oxygen consumed by the body. A very large volume of blood is delivered to the two kidneys under high pressure from the abdominal aorta. Once in the kidney, blood is filtered of its excess water and other chemicals. Some of the filtrate is reabsorbed, but most of it is then excreted.

DISORDERS OF THE URINARY SYSTEM.    The most common abnormalties of the urinary system include kidney stones, usually formed from salt crystals, that can block the passage of urine through the ureter; gout, due to an excessively high level of uric acid in the blood; Bright's disease (also called glomerulo-nephritis), a frequently chronic inflammation of the kidneys often of allergic origin that sometimes leads to severe kidney disease and kidney failure; various infections of the bladder and other organs in the urinary system; and polycystic disease caused by defects in the internal anatomy and functioning of the kidneys. Treatment for severe kidney disease sometimes includes kidney transplants and hemodialysis, a procedure whereby the blood is withdrawn from one of the radial arteries in the arm, circulated through an artificial device external to the body that acts as the kidneys by cleaning, filtering, and enriching the blood, which is then returned to the body via the saphenous vein located in the abdomen.

### The Endocrine System

The endocrine system consists of a group of glands located throughout the trunk and head that produce hormones that are delivered directly into the blood stream (see Figure 1–5). These hormones regulate growth and development, as well as cell and tissue activity. The glands in the endocrine system are thought of as an organ system because they work together, rather than because they are anatomically related or directly connected to each other as are the organs that comprise the other organ systems. Each of the endocrine glands is enormously complex, both anatomically and physiologically. The principal endocrine glands are the pituitary, thyroid, adrenals, gonads, pancreas, and parathyroids.

About thirty-five different hormones have already been identified in the body. These hormones are divided into three groups—steroids, proteins, and catecholamines. Glands that secrete steroids include the ovaries, testes, and adrenal cortex. Protein hormones are secreted by the thyroid, parathyroid, and pancreas, among others. Catecholamines are secreted by the adrenal medulla.

The endocrine glands work with the nervous system to help coordinate body functioning. While the nervous system works quickly, producing immediate but short-lasting effects, the endocrine system works slowly and produces relatively long-lasting effects. The nervous and endocrine system are linked together in the hypothalamus, in the inner portion of the brain, where appetite, temperature, water balance, sleep, sexual activity, and blood vessel diameters, among other bodily functions, are regulated. We will return to a discussion of the hypothalamus later in this chapter and again in Chapter 3 when we examine the response of the body to stress.

DISORDERS OF THE ENDOCRINE SYSTEM.    Endocrine glands do not malfunction very often, but because of their importance as overall regulators of bodily functioning, when they do, extreme abnormalities can occur. Thus, particularly during childhood, malfunctioning of the pituitary gland can result in acromegaly (a permanent enlargement of the bones of the head, hands, and feet) if too much hormone is secreted, and in dwarfism, if too little hormone is

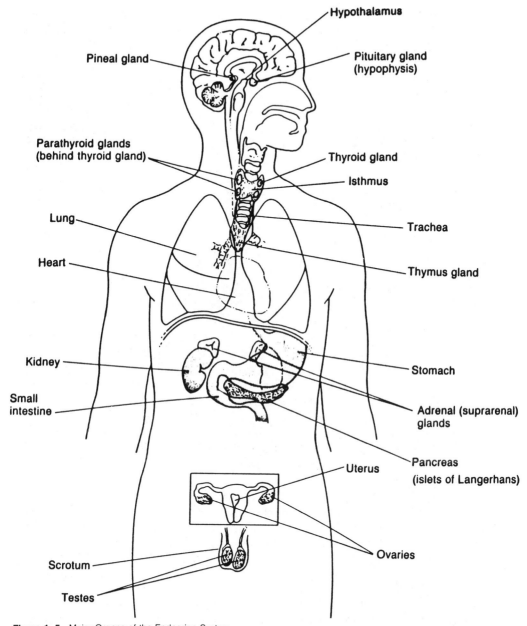

**Figure 1–5** Major Organs of the Endocrine System

From *Principles of Human Physiology* by Gerard J. Tortora, Ronald L. Evans, and Nicholas P. Anagnostakos. © 1982. Reprinted by permission of Harper & Row, Publishers, Inc.

secreted. Thyroid deficiency can result in other types of growth disorders, again particularly during childhood, as well as heart disorders and low intellectual performance. Abnormalities of the parathyroid can result in severe muscular disorders that can be life-threatening.

Abnormalities of the adrenal cortex can result in a variety of chemical imbalances in the body, and of such relatively rare diseases as Addison's disease and Cushing's syndrome. Addison's disease—due to undersecretion of the adrenal cortex—results in severe weight loss, mental lethargy, low blood pressure, dehydration, and muscular weakness. Cushing's syndrome, resulting from oversecretion of the adrenal cortex, produces pathological fat distribution throughout the body that results in spindly legs and excess fat on the stomach and back. Insulin is secreted by the pancreas, and abnormalities of the pancreas can result in diabetes or hypoglycemia.

### The Reproductive System

In the male, the organs of reproduction include the testes, where sperm is produced; a variety of ducts where sperm is stored and transported; the prostate, seminal vesicles, and Cowper's glands where semen is produced to help in the transport of the sperm; and the penis, through which the seminal fluid that includes sperm flows during sexual intercourse (see Figure 1–6). In the female, the organs of reproduction include the two ovaries, where eggs are produced, ordinarily at the rate of one each month; the fallopian tubes through which the eggs are transported to the uterus, where the egg is stored for a brief period of time and where pregnancy is carried out in the event of the egg being fertilized; and the vagina and associated external organs (see Figure 1–7).

Once sperm are ejected into the vagina during sexual intercourse, they have a life expectancy of about 48 hours. Sperm are highly adapted for reaching and penetrating the female egg, being composed of a head that contains the nuclear material, a midsection that provides energy for locomotion, and a tail that helps them to move.

In the female, two sex hormones, estrogen and progesterone, are produced in the ovaries. Estrogens function in the development and maintenance of the female reproductive organs, especially the lining of the uterus (the endometrium) and the secondary sex characteristics; in the distribution of fat to the breasts, abdomen, and hips; and in the development of voice pitch and hair patterns. Progesterone works with estrogens to prepare the endometrium for implantation and to prepare the breasts for milk secretion.

The reproductive cycle in the female is a complex process. Each month the endometrium is prepared to receive a fertilized egg. If an egg is fertilized, it remains and grows in the uterus until delivery. If no fertilization takes place, a portion of the endometrium is shed in the form of blood, mucus, surface cells, and other fluids at the time of menstruation.

DISORDERS OF THE REPRODUCTIVE SYSTEM. Disorders of the reproductive system can be divided into three categories: (1) sexually transmitted

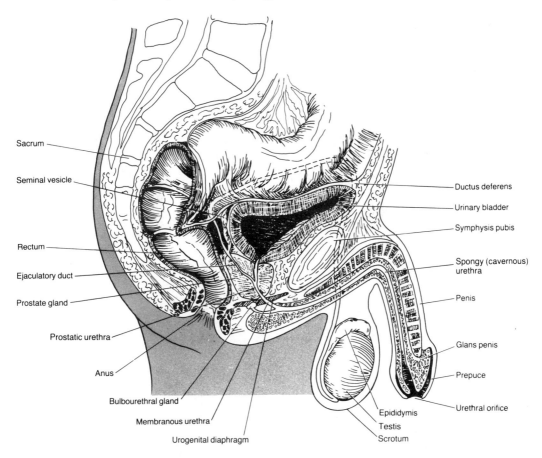

Sacrum

Seminal vesicle

Rectum

Ejaculatory duct

Prostate gland

Prostatic urethra

Anus

Bulbourethral gland

Membranous urethra

Urogenital diaphragm

Ductus deferens

Urinary bladder

Symphysis pubis

Spongy (cavernous) urethra

Penis

Glans penis

Prepuce

Urethral orifice

Epididymis

Testis

Scrotum

**Figure 1–6**   Organs of the Male Reproductive System
From *Principles of Human Physiology* by Gerard J. Tortora, Ronald L. Evans, and Nicholas P. Anagnostakos. © 1982.
Reprinted by permission of Harper & Row, Publishers, Inc.

diseases; (2) gender-specific reproductive diseases; and (3) disorders associated with sex physiology that appear to have a particularly significant psychological and interpersonal component in their perpetuation. Among sexually transmitted diseases, the most common are gonorrhea, an easily treated but easily transmitted bacterial infection; syphilis, a long-lasting bacterial infectious disorder that is treated with somewhat greater difficulty; and genital herpes, a milder disorder caused by the herpes virus that is very difficult to treat successfully. Less common but far more alarming is the acquired immune deficiency syndrome (AIDS)—a currently untreatable sexually transmitted disorder (see next section).

The most common male disorders of the reproductive system include prostitis, a chronic inflammation of the prostate gland; tumors of the reproductive system, most commonly of the prostate; and infertility. In the case of women, the most common disorders of the reproductive system include abnor-

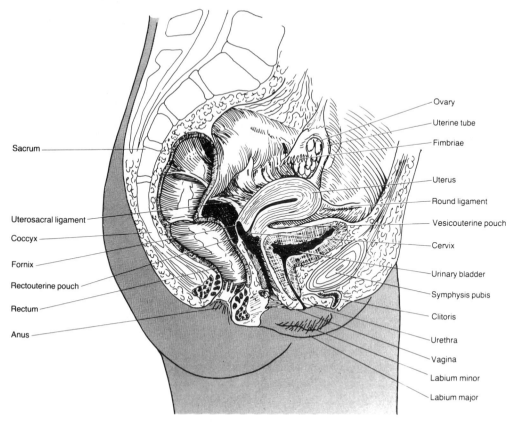

**Figure 1–7**    Organs of the Female Reproductive System
From *Principles of Human Physiology* by Gerard J. Tortora, Ronald L. Evans, and Nicholas P. Anagnostakos. © 1982. Reprinted by permission of Harper & Row, Publishers, Inc.

malities of menstruation, such as amenorrhea (the absence of menstruation), dysmenorrhea (painful menstruation), and premenstrual syndrome (severe physical and emotional distress associated with the menstrual cycle); toxic shock syndrome, a rare but serious condition that appears to be associated with the use of tampons during the menstrual cycle; ovarian cysts, usually benign fluid-containing tumors of the ovaries; cervical cancer; and infertility.

Among the disorders of the reproductive system that appear to have a particularly significant psychological or interpersonal component, four are especially common. These include, in the case of men: (1) impotence, the inability to have or to sustain an erection; and (2) premature ejaculation, often defined as the inability of the male to delay ejaculation long enough to satisfy his partner 50 percent of the time. In the case of women, these psychologically linked reproductive disorders include: (1) orgasmic dysfunction, the inability to achieve orgasm; and (2) vaginismus, involuntary contractions of the muscles surrounding the vagina that make insertion of the erect penis impossible or extremely difficult.

AIDS: THE ACQUIRED IMMUNE DEFICIENCY SYNDROME.   The acquired immune deficiency syndrome (AIDS), first identified in 1981, is caused by an infection due to a newly discovered virus, human T-cell lymphotropic virus, type III (HTLV-III). More than 30,000 cases have already been diagnosed in the United States, of whom 60 percent of victims have already died, and the number is continuing to increase very rapidly. It is currently estimated that by 1990 there will be more than 250,000 identified cases (Morgan & Curran, 1986).

AIDS is understandably generating an enormous amount of anxiety because it cannot yet be controlled. The average survival time is about 1 year, and, on the basis of current figures, about 70 percent of people with AIDS die within 2 years of diagnosis. There is no question about the fact that AIDS has become a public health emergency (Batchelor, 1984; Coates, Temoshok, & Mandel, 1984; Joseph, Emmons, Kessler, Wortman, O'Brien, Hocker, & Schaefer, 1984; Martin & Vance, 1984; Scitovsky & Rice, 1987).

As its name suggests, AIDS is a reduction in the ability of the body's immune system to defend itself against the introduction of any foreign matter. Studies of patients with AIDS indicate that prior to the infection with the AIDS virus their immune system appears to have functioned normally. While most people infected with the virus remain in good health, many develop symptoms that can range in severity from quite mild to very extreme. Symptoms of the disorder may include a variety of unusual infections and malignancies, profound fatique, low-grade fever, loss of appetite and weight, chronic diarrhea, night sweats, and persistent swollen glands in the neck, armpits, or groin. The course of the disease is marked by numerous life-threatening episodes, including a rare form of severe pneumonia, several varieties of severe infections and of cancers, loss of physical strength and mental acuity, and severe and chronic pain. The onset of symptoms can take from 6 months to as long as 5 years.

People infected with the virus are infected for life, and it is not yet known what proportion of them will become ill. Some people who are infected may have many AIDS symptoms but not develop the defining characteristics of AIDS. These people are said to have the AIDS-related complex (ARC). The defining characteristics of AIDS itself include: (1) a positive test for the HTLV-III antibody; (2) a profound dysfunction of the immune system; and (3) significant loss of white blood cells that play an important role in the immune response.

The vast majority of AIDS victims are in the prime of life—between the ages of 20 and 50, and are either homosexual or bisexual men or intravenous drug abusers. It seems only a matter of time before AIDS will infect the heterosexual and nondrug using population as well, and this predicted spread into the general population is helping fuel the growing alarm about the disease.

To date, no way has been found to restore the immune response in persons with AIDS. There are no drugs currently known that cure AIDS, and no vaccine that prevents AIDS, and practically no one who is working on the problem of AIDS believes that a cure or a vaccine will be found very soon. Drugs that inhibit HTLV-III do not result in clinical improvement when administered to AIDS patients. Because the disease cannot be controlled, there is great private uneasiness on the part of people who are at high risk of developing the disorder, and growing public fear of the disease. In addition, there is growing concern on the part of health workers who are responsible for the treatment of AIDS victims for their own safety, and on the part of employers and insurance companies to minimize its economic consequences (U. S. Department of Health and Human Services, 1986a).

HTLV-III infection is spread by direct sexual contact, needle sharing, or, less commonly, through transfusion of infected blood. The virus can be transmitted from a mother to an infant, and about 1 percent of AIDS victims are infants. It is anticipated that the number of infant cases will increase as the number increases among heterosexual women. The most prevalent current theory of AIDS transmission is that the virus travels from host to host inside a special type of white blood cell that can cross through the mucous lining of the inside of the penis and vagina.

The risk of transmitting AIDS from daily contact at work, school, or at home appears to be nonexistent. There appears to be no risk of infection for health professionals if standard safety procedures are used in the handling of blood and tissue samples from AIDS patients. No cases have been found where AIDS has been transmitted by casual household contact, and health care professionals have not developed AIDS from routine care of AIDS patients.

Recommendations for the prevention of AIDS have been promulgated, and follow logically from the current understanding of the transmission of the disease. In order to prevent AIDS, it is recommended that a person should not have sexual intercourse with multiple partners, or with persons who have had multiple partners. If a person has sex with a person who might be infected, precautions to follow include the use of condoms and the avoidance of anal intercourse, oral-genital contact, and open-mouthed kissing. In addition, blood donors and blood that is collected for transfusions should be examined for the presence of the HTLV-III antibody, and intravenous drug use involving needle-sharing should be avoided at all costs. Like lung cancer, AIDS is a disease that can be prevented but cannot be cured.

The emotional well-being of people with AIDS is undermined by physical disease, weakness, and pain, by the likely imminence of death, and by stigmatization, social oppression, and frequently by a pervasive loss of a supportive social network. People who are at risk of AIDS are subject to severe anxiety and depression, and often by a self-imposed social isolation. Currently available drug treatments for AIDS may themselves cause psychological symptoms including listlessness, depression, and anxiety.

In summarizing psychosocial considerations in serving persons with AIDS or at risk for AIDS, the staff at the National Institute of Mental Health has suggested that health care professionals should (1) be alert to the possibility of motor, behavioral, and cognitive changes that might indicate the involvement of the central nervous system in the disease; (2) focus on the need that patients have for strong social support networks; (3) be responsive to the varying and ever-changing psychological reactions to the disorder; and (4) be aware of their own anxieties and fears in working with fatally ill persons who suffer from a stigmatizing and contagious disorder, and seek consultation from mental health professionals on behalf of their patients or themselves (U. S. Department of Health and Human Services, 1986a).

### The Nervous System

The nervous system is the control center and communication network of the body. In conjunction with the endocrine system, the nervous system regulates all bodily movements, maintains homeostasis, and allows us to be what we think of as uniquely human. It is because of our complex and highly developed nervous system that we can think, evaluate, plan, remember, and behave on the basis of our past, present, and hoped-for future. The overall nervous system includes the sense organs, the central nervous system, and the peripheral nervous system. The central nervous system includes the brain and spinal cord. The peripheral nervous system includes the linking pathways between the central nervous system and the sense organs, muscles, and glands (see Figure 1–8).

The brain consists of four principal parts: the brain stem, the diencephalon, the cerebellum, and the cerebrum. The lower end of the brain stem is anatomically a continuation of the spinal cord. Above the brain stem is the diencephalon. Behind the diencephalon is the cerebellum, and completely surrounding the cerebellum and diencephalon is the cerebrum. The cerebrum makes up nearly 90 percent of the total weight of the brain and occupies most of the skull.

All of the ascending and descending nerve tracts that connect the brain with the spinal cord pass through the brain stem. Two principal organs comprise the diencephalon: the thalamus and the hypothalamus. These organs serve as relay stations for sensory impulses. Conscious recognition of pain and temperature, and, to a certain extent, touch and pressure take place in the thalamus. The hypothalamus is partly responsible for the maintenance of homeostasis, as well as for the awareness of smell, sound, taste, and inner bodily sensations. Groups of cells in the hypothalamus regulate heart rate, movement of food through the digestive tract, and contraction of the urinary bladder. As was already mentioned, the hypothalamus serves as the functional junction of the nervous and endocrine systems. Furthermore, the hypothalamus is responsible for such relatively primitive emotions as rage and aggression, and plays a role in the sensations of hunger and thirst, and in the maintenance of body temperature. In the cerebellum are found nerve cells that help coordinate posture and balance, and maintain normal muscle tone.

The most highly developed part of the brain, and the part that distinguishes human beings from lower animals, is the cerebrum. The surface of the cerebrum is composed of billions of cells that form a thin highly convoluted gray layer called the cerebral cortex. Beneath that gray layer lies the white

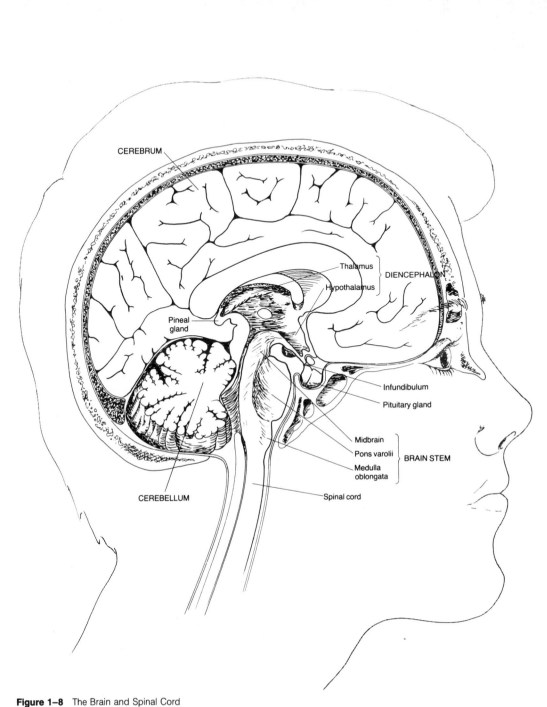

**Figure 1–8**  The Brain and Spinal Cord

From *Principles of Human Physiology* by Gerard J. Tortora, Ronald L. Evans, and Nicholas P. Anagnostakos. © 1982. Reprinted by permission of Harper & Row, Publishers, Inc.

matter—nerve fibers that connect cerebral areas with each other and with the cerebellum and other parts of the brain and spinal cord. Particularly notable in these connective pathways is the limbic system that comprises interconnected parts of the cerebrum and diencephalon. The limbic system is concerned with developmentally primitive emotions such as fear and anger, pleasure and pain, and with certain aspects of sexual behavior, as well as wth visceral responses to emotions. In addition, there is evidence that the limbic system plays an important role in the maintenance of memory.

The cerebrum is divided into motor areas that control muscular movement throughout the body, sensory areas that interpret sensory impulses from the sense organs as well as from a variety of receptors throughout the surface and interior of the body, and association areas that are concerned with emotional and intellectual processes including memory, reasoning, will, judgment, as well as many personality traits.

The spinal cord lies inside of and is protected by the spinal column. It serves not only to convey sensory impulses to the brain and motor impulses from the brain to the peripheral parts of the body, but also provides the needed nerve connections for many bodily reflexes, such as the knee jerk or the rapid withdrawal of the hand when it touches an intolerably hot surface.

The portion of the peripheral nervous system than conveys information from the central nervous system to the muscles and glands is further subdivided into the somatic nervous system and the autonomic nervous system. The somatic nervous system conveys information to the skeletal muscles. The autonomic nervous system automatically controls the glands and the smooth muscles of the heart, the blood vessels, the lining of the stomach, and the intestines (see Figure 1–9).

The autonomic nervous system is further divided into the sympathetic and parasympathetic nervous systems. In times of stress, the sympathetic nervous system dominates bodily functioning. It speeds up the rate and strength of the heart beat. increases the blood supply, releases glucose, directs blood from the skin and internal organs to the brain and muscles, dilates the pupils of the eye, and dilates the bronchi of the lungs, to name but a few of its functions. These automatic actions prepare the body to deal with threat. The parasympathetic nervous system is dominant during periods of relaxation and recuperation, and it functions to maintain the body in a condition of rest.

Nerve impulses are relayed within the automatic nervous system with the help of chemicals called neurotransmitters that are produced within the body and that facilitate the crossing of the junctions (usually called synapses) where nerves come together. The two most important neurotransmitters in the movement of nerve impulses through the autonomic nervous system are acetylcholine and norepinephrine. Other naturally occurring neurotransmitters that are being studied include serotonin, dopamine, gamma-aminobutyric acid, and glutamate. All of these substances, found in varying concentrations in different parts of the central nervous system, are believed to play important roles in the

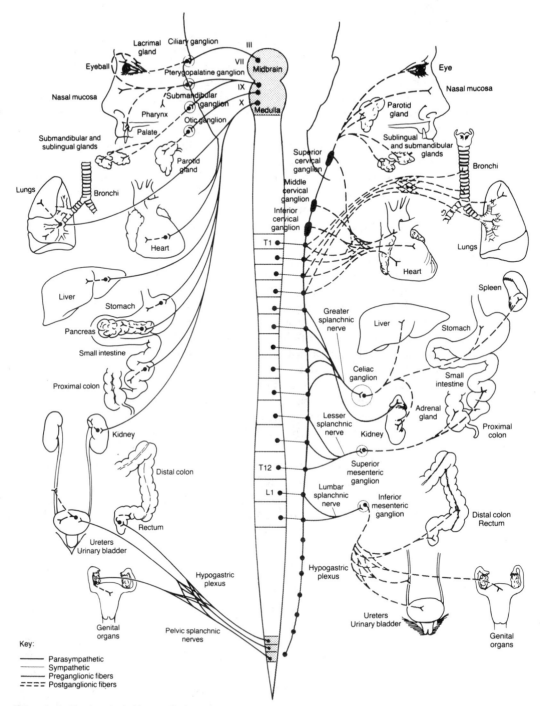

**Figure 1–9** The Autonomic Nervous System

From *Principles of Human Physiology* by Gerard J. Tortora, Ronald L. Evans, and Nicholas P. Anagnostakos. © 1982. Reprinted by permission of Harper & Row, Publishers, Inc.

transmission of impulses from one part of the nervous system to another. The effect of neurotransmitters is very short-lived; the effect can be minimized or even blocked by a variety of chemicals, such as monoamine oxidase, that are produced and stored throughout the body, and by a variety of drugs. We will return to the study of the autonomic nervous system in Chapter 3 when the physiology of stress will be examined.

DISORDERS OF THE NERVOUS SYSTEM.   With the complexity of the central and peripheral nervous systems, it should not be surprising that a great variety of abnormalities can occur. Within the spinal cord the most common problems are due to spinal cord injury; neuritis, a painful chronic inflammation of nervous tissue; and sciatica, a particular type of neuritis that affects the sciatic nerve and its branches in the thighs and legs.

Primarily within the brain itself, common disorders include syphilis, a sexually transmitted infectious disease that can attack most portions of the brain; cerebral palsy, an irreversible motor disorder that generally originates prior to birth and affects the control of the extremities, facial muscles, and the speech centers; Parkinson's disease, a progressive disorder associated with aging of nerve cells that manifests itself in hand tremors, stiffness and slowing of arm and leg movement, and increasing difficulty with speech; multiple sclerosis, due to the deterioration of the protective sheath around nerves in the central nervous system resulting in the progressive loss of bodily functions, becoming finally so severe that the patient is bedridden; epilepsy, uncontrolled nervous discharge that can result in periodic seizures and loss of consciousness; and cerebrovascular accidents, due to the destruction of vital nerve tissue as a consequence of hemorrhaging of blood vessels in the brain.

## CONCLUDING COMMENTS

Formal interest in the newly emerging field of health psychology on the part of the American Psychological Association dates from the report on the role of psychology in the delivery of health services prepared by Schofield (1969). In 1973, the American Psychological Association established a Task Force on Health Research (American Psychological Association, 1976).

In the ensuing decade, psychologists have joined the ranks of sociologists (Enos & Sultan, 1977; Freidson, 1970; Hart, 1985; Petersdorf & Feinstein, 1981; Ruderman, 1981), economists, and anthropologists in developing greatly increased interest and involvement in the study of health and illness from the special vantage point of the social scientist. The Yale Conference on Behavioral Medicine, cohosted by Yale University and the National Heart, Lung and Blood Institute was held in early 1977 and brought together the perspectives of physicians, epidemiologists, sociologists, and psychologists in a collaborative dialogue (Gentry, 1984, pp. ix–x; Schwartz & Weiss, 1978a). The following year saw the establishment of a research and training grant program in behavioral medicine within the National Institutes of Health.

Psychologists have contributed to the scientific understanding of how illness develops and is maintained, how the health care delivery system helps and hinders the recovery process, and how health can be enhanced and illness prevented. In addition, psychologists have begun to make their own special contributions to the treatment of patients with physical illnesses and to the maintenance of wellness in the general population. Psychologists are now employed in large numbers in medical schools, schools of public health, and in a variety of health service and health planning agencies, and graduate programs that prepare psychologists for careers in health psychology are being established throughout the United States (Gentry, Street, Masur, & Asken, 1981; Matthews & Avis, 1982; Olbrisch, Weiss, Stone, & Schwartz, 1985; Silverman, 1980; Thompson & Matarazzo, 1984).

As indications of the magnitude of this level of activity on the part of social scientists, in 1979 the *Journal of Social Issues* devoted an entire issue to the topic of interpersonal relations and health care (DiMatteo & Friedman, 1979). In 1982, the *Journal of Consulting and Clinical Psychology* devoted an entire issue to the field of behavioral medicine (Garfield, 1982). The field of health psychology is now regularly reviewed in the *Annual Review of Psychology* (Krantz, Grunberg, & Baum, 1985; Miller, 1983). The Division of Health Psychology of the American Psychological Association (APA) was founded in 1979, and now has about 3000 members.

A major conference on education and training in health psychology was held in 1983 sponsored by that APA division (Stone, 1983). Recommendations of this working conference will likely serve as the principal guidelines for the development of the field of health psychology in the next decade or two. Health psychology is thought of as having two overlapping training options—one concentrating on preparing the student for a role in health psychology research, and the other in health psychology practice. As was the case when the field of clinical psychology was professionalized 40 years earlier, practitioners are expected to have a strong background in scientific psychology. Thus, training of health psychologists in both research and practice needs to (1) include experience and course content stressing the role of diverse demographic characteristics, such as cultural, ethnic, gender, life style, and age in determining health-related behavior of both clients and health care providers; (2) provide an integrated mixture of theory, practice, and research; (3) place a strong emphasis on research methodology; (4) provide instruction and training in the formulation of health care policy, ethical issues, assessment, and intervention; and (5) stress interdisciplinary collaboration.

In addition, students interested in the practice of health psychology should serve an internship of at least one year in duration. Undergraduates who are interested in exploring a career in health psychology would be well advised to examine the report of this conference.

The past several years have witnessed the publication of a surprisingly large number of edited volumes that have served to review various components of the field of health psychology, the first undergraduate textbooks in the field of health psychology (Gatchel & Baum, 1983; Taylor, 1986), and the establishment of a number of new professional journals devoted to some aspect of health psychology. Among these journals (with first year of publication in parentheses) are the *Journal of Human Stress* (1975), *Journal of Community Health* (1975), *American Journal of Health Planning* (1976), *Journal of Pediatric Psychology* (1976), *Journal of Behavioral Medicine* (1978), *Family and Community Health* (1978), *Journal of Sport Psychology* (1979), *General Hospital Psychiatry* (1979), *Journal of Public Health Policy* (1980), *Journal of Preventive Psychiatry* (1981), *Health Psychology* (1982), and the *Journal of Psychosocial Oncology* (1983).

### Organization of This Book

The fundamental purpose of this book is to explore the major avenues opened by social scientists, primarily psychologists, who have made significant contributions to the field of health psychology.

This volume is divided into thirteen chapters. As part of the overview of health psychology, following this introductory chapter, a second chapter is devoted to a statistical and social policy examination of health and illness in the United States.

In Chapter 3 through 6 of the book we will examine the body of research and theorizing that has sought answers to the complex question, How do psychosocial factors play a role in keeping people healthy and in predisposing them to illness? That is, what part do psychosocial factors play in making certain people unusually vulnerable to illness; in precipitating illness in people who are vulnerable; and in perpetuating illness in people already ill? In particular, we will look at the role of stress in inducing illness (Chapter 3), consumer health education as a major strategy for preventing illness and helping to create informed users of health services (Chapter 4), and lifestyle risk factors that increase our vulnerabilities to illness (Chapters 5 and 6).

In Chapters 7 through 11, we will examine four important topics related to psychosocial aspects of illness. We will study how people become ill—from a psychosocial point of view—and how the medical care system can induce stress that may further complicate their illnesses (Chapter 7), and we will explore the contributions that social scientists have made to our understanding of specific symptoms and specific illnesses (Chapters 8, 9, 10, and 11). Five specific disorders will be examined—chronic pain, heart disease, hypertension, cancer, and asthma.

Finally, in Chapters 12 and 13, attention will be devoted to an examination of two important aspects of health service delivery—the problems of adherence to medical treatment programs (Chapter 12) and to a psychological portrait of physicians and nurses, the two groups of health service providers most directly concerned with patient care (Chapter 13).

## SUMMARY

- The field of health psychology can be defined as the scientific study of behavior, thoughts, attitudes, and beliefs related to health and illness.
- In any field, scientific study requires the use of methods of data collection and analysis that permit hypotheses to be supported or refuted and that provide satisfactory answers to two fundamental questions (1) What do you mean? and (2) How do you know?
- The basic scientific approach to the study of health and illness is encompassed within the field of epidemiology, the general approach to the study of disease distribution and to the identification of causative factors in the development of disease.
- Three general approaches are invoked in the study of health- and illness-related behavior. One approach views such behavior as being like any other habit that is learned, and, at least theoretically, that a behavior can be unlearned. A second approach views these behaviors as the result of an often complex cognitive process. A third approach views them as the reflection of underlying personality characteristics or of unresolved emotional issues.
- The earliest theory of health and illness was fundamentally environmental in nature. It postulated that disease was caused by poisonous substances (miasmas) that came from the earth and were spread by the wind.
- Miasma theory led to practices that attempted to prevent disease by providing healthful environments.
- Germ theory, which gradually replaced miasma theory in the nineteenth century, was appealing because it was more in tune with the emerging field of medicine, in that it was disease-specific and biological in nature. Germ theory led to efforts to change the body rather than the environment.
- With the subsequent biologizing of medicine, professional concern turned to treatment and away from preventive intervention.
- Current theories of health and illness are multidimensional and stress the interaction of biological, psychological, and sociological factors in health maintenance and disease development.
- The contemporary biopsychosocial view of health and illness focuses on preventive intervention as much as on treatment.
- The field of health psychology has emerged out of the growing understanding of the interdependence of biological and psychological functioning, and the realization that the fundamental beliefs and practices of clinical and community psychologists are directly pertinent to general health and illness.
- Special subfields of health psychology are being created that focus on behavior modification as a technique for improving health and treating illness, on the development of psychological explanations of medical phenomena, and on improving the health care delivery system by analyzing and modifying its psychological properties.
- All illnesses are psychosomatic, in that psychosocial and biomedical factors are invariably involved to some degree in their predisposition, precipitation, or perpetuation.

- Physical and mental health are powerfully interdependent, and each influences the other.
- A useful framework for viewing health and illness is the health field, and its four components—human biology, the environment, lifestyle, and the health care organization.
- Psychosocial factors play a significant role in producing much of disease mortality and morbidity that is of concern to health care providers.
- Two competing views of health exist—One that emphasizes health as a process, as the end result of living a life of reason, and the other that emphasizes health as a state, synonymous with the absence of pathology.
- Health is a complex concept, requiring complex procedures for its assessment—procedures that involve the measurement of biological health, psychological health, and social health.
- Procedures for the maintenance of health and for the treatment of disease have political and value components about which there may be considerable controversy.
- Health cannot be understood without being familiar with human anatomy and physiology. Accordingly, a brief overview of the structure and functioning of the human body has been presented.

# Health and Illness in the United States

# 2

## INTRODUCTION

In this chapter, important facts about health and illness in the United States will be presented, wherever possible in a historical perspective. One set of facts is demographic in character—birth rate, life expectancy, major causes of illness and death, mortality rates, and so forth. A second set of facts is concerned with expenditures for health care—how much is being spent for health care, and where the money comes from (National Center for Health Statistics, 1985f). A third set of facts has to do with how medical care is organized and delivered. These three sets of facts are closely interrelated. Changing demographic and health characteristics of the American population have an impact on both the cost and the organization of health services, and changes in the organization of health services are coming about primarily as a way of containing costs.

# BIRTH RATE, MORTALITY RATE, AND LIFE EXPECTANCY

At the start of the twentieth century, the total population of the United States was about 75 million. That number has increased by between 0.5 percent and 2 percent every year ever since. It reached 100 million in about 1920 and 200 million in 1968. The total population in 1984 was about 236 million. As of the year 2000, it has been estimated that the total United States population will be about 268 million people (National Center for Health Statistics, 1984a).

The population of the United States is increasing partly as a consequence of immigration, but mainly because there are more births than deaths. During 1984, for example, there were about 3,700,000 live births and 2 million deaths. Thus, an estimated 1,700,000 persons were added to the population, representing a 0.7 percent increase in population over the previous year (National Center for Health Statistics, 1985b).

### Birth Rate

Rates of birth are calculated in two different ways according to the denominator that is used. In both cases, the numerator is the number of live births. In the case of what is officially called the *birth rate*, the denominator is the total population. In 1984, for example, the birth rate was 15.5 births per 1000 population (National Center for Health Statistics, 1986c). The second measure of birth rate is the *fertility rate*. defined as the number of live births divided by the number of women in the population of child-bearing age, usually considered as between 15 and 44. In 1984, the fertility rate in the United States was 65 births per 1000 women of child-bearing age. Provisional data for 1985 suggest that both birth rate and fertility rate increased by 1 or 2 percent over the 1984 figures.

In 1930, there were about 88 births per 1000 women of child-bearing age. The fertility rate dropped to between 77 and 80 in the period from 1932 to 1940, then climbed irregularly to a high of 122 in the late 1950s, the midpoint of the post–World War II era of the so-called baby-boomers, and then began a fairly steady drop to its present low (U. S. Department of Health, Education, and Welfare, 1978; National Center for Health Statistics, 1986c). Thus, the current fertility rate is only half of what it was 30 years ago, and lower than it has been in more than 50 years.

A number of different factors appear to account for the variation in birth rate over time. Economic considerations undoubtedly played a role in the drop in birth rate during the Depression in the 1930s, and the current drop in birth rate is due, in part, to the delays in marriage among young people who are interested in achieving a higher level of education, as well as in having smaller families.

Birth rate is generally higher among nonwhite women than white women (U. S. Department of Health and Human Services, 1980a). As a result, while in 1950 nonwhites constituted 10.7 percent of the population, by the year 2050, it is estimated that 23 percent of the United States population will be nonwhite (U. S. Bureau of the Census, 1984a).

In 1984, more than one out of every five births was to an unmarried mother. The rate of unmarried births is higher among black women than among white women, but the differential has been declining in recent years, as the rate has been increasing among white women and decreasing among black women. Particularly interesting in these births to unmarried women is that the age of the mothers is increasing. While most unmarried women who gave birth to children used to be under the age of 20, today 65 percent of such births occur to women who are no longer teenagers. This phenomenon is associated with the increase in the number of unmarried women in the population, due largely to the growing tendency to delay marriage and to the increasing number of divorces (National Center for Health Statistics, 1986c).

### Mortality Rate

Mortality rates have decreased slowly but consistently during the twentieth century from a high of about 18 deaths per 1000 population in 1900, to 11 in 1930, to 5.5 as of 1983 (National Center for Health Statistics, 1984a, 1985g; U. S. Department of Health and Human Services, 1985b). Mortality rates are consistently higher for men than for women, regardless of year of data collection, or race, or age. Within most age groups, mortality rates are higher for blacks than for whites.

### Life Expectancy

Paralleling the decline in mortality rates has been an increase in life expectancy. *Life expectancy* refers to anticipated remaining length of life, and it can be calculated as of any age. Life expectancy at birth is defined as the average number of years that a group of infants would be expected to live, if, throughout their life, they were to experience the age-specific death rates prevailing during the year of their birth (National Center for Health Statistics, 1985b). Statistical reports from the U. S. Department of Health and Human Services (see, for example, 1980b) provide information as to average remaining lifetime at any specified age, and report this information separately for men and women within white and nonwhite populations. Life expectancy at age 65 is similarly defined as the average number of additional years that a group of persons aged 65 would be expected to live, if, throughout the remainder of their lives they were to experience the age-specific death rates prevailing during the year they became 65.

In Table 2–1, life expectancy at birth in the United States can been seen as a function of year of birth, gender, and race. The astonishing increase in life expectancy during the twentieth century is quite remarkable, but almost as remarkable is the constant superiority of life expectancy of women as contrasted with men and of whites as contrasted with nonwhites.

**Table 2–1** Life Expectancy at Birth by Gender and
Race: Total United States, 1900, 1950, and 1984

|  | YEAR | | |
| --- | --- | --- | --- |
|  | 1900 | 1950 | 1984 |
| Total Population | 47.3 | 68.2 | 74.7 |
| Gender |  |  |  |
| Male | 46.3 | 65.6 | 71.2 |
| Female | 48.3 | 71.1 | 78.2 |
| Race |  |  |  |
| White | 47.6 | 69.1 | 75.3 |
| Nonwhite | 33.0 | 60.8 | 71.3 |

(*Source:* National Center for Health Statistics, 1986d.)

If we examine life expectancy at age 65, the figures indicate that in 1900 average remaining lifetime was 11.9 years. By 1950, life expectancy at age 65 had increased to 13.9 years. Currently, life expectancy at age 65 is about 17 years (National Center for Health Statistics, 1984a, 1986d). What is clear from the comparisons of changes in life expectancy at birth and at age 65 is that medical and social progress have had a far smaller impact on life expectancy at age 65 than on life expectancy at birth.

## MEASURES OF MORBIDITY

It is a relatively easy matter to gather and analyze death certificates in order to determine causes of death and to identify demographic factors that may be associated with differential mortality rates. Analysis of causes of illness, that is, morbidity, is far more complex, because no compulsory system exists for reporting illness. Yet, information regarding illness patterns is crucial for understanding the health of a community or a nation, particularly since illnesses and their consequences last far longer today than they did at the start of the twentieth century.

The federal agency responsible for collecting and analyzing information about morbidity (as well as on mortality) is the National Center for Health Statistics of the U.S. Department of Health and Human Services. Each year a systematic 10 percent sample of death certificates is sent to the National Center for Health Statistics, from which subsamples are selected for analysis.

The principal source of information on the health of the population of the United States comes from the National Health Interview Survey, authorized by the National Health Survey Act of 1956. This act provides for a continuing survey as well as special studies to secure on a voluntary and confidential basis accurate and current statistical information on the amount, distribution, and effects of illness and disability, and on the services rendered for such conditions.

Data for the National Health Interview Survey are obtained by means of household interviews that are conducted weekly throughout the year on a carefully chosen stratified random sample of households. A different sample of households is selected each week, and over the period of a year data are collected from about 40,000 households representing about 110,000 persons. Questionnaires are forwarded to the National Center for Health Statistics in Hyattsville, Maryland, for coding and data processing. Results are released in the form of printed publications and data tapes that are available for computer analysis by the public.

### Physician Visits

One of the best measures of morbidity, certainly of serious morbidity, is the use of physician services. Information collected in 1980 (National Center for Health Statistics, 1983c; 1987) indicates that about 75 percent of the total civilian, noninstitutionalized population was seen by or talked with a physician during the year prior to the week of the interview. About 20 percent of the population had five or more physician visits. In all, there were about 1 billion physician contacts during the previous year, averaging 4.8 contacts per person per year of which 2.7 were office visits. These figures have been very stable over time. Perhaps the only significant change in the nature of these visits is that there has been a decrease in the number of visits to general practitioners from 62.9 percent of all visits in 1967 to 47.4 percent in 1980, and a corresponding increase in the number of visits to specialists, particularly internists and obstetricians and gynecologists. A higher proportion of females than males saw a physician within the previous year (79.5 percent vs. 69.9 percent). A greater proportion of children under the age of 5 visited physicians than any other age group, and physician visits were more frequent among better-educated persons.

### Hospitalization

While about 35 million people were hospitalized in 1985, the number of patients admitted to general hospitals has dropped quite dramatically since 1980, as has the average length of hospitalization. Between 1983 and 1985 there was an 11 percent decrease in the number of hospital discharges—from more than 38 million in 1983. At the same time the average duration of hospitalization has dropped from 6.9 days to 6.5 days, a decrease of nearly 6 percent (National Center for Health Statistics, 1985d, 1986e). Almost regardless of diagnosis, length of stay has shown a steady decrease in the past two decades. In addition, many procedures formerly performed in hospitals are now performed in outpatient facilities.

Just as in the case of physician visits, women were hospitalized far more commonly than men (193 versus 139 discharges per 1000 population per year). In part, of course, the greater use of hospital facilities by women is accounted for by childbirth—an event that accounts for about 10 percent of all discharges of women from hospitals (National Center for Health Statistics, 1984a).

*Injuries*

According to the most recent report of the National Center for Health Statistics on the topic of injuries, covering the 2-year period 1980–1981 (National Center for Health Statistics, 1985c), about one in every three persons in the United States (69.2 million persons per year) sustained injuries requiring medical attention or causing restriction of activity for 2 days or more. Between 1970 and 1981, the rate of injury increased by 11 percent.

More injuries occurred around the home than in any other place (38 percent of all injuries). Injury rates were higher among males than females (37.0 versus 25.9 per 100 persons per year); highest among persons aged 17 to 24 regardless of gender (41.7 per 100 persons per year); and higher among never married, divorced, and separated persons than among the married and widowed (36.0 versus 26.3 per 100 persons per year). About 80 percent of injured persons received medical attention, requiring more than 100 million visits to physicians each year, and injuries resulted in an average of 3.6 restricted activity days per injured person.

In an interesting study examining one significant cause of injury, Baker, Moore, and Wise (1986) evaluated the effect of the enactment of the "bottle bill" legislation on injuries caused by glass-related lacerations that occurred outside the home. They conducted the study in Massachusetts, where, in 1983, a bill was enacted requiring mandatory monetary deposits on beverage containers. The bill was expected to have a significant environmental impact, but Baker and associates were interested in determining whether it might also result in a reduction in glass-related injuries. They contrasted emergency room visits for lacerations and fractures at the Children's Hospital in Boston for a 2-year time period immediately prior to the enactment of the legislation with the 1-year period immediately after the enactment of the legislation; they found a 60 percent drop in emergency room visits for bottle-related lacerations occurring outside of the home. Their conclusion that the legislation played a significant role in reducing these injuries was strengthened by their observation that during the same time period there was no reduction in the total number of non-glass-related injuries or of glass-related injuries occurring inside the home.

# CAUSES OF DEATH

At the start of the twentieth century, the leading causes of death in the United States were infectious diseases to which young children were unusually vulnerable—influenza, pneumonia, tuberculosis, and diarrhea and related disorders. Since then, the annual mortality rate from these diseases combined has dropped from 521 per 100,000 to 21 per 100,000 (National Center for Health Statistics, 1983a, 1984a).

The pattern of mortality in the United States is dramatically different today from what it was at the start of the century. The major sources of mortality and morbidity are now to be found in the chronic diseases, and in the residuals of injuries and accidents. As of 1982, the four major causes of death in the United States were heart disease, cancer, accidents, and cerebrovascular diseases. These illnesses and accidents accounted for three of every four deaths.

Of these four causes of death, those attributed to heart diseases have shown a remarkable 40 percent decrease in the past 25 years. As a consequence, it now appears that cancer will shortly become the leading cause of death among adults (Levy & Moskowitz, 1982).

Examination of the changes in mortality rates and causes of death since the turn of the century reveals several important trends. As infectious diseases were conquered, death rate among children began to decrease, life expectancy began to increase, and with that increase came an increase in the number and proportion of older Americans along with an increase in the number and proportion of diseases of adults and the elderly.

The extent of these demographic changes can be seen in comparing the age distribution of the United States population in 1900 and 1980. In 1900, 54 percent of the total population was below age 25. In 1980, 41 percent of the total population was below age 25. At the older end of the age spectrum, the proportion of the population has increased since 1900. In 1900, 9.4 percent of the population was 55 years old or older. In 1980, 20.9 percent of the population was 55 years old or older (U.S. Bureau of the Census, 1975; 1983).

Behavioral factors, such as smoking, dietary preferences, and alcohol abuse play an increasingly significant role in today's deaths. It is now estimated that half of the mortality from the ten leading causes of death in the United States can be traced to lifestyles (see Chapters 5 and 6) (U.S. Public Health Service, 1980).

With the increasing evidence that many different diseases may be due to similar self-destructive lifestyles, there is a growing interest on the part of health service providers in creating a late-twentieth-century version of miasma theory. Such a version would search for preventive and therapeutic strategies that appear to be effective across a broad array of disorders. It is exactly in this context that the growing interest in psychological and sociocultural aspects of health and illness can be understood.

## SELF-ASSESSMENTS OF HEALTH

Since 1972, the National Health Interview Survey has included one question that asks the respondent to assess his or her health (or that of family members) in comparison with others of his or her age as excellent, good, fair, or poor. Initially the National Center for Health Statistics had relatively little confidence in this one-item self-report measure, but recent evidence has suggested that the self-assessment is highly correlated with actual health status and with utilization of health care services. In recent years, more confidence has been placed in this self-assessment measure, as a kind of summary statistic, and the first detailed report regarding this self-assessment appeared in 1983 (National Center for Health Statistics, 1983b, 1984a).

As a summary statistic, self-assessments of health can serve three useful purposes: (1) to determine how health care utilization patterns differ among people who differ in self-assessments of health; (2) to determine whether certain subgroups of the population differ in self-assessed health status; and (3) to serve as a control variable when subgroups who differ in their overall health status are compared. An example of the use of self-assessed health status as a control variable would be to contrast life expectancy of persons with a particular disease who consider themselves in poor health with persons with the same disease who consider themselves in good health.

As of 1978, 12.4 percent of the almost 110,000 persons sampled reported that they were not in good health, that is, that their health was fair or poor. The proportion of people reporting being in fair or poor health was significantly greater among persons with lower education and income. Thus, among persons age 17 and over, 35.8 percent with less than a high school education reported being in fair or poor health. In contrast, among college graduates, 5.9 percent reported being in fair or poor health. In the case of income, the same general findings were obtained—of course, education and income are significantly correlated. Among persons with family incomes below $5,000 per year, 31.6 percent reported being in fair or poor health. Among persons with family incomes between $10,000 and $15,000 per year, 12.6 percent reported being in fair or poor health, and among persons with family incomes in excess of $25,000, the proportion reporting being in fair or poor health decreased to 6.8 percent.

Blacks generally report poorer health status than whites (18.9 percent versus 11.5 percent), and this difference occurs within every age group. As for marital status, widows report being in poorest health. But since marital status and age are correlated, with widows being significantly older than any other marital status group, analyses of health and marital status need to be examined in specific age categories. When this is done, widowed, divorced, and separated persons fairly consistently report being in poorer health than do married and never-married persons of the same age. Finally, as for employment status, persons who are employed tend to report better health than persons who are not employed, a finding that is, as you will see, very pertinent to the development of health insurance programs.

## HEALTH STATUS OF CHILDREN

The health of children in the United States has improved dramatically in recent decades. The death rate among fetuses of 20 weeks or more gestation and among newborn infants less than 28 days old, has decreased from 39.7 per 1000 live births in 1950 to 17.0 per 1000 live births in 1981 (National Center for Health Statistics, 1986a). Mortality rate has declined among children age 1 to 4

**Table 2–2**   Infant Mortality Rates—Total, United States

| | YEAR | | | | |
| --- | --- | --- | --- | --- | --- |
| | 1935 | 1950 | 1970 | 1976 | 1982 |
| Fetal Mortality Rate[1] | na[4] | 19.2 | 14.2 | 10.5 | 8.9 |
| Neonatal Mortality Rate[2] | na | 20.5 | 15.1 | 10.9 | 7.3 |
| Infant Mortality Rate[2] | 55.7 | 29.2 | 20.0 | 15.2 | 11.5 |
| Maternal Mortality Rate[3] | 582 | 83.3 | 21.5 | 12.3 | 7.9 |

[1]Per 1000 births.
[2]Per 1000 live births.
[3]Per 100,000 births.
[4]Not available
(*Sources:* National Center for Health Statistics, 1984a; U.S. Bureau of the Census, 1986.)

from 5.6 per 1000 in 1930 to 0.7 per 1000 in 1978. Infectious diseases such as diphtheria, polio, and pneumonia that used to be the major causes of death and disability have largely disappeared. Even in the 5 to 14 year range, where mortality rate has always been lowest, that rate has dropped from 1.0 per 1000 per year in 1940 to 0.3 per 1000 per year in 1978. The dramatic decreases in all of these measures of infant mortality can be seen in Table 2–2.

### Measures of Childhood Mortality

In assessing deaths among infants and children, four different mortality rates are traditionally calculated, depending, in part, on the age of the infant or child at the time of death. Fetal deaths refer to babies that are born dead, and are usually reported as the *fetal mortality rate*, that is, as the proportion of total births. Biostatisticians believe that many fetal deaths are not reported, and accordingly, that fetal mortality rates are considerably understated (Kleinman, 1986).

The second measure is *neonatal mortality rate*—deaths to babies born alive that occur under 28 days of age, expressed in relation to live births. The third measure calculated is *infant mortality rate*—deaths to babies born alive that occur under 1 year of age, again expressed in relation to live births.

The fourth measure of deaths associated with childbirth is *maternal mortality rate*, that is, deaths to mothers arising from complications of pregnancy, childbirth, or the period immediately after childbirth. This measure is typically reported as a rate per 100,000 live births. Just as in the case of fetal mortality rate, there is some evidence that maternal mortality rate is underreported. Of all these measures, the most commonly analyzed is the infant mortality rate.

While infant mortality rate is very low in the United States, being 11.5 deaths per 1000 live births as of 1982, international comparisons indicate that fourteen countries have even lower rates. Among these countries—along with their infant mortality rates as of 1981—include Sweden (7.0), Japan (7.1), Finland (7.6), Norway (8.1), Netherlands (8.2), Denmark (8.4), Switzerland (8.5), and France (9.6).

Brandt (1984) has recently reviewed the progress that has been made in reducing infant mortality and the problems that still remain. Certain babies are at especially high risk of not surviving. Included in this group in Brandt's review were the babies born to adolescents under 18 years of age, including nearly 10,000 babies born to girls under age 15; babies who weighed less than 2,500 grams (5 pounds 8 ounces) at birth; and infants born to women who smoked or drank alcoholic beverages during their pregnancy.

Brandt, who was Assistant Secretary for Health in the U.S. Department of Health and Human Services at the time he reviewed infant mortality, noted that infant mortality rates are still nearly twice as high for black infants as for whites. Low birth weight, the most important risk factor associated with infant mortality, is thought to be due to a combination of many maternal factors, including medical and obstetric history, physical stature, smoking and alcohol use, anemia, hypertension, and poor nutrition. Among black mothers, many births are to teenagers, many mothers have multiple and out-of-wedlock births, and, in addition, this group is frequently poor in both socioeconomic and nutritional status. These factors, which help explain why infant mortality rate is higher among black than among white mothers, are another example of the crucial role of psychosocial factors in determining health levels.

### Infant Mortality

In discussing the causes of death among children, it has been found useful to distinguish among three different categories: (1) infant deaths, that is, among children less than one year old; (2) childhood deaths, that is, among children between the ages of 1 and 14; and (3) adolescent and young adult deaths, that is, among people aged 15 to 24. Among children and young adults, mortality rates and causes of mortality vary by age. In 1982, mortality rate among infants was 1152 per 100,000 live births. Among children aged 1 to 14, the mortality rate was 36.7 per 100,000 population, and among adolescents and young adults age 15 to 24, it was 101 per 100,000 population.

Among infants, the three leading causes of death are congenital anomalies (245.2 per 100,000), sudden infant death syndrome (SIDS) (143.4 per 100,000), and respiratory distress syndrome (109.7 per 100,000) (U.S. Department of Health and Human Services, 1985b). Congenital anomalies are anatomical defects—such as microcephalus, spina bifida, or hydrocephalus—attributed to developmental or genetic problems rather than to injuries in utero or during birth; they comprised more than 20 percent of all infant deaths in 1982. In all three cases, the death rate has decreased over time.

### Childhood Mortality

Death rate among children aged 1 to 14 has decreased from 88 per 100,000 population in 1950 to 37 per 100,000 in 1982. The three leading causes of childhood deaths are accidents, cancer, and congenital anomalies (Baker, 1981). In 1950, pneumonia and influenza were ranked as the second leading cause of death. Today, these diseases are no longer among the top five causes—mainly as a consequence of improvements in access to health care, in living conditions for low-income and minority groups, in medical treatment, and in immunization rates (U.S. Department of Health and Human Services, 1985b). Deaths from childhood cancer have been reduced by nearly 50 percent from 1950 to 1982, mainly as a consequence of improvements in treatment.

Accidents are now the leading cause of death among children, accounting for 42 percent of deaths between ages 1 to 4 and 51 percent of deaths between ages 5 to 14. Of these deaths in the age group 5 to 14, about half are due to motor vehicle accidents. At every age, death rates for boys exceed those for girls. Boys under the age of 6 are 40 percent more likely to die of poisoning, accidents, or violence than girls of the same age. Mortality rates are higher for black children than for white children, and higher for the poor than for the affluent. Most of these excess deaths are due to accidents. Of all major diseases, cancer, particularly acute lymphatic leukemia, results in more deaths than any other cause, even though the probability for survival has improved greatly in the past decades.

### Adolescent and Young Adult Mortality

The overall mortality rate among adolscents and young adults (ages 15 to 24) has declined about 20 percent since 1950. Most common causes of death are accidents, homicide, suicide (particularly by firearms—see Boyd & Moscicki, 1986), cancer, and heart disease, with accidental deaths accounting for about half of all deaths, and motor vehicle accidents accounting for more than 70 percent of all accidental deaths. Young men ages 16 to 17 are twice as likely to die from accidents and violence than young women of the same age.

Of all the causes of death among young people, none is currently of greater concern than deaths from homicide, particularly among black males, where it is the leading cause of death and six times more common than among white males (Homicide Among Young Black Males, 1985). In the case of females, the death rate figures are all lower, but the same differences as a function of race are found.

Among black males in the 15 to 24 year age group, the death rate from homicide amounts to about 70 per year per 100,000 population. More than 70 percent of the deaths are caused by guns, and of these deaths, about three-quarters are due to handguns. Most homicide victims, including black males, are killed during arguments with acquaintances rather than by strangers or by family members.

Lifestyle factors play a particularly important role in the health of adolescents. Included in this category are those risk-taking behaviors that are so often the cause of motor vehicle accidents, and risk-taking sexual behaviors that can result in the development of sexually transmitted diseases as well as unwanted pregnancies. Smoking and drinking are associated with shortened life expectancy. Alcohol often plays a role in motor vehicle accidents. Crime and violence can result in injury or death. Finally, failure to seek medical care when indicated can obviously result in increased risk of significant illness or in unnecessary death.

## HEALTH AND FAMILY INCOME

As has already been noted, persons in families with incomes of less than $5000 a year are four times as likely to be assessed in fair or poor health as are persons in families with incomes of $25,000 or more. Insofar as measures of morbidity or mortality are concerned, either among children or adults, there are strong associations with income (Andersen, Giachello, & Aday, 1986; Markides & Coreil, 1986). In 1976, for example, while about 2 percent of children in families with annual incomes of $15,000 or more were in fair or poor health, among families with annual incomes of less than $5,000, 9 percent of children were judged to be in fair or poor health.

The relationship of socioeconomic status and health services is also true in the case of dental care (Reisine, 1985). Persons in families with $25,000 or more in annual income have almost twice as mnay dental visits per person per year as do persons in families earning less than $5000 per year.

Starfield (1982) recently reviewed the evidence linking poverty and illness among children. The relationships seem very powerful indeed. Family income is more strongly related to health status than any other sociodemographic characteristic. In comparison with children from more affluent families, poor children are 75 percent more likely to be admitted to a hospital, 40 percent more likely to miss school because of illness, more likely to have reported chronic health problems, and to have these problems interfere with their school work. Illness, when it does occur, is also more severe among poor children than among the nonpoor (also see Brown, 1983; Bumpers, 1984; Hart, 1985; National Center for Health Statistics, 1985e; Somers, 1984).

According to these studies, mortality rates are higher for poor children than for nonpoor children in every age group. When children are hospitalized, length of stay is twice as long for poor children as for the nonpoor. Poor children not only have more medical illnesses, they also suffer more severe consequences from those illnesses. Finally, children from poor families appear to receive generally poorer medical care than children from more affluent families. These differences in health status of children, a function of socioeconomic affluence, are cumulative and compound the difficulties these children have when they become adults.

## EXPENDITURES FOR HEALTH CARE

The growing cost of medical care in the United States has been front-page news for the past decade. Between 1965 and 1983, health care expenditures increased an average of 12.8 percent every year—a rate increase that far exceeds the annual inflation rate. Part of the reason for the growing cost of medical care can be found in physicians' income. Average annual net income of physicians doubled from $48,600 in 1973 to $99,500 in 1982 (Reynolds & Abram, 1983). Information regarding the increase in health care expenditures can be seen in Table 2–3.

Starting in 1929, it took about 20 years for per capita health expenditures to double. The next doubling took only 10 years, and since then, health expenditures have doubled every 6 years. The Center for Health Policy Studies at Georgetown University in Washington, D.C., forecasts that total health expenditures will rise at an annual rate of between 10 and 11 percent and will reach $1.9 trillion (13.8 percent of the gross national product) by the year 2000 (Tyson & Merrill, 1984).

Expenditures for health are divided into two categories—(1) health services and supplies, and (2) research and construction. The first category accounts for nearly 96 percent of all health expenditures. Personal health care accounts for 92 percent of the health services and supplies category, and thus, 88 percent of all health expenditures (National Center for Health Statistics, 1984a).

Insofar as the source of funds for total health expenditures, the share that comes from public tax revenues—that is, from money paid in taxes to local, state, or federal government—has steadily increased from 13.6 percent in 1929 to 42 percent in 1983. Of the total of $313.3 billion expended just for personal health care in 1983, 40 percent came from public tax revenues, three-quarters of which came from the federal government and one-quarter from state and local governments.

Private health insurance has paid an increasing proportion of the personal health care bill since its inauguration after World War II, although it is far lower than most people imagine. In 1950, private health insurance paid 9.1 percent of personal health care costs. By 1960, the proportion had increased to 21.1 percent; by 1975, to 26.7 percent; and by 1983, to 32 percent. The remainder of the health bill is paid by patients themselves through direct payments, or what are often called out-of-pocket expenditures. That is, about 40

**Table 2–3**   Health Care Expenditures: Total, United States

| TYPE OF EXPENDITURE | YEAR | | | |
| --- | --- | --- | --- | --- |
| | 1929 | 1955 | 1978 | 1983 |
| Total Health Care Expenditures (in Billions of Dollars) | $3.6 | $17.7 | $188.6 | $355.4 |
| Per Capita Health Care Expenditures (in Dollars per Year) | $2 | $10 | $822 | $1459 |
| Health Care Expenditures as a Proportion of Gross National Product | 3.5% | 4.4% | 8.8% | 10.8% |

(*Sources:* Gibson, Levit, Lazenby, & Waldo, 1984; National Center for Health Statistics, 1984a.)

percent of the personal health care bill is currently being paid out of public tax revenues, about 32 percent by prepaid health insurance, and about 28 percent by the patients themselves in the form of direct payments.

Much of the cost of private insurance comes from employers who either share with their employees the cost of health insurance premiums or who pay the entire health insurance premium as part of a negotiated labor-management contract. Of the more than $300 billion that was spent on health care in 1982, corporations paid more than $77 billion. An astonishing illustration of the costs of health care can be found in a recent report that indicated that expenses paid by the Chrysler Corporation in 1982 for health care for its employees added more than $500 to the price of each vehicle they manufactured (Rosen, 1984).

Unless a person has recently been directly involved in paying medical bills, it is hard to conceive of the costs involved in obtaining medical care. As medical knowledge and technology improves, many people now survive who would have died earlier. But these saved lives often come at great financial cost, that often involves enormous personal anguish.

Costs associated with illness are defined as costs that would not have been incurred had the illness not existed. By this definition, costs represent far more than doctor and hospital bills. Medical costs also include, for example, illness-related out-of-pocket expenses not covered by medical insurance, and income lost as a direct or indirect consequence of the illness.

In a recent effort to determine the true costs associated with one type of medical illness, Bloom, Knorr, and Evans (1985) attempted to identify all illness-related expenditures as well as lost income over time in a group of 569 fairly affluent families in which a child had a malignant neoplasm being treated at the Children's Hospital of Philadelphia.

Illness-related costs were grouped into three categories—(1) direct medical expenses, including hospital, physician, and pharmaceutical services; (2) direct nonmedical illness-related expenses, such as transportation to and from the hospital, special diets, tutors, and necessary home remodeling; and (3) indirect illness-related costs in the form of lost wages by family members directly due to the child's illness, such as the need to accompany the child to the hospital. Out-of-pocket expenses, that is medical expenses not covered by private or public reimbursement programs were separately determined in each of the three categories.

Most indirect costs could not be fully estimated. Psychosocial costs were excluded, as were the costs entailed because, for example, parents could not accept promotions that required them to move. In addition, costs in time rather than in money could not be calculated, nor were costs to collateral family members included such as, for example, the cancellation of advanced educational plans.

Illness-related costs tended to decrease with time after diagnosis. On the average, annual costs across all patients was nearly $30,000, of which nearly $10,000 was not reimbursed. That is, even with public or private insurance, the average family of a child with cancer had illness-related expenses of nearly $10,000 per year that they had to pay themselves.

## HEALTH CARE PERSONNEL

As of 1983, there were nearly 8 million people employed in the health service industry, most of whom worked in hospitals. Between 1970 and 1983, the total number of people employed in the health service industry increased by 85 percent, with the biggest increase taking place in convalescent institutions. Among these 8 million health service providers were about 500,000 physicians, 130,000 dentists, 24,000 optometrists, 150,000 pharmacists, and 1,400,000 registered nurses. The numbers of people in each of these professional groups are increasing at about the same rate as that of health service personnel as a whole. There is some evidence that a surplus is developing in many of these health care provider categories, including physicians. This developing surplus is further complicated by the relatively recent provision of federal support for the creation of three new professional groups—the physician assistant, the nurse practitioner, and the nurse midwife (Yankauer & Sullivan, 1982)—designed to compensate for the physician shortage of some years ago. At the moment, the future of these new professional groups is uncertain, primarily because of the growing surplus of physicians (Stimmel & Graettinger, 1984; Swanson, 1985; Weiner, Steinwachs, & Williamson, 1986).

The number of physicians is increasing at a greater rate than the total population, with the result that while in 1950 there were about 14 active physicians per 10,000 population, in 1985 there were about 22 per 10,000 population. It is now estimated that in the year 2000 there will be about 26 active physicians per 10,000 population. This increase is attributable, in part, to the recent growth in the number of medical schools—from 79 in 1950 to 126 in 1985 in the United States alone. It is now estimated that nearly three times as many physicians will be graduated from medical schools in the year 2000 as were graduated in the year 1950 (National Center for Health Statistics, 1984a).

## ORGANIZATION AND DELIVERY OF HEALTH SERVICES

Behind the figures in the sections on expenditures for health care and on health care personnel lies an ongoing vigorous social policy debate regarding how health services should be organized, delivered, and supported. First, is health care a right that should be available to all, or a privilege that should be available to people who can afford it? Second, should there be a single level of health care that provides equitable care to everyone at the highest possible level, or should different levels of health care exist that differ in quality, cost, and accessibility, with people who can pay for better quality care having it available to them? And third, how should health care services be organized and provided in this large and populous country?

If we examine the current practice of health care delivery in the United States, to deduce the present answers to these questions, we would most probably conclude: (1) health care is more a privilege than a right; (2) levels of health care that differ in quality should exist, and people should be able to have access to the best health care they can afford; (3) the provision of health care should be in the hands of the private sector, even though a significant proportion of it is paid for by public tax revenues (Hyman, 1986; Iglehart, 1985b; Schlesinger & Dorwart, 1984; Woolhandler et al., 1983). Yet, these answers, however accurate they may be as a reflection of contemporary social policy, fail to capture the ferment that characterizes the current health care debate.

### A Brief History of Medical Care in the United States

In his review of the history of health care in the United States, Brown (1983) has made a number of important general observations. First, the more affluent have historically always been able to obtain more and better health care, while the poor have had to manage with less and lower quality health services. Second, except for people who were unusually affluent, obtaining needed health care has easily impoverished many families, rendering them indigent. Third, in the recent past the unstable nature of the economic system has created situations where the entire health care system has been jeopardized. During significant downturns in the economy, such as during times of high unemployment, it was difficult and sometimes impossible for patients to pay their medical bills, for physicians to make a living, or for hospitals to keep their doors open.

Thus it had been clear for some time that a way had to be found to minimize the catastrophic costs of medical care and, at the same time, to assure predictable income for health care providers. In the United States, the choices appeared to be between some form of public or private health insurance.

Efforts to establish some form of public national health insurance began during World War I and continued in the 1930s, at the time the original Social Security Act—designed to provide a measure of economic security for the elderly—was created (Roemer, 1985). Professional medical organizations were firmly opposed to any form of national health insurance (see Tunley, 1966), an opposition so formidable that President Roosevelt abandoned his efforts to link national health insurance to social security in order to assure the passage of the Social Security Act. Efforts to establish a national health insurance program continued without success until well after World War II.

In these unsuccessful efforts, a distinction was made between the so-called "deserving poor" who were poor despite all their efforts to escape poverty, and the "undeserving poor," who appeared to be making little effort to escape poverty. The Social Security Act provided security in old age for those who worked and who contributed to the system, that is, for the group of Americans that included the deserving poor. A second distinction was made between *social insurance,* that is, benefits that were available as a matter of right, and *public assistance,* that is, benefits that were discretionary and required that a person demonstrate need before being declared eligible for assistance. The distinction between social insurance and public assistance had a life of its own, perpetuated by a general prejudice against the poor in the United States, becoming especially important in 1965 when a public health insurance program was finally enacted.

Private health insurance plans had been originally introduced in 1929, first in the form of prepaid insurance for hospital bills (Blue Cross), and then in the form of prepaid insurance for physicians' bills (Blue Shield). These insurance programs became very popular and, by 1945, 24 percent of the population was covered by some form of private health insurance that paid a portion of personal health care costs. But even by 1950, at which time about half of the population was covered by some form of health insurance, private health insurance plans covered only 37 percent of hospital bills and 12 percent of physician bills. It was clear that while private health insurance could meet some of the personal health care expenses of the affluent, the relatively healthy, and the employed, it was not meeting the health-related needs of the unemployed, the poverty-stricken, the disabled, and the aged (Roemer, 1980a).

Because the Social Security Act provided financial support to people when they reached age 65, that is, ordinarily upon retirement, and because the aged as a group were shown to be unusually affected by the high costs of illness, continued attempts to introduce public health insurance concentrated on the elderly. Most of these efforts linked proposed public health insurance to eligibility for support under the Social Security Act.

In 1965, a public health insurance program was finally enacted, in a form that maintained the distinction between mandatory social insurance (called the Medicare program) and discretionary public assistance (called the Medicaid program). The Medicare program included both a compulsory hospital insurance program and a voluntary program to cover a portion of the cost of physicians' services. It was a national program, available to all persons who had reached the age of 65 who were covered under the Social Security Act, with the same set of eligibility requirements and benefits across the entire country. While the original social security system did not cover all persons over age 65, by 1965 virtually all working persons in the population were protected.

In addition to making it possible for the elderly to receive medical care regardless of their ability to pay, the Medicare program was also intended to eliminate differences between the nature and setting of medical care for the poor and the affluent. That is, the Medicare program was designed to make it possible for the poor to obtain their health care from the same sources that provided care for the affluent, as long as they were covered by Social Security. Reimbursement procedures were similar to those in traditional private practice. Hospitals and physicians sent bills for services rendered and were ultimately reimbursed by the appropriate federal and state agencies. Medical costs incurred by the patient that were not covered by Medicare were billed directly to the patients.

The Medicaid program, on the other hand, was public assistance, or what has historically been called "welfare"—a term that has developed a curiously pejorative connotation in the United States. Medicaid programs, designed to help defray the costs of medical care to indigent persons regardless of age as well as to pay for health services not covered by Medicare, were optional with each state, although they were generously subsidized by the federal government. States could not only choose whether to participate in the program, but each state could, within broad limits, establish its own eligibility requirements and levels of payment. States with more generous allowances to families with dependent children or to families with unemployed male heads of household tend to have larger proportions of their poor inhabitants eligible for Medicaid.

Thus, a serious built-in problem exists because of these two components of the public health insurance program. Both Medicare and Medicaid are funded by tax revenues that come from everyone who is employed, yet while Medicare will ultimately benefit virtually everyone as they reach age 65, Medicaid benefits only the poor. Thus, as can be imagined, only the Medicare program has broad popular support.

A very large proportion of poor people are even today not eligible for Medicaid benefits. As of 1982, there was a fivefold variation among states in the ratio of Medicaid recipients to persons below the poverty level, ranging from a high of virtually 100 percent to a low of 17 percent—that is, in the state with the poorest Medicaid coverage, for every 100 persons living below the poverty level, only 17 persons were eligible for Medicaid (National Center for Health Statistics, 1984a). Brown (1983) has estimated that somewhere between 40 and 67 percent of the poor in the United States are ineligible for Medicaid benefits. The ineligibility of so many poor people for Medicaid is crucially important because it was clear almost from the very beginning that Medicare payments would not begin to cover the total costs of health services and that Medicaid would be necessary to pay the portion of health care costs not covered by Medicare.

When Medicare was enacted, the U.S. Congress included the concept of *deductibles* and *coinsurance* patterned after private health insurance programs. Deductibles represented the amount of money that Medicare recipients had to pay for their health care before they were eligible for Medicare payments. Coinsurance represented the proportion of the Medicare-eligible payments that had to be paid by the recipient after the deductible amount had been satisfied. When Medicare legislation was first enacted, a recipient had to pay the first $40 of a hospital bill (the deductible amount) and $10 a day for the sixty-first through ninetieth day of hospitalization as a form of coinsurance. Under the terms of the voluntary portion of Medicare that helped pay physicians' fees, the original Medicare legislation required a premium payment of $3 per month, a deductible of $50, and a coinsurance of 20 percent of the physician's remaining bill.

These figures may not seem very high now, but deductibles and premiums have increased year by year. Currently, the Medicare recipient has to pay the first $492 of the hospital bill plus $123 per day for the sixty-first through ninetieth day of hospitalization—more than a 1000 percent increase over the levels in the original Medicare legislation. As for the voluntary physician insurance, the Medicare recipient now has to pay a monthly premium of $17.90— more than a 500 percent increase—and a deductible of $75. The result of these obligatory costs is that most Medicare patients find themselves needing to purchase supplementary private health insurance to meet those expenses, thus further increasing their out-of-pocket expenditures for health care.

In addition, it should be noted that Medicare does not cover all health-related expenses. Specifically, Medicare does not cover the cost of dentures and routine dental care, eyeglasses, hearing aids, prescription drugs, over-the-counter medicines, routine physical checkups, or custodial care including help with bathing, eating, and taking medications. In addition, only a very small proportion of the cost of nursing home care is reimbursed by the Medicare program. Apparently, inability to chew, see, or hear is considered a tolerable state of affairs for persons over age 65 by the social policy makers in the U.S. Congress, and persons with chronic illnesses simply have to fend for themselves as far as their day-to-day care is concerned. In a recent survey of Americans needing help to function at home, the National Center for Health Statistics (1983f) found that nearly 5 million people with chronic health problems needed help at home either with walking, going outside, bathing, dressing, using the toilet, getting in or out of a bed or a chair, eating, shopping, doing routine household chores, preparing their own meals, or handling their own money. None of the costs associated with these health-related needs is reimbursed by the Medicare program.

Evaluations of the Medicare and Medicaid programs have concluded that their existence has significantly increased the use of health services by the poor. At the same time, however, the need for health care by the poor still far exceeds the amount that they receive, and differentials between the amount and nature of health care received by the affluent and the poor continue to be very significant.

Perhaps the most astonishing finding regarding the effects of Medicare and Medicaid is that the out-of-pocket expenses for health care now paid by the elderly have not decreased materially. Rather, the major consequence of Medicare and Medicaid has been a dramatic increase in total expenditures for health services, far in excess of the inflation rate.

Prior to the enactment of Medicare and Medicaid, there was little reason for physicians or hospitals to increase their charges for medical or hospital care—they were all having difficulty collecting their bills as it was. Once payment for medical care for persons age 65 and above was assured, all forms of medical care began a steep increase in cost. Medicare and Medicaid legislation pumped billions of dollars into the health care system, and the system was quick to absorb it all in the form of increased prices, capital improvements, and profits.

Yet, the financial situation of many health care providers is far from sanguine. From the point of view of many hospital administrators, the Medicare and Medicaid rate schedule (the contracted rate that hospitals will be reimbursed per day of care for patients covered by Medicare or Medicaid) creates problems because the payments do not fully reimburse the actual costs of providing care. This shortfall is further complicated by the fact that emergency care must be provided to people who are both medically indigent and are not eligible for Medicaid payments. As private health insurance programs become increasingly strict about requiring hospitals to justify their bills, there is less surplus to make up for unpaid bills incurred by medically indigent patients. It is only a matter of time before a fiscal crisis in hospital management will arrive.

Out-of-pocket costs for medical care, even for people eligible for Medicare and Medicaid, continue to be a very significant factor in the living expenses of the elderly. As of 1981, those costs amounted to more than 16% of the total income of the elderly with family incomes below $10,000 per year (Brown, 1983). Thus, requiring greater out-of-pocket payments from people who are already strapped by the costs of medical care and normal living expenses does not appear to be a realistic solution to the problems created by the fact that the costs of Medicare and Medicaid are far in excess of original estimates.

As for the settings where the poor obtain medical care, substantial differences continue to exist when they are contrasted with the care settings of the more affluent. Significantly more poor people report that they do not have a regular source of health care, and when they do report a regular source, it tends to be a hospital outpatient clinic rather than a private physician's office. These differences are perpetuated because while physicians are generally willing to treat Medicare patients, they are often unwilling to treat Medicaid patients; under Medicare physicians may bill their patients usual, customary, and reasonable charges, but under Medicaid reimbursement for their services is substantially lower.

Somehow, the great hope that social insurance and public assistance would free the elderly of their anxieties about how they would pay for their medical care has not been achieved (Garrity, Wilson, & Hafferty, 1984; Whitcomb, 1986). Rather, the country is now preoccupied with what to do about the skyrocketing costs of medical care, regardless of how it is paid for—private or public insurance, social insurance or public assistance. That is, public policy concern is no longer focused on equity and quality of medical care. Rather it appears to be focused primarily on cost containment (Dans, Weiner, & Otter, 1985; Eisenberg & Williams, 1981).

DIAGNOSTIC-RELATED GROUPS.    The newest innovation in cost containment is the diagnostic-related group (DRG) system for hospital Medicare payment. Between 1965 and 1983, the Medicare system reimbursed hospitals for all costs judged to be reasonable. That is, hospitals were reimbursed on a fee-for-service basis just as physicians were. Such a cost-based reimbursement system provided no incentive for hospitals to provide cost-effective treatment.

In an effort to introduce some form of cost-containment into the hospital payment structure, in 1983 the U.S. Congress made a very significant change in the way Medicare payments would be made. A so-called *prospective payment* system was introduced. By this system, patients are classified according to their diagnosis, called their *diagnosis-related group* (DRG), and hospitals are paid a fee based on the average costs of medical care for patients with that diagnosis. If a hospital can treat a patient for less than the DRG payment that is allotted, the hospital can keep the savings. If the hospital spends more than the allocated amount for treatment, it must pay the difference itself (Uyeda & Moldawsky, 1986; Weiss, 1986).

While the Medicare program is of primary interest to health care providers serving persons over age 65, Medicare policy changes set an example for the rest of the health service delivery system, including the private insurance industry and Medicaid. Thus, the new DRG prospective payment system is being carefully watched by health economists, and interprofessional battles are being waged because of their anticipated impact on the entire health care delivery system. Initial evidence suggests that some savings are made in the cost of health care. But there is also some evidence that payment ceilings, rather than the patient's medical condition, have become the most significant determinant of when a patient is discharged.

As for the professional battles, perhaps the greatest concern is with who is eligible to receive reimbursement. At the moment, for example, psychologists' and other nonphysicians' services to Medicare patients are reimbursed only if authorized by a physician, a policy that is believed to limit access to health care and that inevitably encourages unnecessarily costly service (DeLeon, Uyeda, & Welch, 1985; Folen, 1985; Roybal, 1984; Tulkin & Frank, 1985; Uyeda & Moldawsky, 1986).

ATTITUDES TOWARD HEALTH CARE.    Public attitudes toward health care costs are complex (Blendon & Altman, 1984; Tyson & Merrill, 1984), and those attitudes help shape public policy. While the public values good health and recognizes the problem of health care costs to be an important one, its attention is diverted by the many other national problems that are thought to be far more important. The public tends to feel that health costs are high but, at the same time, generally supports spending more money for health care, even if tax increases would be necessary. This support is due in large measure to the importance most Americans place on good health. At the same time, although Americans tend to be very critical of the present system of delivering health care, they want it improved without being fundamentally changed. While the public is very critical of physicians in general, most like and have confidence in their own physicians.

Thus, while the public is in favor of cost-containment procedures in the abstract, they do not favor any proposals for containing costs that would change how they themselves obtain medical care. That is, most people are in favor of cost-containment procedures that propose major changes in how medical care is delivered to others, but not for themselves. While most Americans are not in favor of giving up their own personal physicians and obtaining care at more economical physician group practices, for example, they are enthusiastic about poor people using less costly forms of medical care. Under these circumstances, it appears that the poor, who already often receive inadequate medical care, may be unusually vulnerable to being the principal target for cost-containment policy changes.

Two facts seem clear to many social policy experts. First, the original decision to separate the poor from the rest of the population in planning a federal public health insurance program has resulted in very significant problems that have yet to be solved. With the persuasive evidence that reducing health care for the poor may prove incredibly expensive in the long run in both economic as well as human terms, a method of providing expanded preventive and therapeutic health services for the poor has to be found, in spite of the fact that public opinion is opposed to such a solution.

Second, building a health insurance program around traditional fee-for-service medical care, in which payment is received by hospitals and physicians only when services are delivered, has had an inevitable corrupting effect on medical costs (Manning et al., 1984). In 1977, for example, the Subcommittee on Oversight and Investigations of the Committee on Interstate and Foreign Commerce of the U.S. House of Representatives (Committee on Interstate and Foreign Commerce, 1978) investigated the cost and quality of the health delivery system in the United States. Regarding the specific issue of unnecessary surgery, the investigation found that unnecessary surgery was a major national problem that required urgent and accelerated attention. The scope of the problem was enormous, in that, in 1977 alone, there were approximately 2 million unnecessary procedures wasting over $4 billion and costing over 10,000 lives.

The fee-for-service payment system provides no incentives whatsoever for delivering efficient medical care. Indeed, the concept of fee-for-service provides a disincentive for efficiency and parsimony in medical care, since income is directly linked to the amount of services that are delivered. Thus, some change must be found for how medical care is paid for. The answer that appears to be emerging as the United States faces the health service delivery future is some form of organized medical care, and the most common—and at the same time, the most radical—type of medical care system that is being explored is the health maintenance organization.

### The Health Maintenance Organization

A *health maintenance organization* is an organized system of health care that provides comprehensive outpatient and hospital services for enrolled members for a fixed, prepaid annual fee through a single organization and a single payment mechanism. The crucial aspects of the delivery of health services through a health maintenance organization (HMO) are that cost is entirely predictable to the patient, and that the organization makes a profit by reducing unnecessary utilization of medical services. To put it another way, while traditional fee-for-service health providers earn an income by providing service, the health maintenance organization earns its income by providing only the health services that are necessary. As this distinction indicates, a major ingredient in reducing the cost of health care is to reduce overutilization of outpatient and inpatient health services.

HMOs, originally called prepaid group practices, originated early in this century as the west was opened and large numbers of miners, lumbermen, and other workers moved into undeveloped territory where medical services were not available. The first prepaid group practice began in Tacoma, Washington, in 1906, and others spread throughout parts of Washington and Oregon. In each case, small groups of physicians contracted with employers to provide whatever health care services were needed by their employees for an agreed-upon monthly fee.

Whenever HMOs started in a community where physicians were already engaged in the private fee-for-service practice of medicine, a tension soon developed between the private physicians and the HMO physicians, most of whom were salaried (Kahn & Orris, 1982). In many cases, HMO physicians were expelled by the county medical societies, and newcomers who intended to work in HMOs often had inordinate difficulty passing state licensing examinations. These struggles were the start of a 50-year battle between the American Medical Association as well as state and local medical societies, on the one hand, and the proponents of these various forms of prepaid group practices, on the other hand.

These battles often dragged on for years, but were virtually always finally won in the courts by the group practices, most commonly on the grounds that medical associations were engaged in the restraint of trade. The American Medical Association, the principal advocate of the physician in private practice, was strongly opposed to prepaid group practices, ostensibly because its members were opposed to the concepts of consumer control, of prepaid fees, and of physicians working for salaries, but basically because prepaid group practices posed an economic threat to the private practice of medicine (Costilo, 1985).

What is today the largest HMO in the United States, the Kaiser-Permanente Medical Care Program, began in 1933, again in a setting where large numbers of workers were engaged in construction work in an undeveloped and unpopulated area—in this case in the California desert. Other Kaiser-Permanente plans were started at the site of the Grand Coulee Dam in Washington and in the San Francisco Bay Area where 90,000 workers were employed in shipbuilding plants during World War II. When the war ended, enrollment was opened to the public. Today, nearly 5 million people are enrolled in the Kaiser-Permanente plan in nine different geographic areas.

Initial growth of HMOs was slow. By 1970, there were fewer than forty prepaid group practices in the United States, but their number began a period of rapid expansion, as rising health costs began to be of concern to the U.S. Congress, and as what then came to be known as the health maintenance organization was seen as a possible solution to the problem of cost containment. Early research studies contrasting HMOs and traditional fee-for-service medicine had found that while quality of care in HMOs was equal or better than the care delivered by traditional fee-for-service practitioners, overall costs were 15 to 20 percent lower, mainly due to the fact that use of inpatient services was reduced by nearly 50 percent (Meyers, 1981).

In 1971, President Nixon made the HMO the centerpiece of national health policy. More than $25 million in federal money was initially made available to help support new HMOs, and between 1976 and 1981 federal investment in HMOs, in the form of grants and construction loans, exceeded $350 million. In addition, the federal government established standards by which HMOs could become federally qualified to provide health care to federal employees. There are now more than 325 HMOs in the United States serving about 15 million members. It is expected that by 1993, total membership will reach 50 million (Mayer & Mayer, 1985).

Until recently, enrollment in HMOs was through the place of employment. That is, employees at a given organization would have the opportunity to enroll, along with their families, in a local HMO. This practice is similar to what is found in most forms of health insurance coverage. That is, it is more difficult and usually more expensive to enroll in a health insurance program as an individual than as an organizational employee; as has already been noted, people who are employed tend to be healthier than people who are not employed.

Recently, however, the federal government has made it possible for Medicare patients to enroll in federally qualified HMOs, through a contracting mechanism (Iglehart, 1985a). Some states now make it possible for patients who receive Medicaid to obtain their care through HMOs, although growth in that area is very irregular. These further possibilities have opened a new era of problems and possibilities for HMOs. While Medicare was originally modeled after traditional medical practice, it is now being used as an instrument of social change.

Literally billions of dollars are at stake as Medicare and Medicaid turn to the HMO. Now that the federal government has established a mechanism for contracting with HMOs for the provision of health services to persons covered by Medicare, there is the immediate possibility of a one-class medical care system. Except for who pays the premiums, there need be no difference in the nature of medical care received by the affluent and the poor who are part of the same HMO. At the same time, however, Medicare and Medicaid patients tend to be in far poorer health than younger and more affluent people, with the result that meeting their health needs economically will be far more difficult.

The nature of medical practice is undergoing dramatic change, as health service delivery is becoming more competitive. As was mentioned earlier in this chapter, the number of physicians is growing at a faster rate than the total population. As a consequence, physicians are now more willing to work in geographic areas where they were once unwilling to work, and there is some evidence of falling income, particularly for new physicians just completing their medical training (Jencks & Dobson, 1985; Roe, 1985). At the same time, the HMO offers a lifestyle for physicians that allows them to lead a more predictable existence, one less disruptive to themselves and their families. In turn, the changing nature of health care delivery is having a significant impact on the nature of physician training (Smith, 1985).

These are still the early days of HMOs, and HMOs are far from perfect. There have already been cases of poor medical care reported, as well as of overcharging for services rendered. The HMO is turning out to be a very competitive business in many cities. A number of claims of the superiority of HMOs over traditional medical practice have not yet been substantiated (Mechanic, 1976, pp. 83 ff.), and studies of patient satisfaction have yet to yield persuasive results. Given the nature of public attitudes toward their own medical care, HMOs will clearly have to achieve a high level of patient satisfaction as well as provide medical care of high quality in order to be successful. But there seems to be little question about the potential of the HMO to provide responsible preventive and therapeutic medical care, not only at less cost than traditional medical practice but also often with better results (Broskowski, 1981; Carlaw & Di-Angelis, 1982; Donaldson, Nicklason, & Ott, 1985; Hankin & Oktay, 1979; Levin, Glasser, & Roberts, 1984; Squyres, 1982).

Thus, the HMO may be a viable solution to the current problem of controlling the high cost of medical care. Unfortunately, there are also long-term problems for which the HMO will probably not be helpful. As was noted earlier in this chapter, the American population is aging, and with increasing age comes an increasing prevalence of chronic, costly diseases. Second, each technical advance in medical diagnosis or treatment adds significantly to the cost of medical care. At the rate at which these advances are occurring, the cost of medical care will increase independently of how it is financed. Solving these problems will likely require a major increase in national expenditures for health-related services.

### The Preferred Provider Organization

A newer and less radical approach to cost containment is the preferred provider organization (PPO). Most PPOs consist of groups of physicians who form an independent practice association that contracts with employer groups to provide physician services to employees and their families through a negotiated, discounted, fee-for-service mechanism. A built-in utilization review procedure is invariably included to assure a measure of cost containment through monitoring of proposed medical services.

When a PPO form of health insurance is introduced, anticipated cost savings are usually converted into a combination of reduced out-of-pocket expenses to patients and increased services. The most common forms of cost reduction to the patient include reduced monthly premiums, elimination of the annual deductible, and elimination or reduction of the coinsurance portion of the patient's bill. The most common form of increased service is preventive care.

The PPO preserves many of the strengths of traditional medical care. Thus, for example, patients can go to any physician in the PPO that they choose and can see physicians in their own private offices. At the same time, however, it is unlikely that costs will be contained, or that quality of care will be monitored to the same extent that is theoretically true in the HMO, unless the participating physicians exercise considerable control over the utilization of medical care, and over their own charges for services.

### The Comparative Analysis of Health Services

While this chapter deals with health and illness in the United States, the issues in the organization, financing. and delivery of health services that exist in this country have their parallels throughout the world. Indeed, the comparative study of health delivery systems in various countries provides fascinating insights not only into health and illness in other countries, but also into their history, geography, demography, politics, and psychology.

For students who might be interested in an introductory view of health care in other countries, a number of recent reports would be especially useful. Roemer (1980b) has provided an informative worldwide perspective on health care in the twentieth century. Health expenditures in France and the United States have been contrasted in a recent publication of the National Center for Health Statistics (1983d). The British national health service has been reviewed by Kinnaird (1981). South African health care has been examined by Benatar (1986) and by Susser and Cherry (1982), and different aspects of health care in India (Deodhar, 1982), Scotland (Kelman, 1980), Costa Rica (Casas & Vargas, 1980), Yugoslavia (Himmelstein, Lang, & Woolhandler, 1984), and Germany (Light, Liebfried, & Tennstedt, 1986), for example, have been examined. These are but samples of a very large and extremely interesting literature that allows the social scientist and social policy analyst to study health care experiences in various parts of the world and to determine the possible implications of one country's experiences for the design of health care services in other countries.

Of all the countries whose experiences in the organization, delivery, and financing of health care are of interest to social policy planners in the United States, none is of greater pertinence than Canada. Canada and the United States, both very large countries, share not only a common border but also a common age distribution and a common language and recent history. Even more important, the two countries share a common involvement in health care at the local, state or provincial, and federal levels of government; a common pattern of private physicians and voluntary hospitals; and a common complexity of non-profit, for-profit, and public health agencies. Since Canada has recently abandoned a two-class medical care system in favor of a health care system that attempts to make no distinctions on the basis of age or social class, and that attempts to combine health care with social services, it is widely acknowledged that we can indeed learn from their experiences (Iglehart, 1986a, 1986b; Kane & Kane, 1985; Tsalikis, 1982).

The similarities of the two countries should not obscure their differences, however. The United States population is ten times greater than that of Canada. The government structure is simpler in Canada, and there are correspondingly fewer hospitals, medical schools, and nursing homes. Canada has a parliamentary form of government, generally greater public acceptance of the role of government in the provision of social welfare services, less social disequilibrium in general, and a somewhat more homogeneous population. All these factors make it easier for Canada to deal with a problem as complex as health care. Nevertheless, health planners in the United States believe that they may have a great deal to learn from Canada.

Canadian provinces provide universal benefits that include health care, personal care, and social services for functionally impaired persons. Rich or poor, young or old, all Canadians receive health care through its health insurance program. Eligibility for care is based on functional impairment without regard to the individual's income, and if the patient is required to pay a portion of the cost of medical care, the amount that is charged is designed to leave even the poorest Canadian with some disposable income. The Canadian health and welfare program is quite similar to the Medicare program for the elderly in the United States but does not require large premiums, deductibles, and coinsurance. What is even more important is that the Canadian health and welfare program has no age restrictions—it is available for the entire Canadian population (Kane & Kane, 1985). Perhaps as a consequence, the health insurance program in Canada is enormously popular with Canadian citizens, the vast majority of whom feel quite satisfied with the quality of their medical care (Iglehart, 1986b).

The contrast between this statement and the current situation regarding health care in the United States is striking. What is equally striking is that while medical costs in the United States currently consume 10.8 percent of the gross national product and are far from universal or comprehensive, the Canadian health care program manages to provide virtually universal comprehensive care at an expenditure of only 8.5 percent of their gross national product (Iglehart, 1986a). Taylor (1981), writing about that health system from the point of view of a Canadian, has asserted that "the creation of the Canadian health insurance system is viewed by most Canadians as the outstanding social, political, and economic triumph of our history" (p. 177).

THE WORLD HEALTH ORGANIZATION.    In coming to the conclusion of this chapter, it seems fitting to mention the World Health Organization (WHO). No international organization has been more active in its attempts to improve the health status of people around the world than WHO, the health arm of the

United Nations. Headquartered in Geneva, Switzerland, but with worldwide regional offices, WHO has served as the conscience and technical consultant for health officials throughout the world, with particular emphasis on its commitment to improving health status in developing countries. It is in this context that WHO has recently established the goal of facilitating the provision of adequate health care throughout the globe. The goals and ideological position of WHO stand in sharp contrast to the almost single-minded preoccupation with cost containment that characterizes so much of the public policy debate regarding American medical care (Bryant, 1984).

## CONCLUDING COMMENTS

This chapter on health and illness in the United States identifies the subject matter of the field of health psychology. Virtually everything in the remainder of this text can be thought of in the context of the facts and figures presented in this chapter.

This review has underlined the extraordinary improvement in the level of health in the United States in the past 50 years. At the same time, however, adequate medical care is not yet available to all, in spite of the enormity of the expenditures for that purpose.

We have seen how the risk of illness and disability can be enhanced by a variety of disadvantageous demographic, sociocultural and socioeconomic factors. Many visits to physicians' offices are stressful; most hospitalizations are stressful; and unpayable medical bills are stressful—not only for patients but for their families as well. With advances in medical knowledge and technology, many patients are living longer with their diseases—often under conditions of reduced life quality.

Perhaps most surprising in this set of facts and figures is that three-quarters of the entire U.S. population has a professional contact with a physician every year. Physicians' offices thus are probably a major source of information and education about health-related matters, and the nature of patient-physician interaction can help determine not only the prevalence of illness but also of health-oriented behavior in our society.

As will be seen, the role of stress in the development and treatment of illness is increasingly recognized, and psychosocial aspects of many of the most prevalent illnesses are being identified and examined. At the same time, psychosocial approaches to prevention and treatment of physical disorders are being energetically developed and evaluated. Preventive programs, particularly in the case of relatively frequent disorders such as heart disease (Luginbuhl, Forsyth, Hirsch, and Goodman, 1981) have been shown to be economical and cost-effective.

Meanwhile, the medical care service delivery system is undergoing changes of revolutionary proportions, changes that we can only hope are as motivated by the wish to improve the quality and accessibility of health care as they are by the desire to reduce its cost (Cummings, 1986; Iglehart, 1987).

To conclude this chapter by turning to the future, the changes that will be taking place in the demographic characteristics of the United States population in the next two generations will have profound effects on economic aspects of the health delivery system. Only two demographic facts need be examined. First, as has already been noted, the fertility rate is substantially lower for whites than nonwhites. Each year, an increasing proportion of the United States population is nonwhite. Between the year 2000 and the year 2050, the U.S. Bureau of the Census (1984a) estimates that while the number of nonwhites of working age (age 20 to 64) will increase by more than 9 million, the number of whites of working age will *decrease* by more than 2 million.

Second, the difference in socioeconomic status between whites and non-whites is enormous, and there is no reason to believe that any substantial reduction in that difference is going to take place in the near future. In 1983, while 12 percent of the white population lived below the poverty level, 36 percent of the nonwhite population lived below the poverty level (U.S. Bureau of the Census, 1984b).

If we but remember that the U.S. social welfare system, like all social welfare systems throughout the world, is financed by people of working age who are employed, we can quickly understand the implications of these inexorable demographic facts. The financial vitality of the social welfare system will be increasingly dependent on contributions to it that will be made by nonwhites, people who, as we have seen, are disproportionately poor, and disproportionately unemployed. Thus, improving the socioeconomic condition of the entire working-age population will not only serve to improve their lives, but will also be necessary to assure an adequate quality of life for the elderly as well.

## SUMMARY

- In the United States, as throughout most of the developed world, the mortality rate has decreased dramatically in the past century, resulting in a highly significant increase in life expectancy.
- The National Center for Health Statistics, an agency that is part of the U.S. Department of Health and Human Services, is the principal source of information regarding health and illness in the United States.
- About three-quarters of the population of the United States has a professional contact with a physician, and about 15 percent of the population is hospitalized every year.
- Important differences in health and health-care experiences exist as a function of gender, social class, and ethnic group.
- Each year, about one-third of the population receives an injury of sufficient magnitude to require medical attention.
- The average person in the United States has about 19 days a year of restricted activity due to illness or injury.

- Leading causes of death have changed substantially since the turn of the century, from infectious diseases to which children were primarily vulnerable to chronic diseases affecting adults.
- Current leading causes of death are heart disease, cancer, accidents, and cerebrovascular diseases. These diseases account for about three-quarters of all deaths in the United States.
- Self-assessments of health represent a valuable method for measuring general health and well-being. Level of self-assessed health is found to decrease with increasing age and with decreasing social class.
- Childhood mortality rates are calculated in a variety of ways, depending on the age of the child of particular interest. Methods of calculating mortality rates of children include fetal mortality rate, neonatal mortality rate, and infant mortality rate, as well as maternal mortality rate.
- Efforts are currently under way to reduce infant mortality rate, particularly among those groups in which the rate is unusually high, including infants born to mothers under the age of 18 and to mothers who consume excessive amounts of alcohol during their pregnancies.
- Leading causes of death among children and adolescents are accidents, particularly automobile accidents.
- Particular concern is currently expressed regarding the high number of deaths due to homicide among black males.
- Expenditures for health care have risen dramatically in the past 50 years, at a level far in excess of the annual inflation rate. Annual medical care expenditures now amount to nearly $1500 per person, an amount that constitutes nearly 11 percent of the gross national product.
- In spite of the growth of the private health insurance industry, about 40 percent of personal health care costs are paid for by public tax revenues. Slightly more than 32 percent of the costs are paid for by private health insurance, with the balance coming from out-of-pocket expenditures.
- Nearly 8 million people are employed in the health care industry, of whom most work in hospitals.
- The organization of health delivery is undergoing a revolutionary change in the United States, primarily in an effort to contain costs, and secondarily to assure adequate medical care for the entire population. The principal form of health care organization that is emerging is the health maintenance organization (HMO).
- Because all nations are concerned about the delivery of cost-effective, quality health care services, the study of how different countries provide health care to their citizens is particularly pertinent to those people who are developing health-related public policy in the United States. Of particular pertinence is the medical care system in Canada.

# Stress and Health

# 3

## INTRODUCTION

Until perhaps a century ago, illness was thought of in broad rather than in narrow terms, and the living body was viewed as embedded in a total environment of people and places. The mysteries of how the outside somehow got inside were of central interest to physicians of the day, and the study of how environmental events might make a person ill has had a part in medical thinking since time immemorial (Arthur, 1982).

Contemporary interest in stress, both in terms of chronic stressful life circumstances as well as more acute and circumscribed stressful life events represents a fruition of this earlier interest in how external events can become internalized and can make us ill if we fail to cope adequately with the challenges that such events produce.

There is probably no medical term more commonly used in everyday conversation than the word *stress*. Stress is a universal phenomenon, and there are many definitions of the term (Dobson, 1983). The two central elements in most definitions, however, are (1) *stress* is external in origin, and (2) it can produce internal physiological and psychological disturbances. For example, Baum, Singer, and Baum (1981) have defined stress as a "process in which environmental events or forces, called stressors, threaten an organism's existence and well-being" (p. 4).

These external demands or pressures or forces are generally referred to as stress. The internal reactions to these external demands are often referred to as *strain*. The distinction between the terms stress and strain is a very useful one, since it calls attention to the differences of stimulus (stress) and response (strain) (Hobfoll & Walfisch, 1986; Lazarus, 1966). Stress cannot be measured without measuring strain. Since stress, by definition, produces strain, its study is interactional—the study of the individual in the environment.

Virtually all scientists who study stress recognize that different people react differently to external sources of stress. What is one person's threat is another person's challenge. Furthermore, there is general agreement that a number of personal and environmental characteristics can mediate how stress is experienced. These characteristics can make the same external stress seem either more or less severe (Dobson, 1983). Finally, many external demands on the person can have positive consequences. Their successful resolution can make a person stronger and better able to cope with future stresses. Thus, the critical theoretical and empirical issues facing scientists who study stress are to identify the stimulus conditions that produce stress reactions, and the processes that determine whether and in what form those stress reactions will occur (Folkman, Lazarus, Gruen, & DeLongis, 1986; Lazarus, 1966).

## STRESS AND ILLNESS

One finding that has contributed to the development of behavioral medicine is the increasingly strong evidence that psychosocial factors that can be described as stressful can have adverse effects on physical health (Kaprio et al., 1987; Miller, 1983). Stress has been identified as a crucial factor in both physical and emotional disorders, and such stressful life events as job loss, bereavement, and marital disruption have been shown to increase the risk not only of psychological disorders such as depression, but also of minor infections and of many other more serious conditions (Elliott & Eisdorfer, 1982).

Stressful situations are nonspecific in their effect, however. They are generally found to result in an increased risk of a wide variety of medically adverse consequences rather than of any specific disorder. Miller (1983) has included in the list of disorders that appear to be sensitive to stressful situations, gastrointestinal disorders, sudden cardiac death, myocardial infarction, hypertension, stroke, diabetes, cancer, multiple sclerosis, tuberculosis, influenza, pneumonia, headaches, and insomnia—a formidable list indeed.

## SELYE'S GENERAL ADAPTATION SYNDROME

No one was more influential in the renewed twentieth-century interest in stress than Hans Selye. Born in 1907 in Vienna, and educated in medicine in Prague, Selye moved to Montreal, Canada, in the early 1930s and lived there for the rest of his life. He taught at McGill University for 10 years and then moved to the University of Montreal where he directed the Institute of Experimental Medicine and Surgery until his death in 1982 (Malmo, 1986).

While in medical school, Selye found himself struck by the many similarities among patients with very different disorders. That is, while his professors were primarily interested in how patients with different diagnoses differed from each other, Selye was impressed by their similarities—the feeling of being ill, diffuse aches and pains, intestinal disturbances, loss of appetite, loss of weight, and so forth. At first, Selye thought of these common characteristics as a "syndrome of just being sick" (1976, p. 19).

Selye persisted in his study of these general characteristics after moving to Canada, and in 1936 he published his first paper about this phenomenon. He had come to believe that the syndrome was caused by external stress that resulted in three sequential biological reactions. First, the body developed a relatively short-lived *alarm reaction* to the noxious attack. Second, the body adapted to and resisted the attack—the *stage of resistance*. Finally, the toll to the body of continued resistance and adaptation resulted in a *stage of exhaustion*. Casting about for a name for the entire sequence, Selye proposed calling it the *general adaptation syndrome*—a term that has persisted to this day.

One of the consequences of the third stage of exhaustion is that under certain conditions, physical disorders can occur that are caused by this taxing process of defense and adaptation (Bieliauskas, 1982). In a word, then, stress can cause illness.

## THE PHYSIOLOGY OF STRESS

Somehow, external stress gets inside the body. Ader and Cohen (1984) have suggested that "there is probably no major organ system or homeostatic defense mechanism that is not subject to the influence of interactions between psychological and physiological events" (p. 117). Stress has been found to influence neurochemical, hormonal, and immunological functioning (Arnetz & Fjellner, 1986; Burchfield, 1979; Depue & Monroe, 1986; Depue, Monroe, & Shackman, 1979; Herd, 1984; Sklar & Anisman, 1981).

Two interrelated bodily systems—the autonomic nervous system and the endocrine system—play important roles in maintaining the body's stability and flexibility in times of stress, or what, as we learned in Chapter 1, is called, its homeostasis. During the initial stage of alarm tremendous amounts of glucose and oxygen are brought to the brain, skeletal muscles, and heart, that is, to the organs that are most active in warding off danger. These changes in the body result in a number of phenomena, including: (1) an increase in heart rate and strength of heart muscle contraction; (2) a constriction in the blood vessels supplying the skin and internal organs and a dilation in the blood vessels supplying the skeletal muscles and the brain; (3) a rise in production of red blood cells and an increase in the ability of the blood to clot; (4) an increase in perspiration that helps maintain normal body temperature in the face of heightened blood circulation; (5) increased breathing rate and respiration that brings more oxygen into the body; and (6) a decrease in digestive activity. All these changes in the body result in the increase in the body's energy and vigilance, and in the decrease in nonessential activities.

During the second stage—resistance—a variety of complex neurophysiological changes take place in the body that allow the body to continue its defense against a stressor. These second-stage changes provide energy, mainly in the form of additional protein, and cause circulatory changes required for meeting emotional crises, performing strenuous tasks, and fighting infection and bleeding. At the same time the blood chemistry returns nearly to normal.

During the third stage—exhaustion—hormones that have been produced at abnormally high rates can become depleted, as can a variety of important trace minerals, particularly potassium, with the result that cells do not receive enough nutrients and can start to die. Organs of the body that have been weakened by previous illnesses can fail and threaten survival (Dobson, 1983; Herd, 1984; Miller, 1980; Sklar & Ainsman, 1981; Tortora & Evans, 1986).

### Stress and the Immune System

The immune system is a surveillance mechanism that protects the body against disease-causing microorganisms (Jemmott & Locke, 1984). It reduces the body's susceptibility to cancers, infectious diseases, and allergies, among other conditions, and a great deal of current physiological research is concerned with increasing our understanding of how the immune system operates (Strand, 1983).

Two different types of immunity exist—innate immunity that is present from the time of birth and protects us against a variety of bacteria and toxic organisms, and acquired immunity that develops very rapidly after birth in response to specific invading bacteria, viruses, or toxins to which the body does not have an innate immunity (Smith, 1984).

A growing body of research suggests that stress can increase the body's susceptibility to diseases that are under the control of the immune system (Kiecolt-Glaser et al., 1987; Riley, 1981). Stress has been demonstrated to reduce the body's resistance to acute respiratory infections (see, for example, Boyce et al., 1977; Hinkle, 1974; McClelland, Alexander, & Marks, 1982) and tumors (Ader, 1981) and to have measurable impact on the immunological system itself (see, for example, Bartrop et al., 1977; Jemmott et al., 1983; Maier & Laudenslager, 1985). Recent studies have shown that the immune system diminishes in strength with aging (Rogers, Dubey, & Reich, 1979), a finding that can help explain the increasing risk of autoimmune disorders and malignancy in older populations.

Acute, short-term stresses have different immunological effects than chronic long-term stresses. Locke (1982) has postulated that the initial response to a state of mild stress is a transient activation of certain components of the immune system, and that it is not stress itself which is immunosuppressive but stress coupled with poor coping (also see Borysenko & Borysenko, 1982).

## COPING WITH STRESS

Paralleling the increasing acknowledgment of the importance of stress in the development of a wide variety of illnesses, attention has been directed to ways of coping successfully with the daily stresses of life. In general terms, negative reactions to stress can be minimized by a combination of changes made in the environment and inside the person (Hiebert, 1983; Roth & Cohen, 1986; Taylor, 1983; Vinokur & Caplan, 1986; Zastrow, 1984a).

According to Girdano and Everly (1979), stresses have three major causes—psychosocial, bioecological, and personality. Among the *psychosocial* causes of stress, four processes seem most pertinent. These are processes involving (1) the need to adapt or adjust to changing circumstances, (2) the sense of frustration that accompanies the inability to achieve some desired goal or behavior, (3) overload or other forms of overstimulation or excessive demand, and (4) understimulation, usually in the form of boredom or loneliness.

*Bioecological* causes of stress arise in the external environment and produce a stress response that is biologically innate, that is, that depends very little on individual characteristics. Among these stresses are those attributable to such factors as biological rhythms, nutritional habits, and noise pollution. Activity demands that are out of synch with natural biological rhythms, such as our 24-hour internal clock, create stress, as do a number of environmental characteristics such as noise, which in excessive amounts is stressful, apparently primarily on biological grounds. Finally, there is evidence that certain types of dietary intake—caffeine, nicotine, and perhaps sodium, may reduce the capacity to cope with stress.

In the *personality* domain, Girdano and Everly (1979) suggest that certain personality characteristics may make us more vulnerable to stress. Among these characteristics, they identify low self-esteem, fearfulness, and certain specific behavior patterns such as Type A behavior (see Chapter 10). There is also some evidence that coping with stress is more difficult among persons who manifest an external locus of control, that is, the belief that events that occur are primarily the result of factors over which they have little personal control—such as good or bad luck, providence, or God's will (Lester, Leitner, & Posner, 1985; Tyson, 1981)—and that very little can be done to solve whatever problems exist. This latter personaity dimension, sometimes called learned helplessness, is also similar to what has been called a low sense of self-efficacy (Bandura, 1977; Maier & Seligman, 1976).

This analysis of stress sources leads to a series of hypotheses regarding their management. Coping abilities can be enhanced by a variety of cognitive strategies. Among these strategies are (1) developing alternatives for accomplishing desired but frustrated objectives, (2) practicing better time management and other techniques for avoiding overload (see, for example, Shank, 1983), (3) planning ahead to avoid stressful situations, (4) avoiding exposure to environmental stressors, and (5) avoiding or minimizing other changes during periods of time requiring significant adaptation or readjustment.

Stress can be reduced by a variety of strategies including meditation, biofeedback, and other forms of relaxation training (see Chapter 8), and by a number of different forms of physical activity and exercise (Long, 1984; Stevens & Pfost, 1984; Wilson-Barnett, 1984a, 1984b). As a consequence of this recognition, there has been enormous interest in what is called *stress management*, the identification of techniques that can help people cope with acute stress or with the more general and chronic stresses of living.

Most current stress management programs combine many of these components into a multidimensional comprehensive approach. Among these are programs that focus on reducing children's daily life stresses; reducing stresses among university students and professionals, and among low-income women; and programs facilitating weight control efforts, coping with anger, eliminating insominia, reducing dependency on insulin among diabetics, and aiding in the adaptation to cancer treatment. In each of these cases, the programs designed to reduce the negative effects of stress appear to be remarkably successful (Bistline & Frieden, 1984; Bruner, 1984; Charlesworth, Williams, & Baer, 1984; Dougherty & Deck, 1984, Heinrich & Schag, 1985; Kirmil-Gray, Eagleston, Thoresen, & Zarcone, 1985; Kooken & Hayslip, 1984; Lerner, 1985; Marciniak, 1984; Reynolds, 1984; Rosenbaum, 1983; Shaw & Blanchard, 1983; Somerville, Allen, Noble, & Sedgwick, 1984; Starak, 1984; Valdés, 1985; Zastrow, 1984b).

## THE STUDY OF STRESSFUL LIFE EVENTS

The concept of stress has special importance in the field of psychiatry, where today the prevention and treatment of so-called stress-related disorders occupy considerable attention. Much of the present interest in stressful life events comes from the impact that this psychiatric interest has had for the rest of medicine. The person who probably played the most important role in bringing life stress to the attention of psychiatry was Adolf Meyer (1866–1950). Meyer was born and educated in Switzerland and came to the United States in 1892. From 1910 until his retirement in 1941, he founded and then served as the director of the Henry Phipps Psychiatric Clinic at Johns Hopkins Medical School in Baltimore,

Maryland. It is to Meyer that we are indebted for the term "psychobiology"—a term that suggests the equal importance of biology and psychology in developing a full understanding of the patient.

Meyer believed that the only way to gain a valid perspective on the current situation of patients was in terms of their life history. While Meyer acknowledged that it was often time-consuming and unwieldy to collect this information, he nevertheless believed that such an understanding was crucial if the physician was to be successful in helping the patient. Life history experiences that Meyer specifically identified included illnesses, "changes of habitat, of school entrance, graduations . . . , or failures; the various jobs; the dates of possibly important births and deaths in the family, and other fundamentally important environmental influences" (1919/1948, pp. 420, 422).

The field of stressful life event research was given a tremendous impetus by the development of the Social Readjustment Rating Scale by Holmes and Rahe (1967; see also Holmes, 1979; Holmes & Masuda, 1974; Rahe, 1979). Holmes had for a number of years been following Meyer's admonition to search for stressful events in the recent life history of patients. He and his colleagues were persuaded that stressful life events, by evoking such psychophysiological reactions as described earlier, could play a precipitating role in many diseases.

Beginning in 1949, Holmes and his colleagues studied life stressors that were reported by more than 5000 patients as occurring shortly before the onset of their illnesses. From this data pool they assembled a list of forty-three representative life events and scaled them in terms of their judged stressfulness. In this process, they made two critical decisions. First, while most of the items on their list could be considered undesirable events (death of a spouse, marital separation, jail term), the concept of a stressful life event was not limited to such items, but could include desirable events as well (marriage, marital reconciliation, outstanding personal achievement). Stressfulness was defined in terms of the need for readjustment—and desirable events were thought to require a measure of readjustment just as undesirable events. Second, Holmes and his colleagues believed that it was appropriate to develop a rating scale in which stressfulness was judged by outside experts rather than by the persons undergoing the stress themselves. Furthermore, they chose to develop a scale in which each stressful event was given a single, universal weight. The methodological details of the development of the scale are described by Holmes and Masuda (1974).

Thus, while research was continuing to explore the physiological concomitants of chronic stress and stressful life events, there was a remarkably rapid growth in the study of stressful life events per se, stimulated in large measure by the availability of the Holmes and Rahe scale. That scale made it possible to assign weights to events, total these weights across a broad array of such events, and then examine the resulting total scores in terms of their relationships to subsequent illness. Research activity grew at such a pace that only six years after the publication of the Social Readjustment Rating Scale, Barbara and Bruce

Dohrenwend organized an international conference to bring many of the prominent stressful life event researchers together. The report of that conference (Dohrenwend & Dohrenwend, 1974) provides an eloquent review of the state of stressful life event research as of that time.

The major thrust of that report for future research was to underline the complexity of the relationships between stressful life events and subsequent disorders. In particular, the report urged the development of more satisfactory measurement procedures and research designs, greater attention to conceptualization, and examination of the factors that might serve to moderate or potentiate the effects of stressful life events. The field has been extremely responsive to these recommendations (see for example, Cleary, 1980; Rabkin, 1980; Zimmerman, 1983).

### The Assessment of Stressful Life Events

Since the original stressful life event inventory was developed, countless others are now available for different demographic groups. For example, Coddington (1972a, 1972b) has developed a series of stressful life event scales for children of varying ages, precisely following the original Holmes and Rahe procedure. Separate scales, along with their weights, are available for preschool, elementary school, junior high school, and senior high school children. Murrell, Norris, and Hutchins (1984; also see Murrell & Norris, 1984) have developed a stressful life event scale for older adults, and Wolchik, Sandler, Braver, and Fogas (1985) have developed a stressful life event scale for children whose parents are undergoing a divorce. Work has been reported that can lead to the development of a stressful life event scale specifically for people who live and work in a farm community (Olson & Schellenberg, 1986), and attention has been turned to the assessment of less catastrophic, relatively minor, everyday stresses (Zautra, Guarnaccia, & Dohrenwend, 1986).

Holmes and Rahe knew that their list of stressful life events was not comprehensive, and other common stressful life events such as retirement, specific forms of job stress, unemployment, and impending fatherhood are being newly recognized as worthy of study (Ekerdt, Baden, Bossé, & Dibbs, 1983; Linn, Sandifer, & Stein, 1985; Quill, Lipkin, & Lamb, 1984). In addition, atypical stressful life events that would ordinarily not appear on any general scale are being identified and studied, such as the 1979 Three Mile Island nuclear power plant accident (Annas, 1983; Baum, Fleming, & Singer, 1982; Collins, Baum, & Singer, 1983; Hartsough & Savitsky, 1984; Houts et al., 1984) and the Mount Saint Helen's eruption (Adams & Adams, 1984), or stresses associated with the task of body removal following an airplane crash (Taylor, 1984; Taylor & Frazer, 1982).

Perhaps one of the most useful general measures of stressful life events was developed by Horowitz et al. (1977). Their instrument, called the Life Events Questionnaire, maintains the Holmes and Rahe procedure of having stressfulness scored by outside experts, but has two advantages over the original Holmes and Rahe scale. First, item clarity and meaning have been improved, and second, stressfulness weights are assigned as a function of both the nature of the event and the time since the event occurred. More severe events are scored as more stressful, and all events are scored as decreasingly stressful the longer ago they occurred. Sample items from the Horowitz Life Events Questionnaire, along with their weights are shown in Table 3-1.

The more general concept of stress has been subdivided into such terms as "chronic role strain" (Pearlin, 1983), "microstressor" (Monroe, 1983a), and "daily hassle" (Depue & Monroe, 1986; Dohrenwend, Dohrenwend, Dodson, &

**Table 3–1**    Sample Items from the Horowitz Life Events Questionnaire

| EVENT | TIME-RELATED PRESUMPTIVE STRESS WEIGHTS | | | | |
| | *Under 1 Month* | *1–6 Months* | *6–12 Months* | *1–2 Years* | *Over 2 Years* |
| --- | --- | --- | --- | --- | --- |
| Death of husband, wife, lover, or child. | 90 | 81 | 67 | 50 | 32 |
| Legal troubles leading you to be held in jail. | 82 | 65 | 51 | 37 | 27 |
| Death of parent, brother, or sister. | 79 | 70 | 51 | 34 | 23 |
| Divorce from husband or wife, or break-up with lover. | 76 | 63 | 45 | 29 | 16 |
| Separation from husband, wife, or lover because of relationship problems. | 75 | 61 | 41 | 24 | 14 |
| An unwanted pregnancy (you, your wife, or lover). | 72 | 57 | 42 | 25 | 15 |
| A miscarriage or abortion (you, your wife, or lover). | 71 | 53 | 31 | 18 | 11 |
| Death of close friend or other important person. | 70 | 53 | 36 | 22 | 12 |
| Hospitalization of a family member for a serious illness. | 69 | 46 | 26 | 14 | 8 |
| Being fired or laid off. | 68 | 46 | 27 | 16 | 8 |
| Separation from husband, wife, or lover because of job demands. | 65 | 51 | 38 | 26 | 15 |
| Breaking an engagement. | 65 | 47 | 27 | 14 | 7 |
| A love affair outside your primary relationship. | 62 | 50 | 37 | 25 | 17 |
| Involvement in a lawsuit (other than divorce). | 61 | 41 | 23 | 13 | 7 |
| Getting married or returning to husband, wife, or lover after separation. | 60 | 45 | 34 | 23 | 18 |
| Argument with husband, wife, or lover. | 59 | 40 | 26 | 17 | 11 |
| The birth or adoption of a child. | 52 | 39 | 26 | 18 | 15 |
| Move to another town, city, state, or country. | 46 | 32 | 20 | 10 | 5 |
| Move of your home within the same town or city. | 25 | 13 | 7 | 3 | 2 |

Information in this table is provided with the courtesy of M. Horowitz.

Shrout, 1984; Lazarus, 1984; Monroe, 1983a; Zautra, Guarnaccia, & Dohrenwend, 1986). These terms suggest that specific attention is now being paid to the chronicity and severity of stress, and scales are being developed to assess these varying dimensions. Furthermore, it is becoming increasingly clear that stressful life events may vary not only in their chronicity and severity but also in other factors: they may be anticipated or unanticipated, familiar or novel, desirable or undesirable, sudden or gradual, discrete or prolonged, under various degrees of control by the person being studied, and either part of or separated from the signs of impending illness. Finally, measures of strain (see, for example, Cohen, Kamarck, & Mermelstein, 1983) are now available to assess perceived stress, that is, measures of adjustment rather than measures of the stressfulness of the environment.

### Stressful Life Events and Illness

Stressful life events, then, are those external events that make adaptive demands on a person. These demands may be successfully met or may inaugurate a process of internal psychological or physiological straining that can culminate in some form of illness.

The pathway between stressful life events and subsequent illness is a complex one involving a number of important components. A number of different investigators have proposed ways of conceptualizing this process, and there is a reassuring similarity in their proposals. Rahe (1974), for example, has suggested that five separate aspects in this process must be examined:

1. Past experience—how the person has traditionally managed stressful life events so that they are more or less stressful than would generally be the case.

2. Psychological defenses—the abilities a person has to deal with stressful life events so that they have fewer negative consequences.

3. Physiological reactions—the nature of the physiological impact of those stressful life events that are not dealt with by successful psychological defenses.

4. Coping skill—the ability to attenuate or compensate for physiological reactions.

5. Illness behavior—how individuals come to interpret the remaining physiological reactions as symptoms or as illness, and how they decide to seek medical care. (Also see Cobb, 1974; B. P. Dohrenwend, 1979; B. S. Dohrenwend, 1978; Sarason, 1980)

Another proposal suggests that the risk of developing an illness increases as a function of organic vulnerability and severity of stress, and decreases as a function of coping ability, social competence, and strength of the social support system (Albee, 1979, 1985).

Most investigators who study the relationships of stressful life events and illness share three major beliefs. First, they believe that the impact of life stressors can only be understood within a social and psychological context. That context may contain factors that moderate the effects of stressful life events, such as a strong social-support network or personal robustness, or may contain factors that potentiate the effects of stressful life events, such as a history of poor crisis management, characteristic physiological overreaction, or certain personality characteristics such as a sense of external locus of control. Second, they believe that the long-term consequences of stressful life events may not necessarily be deleterious. In fact, coping successfully with a stressful life event may actually strengthen a person's ability to cope with stress in the future. Finally, they believe that in order to evaluate the consequences of stressful life events, help-seeking patterns must be taken into account. In other words, one person may seek help for symptoms that follow a stressful experience while another person may choose not to seek help; the differences may not lie in the reaction to stress but rather to how these two people feel about the medical care system, its adequacy, and its accessibility.

### Consequences of Stressful Life Events

A number of studies have examined the effects of stressful life events on physical well-being. It will be useful to examine several representative examples of these studies to develop a sense of how the consequences of stress are being identified.

Hinkle (1974) has been examining the effects of changes in interpersonal relationships and of changes in the social and cultural milieu on health in a series of studies over the past 30 years. In a study of more than 500 telephone operators who were part of a comprehensive health insurance program and who had worked for 20 years or more, Hinkle found a strong connection between stressful interpersonal and environmental difficulties and illness. He found that a cluster of illnesses coincided with a period when individuals were experiencing many demands and frustrations arising from their social environment or interpersonal relations (also see Aakster, 1974; Cooke & Greene, 1981; Gallin, 1980; Selzer & Vinokur, 1974; Totman, 1979).

Totman, Kiff, Reed, and Craig (1980) examined the relationship of stressful life events to vulnerability to the common cold in a sample of fifty-two persons who were given colds by nasal inoculation with an infecting rhinovirus. These subjects ranged in age from 18 to 49 and included people from many walks of life. Prior to their inoculation with the rhinovirus, they were assessed on a variety of measures of recent life stress and with a number of personality inventories. The severity of the cold was measured by the amount of virus present in nasal washings. These investigators found that certain stressful life events, particularly those associated with changes in general activity level, were significantly related to the magnitude of the subsequent infection.

Cassel (1974b), who studied the effects of stress in a variety of health settings, concluded that one of the psychosocial factors that may play a role in reducing vulnerability to disease is the presence of other members of the same species. His conclusion derives from a review of animal studies as well as studies with human subjects. He has proposed four hypotheses for consideration. First, the social process linking high population density to enhanced susceptibility to disease is not the crowding per se but the

> disordered relationships that, in animals, are inevitable consequences of such crowding. . . . In human populations the circumstances in which increased susceptibility to disease would occur would be those in which there is some evidence of social disorganization. (p. 1041)

Second, persons who occupy subordinate positions in the hierarchy of power or prestige will be particularly vulnerable to disease. Third, biological and social buffers exist (for example, coping capacities and social supports) that can cushion the individual from the physiological or psychological consequences of social disorganization. Finally, Cassel suggested that under conditions of social change and social disorganization, susceptibility to disease is in general increased.

### Moderating Factors

Although there is clear evidence that stressful life events are related to subsequent illness, their relationship is far from perfect. According to Rahe (1979), as well as many others, improved understanding of the relationships of stressful life events to illness onset will require closer examination of potential moderating factors, that is, factors that might change the likelihood that stress will lead to illness. A personal characteristic can be said to function as a moderator if in its presence the relationship of stress and health is weaker than in its absence. Moderating factors are of two general types—personal resources and social resources. Among personal resources, potential moderating factors that have been identified are coping skill, social competence, and a number of specific personality traits. Among social resources, the one moderating factor that is clearly of greatest interest is the nature of the social support network.

PERSONAL RESOURCES.   Cohen and Lazarus (1979; also see Cohen, 1984) have identified five ways in which people draw on their own resources in order to cope with the stresses of illness—information seeking, direct action, inhibition of action, intrapsychic processes, and turning to others. When engaged in information seeking, the person tries to find out what problems exist and what, if anything, must be done. Direct action includes anything that is done about the problem. Since the skillful coper does not engage in impulsive or ill-advised action, inhibition of action constitutes a mode of coping. Intrapsychic processes include all forms of defense—denial, avoidance, or intellectualization, for example. These defenses are particularly useful when the patient can do little about the problem except to allow therapeutic procedures to be applied.

Finally, turning to others constitutes a form of coping, in that there is evidence that persons who are ill do better if they can maintain and use supportive social relationships.

In the case of specific personality traits, the importance of a sense of control over one's life—what is called an inner locus of control—has already been mentioned (Nelson & Cohen, 1983). In a particularly interesting study, Kobasa (1979) examined a number of personality variables in terms of their moderating effects on the consequences of stressful life events. She studied a large sample of executives who, as a group, had undergone considerable stress during the preceding 3 years and was able to isolate two groups of high-stress executives who differed on their reported illnesses—a group of 100 subjects above the median in total stress and below the median for total illness, and a second group of 100 subjects also above the median for total stress but above the median for total illness. These two samples were all males and most were 40 to 59 years old, married, parents, and college educated. Kobasa studied three personality variables related to coping style—the degree to which participants felt that they could control or influence life events, involvement in or commitment to life activities, and the extent to which change was viewed as an exciting challenge to further development. As expected, in the total group, including those executives below the median in stress, there was a significant but modest correlation between total stress and total illness scores.

Kobasa found numerous personality differences between the two groups of high-stress executives, many of which revolved around the concept of internal control. Kobasa noted that in order to remain healthy while encountering great stress, one must have a clear sense of one's values, goals, and capabilities, and a belief in their importance, a commitment toward active involvement in one's environment, an ability to evaluate the impact of any life event on one's general life plan, a belief that one can control and transform the events of one's experience, and an ability to deal with external life stresses without their becoming threats to one's psychological adjustment.

SOCIAL RESOURCES.    At the level of social or environmental resources, enormous activity is taking place around the concept of social support (Andrews, Tennant, Hewson, & Vaillant, 1978; Barrera & Ainlay, 1983; Barrera, Sandler, & Ramsay, 1981; Burke & Weir, 1977; Larocco, House, & French, 1980; Lin, Ensel, Simeone, & Kuo, 1979; Monroe, 1983b; Norbeck, 1981; Norbeck, Lindsey, & Carrieri, 1981; Norbeck & Tilden, 1983; Vaux et al., 1987; Warheit, 1979; Williams, Ware, & Donald, 1981). Cobb (1976) suggested that persons can be said to have social support when they believe they (1) are cared for and loved, (2) are esteemed and valued, and (3) belong to a network of communication and mutual obligation. Cobb has shown that the presence of adequate social support is associated with the lack of complications of pregnancy, particularly among persons high in life stress; with recovery from a variety of illnesses and positive response to a variety of medical procedures; with success in alcoholism recovery programs; with favorable management of the stress of involuntary unemployment; with successful coping with bereavement; and with better management of the illnesses and infirmities associated with aging.

Medalie and Goldbourt (1976) examined the role played by anxiety and psychosocial problems in the development of angina pectoris (a chronic but not life-threatening heart disorder) in a longitudinal 5-year study of 10,000 Israeli male civil servants age 40 and above. The incidence of angina pectoris was found to vary by age, by area of birth, and by a number of physiological variables, but at the same time was found to be higher among persons reporting high anxiety, a high level of family problems, and psychosocial difficulties. Anxiety coupled with psychosocial and family problems appeared to potentiate the relationships found between physiological factors (such as electrocardiographic changes, cholesterol levels, systolic blood pressure) and angina. The risk of developing angina pectoris was found to be about 20 times higher among persons with all risk factors present than among those with none present.

One additional variable was assessed, namely, the perceived love and support of one's wife. The authors found that with high levels of anxiety, the incidence of angina was significantly reduced in the case of those persons who reported having a loving and supportive wife. Medalie and Goldbourt concluded that preventive measures, like stopping smoking, reducing cholesterol and blood pressure levels and weight, probably help to reduce the incidence of myocardial infarction and, to a lesser extent, angina pectoris, but the major sources of risk for angina pectoris are to be found in a detailed investigation of the subject's personal, family, and occupational life situation.

The power of social support has also been studied in the laboratory. For example, Sarason (1980) examined the quality of social supports as a moderating factor in understanding stress responses in an innovative laboratory setting where it was possible to manipulate the nature of social supports experimentally. During a 20-minute period before a difficult anagram task, members of the experimental group participated in a discussion designed to create a social support network and a sense of sharing. Subjects who participated in the group-building discussion and who were high in test anxiety scored significantly higher on the anagram task than high-test-anxiety subjects who were not part of the group-building discussion. In a second experiment, in which social support was generated by a brief empathic comment regarding a subject's inability to solve the anagrams, similar findings were obtained. Sarason has concluded that "under certain conditions social supports function as a moderator by counteracting undesirable consequence of high anxiety" (p. 26).

A number of studies have pointed to the special importance of social resources in the case of the aging population. Lowenthal and Haven (1968), for example, examined the role of strong personal relationships in the maintenance of health and psychological well-being during middle age and senescence. They postulated that having an intimate relationship in the form of a confidant can serve as a buffer against age-linked social losses. It should be noted that being married and having a confidant are not necessarily the same. Some married persons in their study reported not having a confidant. Some unmarried persons in their study reported having a confidant. The sample in this study consisted of 280 persons in San Francisco, aged 60 or above, interviewed annually on three occasions.

Low social interaction and reported social losses in the past year were found to be associated with poor morale. The presence or absence of a confidant had a dramatic attenuating effect on these relationships. Lowenthal and Haven found, for example, that

> if you have a confidant, you can decrease your social interaction and run no greater risk of becoming depressed than if you had increased it. Further, if you have no confidant and retrench in your social life, the odds for depression become overwhelming. . . . An individual who has been widowed within 7 years, and who has a confidant, has even higher morale than a person who remains married, but lacks a confidant. . . . Among those having confidants, only 10 percent more of the widowed than of the married are depressed, but nearly three-fourths of the widowed who have no confidant are depressed, compared with only about half among the married who have no confidant. (pp. 26, 27)

Lowenthal and Haven speculate that part of the reason for the greater life expectancy among older women in contrast to older men (see Chapter 2) is their greater capacity and willingness to develop and sustain intimate relationships (also see Abrahams & Patterson, 1978–1979).

Finally, in a series of recent studies (Kiecolt-Glaser, Garner, et al., 1984; Kiecolt-Glaser, Ricker, et al., 1984; Kiecolt-Glaser, Speicher, et al., 1984) significant relationships between loneliness, stress, and physiological characteristics of the immune response have been reported in samples of medical students and of psychiatric patients. In all three studies, persons in the high-loneliness group had weaker immune responses including weaker cells that have specific antitumor and antiviral functions. In two of the studies, persons in the high-stress group also showed evidence of weaker antitumor and antiviral cells.

## HEALTH-RELATED STRESS IN THE FAMILY

Threats to health are, of course, stressful both for the person and for the family, and have therefore been the subject of a number of studies. Investigators have examined the effects of illness or the risk of illness on psychological functioning, and have evaluated the role of potential moderating factors in reducing or increasing the negative psychological consequences of illness.

### *Threats to Health as Stressful Life Events*

In a particularly interesting examination of how the possibility of severe illness functions as a stressful life event, Hobfoll and Walfisch (1986) interviewed a sample of sixty-eight women who were suspected of having cancer of the body trunk but who, it turned out later, did not have cancer. These women were interviewed immediately prior to undergoing a biopsy for the suspected cancer, a high-stress situation, and again 3 months later. The two interviews assessed level of depression, recent stressful life events, and "mastery"—defined as "the extent to which one imagines onself capable of acting effectively on the environment to meet one's felt needs" (p. 185). This concept is similar to the concepts of self-efficacy and internal locus of control already described.

Hobfoll and Walfish suggested that there were three possible relationships between prior stressful life events, the current crisis (the possibility of cancer), and such reactions as depression. One possibility is that the current crisis is more damaging to psychological functioning if there have been a greater number of prior stressful life events. A second possibility is that regardless of prior stressful life events, the current crisis has a significant impact on psychological well-being. Finally, a third possibility is that frequent prior stressful life events facilitate the mastery of the current crisis.

Each of these hypotheses leads to a different predicted statistical relationship between prior stress and depression. The first hypothesis would be supported if a significant positive correlation between prior stressful life events and current depression were found. The second hypothesis would be supported if no correlation were found between prior stress and current depression. The third hypothesis would be supported if there were a significantly negative correlation between prior stress and current depression. As for the importance of the concept of mastery, Hobfoll and Walfisch predicted that persons with higher sense of mastery would react less negatively to the suspected cancer than people with a weaker sense of mastery.

Hobfoll and Walfisch found that the first model appeared to be more consistent with their results. The extent of depression, measured both immediately prior to the biopsy and 3 months later, was significantly positively correlated with the extent of prior stressful life events. Risk of clinical depression increased linearly with the number of prior stressful life events.

As for the role of the sense of mastery as a mediating factor, Hobfoll and Walfisch found that stressful life events and sense of mastery made independent contributions to depression. Prebiopsy depression scores among women who expressed a low sense of mastery were equally inflated regardless of the extent of prior stressful life events. In the case of women who expressed a high sense of mastery, however, prebiopsy depression scores were substantially lower for women with fewer prior stressful life events than for women with a greater number of prior stressful life events. The only group to escape a significant risk of depression prior to the biopsy were the women with a high sense of mastery and few prior stressful life events. In parallel fashion, in the case of postbiopsy depression scores obtained 3 months after the biopsies, the group with the greatest risk of depression were those with a low sense of mastery and a high number of prior stressful life events. It was in this group that the threat of cancer had a particularly long-lasting effect.

### Caring for an Ill Family Member

Growing interest in the role of the family in health care has come about largely because of two increasing realizations: the importance (1) of the family in medical management and (2) of the use of family-based alternatives as the site for the provision of medical care, particularly in the area of chronic illness. As the family has become increasingly involved in every aspect of medical care—including prevention, treatment, management, and rehabilitation—an increasing degree of collaboration between medical care and family systems has become necessary (Doherty, 1985; Molumphy & Sporakowski, 1984; Stetz, Lewis, & Primomo, 1986). There is no question but that the severe illness of a family member constitutes a stressful life event of the first magnitude, particularly if there is little likelihood of a full recovery.

Doherty and McCubbin (1985) have identified six important ways in which the family plays a role in the health of its members:

1. Health promotion and risk reduction, that is, the role of the family in health maintenance and illness prevention.
2. Family-related stressful life events that precipitate illness.
3. Family-based health and illness appraisal, that is, how the family assesses the health of its members
4. Family response to acute illness, in terms of its interactions and level of functioning.
5. Family role in help-seeking, primarily how the family goes about deciding to seek medical care
6. Family adaptation to illness, including the ways the family copes with illness, cares for its ill members, and assists in seeing that there is appropriate adherence to the prescribed medical treatment.

Two particular arenas in which the family plays a role in the health of its members have been identified in the literature—caring for sick children and caring for physically ill adults, particularly elderly adults. In each of these arenas two questions have been asked: (1) How is family functioning affected by the presence of an illness in one of its members? and (2) How is the ill person's ability to cope with the illness affected by family factors? (See Hymovich, 1976; Masters, Cerreto, & Mendlowitz, 1983; Stein & Riessman, 1980.)

CARING FOR SICK CHILDREN.    Much of the literature on the role of the family in its members' health deals with chronic childhood illness, including diabetes, cystic fibrosis, and cancer. While there is considerable evidence that the chronic illness of a child has an impact on other family members, the specific nature of that impact has not been systematically identified. For example, some studies have shown that relationships between parents are severely strained by a chronic illness in a child, while other studies have shown that the risk of divorce among parents of a chronically ill child actually decreases, suggesting that the illness results in greater solidarity between the parents (see Barbarin, Hughes, & Chesler, 1985; also see Mattsson, 1977; Stein & Riessman, 1980).

A number of recent studies have examined the needs, concerns, and coping strategies of parents with children with cystic fibrosis and have studied the factors associated with compliance with home treatment. Cystic fibrosis is a lethal, genetically transmitted disorder of uncertain course that requires daily treatment and that has the potential for repeated hospitalizations. Obstruction of the pancreatic ducts causes digestive disturbances; thickened bronchial mucus interferes with the normal cleansing action of the lungs; the inability to expell bacteria leads to recurrent respiratory infections that, in turn, lead to irreversible lung damage and eventual death. Average life expectancy of children with cystic fibrosis, while increasing, is only in the 15- to 17-year range. The level of chronic stress for the family is intense and unremitting.

Patterson (1985) examined factors that affected compliance with home treatment procedures designed to keep the lungs clear and to supplement the diet. These home treatment procedures include the administration of oral medications and special diet, aerosol therapy, bronchial drainage, exercise, and mist-tent therapy at night. These procedures are enormously time-consuming and, at the same time, make a substantial difference in life expectancy and quality.

Patterson's subjects included seventy-two families who had a child with cystic fibrosis who was being seen at the University of Minnesota Hospital Cystic Fibrosis Clinic. Compliance was assessed—on the basis of a telephone interview—as the average of the percentages of prescribed home treatments that were actually conducted in each of the areas of home treatment. In addition, Patterson assessed family environment, health-related coping styles, family stressful life events, and general level of health of the child. Six variables were found to account for about half of the variability in compliance—younger-aged child; less active and recreationally oriented family; greater tendency to maintain family integration; if the child was a girl; greater expressiveness on the part of the family; and if the mother was not employed and thus had more time to devote to the child. In addition, compliance with home treatment seemed to increase following improvement in the child's health status (also see Spirito, Russo, & Masek, 1984).

McCubbin and associates (1983) have developed a procedure for analyzing how parents cope with their children who have cystic fibrosis. The scale, called the Coping Health Inventory for Parents (CHIP), consists of forty-five items describing various ways of coping that parents rate in terms of how helpful each of them seems to be. Degree of helpfulness is rated on a 4-point scale from "not helpful," to "minimally helpful," to "moderately helpful," to "extremely helpful."

Statistical analysis of the responses to the forty-five items from a sample of 185 mothers and fathers indicates that the items can be grouped into three coping patterns. The first coping pattern—*maintaining family integration, cooperation, and optimism*—includes such items as (1) "Believing that my child(ren) will get better," (2) "Believing that things will always work out," (3) "Telling myself that I have many things that I should be thankful for," and (4) "Showing that I am strong." The second coping pattern—*maintaining social support, self-esteem, and psychological stability*—includes such items as (1) "Getting away by myself," (2) "Allowing myself to get angry," (3) "Becoming more self-reliant and independent," and (4) "Entertaining friends in our home." The third coping pattern—*understanding the medical situation*—includes such items as (1) "Talking with other parents in the same type of situation and learning about their experiences," (2) "Reading about how other persons in my situation handle things," (3) "Explaining our family situation to friends and neighbors so they will understand us," and (4) "Talking with the doctor about my concerns about my child(ren) with the medical condition."

At the same time that McCubbin and associates obtained responses to the CHIP questionnaire, they had parents also complete a scale that described their family, from which a number of measures of the family environment were obtained. Included among these measures was (1) cohesiveness, the extent to which family members were concerned, helpful, and supportive of each other; (2) expressiveness, the extent to which family members are allowed to act openly and express their feelings directly; (3) organization, the extent to which explicitness of rules and responsibilities are important in the family; and (4) control, the extent to which the family is organized hierarchically, and with fairly rigid procedures. Independently of these two questionnaires, the authors also obtained medical information regarding the children at the time of the completion of the questionnaires and again 2 or 3 months later. Changes in medical condition during the intervening time period were used as a measure of health status.

McCubbin and his colleagues were interested in determining whether parental coping styles were related to self-report measures of family functioning and to changing health status of the child with cystic fibrosis, and, in general, their hypothesis was supported. Specifically, they found that in the case of the mother, greater use of the three coping styles was associated with higher judged levels of family cohesiveness and expressiveness, while greater use of the three coping styles in the case of the father was associated with higher judged levels of family cohesiveness, organization, and control.

In the case of the relationships of the three coping styles to changes in health of the children, again important relationships were found. In the case of both parents, greater use of the first two coping styles (maintaining family integration and maintaining social support) was significantly associated with improvements in health status of the children. On the basis of these results, McCubbin and associates concluded that parents have the need to balance their responsibilities for their ill children with proper attention to themselves as individuals and to the family as a whole. Furthermore, the results underscore the importance of the father and the value of his coping efforts in maintaining family organization and promoting the child's health (also see Hauser et al., 1985).

Involving the family is particularly important in the case of children with cancer. In an effort to learn more about how the family is impacted when a child has cancer, Barbarin, Hughes, and Chesler (1985) interviewed thirty-two married couples who were the parents of currently living children with cancer. Interviews were conducted individually in the home and required between 1 and 1.5 hours to complete. On most dimensions, this sample was very heterogeneous. The age of the children with cancer in this sample ranged from 4 to 21. A variety of forms of cancer were represented.

The interview, although conducted in a semistructured format, did include a structured questionnaire by which it was possible to calculate measures of family cohesion, marital quality, spouse support, medical stress, and involvement in medical care. In addition, the investigators evaluated the extent to which eight different coping strategies were used: (1) information seeking; (2) problem solving—using behaviorally oriented solutions for specific problems associated with their child's illness; (3) informal help seeking with friends and family; (4) maintenance of emotional balance designed to control emotional reactions and to avoid extreme mood swings; (5) prayer and other forms of reliance on religious beliefs; (6) thinking positively and optimistically; (7) denial, in the form of disbelief, refusal to think about the illness, or withdrawal; and (8) fatalistic acceptance.

The most commonly used coping strategies on the part of the couple were acceptance, problem solving, maintenance of emotional balance, optimism, information seeking, and denial. Religion was used somewhat less frequently, and help seeking was used least frequently. Mothers used religion and information seeking more frequently than their husbands, while fathers used denial more frequently than their wives. In spite of these differences, parents generally tended to use the same coping strategies.

Most parents reported that family cohesion was strengthened by their experiences of trying to be helpful to their child and that the spouse was the single most important source of support. But as the number of hospitalizations increased, marital quality and family cohesion tended to diminish. Most parents reported that the wife was primarily responsible for monitoring the child's medical care. If only one parent spent substantial amounts of time in the hospital, it was most likely the mother. Accordingly, wives tended to judge their husband's support by the level of their involvement in the care of their child. Husbands, on the other hand, tended to judge the support provided by their wives by the level of their availability at home.

In a subsequent report, Barbarin and Chesler (1986) presented additional information about the coping strategies used by the parents. These eight coping strategies were not meaningfully correlated with each other, with the exceptions of problem solving and fatalistic acceptance which were significantly negatively correlated. Barbarin and Chesler also examined the quality of the relationship that the parents had with the medical staff in the hospital and found that parent–medical-staff relationships, as assessed by parents, were better in the case of those parents who used more passive and acquiescent coping styles. Specifically, those parents who had better relationships with the medical staff tended to demonstrate fatalistic acceptance, and tended not to use behaviorally oriented problem-solving approaches in dealing with difficulties associated with their child's cancer or to devote energies toward maintaining emotional balance.

Barbarin and Chesler suggest that passivity and acquiescence on the part of parents might not be conducive to establishing a satisfactory long-term adjustment, and they noted that there has been growing criticism of the traditional model of medical practice in which staff "unilaterally establish the rules governing behavior . . . and patients are expected to adopt passive roles" (p. 234; also see Chapter 7). Barbarin and Chesler (1986) believe that "new partnerships among parents and medical professionals require both to experiment with compatible forms of support and education for active parent roles in the medical care of ill children" (p. 234; also see Koch, 1985).

CARING FOR PHYSICALLY ILL ADULTS. Much of the recent research on family coping with illness in elderly adults focuses on the assessment of the burden, both subjective and objective, that the family members face. The subjective burden is assessed in terms of feelings, attitudes, and emotions. The objective burden is assessed in terms of events and activities.

For example, in a study of caregiving to an elderly disabled relative, Montgomery, Gonyea, and Hooyman (1985) distinguished between these two types of burdens. The sample consisted of eighty people caring for an elderly relative in the greater Seattle area. Objective burden was assessed by a nine-item scale that asked about changes since the caregiving began in the areas of available time, privacy, money, personal freedom, energy, and so on. Subjective burden was assessed by a thirteen-item scale that focused on perceived emotions, including the feeling of personal pain, usefulness, fear, strain, pleasure, depression, and so forth. Amount of caregiving was assessed in hours per week in each of twenty-one different caregiving activities. A factor analysis of these twenty-one different caregiving activities resulted in the identification of seven different caregiving tasks types. The two measures of burden were relatively independent of each other.

The subjective sense of burden was found to be significantly greater among family members who were employed and among younger family members. Two of the task types were significantly associated with the objective sense of burden—nursing care, bathing, and dressing, on the one hand; and walking, transportation, and doing errands, on the other. These two types of caregiving tasks appeared to be particularly time-consuming, and the amount of time needed to carry out the caregiving activities may be the critical dimension in determining objective burden. The authors have come to two interesting conclusions from this survey: First, the level of subjective burden is not likely to be reduced through intervention measures since it is related to characteristics of the caregiver that cannot be easily altered. Second, interventions that give the caregiver at least temporary respite might be effective in reducing the level of objective burden.

Two reports dealing with family stresses associated with caring for relatives with Alzheimer's disease have recently appeared. Alzheimer's disease is a degenerative process in the brain. More than 1.5 million American adults are affected by this disease which frequently results in severe, irreversible intellectual impairment. There is no known cause or cure. Alzheimer's patients suffer from progressive cognitive deficits and memory loss during a 3- to 6-year period, during which they must rely increasingly on their families and other support networks to provide care, a frequently exhausting experience for the caregiver. The exhaustion is due to social isolation, lack of time for oneself, career interruptions, financial drain, and unrelieved physical labor, all of which often results in extreme stress and a profound subjective sense of burden. Accordingly, it is important to learn more about how caregivers cope with the need to provide continuous care to their elderly relatives with Alzheimer's disease, and whether any coping strategies reduce the subjective sense of burden (Aronson, Levin, & Lipkowitz, 1984; Pratt, Schmall, Wright, & Cleland, 1985).

## CONCLUDING COMMENTS

Two general approaches exist for reducing the toll that stress causes on health and human welfare—reduction of counterproductive stresses at their source, and increase in the ability to cope with stresses that cannot be prevented. Both strategies have a preventive orientation, but while the former focuses on changes in the social environment, the latter focuses on facilitating changes within people. Most health service providers are drawn to interventions that can result in internal change, leaving to others—social scientists, community psychologists, social workers, and public policy experts—the process of social change.

In all likelihood, both approaches are needed. On the one hand, there is probably no better solution to stress reduction than a satisfying job, an adequate paycheck, and a strong network of friends and family. On the other hand, a supportive environment does not guarantee successful resolution of life stresses in the absence of a healthy genetic foundation and adequate problem-solving skills and self-esteem. The stress-related literature reviewed in this chapter makes a convincing case for the importance of the biopsychosocial orientation to health and illness.

## SUMMARY

- Perhaps the most important concept that has emerged in the study of health and illness in the past quarter century is the concept of stress.

- Excess stress has been identified as a precipitant of a wide variety of illnesses.

- The two people whose work is most clearly identified with the study of the role of stress in illness are Hans Selye and Adolf Meyer.

- Much is being learned about the remarkably complex physiology of stress and about how stress, as an external phenomenon, gets inside the body. Particular attention is now directed to the role of stress in increasing the vulnerability of the body's immune system.

- Paralleling the increasing recognition of the role of stress in precipitating illness has been an increasing interest in studying how people cope with stress and in how to improve those coping responses.

- Stressful life events, as well as chronic stressful life circumstances, have been shown to play a significant role in precipitating illnesses.

- The ways in which stressful life events play a role in the development of illness depend on a number of factors: a person's past experiences with stress; the dominant psychological defenses employed against stress; the nature of the usual physiological reactions to stress; the strength and nature of coping skills; and on illness behavior, including readiness to seek help and characteristics of the medical care system.

- How stress and stressful life events affect health depends upon two groups of moderating factors: (1) personal resources and personality factors, and (2) social resources, particularly the availability of social support.

- Threats to health constitute a source of stress as well as a consequence of stress, not only for persons who are ill but also for their families. Specific attention has been directed toward how families cope with sick children and with sick elderly family members.

- There is some evidence that health service providers want family members to be passive and compliant when an ill family member requires medical care.

- A special source of stress for family members is found in the case of disabled elderly family members, particularly when they require constant personal care, such as is the case with Alzheimer's disease.

- In the case of stress, just as in the case of illness in general, more attention appears to be directed toward treating the condition after it has developed than in preventing the condition from occurring in the first place.

# Consumer Health
# Education

# 4

## INTRODUCTION

The field of health education has two major target populations: (1) the public and (2) health professionals. This chapter will deal with educational approaches directed toward the public that are designed to improve the health of the general population. Another name for this field is *consumer health education,* a term meant to convey the idea that, at one time or another, we are all consumers of health services and that educational approaches can be used to make us more knowledgeable not only about health and illness, but also about how and when to use health services.

It is appropriate to note before moving on, however, that in a field that is changing as rapidly as the field of health care, ongoing education of health professionals is critically important. These educational efforts, often referred to as *in-service training, continuing education,* or *staff development,* constitute the principle means of keeping practitioners up-to-date regarding their technical skills and factual knowledge once they have completed their formal education. Without such continuing education efforts, health service providers can quickly find themselves behind the times, uninformed about current thinking in the field.

In this chapter, you will have occasion to learn about the work of health educators—professionals specifically trained to provide and evaulate educational programs that have the goal of improving physical and mental well-being. Health educators often work in medical settings, but it should not be assumed that only health educators have a role to play in health education and health promotion (Roemer, 1984). Physicians, too, can and should play a key role in educating their patients, and consumers of health services should not hesitate to make sure that their encounters with physicians have an educational as well as a medical component. A successful course of medical treatment should leave a patient wiser as well as healthier. After all, the origin of the word "doctor" is the Latin word *docere,* meaning "to teach."

## DEFINITION AND GOALS OF CONSUMER HEALTH EDUCATION

A number of classic definitions of health education exist in the literature, but perhaps the most comprehensive is the one adopted by the Task Force on Consumer Health Education, jointly sponsored by the National Institutes of Health, the American College of Preventive Medicine, and the John E. Fogarty International Center for Advanced Studies in the Health Sciences:

> The term "consumer health education" subsumes a set of six activities that—(1) inform people about health, illness, disability, and ways in which they can improve and protect their own health, including more efficient use of the delivery system; (2) motivate people to want to change to more healthful practices; (3) help them to learn the necessary skills to adopt and maintain healthful practices and life styles; (4) foster teaching and communication skills in all those engaged in educating consumers about health; (5) advocate changes in the environment that will facilitate healthful conditions and healthful behaviors; and (6) add to knowledge through research and evaluation concerning the most effective ways of achieving these objectives. (Somers, 1976, p. xv, and see also p. 15; also see Dalzell-Ward, 1976; New Definitions, 1974; President's Committee on Health Education 1973)

The field of consumer health education, then, concerns itself with creating an informed public in the areas of health and health practices. The field has three objectives: (1) to provide health-related information, (2) to change health-related attitudes in directions more conducive to good health, and (3) to change health-related behavior in ways that are likely to enhance health. Of these three objectives, changing health-related behavior and attitudes is far more difficult than providing health-related information (Hetherington & Calderone, 1985; Kirscht, 1983; Kreps et al., 1987; Leventhal, 1973). Evaluating consumer health education programs should involve determining the extent to which all three objectives have been met. As you will see, however, many evaluations stop at assessing attitude change, or at even assessing information gain.

In addition to identifying the principal objectives of consumer health education programs, it is important to identify their major target groups. The first target group is the general public. Consumer health education programs designed for the general public serve to inform individuals about health problems and community health resources and about ways of promoting general health. The second target group is composed of at-risk populations. groups of people identified as being unusually vulnerable to some particular disorder or group of disorders. Consumer health education programs for these groups are designed to assist them in preventing these disorders from occurring insofar as possible, as well as in coping with these predictable disorders when they do occur.

The third target group is patients and prospective patients. Educational programs designed for them help them become more knowledgeable health service consumers, by learning more about when to seek health care, how to select health care providers, how to cope with the stresses induced by medical care, and how to improve their adherence to prescribed health care regimens (see Chapter 12). Finally, the fourth target group for consumer health education programs is those people in the community such as elected officials, health agency board members, and governmental authorities who are in a position to influence public policy. Objectives of health education programs aimed at this target population are to develop greater understanding of the impact of public policy on general health and to generate increased support for public policies that promote health.

The general orientation of this book is to treat mental health and general health as different aspects of the same inseparable phenomenon. As was noted in Chapter 1, physical health and mental health tend to go hand in hand. Similarly, general health education and mental health education have much in common. In fact, many of the examples of consumer health education programs that will be described in this chapter have mental health components. There is a specialized field of mental health education, however, that can be thought of as a subfield of general consumer health education (Goldston, 1968; Ketterer, 1981; Swisher, 1976).

### Health Promotion

The term *health promotion* is usually distinguished from the term *disease prevention*, although both activities can take place by means of consumer health education programs. Disease prevention activities are those related to specific diseases, such as spraying malarial swamps to get rid of mosquitoes that carry malaria or fluoridating the water supply to reduce the incidence of dental caries. In contrast, a variety of nonspecific practices—such as providing better prenatal care, crisis intervention services, or social support during times of stress—may have a positive effect on health in general and may, in fact, prevent a variety of forms of disordered behavior. Those practices that have a generally salutary but unspecifiable effect on health are called health promotion (McPheeters, 1976; Perry & Jessor, 1985).

# EXAMPLES OF HEALTH EDUCATION PROGRAMS

It is now appropriate to look at some examples of health education programs in terms of the four target populations of particular interest to health educators—the general public, specific at-risk groups, patients in the medical care system, and policy makers. Health education programs have been directed toward all four groups, although the fewest programs have been reported for policy makers. Nevertheless, it is possible to identify from the literature health education programs in each of the four target-group categories.

### The General Population

Programs directed toward the general population have hardly any choice but to employ the mass media. Most of us obtain health-related information from the media—newspapers, television, magazines, and the radio (see Brawley & Martinez-Brawley, 1984; Maloney & Hersey, 1984; Puska et al., 1987). The Department of Continuing Education at the Harvard Medical School has been publishing a monthly health newsletter for the past decade that is now available on a subscription basis, and the Harvard School of Public Health has recently established a Center for Health Communication, which is designed "to provide the public with reliable health information as a basis for informed personal choices" ("Center Established," 1986). These days, health information is front-page news.

As we have insisted from the outset, however, consumer health education is more than the provision of information. Thus, evaluations of health education programs directed toward the general population must not only determine whether these messages have been received and understood, but must also ascertain the extent to which these messages seem to result in changes in attitudes and behavior.

PREVENTION OF DEPRESSION.   In a study of the effectiveness of a 2-week long television miniseries in San Francisco on behavior and mood, Muñoz, Glish, Soo-Hoo, and Robertson (1982) conducted a telephone survey the week before the series started and the week after it ended, in order to examine its effects on viewers. The series consisted of nine 4-minute segments shown three times daily as part of the local news program. The segments were drawn from a recent volume that dealt with social-learning and self-control approaches to the prevention of depression. Each approach was described and then demonstrated using videotapes of everyday situations portrayed by students.

Telephone numbers were selected at random from the San Francisco telephone directory, and 162 persons aged 18 or older responded to both the pre- and postprogram interviews. The interviews included a set of behavioral questions, a measure of depression, and the determination of which portions of the TV miniseries were watched. The behavioral items, paralleling the themes of the individual segments, included for example doing something pleasant, rewarding onself, relaxing, and trying to think positive thoughts. A twenty-item depressive-mood scale was administered to assess respondents' mood during the past week. In the postprogram interview, after the behavior and mood scales were administered, the respondents were asked whether they remembered watching the segments of the program.

Two of the specific behaviors that were assessed increased significantly during the 2-week period among those respondents who had watched the programs—telling oneself to stop thinking upsetting thoughts and taking time to relax. One general behavior also increased significantly—thinking about how to keep oneself from getting depressed. No significant changes in reported mood were found in the sample as a whole, but when the sample was subdivided according to initial level of depression, the sample with higher initial scores who had watched the segments showed a significant reduction in depressed mood when contrasted with those persons with higher initial scores who had not watched the program.

The authors are cautious in their interpretations of the findings, but they do suggest that the miniseries appeared to have a significant immediate effect on both depression-related behavior and mood.

ENHANCING SOCIAL SUPPORT IN THE COMMUNITY.    In the first state-wide mental health promotion campaign in the United States, in 1982, the California Department of Mental Health launched a mental health education program designed to encourage the public to consider the value of initiating, maintaining, and strengthening personal relationships as a way of enhancing both mental and physical well-being. Entitled *Friends Can Be Good Medicine,* the program combined the use of the mass media with community participation and stressed the health benefits that could accrue from supportive personal relationships (Hersey et al., 1984; Taylor, Lam, Roppel, & Barter, 1984).

The major objectives of the mental health education program were to (1) inform the public about the importance of supportive personal relationships in maintaining mental and physical health, (2) encourage the public to devote more time and energy to enhancing their personal relationships, and (3) create opportunities for communities to come together in order to strengthen their supportive personal relationships.

In order to accomplish these objectives, a variety of health education materials were developed, including public service announcements for television and radio; films; a self-assessment brochure; a booklet of poems; exercises; photographs demonstrating the interrelationships of health and supportive social relationships; billboards and bumper stickers; bilingual slide and audio-cassette programs; board games; and brochures summarizing the fundamental messages of the program.

The pilot program was tested in a six-county area in California in the fall of 1981. Thousands of booklets and brochures were distributed, and numerous workshops, presentations, and in-service training sessions were conducted, along with TV and radio talk show appearances and public service announcements. An independent contractor was hired to conduct the evaluation study. Pre- and postprogram telephone interviews were conducted with a sample of several hundred area residents in order to assess changes in knowledge and attitudes, and intended changes in behavior regarding the establishment and enrichment of personal relationships.

Survey results indicated that among those people who were reached by the campaign, positive changes were found in the three domains of knowledge, attitudes, and intended behavior. Furthermore, there was some evidence that there were positive qualitative as well as quantitative changes in the nature of interpersonal relationships.

On the basis of this pilot study, plans were undertaken to bring the program to the entire state during the month of May 1982. More than 1300 *Friends* activities were conducted during the month, involving fifty-one of California's fifty-eight counties. The films were screened in theaters throughout the state. Nearly 200 television and radio broadcasts focused on the theme of the health education effort. National coverage of the campaign included articles in newspapers throughout the country, along with appearances of staff members on national TV shows.

A second independent evaluation study conducted a year later obtained essentially the same results as the earlier one. In addition, a reassessment of the pilot study population indicated that the initial gains in knowledge, attitudes, and behavior were maintained over the course of the year. Finally, there was some evidence that the program was most effective when communities used a combination of broadcast media, local activities, and educational materials.

STATEWIDE PREVENTION PROGRAMS.    Analysis of risk factors for heart disease, cancer, and cerebrovascular disease, which together account for about two-thirds of all deaths in the United States, indicates that they have a number of similarities. All three diseases are more prevalent among people who have unhealthy diets, and two of the three diseases are more prevalent among people who smoke, have high blood pressure, are physically inactive, have diabetes, and engage in excessive alcohol intake (see Chapter 5). Thus, it has seemed appropriate in the state of Massachusetts to undertake a statewide prevention program, based on a consumer health education model, that has as its objective the reduction in death rate from all three diseases (Havas & Walker, 1986).

The Massachusetts Department of Public Health established the Center for Health Promotion and Environmental Disease Prevention, supported by a combination of state and federal funds. The center has a multidisciplinary staff and a scientific advisory committee (in which the leading public health and medical schools are represented). The program's goals consist of helping all Massachusetts residents to (1) become nonsmokers, (2) lower their serum cholesterol levels and fat intake, (3) lower their blood pressure, (4) increase their amount of vigorous exercise to a level of 20 minutes per day for three or more times per week, and (5) minimize their exposure to toxic substances.

Using realistic estimates of how long it will take to achieve these objectives, the directors of the program believe that at least 500 lives will be saved annually within 2 years, 2000 lives will be saved annually within 5 years, and 4400 lives annually within 10 years.

The key component of the program is the use of mass media for disseminating information on the relationship between lifestyle behaviors and health. In addition, local high blood pressure control activities are being established that concentrate on nonpharmacologic approaches as the first line of therapy. Statewide educational efforts are being undertaken in order to improve nutrition. Efforts to stop smoking are being encouraged by enacting laws to reduce smoking in public places, especially restaurants and health care facilities, worksites, and schools, restricting advertising and free distribution of cigarettes, encouraging insurance companies to lower health and life insurance premiums for nonsmokers, and supporting the development of smoking prevention and cessation programs at worksites and schools. Worksite and community physical fitness programs are being developed. Supplementing these programs are continuing education programs for first-line health providers, with particular concentration on primary care physicians.

### At-Risk Groups

The second category of consumer health education programs includes those that are directed toward specific at-risk groups, that is, groups of people who are at greater than average risk to engage in behaviors that are judged to be self-destructive. At-risk groups can be defined demographically, such as by their gender, age, or physical attributes; or by the occasion of specific events, such as becoming new parents or entering college; or by specific behaviors, such as smoking or driving while drinking.

Two general approaches have been employed in such consumer health education programs. One approach has been health promotion, that is, enhancing coping skills and general well-being rather than attempting to reduce the risk associated with any particular disease or disorder. The other approach, where epidemiological evidence exists, has been to identify groups of people who are at high risk for some specific disorder, such as coronary heart disease or lung cancer, and then to develop a health education program for these specific high-risk groups based on behaviorally-oriented research findings.

HEALTH EDUCATION FOR HEALTHY CHILDREN.   In the case of children, a very strong case has been made that various types of preventive and health promotional activities are not receiving the emphasis they deserve. The Select Panel for the Promotion of Child Health, created by the U.S. Congress in 1978, is charged with the responsibility of formulating specific goals for promoting the health status of children and expectant mothers and for developing a comprehensive national plan for achieving these goals. According to the Select Panel, many problems will not be resolved by a disease-oriented medical care system, however skilled its personnel and sophisticated its technology, but rather by improving the physical and social environments in which people live and by changing individual behavior (U.S. Department of Health and Human Services, 1981a, 1981b).

The Select Panel called particular attention to a number of underutilized measures of demonstrated effectiveness, including improved prenatal care, immunizations, nutritional care, early childhood screening for visual and hearing disorders, preventive dental care, accident prevention, and family planning. While acknowledging that health promotion and disease prevention activities will not eliminate premature deaths and illnesses, the panel became convinced—on the basis of its analysis of testimony, research findings, and background materials—that nearly all forms of prevention are inexpensive, both absolutely and relative to the costs of subsequent care for problems that arise in their absence, and that to withhold such preventive care in the name of cost containment would be economically foolish, quite apart from its questionable morality and ethics.

The panel noted, for example, that the $180 million spent on measles vaccinations between 1966 and 1974 saved an estimated $1.3 billion in medical and other long-term care by reducing deafness, mental retardation, and other problems. In addition, they reported that the cost of genetic screening at birth plus early treatment for seven common disorders was less than one-eighth the projected cost of caring for an impaired child. Furthermore, for every dollar that was spent in water fluoridation, $50 was saved in reduced costs of treating tooth decay.

With virtually all children and adolescents in public school, a great number of health educators have thought of the school setting as an ideal one for the development of educational programs that have an emphasis on health maintenance. School-based health education programs have been in existence since the early 1900s, many inaugurated as a consequence of the prohibition movement that aimed to outlaw the consumption of alcohol. But in spite of the rather obvious advantages of including health education within the normal public school curriculum, few comprehensive health education programs exist, and few persuasive positive evaluations of the programs that do exist have been reported.

In a critical analysis of the state of school health education, Bartlett (1981) evaluated the published outcome studies of traditional school health education programs in the areas of drug and alcohol, smoking, nutrition, driver education, dental health, and heart health. In summary, Bartlett found that these health education programs needed to be improved. They were very effective in increasing knowledge, less effective in improving attitudes, and generally ineffective in changing health practice behavior.

Bartlett identified a number of constraints that reduce the number and the effectiveness of school health education programs. First, there are philosophical differences of opinion in many communities regarding the appropriate tasks that should be undertaken by the school and the home, respectively. Second, because of the generally large number of pupils in the typical classroom, health education has had to be communicated through lectures—a format thought to be far less effective than more personal methods that can work only with far smaller groups (also see Gochman, 1982).

ADOLESCENT PREGNANCY AND PARENTHOOD.    One particularly compelling area for school-based health education is that of adolescent pregnancy and parenthood, particularly in view of the fact that only 20 percent of pregnancies among married or unmarried teenagers are intentional (National Center for Health Statistics, 1985i; 1985j). One of the reasons for determining whether a pregnancy is intended is that a number of studies have documented that children unwanted at the time of pregnancy are at excess risk for subsequent developmental disorders (David, 1986; David & Matejcek, 1981).

Even though teenage girls represent only 20 percent of sexually active females capable of becoming pregnant, they account for nearly half of out-of-wedlock births and one-third of all abortions. Among adolescent girls, more than half of unintended pregnancies result in abortions, and nearly 20 percent in miscarriages or stillbirths (Resnick, 1984). Yet, fewer than 10 percent of adolescents receive a comprehensive sex-education program in school (Maslach & Kerr, 1983).

Adolescents are largely uninformed about reproductive physiology and about contraceptive methods and have negative attitudes toward their use. Adolescents tend not to use contraceptives because they underestimate the possibility of pregnancy, because they do not have access to contraceptives, and because they do not anticipate their need (Morrison, 1985). Indeed, in watching movies that deal with sexual themes among adolescents or young adults, it is striking how few films include any scenes in which the young couple discuss contraception or any other issues pertinent to responsible sexual behavior.

Mecklenburg and Thompson (1983) noted that while the rate of contraceptive use has increased among sexually active girls, it is not high enough to contain the rise in premarital adolescent pregnancies. According to a recent survey of contraceptive use (National Center for Health Statistics, 1984c), only 68 percent of unmarried women between ages 15 and 19 who are sexually active and at risk of unintended pregnancy use any form of contraception. Even among unmarried sexually active women age 20 to 44, who are at risk of unintended pregnancy, only 80 percent use any form of contraception.

Pregnancy rates, birth rates, and abortion rates for American girls between ages 15 and 19 are far higher in the United States than in other developed countries where there is approximately the same level of teenage sexual activity. In the United States, the annual pregnancy rate in the 15 to 19 age group is 96 per 1000. In England, Wales, France, and Canada the rate is half that. The pregnancy rate is three times higher in the United States than in Sweden and nearly seven times higher in the United States than in the Netherlands.

According to a recent study undertaken by the Guttmacher Institute (Jones et al., 1985) designed to gain greater insight into the determinants of teenage reproductive behavior in different countries, the most likely explanation of these rate differences was that other countries appeared to have a stronger commitment to providing contraceptives and sex education—two strategies that appear very effective in reducing both the pregnancy rate and the abortion rate.

In addition to its obvious consequences in terms of pregnancy, adolescent sexual activity results in increased incidence of sexually transmitted diseases; often has long-term negative economic implications for the mother and her child; results in unnecessary mortality and morbidity for mothers and their infants, particularly among very young adolescents; and entails enormous social cost in the form of reduced educational and occupational attainment, increased divorce rate, and welfare program dependency (also see Schinke, Gilchrist, & Small, 1979).

Burden and Klerman (1984) reviewed the literature regarding ways of reducing the economic dependence of adolescent parents and concluded that efforts to reduce the adolescent pregnancy rate will require dealing with the issue of the status of women in the United States. Until such time, early motherhood will continue to remain an attractive alternative to the low-paying, dead-end jobs now available to adolescent women (also see Flick, 1986).

The Adolescent Family Life Program, created by the federal government as a response to the disturbingly high rates of pregnancy and parenthood among adolescents, was recently described by Mecklenburg and Thompson (1983). The program has two components—educational and other services designed to prevent pregnancy, and caretaking services to pregnant adolescent girls and their infants. Included among the services that are authorized by this program are pregnancy testing, maternity counseling, family planning services, prenatal and postnatal care, nutrition information and counseling, screening for and treatment of venereal diseases, pediatric care, educational services in sexuality and family life, educational and vocational services, and adoption counseling.

The Adolescent Family Life Program is governed by two principal values—it seeks to encourage abstinence from premarital sexual relations, and it encourages increased parental involvement in guiding sexual practices among adolescents.

Thus, two competing strategies have been proposed for reducing unplanned adolescent pregnancies—the provision of comprehensive sex education and contraceptive information and materials as urged by most sex educators and consumer health educators, on the one hand, and the encouragement of pre-

marital abstinence and parental involvement in guiding adolescent sexual practices and family planning, on the other hand. People tend to favor one set of
options or the other, but rarely both. This tendency is seen most clearly in the
current debates regarding abortion. People who are closely identified with the
antiabortion position are, at the same time, very often opposed to the provision
of contraceptive information and sex education to adolescents (Schwartz, 1985).

One especially controversial way of increasing parental involvement is
the provision, in many state laws, that requires parental consent before an abortion can be obtained by an unmarried woman under the age of 18. Such parental
consent laws were in effect in twelve states as of mid-1985, and Cartoof and
Klerman (1986) have provided perhaps the first evaluation of this law in their
study conducted in Massachusetts. The Massachusetts parental consent law was
implemented in April 1981.

Cartoof and Klerman collected data on the number of abortions that
took place in Massachusetts and in the five surrounding states of New Hamp-
shire, Rhode Island, Connecticut, Maine, and New York, before and after the
enactment of the Massachusetts law. The studied groups were minors and non-
minors who were residents of Massachusetts.

Cartoof and Klerman found that about half as many women under the
age of 18 obtained abortions in the state during the 20 months after the law went
into effect as had done so previously, but that the number of Massachusetts
minors who traveled to one of the five surrounding states for an abortion increased by about the same amount as the in-state decrease. Thus, the major
result of the Massachusetts parental consent law has been to send a monthly
average of between ninety and ninety-five of the state's pregnant minors across
state lines in search of an abortion.

Cartoof and Klerman have concluded that while advocates of parental
consent laws support the concept in the name of family unity, enhanced communication between parents and their children, protection of young adolescents
who are unable to make mature decisions, and a reduction in the rate of abortion
among them, there is little evidence that parental consent laws are having those
effects.

Understanding contraception is useful not only for adolescents, of
course. According to the results of a recent survey commissioned by the American College of Obstetricians and Gynecologists (Gallup Survey, 1985), Americans in general are grossly misinformed about birth control, with millions of
women of childbearing age in the United States choosing to use no contraception
because they incorrectly believe them to be dangerous. In spite of this lack of
accurate information, 74 percent of the more than 1000 women surveyed in this
study agreed that contraceptive services should be available to teenagers.

PRENATAL AND POSTNATAL HEALTH EDUCATION.    With the growing
realization that the lack of prenatal care can place both mother and infant at
increased risk for a very wide variety of disorders, a number of studies have been

undertaken to mount and evaluate prenatal health education programs. These programs can take one of two forms—an ecologic approach that aims at the entire community, and a high-risk approach that aims at subsets of the community on the basis of their being at unusually high risk (Chamberlin, 1984).

Each approach has its advantages and disadvantages. The high-risk approach assumes that it is possible to identify a small number of families who will produce a very large proportion of the child development and child health problems in the community. Unfortunately, the ability to identify this subset of families is quite limited. Thus, either one ends up with a very large group of potential high-risk families most of whom will not have the problem that is the focus of attention, or the high-risk families that are identified will be small in number but will fail to include the bulk of the problem children. The problem with the first approach is that the cost per actual high-risk family is very high. The problem with the second approach is that large numbers of high-risk families will fail to be identified.

The ecologic or community-wide approach targets the entire population and thus will not fail to identify children in need of help. Unfortunately, at least in the United States, such programs are rare because they are so expensive. In part, however, this high cost is because health-related services are typically fragmented, with many different agencies at different governmental levels (for example, federal, state, county, city) all involved independently of each other in the provision of services. In order for the ecologic approach to work, it will be necessary, in Chamberlin's words, to take a "closer look at how to organize these services into a community-wide delivery system that takes into account all we have learned about human development" (1984, p. 194).

One example of a high-risk program was instituted in a health maintenance organization (see Chapter 2) in southern California, and the report of its effectiveness was prepared by Ershoff, Aaronson, Danaher, and Wasserman (1983). The target population was pregnant women who smoked.

In their study, Ershoff and his colleagues assigned essentially at random fifty-seven women—smokers at the time of the pregnancy testing—to an experimental program that included the provision of nutritional counseling and a home-correspondence smoking cessation program provided by a health educator. An appropriately selected control group of seventy-two pregnant women received standard prenatal care.

For the women in the experimental program, as soon as pregnancy was confirmed, same-day appointments were made with a health educator and a nutritionist, and, following these two appointments, with a physician. Nutritional counseling included a review of the medical record and the administration of a 24-hour dietary recall interview. Counseling focused on the importance of diet, of keeping weight gain within optimal limits, and of restricting the intake of alcohol, caffeine, and other drugs. A second nutritional interview was held 3 months later for the purposes of reassessing nutritional status, checking weight gain, reviewing the physician's progress notes, administering a second 24-hour dietary recall interview, and obtaining self-reports of degree of adherence to recommended dietary changes.

The stop-smoking program was based upon the provision of booklets at home each week that presented a comprehensive smoking cessation program, and a program of telephone contact by the pregnant woman with the health maintenance organization on a three calls per week schedule.

Results of the health education program were striking. In comparison with the control women, a greater proportion of experimental-group women quit smoking or reduced their rate of smoking, and adjusted their dietary intake. Infants born to the mothers in the experimental group had a significantly greater birth weight, and hospital treatment-cost savings as a consequence of the reduced incidence of low birth weight infants amounted to twice as much as the cost of the entire prenatal program. Savings amounted to $183 per delivery, while the total cost of the prenatal health education program was only $93 per delivery.

FAMILY LIFE EDUCATION.    Family life education programs, as their name suggests, are aimed at families. They have as their objectives the improvement of family well-being in both a general and a specific sense. The concept of family life education is quite ecumenical in nature, including efforts to enhance not only health but also interpersonal relationships within as well as external to the family. Family life education programs also aim at facilitating child rearing, the establishment of enduring family-related values, and the manner in which people cope with such problems as family planning, personal sexuality and changing sex roles, conflicts of adolescence, marriage and divorce, and the problems associated with aging (Goodwin, 1972).

As an example of the thought that has gone into the problem of how to reach the target audience, Hennon and Peterson (1981) considered consumer health education programs for young families—people aged 19 to 34—who make up about 30 percent of the American population. As analysis reveals, families are frequently unresponsive to invitations to participate in group educational programs but do respond to opportunities to make decisions in the privacy of their own homes. Young families appear to make most of their decisions at home and are influenced in these decisions by magazines, newsletters, and pamphlets that they receive at home.

On the basis of this analysis of previous research, Hennon and Peterson, two Wisconsin specialists in family resources and consumer sciences, developed a series of ten single-theme learn-at-home packets, dealing with such topics as choosing parenthood, family management, consumer decision making, credit, and family nutrition. These packets were made available to university extension-program faculty members in all Wisconsin counties, and an in-depth study of the effectiveness of this approach was undertaken with a sample of eighty-two young families in nine Wisconsin counties. These families agreed to read the materials and participate in a telephone interview to help evaluate their quality and usefulness.

The interviews were conducted 6 months after the packets had been distributed. Fifty-nine families reported having read all ten packets. In general, families found the materials informative and useful. The packets filled some immediate needs and were judged to be practical, helpful, clear, and interesting. The authors also found that the packets that dealt with a particular need that the family had at a given time were evaluated most favorably. Virtually all families liked the idea of having the learn-at-home packets. Younger families living in rural areas found the packets most useful. About two-thirds of the families reported having used at least one of the ideas in the packets in the 6 months since they had received them.

Hennon and Peterson concluded that young families can be reached by learn-at-home packets and that their delivery system was effective and efficient regardless of the educational level, place of residence, or employment status of the adults in the families they reached.

The family life education program in existence for perhaps the longest continuous period in the United States is "Pierre the Pelican," the program for new mothers that was originated in Louisiana in 1946 by the late Loyd W. Rowland. The pelican is the Louisiana state bird and, undoubtedly a consequence of the French influence in Louisiana, has been named Pierre. The educational materials are prepared in pamphlet form, and are designed to be mailed to all parents of firstborn children in Louisiana. The health education information in the pamphlets is intended to be helpful to new mothers by covering the most important principles of child rearing, including but extending beyond good physical care.

Rowland created the pamphlets to be appropriate at the sixth-grade reading level and made them attractive to read. Each pamphlet is illustrated with sketches and features the character Pierre. The pamphlets comprise a series, make use of a question-and-answer format, are long enough without being tedious, and make an effort to cover topics of special interest to young parents (Greenberg, Harris, MacKinnon, & Chipman, 1953).

There are twenty-eight pamphlets in all, distributed one each month during the first year, every other month during the second year, every fourth month during the third and fourth years, and every 6 months during the fifth and sixth years. The titles of some of the twelve pamphlets distributed to new parents during the first year illustrate the topics covered in the series: "Is 'Bright Eyes' Watching You?" "Talking Starts by Listening," "Sitting Up Is Wonderful to Do," "Let's Think about Discipline," and "Even a Baby Needs Friends His Own Age."

An early evaluation of the Pierre the Pelican series was undertaken by Greenberg and his colleagues (1953). In the concluding section of that evaluation study, Greenberg et al. indicated that Pierre was favorably received by parents. They wrote, "After the first three months of distribution, self-addressed return post cards were mailed to recipients. . . . 50.7 per cent were returned, and every answer was in favor of continuing the series. Of those returning the cards, about 90 per cent answered that they were saving the pamphlets, and without being asked, 82 per cent volunteered . . . that they had found Pierre helpful" (p. 1155).

Health education materials for new parents, such as the Pierre the Pelican series, are generally referred to as *age-paced newsletters.* In a recent national survey designed to determine how frequently such newsletters are used and how effective they seem to be, Cudaback and associates (1985) found that ten different newsletter series are in use and that such newsletters are used in about 40 percent of the states. The newsletters are viewed as practical, inexpensive, and efficient, and the great majority of parents who receive them report that the newsletters are "useful in promoting their self-confidence as parents, improving their knowledge of child development and increasing their ability to be effective nurturing parents" (p. 271).

HEALTH EDUCATION WITH THE BEREAVED.    The last two decades have witnessed a growing interest in bereavement, a crucial event for which health education programs might be helpful. Coping with bereavement, even when death is anticipated, can vary in terms of its adequacy, and one aspect of inadequate coping now identified is the excess risk of illness to the survivors (see Kaprio et al., 1987). As a consequence, a number of preventive intervention programs have been designed to be of help to bereaved persons.

Parkes (1981) evaluated the impact of bereavement counseling on family members of 181 patients who died at St. Christopher's Hospice in London during 1970 through 1974. The selection of family members for followup was made on the basis of a questionnaire completed by nurses at the time of bereavement. All family members judged by the nurse as likely to cope badly were followed. All other family members were divided into a high-risk or low-risk group on the basis of their replies to a brief questionnaire. Members of the high-risk group were randomly assigned to either an experimental or control condition. Thus, bereaved persons who were coping reasonably well but who were judged to be at high-risk of coping poorly in the future were the subjects of this intervention program.

Volunteer counselors visited subjects in the experimental group. Contact was established with a key person within families, most frequently the spouse. Most high-risk persons seemed to require help. Two-thirds of the key persons needed to talk about the bereavement, and more than half were evaluated as having benefited from such conversations. Specific problems noted by the volunteer counselors included housing, financial difficulties, disposal of possessions, need for friendship, insomnia, physical illness, keeping the existing home, excessive crying, eating too little, haunting memories, and difficulty maintaining relationships with others.

The study found that high-risk participants who were assigned to the control condition did more poorly than participants for whom services were provided. Members of the high-risk control group had far more symptoms of illness and increased their use of alcohol, tobacco, and other drugs. In the entire sample, several groups coped particularly poorly with bereavement—women, older participants, and those who were found initially to express a good deal of self-reproach.

Bereaved persons who were initially judged to be at low risk did better than high-risk controls but not better than high-risk participants in the experimental intervention program. Thus, Parkes (1981) concluded that "the effect of the service has been to reduce the health risk of the 'High Risk' group to about the same level as the 'Low Risk' group" and that "the service reduces the need for drugs, alcohol and tobacco among the bereaved and reduces the number of symptoms attributable to anxiety and tension from which they suffer. It may also reduce the use which they make of doctors and hospitals and improve their overall level of contentment" (p. 186).

In a 2-year study of postbereavement adaptation of a group of 162 widows, Vachon et al. (1980) contrasted adaptation to death of a spouse in two groups. In the experimental intervention group, widows were paired with another widow for purposes of providing emotional support and practical assistance. These helper-widows had previously participated in a training seminar that examined issues related to widowhood. The widow-to-widow intervention program consisted of supportive telephone calls and both individual and small-group meetings. The other group served as a control, and no special services were made available to them.

The authors found that the intervention and control subjects were equally disturbed one month after bereavement but that widows in the intervention program were less depressed and preoccupied with the past. One year later, the control group had caught up with the intervention group in their personal adjustment, but the intervention group was superior in terms of their resocialization. Two years later, the level of health was substantially better in the intervention group than in the control group. The authors concluded that those widows who received the intervention services followed the same general course of adaptation as the control subjects but that their rate of adaptation was accelerated (see also Raphael, 1977, 1978; Rogers et al., 1980; Silverman, 1967, 1972; Silverman, MacKenzie, Pettipas, & Wilson, 1975; Walker, MacBride, & Vachon, 1977).

### Patients in the Medical Care System

There is hardly any question about the assertion that becoming ill constitutes a significant stressful life event both for the patient and the patient's family, and that entering the medical care system can compound that stress. Later in this volume (Chapter 7), we will examine how the medical care system induces stress in patients, and what efforts have been made to change the behavior of health care providers so that those stresses can be reduced. Some of the stress of entering the medical care system can be reduced by health education programs directed toward the patients themselves, and an increasing number of university-based health education programs are including patient education in their curricula (Pigg, 1982).

Health education programs directed toward medical patients have two objectives. First, these programs are designed to provide information in order to reduce the sense of uncertainty that often accompanies entrance into the medical care system. Second, these programs are designed to provide emotional support in order to reduce the feeling of danger and threat. Nowadays most physicians spread health educational materials for patients throughout their waiting rooms—articles on how to choose a physician and how to make one's needs known to physicians, and on various medical illnesses and medical procedures. These articles are upbeat and designed to help patients become more informed about their illnesses and more actively involved in their medical care program. Health educators interested in patient education are hopeful that such information will encourage patients to change their behaviors in ways that will increase the effectiveness of medical care.

PATIENT EDUCATION.    Havik (1981) recently reviewed twenty-five different published studies examining the effectiveness of providing patient information and education in reducing the duration or disability of physical disease. Most of the studies were done with surgical patients, and all used extremely brief interventions, averaging about 30 minutes in duration. In all cases, control group data were available and it was possible to calculate the effectiveness of the intervention by contrasting outcome measures in the experimental and control groups.

These brief interventions were of three types. First, usually with the use of videotapes or films, patients were shown what the procedures they were to undergo would be like, and what techniques they could use that would minimize the pain or discomfort associated with the procedures. Second, information was provided about what to expect during the procedure in terms of what would be seen, felt, or heard. Third, specialized support was provided during critical periods in the surgical procedure.

Havik found that 96 percent of the measures of effect calculated in these twenty-five different studies favored the group of patients who received the information and education over patients in the control groups. Information and education appeared to have the greatest effect in reducing physical symptoms, complaints, and complications, and in improving psychosocial well-being.

The effects were observed over a broad spectrum, covering emotional, interpersonal, and physiological variables that were of importance for the total well-being of medical patients. In addition, Havik found that the intervention programs were very brief, could be administered to groups of patients, and could be incorporated in standard treatment and care programs without a great need for additional professional expertise (also see Olbrisch, 1977).

Paralleling the growth of health education programs for patients is the increase in the number of programs for family members (see, for example, Aronson, Levin, & Lipkowitz, 1984; Berkowitz, Eberlein-Fries, Kuipers, & Leff, 1984). Such programs have the same set of goals as do all other health education programs: (1) to inform family members about the patient's illness; (2) to explore attitudes and feelings regarding the illness as well as the patient; (3) to encourage the modification of these attitudes and feelings when such changes seem appropriate; and (4) to facilitate behavior change when indicated. As we saw in Chapter 3, illness of an individual family member can have a significant impact on the entire family organization and structure, and can require new forms of adaptation and adjustment. To the extent that family members cope successfully with the problems created by the illness, recovery or adaptation on the part of the patient can be accelerated with minimal disruption to family functioning.

THE SELF-HELP MOVEMENT.    A special approach to patient education that should be mentioned is the *self-help movement* (Gartner & Riessman, 1984). This movement is characterized by the formation of groups by patients, expatients, and family members designed "to provide mutual aid and assistance to members in dealing with adaptive problems resulting from disability due to illness, disease, or other health-related disorders" (Tracy & Gussow, 1976, p. 381). The disorders are typically chronic in nature, although they may consist of recurrent acute episodes.

With the exception of Alcoholics Anonymous, the self-help group phenomenon is a post–World War II development. Self-help groups are available for persons with addictions and drug dependencies, such as smoking or drug abuse, with a varied array of health problems, such as amyotrophic lateral sclerosis (Lou Gehrig's disease), Alzheimers disease, anemia, cerebral palsy, mastectomy, Parkinson's disease, spina bifida, and stroke, and with such disabilities and injuries as amputation, burns, hearing impairment, learning disabilities, and stuttering. In the 1984–1985 self-help group directory, the New Jersey Self-Help Clearinghouse lists more than 3000 such groups.

There is substantial evidence that self-help groups are effective not only in the case of the persons being helped but also for those persons *providing* the help. Traditional health services are often perceived as too big, distant, and bureaucratized, too costly and ineffective, too demanding in terms of their psychological cost to personnel, and populated by staff who are uninterested in how to prevent disorder and disability. In contrast, self-help groups can be inexpensive, responsive, and accessible. While years ago health professionals tended to be suspicious of self-help groups, primarily because the group leaders were insistent on not involving health care professionals, they are beginning to look at self-help groups more favorably and are beginning to explore how the health professional and self-help group can work together to the mutual benefit of people in need of help.

### General Policy Makers

Social policy is made at every governmental level in the United States, from neighborhood organizations to city councils to state governments to the federal government. Policies of private agencies who fund human service delivery systems, such as local United Way organizations, as well as those of agencies that deliver human services, have an enormous impact on the health and welfare of the population. As a consequence, it should be no surprise that efforts are continually made to influence both public and private social policy. While we have chosen to construe such efforts to influence policy makers as being health education, it might be just as appropriate to think of such efforts as politics in action. We have already seen in Chapter 2 that the enactment of a bottle bill (an expression of a social policy) had an unanticipated favorable impact on reducing the number of out-of-doors glass-related lacerations.

THE POLITICS OF HEALTH EDUCATION.    To the extent that such efforts are inherently political in nature, it is important to identify and comment on an assumption that has been implicit in this book, namely, that good health is a value of the highest priority. In fact, in the real world, health as a value competes with other values—notably, economic well-being and civil liberties. In the case of infant and child health, for example, even though it might be clear that medical well-baby clinics enhance health and save money, it is extremely unlikely that attendance at such clinics could be made compulsory. Even though it can be documented that for every dollar spent in prenatal care ten times that much is saved in the cost of providing postnatal care, the possibility that free prenatal care will someday be available throughout the United States seems quite remote. While it might seem self-evident that one way to reduce the problem of alcoholism and the damage associated with excessive drinking would be to reduce its availability and accessibility (Whitehead, 1979), manufacturers, wholesalers, and retailers of alcoholic beverages (among others) are strongly opposed to such actions.

The political complexities inherent in health-related issues are nowhere more evident than in the role of the federal government regarding cigarette smoking. While the Department of Agriculture expends millions of dollars annually in support of the tobacco industry, the Department of Health and Human Services expends millions of dollars annually in an effort to discourage people from smoking.

As this chapter is being written, most state legislatures have concluded the debate on how to respond to new federal legislation that requires states to raise the legal drinking age to 21 in an effort to reduce automobile fatalities and injuries that arise as a consequence of drinking and driving. Federal legislation uses dollars as a motivator—if states do not raise their legal drinking age, they will not receive as much in federal highway funds as they would if they do raise the legal drinking age. The effort to raise the legal drinking age—in order to reduce the catastrophic consequences of vehicular accidents caused by young people who drink and drive—seems to stand on its own merits, certainly from the point of view of the enhancement of health. Yet, this effort is controversial and generates heated debate about the proper role of the federal government, about the violation of civil liberties of young people, about the loss of tax revenues that will occur as less alcohol is sold, and about whether such an action will actually accomplish its objectives.

This debate is reminiscent of the actions of the federal government nearly 20 years ago regarding the requirement that motorcyclists must wear protective helmets. Thousands of persons are killed and hundreds of thousands injured in motorcycle accidents each year, representing a rate seven times greater than in automobile accidents. Head injuries—the major cause of such deaths—are far less frequent among persons wearing protective helmets than among those not wearing them. As a consequence of such facts, when federal funds became available in 1967 for state highway safety programs, states were required to enact motorcycle helmet laws in order to qualify for those funds. By 1975, virtually all states had enacted laws requiring motorcycle riders to wear helmets, and studies of the effectiveness of these laws showed that both mortality rate and degree of severity of nonfatal injuries subsequently decreased. Fatalities fell by about 30 percent (Watson, Zador, & Wilks, 1980); there was an annual reduction of more than 1000 motorcycle fatalities, and of many times that number in nonfatal injuries.

In 1976, the U.S. Congress removed the financial penalty for noncompliance with the helmet-law provisions, influenced in part by the lobbying of organizations such as the American Motorcyclist Association that opposed this requirement. Between 1976 and 1978, twenty-six states repealed their motorcycle helmet laws. Studies in those states showed substantial increases in motorcycle fatalities and injuries following the repeal of these laws. In 1979, nearly 1000 more motorcyclists died in crashes than had died 2 years earlier (Watson, Zador, & Wilks, 1981).

Watson and associates (1980) found a 38 percent increase in motorcycle fatalities in those states in which helmet laws had been repealed when contrasted with geographically and demographically similar states in which the laws had not been repealed. Of the twenty-six states where the helmet law was repealed, fatality rates increased in all but three. Noting that the mortality rate was twice as high among unhelmeted as among helmeted riders, Watson and others (1980) concluded that "the repeals of motorcycle helmet laws have been one of the most tragic decisions made recently in the USA from the standpoint of public health" (p. 583). In a subsequent analysis, Somers (1983) calculated that the annual cost of helmet law repeal in terms of direct cost of caring for the increased number of people who are in accidents, and the indirect costs to society from preventable disability and death, amounts to a total of $675 million. In spite of these studies, however, current efforts to reenact helmet-use laws at the state level have generally been unsuccessful.

In order to exemplify the types of studies that have been undertaken relating health education methods to the development of public policy, two studies will be described. The first deals with public policy regarding the mandatory use of seatbelts or passive restraints in automobiles. The second study deals with the development of public policy regarding the problem of dog litter.

MOTOR VEHICLE RESTRAINTS.    The effectiveness of shoulder harness seat belts in reducing the severity of injuries and the fatality rates associated with automobile accidents is by now well established (Latimer & Lave, 1987). It is currently estimated that 27,400 adults die in automobile accidents each year. Based on statistics from geographic areas that require the use of seat belts, and taking into account a certain level of noncompliance, it is estimated that requiring all persons who ride in automobiles to use seat belts would save approximately 13,350 lives every year. Requiring the installation of automatic seat belts or airbags would save an estimated 17,800 lives every year. Use of some form of seat restraint would reduce the number of serious injuries and permanent disabilities by 50 percent from the current level of 240,000 per year (National Safety Council, 1982).

Little by little, states are enacting compulsory seat belt laws. These laws usually require drivers and front-seat passengers in automobiles to wear seat belts, and sometimes require that children below a certain age ride in the back seat of motor vehicles in protected safety seats. Yet the public is still not generally favorably disposed to the use of seat belts.

Using a sample of 318 graduate students in the fields of law and business administration (two fields that attract a disproportionately large number of candidates for state and federal elective offices), Runyan and Earp (1985) examined the role of health information on attitudes toward making some form of automobile seat belt restraint mandatory.

The authors randomly assigned the students to one of six experimental groups or one control group. The nature of the information that was presented in the experimental groups was varied along two different dimensions to create six different conditions. One dimension had to do with whether the information about automobile accidents was in terms of fatalities or of injuries. The second dimension had to with the format of the information—whether it was in terms of *attributable benefit* (the actual number of injuries or deaths that could be averted if a given policy were instituted), *attributable risk* (the actual number of injuries or deaths that would be expected to occur if a given policy were instituted), and *relative risk* (the number of times greater the risk of injury or death would be under a "no mandatory seat belt" or "passive restraint" policy than under a "mandatory restraint" policy of some kind. All information presented to study participants was current and completely accurate.

In addition, the authors collected information from the study participants regarding their general attitudes toward governmental health regulations, prior crash experiences, seat belt use, and attitudes toward the need to take into account public preferences, potential danger of the abridgement of personal freedom, cost of policy implementation, equity across different population groups, and judged effectiveness of the policy in accomplishing its objectives when enacting public policy. In order to obtain dependent measures, study participants were asked to rate their attitude toward three policies—voluntary seatbelt use (the policy then in effect in the community where the study was undertaken), mandatory seatbelt use, or automatic passive restraints (that is, automatic seatbelts or airbags)—after the appropriate information set was presented to each group. Members of the control group received information limited to a description of the three restraint policies.

These authors based their study upon their understanding of the psychological literature on decision making. This literature suggests that data that express greater certainty (numbers versus rate differentials) are more persuasive, and that data on lives saved and injuries averted are more impressive than data on lives lost and injuries caused.

Comparison of the ratings of the three alternative policies across the seven different groups indicated that the experimental groups were, on the whole, about three times more likely to choose one of the regulatory policies than those in the control group (60 versus 22 percent). Relative risk figures were less effective than attributable risk or attributable benefit figures in leading to support of mandatory regulatory policies. No differences were found among the groups as a function of whether injury or fatality figures were presented.

In addition, it was found: (1) the more that study participants considered the issue of personal freedom important in developing public policy, the less likely they were to be in favor of any mandatory policy regarding seat restraints; and (2) the more important a policy's effectiveness was considered to be, the more they thought they might themselves be involved in an automobile accident in the future—and the more generally favorable their views were toward governmental health regulations, the more likely were the study participants to prefer a mandatory regulation of some kind.

What was most important among the findings was that these personal preferences were more than three times more influential in determining attitudes toward mandatory seat restraint policy than the facts that were presented regarding the risk of injury or fatality. Thus, whatever facts are presented to policy makers appear to be filtered through a set of values. It thus appears that facts that are presented to policy makers in an effort to influence their opinions regarding desirable public policy are influential only if these facts are consistent with their own preexisting personal value system. Value systems are fairly stable, of course, and thus refractory to change, but some values that people hold will be changed when people are faced with enough persuasive data. This phenomenon is particularly true for elected officials whose survival depends on not being out of step with their constituency.

MANDATING POOPER-SCOOPERS.   In order to end this presentation on a somewhat more encouraging, if not more fastidious, note, here is an example of community psychologists dealing with a health-related issue, in this case, the problem of dog litter. Jason, Zolik, and Matese (1979) have described their efforts to encourage the residents of a forty-square-block residential area in northside Chicago to pick up their dogs' droppings; the ultimate objective was the channeling of results of the study to a city alderman who was introducing legislation to require all dog owners to carry "pooper scoopers" when walking their dogs.

In addition to reducing the esthetic quality of a community, dog droppings have been implicated in a variety of health hazards, including round worms; fish tapeworm; brucellosis canis, an infectious disease characterized by fever, headache, sweating, weakness, and generalized aching that can result in pronounced disability; and echinococcosis, an infectious disease that is acquired when flies or the wind transport the organism's eggs from the feces of infected dogs to a home and deposit them on food (see Jason, Zolik, & Matese, 1979, p. 340).

The experiment was conducted on both sides of a 400-foot-long street within the residential area in a series of 1-week phases. These phases included: (1) a base-line measurement of dog and dog owner behavior; (2) the erection of signs reading "Protect Children's Health. Pick Up Your Dog's Droppings"; (3) prompting dog owners by speaking to them directly urging them to pick up their dog's droppings by means of a plastic bag that was given to the dog owner along with a demonstration of its use; (4) a second period of measurement of dog and dog owner behavior; and (5) a reintroduction of the prompting procedure. In addition, a followup assessment of the area in which the interventions were introduced was conducted 3 months after the end of the program, and 2 months after that, in randomly selected control sites within the same forty-square-block area.

Dependent measures of success of the program were derived from observations of the experimental area across the five time periods. Observations included number of dog defecations, number of defecations that were picked up by owners, and number and total weight of dog droppings that were not removed during the preceding day.

The crucial dependent measure of interest was the proportion of dog defecations that was removed by the dog owner. This proportion was about 5 percent during the first base-line observation period, remained virtually the same during the sign-posting period, increased dramatically to 82 percent during the first prompting period, decreased to 63 percent during the second base-line observation period, and then increased to 84 percent during the second prompting period. At the 3-month followup observation of the experimental area, 71 dog feces were counted. This number compared very favorably with the 222 defecations that had been counted in the same area prior to the start of the experiment.

Following presentation of these findings at the Chicago City Hall, and on television, radio stations, and in the newspapers, the proposed "pooper scooper" ordinance became law. In a subsequent report, Jason and Zolik (1980) indicated that a 2-year followup revealed a 69 percent reduction in dog litter in the forty-square block area, and an 89 percent reduction on the block where the experimental intervention took place. In addition, several citizen groups from other areas in Chicago inaugurated their own dog litter reduction programs, with virtually equal success rates.

## HEALTH PROMOTION IN THE WORKPLACE

Although little was mentioned in Chapter 3 about stress in the workplace, no environmental setting has attracted more attention in recent years in terms of being a source of stress and a locus for the development of health promotion programs. The benefits associated with worksite-based health promotion programs—improved productivity, decreased absenteeism, increased morale, improved work quality, decreased cost of workers compensation insurance, decreased employee turnover, improved employee satisfaction, and improved corporate image—all testify to the manifestations of stress in the work setting (Cottington, Matthews, Talbott, & Kuller, 1986; Goldsmith, 1986; House, Strecher, Metzner, & Robbins, 1986).

While the workplace seems a natural setting for the development of health promotion programs, given the high cost of health care, there are other reasons for selecting this setting. With nearly half of all Americans gainfully employed, the work setting provides an already existing organizational structure, a convenient setting, and a potentially supportive environment for such activities. One consequence of these advantages is that health promotion programs set in the workplace appear to be unusually effective. Smoking cessation programs in the workplace, for example, are two to three times more effective than those based elsewhere in the community (Jason et al., 1987; Schilling, Gilchrist, & Schinke, 1985; Windsor & Bartlett, 1984).

Rosen (1984) has noted that worksite health promotion programs have three general objectives—health care cost management, employee health enhancement, and human resource development. These health promotion programs reflect the realization that the nature of illness has changed in the past generation. Acute infectious diseases are no longer the major source of illness. Rather, most illnesses are chronic lifestyle-related disorders, such as cardiovascular disease, cancer, and accidents. According to Rosen, "predisposing risk factors, such as high cholesterol, hypertension, obesity, diabetes, smoking, substance abuse, stress, exposure to toxic substances and lack of exercise are responsible for much of this illness" (p. 2; also see Alderman, 1984; Charlesworth, Williams, & Baer, 1984; McLeroy, Green, Mullen, & Foshee, 1984). It is these very predisposing factors that health promotion programs can serve to mitigate.

The cost to industry of self-destructive lifestyles is overwhelming, and, of course, that cost is ultimately passed on to the consumer. Rosen (1984) notes, for example, that one smoking employee is estimated to cost employers between

$624 and $4611 more annually than a nonsmoking employee in medical costs, absenteeism, replacement costs, maintenance, property damage, and lower productivity. Furthermore, a typical alcohol- or drug-using employee—not an alcoholic or drug abuser, but rather, a recreational user of alcohol or drugs—is late to work three times more often than the average employee, uses three times the normal level of sick leave benefits, is five times more likely to file compensation claims, and nearly four times more likely to be involved in an accident.

### Examples of Workplace Health Promotion Programs

As of 1984, it was estimated that more than 500 corporations had established multidimensional wellness programs (Fielding, 1984). As Fielding has noted, "American business is bullish on wellness" (p. 249). A few of these wellness programs have become particularly publicized, generally because conscientious efforts have been undertaken to evaluate and describe these programs in both the professional journals and public media (Nathan, 1984a).

JOHNSON & JOHNSON "LIVE FOR LIFE" PROGRAM. This program, sponsored by the nation's largest health care products company, is the largest, best-funded, and perhaps most effective workplace-based health promotion program in the United States (Fielding, 1984; Nathan, 1984b). Its objectives are twofold—to help enhance health among its employees, and to control the costs of illness and accidents to the corporation. The major components of the program include health screening, a lifestyle seminar, and a variety of health promotion programs including smoking cessation, exercise, stress management, nutrition, weight control, general health knowledge enhancement, hypertension detection and control, and employee assistance. The program is offered to about 10,000 employees who live and work in central New Jersey and eastern Pennsylvania. Eventually, Johnson & Johnson plans to offer the program to all of its 60,000 employees worldwide.

Preliminary evaluation of this program has contrasted a group of about 700 employees who participated in the program with a group of equal size who did not, and thus suffers from selection bias. That is, participants in this voluntary program are likely to have been initially more interested in health promotion than nonparticipants. Recognizing this methodological weakness, researchers conducting the initial evaluations have nonetheless been very encouraged (Fielding, 1984). During the first year of the program, in comparison with nonparticipants, participants were exercising significantly more, coping with stress significantly more successfully, and had significantly more favorable attitudes toward their work setting. In addition, significantly more participants had quit smoking.

CONTROL DATA CORPORATION STAYWELL PROGRAM. The STAYWELL program was established in 1979 and currently is delivered to 22,000 Control Data Corporation employees in fourteen American cities. The program emphasizes improving health and reducing known lifestyle health risks (Fielding, 1984; Naditch, 1984a, 1984b). Since Control Data Corporation is a major manufacturer of computers in the United States, it should not be surprising that a large proportion of the educational component of the program is computer-based. The program emphasizes smoking cessation, weight control, fitness behavior, stress management, and improved nutrition. Its components include an orientation program for employees and management, behavioral health screening and health risk appraisal, and a series of behaviorally oriented courses in each emphasized program area. Three specific technical advances in health promotion programming have been facilitated by developments in computer technology—health risk appraisal, worksite health promotion program evaluation, and computer-assisted instruction (Goetz & Bernstein, 1984).

Health risk appraisals are automated procedures for assessing health attitudes and health-related behaviors (Weiss, 1984). These procedures are able to develop health risk profiles and can compute the odds that a person with a given set of family and lifestyle risk factors will become ill or die from a particular disease or within a specified time span. On the basis of a health risk appraisal, it is possible for example to identify employees at unusually high risk of illness, evaluate changes in employees' health status over time, develop a specific health promotion program for a specific employee based on the details of the health risk appraisal, and develop financial projections of health costs in future years based upon the analysis of the relationships of health risks and current health care cost data. Because health risk appraisals are computerized, analyses such as those just mentioned can be done very quickly and very economically.

Worksite health promotion program evaluation can be accomplished with the use of standard computer software programs. These programs will facilitate the development of data bases of a wide variety of employee characteristics, create an integrated comprehensive medical record for employees, monitor program compliance and participation, help determine optimal combinations of wellness programs for selected categories of employees, collect and analyze statistics on absenteeism or on productivity and relate these statistics to health-related variables, and perform cost-benefit analyses of alternative health promotion programs.

Finally, the computer can be used for purposes of computer-assisted instruction. The computer is a tireless teacher, and many aspects of health promotion require just such assistance. Computer programs can provide health-related educational content, can give access to relevant health information on demand, and can help personalize health promotion programs based on individual assessment of employee needs.

Developers of the computer-based wellness program believe it has a number of important and compelling advantages. The program is thought to have the potential for maximum individualization, while at the same time it is patient, tolerant, flexible, less expensive, and more readily available to employees as well as to their families, both at the worksite as well as at home. Finally, the wellness program is capable of linking people who make use of the same program into a supportive network.

Preliminary evaluation of the program, based on the collection and analysis of self-report data, is very positive. Because the STAYWELL program is not yet available to all Control Data Corporation sites, it has been possible to conduct two types of evaluations. First, health-related behavior and attitudes have been contrasted between program participants and employees in matched non-STAYWELL sites. Second, within program sites, changes in health-related behavior and attitudes have been studied as a function of extent of program participation. Both types of evaluations have shown the program to be effective in all targeted areas of program emphasis—weight control, smoking cessation, exercise improvement, stress management, and nutritional behavior.

### Other Workplace Health Promotion Program Evaluations

There have been many reports of the evaluations of worksite health promotion programs, and they have been most favorable. General Motors reported a 40 percent decrease in lost time, a 60 percent decrease in sickness and accident benefits, and a 50 percent decrease in grievances as a consequence of their Employee Assistance Program. Kimberly Clark Corporation reported a 70 percent reduction in on-the-job accidents among its participants. Perhaps most impressive are the figures reported by the New York Telephone Company—an annual saving of $663,000 from its hypertension program, $1,565,000 from its alcoholism program, $269,000 from its breast cancer screening program, $302,000 from its back treatment program, and $268,000 from its stress management program (reported in Rosen, 1984, p. 7).

## CONCLUDING COMMENTS

In spite of the persuasive evidence that health education can improve health status, consumer health education is a long way from realizing its potential. Marshall (1977)—remarking that less than 0.5 percent of the money spent on health-related activities in the United States is allocated to health education—notes the tremendous discrepancy between what is known about health and illness and what is practiced about the same. Only 5 percent of women over age 20 undergo Pap smears, in spite of the fact that the procedure represents a simple way to detect cervical cancer. Only half of people with high blood pressure are aware of their condition, even though high blood pressure can be controlled. Marshall believes that part of the reason so few people take advantage of what is known about the prevention, detection, and treatment of disease can be found in the low level of financial support for the health education of the American public, suggesting its low priority in the health care system (also see David, 1986). The easiest and least expensive aspect of consumer health education is the provision of information. Changing attitudes and subsequent behavior, as we have seen, is far more difficult and requires far more in the way of financial resources.

Kaplan (1984) has recently prepared an especially thoughtful overview of the field of health promotion and consumer health education. Kaplan notes that four separate assumptions are made in undertaking health promotion efforts:

> First, we must assume that behavior is a risk factor; second, we must assume that changing risk factors produce changes in health; third, we must assume that behavior can be changed; and fourth, we must assume that behavioral interventions are better alternatives than other medical, social, and policy interventions. (p. 763)

In reviewing the evidence for each of these assumptions, Kaplan has concluded that the belief that certain forms of behavior are a risk factor for serious illness is clearly supported. As examples of such evidence, Kaplan mentions the connections between smoking and lung cancer, between alcohol use and liver disease (as well as traffic fatalities), and, to a somewhat lesser extent, between diet and exercise and heart disease.

As for the second assumption that changes in behavior produce changes in health, Kaplan has determined that the evidence is less conclusive. In the case of smoking, there is clear evidence that stopping smoking results in reduced risk of lung cancer. Similarly, the evidence seems clear that reducing alcohol intake lowers the risk of vehicular accidents and fatalities. But in the prevention of heart disease—currently, the most active area of health-related psychological research—there is less evidence that changes in diet or exercise result in significant decreases in the risk of heart disease. Many studies have found no reduction in the incidence of heart disease; other studies have found very small and statistically insignificant decreases; and a number of studies have found that decreases in deaths attributable to heart disease have been approximately matched with increases in deaths from other causes. Thus, in experimental samples, overall death rate has not decreased.

Mortality rate from heart and circulatory disease has decreased quite dramatically in the past 15 years, but it is not clear what proportion of this decrease can be attributed to changes in lifestyle. Kaplan has suggested that competing hypotheses need to be evaluated as well—the increased use of cardiopulmonary resuscitation, improved intensive care units in hospitals, improvements in surgical methods for treating heart disease, and better emergency medical services.

Since Kaplan's overview was published, new research findings (Grundy et al., 1982; Lipid Research Clinics Program, 1984a, 1984b; National Institutes of Health, 1984) have been reported that lend increased confidence to the suspected link between dietary changes that result in lowered blood cholesterol levels and risk of coronary heart disease (National Institutes of Health, 1984).

As for the third assumption, that health-related behavior can be changed, Kaplan has concluded that the evidence is equivocal. Many studies have failed to find significant changes in behavior (although most studies do find significant increases in health-related knowledge). And among studies where behavior has been shown to change, the changes have been very modest and often not significant.

Finally, the fourth assumption—that behavior change must be shown to be at least equivalent in effect to other efforts to reduce risk of disease—also presents problems in interpretation. Kaplan notes that health psychologists will have to demonstrate that consumer health programs fall within reasonable cost-effectiveness ranges. Frequent dependent measures of cost-effectiveness that have been employed include the cost of preventing one death and the cost of adding one healthy year of life. Using these dependent measures in comparative studies has shown a wide range in cost-effectiveness. In the case of the prevention of death, results across a variety of studies have ranged from a low of $170,000 to a high of $3 million per single death prevented. Given this relatively high cost, in the context of the already high cost of medical care, the importance of well-conducted cost-effectiveness studies becomes clear. In reviewing such studies, Kaplan has identified consumer health education efforts to improve the adherence to antihypertensive medication as clearly cost-effective.

Kaplan concludes his critique by suggesting that health psychologists must, above all, remain realistic regarding the effectiveness of their interventions. The problems are complex and the evidence linking behavioral change with disease prevention is, with certain exceptions, still weak. Under these circumstances, health psychologists must expect that progress, while encouraging, will be slow (also see Dalzell-Ward, 1976).

With proper information and guidance, consumers of health services can do much on their own to improve their health. Furthermore, there is considerable evidence that levels of health among the healthy can be more successfully maintained by helping them become better informed about health-related facts of life. Consumer health educators are becoming more effective at having an impact on the total population as well as on specified subgroups at special risk, and there is reason for optimism about the expanding role of consumer health education in the development of healthier communities.

## SUMMARY

- The principal way of encouraging changes in health-related behavior is through consumer health education programs that attempt to provide health-related information, change health-related attitudes, and modify health-related behavior in directions that are conducive to improved health.

- The four major target groups for consumer health education programs are the general public, at-risk populations, patients and prospective patients, and social and public policy makers.
- Disease prevention programs aim at preventing specific diseases through consumer health education efforts. Health promotion programs aim at reducing general vulnerability to illness by means of consumer health education programs.
- An important component of consumer health education is mental health education, and a number of health education programs have been reported that have a significant impact on mental health.
- Consumer health education programs designed to change behavior often take far longer to demonstrate their effectiveness than is ordinarily anticipated. Long-term commitment to a consumer health education program seems to be necessary in order to assure success.
- The public has an enormous interest in learning about health and appropriate health-related behavior.
- The mass media have been successfully used in changing health-related behavior of the general public, both in terms of individual behaviors such as smoking reduction and prosocial behaviors that strengthen support networks.
- Consumer health education programs are being increasingly targeted toward school-age children, and the school itself is recognized as an appropriate setting for certain types of health-related educational programs.
- With the overwhelming evidence that unintended adolescent pregnancies often have negative health consequences for the mother as well as for the infant, increasing efforts are being made to reduce the incidence of these pregnancies. The issue is not without controversy, but studies consistently demonstrate that American young people are remarkably uninformed about the facts of sexual life and about ways of preventing unintended pregnancy.
- An at-risk group that appears to be particularly receptive to consumer health education efforts is pregnant women. Significant reductions in smoking and alcohol intake, and significant improvements in nutritional status have been found.
- A number of imaginative health education programs, developed for the entire family, have been favorably evaluated. These programs are often referred to as family life education.
- In the case of health education programs for the bereaved, most efforts include some form of personal contact, usually from persons who successfully coped with their own bereavement.

- Consumer health education programs for patients in the medical care system and for their families are designed to provide information that will reduce their sense of uncertainty and provide social support. These programs are inexpensive and have been shown to be remarkably cost-effective.

- Consumer health education programs targeted to policy makers are not often reported in the literature, but, when undertaken, their results have generally been favorable.

- An increasingly attractive setting for consumer health education programs is the workplace, and a number of very comprehensive programs have been developed and evaluated. Evaluations indicate that absenteeism, health insurance claims, accidents, and grievances all decrease dramatically, and that cost savings to employers are considerable.

# Lifestyle Risk Factors:
# Nutrition, Exercise, Alcohol, and Drug Abuse

# 5

## INTRODUCTION

In Chapter 1 you were introduced to the concept of the *health field*, developed by Lalonde (1974). Of the four components of the health field—human biology, the environment, lifestyle, and health care organization—none is more important than lifestyle.

According to Lalonde, lifestyle consists of the "aggregation of decisions by individuals which affect their health and over which they more or less have control. . . . When those risks result in illness or death, the victim's lifestyle can be said to have contributed to, or caused, his own illness or death" (p. 32).

Lalonde analyzed age-specific mortality figures in Canada and came to a number of important general conclusions regarding the importance of lifestyle. First, from age 5 to 35, the principal cause of death is motor vehicle accidents, the second-most common is other accidents, and the third is suicide. These three, taken together, account for 64 percent of deaths for this age group. Since all these causes of death are mainly due to such lifestyle factors as carelessness, impaired driving, and self-imposed risks, and to such feelings as depression and despair, it is evident that changes in these factors are needed if the rates of death are to be lowered.

At age 35 according to Lalonde, coronary-artery disease first appears as a significant cause of death. By age 40 it becomes the principal cause and holds this position through all subsequent age groups. For the age group 35 to 70 diseases of the cardiovascular system account for 44 percent of all deaths. While there are many causes of circulatory diseases, there is little doubt that obesity, smoking, stress, lack of exercise, and high-fat diets make a significant contribution. All of these factors are due to self-imposed risks.

At age 50, the second-most common cause of death in men is cancer of the larynx, trachea, bronchus, or lung. Bronchitis, emphysema, and asthma account for a large number of additional deaths. These diseases together account for nearly 10 percent of all deaths in the 40- to 70-year-old group, and cigarette smoking is a major contributing factor in all of these deaths. Again the root cause is found in a self-imposed risk.

While the mortality figures reported for Canada are smaller than similar figures for the United States (see Chapter 2), the mortality rates are very comparable in the two countries. What is more important, however, is that the role of lifestyle in producing these deaths is no less important in the United States than in Canada.

Writing some years after Lalonde, specifically regarding the United States, Hamburg, Elliott, and Parron (1982) noted that the heaviest burdens of illness—and about half of all deaths—are related to aspects of individual lifestyle. Known behavioral risk factors, according to Hamburg, Elliott, and Parron, include cigarette smoking, excessive consumption of alcoholic beverages, use of illicit drugs, certain dietary habits, reckless driving, nonadherence to effective medication regimens, and maladaptive responses to social pressures (also see Behavioral Risk Factor Prevalence, 1983).

In the next two chapters, we are going to examine the psychological components of the five principal lifestyle risk factors that contribute so heavily to premature mortality and morbidity. In this chapter we will discuss psychosocial aspects of poor nutritional habits, insufficient exercise, alcohol abuse, and drug abuse. Because the literature dealing with smoking and health is so extensive, we will devote the next chapter to a discussion of psychosocial aspects of smoking. At the conclusion of the next chapter, we will make some observations about general problems inherent in lifestyle modification, that is, problems that appear to cut across efforts to reduce all forms of self-destructive lifestyles.

## NUTRITION AND HEALTH

Appropriate nutrition is necessary for health maintenance, optimal growth and development, physical activity, reproduction, lactation, and recovery from illness and injury throughout the life cycle. A variety of health problems can occur when persons have deficits of essential nutrients, such as fiber or iron, or engage in excessive or inappropriate consumption of some nutrients, such as fats (Oster & Epstein, 1986; Seidell et al., 1986) or coffee (LaCroix et al., 1986), many of which are associated with excess risk of coronary heart disease.

Although the role of nutrition in health is not fully understood, epidemiologic and laboratory studies offer important insights that may help people enhance their prospects of attaining or maintaining health by making appropriate food choices. A number of recent surveys indicate that people are increasingly interested in nutrition, are more aware of the actions they can take to maintain health through their daily eating patterns, and have initiated changes in their nutritional practices. Several studies have found that people are consuming less salt as well as less total fat, saturated fat, and cholesterol. And in the case of nutritional aspects of child rearing, from 1972 to 1982, the percent of babies breastfed at 1 week of age has increased from about 26 to 61 percent, and of infants breastfed at 6 months of age, from about 5 to 27 percent (National Center for Health Statistics, 1983).

Current data indicate that—in spite of a growing interest in nutrition—a substantial proportion of the American public is in poor nutritional condition and the public is still generally uninformed about the relationships of nutrition and health. In the report on health promotion and disease prevention issued by the National Center for Health Statistics (1985a, 1986f), the preliminary results of a survey of about 9000 randomly selected households revealed that less than half of those surveyed ate breakfast every day, that 70 percent snacked between meals or in the evening, that nearly half considered themselves overweight, that more than one-third were currently trying to lose weight (far more commonly reported by women than men), and that in only 28 percent of the occasions when respondents visited a health professional for routine care was eating proper foods ever discussed.

The term "obesity" refers to excess body fat, and is usually defined as a body mass index of greater than 30 (Millar & Stephens, 1987). The body mass index is calculated by dividing weight in kilograms by the square of height in meters. A person with a body mass index of less than 20 is considered underweight, normal weight persons are defined as those with body mass indexes of between 20.1 and 25, and overweight is defined as a body mass index of 25.1 to 30. Thus, for example, a person 1.5 meters tall (4 feet 11 inches) who weighs 150 pounds (68 kilograms) would have a body mass index of just over 30. A person 1.8 meters tall (5 feet 11 inches) would not be considered obese until he or she weighed 214 pounds. About 14 percent of men and 24 percent of women 20 to 74 years of age are classified as obese.

Iron and folic acid deficiencies are common among pregnant or lactating women. It has been estimated that 10 to 15 percent of infants and children among migratory workers and certain rural poor populations suffer growth retardation because of dietary inadequacies. Approximately 10 percent of adolescents are significantly overweight, and a substantial number are pathologically underweight. Of the latter group, many suffer from one of two major eating disorders—anorexia nervosa (Ferguson, 1981) or bulimia, both of which are potentially serious and sometimes life-threatening illnesses.

### Anorexia and Bulimia

Anorexia, or pathological undereating, is characterized by (1) weight loss of at least 25 percent of original body weight; (2) intense and chronic fear of becoming obese even when efforts to lose weight appear to be successful; (3) disturbances of body image, or how one thinks about one's own body—for example, such as by feeling "fat" even when actually emaciated; (4) the absence of any known physical illness that would account for the weight loss; and (5) refusal to eat enough to maintain minimal normal weight. As can be imagined, anorexia can be a life-threatening disorder.

Bulimia is generally a longer-lasting eating disorder characterized by (1) a pattern of binging (rapid consumption of a large amount of food in a relatively short period of time) and purging (self-induced vomiting); (2) a postbinge feeling of anguish, depression, and self-depreciation; and (3) awareness that the eating pattern is abnormal combined with a fear that it cannot be stopped (American Psychiatric Association, 1980).

While these two disorders are far from identical, there are a number of similarities in their psychosocial aspects. For example, both of these eating disorders commonly include feelings of depression and anxiety (Toner, Garfinkel, & Garner, 1986), and there is some preliminary evidence (Humphrey, Apple, & Kirschenbaum, 1986) that interactions between bulimic or anorexic daughters and their parents are more disturbed than between normal daughters and their parents. Parents of daughters with either of these two eating disorders tend to be more inconsistent, less helpful, and more detached in their interactions with them than do parents with daughters without these disorders. These data need to be thought of as preliminary, however, because, for example, it is not clear whether such parent-daughter conflicts result in subsequent eating disorders or are the result of preexisting eating disorders.

Both anorexia and bulimia are far more prevalent among women than men, although Striegel-Moore, Silberstein, and Rodin (1986) suggest that the stage is set for the disorder to become more common among men. Bulimia, particularly common among college-age women, is a syndrome that endangers both emotional and physical health. The behavior may be accompanied by a severe sense of guilt and shame, and has been known to lead to antisocial behavior designed to obtain food or to obtain money to purchase food for a binge (Bellack & Williamson, 1982).

In a recent review of risk factors associated with bulimia, Striegel-Moore, Silberstein, and Rodin (1986) identified three questions that appeared fundamental in the understanding of this condition: (1) Why is the disorder more prevalent among women than men? (2) Which women are at especially high risk? (3) Why is the disorder currently increasing in both incidence and prevalence?

Answers to these questions must come, according to these authors, from a variety of perspectives—sociocultural, developmental, psychological, and biological.

Anorexia and bulimia need to be understood within a sociocultural context. We live in a society that values thinness and that stigmatizes obesity, particularly in the case of women. Virtually from the moment of birth, sex-role stereotyping determines how children begin to think of themselves, and girls, far more than boys, think of themselves in terms of how they look. During adolescence, inevitable biological changes in girls are in conflict with this internalized value system. As girls gain weight, primarily from the normal development of new fat tissue, they often struggle to retain their prepubertal thin look. Most research indicates that when adolescent boys complain about their weight, it is due to the fact that they want to be heavier, while girls who complain about their weight want to be lighter and thinner. As a consequence, women generally overestimate their own body size, while men do not.

During the adult years, the problem with body size continues. Pregnancy typically brings with it an increase in fat that is very difficult to lose. Even in middle and old age, women remain preoccupied with their weight and imagined physical appearance. In the words of Striegel-Moore, Silberstein, and Rodin (1986), "women's battle with weight, both psychological and physical, lasts a lifetime" (p. 252).

In recent years, the standard of beauty has become even thinner, as can be judged from the measurements of Miss America contestants, Playboy centerfolds, and female models in magazine advertisements. At the same time, the average weight of women, particularly under the age of 30, has increased. Thus, the discrepancy between actual weight and idealized weight has grown. Furthermore, the fitness movement has redefined the ideal female form as not only thin but firm, and the accelerating rate of women entering the labor force has served to create a special emphasis on thinness among working women. While the maternal figure can be soft and round, the working female figure must be thin and firm.

### Understanding Obesity

Persons who are significantly overweight are at excess risk for diabetes, gall bladder disease, cardiovascular disease, orthopedic problems, and surgery complications (Miller, 1983; Stachnik, Stoffelmayr, & Hoppe, 1983; Straw, 1983). In addition, persons 20 to 30 percent overweight have a 20 to 40 percent greater mortality rate than persons who are not overweight, and persons 50 to 60 percent overweight have a 150 to 200 percent greater mortality risk (Van Itallie, 1979). Happily, there is evidence that when overweight persons lose their excess weight, and maintain that reduced weight, their life expectancy increases to the level of persons who were never overweight (Bray, 1984).

The relationship between obesity and health is not a simple one. In the case of coronary heart disease, for example, it is clear that gross obesity (weighing 50 percent or more above average) is associated with excess risk, but the relationship is not at all clear for persons who weigh less than 30 percent above average. Thus, what might be called mild obesity does not appear to be significantly associated with excess risk of coronary artery disease.

Indeed, it may be that except at extremes of weight, the social and psychological consequences of obesity are as serious as are the physical hazards. Even among children, obesity is viewed very negatively, and there is little doubt that there is significant discrimination against obese persons. General attitudes toward obese persons differ from those toward persons with severe physical handicaps, probably because, in the eyes of many people, obesity is the person's own fault. Obesity is unquestionably stigmatizing.

In high school, obese students obtain poorer grades than students of normal weight, even though they do not differ in academic aptitude or in IQ. When applying to selective colleges, obese women are not admitted as easily as nonobese women, even though their credentials are completely comparable. During the adult years, obese persons have more difficulty in locating employment than nonobese persons and earn less than nonobese persons in similar jobs (Bray, 1984).

Any examination of obesity must begin with a healthy respect for physiology (Striegel-Moore & Rodin, 1985). A number of studies have shown that it is often exceedingly difficult either to lose or gain weight voluntarily, even under extreme conditions (Keesey, 1980; Keys et al., 1950; Sims & Horton, 1968), and there is a very great likelihood that every individual has an ideal biological weight that is regulated with considerable determination by the body. This ideal biological weight is called the *set point,* and in some individuals it may be considerably below or above what is generally thought of as normal (Kolata, 1985).

Sims and Horton (1968), for example, studied a sample of prisoners who volunteered to modify their dietary habits in order to increase their weights by 25 percent. Many participants in the study were absolutely unable to gain that amount of weight no matter how much they ate, and, at the end of the study, the participants all returned to their starting weights even though they were allowed to eat as much as they wanted. Thus, many people who are overweight may be in a hopeless contest with a determined and unyielding biology.

Under more ordinary circumstances, in spite of set-point theory, undesirable nutritional practices usually result in weight gain. Foods containing high fat content have been found to create obesity in virtually all animals that have been studied (Sclafani, 1980) and, unfortunately, this finding tends to hold true for human beings as well. Thus, weight maintenance depends to a certain extent on dietary restraint. People vary in the extent to which they practice restraint in their eating. At one end of the continuum are unrestrained eaters who eat as freely, as often, and as much as they wish. At the other end are those who constantly worry about what they eat and struggle to resist food (Ruderman, 1986).

There is also considerable evidence that prenatal influences and feeding practices during infancy play a significant role in increasing the risk of obesity.

Prenatal influences refer to various aspects of maternal nutrition during pregnancy, including whether the mother is undernourished or overnourished, as well as the quality of her nutrition. Since the human fetus has mature taste buds and has begun regular swallowing by about the fifteenth week of gestation, there is growing interest in determining whether reducing sugar intake during pregnancy, for example, might result in reduced responsiveness to sweet tastes on the part of the infant (Striegel-Moore & Rodin, 1985).

As for feeding practices during infancy, a number of variables are being examined, including amount of food provided, breast- versus bottlefeeding, and the nature of feeding schedules. In their summary review of this interesting literature, Striegel-Moore and Rodin (1985) have concluded that while the relationships are not overwhelmingly powerful, the risk of obesity generally increases with the amount of food provided during infancy, with the practice of bottlefeeding rather than breastfeeding, and with increasing irregularity and unpredictability of feeding schedules.

Research on eating behavior during childhood has concentrated in two areas—the development of food preferences and aversions, and the development of self-regulatory skills. Particular attention has been directed to examining parental practices in manipulating food preferences in their children. As reported by Striegel-Moore and Rodin (1985), the common practice of rewarding the eating of undesired food with the promise of desired food ("You can have dessert if you eat your vegetables and meat") appears to be self-defeating in that it further reduces the degree of preference children have for the undesired food. In contrast, if no contingencies are established—that is, if dessert, or some other reward, is made available whether or not the undesired food is consumed—or if the child simply sees people at the table eating that undesired food, preference for the undesired food tends to increase, with a decreased risk of obesity the result.

Research on obesity during childhood strongly suggests that the risk of obesity is reduced to the extent that children are helped to develop self-regulatory skills, that is, the ability to make their own decisions regarding what they eat, without undue parental control.

At the sociopolitical level, in their analysis of nutritional behavior, Jeffrey and Lemnitzer (1981) have suggested that the most powerful general influence on eating behavior is advertising. Television advertising in particular is a persistent form of persuasion—a crucial aspect of the background against which efforts to reduce obesity and to improve nutrition need to be understood. By the time the average child enters kindergarten, he or she will have seen 70,000 food-related commercials. These commercial messages are not randomly distributed among all food groups. Rather, they are primarily directed toward cereal products, candy, cookies, crackers, and gum. More than two-thirds of all food commercials are for sugared products. Jeffrey and Lemnitzer comment that "the child hardly ever sees anyone on TV talking favorably about meat, eggs, fruit, or vegetables. In addition, snacking . . . is encouraged . . . coupled with a lack of information on the dangers of obesity and the need for proper nutrition" (1981, p. 52).

### Prevention and Reduction of Obesity

Because of the evidence linking overweight with an increased risk of a variety of disorders as well as an excess mortality rate, and because the dependent measure of success (weight loss) is so specific and objective, the reduction of obesity is an attractive goal for persons interested in health improvement.

Straw (1983) has reviewed the various procedures available for the treatment of obesity under five general categories: dietary treatment, anorectic drugs, fasts and modified fasts, surgical interventions, and behavior therapy (also see Wilson, 1984). Dietary treatment is the most common form of treatment for obesity, but, as will be seen, only modest weight losses occur, and even these weight losses are rarely maintained. Second-most common in the treatment of obesity is the use of anorectic drugs, usually derivatives of phenylethylamine, that act within the brain to suppress appetite. Weight loss tends to be slightly greater with the use of these drugs than without their use, but again, there appear to be frequent failures in the maintenance of the weight loss after the drug treatment has ended. Brownell and Stunkard (1981), for example, found in their sample of 124 obese men and women who were randomly assigned to medication and no-medication groups, that while the medication group lost an average of 10.8 kg during the 16-week treatment program, a year later they had regained 6.1 kg. In the case of the no-medication groups, weight loss was only 7.1 kg during the treatment program, but a year later this group had regained only 3.1 kg.

Total fasts are usually undertaken on an inpatient basis, while modified fasts (involving specially prepared foods having a caloric content of from 400 to 600 calories per day) can usually be managed on an outpatient basis. Total fasts frequently result in medical complications, and even modified fasts have certain undesirable medical side effects. Again, maintenance of weight loss is a problem, and in one 2-year followup study of forty-seven persons who successfully completed a modified fast program, Genuth, Vertes, and Hazelton (1978) found that more than half of the sample had regained more than half of the weight that they had lost.

Surgical interventions involve either bypassing most of the small intestine, or reducing the size of the stomach (gastric bypass), in order to reduce the absorption of nutrients as well as caloric intake. Surgical intervention is used most commonly in severe cases of obesity—when weight is at least double its ideal level. Results of either type of bypass surgery are superior to all other obesity treatments, averaging nearly 100 pounds in weight loss within the first year of the surgery, with excellent maintenance of weight loss. In addition, there are frequent reports of improved self-esteem. There are medical risks to the surgery, however, including a mortality rate of somewhere between 3 and 10 percent and chronic diarrhea, with the risks somewhat smaller in the case of the gastric bypass than the intestinal bypass.

Finally, behavior therapy involves such procedures as cognitive restructuring, relaxation and assertiveness training, nutrition counseling, and changes in eating style. Most studies have found that the average program lasts about 10 weeks and results in a weight loss of about 1 pound per week. In the case of behavior therapy approaches to obesity treatment, weight loss is not great, but the maintenance of weight loss appears to be good.

Brownell, Stunkard, & McKeon (1985) have reported on weight reduction programs based at the worksite. In general, these programs appear to have lower attrition rates than those conducted in other settings and seem to be as effective when conducted by lay leaders as by professional therapists. One form of weight loss program that appears to be particularly effective at the worksite is the weight loss competition, either between several similar employee groups or among several different divisions within the same industry. Brownell and associates (1984) have described three such programs. In all cases, attrition was very low, weight loss was adequate, averaging 5.5 kg, and positive changes in morale and in employee-management relations were reported by both employees and management personnel.

OBESITY IN ADULTS.    Nearly all people who are obese are aware of the unhealthy nature of obesity, yet they find it extremely difficult to lose weight (Hagen, 1981; Hirsch, 1982). Brownell (1982) has noted that if one defines cure from obesity as the achievement of ideal weight and then the maintenance of that ideal weight for a 5-year period—a definition analogous to a "cure" of cancer being survival for five years—then a person is more likely to recover from most forms of cancer than from obesity.

Weight reduction programs tend to have only temporary success, at best, with an eventual failure rate of about 95 percent (Bellack & Williamson, 1982). In other words, short-term weight loss in a dietary regimen is relatively common, but long-term maintenance of the weight loss is almost impossible to achieve. In his recent review of weight control treatments, Wilson (1984) found that far too many obese individuals are trapped in a recurring cycle of losing and regaining weight, a pattern that can have deleterious consequences for the person's physical health and psychological well-being. Complicating this low success rate is the evidence that failure in a weight control program can lead to a sense of guilt, self-blame, depression, a feeling of helplessness or hopelessness, and a weakened sense of self-efficacy (also see Hochbaum, 1979).

According to Wilson (1984), the most extensively studied and widely used psychological method among adults for losing weight is behavioral treatment. Here, the emphasis is on (1) changing behavior in order to decrease caloric intake, and (2) increasing caloric expenditure. Most people believe that behavioral methods of weight control are the preferred form of treatment for mild and moderate cases of obesity.

As for restricting caloric intake, behavioral treatment methods include four elements: (1) self-monitoring and goal-setting; (2) stimulus control of external cues for eating; (3) changing the characteristics of eating patterns; and (4) reinforcement of the resultant altered behavior. Self-monitoring of behavior, thoughts, and feelings associated with eating, as well as of actual caloric intake, is the single most important element in the behavioral treatment of obesity. Self-monitoring allows people to regulate their eating-related behaviors in light of the goals they have set for themselves. Goals, in turn, are best when they are simple, short-term, and specific.

Stimulus control of external cues—for example, always eating in the same place—has not been studied by itself as a behavioral treatment approach to weight reduction, since most researchers believe it is not effective when used alone. Similarly, modifying the topographic characteristics of eating, for example, eating more slowly or chewing a certain number of times before swallowing, has not been found to be effective by itself.

Reinforcement of goal attainment in a weight control program has typically helped to modify eating behaviors. Monetary rewards or punishments—for example, returning versus retaining deposits of money made at the start of a weight control program—have been found to result in short-term weight loss and to some increase in the duration of the weight loss.

When we look at physical activity as used in the behavioral treatment of obesity, we can see that the principal focus is on increasing the level and consistency of physical exercise. Exercise consumes calories, of course, which adds to the effectiveness of the program. But in addition, exercise helps counteract some of the ill effects of obesity, tends to suppress appetite, increases basal metabolism (a biological phenomenon that accounts for a very large proportion of total energy expenditure), maximizes the loss of fat tissue, and minimizes the loss of lean tissue. Weight control programs typically employ systematic booster sessions to increase participation in a physical exercise regimen, and also try to invoke a special social support network (usually other dieters) in restoring interest when it weakens. Couples generally have greater success than individuals when undertaking a weight control program, in part because they can support each other during the times when motivation flags.

As can be inferred from what has just been said, most behavioral treatment programs employ several strategies at the same time. Perhaps the most common multidimensional programs combine drug therapy with behavioral treatment. Drug treatment often results in rapid and substantial weight loss, but a very high relapse rate is often found. Combining the use of drugs with behavioral treatment may reduce the relapse rate, particularly if the two treatments are sequenced properly.

Even when there is weight loss, there are a number of suspected undesirable psychological effects that often accompany dieting, particularly depression and anxiety. In fact, little is known about the negative social and psychological effects of weight loss or of attempts at weight loss, but it is thought that unsuccessful weight loss attempts result in reductions in self-esteem, marital satisfaction, social interrelationships, work performance, and psychological adjustment (Brownell, 1982).

OBESITY IN CHILDREN.   Obesity in children is not only serious in its own right, but obese children usually become obese adolescents, and obese adolescents usually become obese adults. It has been estimated that if an obese junior high student has not achieved normal weight by the end of adolescence, the odds against that person ever achieving normal weight are 28 to 1 (Stunkard & Burt, 1967).

Multifaceted programs for helping obese children lose weight appear very promising, particularly if the programs involve the family, exercise, changes in nutrition, as well as traditional behavior modification techniques (Epstein & Wing, 1987). These are techniques that set up a systematic pattern of rewards for achieving each step in the weight loss program. The role and contribution of the parents to the success of a child's weight loss program is particularly remarkable when the parents are themselves interested in losing weight and are able to join in a mutually supportive weight loss program with their children.

The school is a natural setting for implementing weight loss programs. Such programs can be built into an educational model, can reach a very large number of children, are relatively inexpensive, can be continuous, can include appropriate counseling and social support, and can be inaugurated before the problem becomes too serious. When these programs have the same multifaceted character as has just been described, they appear to be unusually effective.

The other natural setting for weight loss programs in the case of children and adolescents is the home. Becker and others (1977) examined the extent of compliance of parents of obese children with a dietary regimen designed to help their children lose weight. These researchers had earlier developed a way of thinking about preventive health behavior that they called a health belief model. The model is based upon the hypothesis that whether or not preventive health behavior occurs depends on four sets of beliefs: (1) how susceptible people think they are to the disorder, (2) how threatening or dangerous the disorder is thought to be, (3) how much the preventive action is thought to reduce the danger or threat, and (4) what barriers people think exist that might prevent the preventive health behavior taking place. Note that this view of health behavior is entirely cognitive—health behavior is seen as explainable in terms of preexisting attitudes. Reviewing the literature on the relationship of behavior to attitude shows considerable evidence that if the examined attitudes are directly pertinent to the behaviors that are to be predicted, attitudes do predict later behavior rather well (Ajzen & Fishbein, 1977).

The health belief model has been used in studying such preventive health behaviors as participating in a tuberculosis screening program, undergoing polio vaccinations, taking part in preventive dental care, inaugurating a breast self-examination program, reducing smoking, and undergoing genetic screening, as well as dieting in an effort to reduce obesity (see Chapter 12; also see Becker & Maiman, 1975; Becker et al., 1977; Calnan & Moss, 1984; Kirscht, 1983; Stone, 1979b).

In the case of parental compliance with a dietary regimen for their obese children, the variables in this model were assessed at the start of the study. Among these variables were measures of motivation, attitudes toward obesity as a threat to health, feelings of control over health matters, faith in medical care, and intention to comply. In addition, a number of demographic variables were assessed at the start of the experiment.

A group of 182 mothers and their obese children began the experiment, but attrition was high, with only 113 mother-children pairs completing the 2-month program. The original sample was divided into three groups: (1) a control group; (2) a high fear-inducing experimental group (oral and written information about the possible unfavorable consequences of obesity was given as part of the initial interview); and (3) a low fear-inducing experimental group (less threatening oral and written information about the dangers of obesity was included in the initial interview).

The most powerful predictor variable was the degree of concern the mother expressed about the child's general health—greater concern resulted in greater weight loss. Other variables that were significantly related to subsequent weight loss were (1) mother's perception of how easily her child gets sick, (2) perceived severity of the child's obesity, and (3) a greater sense of control over obesity and its consequences. High fear arousal was associated with greater weight loss than the low fear-arousal procedure, and there was virtually no weight loss in the control group. Demographic variables—such as age and sex of child, race, number of siblings, and income—were generally unrelated to subsequent weight loss.

## EXERCISE AND HEALTH

Although the past decade has witnessed a remarkable growth of interest in physical fitness and exercise in the United States (see, for example, Berger & Owen, 1983), the American lifestyle is still relatively sedentary. The most recent data available estimate that only about one-third of adults exercise regularly, only one-third of children participate in daily physical education programs, and only one-third of adults over 65 years of age take regular walks. Most people do not exercise in the manner necessary to achieve maximum benefits. The therapeutic benefits of exercise have largely been ignored by traditional health professionals. Although the health benefits derived from exercise have not been fully defined, continuing research suggests that appropriate physical activity can enhance the effectiveness of programs designed to treat and prevent heart disease (Haskell, 1985; Taylor et al., 1986), obesity (as was described in the previous section), hypertension, diabetes, musculoskeletal problems, stress, anxiety, and depression (Epstein & Wing, 1980; National Center for Health Statistics, 1983a; Sime, 1984).

Most benefits of exercise result from the energy expenditure that is required for skeletal muscle contraction. Thus, the most direct result of the increased metabolism is in enhancing the efficiency and capacity of muscles to perform work. Secondarily, changes occur in those body systems that make it possible to provide that increased energy—the nervous system, the endocrine system, the cardiovascular system, and the respiratory system (also see Siscovick, Laporte, & Newman, 1985).

### Exercise and Mental Health

Insofar as the effects of exercise on mental health are concerned, Sime (1984) has noted that avid exercisers frequently report improved quality of life; increased sense of accomplishment, worth, and well-being; and feelings of relaxation, euphoria, and elation during and after exercising. Well-controlled studies, however, have not always found these effects in persons who are free of psychopathology or physical illness (Haskell, 1985; Hughes, Casal, & Leon, 1986; Sinyor, Golden, Steinert, & Seraganian, 1986).

As for specific psychological disorders, exercise has been shown to reduce anxiety and depression. In the case of anxiety, while research studies can be improved, there appears to be evidence that it is state anxiety (transitory anxiety related to specific life events) rather than trait anxiety (persistent anxiety that appears to be characterological in nature and not particularly related to specific life events) that is most responsive to exercise. An exercise program of moderate intensity, frequency, and duration appears to be far more effective than a single episode of exercise in reducing anxiety and tension, and the effects appear to be similar among men and women.

Taylor, Sallis, and Needle (1985; see also Sime, 1984) maintain that evidence of the effectiveness of exercise also exists in the case of mild to moderate depression. Physical activity and exercise appear to alleviate some of the symptoms of depression, particularly in the case of people whose level of depression is higher than normal prior to the start of an exercise program. The research also suggests that physical exercise may provide a beneficial adjunct for alcoholism and substance abuse programs, improve self-image, social skills, and cognitive functioning, and reduce the symptoms of anxiety and stress.

### Exercise Programs in Action

Preventive and therapeutic exercise programs are increasingly found in the community at large, in the school, and in the worksite (Iverson, Fielding, Crow, & Christenson, 1985). Very few formal exercise programs are available in medical care settings such as hospitals or outpatient clinics. Physicians prescribe exercise programs to less than 10 percent of patients they see, and a number of studies suggest that part of the reason is that physicians do not believe that they can alter the behavior of their patients. Interestingly, patients want their physicians to be concerned about their health habits, and it seems quite likely that the influence physicians have over their patients' behavior is substantially greater than physicians believe.

Most people who consider where to locate physical activity programs for maximum benefit conclude that the single most important setting for such programs is the school. Well-run physical education programs for school-aged children can set the stage for a lifetime of interest and involvement in exercise. Yet, in spite of the fact that most states require the teaching of physical education at some point in the school curriculum, only about one-third of young people between age 10 and 17 participate in daily physical education programs in school (Iverson et al., 1985).

The newest setting for the development of physical activity programs is the worksite. With the rapid entrance of women into the labor force, the worksite has the same compelling quality as a setting for adults that the school has for children. Nearly three-quarters of adults between the ages of 18 and 65 are now employed, and worksite physical activity programs have been shown to result in health and social benefits to employees, and in both economic and noneconomic benefits to employers (Iverson et al., 1985; also see Chapter 4).

### Adherence to Exercise Programs

Regardless of the setting in which physical activity and exercise programs take place, major concern is consistently expressed for the low rate of adherence to such programs (Epstein & Wing, 1980; Haskell, 1985; Mirotznik, Speedling, Stein, & Bronz, 1985; Oldridge, 1984; also see Chapter 12). Fewer than half of people who start out in what is intended to be a continuous exercise program are still in the program 6 months later, with most dropouts occurring within the first 3 months. In a study undertaken in Finland, Kentala (1972) found that in a sample of 298 postmyocardial infarction patients, only 77 chose to enter a recommended exercise program and, of those, only 39 percent were active in the program 5 months later. Even more discouraging was the fact that only 13 percent were active 1 year later.

Three sets of factors have been studied in terms of their roles in understanding adherence—personal factors, social-environmental factors, and characteristics of the exercise program itself. Unfortunately, the most obvious personal factor—attitude toward exercise—appears to be unrelated to whether a person adheres to an exercise program. That is, most people who lead sedentary lives have extremely favorable attitudes toward exercise (Dishman & Gettman, 1980).

As for personal factors, perhaps the most accurate predictor is low motivation. A second important personal factor is the extent to which the person is achieving his or her exercise objectives. Low motivation combined with the failure to appear to be making progress toward one's goals may be a near fatal combination. In the behavioral domain, predictors of dropping out of exercise programs include smoking, inactive leisure-time pursuits, and Type A behavior (Martin & Dubbert, 1982). As for biological factors, a high dropout rate is associated with being overweight. Combining a measure of body weight, motivation, and smoking behavior results in 80 percent accuracy in predicting who will adhere to an exercise program and who will drop out.

The major social-environmental factors that appear to predict adherence to an exercise program include support by family members, geographic stability, absence of family problems, and exercising in a group setting as opposed to exercising alone. Finally, as for characteristics of the exercise program, adherence is highest when the program is conveniently located and moderate in intensity—not too easy and not too hard.

In their general conclusions regarding the current status of exercise programs, Martin and Dubbert (1982) indicate that: (1) aerobic exercise (Cooper, 1968) appears to be beneficial in the treatment and prevention of a variety of health disorders; (2) problems of low adherence rate are so severe that even when the evidence is clear that exercise is helpful, the overall effectiveness of exercise is in doubt; (3) comparison among studies is difficult because of the failure to establish standardized ways of measuring the exercise program and adherence; (4) there is some evidence that behavioral strategies such as self-control procedures can increase adherence, but the effects appear to be temporary; and (5) many of the studies of the effectiveness of exercise programs are methodologically unsound, in that, without appropriately selected control groups, it is not possible to identify the specific effects of the exercise versus the effects of participating in a program of any kind.

## ALCOHOL ABUSE AND HEALTH

Alcohol is the most widely used drug in the United States. In virtually all surveys, a majority of adults report drinking some alcohol during the month prior to the conducting of the survey. Among older adults, 11 percent report drinking on 20 or more days during the past month (Miller & Cisin, 1983). As of 1985 (National Center for Health Statistics, 1985a, 1986f) only 14 percent of adults reported having had no alcoholic beverages during the previous 2 weeks, and nearly one-quarter of adult men reported having five or more alcoholic drinks on 10 or more days during the past year, a figure about four times higher than in the case of women. Average consumption of alcohol in the United States for all persons over 14 years old is equivalent to about 2.75 gallons of pure ethanol per person per year, and is 10 percent higher than a decade ago. In fact, the consumption of alcohol has been increasing worldwide. In the United States, it is currently estimated that there are about 8 million persons who suffer from some form of alcohol abuse or alcohol dependence.

Among high school seniors, more than 90 percent report having consumed alcohol at some point in their lives, about 87 percent report having consumed alcohol during the past year, and more than 70 percent in the past month (Johnston, O'Malley, & Bachman, 1984). Attitudes toward alcohol consumption among high school seniors have not changed significantly in the past decade and appear to be remarkably sanguine. Only about 20 percent of high school seniors believe that taking one or two drinks nearly every day is harmful, and only 65 percent believe that taking four or five drinks nearly every day is harmful.

The relationship of drinking and driving, especially among teenagers, is of major public concern. Between 50,000 and 200,000 people die each year from alcohol-related illnesses, accidents, and violence—representing perhaps 10 percent of all deaths in the United States (Healey, 1986; Waller, 1986; Waller, Stewart, et al., 1986). Liver disease—most commonly cirrhosis of the liver—ranks among the ten leading causes of death and is largely attributable to alcohol consumption. Alcohol abuse is associated with cancer of the liver, pancreas, esophagus, and mouth, with brain damage, with suppression of the normal immune response, with depression and hypertension, and with physical and mental abnormalities in the children of alcoholic women (Alcohol-Associated Premature Mortality, 1985; Blume, 1986; Cushner, 1981; DeFrank et al., 1987; Deykin et al., 1987; Gill et al., 1986; MacGregor, 1986; Surveillance and Assessment, 1985).

The misuse of alcohol leads to increased risk of injury and death to the self, family members, and others, especially by fires and motor-vehicle and other accidents. The level of family disruption and chronic family misery in families with an alcoholic member is beyond calculation. Alcohol misuse cost society an estimated $49.4 billion in 1977 (Berry, Boland, Smart, & Kanak, 1977; Miller, 1983; National Center for Health Statistics, 1983a). On a positive note, there is considerable evidence that treatment for alcoholism results in a dramatic and long-lasting decrease in both inpatient and outpatient medical care utilization (Cohen, 1986g; Holder & Blose, 1986; Miller & Hester, 1986).

Both environmental and genetic factors appear to be involved in alcohol abuse, and there is some evidence (Institute of Medicine, 1980) that there are common elements in alcohol abuse, drug abuse, risk-taking behavior, and cigarette smoking in terms of both environmental and genetic factors.

### Risk Factors in Alcoholism

There is a strong genetic component to alcoholism. In a series of extraordinary studies conducted in Stockholm, Sweden, in the late 1970s (Bohman, 1978; Cloninger, Bohman, & Sigvardsson, 1981), official records of alcoholics were used in a study of more than 2000 persons born between 1930 and 1950 who were adopted at an early age by nonrelatives. Supplemental information regarding alcohol abuse was available from a national register of alcohol treatment records. Thus, it was possible to identify people who were adopted at a very early age and to study their drinking behavior as it related to the drinking behavior of their biological parents (a genetic link) and their adopting parents (a psychosocial link). Parenthetically, it should be mentioned that Sweden is one of the few countries in the world where accurate centralized records of this kind are available that make such a study possible.

While 39 percent of male adoptees whose biological fathers were registered as alcohol abusers were in the alcohol treatment register, only 13 percent of adoptees whose biological fathers were not registered were listed in the register. That is, sons of alcoholics are three times as likely to become alcoholics, even if they are not reared by their biological parents, as do men who do not have alcoholic parents.

If mild alcohol abuse is reported for the adopted son, there is a greater probability that the adopting father's name will appear in the alcohol register than if moderate alcohol abuse is reported for the son. In the case of mild alcohol abuse of the son, only if both the biological and adopting father are in the register is the risk of alcoholism on the part of the adopted son significantly elevated. In the case of moderate alcohol abuse, however, whether or not the adopting father is in the register, if the biological father is in the register the risk of the son being in the register is more than four times greater than if the biological father does not appear in the register. It thus appears that moderate alcohol abuse is primarily a genetic trait, while mild alcohol abuse can be transmitted either genetically or as a function of the social environment.

Other research supports the role of inheritance in the transmission of alcoholism. Identical twins, who by definition share a common genetic inheritance, have a greater concordance rate for alcoholism than do fraternal twins, who, by definition, are twins who do not share an identical genetic inheritance. These findings—combined with those from animal studies, which also provide clear-cut evidence of a genetic factor in alcohol preference—have led to the ongoing search for the specific genetic basis of alcoholism risk (Blume, 1986; Institute of Medicine, 1980; Zucker & Gomberg, 1986).

There is no question that psychosocial factors also play a role in determining the risk of alcoholism. Not all identical twins are concordant for alcoholism. Alcoholism is particularly infrequent in those cultures where drinking customs and values are well known and generally agreed upon. Basic attitudes toward drinking among children are clearly related to parental behavior, and social norms and group pressures play a particularly strong role in determining alcohol-related behavior (Cohen, 1986f; Critchlow, 1986; Hull & Bond, 1986; Zucker & Gombert, 1986).

Recent surveys have shown a significant increase in drinking among young adolescents between ages 10 to 15. While girls drink less—and less often—than boys, their drinking behavior has increased more rapidly in recent years than in the case of boys. A number of social and psychological factors, such as low self-esteem, high egocentrism, poor time perspective, and high readiness to be influenced by others, are associated with greater risk of drinking among adolescents.

Alcohol use may appear to be stimulating, but it actually depresses and anesthetizes the central nervous system. Perhaps because of this effect there is in the case of adolescents a strong association between alcohol use, on the one hand, and poor school performance and excessive risk of driving accidents, on the other.

Jessor (1984), writing about adolescents and with particular reference to alcohol intake, has suggested that lifestyles that compromise health may be understood as: (1) inappropriate efforts aimed at achieving independence from parental control when more appropriate methods are unavailable or unattainable; (2) ways of expressing opposition to adult authority; (3) coping mechanisms for dealing with anxiety, frustration, or failure; (4) ways of gaining admission to peer groups or gaining acceptance among peer groups; (5) confirmation of important aspects of personal identity; or (6) symbols of having made a developmental transition from a less mature to a more mature status.

Alcoholism has recently been recognized as an important problem among women, although rates of alcoholism are considerably lower among women than men. There is evidence that genetic factors exist in the case of female alcoholics (Blume, 1986; Bohman, Sigvardsson, & Cloninger, 1981), although to a somewhat lesser extent than in the case of male alcoholics.

In a recent national survey of drinking and drinking-related psychosocial problems among women, Wilsnack, Wilsnack, and Klassen (1984) found that alcohol-related difficulties were particularly prominent among women aged 21 to 34, among women who were unmarried or who had disrupted marriages, and among women who were married to men who were themselves frequent drinkers. Long-term research suggests that young women who drink in order to relieve shyness, to have fun, and to get along better on dates are at excess risk for the development of later problems of alcoholism (Blume, 1986).

### Prevention of Alcoholism

In reviewing social models of alcoholism prevention, Tuchfeld and Marcus (1984) have identified three specific approaches: (1) the sociocultural model; (2) the social-structural model; and (3) the public health model (also see Frances & Franklin, 1986). The major sociocultural model examines normative patterns of alcohol use, and has as its fundamental assumption the belief that the rate of alcoholism should be relatively low in those cultures in which drinking practices are well integrated into accepted ways of behaving, and in which the rules and contexts for drinking are clearly defined.

Three implications for prevention can be derived from the sociocultural model. First, efforts should be made to change normative acceptable behavior in a group in which alcohol use is considered excessive. Second, drinking of alcoholic beverages should be integrated into other social activities, such as meals or religious practices, rather than engaged in for its own sake. Third, alcohol should be introduced to children at an early age (in controlled amounts, to be sure) in order to facilitate the identification with a culture's normative drinking practices.

Prevention of alcoholism may also depend on developing an understanding of why people drink, and then on developing alternative, less destructive ways of dealing with these motivational needs (Engstrom, 1984). One of the theoretical by-products of a study of the motivations that are the antecedents of drinking is increased self-awareness. It is generally believed that increased self-awareness results in increased ability to control one's own behavior.

The social-structural model is based upon the assumption that structural conditions can be created that can reduce alcohol consumption. Among these potential structural changes are (1) restricting the availability of alcohol; (2) enacting laws restricting drinking of alcohol, such as by raising the minimum drinking age; (3) regulating alcohol advertising; and (4) encouraging practices that make excessive consumption of alcohol less prevalent and less dangerous, such as by training bartenders to recognize when their patrons have had enough to drink or by providing rides for persons who have consumed excessive amounts of alcohol and who thus should not be allowed to drive their own motor vehicles.

There is some evidence from other countries that raising the cost of alcohol as a way of reducing alcohol consumption has been moderately effective. In the United States, some evidence has already been reported to suggest that raising the drinking age combined with the enactment of a mandatory bottle deposit law results in a modest reduction in sales of alcoholic beverages. Unfortunately, there is no evidence that these public policy changes result in reduced consumption of alcohol among the heaviest drinkers.

Two other public policy approaches to alcohol availability have recently been examined. First, efforts have been made to repeal the tax laws that allow businesses to claim deductions for alcohol consumed in business-related activities—the so-called three-martini lunch. Such expenses amount to over $10 billion per year, resulting in a loss of tax revenues in the amount of between $3 and $5 billion annually. Second, programs designed for servers of alcoholic beverages have been inaugurated to limit the amount of alcohol that can be served to a patron in order that he or she does not become intoxicated, and to allow servers to take action to insure that an intoxicated patron does not leave the premises in an automobile. These approaches are promising but not yet tested (Mosher, 1982, 1983a, 1983b).

Efforts to reduce the consumption of alcohol by restricting its availability or by regulating the nature of alcohol advertising, or by any other method, conflict with the principal objective of the alcohol industry, that is, the sale of alcoholic beverages and the generation of profit. Mosher and Wallack (1981) recently described the work of the Bureau of Alcohol, Tobacco, and Firearms (BATF) in developing changes in the regulations regarding alcohol advertising. The BATF has both statutory and constitutional authority and responsibility to regulate alcohol advertising in order to prevent deception, but, as Mosher and

Wallack have documented, the BATF "has shown a disregard for its public health responsibilities and an unwillingness to act in the public interest" (p. 334). Rather, the BATF, showing little if any awareness of the evidence that alcohol abuse is a major public health problem, permits the alcohol industry to continue its massive advertising campaign that falsely portrays alcohol as a positive force for a socially, sexually, and economically fulfilling lifestyle. Mosher and Wallack have concluded that the BATF actually functions as a mediator of competing alcohol industry interests rather than an agency with the responsibility to protect the public's health.

The public health model is based upon the assumption that if alcoholism were viewed as a disease, then all of the traditional disease prevention approaches would be appropriate. Such measures would include genetic counseling, the search for biological blocking agents that could be added to alcohol to inhibit intoxication, the identification of groups at excess risk of developing destructive drinking behavior, and the subsequent development of preventive approaches directed specifically at these groups.

Nathan (1983) has recently reviewed the status of alcoholism prevention programs in the United States. Most preventive intervention efforts aimed at high-risk groups have not been remarkably effective. In recent years programs have been designed for women, whose alcoholism rate has been climbing since the turn of the century. Some programs are based on the theory that women who drink have deficits in assertiveness, self-esteem, stress-management skills, and social skills. Accordingly, these programs provide training in these areas. Other programs are based on the belief that women who drink have inadequate information about alcohol and its effects, and so seek to provide that information. There is some evidence that these programs enhance information and often modify attitudes toward drinking. Unfortunately, as Nathan has indicated, reduction in the amount of alcohol consumption has rarely been assessed and, where assessed, has rarely been achieved.

Another group identified as a target for preventive intervention programs, according to Nathan (1983), is adolescents. While some preventive intervention programs are aimed at elementary school children, most are designed for young people aged 12 and above. Some of these programs are limited to the provision of educational content, while others are far more comprehensive in nature, and include counseling and staff educational services.

One of the most successful of these programs was developed by Goodstadt, Sheppard, and Chan (1982) in which a broadly based educational effort resulted in decreased alcohol consumption. Goodstadt and associates developed two sets of ten self-contained lesson plans, one for students in seventh and eighth grades, and the other for students in ninth and tenth grades. Topics in the lesson plans included myths about alcohol, information about advertising, reasons for drinking, and effects of alcohol on the family, driving, sports, fitness, and sexuality. Three lessons or more were taught on a daily basis in eight elementary and secondary schools in an urban Canadian public school system. Classes in other

schools did not participate in the special teaching curriculum and served as a control group.

In general, Goodstadt and associates found that the program increased the participants' knowledge about alcohol, had little consistent effect on their attitudes toward alcohol, but did produce decreases in both present alcohol use and in predictions of future alcohol use. In contrast to these findings at the level of junior and senior high school, efforts to mount comprehensive programs at the college level have not resulted in significant decreases in drinking behavior.

Special programs have been developed for pregnant women in the hopes of reducing the incidence of fetal alcohol syndrome, a disorder that appears in newborn infants whose mothers have been abusing alcohol during their pregnancies. In a recent report from one such program (Lowman, 1982), an educational effort designed for pregnant women in Seattle appears to have resulted in a decrease in alcohol use.

According to Nathan (1983), efforts to reduce the prevalence of drunken driving are quite new and include changes in the law and in patterns of law enforcement. These programs have not yet been evaluated in terms of their long-term effectiveness, although there is some evidence of short-term decreases in drunken driving.

Since there is considerable evidence that alcoholism results in significant reductions in work productivity, it would seem natural to establish alcoholism prevention programs in the workplace (see Chapter 4), Nathan (1983) has reported that in recent years, industry, through its Employee Association Programs, seems to be recognizing the necessity of providing treatment programs for its employees with alcohol-related problems. Industry has not, however, yet recognized the cost-effectiveness of programs designed to prevent these problems from occurring.

## DRUG ABUSE AND HEALTH

While illicit drug abuse, particularly among adolescents and young adults, has declined from its high levels in the late 1970s, it continues to be a serious health problem (Brunswick & Messeri, 1986). Currently, some 20 million people use marijuana, and there is some evidence that that number is underestimated (Hingson et al., 1986). The popularity of cocaine continues, with more than 22 million Americans having tried cocaine at least once and an estimated 4 to 5 million current users. Around 1986, a new, far less expensive form of cocaine called "crack" appeared that has increased cocaine's availability and threatens to increase its use (Cohen, 1986e). There is considerable evidence that cocaine use endangers the health not only of the user but, in the case of pregnant women, the health of the baby as well (Chasnoff, Burns, Schnoll, & Burns, 1985). In addition, the abuse of stimulants, sedatives, hallucinogens, inhalants, and other psychoactive drugs remains a problem. It is currently estimated that more than 3

million Americans suffer from some form of drug abuse or drug dependence, and efforts are currently under way to test for drug use in a very wide variety of settings, particularly in the workplace (Cohen, 1986d).

Heroin addiction is considered by many to be the most serious drug problem in the United States. The toll from heroin includes premature death and severe disability, family disruption, and crime. The increased use of heroin with alcohol and cocaine is also of concern. The destructive intensity of cocaine on health is worsening as more and more users experiment with smoking and intravenous administration (National Institute of Drug Abuse, 1985). The widespread prevalence of marijuana use, especially among the young, has raised concerns about the short- and long-term effects of its use on health, particularly with the recent availability of marijuana that is ten times more potent than that smoked only a decade ago (Cohen, 1986a). Special concern has begun to be expressed regarding the relationship of marijuana to automobile accidents, especially when marijuana is used in combination with alcohol (National Center for Health Statistics, 1983a).

Annual surveys of drug use and attitudes toward drug use among high school seniors have been conducted since 1975 by the Institute for Social Research at the University of Michigan (Miller & Cisin, 1983). The use of virtually all drugs increased markedly from 1975 until their peak in 1978. Since then there has been a substantial decrease. For example, between 1978 and 1982 there was a drop from 10.7 to 6.3 percent in the proportion of high school seniors describing themselves as daily users of marijuana. At the same time, the proportion of high school seniors who disapprove of regular use of marijuana has increased from 65 percent in 1977 to 85 percent in 1984.

### The Drug-use Career

Three stages have been identified in the typical drug-use career (Miller & Cisin, 1983). The first involves the use of the two principal legal drugs—alcohol and cigarettes. The second stage includes the use of marijuana. The third includes the use of illicit drugs other than marijuana, including cocaine, hallucinogens, and heroin.

Each stage seems almost to be a necessary but not sufficient condition for graduation to the next stage. Alcohol or cigarette use precedes second-stage marijuana use in almost 95 percent of marijuana users; marijuana use precedes the use of third-stage illicit drugs in about 90 percent of third-stage drug users. On the other hand, far more than half of young adults who have used alcohol or cigarettes have not gone on to use marijuana, and a far smaller proportion of marijuana users have gone on to use other illicit drugs or to use licit psychotherapeutic drugs for nonmedical purposes.

While this view of the stages in drug use is undoubtedly accurate, the causal relationship between the use of drugs at each stage and at each subsequent stage is unclear. In all likelihood, for example, nearly 100 percent of alcohol users previously drank milk. It would be absurd, however, to suggest that

drinking milk causes the subsequent use of alcohol. The difficulty with the causal interpretation lies in the fact that the presumed cause exists in virtually the entire population.

As for concurrent use of drugs at different stages, recent studies have established that virtually all marijuana users also use alcohol and cigarettes, and that about 75 percent of current users of stage-three drugs also report using marijuana. In addition, nearly all stage-three drug users also report using alcohol. Thus, advancing to a new stage in drug use generally means bringing the earlier stage behavior along. In fact, many stage-three drug users advertently combine marijuana use with stage-three drug use.

### Risk Factors in Drug Use

Among young people, drug use is more common among those who date and those who are exposed to drug use by older family members. In the case of adolescent drug use, dating and drug use may be two aspects of the syndrome of precocious peer-oriented behavior identified by Jessor and Jessor (1977). Among adults, drug use is particularly common among those who have a low level of involvement with their families. Drug use continues to be more common in large metropolitan areas than in other types of communities, although differences attributable to geography are diminishing. There are no remarkable differences in drug-use practices as a function of gender, race, or educational level, except for the one significant finding that daily use of marijuana is more commonly reported by men ages 18 to 25 than among women in the same age group.

Characteristics of family life are also associated with drug-use patterns. Illicit drug use is lowest for those who are already married and forming a stable family of their own (16 percent) and highest for those young adults who live with roommates or friends or who are cohabiting (43 percent). Young adults who live alone or who live with their parents report intermediate levels of drug use.

### Prevention of Drug Abuse

Control of drug abuse is complex because drug abuse is thought of from different points of view. O'Connor and Ahmed (1979), for example, have noted that in the United States drug abuse is thought of simultaneously as an illness, a crime, and as a social behavior. Each of these views brings with it different modes of control. That is, control of drug abuse can be thought of as requiring either treatment, punishment, or regulation. In most communities, each of these modes of control are employed from time to time, and often simultaneously.

Three types of prevention strategies have been identified and evaluated in the literature—media campaigns, school programs, and multidimensional approaches. Public information media campaigns designed to convey information about the harmful effects of drugs were initiated in the 1960s and 1970s, but it is the general opinion that those early health education programs were not successful because they were not credible. The harmful effects of drugs were sometimes unrealistically exaggerated, and the use of these media campaigns often resulted in an increase in the already high level of polarization between the establishment, on the one hand, and youth—regardless of their drug use patterns—on the other hand (U.S. Department of Health, Education, and Welfare, 1977).

Drug education programs mounted in the schools appear to increase information about drugs but do not appear to modify behavior. In some cases, school-based education programs seem to have actually increased drug use, by reducing the anxiety associated with drugs and drug use. In spite of these negative findings, most schools continue to provide drug and alcohol education programs for their students, undoubtedly in the hopes that in the long run drug-related behaviors will change. Perhaps the single best source of current information about drug and alcohol abuse is the *Drug Abuse & Alcoholism Newsletter,* published continuously since 1971 by the Vista Hill Foundation (see, for example, Cohen, 1985a, 1985b).

Generic, multidimensional drug-abuse prevention programs began to appear in the mid-1970s. These programs take into account the research findings that distinguish drug users from non-drug-users and attend to such matters as low self-esteem and alienation from authority figures without dealing directly with drug abuse. These programs—focusing on what is called affective or emotional education—attempt to raise self-esteem and to reduce the sense of alienation in the hopes that one of the by-products will be a reduction in drug abuse. Evaluation of these generic programs, not very encouraging, suggests that non-drug-specific affective education approaches alone are not sufficient to prevent the onset of drug use (see, for example, Schaps, Moskowitz, Malvin, & Schaeffer, 1984).

While these three types of prevention strategies do not seem to be remarkably effective, recent results with programs that attempt to deal with the social environment seem to offer considerable promise. These drug abuse prevention programs focus on the entire environment within which the child is living, including modifying the nature of peer pressure, creating a non-drug-use climate, and involving parents and school personnel (Durell & Bukoski, 1984).

Perhaps the most recent—and in some ways the most interesting drug abuse prevention program—is the "Just Say No" program that began in 1985 in a grade school in Oakland, California (Cohen, 1986b). A group of grade-school children were discussing with their teacher how young people could resist the pressure to use drugs. The students seemed to agree that the simplest way was just to say no. A number of students suggested that they could start a Just Say No Club, and from those suggestions has come a remarkable, rapidly growing national movement. While it is impossible to determine what its effects have been or to predict what will happen to the movement, it can become an important deterrent to the peer pressures that push youngsters into drug-taking careers (Cohen, 1986b).

## CONCLUDING COMMENTS

The cost to our society of destructive lifestyles—in health, social, and financial terms—is enormous. In the case of alcohol and drug abuse among persons in the labor force, the cost associated with excess health care, days away from work, and lost productivity is in excess of $30 billion per year (Quayle, 1983). Employees with a drinking or drug abuse problem are absent sixteen times more often than the average employee, have an accident rate that is four times greater than the average employee, and have five times as many compensation claims.

Our review of preventive intervention programs suggests that the task of changing behavior in the direction of reducing the prevalence of destructive lifestyles is very complex. Yet, on the positive side, Kandel and Logan (1984) have found that the period of major risk for initiation to cigarette smoking, alcohol abuse, and drug abuse is prior to age 20 and for most illicit drugs prior to age 21. People who have not experimented with these substances prior to age 20 or 21 are unlikely to do so thereafter. The significance of this observation cannot be exaggerated. Preventive intervention programs, in the case of health-compromising lifestyles, need not be designed for the entire life span. There is reason to believe that successful preventive intervention programs designed for preadolescents, adolescents, and very young adults may be all that is needed. That is, prevention may be successfully accomplished by delaying the onset of the self-destructive behavior.

One general conclusion that follows from this age-specific observation is that the school setting may be the most important single location for the development and implementation of preventive intervention programs designed to modify lifestyles. Such programs can be embedded within physical education or health education classes, although their principles can pervade the entire curriculum. In order to enhance their effect, these programs could also involve parents.

A second general conclusion that seems justified from this review of lifestyle risk factors is that the short-term impact of programs designed to modify these factors is far greater than long-term impact. That is to say, adherence to programs designed to reduce the frequency of destructive lifestyles is very limited. This conclusion reinforces another observation—prevention of the undesirable behavior is probably easier to accomplish than cure of the undesirable behavior. In addition, as will be seen in Chapter 12, adherence is a more general variable that includes adherence to medical regimens as well.

## SUMMARY

- Four lifestyle factors have been shown to have a substantial impact on morbidity and mortality—poor nutritional habits, insufficient exercise, alcohol abuse, and other forms of drug abuse.

- The principal nutritional problem in the United States is obesity, a problem that affects about 20 percent of the population. Less common—but equally serious when they occur—are dietary inadequacy, bulimia, and anorexia. With the exception of dietary inadequacy, these problems are substantially more common in women than in men.

- Except at the extremes of obesity, the psychosocial consequences of obesity are as important as physical consequences. At the extremes, when weight is 50 percent above normal, physical health consequences are very considerable.

- A strong genetic component to weight exists, that serves to limit the effectiveness of diet or other forms of weight control.

- Weight reduction programs have far better short-term success than long-term success, and it has been judged that most programs ultimately fail to achieve their desired objectives.

- Adequate physical activity plays an important role in health maintenance and is particularly important in today's sedentary society.

- Physical activity has been found to have a favorable effect on mental health, particularly on reducing depression, and to reduce the risk of obesity, hypertension, diabetes, and musculoskeletal problems.

- A special problem in efforts to increase the level of exercise is low rate of adherence to such programs. Rate of adherence is generally so low that the effectiveness of such programs is thrown into doubt.

- Alcohol is the most widely used drug in the United States, and its abuse has enormous negative consequences for health and well-being. Alcohol use is directly involved in about 10 percent of all deaths.

- Alcohol abuse has a strong genetic component, particularly in the case of men, with children of alcoholics found to be at excess risk, even if they have been raised by nonalcoholic foster parents.

- Most investigators believe that reducing the prevalence of alcohol abuse will require substantial public policy changes as well as changes in societal values and standards of acceptable behavior.

- While alcoholism prevention programs have shown some successes, considerable work remains to be done before the prevalence of alcohol abuse will significantly decrease.

- Other forms of drug abuse—licit as well as illicit, including heroin, cocaine, marijuana, stimulants, inhalants, sedatives—are somewhat less common than was true a few years ago. Nevertheless, more than 3 million Americans suffer from some form of drug abuse or drug dependence.

- Controlling drug abuse is complex because drug abuse is simultaneously viewed as social behavior, illness, and, in the case of illicit drugs, a crime.

- Drug-related health education programs in the schools, apparently quite successful in communicating information about drug abuse, are far less successful in reducing the prevalence of the problem.

- Drug abuse prevention programs are more successful if they are multidimensional in nature, and if they involve the family and include efforts to reduce peer pressure and to create an influential group of nondrug users.

- One encouraging finding from a number of different studies of self-destructive lifestyles is that if they do not occur before the age of 20 or 21, they are very unlikely to develop at all. Thus, efforts to prevent or end self-destructive lifestyles need to be introduced early with the assurance that if these efforts are successful through high school and early college years, there may be little further need for their continuation.

# Lifestyle Risk Factors: Smoking and Health

# 6

## INTRODUCTION

Cigarette smoking is the largest single preventable cause of illness and premature death in the United States. It has been called the most addictive and dependence-producing form of self-administered gratification that exists (Pechacek & McAlister, 1980). Cigarette smokers have a 70-percent higher overall death rate than nonsmokers, and tobacco is associated with more than 300,000 premature deaths per year—about 15 percent of all deaths in a given year (Mattson, Pollack, & Cullen, 1987). Studies that examine why women live substantially longer than men consistently find that about half of the difference in life expectancy is due to the fact that fewer women than men smoke (Miller & Gerstein, 1983; Waldron, 1986). Each premature death that has been averted by not smoking has resulted, on the average, in 23 additional years of life (Warner & Murt, 1983). In terms not only of premature death, but of increased medical bills and time lost from work, this excess death rate among smokers and even their nonsmoking spouses (Humble, Samet, & Pathak, 1987) currently costs the United States about $65 billion annually, or $2.17 for each pack of cigarettes sold (Office of Technology Assessment, 1985).

The major single cause of cancer mortality in the United States is cigarette smoking, accounting for more than 100,000 cancer deaths annually, representing about 30 percent of all cancer deaths. Smoking is a causal factor in coronary heart disease and arteriosclerotic peripheral vascular disease, and is also the most important cause of chronic obstructive lung disease (National Center for Health Statistics, 1983a). A probable relationship has been found between risk of cancer among nonsmokers and their exposure to other people's smoking. The 5-year survival rate for lung cancer is less than 10 percent and has not changed in the past 25 years. Early diagnosis and treatment do not improve the chances for survival.

In 1950, lung cancer accounted for 18,300 deaths in the United States. In 1982, 32 years later, lung cancer accounted for about 110,000 deaths. Lung cancer accounts for 25 percent of all cancer deaths in the United States and, while it is not successfully treatable, it is largely preventable. It is currently estimated that 85 percent of lung cancer deaths could have been avoided if the persons involved had not taken up smoking.

When combined with alcohol, cigarette smoking increases the likelihood of cancer of the larynx, esophagus, and oral cavity. Combined with other coronary risk factors such as high cholesterol, cigarette smoking increases cardiovascular risk. During pregnancy, cigarette smoking can increase the risk of spontaneous abortion, retarded fetal growth, and even fetal or neonatal death. In addition, cigarette smoking is the major identifiable cause of residential fire deaths and injuries as well as a contributor to accidental injuries.

Although this chapter will not discuss the topic of "smokeless tobacco" (chewing tobacco and snuff), it would be appropriate to mention that a report of the Advisory Committee to the Surgeon General was issued in 1986 on the topic of the health consequences of using smokeless tobacco (U.S. Department of Health and Human Services, 1986b). In that report, the Committee concluded that the oral use of smokeless tobacco represents a significant health risk, that it is not a safe substitute for smoking cigarettes, that it can cause cancer and a number of noncancerous oral conditions, and that it can lead to nicotine addiction and dependence.

Since 1968, the Department of Health and Human Services has issued an annual annotated bibliography of published research studies on the topic of smoking and health. The most recent edition, covering publications in 1984, lists and summarizes more than 2000 published research studies from around the world (U.S. Department of Health and Human Services, 1985a). Publications are divided into sixteen different sections, including such topics as pharmacology and toxicology, mortality and morbidity, neoplastic diseases, cardiovascular diseases, pregnancy and infant health, behavioral and psychological aspects, smoking prevention and intervention, smoking cessation methods, tobacco product additives, tobacco manufacturing and processing, tobacco economics, and legislation. Given the magnitude of this literature, this book must limit itself to identifying and discussing the major issues and conclusions in this important field from the point of view of social scientists. At the outset, however, it should be noted that the harmful effects of tobacco have been suspected for centuries. King James I of England, who died in 1625, in his *Counterblaste to Tobacco,* wrote:

> A custom loathsome to the eye, hateful to the nose, harmful to the brain, dangerous to the lungs, and in the black, stinking fume thereof nearest resembling the horrible Stygian smoke of the pit that is bottomless. (Evans, 1968, pp. 698–699)

## SURVEYS OF TOBACCO USE

National surveys of tobacco use have been conducted periodically under the auspices of the National Center for Health Statistics and the National Clearinghouse for Smoking and Health since 1965 (National Center for Health Statistics, 1985a, 1986f; U.S. Department of Health and Human Services, 1984a; see also Pechacek & McAlister, 1980; Shopland & Brown, 1987). These surveys, based on very large samples of adults randomly selected across the United States, have examined current smoking behavior, smoking history, and previous attempts to quit smoking as a function of age and gender. Because a number of surveys were conducted between 1966 and 1985, it has also been possible to report on trends across time. The results of these surveys can be summarized as follows:

1.  The proportion of current regular smokers declined steadily between 1965 and 1985. The decline was steeper among males (from 52 to 33 percent) than among females (from 34 to 28 percent), and was greater among persons who had higher levels of education (Terris, 1984).

2.  The proportion of adults who never smoked increased steadily from 1965 to 1985. As of 1985, among males, 36 percent have never smoked; among females, 54 percent have never smoked.

3.  The mean number of cigarettes smoked per day by current smokers increased slightly from 1970 to 1980 (from 20 to 21.7 cigarettes). The increase was greater in the case of females than males, with the result that differences in smoking behavior between men and women—both in terms of whether they are smokers and, if so, in terms of how much they smoke—are diminishing.

4.  Smoking rates were higher among currently divorced or separated persons than among people who were currently married or who had never been married. Smoking rates decreased with greater education and income.

5.  The greatest average increase in daily cigarette consumption between 1970 and 1980 was observed among women aged 35 to 44.

6.  The proportion of current smokers who attempted to quit during the previous year increased from 1966 to 1980 (26.0 to 36.7 percent).

7.  Among current smokers, younger persons and females were more likely than older persons and males to have attempted to quit during the previous year.

Surveys of high school seniors—conducted annually since 1975—indicate that reported daily use of cigarettes among high school seniors has dropped from its high of 28.8 percent in 1977 to 21.1 percent in 1982 (Johnston, O'Malley, & Bachman, 1984).

## ESTABLISHING THE SMOKING–LUNG CANCER LINK

Since 1951, when the first prospective study (see Chapter 1) of smoking and health was conducted, a number of major prospective studies have been conducted in the United States, Great Britain, Sweden, Canada, and Japan. In total, these studies have amassed more than 17 million person-years (data collected about one person for one year) of observation that included more than 330,000 deaths. In every one of these studies, cigarette smokers had significantly higher mortality rates than nonsmokers, not only for cancer but for a number of other chronic diseases as well.

In these prospective studies, the mortality rate has been invariably higher among smokers than nonsmokers for cancer of the lung, larynx, oral cavity, esophagus, bladder, kidney, and pancreas. The greatest difference in mortality rate is in the case of lung cancer, where the risk of death has been found to be about ten times higher among smokers in general than among nonsmokers. In the case of those who smoke more than one pack of cigarettes a day, the risk of lung cancer is 15 to 25 times greater than in the case of nonsmokers.

In addition to these prospective studies, hundreds of retrospective studies have examined almost every aspect of the potential association between smoking and cancer. Researchers have studied, for example, type and quantity of tobacco smoked, duration of smoking, and inhalation practices. Findings in these retrospective studies have consistently supported the results of the prospective studies.

The most direct measure of the association between cigarette smoking and lung cancer is the comparison of death or morbidity rates from the disease between smokers and nonsmokers. As has been noted, such comparisons require prospective studies. The greater the difference in those rates, the more likely is it that the suspected causative factor is implicated.

In an 11-year study of 4000 men and women aged 35 to 64—divided into three categories according to their smoking history: smokers, exsmokers, and nonsmokers—Friedman, Dales, and Ury (1979) found that the death rate was consistently and, in most cases, significantly higher among smokers than among exsmokers, and among exsmokers than nonsmokers, for every cause of death examined. In addition, the relationship of smoking to death rate from all causes combined persisted even after excluding from the analysis the relationships of major demographic variables, most of which were correlated with smoking history, such as education, alcohol use, marital status, presence of serious disease, occupational exposure, emotional disturbance, and coronary-disease risk factors.

As was noted in Chapter 1, criteria for establishing cause in epidemiological research include not only consistency and strength of the relationship between the presumed causal factor and the presumed disease consequence, but also specificity of the relationship, temporal sequence of the relationship, coherence of the relationship in terms of dose-response studies, and the findings of experimental preventive trials based on the presumed causal relationship.

Specificity is judged by how frequently the presence of one specific variable will predict the presence of a specific disease. In the case of cigarette smoking, there is relatively little specificity, because smoking is associated with excess risk of illness and death from a very broad number of diseases. But because cigarette smoking seems to be associated with higher than average death and morbidity rates from many different disorders including lung cancer does not mean that its association with lung cancer is any less persuasive.

In the case of cigarette smoking, varying degrees of association have been found with various cancers. The differing degrees of association tend to be stable and, thus, the consistently powerful association of smoking with lung cancer is even more persuasive.

The temporal-relationship criterion requires that exposure to the suspected causative factor must precede the disease. Prospective cohort studies appear to meet this criterion since, by design, they identify study samples in terms of the presence or absence of the presumed prior causative factor—in this case, cigarette smoking. Having identified two groups of people who differ in terms of their smoking histories, it would seem that determining the risk of lung cancer or any other disease in the future would, on the face of it, keep everything in proper temporal sequence.

But it is important not to underestimate the complexity of this criterion. It is, after all, perfectly logical to argue, as once was true of the American tobacco industry, that lung cancer causes smoking. One need only take the position that prodromal symptoms of lung cancer, that is, warning symptoms that indicate that lung cancer has already begun, exist long before the biological evidence of the disease can be found, and that one of these prodromal symptoms is the propensity to smoke. A parallel argument could be made, for example, in explaining the relationship of marital disruption as a stressful life event and physical illness. One could argue, as we have done in Chapter 3, that stressful life events such as marital disruption can precipitate illness in people who are healthy but vulnerable. On the other hand, it is just as logical to argue that preexisting physical illness can lead to marital disruption. The fundamental question really is one of evidence: What evidence can be assembled to test either of these hypotheses? In part, the evidence rests on unequivocal determinations of the temporal relationship, that is, of which came first—the physical illness or the marital disruption.

In the case of smoking and lung cancer, while it is logical, although markedly convoluted, to argue that lung cancer causes smoking, the hypothesis that the propensity to smoke is a prodromal symptom of lung cancer cannot be tested and, hence, cannot be evaluated. In order to test the hypothesis that lung cancer causes smoking, it would be necessary to be able to distinguish between smoking that is a prodromal symptom of lung cancer and smoking that is not, since not everyone who smokes develops lung cancer. If such a distinction could be made, it would be possible to label smoking into two types—lung-cancer type and non-lung-cancer type. Then one could convincingly test the hypothesis that lung cancer causes smoking by showing that the lung-cancer type of smoking is associated with subsequent biological evidence of lung cancer significantly more often than the non-lung-cancer type of smoking. This crucial distinction between the two postulated types of smoking cannot be made, however, and hence there is no way to test the hypothesis. In this case, an untestable hypothesis is hardly better than no hypothesis at all.

The coherence criterion for the evaluation of causal significance of an association is based upon its degree of agreement with known facts in the natural history of the disease. One of the most important aspects of the coherence criterion is evidence that risk of the disease increases with degree of exposure to the suspected agent. As was already noted, dose-response relationships between the suspected agent and the disease have been consistently found in the case of smoking and lung cancer—the more a person smokes and has smoked, the greater is the risk for lung cancer.

The final epidemiological link in the establishment of a causal connection between a suspected agent and a subsequent disease is to demonstrate that if there is a reduction in the frequency or intensity of the suspected agent, a subsequent reduction in the incidence or severity of the disease will be found.

The evidence linking smoking cessation and risk of lung cancer is very reassuring. An association has been found for all types of cancers. The ex-smoker's risk of dying from lung cancer gradually decreases with the number of years off cigarettes and after 20 years of not smoking, comes very close to that of the nonsmoker. For the continuing cigarette smoker the lung cancer risk consistently remains more than ten times that of the nonsmoker. The exsmoker's risk for laryngeal and oral cavity cancers decreases gradually with the number of years since cessation of smoking, approaching that of nonsmokers after 10 to 15 years. Exsmokers have only about one-third the risk of esophageal cancer of current smokers, and their disease rates approach those of nonsmokers after only 4 years.

In the 1982 report of the Surgeon General on the health consequences of smoking (Koop & Luoto, 1982; U.S. Department of Health and Human Services, 1982), a comprehensive evaluation of the relationship between cigarette smoking and cancer was undertaken. In the words of that report,

> Since 1937, cancer has been the second most important cause of death in the United States and will account for an estimated 430,000 deaths this year. Surveys have shown that Americans fear dying of cancer more than any other disease. We have yet to observe, however, a decline in the cancer mortality rate as is currently occurring for other chronic diseases, such as the 30 percent decline in the cardiovascular disease mortality rate and the 50 percent decline in the cerebrovascular disease mortality rate observed over the last three decades. The mortality rate for cancer has changed little over two decades, and that change has been a small, but measurable increase. This increase in mortality has occurred in the face of remarkable improvements in survival rates for some cancer sites through earlier or better diagnosis and treatment. Unfortunately, however, these advances have failed to counter the remarkable increases in mortality from smoking-related cancers, many of which have a poor prognosis for long-term survival or cures. (U.S. Department of Health and Human Services, 1982, p. v)

## CONTROL OF SMOKING: A PSYCHOLOGICAL PERSPECTIVE

Writers who have examined the control of smoking from a psychological point of view (see, for example, Benfari, Ockene, & McIntyre, 1982; Lichtenstein, 1982) have concerned themselves with the development of a theory of smoking and with improving the methodological sophistication of the study of smoking control programs. These two interests—in model and theory building and in methodological soundness—probably characterize psychological interests in a variety of other areas as well.

### Psychological Smoking Models

Psychologists have developed three theoretical models for understanding smoking behavior—a psychological model, a psychosocial model, and a pharmacological model. The psychological model focuses on needs, drives, and emotions. This model views smoking behavior as serving to minimize negative emotions, such as distress, anger, fear, and shame, and as reinforcing and persistent because it is successful in warding off these feelings (Tomkins, 1966). This model has been elaborated and evaluated, and there is considerable evidence that an association exists between the amount of smoking and the extent to which cigarettes are used to ward off feelings of negative emotion. In addition, heavy smokers have been found to manifest more psychological disturbances than lighter smokers (Benfari, Ockene, & McIntyre, 1982).

The psychosocial model views smoking behavior as a means of coping with stress or with stressful life events. Successful coping with stress serves as the reinforcer for smoking behavior. Laboratory studies have tended to support the hypothesis that smoking facilitates coping (Hemistra, 1973; Nesbitt, 1973; Ockene et al., 1981). Smoking has been found to reduce fluctuations or changes in mood during stress and serves as a successful means for enduring a stressor, such as electric shock. When compared to nonsmokers, people who smoke more than a pack of cigarettes per day have been found to have a lower tolerance for stress if they are not permitted to smoke and a greater tolerance for stress if they are permitted to smoke. Thus, persons under high stress may have unusual difficulty in trying to quit smoking.

Another aspect of the psychosocial model is the concept of psychosocial assets—those personal attributes that may provide special strength in developing more satisfactory long-term coping mechanisms. Included in the concept of psychosocial assets are such attributes as self-efficacy, internal locus of control, and a strong social support network (see Chapter 3). These personal assets may make it easier for a person under high stress to quit smoking.

The pharmacological model seeks a specific chemical agent within the cigarette itself to which a smoker might become dependent or addicted. The most likely agent appears to be nicotine. A number of studies have supported this hypothesis—studies that have shown that smokers smoke more when the amount of nicotine in their cigarettes is reduced and that smoking is decreased when nicotine is provided in other ways, such as by means of nicotine gum, particularly as part of a comprehensive smoking cessation program.

### Methodological Issues

In reviewing the large variety of studies that have sought to evaluate alternative smoking cessation programs, psychologists have noted five methodological problems that keep appearing in these studies. These problems consist of (1) difficulties in verifying self-reports of smoking behavior, (2) lack of control groups in the evaluation of smoking cessation programs, (3) difficulties in classifying level of previous smoking or level of smoking reduction, (4) lack of agreement regarding optimal length of followup, and (5) methodological differences in determining outcome of smoking cessation programs (see, for example, Pechack & McAlister, 1980).

Since the dependent variable in evaluating smoking control programs is the amount of smoking, it is critically important that the measure of amount of smoking be a valid one. Accordingly, it is always important to be able to verify self-reports of smoking behavior. Three objective measures of smoking behavior have recently been developed that differ in intrusiveness, cost, and sensitivity— carbon monoxide, thiocyanate, and cotinine. Smoking involves the intake of carbon monoxide, which, in turn, increases carboxyhemoglobin in the blood. The amount of carboxyhemoglobin can be measured directly from blood samples and also, indirectly but somewhat more crudely, by analyzing the amount of carbon monoxide in the breath. These measures are crude because carbon monoxide can enter the body in smoky rooms or from car exhaust. In addition, carbon monoxide lasts a very short time in the body, so that if the subject has not smoked for several hours, none will be detected. Thus, the measurement of carbon monoxide is particularly useful in providing feedback to heavy-smoking subjects who are interested in cutting down their smoking, but is not useful as part of a smoking cessation program.

Thiocyanate, a by-product of the small and nontoxic amounts of cyanide in tobacco, can be detected in the saliva. Thiocyanate lasts longer than carbon monoxide (approximately 2 weeks), and only very rarely comes from any sources other than tobacco. Saliva samples are easy to obtain, and they can be frozen and shipped elsewhere for analysis at a later date. Thus, thiocyanate is particularly useful in studies designed to assist smokers to become abstinent. Combined with the measure of carbon monoxide in the breath, the two measures are a powerful test of smoking behavior.

Nicotine, through its derivative, cotinine, can be reliably detected in the urine, and its measurement validly discriminates smokers from nonsmokers (Sepkovic & Haley, 1985). With these three excellent measures available to detect the physiological by-products of smoking, and with the occasional low validity of self-reports of smoking behavior, most researchers now believe that any study of smoking behavior must include one or more of these physiological measures.

There are two aspects to the control group problem. First, without a matched randomly assigned control group, it is simply impossible to make any credible assertions regarding the success of a particular stop-smoking program. When such programs were first established and evaluated, they rarely included control groups in their design. Currently, however, virtually all smoking cessation studies have included control groups. Second, when control groups are included in evaluation studies, there is considerable evidence that significant smoking reduction occurs in the control group as well as in the experimental group. Nonspecific factors, such as simply being part of an important treatment study, are ordinarily thought of as responsible for this decrease in smoking among members of the untreated control group. Thus, it becomes more difficult to document the specific effectiveness of the intervention program under investigation without assessing other factors besides the probability of stopping smoking. Among such other factors should be, for example, whether people in the experimental group stop smoking for longer periods of time than people in the untreated control groups.

If there is no general agreement about how to classify smoking behavior and decreases in smoking behavior, it becomes impossible to compare and contrast different outcomes of smoking control program. As for smoking behavior, most researchers assess number of cigarettes smoked per day, but it is clear that one needs also to take into account such past factors as how long persons have smoked, and such present factors as their specific smoking behavior, in terms of how many puffs are taken per cigarette and how much they inhale when they smoke. As for assessing degree of smoking reduction, each study seems to use its own criteria—no cigarettes for the previous week, no more than six cigarettes in any given week, and so forth.

Similarly, there are differences in the duration of followup studies in smoking control program evaluations, and, again, it would be useful to have a general research paradigm that everyone could rely on. Since there is a high recidivism rate during the first year following participation in a smoking control program, smoking behavior should be assessed, at minimum, immediately post-treatment, and again in 1 year.

Finally, there are no agreed upon strategies for conducting followup studies. Studies have used telephone calls, in-person interviews combined with appropriate laboratory analyses, and mail-out questionnaires. In the case of mail questionnaires, for example, it has been found that subjects who respond most quickly are more often exsmokers, while those who take longer to respond or who must be contacted repeatedly before they respond tend to be smokers. Thus, the nature of the results of such a followup study will depend, in part, on how conscientious the researcher is in obtaining responses from all study subjects. The less conscientious the researcher is, the better the results of the smoking control program under investigation will appear.

## CONTROL OF SMOKING: A SOCIAL PERSPECTIVE

Scientists who take a social perspective in studying smoking and the control of smoking behavior concern themselves with understanding how social and cultural forces influence the establishment of smoking behavior, and how such forces can be used to prevent smoking or to help people stop smoking once they have started (Syme & Alcalay, 1982). Particularly when dealing with a behavior that characterizes millions of people, such as smoking, a social perspective has the potential of being far more useful than one that deals with smokers one at a time. In addition, only a social perspective can be of use in thinking about the prevention of smoking behavior among the entire nonsmoking population.

Another compelling reason for approaching the question of smoking from a sociocultural point of view is that there is considerable evidence that some groups consistently smoke more than others. Thus, men smoke more than women, and both men and women in the age group 25 to 44 smoke more than those in any other age group. More blacks than whites smoke, regardless of gender. Persons with less education smoke more than those with more education. White-collar workers smoke less than blue-collar workers. Divorced and separated persons smoke far more than persons who are in intact marriages. Only a social perspective can help understand why such group differences exist.

### Interpersonal Influences

Two major social influences on the establishment of smoking behavior have been noted: the influence of others, and the influence of media advertising. During adolescence, when most smoking starts, smoking plays a symbolic role in the three great issues that teenagers face—the deemphasis of parental identification, the establishment of bonds with peers, and the establishment of an independent self-identity. Teenagers who have parents, older siblings, and friends who smoke tend to smoke more often themselves. In fact, those who have two parents who smoke are twice as likely to smoke as those who have no parents who smoke.

Smoking is thought of by teenagers as adult behavior normally off limits to children. Thus, smoking by teenagers is a sign of emerging adulthood and, to some extent, defiance of parents. On the other hand, smoking behavior of teenagers has diminished in recent years, partly because of their increasing concern with health and partly because smoking does not have the peer acceptance it used to have. Thus, the reduction of smoking behavior is synergistic—as fewer teenagers smoke, fewer teenagers will begin to smoke.

### Social Perspectives on Influencing Smoking Behavior

Social scientists have developed a number of very useful principles in developing smoking prevention programs (Gray & Daube, 1980). Those principles that rely on social perspective include the following:

1.  Smoking behavior should be placed within the total context of health, sex, school, authority figures, and personal growth.
2.  Nonsmoking should be viewed positively rather than negatively, by associating it with such values as independence, freedom, and emancipation.
3.  Nonsmoking needs to be viewed as acceptable by peers.
4.  Significant and popular figures from the world of entertainment or politics who do not smoke can make a special contribution in media campaigns for nonsmoking.
5.  Desirable alternatives to smoking—such as exercise, nutrition, or friendship—need to be presented as part of a program designed to encourage nonsmoking.
6.  The approach needs to stress the advantages of nonsmoking in the here and now, rather than the dangers of smoking in the distant future.
7.  A nonsmoking program should be tailored to the intended audience. Thus, in the case of adolescents, for example, factors such as popularity or attractiveness need to be stressed rather than the dangers of lung cancer or the advantages of reduced life insurance premiums.

Considering these seven principles is important not only for thinking about smoking prevention programs but for any efforts designed to create behavior change (see, for example, Mider, 1984). In addition, it would be useful to think about these principles in the context of any effort to create social policy.

One of the most interesting—and at the same time, most discouraging—aspects of smoking is that while there has been an enormous increase in the proportion of people who are aware of the harmful effects of smoking, there has been only a relatively small decline in the number of smokers. Social scientists have, as one can well imagine, given a good deal of thought to why so many people continue to smoke, and three reasons have been advanced.

First, cigarette smoking appears to be socially and psychologically—if not biologically—addictive, and quitting is far more difficult than most smokers care to admit. Second, smoking is viewed as pleasurable and relaxing. As was noted in the discussion of psychological perspectives on smoking control, there is considerable evidence that smoking reduces anxiety. Third, smoking is associated with sociability and provides powerful reinforcements in social situations.

At the present time, our society, including the mass media, continues to encourage smoking, although there is considerable evidence that societal values are changing and that cigarette advertising is having less of a persuasive impact on smoking behavior. As for discouraging smoking, educational efforts have been fairly successful. Further advances will need to include the social perspective, that is, the examination of the social context within which smoking occurs.

Most successful smoking cessation programs include a variety of different approaches. If social factors play a significant role in smoking, then smoking cessation programs need to provide alternative methods for meeting these social needs. At the same time, there are social policies that need to be changed. For example, as Syme and Alacalay (1982) have pointed out, current Internal Revenue Service rules permit including the cost of programs designed to reduce alcohol or other drug abuse as medical expenses, but not the cost of smoking prevention or smoking cessation programs. This rule seems absurd on the face of it, given the absolutely incontrovertible evidence that smoking is far more dangerous to one's health than either alcohol or illicit drugs.

Scientists who emphasize the importance of a social perspective in considering smoking cessation, stress four general points:

1.  Efforts to inform the public about the dangerous health consequences of smoking will probably need to continue indefinitely.
2.  In terms of its prevalence, smoking must be presented for what it is—atypical behavior of a minority of the population. The increasing constraints on smoking behavior and the increasing attention being accorded to the rights of nonsmokers help keep smoking in its proper demographic perspective.
3.  Constant attention needs to be devoted to the influence of public policy

and of public policy makers in order to counteract the efforts of the tobacco industry in encouraging smoking.

4. In spite of their high cost, and the enormous effort involved, antismoking advertisements must be revived, maintained, and increased.

Perhaps the best antismoking advertisement is the nonsmoker, and as the number and proportion of nonsmokers continues to increase, smoking will be increasingly seen as deviant and unacceptable. It will become increasingly difficult to smoke as a larger and larger proportion of the population think of smoking as not only unhealthy and unpleasant, but also as stupid (Syme & Alcalay, 1982).

## CONTROL OF SMOKING: A PUBLIC POLICY PERSPECTIVE

Prior to 1950, when the first evidence regarding the harmful consequences of cigarette smoking began to appear, there was no significant public policy debate regarding smoking. In the United States the tobacco industry was subsidized by the Department of Agriculture's price support system, and tobacco products were taxed to raise public revenues (practices that continue to this day). The tobacco industry responded quickly to the reports of the harmful effects of smoking that were beginning to appear. In 1954, the Tobacco Research Institute (TRI) was created for the purposes of supporting research that might refute these reports and of serving as the public relations arm of the industry.

For the next several years, the TRI made serious efforts to influence and downplay the statements that were emanating from such groups as the American Cancer Society as to the harmful effects of smoking, and it was not until about 1960 that the scientific views began to prevail. In 1959, the Surgeon-General of the U.S. Public Health Service issued a statement regarding the harmful effects of smoking. In 1962, the Advisory Committee on Smoking and Health was created. And in 1964, the first official report linking smoking and lung cancer was published.

After this report was issued, the scientific arguments became less prevalent and the debate turned to its current form—a debate between health and economic interests. Unobtrusive health hazard warnings on packages of cigarettes were mandated by the Federal Trade Commission in 1965, but these were balanced by a 4-year moratorium on any further action regarding advertising. In 1967, following a successful court test calling for equal time in advertising, broadcasting stations were required to air one antismoking message for every five tobacco advertisements. In 1969 federal legislation banned cigarette advertising on TV and radio but, at the same time, banned antismoking messages. In all of these actions, the power of the tobacco industry can be seen.

The role of the media in the inauguration of smoking may be less important than in the perpetuation of smoking once it has begun. Smoking is presented as glamorous, fun, and relaxing, of course, but the evidence suggests that antismoking advertising is more effective in getting people to stop smoking than prosmoking advertising is in getting people to start smoking. Most social scientists believe that this is why the tobacco industry agreed to give up its radio and television advertising in return for the reduction of the antismoking commercials in those same media (Syme & Alcalay, 1982).

By the mid 1960s, however, the movement against cigarette smoking was gaining in momentum, and that momentum has continued until today. It is now seen in the regulations regarding no-smoking areas in airplanes, places of employment, and restaurants, for example; in the banning of smoking in many public buildings, grocery stores, and hospitals; and in the expansion of public education programs designed to reduce the prevalence of cigarette smoking. Such public education programs are now spreading around the world, and there is reason to believe that the prevalence of smoking will continue to diminish worldwide until it becomes virtually nonexistent.

In his recent review of the public policy aspects of smoking control efforts, Breslow (1982) has indicated that on a worldwide basis the "fundamental conflict that public policy must resolve is between the long-term health and the short-term economic interests involved in cigarette smoking" (p. 130). Tobacco sales in the United States amounted to $15.7 billion in 1975. In 1983, $1.5 billion was spent by the tobacco industry in promoting cigarette smoking (Warner, 1985). The tobacco industry promotes cigarette smoking not only in developed countries throughout the world but in developing countries where the standard of living is increasing sufficiently so that people can now afford to buy cigarettes. Sales are rapidly increasing in developing countries. For years, in spite of strong objections by many members of the U.S. Congress, the United States has been giving millions of dollars worth of tobacco to developing countries as part of our "Food for Peace" program, with one of its objectives being the opening of new markets for the American tobacco industry.

An example of how the struggle of health versus economics plays itself out can be seen in the case of special supplements on personal health care recently published by major news magazines. On November 7, 1983, *Newsweek* published such a supplement prepared by the American Medical Association. The supplement was designed to provide information on good health from the medical profession itself. Yet, in spite of the overwhelming evidence linking smoking to poor health, no mention was made of the health hazards of smoking in the entire sixteen-page document. That same issue of *Newsweek* contained twelve pages of cigarette advertisements, worth close to $1 million in revenues (Warner, 1985). The intention of the American Medical Association was to include a strong statement about smoking, but *Newsweek* resisted any mention of cigarettes.

One year later, *Time* published a similar supplement, with the assistance of the American Academy of Family Physicians (AAFP)—again containing no references to cigarette smoking. According to the AAFP, *Time* removed discussion of the health hazards of smoking without the knowledge of the Academy. That issue of *Time* contained eight pages of cigarette advertising.

While the legal and philosophical issues regarding freedom of the press are complex, it does seem clear in these instances that the medical profession has indirectly permitted itself to be part of a process that has been contrary to its fundamental aim, the enhancement of health. This dilemma is not limited to the medical profession. The American Psychological Association recently purchased the monthly magazine *Psychology Today*—a magazine that derives considerable revenue from its cigarette advertising. The purchase touched off an acrimonious debate among members of the American Psychological Association as to whether the magazine should continue to accept such advertising. At the present time, in spite of objections to the contrary, the magazine continues to accept cigarette advertising.

American corporations involved in the growing of tobacco or the manufacture of cigarettes are beginning to diversify their interests, as they note the increasingly successful efforts being made to encourage the public not to start smoking or to stop smoking if they have already started. In socialist countries—such as China, Yugoslavia, or the Soviet Union—on the other hand, the tobacco industry is in the hands of the government. Revenue from the sale of tobacco products constitutes a significant proportion of their total income and, until very recently at least, the short-term economic interests of these countries have prevailed.

Breslow has suggested that if cigarettes were being introduced today, they would more than likely be banned, in view of the clear evidence of their cancer-producing potential. But cigarettes were introduced more than a century ago, and the 300,000 deaths every year that occur in the United States as a direct consequence of smoking have occurred for so long that they do not create a sense of urgency. This phenomenon of adaptation, combined with the powerful countervailing economic interests that have already been described, makes it impossible to consider banning cigarettes today.

On the other hand, banning smoking is only one among a large variety of strategies that can be invoked, and there is a general sense that health interests are slowly gaining the upper hand in their struggle with economic interests in the establishing of public policy regarding cigarette smoking.

### Public Policy Strategies

The list of potential antismoking strategies is remarkably long, and many can be used in combination. In addition to the general prohibition of smoking (a strategy that few if any people believe will be effective), other strategies that have been suggested include (1) restricting where people may smoke (and, in some cases, who may smoke); (2) identifying and reducing the haz-

ardous substances in cigarette smoke; (3) restricting advertising of tobacco products; (4) increasing, through consumer health education, knowledge of the
harmful effects of smoking, particularly among such groups as preadolescents
and pregnant women; (5) incorporating information about the dangers of smoking in the public school curriculum; (6) expanding smoking cessation programs
for people who want to quit smoking; (7) increasing taxation on tobacco products; (8) finding other uses for tobacco, such as in animal feed, or in the manufacture of pesticides or medicinal products; and (9) retraining tobacco farmers
for other ways of earning a living.

The issues are far too complex to believe that any single measure will
suffice. Legislative action will be needed on the federal, state, and local levels,
and priority must be given to dealing with the economic aspects of cigarette-
smoking control at the same time as dealing with the health aspects.

## SMOKING CESSATION AND SMOKING PREVENTION

With the evidence linking smoking to subsequent excess risk of a variety of
illnesses, considerable attention has been directed to ways of discouraging people from starting to smoke and to encouraging people who do smoke to stop
(National Cancer Institute, 1986). In the case of quitting smoking, two separate
efforts can be distinguished—attempts to persuade people to quit smoking, and
attempts to persuade people who have quit smoking to stick to their decision.

As of 1981, when Evans and his colleagues (Evans, Hill, Raines, & Henderson, 1981) published their critical review of programs designed to control
smoking, a surprisingly large number of reports included no evaluations of
program effectiveness at all. Relatively few of the published studies included
carefully designed and described treatment programs and planned evaluation
procedures. Most published reports were characterized by weak methodologies,
including inadequate assessment of program participation, poor data collection
procedures, lack of control groups, and incomplete or nonexistent followup
procedures. More recent studies seem to be more carefully conceptualized and
designed, and there is greater recognition of the need for long-term followup
evaluation of program outcomes (see, for example, Evans, 1985).

For example, Midanik and associates (1985) reported on a 5-year followup of participants in an 8-week smoking cessation program that was offered
as part of a prepaid medical plan. They reported that the best predictor of
smoking cessation was attendance during the program. Those participants who
attended fewer sessions were more likely to smoke during the entire followup
period. Virtually all of those participants who attended no more than half of the
sessions reported smoking at every one of the five annual followup interviews,
while only about half of participants who attended all of the sessions reported
smoking at any time during the 5-year followup.

### Smoking Cessation

Five different smoking intervention strategies designed to encourage people to quite smoking have been identified in the literature: (1) aversion, (2) self-control, (3) a combination of aversion and self-control, (4) pharmacological, and (5) health education (Altman et al., 1987; Evans, Hill, Raines, & Henderson, 1981; Flay, 1987; Pechacek & McAlister, 1980).

Aversion programs are based upon the psychological principle that if smoking is followed by aversive (unpleasant) consequences, a desire not to smoke should develop and should ultimately become stronger than the desire to smoke. Four aversion strategies have been reported in the literature—electric shock, rapid smoking, satiation, and cognitive sensitization.

Electric shock as an aversion therapy has been used either in the laboratory or in the natural environment and is administered when people experience an urge to smoke or while they are actually smoking. The rapid-smoking technique requires the smoker to chain smoke as many cigarettes as possible and to puff every 6 seconds. Between rapid smoking sessions, the smoker is to remain abstinent. While there can be some undesirable side effects of rapid smoking, none appears to be clinically significant. The satiation strategy requires the smoker to double or triple his or her usual smoking rates for several days. Cognitive sensitization uses imagination, and creates a situation where smokers imagine themselves preparing to smoke and then throwing up or experiencing some other unpleasant behavior.

None of these four aversion methods has been found to be remarkably effective. Electric shock—administered either in the laboratory or in the natural environment, whenever there is an urge to smoke—has been found to be ineffective. A very large number of evaluation studies of rapid-smoking programs have been reported. Positive results tend to outweigh negative results, but not by a magnitude that would provide unequivocal support for the rapid-smoking procedure. Evaluation studies of satiation programs have often yielded positive results, particularly when combined with other approaches. The research literature on cognitive sensitization programs has yielded mixed results.

Self-control methods are those that place the direction of the program in the hands of the smoker, although the smoker can work with a counselor during the early phases of the program. Three specifically identified aspects of a self-control program are thought to make such programs more effective: (1) environmental planning, (2) behavioral programming, and (3) cognitive control.

In the case of environmental planning, an attempt is made to modify smoking behavior by changing the circumstances in which it occurs, or by working with others who also wish to stop smoking in order to reinforce each other's smoking cessation efforts. In the case of behavioral programming, the smoker institutes a self-directed system of rewards and punishments to facilitate smoking cessation. In the case of cognitive control, the smoker attempts to limit smoking behavior by how he or she thinks about smoking. Most formal stop-smoking programs in existence today tend to include several of these different components, in the hopes that such an approach will increase the success rate. Some programs include hypnosis in addition to cognitive and behavioral components, often with good results (see, for example, Jeffrey, Jeffrey, Greuling, & Gentry, 1985).

Foxx and Brown (1979) have reported on a comparative analysis of four approaches to smoking reduction: (1) nicotine and tar fading, by changing cigarette brands weekly to ones containing progressively less nicotine and tar; (2) a self-monitoring approach involving daily plotting of nicotine and tar intake; (3) a combination of nicotine and tar fading and self-monitoring; and (4) a slightly modified version of the American Cancer Society Stop Smoking Program.

The American Cancer Society Stop Smoking Program involves three phases that all occur within a deliberately created supportive group atmosphere. The first phase includes the presentation of a set of suggestions and ideas from exsmokers, and the completion of a questionnaire designed to provide information about what is particularly satisfying about smoking to the smoker. Given those sources of satisfaction, suggestions for quitting smoking are developed. In the second phase, efforts are made to help the participants abstain from smoking. A 48-hour no-smoking period is scheduled, and participants are given a list of forty suggestions for quitting smoking. The final phase begins after the formal program has ended and involves the organization of an I Quit Club as a form of group support for exsmokers.

A total of forty-four subjects were involved in the Foxx and Brown study and were randomly assigned to the four treatment conditions. Subjects had smoked for an average of 14 years, with none smoking less than 1 year, and all subjects smoked at least one pack of cigarettes per day at the start of the smoking reduction program. All four programs required a total of 5 weeks, with meetings taking place once each week. The treatment programs were designed so that subjects would quit smoking after the fifth session, regardless of which program they were in. Followup interviews were conducted five times over the next 18 months. Self-reported smoking behavior was checked against smoking behavior as assessed by another person in a close relationship with the study participant.

The results of this study were very significant. No one in the self-monitoring group ever quit smoking. At 6 months, 50 percent of the combined nicotine-reduction and self-monitoring group had quit smoking—a figure that dropped to 40 percent at the time of the final 18-month followup assessment. No more than 10 percent of either the American Cancer Society or nicotine reduction groups ever quit smoking. According to the authors, the combined nicotine-reduction and self-monitoring program was most successful because it produced a reasonable abstinence level and an alternative goal for those who continued smoking. In addition, nicotine dependence was reduced and positive feedback was provided, and no aversive procedures were used. The program was simple to implement, it provided a built-in success mechanism in the form of reduced nicotine and tar intake, and it combined the strengths of an individual and a group approach to smoking reduction.

Unfortunately, as Benowitz, Jacob, Kozlowski, and Yu (1986) have reported, reducing the number of cigarettes smoked makes less difference than might be predicted in the intake of nicotine, tar, and carbon monoxide, because of the tendency of people who are trying to reduce the number of cigarettes they smoke each day to oversmoke, that is, to smoke cigarettes to shorter butt lengths. The result of oversmoking is that there is a significant increase in the amount of tar, nicotine, and carbon monoxide inhaled per cigarette.

Pharmacologic approaches to smoking cessation are based upon the premise that the smoker has become addicted to nicotine. Accordingly, this approach provides nicotine to the smoker, mainly in the form of a special chewing gum. There is considerable evidence that chewing nicotine gum is an effective adjunct in smoking cessation programs (Oster, Huse, Delea, & Colditz, 1986). An aspect of this approach that defies logic is that while cigarettes, containing considerable nicotine, of course, are freely available to the public, a physician's prescription is currently needed to purchase nicotine gum.

The health education model for smoking cessation represents an attempt to encourage smokers to stop smoking by using traditional educational approaches, such as by curricula that point out the harmful aspects of smoking. In an unusually well-designed recent evaluation of two different health education methods, Windsor and colleagues (1985) randomly assigned a total of 300 pregnant women from three public health maternity clinics to three different groups—a control group and two experimental groups which received different health education materials.

The first experimental group received a 10-minute health education counseling session, were given a booklet entitled "Because You Love Your Baby" presenting information on the dangers of smoking and the benefits of quitting, and were taught how to use the American Lung Association "Freedom from Smoking Program Manual." This manual presents a 17-day self-directed plan to quit smoking.

The second experimental group received the 10-minute health education counseling session and the same booklet describing the dangers of smoking, but were given a different self-help manual specifically designed for pregnant women, called "A Pregnant Woman's Self-Help Guide to Quit Smoking." This manual describes a 7-day plan for quitting smoking that covers such topics as discovering why you want to stop smoking, learning why you smoke cigarettes, learning smoking signals, making a stop-smoking contract, learning breathing exercises and how to relax, and learning how to deal with physical reactions to quitting.

Using a pretest-posttest design—in which smoking behavior was assessed initially, at midpregnancy, and at the end of pregnancy both by means of self-report and by a saliva thiocyanate (SCN) test—the authors found that both health education programs were superior to no program at all and that the manual designed for pregnant women was superior to the more generic manual. In the control group, 2 percent of the sample quit smoking and 7 percent reduced their SCN levels; in the generic manual group, 6 percent quit smoking and 14 percent reduced their SCN levels; and in the specific pregnancy-related manual group, 14 percent quit smoking and 17 percent reduced their SCN levels. Differences among each pair of groups were statistically significant.

In their general summary of smoking cessation program evaluations, Benfari, Ockene, and McIntyre (1982; see also Evans, Hill, Raines, & Henderson, 1981) have concluded that while almost any intervention can be effective and can have short-term success rates as high as in the 70 to 80 percent range, long-term success rates deteriorate to a level often no better than 30 to 40 percent. In addition, these authors have indicated that programs which include several different approaches to smoking cessation tend to be more successful than one-component approaches.

Clearly then, a major problem is that smoking cessation does not usually last very long, many smokers becoming exsmokers for a relatively short period of time before resuming smoking. More recent approaches to smoking cessation have begun to deal with the more complex question of whether there is some way of thinking about smokers and why they smoke so that smoking cessation strategies can be selected by analyzing salient characteristics of specific smokers, in order to increase the likelihood of success when applying the selected strategy.

In terms of more ambitious recent smoking cessation efforts, the North Karelia Project in Finland (McAlister et al., 1980) is perhaps the most interesting. This study examined the effectiveness of a seven-session televised smoking cessation clinic. Smokers in the Province of North Karelia were encouraged to watch the program in groups. What is especially impressive about this program is its cost-effectiveness.

The program was evaluated by contrasting its effect in North Karelia—where intensive publicity efforts resulted in 9 percent of the adult male population aged 30 to 64 watching four or more of the televised programs—with results in a neighboring province—where, without the publicity, 4.8 percent of the comparable group watched the same proportion of programs. In total, 2.3 percent of the North Karelia smokers reported abstinence at the 6-month followup while 1.3 percent of the control province smokers did. In both provinces combined, 27 percent of those men who watched at least four programs and who attempted to stop smoking were abstinent at the 6-month followup.

An additional followup survey repeated a year after the program indicated that about 1 percent of those smoking at the time of the original program were still abstinent. The original TV series had been repeated about 3 months prior to the 1-year followup, and between the two exposures of the program about 2 percent of smokers nationwide remained abstinent for from 3 months to 1 year. The authors estimated that somewhere between 10,000 and 30,000 people were abstinent. Since the cost of production of the TV program was about

$8000, it was estimated that the cost of this smoking prevention program was less than $1 per subsequently abstinent smoker.

In general, recent studies of smoking cessation programs suggest that their impact is related (1) to the level of motivation to stop smoking, (2) to the developing of better physical and psychological well-being, and (3) to the achieving of milder smoking habits. People who have better problem-solving skills and who make greater use of self-reward in controlling their own behavior appear to be most successful in smoking cessation.

As for programs designed to reduce the risk of relapse among persons who have stopped smoking, maintenance rates appear to have improved from their average a few years ago of 25 to 30 percent to current rates that average closer to 50 percent. Since the presence of group support, nonsmoking spouses, and professional contact reduces the risk of relapse, smoking cessation programs based in the workplace, with the possibility of continuing reinforcement of nonsmoking behavior at work and at home, seem particularly promising.

The development of successful programs to assist adults to stop smoking once they have started is complicated by the fact that about 95 percent of adults who have stopped smoking have done so on their own, that is, without participation in any organized formal program. Undoubtedly, the most cost-effective method of successfully encouraging adults to stop smoking is exhortation on the part of their physicians (Wells et al., 1986). The vast majority of physicians rank the elimination of cigarette smoking as the single most important health-promoting behavior that their patients can inaugurate (Sobal et al., 1985). Indeed, a surprising number of articles on the topic of smoking prevention during the past several years, worldwide, encourage physicians to urge their smoking patients to give up the habit. This method is cost-effective because it takes but a moment or two on the part of the physician. Studies (see, for example, Russell, Wilson, Taylor, & Baker, 1979) have suggested that if all physicians would take a moment to urge their smoking patients to stop smoking, their aggregate efforts would produce more exsmokers than do all of the intensive smoking cessation clinics, and at virtually no cost.

### Smoking Prevention

Smoking prevention programs aimed at youth have a number of compelling justifications. First, the public school system provides a vehicle whereby young people can be reached prior to the time they might start smoking; second, preventing the onset of smoking may be easier than persuading adolescents to stop smoking once they have begun; third, smoking, even of short duration, appears to be harmful to health; and finally, health benefits will occur even if such programs only delay the onset of smoking rather than eliminate it altogether (Evans, Smith, & Raines, 1984).

Successful adolescent smoking prevention programs have a number of aspects in common—all have been based on sound social-psychological theory, and all have taken place in schools, mostly with seventh-grade students. Most smoking prevention programs emphasize short-term negative consequences of smoking such as bad breath or yellow teeth, and employ role models (either live or on film) to depict typical pressures to smoke that come from peers, parents, and the media along with techniques for resisting smoking pressures (see, for example, Schinke, Gilchrist, & Snow, 1985). Such programs have shown a 50-percent or more reduction in smoking onset (U.S. Department of Health and Human Services, 1982).

Warner and Murt (1982) have contrasted current smoking rates with those that would have been expected had antismoking programs never existed, that is, had the increases in smoking behavior during the years before the development of antismoking programs continued. Their conclusions are cautiously optimistic: (1) The response to antismoking programs is more substantial than conventional comparisons would suggest. (2) The positive response to antismoking programs has come from women as well as from men, although smoking reduction occurred earlier among men. And (3), if people born after 1960 smoke at the same rate as today's young people, there will be a further reduction in the proportion of the population who smoke, as tomorrow's lighter-smoking adults gradually replace today's heavy-smoking adults.

## CONCLUDING COMMENTS

Chapters 5 and 6 have been organized in terms of five specific lifestyle risk factors. But it should be made clear that these lifestyles are not independent of one another. Jessor (1982), for example, has noted that "one of the clearest facts to have emerged from the past decade of research . . . is that there is *substantial covariation* among many of these health-related behaviors. That is, they tend to occur together within the same adolescent" (p. 453; also see Jessor, 1984). In a recent examination of risk factors for drug use among adolescents, for example, Newcomb, Maddahian, and Bentler (1986) found that in the case of high school students a single set of risk factors was significantly associated with use and abuse of cigarettes, alcohol, marijuana, and hard drugs.

Lifestyles that increase the risk of illness appear to constitute a *syndrome* rather than separate independent behaviors. Thus, another basis for optimism in the control of lifestyle risk factors is that successful reduction of the intensity or prevalence of one risk factor is likely to be accompanied by parallel reduction of other risk factors as well. Once again, the potential usefulness of the generic view of health and illness can be seen.

A second conclusion that seems to have general validity across the entire lifestyle spectrum is the important role of the primary care physician. As was indicated in Chapter 2, the average American visits a physician between two and three times each year, and each of these visits presents an unparalleled opportunity for a preventive intervention that is remarkably cost-effective. Physicians need to believe what many surely must suspect is true, namely, that they can have an enormously significant impact on the behavior of their patients.

Understanding lifestyles that increase the risk of illness requires an interactionist view of behavior—a view that examines how personality factors interact with situational variables in increasing the likelihood of self-destructive behaviors. We have seen this view in our earlier discussion of adherence to exercise programs and in our presentation of psychological models of smoking behavior.

A final aspect of the general nature of lifestyle modification is concerned with the common problem of relapse, that is, the return to a self-destructive lifestyle after some period of abstinence, a process sometimes called "backsliding" (Brownell, Marlatt, Lichtenstein, & Wilson, 1986; Cohen, 1986c). While there are, of course, important differences between many characteristics of the five lifestyles these last two chapters have been concerned with, there are a number of striking similarities. Among these is the striking frequency of relapse.

Most relapses, regardless of the lifestyle in question, seem to occur after a negative emotional state, such as intense anxiety, anger, or frustration associated with stress. Persons who relapse appear to be less motivated, generally have a less favorable response to the program designed to change their lifestyle, seem to have poorer coping styles, and seem to have less sense of self-efficacy and lower self-esteem.

Physiological factors, in the form of withdrawal symptoms, may also be involved in relapse (Cohen, 1986c; Kraus, Gottlieb, Horwitz, & Anscher, 1985). That is, certain lifestyles can be thought of as a form of addiction, and their modification can result in a variety of well-known and lesser-known withdrawal symptoms such as delirium tremens following withdrawal from alcohol; agitation, sweating, convulsions, and so forth following withdrawal from opiates; depression following withdrawal of stimulants; and a number of nonspecific and non-life-endangering reactions following withdrawal from tobacco.

Social factors, such as the absence of social support, and environmental factors, such as social pressure, can also play a significant role in all forms of relapse. These three sets of factors—individual, physiological, and social—can interact with each other to potentiate the risk of relapse. Traditional approaches to minimizing the relapse rate—by providing booster sessions, by adding new components to the lifestyle modification program, or by lengthening the duration of the intervention—have generally been ineffective.

Brownell and associates (1986) have examined the relapse-related research across three particular conditions—alcoholism, smoking, and obesity—and have identified a number of different strategies that might reduce relapse rate during each of the three stages of the lifestyle change process, namely: (1) the early stage of high motivation and commitment to change, (2) the initial period of behavior change, and (3) the maintenance period following the initial behavioral change.

During the early high commitment and motivation stage, Brownell and associates suggest that it is important to screen program participants in order to identify those with insufficient motivation and to enhance the level of motivation wherever needed. During the second, initial behavior change stage, special attention needs to be directed toward the prevention of relapse by the addition of a series of general coping skills to the specific skills needed for reducing the frequency of the specific lifestyle in question. Finally, during the maintenance stage, it appears to be important to enhance levels of social support, broaden the range of lifestyles that are being modified, and to institute a constant process of monitoring. Brownell and colleagues also suggest that there is some evidence that physical exercise reduces relapse, not only in the case of persons who are trying to reduce their obesity but also in the case of persons who are trying to quit smoking or drinking.

Illness prevention takes on a particularly salient role in the health care system when health care professionals are rewarded for keeping people healthy rather than for treating people who are sick, as is now the case. As was indicated in Chapter 2, there is reason to hope that the medical care system in the United States is moving toward one that rewards health rather than rewarding illness. Accordingly, we can expect that health care professionals will find themselves turning their attention increasingly to prevention of illness and maintenance of health. With that new emphasis, we can expect that they will devote more of their energies to helping reduce the incidence, prevalence, and duration of risk-producing lifestyles.

## SUMMARY

- The role of smoking in morbidity and mortality is firmly established. It is estimated that about 300,000 deaths every year, that is, about 15 percent of all deaths, could be prevented if there were no cigarette smoking.
- The addictive nature of cigarette smoking must not be overlooked. By all standards of definition, smoking may be an addiction.
- Smokeless tobacco (snuff and chewing tobacco) has been found to increase the risk of cancerous and noncancerous oral cavity disease, and is clearly not a safe substitute for cigarette smoking.
- Cigarette smoking has been declining slowly since 1965, particularly among men.
- The causal connection between cigarette smoking and lung cancer is firmly established, a matter of particular importance in view of the fact that lung cancer cannot be successfully treated once it has occurred.
- Consumer health education efforts to reduce or eliminate smoking are showing signs of success, but it has taken years of dedicated research and program implementation to yield these results. Examination of this literature presents an important lesson regarding the virtues of persistence.
- As in the case of other lifestyle factors, smoking can be investigated from a biological, psychological, or sociological point of view. Each approach adds to our understanding of the problem and of ways to reduce it.

- Smoking cessation programs appear to be increasingly successful, as are smoking prevention programs, although their success appears to be limited and best understood in the context of slowly changing societal values that are making smoking increasingly unacceptable as social behavior.

- Efforts to prevent and reduce cigarette smoking have important public policy implications. The federal government continues to subsidize the tobacco industry, a multibillion dollar industry with an advertizing budget alone well in excess of $1 billion providing a livelihood for tens of thousands of workers in the United States.

- Evaluation of smoking cessation and smoking prevention programs presents a number of complex methodological issues that can be examined not only in their own right but also because these issues are of general importance in the evaluation of most preventive intervention programs.

- There is substantial evidence that the five lifestyle factors examined in Chapters 5 and 6 are significantly correlated with each other and that, for example, if programs are successful in reducing smoking, subsequent changes can be expected in the reduction of other illness-producing lifestyles.

- Interest in reducing the prevalence of lifestyles negatively affecting health is increasing on the part of health care providers, as prevention of illness is becoming more pertinent to their ways of thinking about health service delivery.

# Becoming and Being Ill

# 7

**INTRODUCTION**

As indicated in Chapter 1, having a disease and being sick are two very different concepts. Having a disease is a biological phenomenon; there is some significant deviation of the body from its normal state. Being sick is a psychosocial phenomenon, meaning that you act like and are treated like a sick person, or, as Parsons (1958) has written, you have petitioned for and have been granted the sick role (also see Birenbaum, 1981, pp. 48–53). Thus, a person can have a disease and not be sick; conversely, a person can be sick without having a disease. People can have diseases all by themselves, but it takes someone else to assign them the role of being sick. In western society, it is the physician who is given that responsibility.

The sociological concept of the sick role is a very important one, since it emphasizes the idea that being sick has some specific role requirements. According to Parsons (1958), once people enter the sick role, a series of changes take place in terms of what they believe is expected of them and what they can expect of themselves. People who are considered sick are generally not thought of as responsible for their illnesses. People who are given the sick role are exempt from the activities and obligations normally expected of them, such as going to work or to school, or taking care of their children. At the same time, however, there are certain limitations and requirements to the sick role. The role cannot be assigned indefinitely, particularly if the person makes no effort to seek help. Furthermore, the person is expected to feel uncomfortable about being sick and to cooperate in the process of getting well.

The concept of the sick role is limited in its usefulness, however. First, the concept does not match the facts in accounting for many psychiatric disorders, since psychiatric patients are often thought to be responsible for their own illnesses and sometimes do not seem to cooperate in trying to get well. Second, the concept does not describe the sickness behavior of the aged or of persons with physical disabilities or chronic illnesses, since the sick role must sometimes be assigned virtually indefinitely. Finally, it does not account for sociocultural differences in sickness behavior, since cultures vary in terms of how and when people seek help, how they respond to their symptoms, and how they go about trying to get well. Thinking about the sick role appears to be useful primarily in the case of acute illnesses, or in the acute phase of more chronic disorders.

Mechanic (1982, p. 1) notes that "illness usually refers to a limited scientific concept denoting a constellation of symptoms or a condition underlying them" (also see Mechanic 1962, 1966, 1976), while "illness behavior . . . describes the manner in which persons monitor their bodies, define and interpret their symptoms, take remedial actions, and utilize the health-care system" (1982, p. 1). Clearly, from the point of view of the field of health psychology, the concept of greatest interest is that of illness behavior.

Illness behavior can vary in terms of its appropriateness. Thus, according to Pilowsky (1978c) there can be normal illness behavior or abnormal illness behavior. Normal illness behavior is appropriate to the objective pathology detected by the health service provider, while abnormal illness behavior is diagnosed on the basis of evidence of inappropriate or maladaptive ways of "perceiving, evaluating and acting in relation to one's own state of health . . . taking into account the individual's age, educational and sociocultural background" (Pilowsky, 1978c, p. 133). The concept of abnormal illness behavior identified by Pilowsky, it should be noted, essentially assumes that it is always the patient and never the physician who is in error, that is, that if the physician fails to find a disease that matches the patient's symptoms, the fault lies with the patient. There is a sense, then, in which the concept of abnormal illness behavior is a kind of patient-blaming.

In this chapter, we will examine the complex psychosocial processes by which people become ill, seek help, and become patients in the medical care system, and we will examine that system in terms of how it may add to the stresses inherent in being ill, and what can be done to reduce those stresses.

# HEALTH AND ILLNESS BEHAVIORS

The concept of illness behavior includes three different behavioral components (Rosenstock & Kirscht, 1979)—*preventive health behavior,* the activities undertaken by individuals who believe themselves to be healthy, for the purpose of preventing disease; *diagnosis seeking,* those activities undertaken by individuals who feel ill for the purpose of detecting and defining their illness and of discovering a suitable remedy; and *treatment seeking,* the array of activities undertaken by those who consider themselves ill for the purpose of getting well.

### Preventive Health Behavior

Activities on the part of healthy people that are designed to maintain health and prevent illness are referred to as preventive health behavior. While one might think that preventive health behavior is a generalized trait—that is, that the degrees to which people engage in various forms of health maintenance tend to be highly correlated with each other—the research evidence suggests just the opposite. Studies have shown that health maintenance behaviors are surprisingly independent of each other.

Thus, people who seek medical checkups in the absence of symptoms, for example, are not more likely to use seat belts regularly than people who do not seek medical checkups. Similarly, it has been found that there is very little relationship between whether people use seat belts, buy insurance, or keep a fire extinguisher in the home, or whether they are careful about their diets, exercise regularly, or engage in preventive dental care. Preventive health behavior is learned, and specific forms of preventive health behavior seem to have been learned individually in a variety of different settings, often in childhood, and often for reasons that have little to do with concerns about health (Rosenstock & Kirscht, 1979). For example, people may have developed the habit of brushing their teeth as children without being consciously aware of the connection between toothbrushing and dental health. Similarly, many eating habits may have developed in childhood independently of any concern with nutritional health.

In their recent review of demographic variations in preventive health behavior, Rosenstock and Kirscht (1979) have noted that preventive health behavior seems more common among younger than older people, among women than men, and among people who are better-educated and have higher incomes than among people who are less well educated and have lower incomes. Even when preventive services, such as immunizations, are free of charge, middle-class people still tend to take advantage of the opportunity significantly more often than do the less affluent.

Since it has usually been found that hospital utilization is higher among poorer people, it has been thought that if ways could be found to make preventive health care more accessible and affordable to the poor, their rates of hospitalization might be reduced. But the poor may have little alternative other than to wait until illnesses are significantly disabling before seeking medical care. Preventive health care may simply be a luxury they cannot afford.

### Diagnosis-seeking Behavior

The same set of demographic factors associated with preventive health behavior are associated with diagnosis-seeking behavior, that is, activities of persons who feel ill and who want to find out what is wrong and what to do about it. Diagnosis-seeking behavior is more common in higher socioeconomic groups, more common in women than in men (even when medical care associated with pregnancy is excluded), and more common among whites than among nonwhites.

There is enormous variation in the ways which people deal with feeling ill. Some of that variation is accounted for by the nature of the illness, of course. Even though some people may characteristically ignore or deny illness, it is far harder to do nothing in the face of a compound fracture of the leg than it is to do nothing in the face of vague intestinal symptoms. In general, however, people vary in terms of how they experience symptoms and how ready they are to find out what is wrong and decide what to do about it.

Seeking medical care is far less common than administering self-care or obtaining lay care within the family; it is more common where there is a greater perceived sense of urgency and where care is accessible and affordable (Aday & Andersen, 1974). The matter of affordability is clearly part of why more affluent people have higher readiness to find out what is wrong with them. Yet, even when all these conditions are met, there are still great variations in the readiness to seek care. In contrast to preventive health behavior, which does not appear to be consistent across many different situations, readiness to seek help in the face of symptoms is a far more stable and general trait. It has been found, for example, that readiness to seek help for symptoms of what might be cancer is highly associated with readiness to seek help for other symptoms as well (Tracey, Sherry, & Keitel, 1986).

In the case of cancer symptoms, and probably other symptoms as well, there is an interesting interaction of knowledge and anxiety. Knowledge about the symptoms of cancer combined with a high level of anxiety results in long delays in seeking help, while knowledge combined with a low level of anxiety leads to seeking medical care far more promptly (Antonovsky & Hartman, 1974).

### Treatment-seeking Behavior

Actions that people take to aid recovering from illnesses are referred to as treatment-seeking behavior. Medical care can be both underutilized and overutilized, and both cases represent deviations from appropriate treatment-seeking behavior. Underutilization takes place when patients do not follow up on medical referrals or do not adhere to medical care programs (see Chapter 12). Overutilization takes place when, from the point of view of the health service provider, a person seeks more care than is justified (see Chapter 13). Determining what is appropriate depends, however, on one's point of view. Since people often seek medical care when they are worried about their health status, the worry needs to be dealt with as much as does the illness that precipitates it. Thus, from the point of view of the health care provider, a person may overutilize health care, while from the point of view of the patient, there is no overutilization. People who ostensibly overutilize health care services are worried, and until the worry is effectively dealt with the demand for services may appropriately continue.

Seeking medical care has been found to be more common among people who have a greater sense of personal efficacy and internal control. Indeed, a low sense of internal control has been reported to be associated with less self-initiated preventive care and less optimism concerning the efficacy of early treatment (Seeman & Seeman, 1983). Specific situational factors found to play a role in determining the readiness to seek medical care include financial and other pertinent resources available to the person, geographic availability of health care, and degree of perceived stress.

Richardson (1970), who examined factors associated with seeking medical services among the urban poor, found that when perceived severity of the condition was thought to be high, it was the single most significant factor in determining whether help was sought. As symptoms diminished in perceived severity, cost and accessibility became more important in determining whether they would seek medical care.

### Explaining Health-related Behavior

McKinlay (1972) has identified six different approaches that have been used in an effort to understand health-related behavior: (1) economic, (2) sociodemographic, (3) geographic, (4) sociopsychological, (5) sociocultural, and (6) organizational. People who study economic aspects of illness behavior are interested in such problems as identifying financial barriers to seeking health services. Research has indicated, interestingly, that these financial barriers are not all that prevent people from seeking medical care. Even when such barriers are reduced or even eliminated, there are still wide variations by social class or by ethnic group in the utilization of health services (Rosenstock & Kirscht, 1979).

People who study sociodemographic aspects of illness behavior examine variations in the use of medical care among different demographic groups. Such studies have shown, for example, that women make more use of medical care than men, that whites make more use of medical care than nonwhites, and that use of health services increases with age, with income, and with education. In the case of gender differences in the use of medical care, Marcus and Siegel (1982) have found support for the hypothesis that one reason women make more use of health services than men may be because a smaller proportion of them are in the labor force; it may be easier for women who are not working outside the home to reschedule their activities in order to visit a physician. As an increasing proportion of women join the labor force, we should find a decreasing gender difference in the use of medical services. The sociodemographic approach to the study of variations in medical care use is not sufficient by itself, however, since it provides no way of understanding why variations in health behavior occur within any particular sociodemographic group.

There is an important sense in which use of health care is related to geographic factors, most notably, proximity to available services. People who take the geographic approach to the study of health care use examine how that utilization differs in different parts of the world, as a function of such geographic factors as urban versus rural setting and, as has been indicated, of proximity (see, for example, Aday & Anderson, 1974; Eyles & Woods, 1983; McGlashan & Blunden, 1983). Within urban areas, there appears to be very little relationship between proximity and health care utilization. In rural areas, however, proximity of services seems to play a far more important role in determining who makes use of those services.

The sociopsychological approach to the study of health care utilization examines the ways in which use of health services is related to motivation, perception, learning, beliefs, and other sociopsychological factors (see, for example, Becker, 1974). The sociocultural approach focuses on such factors as values, norms, beliefs, and lifestyles in understanding differential use of services. One of the most important independent variables from the sociocultural perspective is social class (see, for example, Zola, 1964).

Last, but by no means least, people interested in organizational factors that are associated with health care utilization study how such utilization is related to characteristics of the health service delivery system, such as its hours of operation, its convenience to the patient, the quality of the encounters between service providers and clients, and continuity of care (see Becker, Drachman, & Kirscht, 1974; Levine, Scotch, & Vlasak, 1969).

## SEEKING HEALTH CARE SERVICES

While psychological or medical symptoms may be a necessary cause for the use of health care services, they are clearly not a sufficient cause. Only about one-fourth to one-third of persons who experience what they identify as an episode of physical or psychological illness—including evidence of disability, need for medication, or limitation of activity—consult a physician for help (Locke & Slaby, 1982). Thus, there has been considerable attention devoted to attempting to understand how people make the decision to seek medical care in our complex medical care system.

### The Medical Care System

No medical care system in the world is more complex than that of the United States. We have already commented on the extraordinary number of people (nearly 8 million) employed in the health care industry (see Chapter 2), but the cast of characters includes, in addition to physicians and nurses, such allied health professionals as audiologists, chiropractics, chiropodists, dietitians, licensed practical nurses, medical technologists, occupational therapists, opticians, paramedics, pharmacists, physical therapists, physician assistants, podiatrists, recreational therapists, respiratory therapists, and speech pathologists.

Physicians, in turn, can become specialists in specific diseases or in the treatment of specific portions of the body, and the medical lexicon now includes such terms as anesthesiology, dermatology, gynecology, immunology, internal medicine, neurology, obstetrics, oncology, opthalmology, otolaryngology, pathology, pediatrics, proctology, psychiatry, radiology, surgery, and urology.

Furthermore, these health professionals work in a far greater variety of settings than we realize. These settings include not only the solo practices of self-employed physicians but also physicians in partnerships or those who share overhead expenses in a form of group practice. Physicians' settings also include a variety of inpatient facilities, hospital outpatient departments, free-standing emergency centers, ambulatory surgical centers, medical schools, well-baby clinics, school and college health programs, industrial health programs, public health screening units, neighborhood health centers, disease prevention facilities, hospices, rehabilitation facilities, and nursing homes.

Inpatient medical facilities are particularly complex, both in terms of their variety and their inner workings. Hospitals were originally established to care for the poor. People who could afford a higher level of medical care were cared for at home. It is because of the historical connection of hospitals with poverty that so many hospitals were originally established and staffed by members of charitable religious orders. Until a century ago, hospitals had a deservedly bad reputation. Hospitals were places where impoverished sick people went to die.

With the development of modern medical technology that began a century ago, particularly in the areas of anesthesia, antisepsis, and the currently bewildering array of diagnostic procedures, and with the improvement of the quality and the success of hospital care, the image of the hospital has undergone an equally well-deserved transformation, although not always without struggle (Weiss, 1985; Young, 1984). In most communities, the general hospital is the locus of the highest available quality of medical care.

The most common type of hospital is the community (or general) hospital. Most people in the United States who are hospitalized use such a facility. Traditionally, community hospitals have been run as nonprofit corporations, with an elected community board of directors and a number of different sources of both public and private support to supplement the income derived from patient charges. Today, traditional community hospitals are being transformed from nonprofit corporations into investor-owned corporations that intend to be profit making—or, to use the technical vocabulary, from eleemosynary to proprietary organizations. Weiss (1985) estimates that by 1990 over 90 percent of community hospitals will have some association with one of the growing number of investor-owned hospital chains.

Hospitals have two parallel functions—healing and housing—and each function has its own administrative hierarchy. In community hospitals, the healing function is in the hands of an elected or appointed medical director (often called chief-of-staff) and a number of private-practice (usually fee-for-service) physicians appointed to the medical staff who spend part of their time caring for their hospitalized patients. In traditional community hospitals, physicians derive income only from patient billing. With the advent of health maintenance organizations, a growing number of physicians are salaried. Complementing the work of the physician is the registered nurse and members of the large group of specialized ancillary medical professions that have already been identified. In the vast majority of cases, hospital-based nurses and ancillary health care providers are salaried. Hospitals that engage in teaching functions also have a variety of students—student nurses, dietitians, medical interns and residents, among others.

On the housing side of the hospital can be found the hospital administrator—increasingly a person with advanced training in the specialty field of hospital administration rather than a physician—business and clerical personnel, and the housekeeping and kitchen staff. Housing and healing functions are interdependent, and in a well-run hospital conflicts between housing and healing personnel are infrequent and quickly resolved. The patient is rarely aware of the organizational character of the general hospital, except perhaps when there is some disequilibrium in the system, but it is safe to say that there is probably no organization more complex and stress-laden than the busy community hospital.

### Sociocultural Factors in Seeking Medical Care

Readiness to seek medical care has been found to be associated with cultural background as well as with specific situational factors. Cultural factors help determine how symptoms are interpreted and how the norms for behavior in the face of perceived symptoms are developed.

According to Mechanic (1978, 1982), becoming ill is a complex form of adaptation, in which people need to create a better fit between themselves and the surrounding social environment. On the one hand, sociocultural factors help determine whether a given set of symptoms qualify as an illness from the point of view of the physician; on the other hand, sociocultural factors help determine the circumstances under which potential patients become willing to consider themselves ill, that is, as deviating in some significant degree from normal. A complex and subtle negotiation process often takes place between the medical caregiver and the potential patient.

While only physicians can confer the sick role, people themselves have an important role in the decision to become ill. Mechanic (1962, 1966, 1976; also see Rosenstock & Kirscht, 1979) has identified eight variables important in the process of deciding to become ill: (1) characteristics of the symptoms, (2) ability to recognize the symptoms, (3) judged severity of the symptoms, (4) extent of disability associated with the symptoms, (5) degree of expected stoicism in the cultural background of the person, (6) amount of medical information available to the person, (7) availability and accessibility of help, and (8) acceptability of help seeking in the cultural and social milieu.

Assessing the strength of these eight variables is crucial for increasing the likelihood that people in need of health services will seek them out. If health planners believe that a group of people will not make use of health services because they value stoicism, or because available help is not acceptable, it will be difficult for public policy makers to improve the accessibility of those services or provide effective consumer health education to that group unless they are responsive to those particular values.

It has long been known that there are dramatic sociocultural differences in attitudes toward illness, with persons in upper social classes more likely than persons in lower social classes to perceive themselves as ill and to seek help under apparently identical circumstances (see Koos, 1954, for example). In addition, there are marked cultural differences in attitudes toward illness and toward medical care. We have already noted briefly in Chapter 2 that attitudes toward traditional or folk medicine vary dramatically in different parts of the world. A belief in folk medicine includes a belief in the efficacy of the folk practitioner—the *curandero* or the *shaman*—who is especially trained to treat the patient in that special cultural context.

Other aspects of the role culture plays in becoming ill can be found in cultural differences in attitudes toward pain, toward the readiness to acknowledge symptoms, toward interpreting symptoms as a sign of illness, and toward seeking help (Zborowski, 1969; Zola, 1966, 1972). Not only are there ethnic differences in symptom expression, but these differences in turn result in different treatment decisions by physicians.

Because the evidence is clear that different people in the same sociocultural group respond differently to the same physical condition, another line of reasoning has sought to identify social factors that might influence illness responses. Petitioning for the sick role is a social act, and awarding that role to a petitioner is a social response. Since the physician acts for society in awarding the sick role, societal values place restrictions as well as liberties on the set of circumstances that will allow the sick role to be assigned.

In societies where being ill is stigmatizing, people may hide their symptoms for as long as possible, or they may deny their diseases because of a reluctance to be known as ill. Similarly, different diseases may have different social meanings or different degrees of social desirability. In these circumstances it may be more acceptable to be assigned the sick role because of one disease than another and, thus, it may be easier to petition for the sick role because of one set of symptoms than another.

Another factor that is operative in determining illness behavior is social conformity. Each social group defines acceptable and unacceptable illness behavior, and people embedded in a given social group quickly learn that certain kinds of behavior—such as crying—may be unacceptable or that it is all right to stay home from work with symptoms of influenza.

### Perceptual and Attitudinal Factors in Seeking Medical Care

Since being ill is imperfectly correlated with having a disease, and it depends on one's perception of and attitudes toward one's symptoms, the sick role is not assigned in perfect relationship to the presence of disease. The sick role is more likely to be assigned to persons who are more acutely attuned to the sensations that emanate from their bodies, and less likely to be assigned to persons who seem, for whatever reasons, oblivious to internal sensations. The sick role can be assigned to one person because that person petitions for it, and can fail to be assigned to another person, with the same symptoms, because those symptoms are more easily tolerated or denied. Similarly, the sick role can be assigned to a person who would rather stay home than go to work and who calls in requesting sick leave.

SYMPTOM PERCEPTION.    Symptom reporting appears to be a stable personality trait, with some people consistently more likely to report symptoms than other people. People who generally attend to their internal bodily state tend to be high symptom reporters, to take larger amounts of medication, and to make more frequent visits to physicians than do people who do not attend to their internal bodily state. High symptom reporters are generally more anxious and have lower self-esteem and internal locus of control than low symptom reporters (Pennebaker, 1982). Again, it is important to note that these relationships do not spell out a causative sequence. It is entirely possible that reporting symptoms causes people to feel anxious, to have reduced self-esteem, and to feel less in control of their immediate environment.

In a sample of 400 undergraduates enrolled in psychology courses (Pennebaker, 1982), high symptom reporters were found to exercise and to sleep less, and to use more caffeine than low symptoms reporters. High symptom reporters also were found to eat less and have more irregular eating habits than low symptom reporters. Background data contrasting people who differed in symptom reporting indicated that high symptom reporters came from disrupted homes significantly more often than low symptom reporters, and significantly more often reported traumatic sexual experiences prior to the age of 17. In addition, there were a number of differences in self-image between high and low symptom reporters, with high symptom reporters being significantly more concerned about their physical appearance and attractiveness.

Some of the findings in this study have been replicated in other studies as well, and Pennebaker (1982) has identified the four major background factors that appear to be present in the case of high symptom reporters: (1) family conflict that can serve to undermine the child's self-confidence and force the child to become more self-attentive; (2) social insecurity including extreme approval-seeking from others; (3) reinforcement for symptom reporting, in the form of anxiety and conflict reduction, and secondary gain; and (4) greater attentiveness to bodily functioning.

Costa and McCrae (1985) have recently reviewed the literature regarding symptom reporting among the elderly. Medical complaints among the elderly are often thought to be unfounded. Hypochondriasis—the conviction that one is ill and the persistent preoccupation with physical health, out of proportion to any existing justification—is often thought to increase with age. The danger in this point of view is that health care providers will tend to dismiss the complaints of their elderly patients as being unrelated to objective disease.

Costa and McCrae (1985) have concluded that the stereotype that older people are hypochondriacs is unfounded. It is true that older people have more physical complaints and make more use of medical care services than younger people, but older people are, in fact, less healthy. In addition, the research evidence suggests that frequency of medical complaints is, in fact, a stable personality trait over time (also see Leventhal, Nerenz, & Steele, 1984).

Deciding to seek health care services (whether preventive or clinical) is thus a decision-making process that has complex rational elements. A number of investigators have applied general decision-making theory to the examination of how people decide to ask for medical help. Theories of rational decision making suggest that help seeking comes about following a process of weighing the pros and cons of seeking and of not seeking help. The most common term applied to this decision-making model is *subjective expected utility* (SEU). Janis (1984b) describes this model as follows:

> The SEU model assumes that a decision maker arrives at an overall utility estimate for each alternative by multiplying his or her subjective estimate of the utility values for each outcome by his or her subjective estimate of the probability that it will occur. The decision maker then selects the outcome with the highest positive value. (p. 328)

In order to examine the validity of such a model, it would be necessary to identify as complete a list as possible of factors that might be pertinent in a pending decision. Then subjects would be asked to assign estimated probabilities of occurrence and estimated levels of desirability (both in terms of direction and magnitude) to each one of these factors. Sociocultural factors would, of course, play an important role in determining desirability. Multiplying desirabilities by probabilities across all of the factors and summing these products would provide the total SEU. The theory of rational decision making would predict that the decision with the greatest SEU would be the one with the greatest probability of being made.

A simple example of such a decision-making process is in the case of buying health insurance. Most people would tend to argue that while the probability of developing an illness might be substantially lower than the probability of remaining healthy, the negative financial consequences of something going wrong (in terms of the cost of medical care) would be far greater than the positive financial consequences of something not going wrong. Accordingly, most people who can afford it do buy health insurance when they have the chance; interestingly, they may count themselves fortunate even if they become ill (because their insurance will pay a large proportion of the cost), as well as if they do not become ill (because they are healthy).

The inadequacy with the SEU model of decision making is that it assumes that a completely competent and completely rational process takes place. In anxiety-provoking situations, such as in the case of suspected illness, people cannot be expected to proceed in an entirely rational manner. Accordingly, Janis has expanded the theory of decision making to include situations where there is anxiety and conflict.

## ILLNESS AND THE MEDICAL CARE SYSTEM AS SOURCES OF STRESS

Being ill can involve threats not only to life and physical well-being but also to one's self-concept, belief systems, social and occupational functioning, and emotional well-being. Among these threats, Cohen and Lazarus (1979) specifically note (1) threats to life and the fear of dying; (2) threats to bodily integrity and comfort that are caused by the illness, the diagnostic procedures, or the treatment; (3) threats to one's future plans, caused by the uncertainty regarding the course of the illness and the resulting loss of autonomy; (4) threats due to the sharp increase in anxiety, anger, and other negative emotions; (5) threats associated with the interruption of normal social roles and activities; and (6) threats resulting from the need to adjust to a new physical and social environment, in the case of hospitalization.

### Becoming a Patient

In addition to the reality-based stresses associated with the illness, the medical care system itself induces stresses both in outpatient as well as in inpatient settings. Many medical patients are dissatisfied with one or another aspect of their medical care, and most have no great enthusiasm for repeating the experience (Weiss, 1985).

OUTPATIENT EXPERIENCES.  There are numerous reports of insensitivity on the part of health service providers to outpatients. Baruch (1981) among others, who calls these reports "atrocity stories," has collected and analyzed samples of such stories as a way of examining the interactions between patients and physicians. What is important about these interactions is that they represent largely unnecessary sources of stress which serve to complicate the normal stress associated with the illness.

One very useful approach to the examination of sources of stress associated with obtaining medical care is to evaluate factors that appear to result in varying levels of patient satisfaction. Such studies generally examine how four factors—patient characteristics, organizational characteristics, physician characteristics, and physician-patient interactional characteristics—are related to patient satisfaction.

Greenley and Schoenherr (1981), for example, examined the relationships of patient and organizational characteristics to patient satisfaction across a variety of human service organizations, including medical facilities, and found first that patient characteristics were more powerfully related to measures of expressed satisfaction than were organizational characteristics. Of the patient characteristics, the one that was most closely related to level of satisfaction was anticipated level of satisfaction. In other words, to a certain extent low patient satisfaction was a self-fulfilling prophecy, although as we will soon see, there is evidence that with continuing contact with a health care facility, level of satisfaction can change on the basis of experience. The one organizational characteristic associated directly with patient satisfaction was what was called perceived role discretion. Patient satisfaction was higher in those agencies where patients believed that staff members had enough discretion to be able to make autonomous work-related decisions, particularly decisions that led to their receiving services more promptly. The implication of this finding is clear—reduce waiting time to a minimum if you want a satisfied patient.

Ross and her colleagues (Ross & Duff, 1982; Ross, Mirowsky, & Duff, 1982; Ross, Wheaton, & Duff, 1981) have examined a number of factors that are thought to play a role in determining patient satisfaction in a study of sixty-one pediatricians in the New Haven, Connecticut, area. In their ambitious 2-year study, Ross and associates interviewed all of the pediatricians, observed their practice, and later interviewed a sample of families. The pediatricians practiced in two different settings—some were in solo or small-group fee-for-service practice, while others were part of large prepaid multispeciality groups. In addition to interviewing the physicians, these investigators observed more than 1200 physician visits and interviewed 376 mothers of children who had been seen in these physician visits. It was the mothers who provided the judgments of patient satisfaction.

Ross and her associates were interested in identifying factors that seemed to be predictive of whether mothers revisited the same doctors when their children required additional medical care. The investigators examined the extent to which demographic characteristics of the child and the mother, type of medical practice, and two aspects of the doctor-patient relationship (quality of technical care and quality of psychosocial caring) were associated with the number of return visits (a number that ranged from 0 to 45) that served as the principal dependent variable. Four independent measures were significantly related to the number of return visits—poor health of the child, young age of the child, a high level of psychosocial caring on the part of the physician, and being a patient of a physician who practices in a large prepaid group practice. Return visits to the physician were more common, quite understandably, when children were sicker and younger (presumably because a variety of preventive services such as immunizations were made available at younger ages), but return visits were also common when accessibility was easier and physicians were more caring. The implications for enhancing patient satisfaction are quite clear from these findings. Make it easy for patients to have access to the health care provider and provide care that is not only competent but also compassionate and supportive.

Ross and associates also hypothesized that personal characteristics of the physician would play a significant role in determining patient satisfaction in cases of large prepaid group practices where physicians are assigned to patients but would not in small fee-for-service practices where clients select their own pediatrician. Specifically in the case of the prepaid group practice, the investigators hypothesized that patient satisfaction would decrease—somewhat irrationally—as the physician was increasingly atypical, from a demographic point of view, that is, not a relatively young man from a Protestant or Jewish background, as were most of the physicians on the staff. This general hypothesis was supported. In the small fee-for-service practices, where patients freely chose their own physicians, demographic characteristics of physicians were unrelated to patient satisfaction. In the prepaid group practice, however, where physicians were assigned rather than selected, patients were less satisfied with older physicians, women physicians, and physicians from Catholic backgrounds. One important implication of these findings, from the point of view of large multi-speciality group practices, is that it may take time to develop a high level of patient satisfaction when demographically atypical physicians are employed and assigned to patients.

Finally, Ross and colleagues were interested in the relationship between patient satisfaction and the nature of the medical practice organization—that is, whether the practice was solo fee-for-service, a two-physician fee-for-service partnership, a small group of three to five fee-for-service physicians, or a large prepaid group. The findings in this analysis dovetail in important ways with the findings in the previous analyses. In this study, the most striking finding had to do with changes in patient satisfaction over time. Both expectation and experience played significant roles in patient satisfaction. Mothers whose children were treated by solo fee-for-service physicians began their relationship with very high levels of satisfaction, presumably in part because they chose the physicians themselves; these levels of satisfaction, however, deteriorated over time. Conversely, mothers whose children were treated by physicians in large prepaid group practices started out having low levels of satisfaction. But the longer the patients attended these large prepaid groups, the more satisfied they became. Thus, level of patient satisfaction appears to be very responsive to the experiences that patients have with health care providers. Health care facilities that attend to the quality as well as to the competence of their medical care can realistically expect an increasing level of patient satisfaction with increasing exposure to the treatment services.

INPATIENT EXPERIENCES.    Hospitalization is virtually always a stressful life event, and in most cases more stressful than obtaining outpatient care. Not only does hospitalization occur in association with illness and with procedures and risks that are sometimes dangerous and unpleasant, but the role of patient is fundamentally different from most other life roles. Lorber (1975) has suggested that most hospital patients quickly learn that they should be quiet, submissive, obedient, and anonymous, and Weiss (1985) has suggested that these role requirements are part of the reason why some pregnant women choose to have home births rather than give birth in the hospital, and why some people who are terminally ill choose to spend their last days at home rather than in the hospital.

Taylor (1979) has distinguished the "good" hospital patient from the "bad" hospital patient and defines the bad patient as one who acts like a consumer (also see Barr, 1983; Haug & Lavin, 1981). These patients want to know what is being done to them and why, and are unwilling to give up their accustomed life roles any more than is absolutely necessary. From the point of view of hospital personnel, "good" patients are ones who add no stress to an already highly charged social system. These patients deal internally with the stresses associated with their hospitalization. From the point of view of most hospital patients, on the other hand, "good" staff members are those who help them cope with the stress of hospitalization.

The hospital environment increases a sense of helplessness on the part of the patient, and thus presents particularly complex demands in the case of those patients who are accustomed to being in charge of their own lives (Taylor, 1982). The concept of locus of control, introduced by Rotter (1966), describes an important general personality characteristic, namely, the extent to which people believe that they are in control of their lives. At one end of this continuum are people with a strongly internal locus of control. These people believe that their fate is in their own hands. At the other end of this continuum are people with a strongly external locus of control. These people believe that most of what happens to them is the result of luck, powerful others, or providence. Since adapting to the role of hospital patient generally requires people to put themselves and their fates in the hands of others, the role appears to be particularly difficult for persons who have a strong internal locus of control.

In addition, the role of hospital patient often results in a sense of dehumanization and deindividualization. The patient—accustomed to being thought of as "John Jones, the plumber" or "Tom Smith, the computer programmer" or "Professor Bourne"—is suddenly "the gallbladder in Room 304." Strangers continually walk in and out of patients' rooms, undermining any possibility of maintaining a modicum of privacy. Conversations are held in front of and about patients as if they were not there. Patients' questions are frequently viewed as intrusions into the normal functioning of the hospital ward. It does not take very long before a hospital patient becomes socialized into what might be a very new role—the passive, obedient nonperson (Birenbaum, 1981).

### Reducing the Stresses of Medical Care

Interest in the development and evaluation of intervention programs designed to reduce the stresses associated with illness and with medical care now tends to be interdisciplinary, and many innovative supplementary treatment programs have been developed and evaluated by psychologists and by nurses. Janis (1958; also see Wilson-Barnett, 1984a) was perhaps the first person to examine the stresses associated with surgical procedures from a psychological point of view. Janis assessed the level of anxiety in a sample of patients based upon interviews conducted the evening before surgery; surgical outcome was found to be best among the group that was moderately worried, with a generally poorer outcome among patients who were either excessively worried or who appeared not to be worried at all. On the basis of these findings, Janis developed a number of information-based intervention procedures that helped surgical patients do an appropriate amount of worrying.

Janis' fundamental hypothesis linking the presentation of information with surgical outcome has not been consistently supported, and the relationships that have been found are somewhat more complex than his hypothesis would suggest (Johnson, 1984). Yet, despite these findings, Janis' work has proved to be seminal in the study of psychological factors in coping with surgery.

Intervention programs targeted to medical patients that are designed to reduce the stresses associated with medical care now tend to group themselves into different categories (Kendall & Watson, 1981): (1) interventions designed to provide psychological support, (2) interventions that seek to reduce stress by providing information, (3) interventions that enhance coping skills by providing opportunities for modeling successful coping behavior or by other forms of cognitive behavior change, and (4) interventions that seek to reduce anxiety directly by increasing the level of relaxation.

Research studies that have examined stress-reduction techniques in the case of patients undergoing medical care have nearly all been conducted with hospitalized patients (see, for example, Wilson-Barnett, 1984b).

HOSPITALIZED CHILDREN. Hospitalization of children is being increasingly acknowledged by health care practitioners as potentially very stressful. The term "psychologic upset" has been used to refer to the immediate and long-term problems associated with this stress.

DiMatteo and Friedman have noted that hospitalization "is a threat to most young children, primarily because they feel betrayed and deserted by their parents. These children are usually too young to understand assurances that their parents will return for them and they will soon be able to go home" (1982, p. 303). In addition to the growing tendency to avoid hospitalization of children whenever possible, DiMatteo and Friedman have noted that parents are commonly encouraged to remain in the hospital with their young child, that hospitalized children are encouraged to keep in touch with their homes by telephone, and that hospital personnel are urged to help children maintain all possible independence and autonomy, that is, all possible internal locus of control.

Among experimental preventive intervention programs that have been reported in the literature, the results of evaluations of programs designed to reduce the stresses to children that are associated with illness and medical care are unusually sound and compelling. The amount of research regarding specific medical procedures is associated with the frequency of those procedures. Thus, a number of studies exist in which efforts have been undertaken to reduce the stresses associated with elective surgery for tonsillectomies, hernias, or urinary-genital tract surgery.

In one such study, Melamed and Siegel (1975; also see Agras, 1984) randomly assigned sixty children between the ages of 4 and 12 about to undergo surgery for one of these three disorders into two groups. Both groups received the usual explanations and demonstrations of many of the hospital procedures they were about to undergo. In addition, however, while the control group children watched an interesting film that was unrelated to the hospital experience, children in the experimental group watched a special film showing a child successfully coping with the hospitalization. The film, entitled *Ethan Has an Operation,* is 16 minutes in length and depicts a 7-year-old boy who has been hospitalized for a hernia operation. The film includes scenes showing most of the events that children encounter when hospitalized for elective surgery—admission, orientation to the hospital ward, introduction to the medical personnel, administration of a blood test, separation from the mother, and scenes of what occurs in the operating and recovery room. Much of the film is narrated by a child who describes his feelings and concerns at each stage of the hospital experience. The authors hoped that children in the experimental group would model themselves after the child in the film.

A variety of measures of anxiety as well as certain physiological measures were obtained at four points—prefilm, postfilm, preoperative, and 3 to 4 weeks postoperative at the time of the surgeon's followup examination. On all measures, children in the experimental group demonstrated significantly fewer difficulties. In the author's words, "the efficacy of preoperative preparation using a film of a child undergoing hospitalization for surgery was demonstrated on all measures of transitory, situational anxiety. The experimental subjects . . . showed lower sweat gland activity, fewer self-reported medical concerns, and fewer anxiety-related behaviors than the control subjects at both the preoperative and postoperative assessments" (p. 518). In addition, fewer children in the experimental group required pain medication after the surgery, fewer were nauseated or vomited, and more ate solid food earlier.

Measures of the children's adjustment were paralleled by reports from the parents. When parent reports were contrasted, parents of the children in the control group reported that their children had significantly more behavior problems during the posthospitalization period, a greater number and intensity of fears related to their hospitalization, and more anxiety at the time of the surgery and the followup visit than did the parents of the children in the experimental group. It is particularly noteworthy that the intervention—watching a 16-minute film—is remarkably inexpensive and, thus—given its positive impact—is very cost-effective.

In a subsequent study involving a different sample of children, Melamed, Meyer, Gee, and Soule (1976) were able to show that their original results could be successfully replicated, and that the film alone was about as effective as the film accompanied by extensive preoperative preparation, even if the film was shown a week before surgery. Finally, Melamed and her colleagues found that the film was particularly effective if the young narrator in the film resembled the patient in age, gender, and race.

In a similar study, Wolfer and Visintainer (1975) examined the effects of psychologic preparation and supportive care by nurses on mothers' and children's reactions to pediatric hospitalization. Their sample comprised eighty children aged 3 to 14. The children were scheduled for various types of elective minor surgery, and none of them had experienced a previous hospitalization during the past year, suffered from any chronic disease, or had other medical or psychological conditions. Five categories of real or imagined dangers were identified: (1) the fear of discomfort, pain, or death; (2) anxiety associated with separation from parents and friends; (3) fear of the unknown; (4) uncertainty about limits and expectations; and (5) relative loss of control, autonomy, and competence.

Relevant information about procedures was provided in developmentally appropriate form to the children and parents during stressful points. Information, instruction, and support designed to minimize stress and facilitate coping on the part of the child were provided by one nurse who was present at all critical times during the hospitalization. Regular nursing care was provided to the control group.

Both behavioral and physiological dependent measures were used, including ratings of the children's emotional state, cooperativeness, ease with which fluids were taken postoperatively, and of recovery room upset as reflected in medication decisions. Pulse rates and time to first postoperative voiding were also measured. Adjustment after discharge was measured by means of a posthospital behavior questionnaire. Using this instrument, the parent compared the child's pre- and posthospital behavior in terms of six factors: general anxiety and regression, separation anxiety, anxiety about sleep, eating disturbance, aggression toward authority, and apathy-withdrawal. The parent's experience was assessed in five ways: manifest upset; coping and cooperation, both rated upon admission; anxiety; satisfaction with care; and adequacy of information received. These ratings were assessed by means of a questionnaire administered prior to discharge.

The authors found that the experimental group suffered from less upset and fewer cooperation difficulties during hospitalization than did the control group. They also reported fewer posthospital problems. Experimental group children demonstrated greater ease of fluid intake, less time to first voiding, lower heart rates, lower incidence of resistance to anesthesia induction, and better postdischarge adjustment scores. Moreover, experimental group parents emerged as less anxious and more satisfied. Wolfer and Visintainer suggested that "these results seemed to provide strong support for the beneficial effect of systematic preparation and support for hospitalized children and patients" (1975, p. 254; also see Johnson, Kirchhoff, & Endress, 1975; Skipper & Leonard, 1968).

HOSPITALIZED ADULTS.    As was noted in Chapter 2, nearly 40 million people were hospitalized in 1983, most of whom were adults. More than half of these patients underwent some surgical or diagnostic procedure, and there is every reason to believe that a good deal of anxiety was associated with those processes. Numerous investigators have concerned themselves with ways of reducing that anxiety.

Egbert, Battit, Welch, and Bartlett (1964), for example, divided a sample of ninety-seven patients undergoing abdominal surgery into two randomly selected groups. Members of the control group were treated in a routine preoperative manner. In particular, as was routinely the case, they were not told about postoperative pain or its management. Members of the experimental group were given a good deal of information about postoperative pain, its characteristics, and its management. These conversations were conducted by the anesthetists. Surgeons did not know which patients were receiving the special information and continued their practices as usual. In comparison with the control group, the experimental group used significantly less narcotic medication postoperatively, gave fewer indications of pain on the first postoperative day, and were ultimately discharged nearly 3 days earlier.

Langer, Janis, and Wolfer (1975) examined the effectiveness of two alternative coping strategies in dealing with postoperative surgical recovery. They created four groups of fifteen patients each who were undergoing elective surgery for which the prognosis was generally favorable. Groups were created by a stratified randomization procedure that equated them for type and severity of the operation, age, gender, and religious affiliation. One group was given preoperative instruction in alternative styles of coping with stress; the second group was given information regarding the impending surgical procedures; a third group received both information about the surgical procedure and coping instructions; and the fourth group received time-matched neutral interviews that were related to their illnesses but not to coping with surgery.

While differences among the four groups were not dramatic, the mem bers of the control group requested more medication following surgery than either of the experimental groups and tended to stay in the hospital longer. Of the two intervention strategies, the procedure designed to increase coping skills tended to be more effective than the one that concentrated on providing information.

NOXIOUS MEDICAL PROCEDURES.  Many medical diagnostic procedures are dangerous, painful, or uncomfortable, and generate significant amounts of stress and anxiety in patients. A small number of studies have been reported in which efforts to reduce that stress have been undertaken.

Johnson and Leventhal (1974), for example, investigated the effects of two different methods for reducing patients' anxiety during a gastrointestinal endoscopic examination. This procedure is designed to allow for the visual examination and photography of the upper gastrointestinal tract. After swabbing the throat with an anesthetic, the physician passes a flexible fiber optic tube about 12 millimeters (about one-half inch) in diameter and about 90 centimeters (about 3 feet) in length through the mouth into the gastrointestinal tract, where it must remain for between 15 to 30 minutes. Patients are sedated but not anesthetized, because they need to follow the physician's instructions throughout the procedure. If the patient follows the physician's instructions, gagging and general discomfort are less frequent. The procedure is clearly a noxious one.

The authors began with the assumption that threatening situations evoke two largely independent types of responses:

> emotional reactions that include subjective and autonomic signs of emotion and behavior to reduce emotion and . . . danger-oriented reactions that include awareness of the objective features of the threat agent and behaviors designed to control the degree of potential danger. (p. 710)

Johnson and Levanthal, however, operationalized these variables in relation to two types of preparatory messages—one involving a sensory description of the experience and the other involving a description of appropriate examination behavior. Four groups of patients were formed on the basis of the presence or absence of these two preparatory messages. A control group comprised patients who received no preparatory information. One experimental group received only the sensory descriptive information; another only the behavioral instructions; and the third both the sensory descriptive information and the behavioral instructions.

A total of forty-eight patients undergoing a gastrointestinal endoscopic examination were assigned to one of these four groups. Two observers who were unaware of group assignments charted the relevant information during the patients' hospitalization. Several dependent measures were used to gauge reactions during the procedure, including amount of tranquilizer administered, changes in heart rate, avoidance movements, gagging, and time required to insert the endoscope. These measures were seen as reflecting the degree to which their instructions helped the patient cope with the procedure.

Johnson and Leventhal found a slight reduction in tranquilizer dosage, in difficulties of stabilization of heart rate, and in prevalence of gagging among those receiving the behavioral instructions. The group receiving only sensory descriptions was given less tranquilizer and showed less gagging and more stable heart rates than did those in the control group, but the differences were statistically significant only for patients under 50 years of age. Subjects receiving both behavioral and sensory information exhibited more stable heart rates and reduced gagging, but an increase in the time required to insert the endoscope. Tranquilizer dosage was slightly reduced among patients under 50 years of age, but was increased among those over 50 years old. Thus, preparatory communication appeared to reduce the distress associated with the endoscopic procedure to a limited extent.

## PSYCHOLOGICAL ASSESSMENT OF MEDICAL PATIENTS

Implicit in almost everything that has been written in this chapter is the general principle that the more that is known about the patient's psychology, the more successful will the health care delivery system be in providing competent, compassionate, and satisfying treatment. Learning about pertinent psychological aspects of a medical patient's condition is one of the major provinces of the health psychologist.

You have already seen on numerous occasions in this book how health psychologists use psychological assessment procedures to establish dependent measures of adjustment in evaluating health status. In particular, you have seen how psychological test instruments have been used to evaluate coping patterns employed by parents of chronically ill children (Chapter 3) and to assess attitudes that are thought to be pertinent to preventive health behavior (Chapter 5). Later, in Chapter 9, you will see how psychologists use test instruments to appraise pain and illness behavior; in Chapter 10 you will see how psychologists measure Type A behavior and anger; and in Chapter 11 you will learn how psychological assessment procedures are used in the development of treatment programs for persons suffering from asthma. At this point, it is appropriate to recognize the role of the health psychologist as an assessor of health attitudes and values, and to illustrate that role by examining two assessment instruments that are often used by health psychologists in medical settings.

Psychologists have a long tradition in the field of psychological assessment. The tradition, begun with the assessment of intelligence in young children, has come to maturity in the field of clinical psychology where psychologists are actively involved in the assessment of cognitive functioning, personality, and psychopathology in patients with emotional disorders.

Psychologists who work in general medical settings rarely find that assessment tools used with psychiatric patients are appropriate with medical patients. Accordingly, one special development that has characterized the field of health psychology has been the creation of assessment procedures that are specifically designed to be pertinent to the field of general medicine. These assessment procedures generally fall into the category of objective self-report instruments rather than projective tests—which attempt to determine health status by assessing patients' reactions to unstructured stimulus materials such as inkblots or drawings. The advantages of these assessment instruments over traditional medical interviews is that the questions are carefully chosen and analyzed in terms of their reliability and validity, and that since a specific set of questions is presented and later scored, it is possible to make reliable and valid analyses of differences between certain patients or groups of patients as well as of changes in patients over time.

### The Millon Behavioral Health Inventory

One of the relatively new assessment instruments developed for examining medical patients is the Millon Behavioral Health Inventory (MBHI) developed at the University of Illinois College of Medicine and reported by Millon, Green, and Meagher (1979). This scale, comprising 150 true-false items, assesses twenty dimensions that are thought of as particularly relevant to general medical settings. The twenty dimensions are divided into four major groups: (1) personality style, (2) psychogenic attitude, (3) psychosomatic correlate, and (4) prognostic index. Eight general personality styles are assessed: introversive, inhibited, cooperative, sociable, confident, forceful, respectful, and sensitive.

Six specific psychogenic attitudes, single dimensions that have been found to be related to the risk of a variety of disorders, are assessed: (1) chronic tension, (2) recent stress, (3) premorbid pessimism, (4) future despair, (5) social alienation, and (6) somatic anxiety.

People who score high on chronic tension, for example, tend to function under self-imposed pressures and have difficulty relaxing since they are impatient and constantly on the go. People who score high on somatic anxiety, to give another example, are overly concerned with bodily functions and are afraid of pain and of becoming ill.

Three specific sets of personality traits found to be associated with certain psychosomatic disorders are assessed—allergic inclination, gastrointestinal susceptibility, and cardiovascular tendency. Finally, three indices that are associated with prognosis have been developed—pain treatment responsivity, life-threat reactivity, and emotional vulnerability. The pain treatment responsivity index measures a set of traits that are similar to those found in patients who fail to respond successfully to treatment programs for the alleviation of chronic pain. The life-threat reactivity index measures a set of traits often found among persons with life-threatening illnesses who are having more than average difficulty coping. The emotional vulnerability index is made up of traits that are commonly found among patients who respond poorly to major surgical procedures or other life-threatening medical interventions.

Thus, the MBHI is a relatively brief general-purpose psychological assessment tool specifically designed to be used in a variety of medical settings. The scales appear to be adequately reliable, and the instrument is being used in pain centers, medical oncology units, in the study of sexual dysfunction, and in rehabilitation settings (Millon, Green, & Meagher, 1982; Murphy, Sperr, & Sperr, 1986).

### The Psychosocial Adjustment to Illness Scale

Another relatively new psychological assessment instrument is the Psychosocial Adjustment to Illness Scale (PAIS) developed at the Johns Hopkins University School of Medicine by Derogatis (1986). This scale, also multidimensional, is designed to assess the psychological and social adjustment of medical patients and members of their immediate families to the patients' illnesses. The PAIS consists of forty-six items and is available in two forms. The principal form, designed to be used by an interviewer, consists of questions to be posed along with a place to check which of several precoded answers comes closest to the answer given by the patient. The parallel self-report version is designed to be completed by patients themselves.

Seven specific aspects of psychosocial adjustment are evaluated by the PAIS: (1) health care orientation, (2) vocational environment, (3) domestic environment, (4) sexual relationships, (5) extended family relationships, (6) social environment, and (7) psychological distress. Health care orientation refers to the nature of the patient's attitudes toward such matters as health care in general, perceptions of health care professionals, and expectancies regarding the current disorder and its outcome. An example of an item on this scale is, "Can you describe for me your general attitude and approach to taking care of your health?"

The vocational environment assesses the impact that a medical disorder may have on such matters as vocational performance, interest, and satisfaction. (Example item: "Is your work as important to you now as it was before your illness?") The domestic environment scale is designed to assess problems in adaptation experienced by patients and their families in the family environment in response to the patient's illness. (Example item: "To what degree has your illness interfered with your duties and tasks around the house?")

The sexual relationships scale is designed to provide an estimate of changes in the quality of sexual relationships that are associated with the patient's illness. (Example item: "When some people become ill, they report a loss of interest in sexual activities. Have you experienced a reduction of sexual interest associated with your illness?") The extended family relationships scale assesses disruption in that area associated with the patient's illness. (Example item: "Do you normally depend on members of your extended family for physical or financial assistance, and has this changed at all since your illness?")

The social environment scale reflects the patient's current social and leisure time activities and whether there has been any impairment in these activities associated with the illness. (Example item: "Have you maintained your interest in social activities since your illness—e.g., social clubs, church groups, going to the movies?") Finally, the psychological distress scale consists of a number of items that assess the level of depression, anxiety, hostility, reduced self-esteem, and so forth that are thought to be the direct result of the illness and its aftereffects. (Example item: "Have you been feeling less adequate, or helpless, or somewhat down on yourself since your illness?")

Each of the seven scales seem sufficiently reliable to be used for research purposes, although since each scale includes items that are not necessarily always answered in the same direction, reliability coefficients are lower than those typically found in longer scales that assess some unidimensional variable such as self-esteem or depression. Furthermore, the scales seem reasonably independent of each other. There is also some preliminary information reported by Derogatis (1986) that suggests that the scales have acceptable validity and a good deal of practical utility in the management of a variety of patient groups.

As can be seen from this description of the MBHI and the PAIS, the development of assessment instruments in the field of health psychology tends to go through a number of regular stages. First, there is consideration given to the concepts that are to be measured and to what they comprise. Then, items are proposed that might be used in the measurement of each of these concepts. Statistical analyses of the items after the preliminary versions of the test are used to determine which items seem suitable; some items are then rejected while others are accepted, and still others can be added. Finally, a decision is made as to which items will be used to measure each concept based upon psychometric analyses of the scales to assure that the scales are reliable and robust. Attention is then concentrated in determining the usefulness and predictive validity of the scales. The process is a long one, as you can see, but the end result can be the development of a very important assessment procedure that can become, like the thermometer, an indispensable instrument in the management of medical patients.

## CONCLUDING COMMENTS

The process of becoming ill is unusually complex, and involves far more than the perception of abnormalities in bodily functioning. If people wait too long before petitioning for the sick role, their health can be endangered. If people are overly vigilant about seeking medical care, they run the risk of receiving inappropriate and costly care and of being discouraged about seeking health care in the future when the situation might be more appropriate to do so. Seeking medical care entails a psychosocial as well as a financial cost, and not everyone in need of care has the strength to go through that process.

Perhaps the single most important psychological attribute that must be present in order that medical help seeking can take place when it is needed is what is called self-efficacy (Bandura, 1977, 1982). Its converse has been called learned helplessness (Abramson, Seligman, & Teasdale, 1978; Maier & Seligman, 1976). People with an adequate sense of self-efficacy believe that they have the power—within certain limits, of course—to affect the course of their lives. People whose past histories have taught them that they can do little about changing their lives have learned to be helpless, that is, have a low sense of self-efficacy. It seems very likely that one important reason why people who are poor or psychologically unsupported or repeatedly unsuccessful hesitate before seeking medical care is that they have learned that they can do very little about bettering their lives.

This kind of helplessness appears to be surprisingly easily learned. It requires merely that a person be subjected to unavoidable and uncontrollable stress. Exposure to such stresses appears to interefere with a person's ability to see a causal relationship between his or her behavior and subsequent events. Exposure to such stresses appears to reduce the subsequent motivation to try to escape these stresses and seems to produce significant emotional disruption. The consequences of the sense of learned helplessness are measurable in a person's intellectual, motivational, and emotional life (Levy, 1985; Sue & Zane, 1980; Viney, 1986).

With the persuasive evidence that some aspects of being ill and receiving medical treatment are unduly stressful, and that remarkably little effort is needed to reduce some of those stresses significantly, it seems likely that research studies examining intervention programs designed to facilitate coping with illness-related stress are likely to continue to be reported. If the results of preventive intervention studies continue to be positive, significant permanent changes in certain aspects of the medical care system may well be undertaken as a consequence of these research reports. Thus, it can be predicted that one of the most fruitful areas of preventive intervention research may be located within the medical care system itself (Johnson, 1984).

## SUMMARY

- While people can develop illnesses or diseases all by themselves, it takes a physician to designate a person as sick or to assign the sick role.
- There are duties and responsibilities that go with being sick, as well as exemptions from responsibilities. The patient's principal exemption is not being required to carry out normal activities. Among the responsibilities associated with the sick role are feeling uncomfortable about being sick and cooperating in the process of getting well.
- Preventive health behavior—behavior designed to maintain health and prevent illness—consists of a number of remarkably uncorrelated com-

Becoming and Being Ill

ponents. There does not appear to be a general trait that might be called preventive health behavior. Rather, such behavior appears to be situation- and issue-specific.

- People seem to differ in their general tendency toward diagnosis and treatment seeking, and there is some consistency about these behaviors across a variety of settings. Most researchers believe, however, that far fewer people seek medical help for either primarily physical or primarily emotional disorders than is optimal.

- Treatment-seeking behavior is more common among younger than older people, among women than men, and among persons who have greater levels of education and greater incomes.

- Treatment seeking occurs more often when a person has a high level of information and a low level of anxiety about the suspected problem.

- Medical care can be overutilized or underutilized, at least from the point of view of the health care provider. There is some question about whether medical care can be over- or underutilized from the point of view of the patient.

- There are a number of very different but equally appropriate perspectives for studying health behavior, including the economic, sociodemographic, geographic, sociopsychological, sociocultural, and organizational perspectives.

- Deciding to seek health services has complex rational components. Seeking medical care is a form of decision making and, like all decisions, takes place following a process of weighing the pros and cons of seeking and not seeking health services.

- A number of variables are important in the decision to seek help, including the nature and severity of the symptoms, the ability to recognize the symptoms, the extent of disability, cultural values regarding stoicism and tolerance for pain, availability and accessibility of information and help, and social acceptability of help seeking.

- There are profound sociocultural differences among groups that result in significant variation in help-seeking behavior. Among these differences are attitudes toward illness and pain, medical care, the stigmatizing nature of illness, and whom it is most appropriate to consult for each type of illness.

- Symptoms tend to be more strongly perceived by people who are bored, live alone, or are socially isolated in other ways, lack self-confidence, and need constant approval from others.

- Among elderly people, the level of symptom reporting tends to increase, but it is not clear whether it increases because people become somewhat hypochondriacal with age, or because they are simply sicker.

- Becoming and being ill constitutes an important and sometimes powerful source of stress, particularly when medical care personnel do not understand psychosocial factors in the illness. As a consequence, there is growing interest in how to reduce the stress associated with illnesses.

- Four broad classes of variables have been found to be related to degree of satisfaction with medical care—demographic characteristics of the patient, how the medical practice is organized, personal characteristics of the physician, and the nature of the patient-physician interaction.
- There is considerable research that clearly indicates that much can be done psychologically to reduce the stress associated with becoming ill. One of the stresses of illness that is commonly reported, particularly when the patient is hospitalized, is the loss of the sense of being a person.
- Hospitalization of children is clearly thought of as stressful, for children and for their parents. Many hospital personnel have been trained to reduce that stress using a variety of educational and support-building procedures.
- Studies evaluating the effectiveness of nursing procedures designed to reduce the stresses of hospitalization and surgery are unusually well designed. They virtually always indicate that significant reductions of discomfort following surgery and more rapid recovery can be obtained quite easily.
- Educational procedures can be effective in reducing the discomfort associated with noxious medical diagnostic techniques and with surgery.
- Central in the task of improving the quality and success of medical treatment is a better understanding of the psychology of the medical patient. Health psychologists have developed a number of very useful assessment procedures for learning about health-related aspects of patients' attitudes and values. These assessment procedures form an important aspect of the practice of health psychology.

# Psychosocial Aspects of Specific Disorders:

# Introduction

# 8

## INTRODUCTION

In this and the next three chapters we will examine psychological aspects of five specific disorders—chronic pain, heart disease, hypertension, cancer, and asthma. While a great many disorders have been considered from a psychosocial point of view, these five disorders have attracted the greatest attention in the empirical literature.

It should be noted, however, that other disorders are beginning to be examined from a psychosocial point of view including rheumatoid arthritis (Anderson et al., 1985); Parkinson's disease (Dakof & Mendelsohn, 1986); diabetes (Epstein et al., 1981; Fisher, Delamater, Bertelson, & Kirkley, 1982); the irritable bowel syndrome (Ford, 1986); infectious mononucleosis (Kasl, Evans, & Niederman, 1979); the acquired immune deficiency syndrome (Martin & Vance, 1984); insomnia (Borkovec, 1982; Borkovec, Grayson, O'Brien, & Weerts, 1979); gastrointestinal disorders (Brooks & Richardson, 1980; Whitehead & Bosmajian, 1982); and Raynaud's disease, a painful vascular disease mainly in the hands and feet that is often precipitated by cold weather (Keefe, Surwit, & Pilon, 1979; Surwit, 1982; Surwit, Pilon, & Fenton, 1978).

This chapter will provide introductory material regarding the two areas of central interest to health psychologists—what is known about how people become and remain vulnerable to these disorders, and what can be done to be of help once the disorders develop. While there will be a summary at the end of each of these four related chapters, because the chapters are all part of a single theme, we will wait until the end of the four chapters before providing concluding comments.

## HISTORICAL AND THEORETICAL OVERVIEW

Examining psychological aspects of specific illnesses requires great care in avoiding the psychosomatic fallacy. That fallacy has two components. First is the belief that some disorders have a psychological etiology and some do not—a false belief that you were introduced to in Chapter 1. Second is the belief that many illnesses can be distinguished from one another on the basis of their unique psychological characteristics, that is, that there are psychological characteristics that go hand in hand with certain specific disorders. Neither of these assumptions has been shown to have any empirical justification.

The task in discussing psychosocial aspects of specific disorders is to show proper respect for the evidence that links the social, psychological, and biological sciences with each other, while carefully steering clear of the twin dangers of the psychosomatic fallacy.

The term *psychosomatic medicine* dates from the early nineteenth century, but the interest in understanding bodily symptoms in terms of psychological factors began in earnest about a hundred years later, at the start of the twentieth century. The movement was initially dominated by psychoanalysts whose concern was with diseases that appeared to have psychological stress as a prominent feature (Stone, 1979b). Among the conditions that attracted the attention of persons associated with the field of psychosomatic medicine during its early development were hypertension, rheumatoid arthritis, menstrual problems, peptic ulcer, ulcerative colitis, migraine, skin disorders, allergies, diabetes, asthma, and intestinal, kidney, and respiratory disorders.

Psychosomatic theory was, at first, a rather narrow and somewhat constricting concept in which efforts were made to understand a limited set of specific diseases in relation to psychoanalytic theories of repression and psychosexual conflict. These early theories were driven by the fundamental belief that a unique set of psychological determinants (experiences, unresolved conflicts, persistent needs, attitudes, or character structure) formed the necessary precursor for a great many unique physical diseases. It was the belief of the early psychosomaticists that certain disorders stood in a symbolic relationship to certain personality traits or unresolved psychological conflicts. Research studies have virtually never substantiated this belief (see, for example, Schmidt, Carney, & Fitzsimmons, 1986). An example of the specificity of this generally discredited belief system can be found in Table 8–1.

Two names are prominently associated with these unsupported early

**Table 8–1**    Psychosomatic Disorders and Hypothesized Personality Characteristics

| DISORDER | HYPOTHESIZED PERSONALITY CHARACTERISTIC |
| --- | --- |
| Acne | The person feels he or she is being picked on and wants to be left alone. |
| Asthma | The individual feels left out, unloved, or ignored, and wants to screen out another individual or the situation. |
| Hypertension | The person feels threatened with being harmed by an ever-present danger. As a result, he or she feels the need to be on guard and prepared to meet all threats. |
| Hives | There are feelings of taking a beating (or being mistreated) and being helpless to do anything about it. |
| Migraine | The individual feels that something has to be accomplished or achieved or some goal reached. The person then relaxes after the effort is exerted. |
| Duodenal ulcer | The individual feels deprived of what is due him or her and wants to seek revenge or get even. |
| Rheumatoid arthritis | The person feels tied down, restrained, or restricted and wants to restore freedom of movement. |
| Hyperthyroidism | The individual feels he or she might lose a loved person or object and takes care to prevent such a loss by holding on or by possessiveness. |
| Low back pain | The person wants to run away, walk out, or escape from the situation. |

(Adapted with permission from D. S. Krantz and D. C. Glass (1984, p. 43). Also see Graham et al., 1962).

theories—Franz Alexander (1891–1964) and Flanders Dunbar (1902–1959). Flanders Dunbar's textbook, *Emotions and Bodily Changes,* went through four editions between 1935 and 1954, and in her last edition (1954) eight "psychosomatic diagnostic groups" were described. Persons in these psychosomatic diagnostic groups were fearlessly portrayed not only in terms of their unique areas of focal conflict and characteristic reactions, but also, for example, in terms of their unique neurotic traits, attitudes toward the family, patterns of addictions and interests, reactions to illness, and their life situation immediately prior to onset of the disorder.

In the case of hypertension, for example, the areas of focal conflict and characteristic reaction were thought of as involving aggression and passivity in the form of rivalry and self-defeat. Neurotic traits associated with hypertension were believed to include temper tantrums, nailbiting, obsessive doubts, compulsive traits, perfectionistic inclinations, dependence on food, and dependence on someone in a parental role. Attitude toward the family involved ambivalence toward father and a passive but hostile and fearful attitude toward mother. Unique addictions and interests included excessive use of coffee, cigarettes, and alcohol; interest in such athletic pursuits as golf, hunting, and riding; and interest in wine, women, and song. The unique reaction to the hypertension was giving in to passive tendencies and using the illness as an alibi for failure. The life situation prior to onset was described as involving the death of or separation from a loved one, or a setback in a field in which the patient has a particularly high level of aspiration.

Alexander's work, in contrast to that of Dunbar, seems, in retrospect, somewhat more sophisticated—although, as it turned out, it was no more valid. His group searched for personality types and psychological conflict patterns associated with specific diseases. Alexander and associates based their theories on earlier Freudian psychoanalytic views of normal development. Specifically, Alexander examined three aspects of this view: (1) the wish to incorporate, receive, or take in; (2) the wish to eliminate, to give, to expend energy for accomplishing something; and (3) the wish to retain or accumulate.

For example, gastrointestinal disturbances, such as ulcers, were thought to have parallels in personality. Thus,

> stomach functions . . . seem to be disturbed in some patients who re-acted with shame to their wish to receive help or love or to lean on another person. In others the conflict expressed itself as guilt about wanting to take something away from another person by force, as occurs in sibling rivalry among children who want to possess parental love alone and who also envy the possessions of their siblings. The reason why the stomach functions are vulnerable to this type of conflict was found in the well-established finding that eating constitutes the first gratification of the receptive incorporating urge. In the child's mind the wish to be loved and the wish to be fed become deeply linked. When in later life the wish to be helped by another person provokes shame, which is not an unusual reaction in a society that places a premium on the self-made man, the wish to be helped finds regressive gratification by an increased urge toward oral incorporation. This urge stimulates stomach secretion, and chronic hypersecretion in disposed individuals may eventually lead to ulcer formation. (Alexander & Selesnick, 1966, pp. 482–483)

In addition to developing a psychoanalytic theory of ulcers, Alexander and his group developed other theories to account for ulcerative colitis, asthma, hypertension, rheumatoid arthritis, neurodermatitis, and hyperthyroidism. Colitis was thought to be associated with unconscious dependent tendencies and a lack of self-confidence. Rheumatoid arthritis was thought to be associated with tightly controlled muscular expression of emotions. Asthma was thought to be associated with disturbed mother-child relationships and the suppressed impulse to cry. Hypertension was thought to be associated with an inhibition against the free expression of resentments felt toward other people because of a desire to be loved.

While Alexander was careful to point out that these alleged characteristic emotional conflict patterns, even when combined with the idea that there might be certain biological organ vulnerabilities, were not enough to account for the onset of symptoms, the field of psychosomatic medicine was irresistibly drawn to these appealing psychodynamic theories (Krantz & Glass, 1984).

## CONTEMPORARY PSYCHOSOMATIC THEORY

Compared to the earlier view of psychosomatic theory just described, contemporary psychosomatic theory is remarkably liberating. The view that specific diseases are somehow connected with specific personality types or emotional conflicts has largely been abandoned. The belief that illness is, in part, a consequence of personality is as strong as ever, but no longer is there any assertion that knowing about the personality of an individual or about the person's unresolved emotional conflicts will make it possible to predict the specific illness that is likely to occur.

A second noteworthy aspect of contemporary psychosomatic theory is that all the links between physical and psychological well-being are legitimate areas of inquiry, and that the relationships are recognized as bidirectional. No longer is it thought that certain disorders are psychosomatic while other disorders are not. It is now perfectly legitimate to be interested in the roles played by psychosocial factors in potentiating or moderating infectious or nutritional diseases as well as other diseases of known biological etiology. Contemporary psychosomaticists are interested in how psychosocial factors play roles in all illness, and in how physical illnesses of any kind can result in psychological stress. The entire mind-body interaction defines the domain of current interest to psychosomaticists (Lipowski, 1976).

A third noteworthy aspect of the new psychosomatic theory is the attention that is now paid to the social environment in addition to the psychological environment in understanding illness (Jenkins, 1972). Psychosomaticists are interested in how aspects of the physical environment, such as noise (Tarnopolsky & McLean, 1976) or environmental toxins (Greenberg, 1983), affect health and illness, and in how cultural and anthropological characteristics of societies play a role in health and illness (see, for example, Logan and Hunt, 1976; Ramesh, 1983). Geographers have been interested in health since perhaps World War II, and there is now a field of medical geography that concerns itself with how the physical and sociocultural environment affect and are affected by health and illness (see, for example, Eyles & Woods, 1983; McGlashan & Blunden, 1983; Pyle, 1983).

Finally, the new psychosomatic theory is far more biologically sophisticated than was the case a generation ago. Recent progress in the study of general nonspecific biological reactions to illness, for example, have resulted in considerably increased understanding of the role of biological factors in producing the somatic response to psychosocial events. These biological responses to psychosocial events are normal and healthy, but may, in the short run, be too great for a weak and vulnerable organ. In the long run, sustained biological responses to psychosocial events may produce bodily changes that signal the presence of a diagnosable disease (Krantz & Manuck, 1984; Ursin, 1980).

Thus, contemporary interest in psychosomatic theory is far broader than was the case two or three decades ago. It now includes such topics as the psychobiology of separation and loss, psychosocial effects of surgery, physical illness as a stressful life event, and psychosocial aspects of chronic and terminal illnesses. With this modified and broadened agenda, the social sciences have an increasingly important role in the overall effort to understand health and illness. In summary, contemporary psychosomatic theory is virtually synonymous with the scope of this text in that it concerns itself with the psychosocial approach to the study of health and illness.

Two different groups of hypotheses linking psychological variables and illness have been identified—generalized susceptibility hypotheses, and specific illness hypotheses (Cohen, 1979). In the first group are those hypotheses that hold that psychological factors (such as a sense of helplessness or hopelessness, the accumulation of stressful life events, or how one appraises and is able to adapt to certain stressful life situations) increase the overall risk of illness but do not determine the specific illness that will develop. The generalized susceptibility hypothesis suggests that there are "disease-prone" personalities (Friedman & Booth-Kewley, 1987). In the second group are those hypotheses that hold that certain psychological factors are significantly linked to the increased risk of developing specific illnesses or groups of illnesses (such as cancer or coronary disease). It is this second group of hypotheses that appears to have little support in the research literature.

There does not appear to be a simple relationship between stress or personality factors, on the one hand, and the development of illness, on the other hand. The effects of early experience on later illness susceptibility depend on a variety of moderating factors, such as characteristics of early childrearing, or the acuteness or chronicity of stress. Biological reactions (some of which are often thought of as illnesses) to stressful life circumstances are very complex, and it may be unrealistic to search for simple relationships between certain forms of stress and certain bodily reactions. Finally, certain psychological factors may be linked to precursors of a disease, while others may be linked to the development of the disease, and still others may be linked to when the disease actually manifests itself, that is, when it is precipitated.

Health psychologists who work in medical settings spend significant portions of their time working directly with medical patients carrying out activities that are referred to, in general terms, as "psychological intervention." The term is a broad one and includes any approach based upon psychological principles that is designed to change behavior. Thus, the term includes not only most forms of psychotherapy, but also includes the use of contingency management based on operant conditioning principles, and procedures designed to modify the nature of the stimulus through such counterconditioning procedures as relaxation training, hypnosis, and biofeedback either alone or in combination with each other. All forms of psychological intervention assume that illness behavior is learned and that it can, under the right circumstances, be unlearned (Berni & Fordyce, 1977; Fordyce, 1978; Roberts, 1981; Sternbach, 1976; Turk, 1978).

## AN OVERVIEW OF PSYCHOLOGICAL
## INTERVENTION APPROACHES

In Chapter 1 you were introduced to the general theoretical approaches that are employed in conceptualizing health and illness behavior and its modification. As was mentioned in Chapter 1, health and illness behavior is developed and maintained by three interacting and overlapping regulatory processes—stimulus perception, reinforcement patterns, and cognitive mediating processes (Bandura, 1977). These approaches have important implications for psychological intervention.

Behavior and disease are linked together like a two-way street (Agras, 1984). First, certain forms of behavior can lead to disease. The most obvious examples of this relationship are in the area of illness- or accident-producing lifestyles, such as smoking or alcohol abuse (see Chapters 5 and 6). When it is clear that a particular type of behavior can result in some form of illness, the task of a psychological approach to illness reduction is to try to reduce or eliminate the illness-producing behavior (see Chapter 4).

The second way in which behavior and illness are related is that under certain conditions, illness can cause certain forms of counterproductive behavior. For example, as we saw in Chapter 3, juvenile diabetes creates stresses for adolescent patients that can result in disturbed interpersonal relationships. Life-threatening illnesses can result in severe depression and withdrawal from other people. We have also seen that certain types of medical procedures can cause extreme anxiety that can, in turn, delay the process of recovery (Chapter 7). When it is clear that certain forms of behavior have begun as a secondary consequence of an illness that appear to be retarding recovery, psychological treatment approaches become part of the general medical treatment program and may involve the patient, the patient's family, and the health service delivery team in efforts to reduce that behavior. When the relationships of behavior and illness are not clearly understood, the development of an effective psychological intervention program is more difficult.

How one reacts to illness or to the medical procedures that are designed to treat the illness may be a function of characteristics of or reactions to the stimulus, such as how a person responds to the sensation of pain or to impending surgery. Psychological intervention in this context can be used to modify characteristics of the stimulus or of reactions to the stimulus by such procedures as relaxation training, biofeedback, health-related information, or social modeling. For example, the provision of information that sets the stage for constructive modeling on the part of the patient is particularly useful in reducing anxiety prior to impending surgery or other noxious medical procedures, as we have seen in Chapter 7.

From the point of view that stresses that health and illness behavior is learned and that it can be unlearned, the basic principles of behavior modification can be employed in carrying out psychological interventions. These interventions basically attempt to modify illness behavior by various forms of contingency management designed to reinforce desired behavior and to extinguish undesired behavior.

If one stresses cognitive mediating processes in interpreting some specific health or illness behavior, then modifying that behavior will involve psychological interventions that focus on changes in attitudes or beliefs, and on increasing the range of alternatives that are open to patients in their efforts to cope with their illnesses. The two most common forms of intervention that are designed to change attitudes or beliefs are psychotherapy and consumer health education. Some form of psychotherapeutic intervention may be needed in helping patients come to grips with underlying psychological aspects of their efforts to cope with their illnesses. Educational approaches may be needed when it is clear that behavior will not likely change without the provision of additional information.

### Becoming Part of the Treatment Team

Adding psychological treatment modalities to the traditional medical setting, such as a hospital or outpatient clinic, is not a simple procedure. Medical settings are unusually complex and have strong traditions, and Tefft and Simeonsson (1979) have described some of the problems inherent in changing them (also see Sarason, 1972). The assumptions under which most medical care settings operate are rarely appropriate when considering the medical disorders for which psychological interventions are undertaken. Among these assumptions are that: (1) patients should turn themselves over to the medical experts and simply do what they are told; (2) treatment procedures should be dictated primarily by the patient's physiological condition, without significant regard for the accompanying psychosocial facts; and (3) the physician is in charge and gives the directives that are to be followed by nurses and other "ancillary" health service personnel.

In order for psychologists to take their place successfully in medical settings, Tefft and Simeonsson (1979) urge psychologists to develop a greater appreciation of the history of medical care settings and how they have come to be what they are, and to maintain a realistic time perspective on how long the process of becoming a necessary part of the health care team will likely take.

### The Placebo Effect

Before discussing any specific psychological intervention procedure, it is important to discuss the placebo and the placebo effect. A *placebo* is any medication or procedure that has a therapeutic effect independent of its pharmacology or other specific properties. The placebo effect can be seen when a pharmacologically inert substance is administered to a patient and consequently the patient reports improvement. In such a circumstance, health care providers generally conclude that improvement has taken place simply because the patient believed that a valid treatment was being provided, that is, because the patient had what Frank (1982) calls "expectant faith" (p. 450). The placebo effect may be based on environmental factors, such as where and in what form the therapy is administered; therapist characteristics, such as persuasiveness and enthusiasm; and patient characteristics, such as past experiences with medication or medical procedures or readiness to be helped. The placebo effect is surprisingly common and remarkably ubiquitous.

There are two important reasons for studying placebos. First, there is no question about the fact that placebos are frequently helpful in reducing symptomatology, and the mechanisms of that effectiveness need to be uncovered. Second, the placebo effect is a measure of the nonspecific benefit of any therapy; if a specific medication or psychological intervention, such as those that will be discussed in this chapter, is thought to have special properties, it must be shown that its effectiveness significantly exceeds that of a placebo.

Many health care providers underestimate the effectiveness of placebos; they tend to think that if a placebo results in symptom reduction it means that the symptom was imaginary rather than real (Goodwin, Goodwin, & Vogel, 1979). Yet, a great variety of symptoms, such as postoperative pain, cough, hypertension, and nausea, appear to respond to placebo treatment (Agras, 1984; Frank, 1982).

As for the physiological basis for the placebo effect, evidence is converging that endogenous opiate-like substances, called *endorphins* (Maier & Laudenslager, 1985) are produced by the body and released when placebos are administered. These endorphins appear to reduce pain and produce euphoria; they appear to be similar to opiates in how they act on the central nervous system. Furthermore, it has also been found that drugs that block the effect of artificial opiates appear to reduce the effect of naturally produced endorphins as well.

In an interesting example of this line of research, Levine, Gordon, and Fields (1978) studied postoperative pain in a group of patients who had undergone extraction of impacted wisdom teeth. A total of fifty-one patients was divided according to the drugs they received 2 hours and again 3 hours after the extraction. All patients were normally anesthetized during the extraction itself. One group received placebos at both points after the extraction. A second group received placebo at 2 hours and naloxone (a drug that blocks the pain-reducing effect of an opiate) at 3 hours. A third group received naloxone 2 hours and the placebo 3 hours after the extraction. These investigators examined the hypothesis that if placebo-induced pain relief is mediated by endorphins, then the opiate-antagonist, naloxone, would be expected to block that pain relief.

Pain was assessed by means of two different but highly correlated self-report measures, and the results were consistent with the hypothesis that endorphin release mediates placebo pain relief. Patients given naloxone reported significantly greater pain than those given a placebo. Furthermore, among the group of patients who received a placebo as their first postoperative drug and who reported either no increase in pain or an actual reduction of pain, the subsequent administration of naloxone produced a pain increase. Among those patients who were initially given a placebo and who reported an increase in pain, the subsequent administration of naloxone produced no further pain increase. Finally, among those patients who initially received naloxone following the extraction, the subsequent administration of a placebo rarely produced any significant pain reduction.

### Modifying How the Stimulus Is Perceived

As we have suggested, behavior can be changed by: (1) modifying the perception of the stimulus that precedes the behavior; (2) modifying the contingencies that reinforce the behavior itself; or (3) changing the nature of cognitive mediating processes, such as attitudes or values that take place between the perception of the stimulus and the behavioral response.

We will begin our examination of psychological intervention techniques by exploring that large group of activities that are designed to modify the nature of and the reaction to the perceived stimulus. These interventions sometimes are referred to as counterconditioning (Price, 1974; Rickles, Onoda, & Doyle, 1982).

HYPNOSIS. Hypnosis is a process of suggestion that can sometimes achieve very great levels of relaxation as well as remarkable instances of behavior change. It is not clear whether being hypnotized represents an altered state of consciousness or whether it is little more than a state of heightened suggestibility. In spite of the fact that hypnosis has been an officially accepted psychological intervention procedure since 1960 when its use was endorsed by the American Psychological Association (Agras, 1984; Hilgard, 1968), hypnosis remains a poorly understood and somewhat mysterious phenomenon; and, just as in the case of the placebo, there is some suspicion about its use on the part of many health care providers (Hilgard, 1971, 1978).

Three disorders have been thought to be particularly responsive to hypnosis—skin disorders, headaches, and asthma (De Piano & Salzberg, 1979), although studies using hypnosis have been reported for a wide variety of other conditions as well, particularly in reducing the discomfort associated with both acute and chronic pain. Many published reports have been based on single case studies, however (see, for example, Fung & Lazar, 1983; Smith & Balaban, 1983), and others have failed to include control groups, or failed to make random assignment to treatment conditions. These methodological inadequacies tend to be more common in older studies than newer studies, however, and there is a growing interest in the development of cooperative studies in which scientists in a number of different settings agree to pool their data in order to increase the number of cases in their sample (Miller, 1983). There is probably no area in health psychology where there is greater need for well-controlled and well-executed studies than in the study of hypnosis and its role in the treatment of physical disorders. A significant increase in the number and quality of such research studies should go a long way toward reducing the uncertainty about its use (LeBaron & Zeltzer, 1984).

A number of studies have demonstrated that degree of hypnotizability is associated with greater success in the treatment of a number of different disorders, including obesity and facial pain (Andersen, 1985; Miller & Cross, 1985; Stam, McGrath, Brooke, & Cosier, 1986). There is some overall evidence that hypnosis can facilitate insight into the origins and psychological role of symptoms and can reduce the perceived discomfort associated with certain physiological processes. Evidence that hypnosis can alter physiological functioning is not as convincing (De Piano & Salzberg, 1979). Of the conditions for which hypnosis has been most commonly used and studied, asthma has obtained the most promising results.

RELAXATION TRAINING.    Relaxation is nearly universally thought of as a desirable and pleasant state, and efforts to encourage relaxation as a way of coping with stress-induced physiological arousal have been reported for centuries. The value of taking time to relax is being increasingly recognized, and there is considerable evidence that many people who are physically ill suffer from an inability to relax (Agras, 1984; Anderson, 1982; Andrasik, Coleman, & Epstein, 1982; Tarler-Benlolo, 1978; Tolman & Rose, 1985). Among the techniques that have been used to help with the process of relaxation are progressive relaxation, meditation, autogenic training, and biofeedback.

Preceding the modern era of relaxation training, treatment of the physically ill often included other forms of prescribed relaxation, most notably, the use of spas and their healing waters. Since antiquity, certain naturally occurring waters in different parts of the world have been thought to possess healing properties. Americans traveling in Europe today can easily find spas that combine natural beauty, a relaxing atmosphere, an organized healthful lifestyle, especially from a nutritional point of view, and an astonishing array of naturally occurring substances, including waters, vapors, and muds that purport to have healing properties.

The study and use of naturally occurring materials in the service of health is called *balneology*, a term almost unknown in the United States. Specific waters are well known for their curative properties for specific illnesses. Many European physicians prescribe the use of healing waters, and most health insurance programs in Europe reimburse patients for the costs associated with visiting spas for their healing properties. While most Europeans seem to believe that spas are healthful, there is disagreement among health care providers as to whether their therapeutic value is based upon disorder-specific healing properties of the waters, the general therapeutic value of relaxation, or the placebo effect (Addison, 1951; Bannerman, Burton, & Wen-Chieh, 1983).

In 1669, Jorden introduced his discourse on natural baths by noting that "these kind of watry and vaporous Bathes have been in use from all antiquity, and held in great esteem, both for pleasure, and for preservation of health. For there is no form of Remedy more comfortable to mans body, or which easeth pain and weariness more speedily, and more effectually" (p. 2). A few years later, in 1683, Haworth introduced his description of one of the contemporary baths by noting that "amongst the many excellent Helps and useful Inventions where-with the Industry of Ancient and Modern Physicians hath supported the totter-ing Fabric of Mens Bodies, the Practice of Bagnios deservedly claims an honour-able Mention, and justly challenges a venerable Esteem" (p. 31).

There was a time when health spas were as well known in the United States as they were in Europe. Perhaps the most famous spa in the United States was the one located in Saratoga, New York. In 1821, the formidable benefits of the waters at Saratoga were described as follows:

> The most prominent and perceptible effects of these waters when taken into the stomach are Cathartick, Diuretick and Tonick. They are much used in a great variety of complaints; but the diseases in which they are the most efficacious are, Jaundice and billious affections generally, Dys-pepsia, Habitual Costiveness, Hypochondriacal Complaints, Depraved appetite, Calculous and nephritic complaints, Phagedenic or ill condi-tioned species or states of gout, some species of dropsy, Scrofula, paral-ysis, Scorbutic affections and old Scorbutic ulcers, Amenorrhea, Dys-menorrhea and Chlorosis. (quoted in Amory, 1948, p. 410; also see Willis, 1856)

American medicine tends to be particularly skeptical regarding the therapeutic properties of naturally occurring substances; modern medicine tends to be equally skeptical regarding the practice of most forms of what is sometimes called traditional medicine—and sometimes referred to as indige-nous, alternative, folk, or ethno-medicine. These terms are used to describe the culture-bound health care practices that existed in the prescientific era, that is, prior to the beginning of the nineteenth century.

However, Bannerman, Burton, and Wen-Chieh (1983), writing on be-half of the World Health Organization, remind their readers that practitioners of traditional medicine define life as "the union of body, senses, mind and souls," and describe positive health as "the blending of physical, mental, social, moral and spiritual welfare" (p. 9). Indeed, one of the more interesting contem-porary developments in the field of health care is the renewed interest in tradi-tional medicine, now often called holistic medicine. Twentieth century versions of these earlier forms of therapy that include a strong relaxation component now exist, but with little of the charm attributed to the spas of an earlier time.

PROGRESSIVE RELAXATION.    The earliest modern form of relaxation training was developed by Jacobson (1929, 1970, 1977), who was persuaded of the importance of relaxation in the treatment of stress-related disorders, but who soon learned that merely telling a patient to relax was rarely successful. Rather, a more structured procedure appeared to be necessary, and Jacobson developed such a procedure. In this system, a patient is taught to recognize and relax muscle tension through successive tensing and relaxing of fifteen specific muscle groups. The procedure is quite time-consuming, taking as much as 2 hours a day, but patients can increase their awareness of muscle tension and their abilities to reduce that tension. Audiotapes of the therapist's instructions appear to be quite effective, thus making it possible for the patient to practice relaxation at the most convenient times. Progressive relaxation has been found to be effective in the treatment of insomnia, hypertension, certain forms of headaches, and anxiety.

Progressive relaxation techniques have been included in systematic desensitization procedures, such as those developed by Wolpe (1958), because of their potential for inhibiting anxiety responses. In a systematic desensitization procedure, the patient and therapist work together to develop a list of anxiety-provoking situations that seem to trigger the undesired response. The list is then arranged in a hierarchy from those situations that appear to be less stressful to those that are more stressful; then, by a process of guided suggestion, relaxation, and practice, the patient is taught to master, that is, to become desensitized to, each anxiety-provoking situation starting with the mildest.

TRANSCENDENTAL MEDITATION. Among the various approaches to relaxation, none has a more dedicated following than transcendental meditation. The transcendental meditation technique, adapted from the Indian yogic tradition, is a "procedure for experiencing the *mechanics* of the thinking process in a new direction" (Domash, 1977, p. 19; see also Carrington, 1982). The technique of meditation aims at increasing the awareness of thought prior to the emergence of its fully developed form; it uses a set of sounds (*mantras*, in Sanscrit) to facilitate this new awareness. According to Tarler-Benlolo (1978), the technique is easily learned and simple to perform.

Domash describes the experience of transcendental meditation as follows:

> To practice the Transcendental Meditation technique, the subject simply sits comfortably with eyes closed and begins to use the thinking process, with the mantra as a medium, in the precise but restful way he has been taught. Subjectively, the meditator usually reports an immediate sense of bodily quiet and relaxation along with a "settling down" of thought activity. Often, there is a loss of bodily sensation—yet full conscious awareness is maintained and in fact is reported to be experienced as "expanded" or "clarified." At certain moments in the period of the TM technique there may occur shorter or longer intervals when thought activity is reported to cease completely, and the mind then simply experiences conscious awareness alone, without content. This condition, which is difficult to imagine or describe precisely just because it is a novel fourth mode of consciousness, is the state given the name "pure consciousness." . . . The process is described as a restful, deeply enjoyable one, and afterwards there is typically a feeling of refreshment, liveliness, strength, and clarity of mind. (Domash, 1977, p. 21)

A remarkably large research literature exists examining the effects of transcendental meditation. In part, this fact is due to the systematic and standardized description of TM that makes it relatively easy to know when the technique is being used. In addition, the leaders of the TM movement have clearly advocated and encouraged the scientific study of the technique. Among this literature are papers examining basic physiological aspects of TM (Badawi, Wallace, Orme-Johnson, & Rouzere, 1984; Farrow & Hebert, 1982; Singh, 1984; Wallace, 1970), and papers evaluating TM as a technique in the treatment of hypertension (Wallace et al., 1983), high levels of cholesterol (Cooper & Aygen, 1979), aging (Wallace, Dillbeck, Jacobe, & Harrington, 1982), anxiety (Dillbeck, 1977; Hjelle, 1974), and in the prevention of alcohol and marijuana abuse (Shafii, Lavely, & Jaffe, 1974, 1975). Each of these studies employed some form of control or comparison group, usually a group of subjects who practiced some other form of relaxation, and these studies have found that the TM group is superior for reducing cholesterol level, anxiety level, alcohol and marijuana use, systolic blood pressure levels, as well as retarding physiological changes associated with the aging process.

AUTOGENIC TRAINING.    Autogenic training, a system of relaxation that combines elements of hypnosis, yoga, and passive nonmuscular relaxation exercises, was developed by Schultz and Luthe (Luthe, 1963, 1969; Schultz & Luthe, 1959). The technique is a complex one, and an international organization exists that trains and accredits autogenic practitioners. Autogenic training appears to be associated with a variety of important physiological changes, including decreased respiration rate, heart rate, and blood pressure, and appears to be effective in the treatment of a variety of stress-related disorders (Tarler-Benlolo, 1978). The method has been combined with biofeedback into a system of autogenic feedback training (Green, Green, & Walters, 1970; Sargent, Green, & Walters, 1973) that has been found to be successful in the treatment of migraine and muscle tension headaches.

BIOFEEDBACK.    The term *biofeedback* refers to a procedure in which individuals are given information regarding their physiological functioning, such as muscular tension, in order to help them regulate that functioning and reduce physical symptoms thought to be associated with that tension (Andrasik, Coleman, & Epstein, 1982; also see Miller, 1978; Turk, Meichenbaum, & Berman, 1979, pp. 1322–1323). Biofeedback can be thought of in general or in specific terms. In the case of the general conceptualization, biofeedback is seen as a method of teaching stress management skills, typically focusing on the relation between high levels of anxiety and stress on the one hand and physical symptoms such as headache, hypertension, asthma, and chronic pain on the other hand (Dolce & Raczynski, 1985). In more specific terms, in the case of the modification of muscular tension, for example, biofeedback seeks to identify specific muscular problems, such as abnormal paraspinal muscle activity during movement, and then tailor-make a program to alleviate the specific faulty neuromuscular behavior pattern. Biofeedback procedures can be used to increase the effectiveness of other relaxation programs.

The development of biofeedback dates from the work of Budzynski and Stoyva (1969) who were concerned with improving the effectiveness of relaxation training. They felt that the training could be improved by providing a process for detecting muscular tension level and feeding this information back to the subject. They reasoned that this information feedback would make it possible for the subject to relax more quickly and more thoroughly (Tarler-Benlolo, 1978).

Budzynski and Stoyva developed an instrument that assessed muscle tension and emitted a tone that varied in pitch according to the level of muscle activity that was detected. With this instrument it was possible to: (1) detect and amplify some biological response, such as muscle tension; (2) process that response into a form that was interpretable by the subject; and (3) immediately feed back the processed response to the subject. Thus, a closed feedback system could be established. A physiological response is generated by a subject; the response is detected, amplified, processed, and fed back to the subject. The subject then uses this information in order to change the physiological response which is again detected, amplified, processed, and fed back to the subject, and so on.

Biofeedback procedures make it possible to speed up the rate at which relaxation can occur. With increased relaxation comes decreased anxiety, and both can result in reduced symptomatology. Biofeedback procedures are particularly helpful in conjunction with contingency management programs, specifically when symptoms are associated with muscular tension (Stroebel & Glueck, 1976; Weisenberg, 1977), and a number of studies have been reported indicating that biofeedback can have very positive consequences, particularly for pain reduction (see, for example, Nouwen & Solinger, 1979; Peck & Kraft, 1977; Sherman, Gall, & Gormly, 1979). The original biofeedback instrument has served as the prototype for other measurement and feedback devices that have since been developed for use in the modification of skin temperature, blood pressure, galvanic skin response, and brain waves.

Writings on the topic of biofeedback underwent a period of very rapid growth during the 1970s, followed by a leveling off or perhaps a slight decline in the 1980s. According to Hatch and Riley (1985) who made a careful search of the worldwide literature on the topic of biofeedback, there is some evidence that the slight decline in publications about biofeedback has been particularly evident in psychological journals, in books, in popular magazines, and in dissertations, but that the number of publications on the topic of biofeedback has shown no decline in medical journals. This level publication rate in medical journals may reflect the steady interest in the application of biofeedback to the treatment of medical disorders.

There is some clinical evidence that biofeedback procedures may need to be employed in conjunction with other procedures (Ford, 1982; Rickles,

Onoda, & Doyle, 1982). Indeed, biofeedback is rarely used alone, and according to Miller (1985) biofeedback is typically combined with "other techniques for inducing relaxation and with procedures for dealing with special problems, such as lack of assertiveness or fear of losing control, that are encountered during the treatment" (p. 5). Evaluating the effectiveness of biofeedback procedures is complicated by the fact that it is so frequently combined with other therapeutic interventions into a set of interacting interventions (Kewman & Roberts, 1983; Steiner & Dince, 1981, 1983). There is some growing sentiment that biofeedback has not lived up to its early promises, but this may be because those early promises were unrealistic, rather than because biofeedback procedures are not efficacious.

A particularly interesting aspect of biofeedback is that it may involve psychological processes that are antithetical to the processes that are involved in the case of hypnosis. Both Miller and Cross (1985) and Qualls and Sheehan (1981) in their studies of alternative approaches to the treatment of chronic pain have found that measures of hypnotizability are associated with differential response to hypnosis and biofeedback. Persons who demonstrate high hypnotizability are more helped by hypnosis than by biofeedback, while persons who demonstrate low hypnotizability are more helped by biofeedback than by hypnosis. Qualls and Sheehan (1981) have hypothesized that biofeedback procedures help people focus their attention, and thus are especially useful to people who are generally unable to concentrate in the ways thought necessary to be hypnotizable.

### Contingency Management Techniques

Perhaps the most systematic and well-specified procedure for modifying health behavior is what is generically referred to as *contingency management*. Using the fundamental principles of reinforcement and extinction that are derived from traditional conditioning theory, it has been found possible to facilitate those behaviors that are health-inducing and to discourage those behaviors that are illness-producing or illness-maintaining. Contingency management techniques are often used in conjunction with other forms of psychological intervention as part of multidimensional treatment programs.

The basic principles of reinforcement and extinction are simply stated. Behaviors that are reinforced tend to increase in their occurrence; behaviors that are extinguished, or negatively reinforced, tend to decrease in their occurrence. In order to develop a contingency management program for a given person, it is only necessary to determine: (1) what behaviors need to be increased or decreased in their frequency, or what goal needs to be attained; and (2) what consequences serve as effective reinforcers or extinguishers.

For example, Taylor, Pfenninger, and Candelaria (1980) were faced with the need to reduce the overutilization of medical services by a specific patient, in this case, the client was a 30-year-old separated woman with two children who had made 280 visits, including 146 emergency room visits, to 159 different members of a teaching hospital in a 13-year period; Taylor and associates developed a written contract with her. Initial analysis of her situation revealed that there were two health professionals—a family practice resident and a psychiatrist—she particularly liked among those whom she contacted from time to time. On the basis of this information, a contract, including both reinforcement and extinction contingencies, was written and agreed upon. The contract had a number of specifications including, for example:

1.  In exchange for a one-half hour appointment every other week with the family practice resident, during which time any problem could be discussed, the patient agreed to keep her appointment, follow instructions that she agreed to during the visit, and not call between visits.
2.  If the patient was 10 minutes late for her appointment, the appointment would be canceled and no appointment scheduled for 2 weeks.
3.  If the patient called the family practice resident between visits, the next appointment would be canceled.
4.  If the patient saw another physician without informing the family practice resident, except in the case of an emergency, the family practice resident would turn her over to that physician for all subsequent care.
5.  In exchange for going to lunch with the psychiatrist, the patient agreed to enroll in a high school diploma class and attend 80 percent of the classes for 2 months.

The results of the contractual procedure were quite remarkable, at least from the point of view of the medical care provider. Use of medical care dropped to about one-fifth of its initial level. Subsequently, during a trial period in which the contract was not enforced, use of medical services again increased to the initial precontract level. Unfortunately, no information was presented regarding the consequences of the contract mechanism from the point of view of the patient. The authors are sensitive, however, to the fact that the contract mechanism can be abused, particularly when psychosocial and medical system factors may be significantly responsible for the behavior that is thought to be inappropriate.

In another case, Alford, Blanchard, and Buckley (1972) developed a contingency management program for a 17-year-old girl who, for the past 10 years, had been vomiting immediately after meals, and who was being treated in an inpatient setting. The investigators hypothesized that social attention was reinforcing the behavior. As a consequence, after initial baseline measures were obtained, the patient was given six small meals each day in her room, and nurses who were with her when she ate were instructed to leave the room as soon as the vomiting took place. Within a very short time, the latency period between the time of eating and vomiting began to increase from its initial level of less than 15 minutes to 1 hour, after which time the vomiting seemed to disappear. Subsequently, the patient was returned to a normal three meal per day schedule in the dining room and began to eat in the presence of other patients who had been taught to ignore her should vomiting occur. Followup evidence, 7 months after the treatment ended, revealed that vomiting had occurred only once during that period.

### Modifying Cognitive Mediating Processes

Psychotherapeutic and educational procedures have been used for decades as part of the treatment of those medical disorders that have been thought to have a psychological origin, that is, the so-called psychosomatic disorders. More recently, psychotherapeutic intervention has been employed in order to reduce the overuse of medical services, to help patients cope with noxious or poorly understood medical or surgical procedures, and in rehabilitation (Olbrisch, 1977).

In view of the fact that responses to physical illness are mediated by cognitive processes, psychotherapy, particularly the varieties that lead to cognitive restructuring, has a potentially important role to play in the treatment of physical illnesses (Tolman & Rose, 1985). Among the best known forms of psychotherapy that are designed to change cognitive belief systems are Ellis' rational emotive therapy (Ellis, 1970, 1977), Beck's cognitive therapy (1963), and Meichenbaum's cognitive behavioral approach (1977). These approaches can change important aspects of belief systems that are the basis of negative physical reactions to emotional problems, can modify maladaptive thought patterns, and can reduce the extent to which patients make self-defeating statements.

Although there is little evidence that the use of psychotherapy in order to treat an illness by interpreting its psychodynamics is effective, there is growing evidence, as will be seen in the following, that brief psychotherapy can play a useful role in patient care. In addition, there is considerable evidence that a psychotherapeutic orientation to the physically ill patient can have substantial cost offset benefits. In other words, the cost of providing brief psychotherapeutic contacts with ill patients is more than offset by subsequent reductions in the use of medical care.

Cummings and Follette (Cummings, 1977a, 1977b, 1986; Cummings & Follette, 1968; Follette & Cummings, 1967) undertook a series of studies designed to investigate the role of psychotherapy in reducing medical care utilization in a prepaid health plan setting. They believed that clients often converted emotional problems into physical ones and thus overutilized medical facilities. They estimated that "60 percent or more of the physicians' visits are made by patients who demonstrate an emotional, rather than an organic, etiology for their physical symptoms" (Cummings, 1977a, p. 711). Among the groups they studied was a sample of eighty emotionally distressed patients who were assigned to receive a single psychotherapeutic interview. They found, totally unexpectedly, that one interview, with no repeat psychological visits, reduced medical utilization by 60 percent over the next 5 years, as a consequence of resolving the emotional distress that was being reflected in physical symptoms.

Other studies provide additional, equally startling findings. Goldberg, Krantz, and Locke (1970) studied the effects of short-term outpatient therapy on the utilization of medical services. Their sample consisted of 256 persons enrolled in the Group Health Association prepaid medical program in Washington, D. C., who had been referred and found eligible for and in need of outpatient psychiatric care. In the year following referral, this group showed an average reduction of 31 percent in physician visits and 30 percent in laboratory and x-ray visits from the previous year. But this reduction was independent of whether those referred for care had actually received it. In fact, the reduction in physician visits was 23 percent among those who had had ten or more sessions of psychotherapy and 30 percent among those who had had between one and nine sessions, but 39 percent among those who had had no psychotherapy at all.

Rosen and Wiens (1979) examined the same issue at the University of Oregon Health Sciences Center. Four groups of patients were compared: (1) those who received medical services but were not referred for psychological services; (2) those who were referred for psychological services but did not keep their scheduled appointments; (3) those who were referred for psychological services but received only an evaluation; and (4) those who were referred and who received both an evaluation and subsequent brief psychotherapy. Groups 1 and 2, that is, those who received no psychological services, showed no subsequent reduction in the utilization of medical care, including number of outpatient visits, emergency room visits, days of hospitalization, diagnostic procedures, and pharmaceutical prescriptions. Groups 3 and 4, those receiving only an evaluation or an evaluation and brief psychotherapy (averaging seven interviews), showed significant reduction in the utilization of medical care. The group receiving only the evaluation showed the most consistent reduction in, among other things, medical outpatient visits, pharmaceutical prescriptions, emergency room visits, and diagnostic services.

The one fact that links the findings of all these studies is that a single contact with a mental health professional, virtually regardless of its purpose, appears to have salutary consequences for physical well-being, as reflected by the use of medical care. It appears to make little difference whether that contact is designed to be primarily evaluative or therapeutic.

## SUMMARY

- While psychosocial aspects of a great many specific disorders have begun to be investigated, the five disorders that have attracted the greatest attention in the health psychology literature are chronic pain, heart disease, hypertension, cancer, and asthma.
- In discussing psychological aspects of specific illnesses, it is important to realize that all disorders have biological, psychological, and sociological

components and that there is no isomorphic relationship between specific disorders and specific personality types.

- Early psychosomaticists believed that there were a small number of disorders that were "psychosomatic," that is, that stood in a symbolic relationship to a very specific constellation of personality traits or experiences. While this belief is still prevalent among many health service providers, there is no evidence that it is true.

- Contemporary psychosomatic therapy holds that psychosocial factors play an important but nonspecific role in illness and that links between physical and psychological well-being are complex and omnidirectional.

- Contemporary psychosomatic theory is interested in the role of the physical and social environment in all illness and in how biological processes function interdependently with psychosocial phenomena in producing physical illness.

- Physical illnesses can be a powerful source of stress, and health psychologists are increasingly interested in reducing those stresses by assisting people to cope with illness.

- Psychologists have developed a wide variety of interventions designed to help people cope with illnesses and reduce their duration and associated disability.

- In thinking about psychological interventions in the case of illness, it is assumed that illness behavior is, in part, learned, and that therefore it can be unlearned, and that behavior and illness are linked together, that is, that illness can undesirably affect behavior and that behavior can lead to illness.

- Instituting psychological interventions in medical care settings usually requires changes in the setting that may be unusually difficult to achieve. Accordingly, it is important for social scientists who hope to become part of the medical care system to understand how hospitals and other medical settings operate and how effective interventions in those systems can be introduced.

- The effectiveness of any psychological intervention must be measured against the placebo effect, that is, the benefit that occurs from any medication or procedure that is unrelated to its pharmacology or other specific properties.

- Placebos appear to benefit patients by virtue of the fact that their administration causes the body to generate endorphins that reduce pain and generate euphoria.

- While empirical evaluation studies of the effectiveness of hypnosis have generally been methodologically weak, there is some evidence to suggest that hypnosis may be helpful in the treatment of skin disorders, headaches, and asthma.

- Interest in rest and relaxation as psychosocial treatment strategies has a long and respected history, particularly in Europe, where healing waters and other naturally occurring substances have long constituted part of the medical care armamentarium.

- A variety of more directed relaxation procedures has been in existence for more than 50 years, and there is considerable evidence that such procedures can have a remarkable effect on anxiety reduction and on the elimination of phobias and other symptoms.

- Unquestionably, the most carefully studied and evaluated form of relaxation is transcendental meditation, a procedure that has clearly demonstrated effectiveness in reducing the disability associated with a very wide variety of physical disorders.

- Biofeedback procedures are designed to help patients develop increased control over their physiological functioning and hence over the symptoms associated with certain illnesses. It is particularly helpful in enhancing stress management skills and in reducing anxiety.

- Traditional reinforcement-based learning theories have been used to develop contingency-management techniques for controlling illness behaviors.

- Brief psychotherapy, often as brief as a single interview, has been found to be remarkably helpful in assisting patients to cope with their illnesses and in reducing the costs of medical care.

# Psychosocial Aspects of Chronic Pain

# 9

## INTRODUCTION

Untold numbers of Americans suffer with chronic pain, a condition that is so severe that it immobilizes a million or more Americans on any given day (Roberts, 1981). As should not be surprising, the most common demand patients make of physicians is for the relief of pain (Black, 1975). More than 70 million office visits to physicians, representing more than 6 percent of all visits, were made in the 2-year period 1980–1981 with pain as the chief symptom (National Center for Health Statistics, 1984b). Pain relievers constitute 9 percent of all drugs prescribed in office practice (National Center for Health Statistics, 1983e; 1983g; 1985h). Chronic pain ranks among the most costly medical conditions not only in terms of expenditures for outpatient treatment and hospitalization, but also because of the large disability payments often made to people who are no longer able to work (Brena, 1978; Keefe, 1982; Roberts, 1981).

Not only is chronic pain common, but it is also one of the most difficult problems treated by the health service provider. Chronic pain imposes severe emotional, physical, economic, and social stress on patients, on their families, and on society, and is more common and much less effectively managed than acute pain. Because of its long-standing nature, chronic pain often results in

severe depression, narcotic or sedative dependence and tolerance, multiple surgical interventions, and a sense of hopelessness, helplessness, discouragement,
anger, loss of self-esteem, despair, and demoralization (Cohen, 1984; France et
al., 1986; Romano & Turner, 1985). These problems feed on each other and
often result in family stress and bitterness toward health service providers—and
ultimately, in a person who is thoroughly disabled.

The management of chronic pain is one of the most unrewarding tasks
of the physician. While acute pain (discussed in the next section), even though it
is anxiety-producing, can have certain beneficial effects, chronic pain, on the
other hand, is almost wholly negative in its effects. Unable to heal patients and
even to provide much relief, physicians are denied their most important sources
of professional satisfaction (National Center for Health Statistics, 1986g).

Chronic pain is associated with many different disorders, including arthritis, some malignancies, and degenerative spinal disc disease (Lichtenberg,
Swensen, & Skehan, 1986; Roberts, Bennett, & Smith, 1986); at the same time, it
is sufficiently independent of specific disorders to be thought of as a health-
related problem in its own right (Holden, 1979). As such, chronic pain has
attracted the attention of social scientists who are actively exploring psychosocial
aspects of its causes, prevention, and treatment.

Pain is, at one and the same time: (1) a subjective experience; (2) an
unpleasant stimulus; and (3) a form of self-protection (Bradley et al., 1981;
International Association for the Study of Pain, 1979; Sternbach, 1968). Pain
cannot be assessed in the same objective way that blood pressure or body temperature is measured. All pain is psychological, a subjective experience that is
virtually impossible to verify objectively (Pinkerton, Hughes, & Wenrich, 1982;
Weisenberg, 1977, 1980; Ziesat, 1981). Accordingly, in the study of pain, scientists either use self-reports as their principal dependent measures of interest, or
else study what is usually called *pain behavior,* that is, the observable behaviors
that are associated with self-reports of pain.

The expression of pain can have different significance to different people and can have different meanings to the same person at different times. Thus,
pain can mean "Don't hurt me," or "Help me," or "I don't have to go to work,"
or "I am being punished," or "I am a real man," or "I am still alive" (Weisenberg,
1977, 1980; Zborowski, 1969). A moment's reflection will demonstrate that these
six phrases are very different from each other from a psychological point of
view. The sensation of pain can signify hope or hopelessness, self-worth or
worthlessness, strength or weakness. Hence the importance of viewing pain in a
psychosocial context.

## DIMENSIONS OF PAIN

### Acute versus Chronic Pain

In considering the topic of pain, most writers make a number of important distinctions among types of pain. Perhaps most important, there is a distinction made between *acute* and *chronic* pain. Acute pain is ordinarily of biological

origin, and of short duration, and alerts a person that something is wrong with the body and that something needs to be done to alleviate the problem. Thus, acute pain has a beneficial aspect. In contrast, chronic pain is that pain that continues long after the person has been alerted, by which time the pain serves no further constructive purpose. Chronic pain begins when treatment procedures have not resulted in a significant reduction of pain associated with an acute episode. Chronic pain is persistent, and the label is usually not assigned until pain has lasted for 6 months or longer (Ziesat, 1981).

Thus, chronic pain always begins with acute pain. At some point in the history of a person's pain it can move from being acute and primarily the result of biological factors, to chronic and, hypothetically at least, increasingly the result of significant psychosocial factors.

According to Pinkerton, Hughes, and Wenrich (1982), acute and chronic pain differ in the nature of the anxiety they produce. In the case of acute pain, anxiety increases as pain intensity increases. When diagnosis and treatment are instituted, anxiety usually decreases. This reduction in anxiety is not only an indication that the treatment is effective, but also serves to reduce pain itself. In the case of chronic pain, however, the initial anxiety level persists and may, in addition, be supplemented by a growing sense of hopelessness and despair. Thus, acute pain may be thought of as an event, while chronic pain becomes a state of existence, a sometimes senseless, unending nightmare (LeShan, 1964).

Another reason for distinguishing between acute and chronic pain is that they differ in their responsivity to medication. The most effective remedies for acute pain (usually narcotics or analgesics) are usually not only ineffective for chronic pain, but they also commonly cause severe side effects, such as habituation, that further complicate its management (Melzack & Wall, 1983).

### Malignant versus Benign Pain

A second distinction that is made in the literature is between *malignant* and *benign* pain. Malignant pain is pain that is associated with a malignant disorder. This type of pain is common for between one-third and two-thirds of cancer patients, for example, depending on the stage of the disease. Pain associated with malignancies responds to a special set of treatment procedures, and the prevention and treatment of malignant pain constitutes a highly specialized field of its own. Benign pain, on the other hand, is unrelated to any malignant process. This distinction between benign and malignant pain is not to suggest, however, that benign pain is not severe, or that it has no biological basis. Indeed, benign pain may involve various forms of organic disease, and, as will be seen, can be very severe.

### Psychogenic versus Biogenic Pain

A third distinction in the literature of pain, made somewhat less commonly today than was the case a generation ago, is that between *psychogenic* and *biogenic* pain. Psychogenic pain, as its name suggests, is pain whose origin is thought of as primarily psychological; biogenic pain is that pain whose origin is thought of as primarily biological. The category of Psychogenic Pain Disorder appears in the current American Psychiatric Association Diagnostic and Statistical Manual of Mental Disorders (1980), where it is defined in terms of "a clinical picture in which the predominant feature is the complaint of pain, in the absence of adequate physical findings and in association with evidence of the etiological role of psychological factors" (p. 247). The concept of biogenic pain suggests that there will be pain only if there is a lesion. The concept of psychogenic pain suggests that there will be pain only if there is a reason (conscious or unconscious) for it.

The fundamental implication of this conception of psychogenic pain is that its relief requires psychological intervention. To put it another way, the concept of psychogenic pain requires that in trying to help a person in pain, one attend first to the person, and only second to the pain. Attending to the person rather than to the pain generally means that health psychologists will concentrate on helping patients so that they can find better alternatives to their suffering, if they choose to do so.

The concept of pain as caused primarily or solely by psychological factors (or primarily or solely by biological factors, for that matter) is contrary to contemporary thinking regarding health and illness; as Zlutnick and Taylor (1982) have recently commented, efforts to make such determinations can quickly degenerate into questions regarding the patient's integrity and reliability. Clinicians are frequently driven to wonder, for example, whether the patient is faking, or whether the patient is just a chronic complainer. Therefore, the issue becomes whether the pain is real or imaginary rather than how to best go about treating it (Szasz, 1968).

Paralleling the early history of psychosomatic medicine in which specific disorders were thought to have powerful symbolic relationships with specific personality traits or specific unresolved psychological conflicts, a generation ago there was literature on the symbolic nature of the symptom of pain. Thus, for example, Engel (1959) identified some of the possible psychogenic aspects of pain—pain could be a psychological warning or form of self-protection, or part of a dependent interpersonal relationship, or a way of punishing oneself and of relieving guilt, or a way of expressing aggression, or a way of internalizing a loved object when loss of that object is threatened, or part of a complex sexual experience, or the expression of an unconscious need to suffer, or a form of identification with an important person in the patient's psychic life (also see Pilowsky, 1978a).

Research evidence that has accumulated in the past two decades attempting to link pain as such with specific psychodynamic characteristics parallels the findings of the general psychosomatic literature. That is, the evidence of the symbolic nature of chronic pain is skimpy at best, there is little evidence that persons with different types of chronic pain differ significantly from each other in terms of personality characteristics, and there is little evidence that psychotherapeutic approaches specifically designed to control chronic pain are effective (see, for example, Andrasik et al., 1982).

While pain may not have specific symbolic functions, however, it is certainly a psychosocial as well as a biological phenomenon, and its reported severity depends very much on the context in which it occurs. For example, Beecher (1956) reported that in a sample of more than 200 men seriously wounded in battle, only 25 percent wanted pain-killing drugs. In the case of similar surgical wounds made under anesthesia in a group of 150 male civilians, more than 80 percent wanted drug relief. According to Beecher, the difference was due not to the nature of the tissue damage, but to the significance of the wound, that is, to what the pain meant to the patient. In battle, the wound meant survival, escape from overpowering anxiety and fear of death, and the end of military service; in civilian life, the surgery most often spelled disaster and was seen as a calamitous, depressing, and anxiety-provoking event. There is some additional evidence that a high level of hypochondriasis (being preoccupied with the fear or the belief of having a severe disease) is associated with a poor response to most forms of treatment designed to reduce the severity of chronic pain (Williams et al., 1986).

Pain is also a complex cultural phenomenon. Illich (1976), in his sociopolitical critique of the medical establishment, has commented that traditional cultures confront pain by interpreting it as a challenge to the individual to make it appropriately tolerable. Illich is not recommending that people go out of their way to find pain, of course, but rather is suggesting that in the process of learning to tolerate pain, individuals can develop patience, courage, forbearance, compassion, perseverance, and even resignation.

In contrast, according to Illich, modern medicine turns pain into a demand made by individuals on the medical community to have the problem managed out of existence. The medical establishment, treating pain as a technical matter, diminishes the uniquely human experience of suffering by depriving people of the opportunity to come to grips with its inherent personal meaning.

## THEORIES OF PAIN

Because acute and chronic pain are clinically and psychologically different from each other, the theories that have been proposed to account for their origins are now also different. Melzack and Wall (1983) have provided a very useful historical review of pain theories, with particular reference to their own gate-control theory.

The earliest theory of pain was developed by Descartes in the midseventeenth century. Descartes' theory was a form of specificity theory, a view of how pain occurs that still occupies a position of considerable importance in the medical literature. According to specificity theory, specific pain receptors in the skin or in other parts of the body sense pain and deliver messages regarding those sensations to the pain center in the brain. As can be seen, specificity theory is essentially a theory of acute pain.

Specificity theory remained largely unchanged for two hundred years until it became appropriate to take into account advances that were made in the seventeenth and eighteenth centuries in the understanding of central nervous system anatomy and physiology. In particular, a great deal had been learned regarding the nature of nerve impulses and the physiology of the cerebral cortex. As a consequence, nineteenth century pain theory held that nerve sensations were identical whether one was talking about vision or taste or pain, and that what made any of these sensations the special experience it was had to do with where the sensations ended up in the cortex of the brain. That is, there was a visual center in the cortex, a hearing center, a taste center, a pain center, and so on. Indeed, it was thought that if auditory nerves could be connected to the visual cortex and visual nerves connected to the auditory cortex, we would see thunder and hear lightning.

Specificity theory was further modified during the last half of the nineteenth century, and by the end of the century it had become even more complex—largely as a consequence of further advances in the understanding of the peripheral and central nervous systems. A variety of different types of nerve endings had been identified. Free nerve endings were discovered virtually everywhere in the upper layers of the skin that were thought to serve as pain receptors. Three other types of nerve endings were also identified and thought to be associated with the sensations of touch, cold, and warmth. In addition, studies of the central nervous system had concluded that the pain center was located in the thalamus (see Chapter 1).

It is now known that specificity theory is only partially correct. While the general formulation that postulates that there are skin receptors with specialized physiological properties is correct, it is clear that there is much greater variety in the nature of these receptors than was originally suggested. There are far more than four different types of skin receptors. Furthermore, sensations of pain are very imperfectly related to the body's physiological responses, and psychological factors play a very significant role in determining how people will react to sensations that originate in pain receptors.

A significant modification in the nature of pain theory began at the end of the nineteenth century and continued into the midtwentieth century. This revision focused on the concept of summation. According to this theory, sensations are transmitted from peripheral nervous system pain receptors to the spinal cord where they accumulate until they reach a critical level of intensity, at which time they are transmitted to the pain centers in the brain. Thus, pain is thought of as the end result of a special pattern of intense stimulation that begins in the peripheral nervous system and is modified in the spinal cord.

It has also been postulated that there is a specialized control system, probably located in the brain, that prevents summation from taking place, and that when this control system is destroyed, pathological chronic pain results. Furthermore, it has been postulated that pain sensations themselves are carried by nerves in which the speed of conduction is relatively slow, while the control system that prevents or delays summation is made up of rapidly conducting nerves. Damage to that rapid system results in chronic intractable pain.

The gate-control theory of pain, introduced by Melzack and Wall in 1965, represented a way of explaining how these psychological factors played a role in pain perception. Melzack and Wall postulated that a special set of nerve impulses that descend from the brain to the spinal cord serve to open and close a "gate" which, in turn, determines whether the sensation of pain is perceived.

Melzack and Wall have explored their gate-control theory for the past two decades, and their work continues to expand our understanding of pain and its vicissitudes. The experience of pain is far more complex than was originally thought when early forms of specificity theory were advanced, although that theory still is true for certain forms of acute pain.

As is invariably true with theories of this kind, at first more questions are raised than answered, but with continued investigation these questions slowly yield, even though the answers can often become highly technical. This is certainly the case with Melzack and Wall's gate-control theory; advances are described in their 1983 book, entitled *The Challenge of Pain,* with the full realization that there is much more that needs to be learned about exactly how sensations of pain are felt in the body.

## TYPES OF CHRONIC PAIN

Melzack (1973) has identified four major types of chronic pain on the basis of their original biogenic sources—phantom limb pain, causalgia, neuralgia, and posttraumatic pain syndromes. All four types share a common history: (1) they all begin as signals of bodily damage (that is, as acute pain); (2) they persist, spread, and increase in intensity over time so that they become illnesses in their own right; and (3) the pain may gradually become far more intense than was the case initially.

### Phantom Limb Pain

Phantom limb pain is pain that appears to originate in a limb that has been amputated—that is, in a so-called "phantom limb." Phantom limb pain is common and ultimately subsides and eventually disappears, usually within a year. But in about 10 percent of persons who have limb amputations, the pain persists and becomes worse with time. The bizarreness of phantom limb pain should not result in our thinking of the pain as trivial.

Phantom limb pain endures long after the injured tissue at the site of the amputation has healed and can spread to healthy tissue. It appears to be most common in people who have suffered pain in the limb prior to amputation and can sometimes be relieved by injections of local anesthetics in the site of the stump. Efforts to explain phantom limb pain have resulted in the somewhat unsatisfactory conclusion that it "cannot be satisfactorily explained by any single mechanism such as peripheral nerve irritation, abnormal sympathetic activity, or psychopathology" (Melzack, 1973, p. 60). All three levels of analysis interact in some way to produce the phenomenon.

### Causalgia

Causalgia, a term that means "burning pain," is a chronic severe pain that occurs after the infliction of bullet wounds or wounds caused by other high-velocity objects. The pain can be unrelenting and of very high intensity and has been called "the most terrible of all tortures which a nerve wound may inflict" (cited in Melzack, 1973, p. 61). Causalgia occurs in about 5 percent of cases of peripheral nerve injury and persists for 6 months or more in about 85 percent of cases. A year after the injury about 25 percent of people who complained about the pain initially still report pain.

As in the case of phantom limb pain, causalgia appears to have multiple interacting causes. Peripheral nerve surgery to remove the offending nerve endings is rarely successful. Two remedies appear to be of some help. First, as in the case of phantom limb pain, infusion of local anesthetics appears to be helpful well beyond the known duration of the anesthetic agent. Second, a slow program of training to tolerate sensory stimulation of the affected body part along with training to learn to reuse the limb, have been found to be helpful.

### Neuralgia

Neuralgic pain is pain that is severe and unremitting, caused by viral infections of the peripheral nerves, nerve degeneration associated with diabetes or other illnesses, or poor circulation. Almost any infection that affects peripheral nerves may cause neuralgia.

Neuralgia that is caused by viral infections has two other characteristics that are quite unusual. First, reaction to sensory stimulation is slow, with a marked delay in the onset of pain after stimulation. Second, contrary to the reaction in a non-neuralgic site, stimulation is cumulative so that mild heat applied to the site of the neuralgia will feel comfortable at first and gradually intensify in discomfort until it finally becomes unbearable.

Neuralgia is particularly common in older people, and is thought to be related to the loss of myelinated peripheral nerve fibers which tend to degenerate with aging. Surgical procedures rarely are successful in reducing this pain, in spite of the fact that the pain is associated with changes in the anatomical character of peripheral nerves. Changes in the central nervous system must also occur to help account for the cumulative reaction to stimulation, the delays in responding, and the persistence and spread of the pain.

### Posttraumatic Pain Syndromes

Related to neuralgia are posttraumatic pain syndromes that occur after accidents or other injuries. Both syndromes last far longer and are far more severe than would have been expected on the basis of the original infection or injury and tend to spread to neighboring tissues. The causes of posttraumatic pain syndromes are not known, but, as in the case of phantom limb pain and causalgia, local infiltrations of anesthetics are often helpful and sometimes permanently so.

In providing an overview of these four types of chronic pain, Melzack (1973) has identified three common features. First, the phenomena of summation (whereby gentle touch, for example, can trigger extreme pain if the stimulus persists), the delay between the stimulus and the resulting pain, the spread to surrounding tissues, and persistence all suggest that the central nervous system as well as the peripheral nervous system is involved in the pain. Second, chronic pain has multiple causes that are biopsychosocial in nature. Thus, strategies for the relief of chronic pain must be biopsychosocial as well. Third, surgical procedures are rarely successful in relieving chronic pain. From a biological point of view, local anesthetics seem most helpful. But clearly more research is needed, and as will be seen later in this chapter, psychologists have been very active and remarkably effective in relieving chronic pain that does not respond to medical procedures.

### Chronic Low Back Pain

Perhaps the most common form of posttraumatic pain is chronic low back pain. An estimated 80 percent of the general population suffer from back pain at some time in their lives, and the annual incidence of lower back pain is about 50 per 1000 persons. It has been estimated that more than 1 million Americans injure their backs every year and of these, some 65,000 become permanently disabled (Beals & Hickman, 1972; Dolce & Raczynski, 1985). A patient with low back pain who has been out of work for 6 months or longer has only a 50 percent chance of ever returning to work (Roberts, 1981). De Andrade (1978) believes that in the United States, in the 30–60 age group, low back pain is the single most costly illness in existence. Chronic low back pain results in the expenditure of billions of dollars each year and causes "incalculable damage on sufferers and their families" (Holden, 1979, p. 984).

Craig (1978) has suggested that there might be reason to suspect a familial factor in low back pain, since about 60 percent of low back pain patients report that at least one close family member suffers from the same or a similar condition. More data will be necessary to establish the familial factor, however, since if 80 percent of the general population suffers from back pain, the chances are that about 64 percent (.80 × .80) of any two people chosen at random would report suffering from back pain at some time in their lives.

Persons with chronic lower back pain constitute a large proportion of the cases at the more than 1000 pain treatment centers that currently exist in the United States (Stieg & Williams, 1983). On the physical side, chronic lower back pain is associated with spinal disc deformities, neoplasms, infectious diseases of the spine, and lesions of ligaments and muscles. In perhaps a majority of these cases, however, no discernible physical basis can be found for the pain (White & Gordon, 1982).

Efforts to identify personality attributes of low back pain patients that might be associated with the presence of organic lesions have not been successful. Freeman, Calsyn, and Louks (1976), for example, administered the Minnesota Multiphasic Personality Inventory to three groups of twelve patients each—an organic group (an organic disease process sufficient to account for the pain was found), a functional group (no organic basis for the pain could be found), and a mixed group (some organic basis for the pain was found, but not sufficient to account for the severity of the pain). Of the twenty-nine scales that were examined, only one significantly differentiated the three groups from each other. Obtaining only one significant finding out of twenty-nine statistical analyses could have occurred by chance so easily that ordinarily an investigator would not trust the specific finding. Attempts to sort the thirty-six patients into the three groups on the basis of MMPI scores yielded large numbers of false positives, and no attempt was made to replicate the sorting procedure on a new sample of patients.

Treatment success is so low in the case of back pain, that Sternbach, Wolf, Murphy, and Akeson (1973) have coined the term, "low-back losers" to describe these treatment failures. Raskind and Glover (1975) use the term, "low back derelict"—hardly any less pejorative. Such patients report back pain for months, are unable to work, receive some form of disability compensation, and continue to search for relief even after numerous surgical failures. Studies have been undertaken to identify psychological factors that seem predictive of good outcome following surgical intervention for low back pain, and in a recent study of coping strategies, only the measure of self-reliance contributed to the ability to predict outcome following a laminectomy (Gross, 1986). There is no reason to think that the relationship between higher self-reliance and better surgical outcome is limited to back surgery, of course.

Lower back pain has most recently been viewed as the result of abnormal neuromuscular activity. Three etiological theories of this abnormal neuromuscular activity are most prevalent in the study of chronic lower back pain— physical stressors, psychosocial stressors, and biomechanical stressors (Dolce & Raczynski, 1985).

The physical stressor theory attributes chronic lower back pain to some organic or mechanical stressor that triggers painful muscle spasms (Kelsey & Ostfeld, 1975). The psychosocial stressor theory attributes this pain to increased muscle activity due to ineffective coping with stress. The biomechanical theory attributes pain to asymmetrical and abnormally low levels of neuromuscular activity of the back muscles. The theories are clearly not mutually exclusive.

Paralleling this recently increased understanding of muscular activity of the back has been the development of specific biofeedback treatment programs designed to sensitize patients to the neuromuscular activity that is taking place in their backs. These studies have yielded mixed results, in part because there is an imperfect relationship between measured neuromuscular activity and pain. Thus, some treatment programs have yielded modifications in neuromuscular activity but not in pain. The results of biofeedback studies have been encouraging, however, and increases in their effectiveness can undoubtedly be expected as more precise measures of muscular activity are taken, resulting in the establishment of more precise biofeedback program objectives (see, for example, Nouwen & Solinger, 1979).

## SOCIOCULTURAL ASPECTS OF PAIN

There is a substantial literature examining cultural differences in the experience and management of pain. As of 1968, however, when Wolff and Langley prepared a review of the literature that had been reported prior to that time, the basic question of whether there were ethnocultural differences in the experience of pain had not yet been satisfactorily answered. Wolff and Langley suggested that there were very few controlled studies and that those that had appeared yielded equivocal findings. Indeed, even among studies reported since that review, authors have been invariably tentative in their interpretations of their data.

For example, Zola (1966) contrasted a group of eighty-one Irish and sixty-three Italians who lived in Boston and who were new admissions to the Massachusetts Eye and Ear Infirmary and to the eye, ear, nose, and throat and medical clinics of the Massachusetts General Hospital. A number of differences between the two ethnic groups were found. Italians, for example, complained of pain significantly more often than did the Irish. Italians had significantly more presenting complaints upon admission and significantly more complaints of a diffuse nature than did the Irish. Zola speculated that Italian and Irish ways of communicating illness reflected traditional ways of handling problems within the culture. Italians, according to Zola, are generally thought of as expansive, expressive, and dramatic. In contrast, the Irish tend to survive by ignoring problems and denying their significance, and by tolerating suffering.

Sternbach and Tursky (1965; Tursky & Sternbach, 1967) contrasted four groups of housewives—Americans of British descent, native-born Italians, Jews, and Irish—in terms of their responses to electric shock in a laboratory situation and their attitudes toward pain as reflected in standardized interviews. There were fifteen women in each group. Significant differences were found in some aspects of their reactions to shock. British housewives adapted more quickly to shock; Italian housewives had lower thresholds for tolerable shock intensity; and Irish housewives reported more anxiety and greater unwillingness to express it. In general, British housewives tended to have a matter-of-fact orientation toward pain, Jewish housewives were unduly concerned about the significance of their reactions to pain, Italian housewives expressed a desire for pain relief, and the Irish housewives tended to inhibit their expression of pain. These findings were thought to be consistent with fundamental cultural norms.

In a more extended study of cultural differences in response to pain, Zborowski (1969) conducted a structured interview with 146 men who were patients at the Veterans Administration Hospital in the Bronx, New York. These men were grouped according to their ethnicity—approximately equally divided among Anglo-Saxon Old Americans, Irish, Italians, and Jews.

A number of significant ethnic differences were found which were remarkably consistent with the findings reported in the earlier studies just reviewed. For example, Jewish and Italian patients tended to be more emotional than the Anglo-Saxon Old Americans or the Irish, and less specific in their descriptions of pain. Jews and Italians tended to consult physicians more quickly and yet to be more apprehensive about physicians than either Anglo-Saxon Old Americans or Irish patients.

In spite of the ethnic differences found in this study, the nature of the illness was substantially more important in affecting patients' responses to the interview than was ethnic group membership. In order to examine the independent effects of ethnic group, Zborowski selected all patients suffering from herniated discs and backache and examined ethnic group differences within this diagnostic subgroup. He found that the Italian and Jewish patients showed their pain more than did the Irish and Anglo-Saxon Old Americans. Along with the major role played by the specific pathology in influencing response to pain, Zborowski found that the cultural background of the patient had an important, if not determining, role in shaping his behavior in pain and illness (also see Johnson & Rice, 1974; Marbach & Lipton, 1978; Weisenberg, Kreindler, Schachat, & Werboff, 1975).

Studies of ethnic group differences in pain perception and in pain management have become less common in recent years. The studies that have been reported here were published in the 1960s and early 1970s and are reasonably representative of studies conducted at that time. These studies tend to show, in general, that a small proportion of the variance in pain-related behavior can be accounted for on the basis of ethnic or racial group membership, but that the nature of the illness, on the one hand, and individual differences, on the other hand, are more powerful predictors of reactions to pain. Accordingly, while it is important to sensitize health service providers to ethnic differences that may be significant in determining how their patients react to health care and the health service delivery system, it is apparently unlikely that additional research will add substantially to our ability to control pain by attending to these ethnic and cultural issues.

In more recent years, increasing attention has been paid to how societal factors seem to perpetuate pain, particularly chronic pain. Chronic pain develops and is perpetuated by processes that have a clear psychosocial component. Cohen (1984) has identified three major perpetuating factors including: (1) a medical and legal system that provides strong incentives for the persistence of pain—mainly by providing financial rewards for its continuation; (2) secondary gain from the disability associated with chronic pain including increased availability of social support, more satisfying meeting of dependency needs, and liberation from the need to solve other difficult life problems; and (3) a cycle of events in which medical or surgical treatments that are designed to relieve the chronic pain produce side effects that serve to intensify and perpetuate the pain (also see Brena, 1978).

Stieg and Williams (1983) have similarly identified a number of societal factors that increase the number of chronic pain patients—"the medical profession itself . . . , changing family roles, economic stress with rising unemployment, reduction of individual buying power, and a welfare and disability system that increasingly appears to reward illness rather than health" (p. 372; also see Fordyce, 1985).

## DEMOGRAPHIC AND PERSONALITY ASPECTS OF PAIN

The reaction to pain varies with a number of different demographic factors, although again the relationships tend to be quite limited (Weisenberg, 1977). In the case of gender, wherever significant differences have been found, women tend to show lower pain threshold and pain tolerance than men in the laboratory as well as in the clinical setting. In many studies, however, gender differences in reactions to pain are small and insignificant. Pain threshold appears to increase slightly with age.

Tolerance for pain has been found to be significantly positively correlated with extroversion and negatively correlated with neuroticism in laboratory studies. That is, higher tolerance for pain is associated with higher extroversion and with lower neuroticism. In addition, tolerance for pain is greater among people who practice a certain amount of self-deception as a defensive style (Jamner & Schwartz, 1986). Among a clinical population, level of pain has been found to be significantly correlated with neuroticism—as neuroticism increases, so does pain. Pain is found as a symptom in about half of psychiatric patients, most commonly among patients with a diagnosis of anxiety disorders or hysteria (Merskey, 1978; Weisenberg, 1980).

Other personality traits have also been identified that appear to have some relationship to pain tolerance. Psychologists who study personality have, for example, identified some people, called *augmenters,* who characteristically show a tendency to perceive stimulation as greater than it really is, and *reducers,* who characteristically perceive stimulation as less powerful than it really is. Reducers have been found able to tolerate more pain in laboratory experiments. Another personality dimension that has been identified is the *coper-avoider* continuum. Copers tend to respond to pain by dealing with it directly. Avoiders tend to deal with pain by denial and avoidance. Copers who are given a good deal of specific information about their medical conditions tend to improve more rapidly than those who are not provided with this information. Avoiders, on the other hand, tend to do more poorly when provided with detailed information about their conditions than when provided with general nonspecific information (Goldstein, 1973; Weisenberg, 1977; also see Bradley et al., 1981; Pilowsky, 1978a; Szasz, 1968; Woodforde & Merskey, 1972).

## MEASUREMENT OF PAIN

Pain is investigated in two settings—the laboratory and the clinic. In the laboratory, where pain has been produced chemically, mechanically, electrically, and thermally, pain can be measured by using traditional psychophysical methods (see the following discussion). In the clinic, pain already exists, and its measurement is, in some ways, more complex (Wolff, 1978). In either setting, the laboratory or the clinic, measurement implies quantification. The ability to assign numbers to represent the magnitude of pain is the first step toward its scientific study (Chapman, 1976; Tursky, 1976).

While there are some similarities between laboratory pain and clinical pain, they are remarkably different in a number of important ways. Clinical pain usually includes a strong sense of anxiety associated with the threat of death or disability. In the laboratory, this sense of anxiety is missing. In addition, as Weisenberg (1977), among others, has noted, while morphine is very effective in reducing pain in the clinic, it is almost completely ineffective in reducing pain generated in the laboratory. Similarly, placebos are effective in reducing pain in about 35 percent of cases seen in the clinic, but only in about 3 percent of cases of pain generated in the laboratory.

### Measurement of Pain in the Laboratory

In the case of the laboratory study of pain, two different measurements have been identified—*pain threshold* and *pain tolerance*. Pain threshold refers to the point at which an individual first perceives a stimulus as painful. Pain tolerance refers to the point at which an individual is not willing to accept painful stimulation of a higher magnitude or to continue to endure stimulation at a given level of intensity. The difference between these two measures identifies what is usually called the *pain sensitivity range*.

Beecher (1968) has provided a splendid case history of the first 20 years of investigation in the anesthesia laboratory at Harvard Medical School. This work has put the study of pain on a firm scientific foundation. The principal interest of this group was the study of the effectiveness of various pain relievers both among clinical patients and in the laboratory.

The clinical pain that was studied by this group was postsurgical, that is, pain associated with postoperative wounds. This group was able to show that the pain-relieving power of varying doses of morphine could be accurately assessed, and that postoperative patients could easily distinguish between morphine, aspirin, and a placebo on the basis of their differential pain-relieving power.

In the laboratory, this group of investigators had initially induced pain by the use of radiant heat. But surprisingly, they found that study subjects were unable to distinguish between large doses of morphine and placebos in terms of their effects upon pain threshold or pain tolerance. Later, they tried to induce pain by the use of a tourniquet around the arm. In this case too, neither pain threshold nor pain tolerance was reliably influenced by the use of pain relievers. Finally, they were able to develop a laboratory method for the creation of pain that was more similar to clinical pain in its sensitivity to analgesics.

This method, called the submaximum effort tourniquet technique, produced pain by having the subject squeeze a hand exerciser twenty times after a tourniquet had been inflated around his upper arm. This form of pain simulated more successfully the duration and severity of clinical pain, and the investigators were able to show that administration of pain relievers had predictable and dependable effects on that pain. Furthermore, they also were able to show the presence of dose-response curves, that is, as the amount of analgesic that was administered was increased, the greater was the reported relief of pain. Thus, a laboratory method was found for the production of pain that gave the same results as had been consistently found in the clinic. The drug morphine, for example, that virtually always relieves clinical pain, was found to relieve laboratory pain as well. Yet this apparently simple task of finding a laboratory-generated form of pain that would simulate clinical pain in its response to pain-relieving drugs took nearly two decades of work.

### Measurement of Clinical Pain

In the case of clinical pain, where pain already exists and need not be artificially induced, the measurement of pain is quite different. Fordyce and Steger (1979) distinguish among pain—a sensation; suffering—a negatively toned feeling state; and pain behavior—the visible manifestations of the problem. It is difficult to assess pain or suffering, except by self-report. Pain behavior can, of course, be operationally defined, but it is important for clinicians to keep in mind that they are assessing pain behavior rather than the sensation of pain. The phenomena of pain, suffering, and pain behaviors are undoubtedly imperfectly correlated, particularly in the case of chronic pain.

In the clinical setting, level of pain is most commonly assessed by self-report. These reports are obtained by asking the patient how much it hurts and what the pain feels like. Chapman (1976) makes an important distinction between the terms "measurement" and "estimation." Asking individuals to estimate their weight is very different from weighing those individuals, since estimates are subject to a wide variety of errors. In the case of pain, unfortunately, investigators are limited, by and large, to estimates rather than measures. Clinicians are also becoming increasingly accustomed to determining attitudes toward pain and toward illness in general as part of their assessment of the patient. A number of self-report measures have been developed in the past 15 years for the assessment of pain (see, for example, Black & Chapman 1976; Leavitt, Garron, D'Angelo, & McNeill, 1979). We will examine two of these measures in some detail. As will be seen, the measures are very different from each other in almost every respect, although both are very useful in assessing the subjective qualities of experienced pain.

THE MCGILL PAIN QUESTIONNAIRE.    The McGill Pain Questionnaire (Agnew & Merskey, 1976; Dubuisson & Melzack, 1976; Hunter, Philips, & Rachman, 1979; McCreary, Turner, & Dawson, 1981; Melzack, 1975a; Melzack & Perry, 1975; Melzack & Torgerson, 1971; Van Buren & Kleinknecht, 1979) is designed to allow patients to provide a qualitative systematic description of their pain. The McGill Pain Questionnaire begins with the assumption that pain is a complex, multidimensional concept that cannot be completely assessed by any single variable such as intensity.

As is the case with most test instruments, the McGill Pain Questionnaire has gone through a number of revisions. In essence, however, a list of words is provided to patients, who are asked to circle those words that accurately reflect what their pain feels like. The words are grouped conceptually into three major categories: (1) sensory (such as "throbbing," "shooting," "stabbing," "pinching," "cramping," "wrenching," "burning," "tingling," or "dull"); (2) affective (such as "exhausting," "terrifying," "cruel," "blinding," or "vicious"); and (3) evaluative (such as "excruciating," "annoying," "intense," or "unbearable"). In addition, three other dimensions of pain are assessed: (4) constancy (such as "continuous," or "steady"); (5) rhythmicity (such as "periodic," or "intermittent"); and (6) transience (such as "brief," or "momentary"). The questionnaire can be completed in a few minutes.

A number of different studies have been reported using this scale. First, Melzack and Torgerson (1971) were able to show that there was considerable agreement among patients, physicians, and students as to the level of intensity associated with each of the terms used in the scale. Intensity levels, ranging from 1 = mild to 5 = worst, were assigned to each of the descriptive terms, and Melzack and Torgerson were able to report that while there were small differences in actual scale values among the three groups of judges, there was considerable agreement as to the positions of the words in relation to each other.

Thus, for example, in the sensory dimension, the order of intensity for words denoting thermal properties of the pain was: (1) "hot," (2) "burning," (3) "scalding," and (4) "searing." The order of intensity for words denoting temporal properties of the pain was: (1) "flickering," (2) "quivering," (3) "pulsing," (4) "throbbing," (5) "beating," and (6) "pounding." The order of intensity in the affective dimension for words denoting the punishing qualities of the pain was: (1) "punishing," (2) "grueling," (3) "cruel," (4) "vicious," and (5) "killing."

In another study, Dubuisson and Melzack (1976) administered the McGill Pain Questionnaire to ninety-five patients who were grouped by diagnoses—menstrual pain, arthritis, labor pain, degenerative disc disease, toothache, metastatic carcinoma, phantom limb pain, and postherpetic neuralgia. Using a complex statistical analysis of the 102 terms, the authors were able to show that the quality of the pain was significantly different among each of the diagnostic groups. Thus, for example, the most common terms used by the menstrual pain group in describing their pain were "constant," "sickening," "tiring," "cramping," and "aching." In contrast, the most common terms used by the labor pain group were "rhythmic," "cramping," "sharp," "intense," "shooting," "aching," and "exhausting." (Also see Crockett, Prkachin, Craig, & Greenstein, 1986; McCreary, Turner, & Dawson, 1981; Van Buren & Kleinknecht, 1979).

THE ILLNESS BEHAVIOR QUESTIONNAIRE.  The Illness Behavior Questionnaire (Pilowsky, 1978b; Pilowsky & Spence, 1975, 1976a, 1976b, 1976c) was developed at the University of Washington School of Medicine and consists of fifty-two questions regarding illness behavior and reactions to illness that are answered either "Yes" or "No." Pilowsky and Spence (1975) describe the purposes of the questionnaire in the following words: "The questions are largely not concerned with the presence or absence of physical symptoms. They deal instead with the patient's attitudes and feelings about his illness, his perception of the reactions of significant others in the environment (including his doctor's) to himself and his illness, and the patient's own view of his current psychosocial situation" (p. 281). The questionnaire can be self-administered and takes but a few minutes to complete.

In their first study, Pilowsky and Spence (1975; Pilowsky, Chapman, & Bonica, 1977) administered the questionnaire to 100 patients who were referred to their clinic because of chronic intractable pain; the researchers were able to show that answers to many of the items provided by these patients clustered together to form factors. A total of seven factors, involving thirty-one of the fifty-two items, were identified. For example, the most powerful factor, labeled "general hypochondriasis" factor, included nine items. (Sample question: If you feel ill and someone tells you that you are looking better, do you become annoyed? Answer: Yes.) Answers to these nine items tended to be highly correlated. That is, people who answered one of these items "Yes" tended to answer most of the rest of the items "Yes." Similarly, people who answered one of these items "No" tended to answer most of the rest of the items "No." Thus, a score on the general hypochondriasis factor that would range from 0 to 9 could be calculated by simply adding the number of "Yes" answers to these nine questions.

The six other factors were all less powerful, but each was named and scored in a similar manner as was the first factor. The other factors were named: "disease conviction with somatic preoccupation" (Sample question: Do you think there is something seriously wrong with your body? Answer: Yes); "psychological versus somatic perception of illness" (Sample question: Do you ever think of your illness as a punishment for something you have done wrong in the past? Answer: Yes); "affective inhibition" (Sample question: Can you express your personal feelings easily to other people? Answer: No); "affective disturbance" (Sample question: Do you have trouble with your nerves? Answer: Yes); "denial" (Sample question: Except for your illness, do you have any problems in your life: Answer: No); and "irritability" (Sample question: Are you easy to get on with when you are ill? Answer: No). Finally, the 100 chronic pain patients were grouped according to their pattern of scores on the seven factors. This analysis revealed that chronic pain patients were not all alike in their reactions to their pain. Some patients, for example, were quite realistic and were dealing with their pain without any undue difficulty, while other patients were preoccupied with their symptoms, were angry, depressed, and discouraged.

In a second study, Pilowsky and Spence (1976a) contrasted factor scores obtained by the original group of 100 intractable pain patients with scores obtained by a group of 40 patients who were attending the rheumatology, radiotherapy, pulmonary, and physiotherapy clinics, all of whom answered "Yes" to the question, "Do you experience a lot of pain with your illness?" These latter patients were all thought of as having symptoms of pain that were appropriate to their illnesses. Comparison of the factor scores in the two groups of patients revealed that patients in the intractable pain group obtained significantly higher scores on the disease conviction factor than did patients in the comparison group. Patients with intractable pain were more convinced that they had a real disease, were more preoccupied about their body functioning, and were significantly less able to accept reassurance from the physician than were the comparison group of patients. The authors concluded that this pattern of nonacceptance of reassurance, somatic preoccupation, and need to emphasize a conviction of disease may signify the presence of a maladaptive illness behavior syndrome.

In a later study, Pilowsky, Chapman, and Bonica (1977) contrasted another group of patients with intractable chronic pain with an unselected sample of seventy-eight patients who attended the family medicine clinic at the University of Washington Hospital. Both groups of patients were administered the Illness Behavior Questionnaire, and, in addition, the chronic pain group completed a scale that measured depression. The two groups differed significantly on three of the seven scales—disease conviction, psychologic versus somatic perception, and denial. Pain clinic patients showed greater conviction that a disease was present and greater somatic preoccupation, were more reluctant to consider their problems in psychological terms, and were more likely to deny life problems not directly related to disease. In addition, depression scores were significantly related to four of the seven factor scores on the Illness Behavior Questionnaire—general hypochondriases, disease conviction, affective disturbance, and irritability. These findings suggested to Pilowsky and associates that many chronic intractable pain patients appeared to be manifesting abnormal illness behavior characterized by an excessive preoccupation with their symptoms combined with a pathological level of depression. Under these circumstances, a total psychological, social, and physical evaluation of these patients appeared necessary, and collaborative, interdisciplinary efforts were thought to be needed in the effective management of these patients (also see Keefe et al., 1986).

## PSYCHOSOCIAL APPROACHES IN REDUCING CHRONIC PAIN

We have already seen that in some circumstances, physiological intervention can be of significant help in reducing the discomfort associated with chronic pain. Thus, for example, local infiltration with analgesics and anesthetics seem very promising in the treatment of phantom limb pain. Acupuncture treatment for chronic pain has been reported, although with only limited success (Hossenlopp, Leiber, & Mo, 1976; Kepes, Chen, & Schapira, 1976). Chronic pain has a neurophysiological foundation (Melzack, 1973; Melzack & Dennis, 1978), and, happily, pharmaceutical treatments are often successful in relieving the pain (Cannon, Liebeskind, & Frenk, 1978). Patients with chronic pain are usually referred for psychological treatment following the failure of medical or surgical treatment to attain long-term positive results, or following the decision that such treatments are unsuitable or unlikely to succeed.

Treatment programs that use basic learning theory principles of operant conditioning in contingency management of persons with chronic pain begin by distinguishing between pain *behavior* and well *behavior*. Both forms of behavior are, by definition, observable, in contrast to pain, which is not. Pain behavior includes taking medication, refusing to work, seeking health care, complaining about pain, remaining inactive and bedridden, and so forth. Well behavior is essentially the opposite of pain behavior and includes increased activity level, reduced use of medication and health care services, and reduced expression of symptoms of pain.

Contingency management programs begin with a set of simple principles:

1.  Pain is unobservable. Only pain behavior is observable, and contingency management programs are designed to reduce pain behavior.
2.  Pain behavior can be both a response to an environmental stimulus and a cause of environmental change. For example, environmental demands or frustrations can cause an increase in pain behavior; increased pain behavior can cause increased attention of others or reduced demands on the patient by the outside world.
3.  Increased pain behavior can also be produced by punishment of well behavior. Thus, for example, a patient's efforts to reduce dependence on medication can be unconsciously discouraged by family members, which can, in turn, result in increased pain behavior.
4.  Contingency management programs, then, are designed to exercise control over the environment as well as the patient in order to encourage the increased expression of well behavior and decreased expression of pain behavior on the part of the patient.

These objectives are generally achieved by teaching persons in the environment to reinforce well behaviors and to withdraw reinforcement from pain behaviors (Bradley, 1981; Zlutnick & Taylor, 1982, pp. 276–279).

The earliest studies of contingency management programs with patients suffering from chronic pain were conducted by Fordyce (Fordyce, 1976, 1978; Fordyce & Steger, 1979). These programs were conducted in an inpatient setting, and early results appeared quite favorable. Specifically, Fordyce identified a sample of thirty-six patients who had complained of pain for over 9 months, who had not worked for more than 3 years, and who had had an average of three surgical procedures because of pain. These patients were then hospitalized between 4 and 12 weeks (average length of hospitalization was 7.7 weeks) in a contingency management program followed by an average of 3 weeks of subsequent outpatient treatment. Evaluation of the program indicated that there was a significant increase in well behavior (such as, time spent out of bed, standing, walking, exercising) and a significant decrease in pain behavior (such as, reduced medication intake). Followup data, collected nearly 2 years later, indicated that the gains were generally maintained.

The program that was instituted by Fordyce and associates had three components that followed directly from the contingency management principles identified above. First, nursing staff and family members were taught to withhold social reinforcement of pain behavior. Second, staff and family members were taught to reinforce well behavior, by providing attention and praise. Third, the specific reinforcing value of medication was reduced by providing medication (in the form of a "pain cocktail"—a liquid containing gradually reduced amounts of active medications) on a time schedule, rather than on demand. That is, medication was provided every 4 hours, for example, rather than when the patient reported pain (Fordyce & Steger, 1979; Keefe, 1982).

A large number of similar programs are now in existence, all generally patterned after the original Fordyce contingency management program (see Pinkerton, Hughes, & Wenrich, 1982, pp. 269–272), although the Fordyce approach has not escaped criticism. Melzack and Wall (1983), in reviewing the Fordyce contingency management strategy, have raised a number of cautionary questions. First, while contingency management programs seem to reduce the frequency of pain behavior, it is not at all clear that such programs have reduced the experience of pain. Second, Melzack and Wall (1983) believe that a persuasive case has not yet been made that contingency management programs are superior to other types of pain control programs, partly because of methodological inadequacies in much research. They mention, for example, the chronic absence of control or comparison groups in much of the research, and the high level of selectivity in the choice of participants in such studies combined with the high subject loss during followup studies that severely lower the confidence that one can have in the research results. Third, they are concerned about the cost of contingency management programs and about the issue of cost-benefit. That is, such programs involve relatively long periods of hospitalization and are thus extremely expensive.

Another approach to helping a patient with chronic pain is to help the patient relax, a strategy that can have significant influence on reducing the level of pain. To the extent that tension and stress can be reduced, a drop in anxiety level and an increase in pain tolerance can be anticipated (Guck, 1984). Chronic pain patients can be taught to relax in a variety of ways, including counterconditioning through biofeedback (Christidis, Ince, Zaretsky, & Pitchford, 1986), systematic desensitization (Wolpe, 1969), and hypnosis (McGlashan, Evans, & Orne, 1969; Orne, 1976; Thompson, 1976). Another technique that is commonly used is to modify how patients think about their pain, using such procedures as cognitive rehearsal (Folkins, Lawson, Opton, & Lazarus, 1968; Sherman, Gall, & Gormly, 1979; Taylor, Zlutnick, Corley, & Flora, 1980; Varni, 1981a, 1981b; Varni, Gilbert, & Dietrich, 1981), and social modeling (Craig, 1978), both of which can help patients anticipate pain and prepare for its arrival and for their reactions to it. What is important about all of these procedures is that they are ultimately a form of self-control; as such they do not need the active participation of professional health care providers such as biofeedback specialists and the use of special health care settings.

Most treatment programs that attempt to modify the stimulus properties related to chronic pain tend to include more than one component. For example, Gottlieb and associates (1977) established a comprehensive self-regulation treatment program using a sample of seventy-two patients with chronic back pain. The patients, whose average age was 43, had been disabled an average of 3.6 years, and had already undergone an average of two surgical procedures in an effort to treat their chronic low back pain. Neither surgery nor traditional conservative management approaches had been helpful either in rehabilitating these patients or in providing them relief from pain.

The program included biofeedback training for muscle relaxation, psychological counseling, patient-regulated medication, case conferences, physical therapy, vocational rehabilitation, educational information, and the creation of a therapeutic milieu. The program lasted an average of 45 days, and fifty of the seventy-two patients were judged to have achieved maximum benefits from the program.

A substantial number improved significantly in terms of functional performance and clinical assessment at the conclusion of the program and at the time of a 1-month followup examination. In spite of the fact that none of the patients in this study were employed at the start of the program, most were maintaining a successful level of vocational restoration at the time of the followup; and, in a subsample of twenty-three of the fifty people who completed the program who were contacted 6 months later, most were still either employed or in training.

Turk, Meichenbaum, and Berman (1979) recently reviewed the literature on the use of biofeedback procedures for the regulation of pain, including tension headache and migraine headache. Tension headache is muscular in origin, while migraine appears to be vascular in nature. Blanchard and Andrasik (1982) examined the recent developments in psychological treatment of headache pain. Their two sets of conclusions are very similar. In the case of tension headaches, biofeedback procedures appear to be helpful in reducing pain, but they are no more effective than a variety of other generally less-expensive procedures, including relaxation training and the use of placebos. In the case of migraine headaches, a disorder thought to be due to excessive vasodilation and blood flow in arteries in the head, a wide variety of medications have been found to produce vasoconstriction and to provide relief from migraine, particularly when taken early. The theory that appears most persuasive linking migraine and biofeedback has to do with peripheral temperature. It is thought that if peripheral temperature can be increased, blood flow will increase in the periphery and decrease in the cranial region. Accordingly, a number of studies have sought to treat migraine by using biofeedback procedures to increase peripheral temperature, particularly in the fingers. Evaluation of biofeedback procedures indicates that they are helpful, although there is some debate in the literature whether they are more helpful than less-expensive medications or than the use of relaxation training or placebos (Blanchard et al., 1985; Daly, Donn, Galliher, & Zimmerman, 1983; Turk, Meichenbaum, & Berman, 1979).

A number of other relatively new studies have also shown a high level of equivalence of various approaches (particularly biofeedback and relaxation training) to the treatment of various forms of chronic pain (see, for example, Blanchard et al., 1986). Furthermore, there is some evidence that biofeedback training is effective even when the feedback is manipulated so that it bears an inaccurate relationship to actual changes in muscle activity, as long as the patients are informed that they are achieving a high level of success in manipulating their own physiological functioning (see, for example, Holroyd et al., 1984). These findings have led Blanchard and Andrasik (1982) to advance the ultimate psychosocial hypothesis, namely, that through treatment, patients become sensitive to the factors that precede pain and with feedback reports that serve to increase their confidence, they become more able to control their reactions. As a consequence, their sense of self-efficacy increases (whether or not there is any truth to the feedback reports), which, in turn, allows them to attempt new approaches to coping with pain.

In spite of the considerable attention being given in the mass media to the use of biofeedback, particularly in the regulation of pain, and in spite of occasional positive results of such programs (see, for example, McGrady, Bernal, Fine, & Woerner, 1983), Turk and his colleagues suggest that support for its widely acclaimed benefits is lacking. By way of summary, they suggest that the subtitle of Melzack's (1975b) earlier review of the literature on biofeedback approaches to chronic pain—"Don't Hold the Party Yet"—should be taken seriously.

### Description of a Pain Control Program

As was mentioned earlier, many, if not most, pain control centers use a multimodal approach to pain reduction, that is, a combination of contingency management with some form of relaxation or desensitization, plus some form of psychotherapy with the patient and family members. While the use of such multimodal programs makes it difficult to evaluate the individual components of the program, there is a general belief that a multidimensional program is superior to any one program component alone.

A number of different pain control programs have been described in the literature, including the program at the University of Washington School of Medicine (Bonica, 1976; Fordyce, 1976); the Pain Rehabilitation Center in La-Crosse, Wisconsin (Shealy & Shealy, 1976); the Division of Behavioral Medicine in the Department of Psychiatry at the University of Utah Medical Center (Corley & Zlutnick, 1981); the Portland Pain Center in Oregon (Newman, Seres,

Yospe, & Garlington, 1978; Seres & Newman, 1976); the Rancho Los Amigos Hospital in Downey, California (Cairns, Thomas, Mooney, & Pace, 1976); and Casa Colina Hospital for Rehabilitative Medicine in Pomona, California (Gottlieb et al., 1977).

Zlutnick and Taylor (1982) have recently described the multimodal pain control program at the Pacific Medical Center in San Francisco with which they are affiliated, and a review of their description will provide a good example of a program in action.

Patients are accepted into this inpatient program only upon referral from a physician. After all pertinent medical records are reviewed, the prospective patient receives, in the mail, a 2-week supply of pain diary forms, a pain history questionnaire, insurance forms, and a program description. The diary form provides a place to record activities, medication intake, pain, and mood, on an hourly basis throughout the 24-hour day. After all materials are completed and returned by the prospective patient, an intake evaluation is scheduled in order to determine eligibility and suitability for the treatment program.

Criteria for acceptance into the program include: (1) a history of severe chronic pain for a minimum of 6 months; (2) a complete medical evaluation that rules out the presence of disease processes that might be responsible for the pain; (3) overuse of pain-killing drugs; (4) family or residential circumstances that make outpatient treatment impossible. Criteria for exclusion from the program include: (1) presence of known or suspected organic brain disease; (2) presence of a psychiatric diagnosis, including antisocial personality, manic-depressive psychosis, or schizophrenia; (3) active involvement in litigation regarding disability payments; and (4) concern that a physiological basis for the pain has been overlooked or not adequately treated.

Prior to admission, the patient signs a contract specifying treatment goals and agreeing to drug withdrawal procedures, and makes three deposits of funds—two of which are refundable at the time that the program and the followup visits are completed, and the third that serves as an advance against the deductible portion of the patient's health insurance. During the first 3 to 6 days of the program, baseline data are collected, including the continuation of the daily pain diaries. Medication use is monitored, and urine drug screening tests are conducted. Patients are put on a full medication regime, as needed.

Detoxification, that is, the elimination of accumulated medications from the body, is accomplished at the rate of 20–25 percent per day, unless the pharmacological properties of the addicting drug require a more prolonged detoxification period. All drugs are put into a "pain cocktail." Staff behavior follows the contingency management policies described above. That is, reassurance, support, and understanding are the order of the day, as the staff reinforce well behavior and withdraw reinforcement from pain behavior.

Following detoxification, patients are taught deep muscle relaxation and other anxiety-reduction procedures. Treatment goals and objectives are reevaluated. Ancillary treatment procedures, such as social skills training, job placement, physical therapy, and so forth are undertaken. Prior to discharge, the family is convened to discuss the treatment and their role in its continuation. The referring physician is contacted and apprised of the patient's condition and status. Patients are discharged with instructions to continue to complete the daily pain diaries and to report for the first followup interview in 2 to 4 weeks.

Followup visits are scheduled at 6-month intervals thereafter. Drug urine screens are obtained at all visits, and additional outpatient visits or telephone contacts are scheduled as necessary.

### Cost-effectiveness of a Pain Control Program

In one of the few studies of the cost-effectiveness of a pain control program that has thus far been reported, Stieg and Williams (1983) calculated the estimated cost-effectiveness in a group of fifty-three chronic pain patients with work-related injuries who were treated at the Boulder Memorial Hospital Pain Control Center in Colorado. These patients were treated with a combination of drug detoxification; physical, recreational, and occupational therapies; and individual and group counseling. These patients were, on the average, 41 years old and had completed high school. More than 2½ years had elapsed between their injuries and the pain treatment program, during which time each of the fifty-three patients had had, on the average, 1.7 surgical procedures. More than half of the patients in this study were involved in litigation related to their chronic pain.

Stieg and Williams calculated three cost estimates: (1) the total amount of anticipated medical costs and disability payments until age 72 in the absence of treatment in the pain control center, based on those costs for at least 1 year prior to the pain control program; (2) the total amount of anticipated medical costs and disability payments until age 72 following the pain control program, based on those costs for at least 1 year following participation in the program; and (3) the cost of the pain control program itself. The cost-effectiveness was calculated by subtracting the cost of the program plus the anticipated-treatment medical and disability payments based on posttreatment expenditures from the anticipated medical and disability payments based on pretreatment expenditures. Their conclusions were that participation in the pain control program would save an estimated $256,000 per patient in the years between completion of the program and the time the patients would reach 72 years of age.

## SUMMARY

- Chronic pain disables a million or more people in the United States on any given day and is perhaps the most common reason for seeking medical care.
- Chronic pain is a particularly costly medical problem because of the

large disability payments that are made to people who are no longer able to work.

- Chronic pain often leads to severe depression, drug dependence, discouragement and demoralization, and to despair not only for patients but also for their families.

- Pain is simultaneously a subjective experience, an unpleasant stimulus, and a form of self-protection, and cannot be assessed the way blood pressure or body temperature is assessed. Pain must be assessed subjectively, by self-report, and has different symbolic meanings to different patients.

- Three important dimensions of pain have been identified—chronic versus acute pain, malignant versus benign pain, and psychogenic versus biogenic pain. There is a strong psychosocial and cultural component to many forms of pain.

- Scientists have been developing theories of pain for more than two centuries, and these theories have, in the last quarter century, become more complex as more is learned about the functioning of the central and peripheral nervous systems.

- Four special forms of chronic pain have been identified—phantom limb pain, causalgia, neuralgia, and posttraumatic pain syndromes.

- A special form of chronic pain that is very common and very long-lasting is chronic low back pain. In the 30–60 year age range, chronic low back pain is the most costly illness in existence.

- Tolerance of pain appears to vary as a function of a number of demographic and personality characteristics, but the relationships are not very strong.

- Since pain is not a verifiable phenomenon, its assessment is unusually difficult. Some procedures are now available in the laboratory to assess pain using traditional psychophysical methods.

- Pain studied in the laboratory behaves very differently from pain found among clinical patients. Laboratory pain, for example, reacts very differently to drugs and to placebos than does clinical pain and produces far less anxiety.

- In the pain laboratory, important differences exist between pain threshold and pain tolerance.

- A number of psychological test instruments have been developed to assess clinical and laboratory pain, and these instruments have been productively used in a variety of research programs.

- Psychosocial factors play a very important role in the perpetuation of pain. Included among the psychosocial factors that have already been identified are the medical and legal system that provides strong incentives for the continuity of pain, a secondary gain system that results in rewarding pain, and the use of medical treatments that produce side effects that intensify and perpetuate the pain.

- Systematic multicomponent psychological intervention programs have been developed to help patients cope with chronic pain. These pain control programs are nearly always found to be helpful, and such programs are increasing rapidly throughout the United States.

- Pain control programs appear to be unusually cost-effective and have the potential of substantially reducing subsequent illness and disability.

# Psychosocial Aspects of Cardiovascular Disease

# 10

## INTRODUCTION

Diseases of the heart and blood vessels (cardiovascular diseases) have been the major cause of death in the United States for more than 40 years (Pinkerton, Hughes, & Wenrich, 1982). Together they account for over half of all deaths. Cardiovascular disease accounted for 650,000 deaths in 1978, and of these deaths, 150,000 occurred to people less than 65 years old.

Heart disease (also called coronary artery disease, or ischemic heart disease) accounts for about two-thirds of all cardiovascular deaths. About one-third of all deaths to people aged 35 to 64, and about 40 percent of all deaths to white males age 55 and above are due to coronary disease. At the current rate, one out of every five men, and one out of every seventeen women will experience symptoms of coronary disease before the age of 60 (Keeping Up With Cholesterol, 1985). The total cost of cardiovascular disorders is estimated to be between $60 billion and $80 billion annually—about one-fifth of the total cost of illness in the United States (Levy & Moskowitz, 1982; Lindemann, 1981). The reason why the cost of cardiovascular disease is this low is because heart attacks are often fatal.

In spite of the continuing magnitude of the problem, a remarkable reduction in cardiovascular disease has occurred in the past 30 years. The mortality rate has decreased nearly 38 percent (compared with a decrease from other causes of death of only 21 percent during the same time period), and most of that decrease has occurred in the past decade. While heart disease remains the leading cause of death among persons aged 45 and above, among people aged 25 to 44 the decrease in the number of deaths from heart disease has been so great that the disease has dropped from first to third in the list of leading causes of death. Death rate from heart disease is now lower among people aged 25 to 44 than the death rate from cancer and from accidents (National Center for Health Statistics, 1985g). This decrease in overall cardiovascular mortality rate has resulted in more than 1 million lives being extended between 1968 and 1978, and, as a consequence, there has been an increase in life expectancy of 2 years for both men and women.

It is generally thought that this drop in the death rate due to cardiovascular disease is a result of: (1) improved medical services, including the development of coronary care units along with improved emergency services and surgical and medical diagnostic procedures and treatments; (2) improved control of blood pressure; and (3) changes in lifestyle, including smoking reduction, increased leisure time activity, and modification of eating habits (see Chapters 5 and 6).

It is not at all clear whether the drop in death rate is due more to improved treatment or to improved preventive programs. Since there is no systematic national reporting of nonfatal heart attacks, it is not known whether there have been fewer heart attacks or whether there have been fewer deaths from heart attacks. If there have in fact been fewer heart attacks, that would suggest that preventive programs have been responsible for the reduced mortality figures. If, on the other hand, there have been about as many heart attacks but there has been a lower death rate from those attacks, that would suggest that improvements in treatment procedures have been responsible for the reduced mortality figures (Levy, 1981).

Epidemiologists have been trying to identify risk factors that make certain people particularly vulnerable to coronary disease (Smith, McKinlay, & Thorington, 1987). The need to identify these risk factors is especially important when one realizes that in about 25 percent of deaths from coronary disease, the first heart attack is fatal. Some risk factors that have been identified cannot be modified, such as gender, age, or history of heart disease in the family. Other risk factors can be modified, including, for example, cigarette smoking, hypertension, and cholesterol levels (Lindemann, 1981); another possibly modifiable factor is what is called cardiovascular reactivity, that is, the magnitude of the cardiovascular response to stressful stimuli (Jacob & Chesney, 1984).

As was noted in Chapter 6, the relationship between cigarette smoking and risk of coronary disease is very high. Similarly, the risk of coronary disease is substantially greater among people with high blood pressure and people with excess levels of cholesterol. One particularly interesting aspect of the relationship of cholesterol to heart disease is its changing interaction with socioeconomic conditions. Excess cholesterol levels were, at one time, positively correlated with social class. That is, as social class increased, so did cholesterol levels. In the past few years, however, the correlation has become a negative one. At every age group, cholesterol levels are now lower in the more affluent than in the less affluent members of society. This change is consistent with general findings in the field of health education that suggest that the more affluent and better educated are the first to change their behavior when the evidence of that behavior's harmfulness becomes available.

The decrease of mortality rate associated with cardiovascular disease noted in the United States has not been paralleled by similar decreases in other industrialized countries, although Japan, Australia, and Canada have noted some decrease. In many other countries, including Romania, Poland, Northern Ireland, and West Germany, increases in mortality rates from cardiovascular diseases have been noted.

## PERSONALITY AND HEART DISEASE

A major source of information linking personality traits with risk of coronary disease has come from the Framingham study—a longitudinal study that began in 1948 of more than 5000 men and women in Framingham, Massachusetts who were between ages 30 and 62 and free of coronary disease at the start of the project (Kannel & Gordon, 1970). The role of personality factors can be seen in an early report of that study; this report characterized the person who is a prime candidate for a heart attack as one who is "overweight, with high blood pressure . . . a cigarette smoker, physically indolent yet tense, and a heavy sugar user with a preference for foods that are rich in animal fat" (Lindemann, 1981, pp. 318–319; also see Booth-Kewley & Friedman, 1987).

Crisp, Queenan, and D'Souza (1984) contrasted a group of 26 men with severe myocardial infarctions with a sample of 235 men without the disorder who were similar in age. Of the 26 men with infarctions, 15 had been screened prior to the onset of their disorders, while the remaining 11 men were screened afterwards. The screening included measures of six psychological traits and psychiatric symptom sets—free-floating anxiety, phobic anxiety, obsessionality, functional somatic complaints, depression, and hysteria.

Prior to the infarction, the coronary patients reported significantly more somatic complaints and significantly greater depression than the non-ill comparison group. The items on the self-report scale that most discriminated those men who subsequently developed coronary disease from those who did not included excessive sweating or heart fluttering, presence of crises that required considerable effort to resolve, dislike of going out alone, lessened sexual interest, and being happiest when working. The authors also noted changes in psychological status after myocardial infarction, particularly in higher levels of anxiety, substantial increases in depression, greater social avoidance, and greater introversion.

Lynch (1977; 1985) has been investigating the effects of human relationships on health in general and the functioning of the heart in particular for more than a decade. Lynch introduced his first report—a book entitled "The Broken Heart: The Medical Consequences of Loneliness"—with the following statement:

> This book is about life and death—love, companionship, and health—and loneliness that can break the human heart. This book touches on complex themes that are in some ways as old as mankind itself, but its purpose is simple: to document the fact that reflected in our hearts there is a biological basis for our need to form loving human relationships. If we fail to fulfill that need, our health is in peril. (p. xiii)

Basing the early part of his book on national statistics, Lynch first showed that human relationships are undergoing a significant disruption that is increasing as the twentieth century comes to an end. Lynch identified the increasing divorce rate, particularly among families where there are children, the rise in the rate of illegitimate births, the increase in the number of one-parent households, the increase in the number of married mothers who work outside the house, and the decrease in the remarriage rate among divorced persons.

Lynch went on to document the fact that heart disease is one of the most frequent causes of death in the United States, and that while elevated blood pressure, elevated serum cholesterol, and cigarette smoking are powerful predictors of heart disease, psychological and sociological factors also put people at higher risk of developing coronary disease. Among the demographic factors that are related to the death rate from heart disease, one of the most important is marital status. Death rates from heart disease for never married, divorced, and widowed persons are significantly greater than the rates for married persons. This conclusion holds for both sexes, at all ages, and for both whites and nonwhites. In addition, death rates from heart disease are associated with stressful life events, particularly from events that involve significant personal losses, the most common of which is the death of a spouse.

Lynch did not mean, of course, that marital discord or loneliness causes every myocardial infarction, for clearly such a position would be absurd. And yet, in a surprising number of cases of premature coronary disease and premature death, he found that interpersonal unhappiness, the lack of love, and human loneliness seem to be among the root causes of the physical problems.

Next, Lynch turned to clinical studies of the heart. His review of the literature, regarding normal persons as well as those with heart disease, led him to conclude that human contact, even transient human contact, has a powerful influence on the cardiovascular system. But this relationship of human contact to the functioning of the heart is not only a negative one. Lynch also felt that if the lack of human love or the memory of earlier personal traumas can disturb the heart, then the presence of human love may serve as a powerful therapeutic force, helping the heart to restore itself.

Nowhere is the healing power of human contact more evident than in coronary care units in the general hospital. The importance of human relationships as part of coronary care has, according to Lynch, been documented in study after study, including his own work with hundreds of coronary care patients that he reports in his book. Lynch's work underlined the importance of human companionship, on the one hand, and chronic loneliness on the other hand for general health, cardiovascular disease, and premature death. Human companionship is, in Lynch's words, the "elixir of life; without it we cannot survive" (p. 230).

### The Type A Personality

Of all personality traits thought to be related to the risk of heart disease, the one that has been most actively studied is the so-called Type A personality, originally described by Friedman and Rosenman in 1974. Type A personalities are described as having a sense of time urgency; an exaggerated sense of involvement; and hostile, competitive, and hard-driving tendencies in their relationships with others, as well as being inner directed, self-centered, easily angered, impatient, sexually aggressive, energetic, and tense (Lindemann, 1981; Suinn, 1980). Most research studies, particularly older studies, have found that persons with Type A personalities are significantly more vulnerable to coronary disease than are so-called Type B individuals who do not have these personality traits (Booth-Kewley & Friedman, 1987; Eliot & Buell, 1981; Jenkins, 1981; Miller, 1983; Rosenman, Brand, Sholtz, & Friedman, 1976; Scherwitz et al., 1986). As a consequence, a number of investigations have been undertaken in an effort to reduce the intensity of such behavior patterns (Suinn, 1982).

Type A behavior was originally assessed by means of the structured interview developed by Rosenman and associates (1964)—an individually administered interview requiring about 30 minutes. The original development of the structured interview was based on a sample of more than 3500 men aged 39 to 59 living in the San Francisco and Los Angeles areas who were examined in 1960 and 1961. Included in the sample were 113 men with evidence of coronary disease. The Type A behavior pattern was found to be more common among persons with coronary disease than among those without the disease, although the differences were not dramatic. In the entire sample, 71 percent of the group with coronary disease exhibited Type A behavior, as against 52 percent of the group without coronary disease.

In a 2-year followup study with this group of subjects, Rosenman and associates (1966) found that 70 of the original sample of more than 3300 persons without coronary disease had developed the disorder. Scores on the original behavior pattern scale were examined, and it was found that those persons who had developed heart disease had scored significantly higher than those who had not subsequently developed heart disease.

Some year later, a self-administered version of the structured interview, called the Jenkins Activity Survey, was developed by Jenkins, Rosenman, and Friedman (1967; see also Jenkins, Rosenman, & Zyzanski, 1974; Jenkins Zyzanski, & Rosenman, 1971) with a sample of about 2800 men interviewed in 1965 and again in 1966. The Jenkins Activity Survey is a multiple-choice, computer-scorable measure that originally consisted of sixty-one questions designed to determine the presence and degree of

> excesses of competitiveness, striving for achievement, aggressiveness (sometimes stringently repressed), time urgency, acceleration of common activities, restlessness, hostility, hyperalertness, explosiveness of speech amplitude, tenseness of facial musculature and feelings of struggle against the limitations of time and the insensitivity of the environment. (Jenkins, Rosenman, & Zyzanski, 1974, p. 1271)

In addition to yielding a total Type A behavior score, subscores are available measuring speed and impatience, hard-drivingness and competitiveness, and job involvement. Subsequent studies with the scale have resulted in a shortened nineteenth-item version that appears to combine brevity with fairly accurate prediction. As in the case of the earlier followup studies by Rosenman and his colleagues, scores on the Jenkins Activity Survey were found to be significantly higher among men who subsequently developed heart disease than among men who did not. The Jenkins Activity Survey currently appears to be the most commonly used measure of Type A behavior, although there is considerable evidence that scores on the Jenkins Activity Survey do not correlate as highly with the risk of coronary artery disease as do scores on the original structured interview measure (Booth-Kewley & Friedman, 1987; Rosenman, 1985).

The classification system for designating Type A and Type B personalities is in need of continued study, since individuals do not always conform to all aspects of the hypothesized personality type. In addition, the concepts describe the extremes of various trait distributions, and most people fall closer to the middle of these distributions. Finally, research has indicated that while more Type A than Type B individuals have coronary disease, many Type As do not get heart attacks, and many Type Bs do.

An increasing number of more recent studies have failed to find an association between assessed Type A behavior and any aspect of coronary disease. For example, Dimsdale and associates (1979) did not find a significant relationship between Type A behavior and evidence of coronary artery disease as assessed by an angiogram in two separate samples of patients. Krantz and co-workers (1981) did not find a significant relationship between measures of Type A behavior and cardiovascular response to a stress-inducing social situation in a sample of eighty-three patients scheduled for a cardiac catheterization.

Similarly, Scherwitz and associates (1983; also see Scherwitz et al., 1986) failed to find a significant relationship between Type A behavior and extent of coronary artery disease in a sample of 150 men scheduled for an angiogram. What did turn out to be significant in their study was a relationship between the extent of heart disease and the use of self-references in speech—the use of the words "I," "me," "my," "myself," and "mine." The authors were interested in the phenomenon of self-reference because of previous evidence that one aspect of the psychology of patients with coronary disease was their focus and involvement with themselves, that is, their inner directedness and self-involvement. It would be interesting to study the extent of self-involvement in other samples of persons with life-threatening disorders, since it might be hypothesized that any such disorder would increase one's interest and involvement with the self.

More recently, Case and other members of the Multicenter Post-Infarction Research Group (1985) assessed Type A behavior by means of the Jenkins Activity Survey; their sample was composed of 516 of the total of 866 patients who enrolled in the Multicenter Post-Infarction Program following a heart attack; the program is located in several cooperating hospitals in New York City, and in Manhasset and Rochester, New York. Case and associates were unable to find that Type A scores or subscores were significantly related to general mortality during the next 3 years, mortality from coronary disease, length of survival following the heart attack, or duration of stay in the coronary care unit.

In the Case and co-workers study, however, a serious methodological problem occurred that makes their negative results difficult to interpret. The 516 patients who took the Jenkins Activity Survey differed very substantially from the 350 who did not. A significantly higher proportion of the nonparticipants were female, older, unmarried, less well educated, unemployed, and non-English speaking. In addition, the nonparticipants had more severe heart disease and significantly higher mortality rates—both in general, and due specifically to heart disease. For some reasons, a very select sample of patients were chosen to participate in this study. That is, the participants are clearly not a random sample of the patients in the postinfarction program. Participants were, as a group, younger, healthier, better educated, and more affluent.

ANGER, HOSTILITY, AND AGGRESSION.   Part of the reason that Type A personality scores are not more powerfully related to the risk of heart disease may be that there are several somewhat different personality components that are combined in arriving at a total Type A score; these different components should be examined separately. Of all the aspects of the Type A personality, the variables that have received the greatest attention are anger, hostility, and aggression. The three terms are closely related, of course, but are not identical. Anger is an emotional state commonly associated with a heightened arousal of the autonomic nervous system that can vary in intensity between minor irritation and annoyance to fury and rage. Hostility is an attitudinal set that stems from an absence of trust in others, centers around the belief that others are generally mean, selfish, and undependable, and includes such attitudes as hatred, animosity, and resentment as well as chronic anger. Aggression refers to destructive punitive behaviors directed toward others (Spielberger et al., 1985; Williams, Barefoot, & Shekelle, 1985). Rosenman (1985) has reviewed the literature examining the health consequences of anger, and Williams, Barefoot, and Shekelle (1985) have reviewed the literature examining the health consequences of hostility. Psychometric test instruments that assess anger and hostility are generally found to be significantly correlated with scores on the Type A behavior structured interview, but the correlations are low enough so that they can be productively studied in their own right.

Before examining the literature in order to learn what has been found regarding the relationships of anger and heart disease, it will be useful to discuss how anger is conceptualized and assessed. The tasks of conceptualization and assessment go hand in hand, and, as has been repeatedly demonstrated in this volume, the development of well-elaborated assessment procedures constitutes a significant portion of the work of health psychologists.

Spielberger and his colleagues (Spielberger, Jacobs, Russell, & Crane, 1983; Spielberger et al., 1985) have developed two fifteen-item scales that measure different aspects of these three concepts. The State-Trait Anger Scale (STAS) assesses anger intensity (the state of anger) and anger proneness (the trait of anger). Anger as a state and anger as a trait are not independent of each other. People with a greater disposition to experience anger, that is, people with high scores on the trait scale, will experience higher levels of anger than people who are not disposed to experience anger. Thus, in some ways, the trait of anger is analogous to hostility.

Items in the anger intensity scale include "I am furious," "I feel angry," "I feel irritated," and "I am burned up," and are answered by choosing the most appropriate rating—"Not at all," "Somewhat," "Moderately so," or "Very much so." Items in the anger proneness scale include "I have a fiery temper," "I am a hotheaded person," and "It makes me furious when I am criticized in front of others." These items are answered by choosing the most appropriate rating— "Almost never," "Sometimes," "Often," or "Almost always." Subsequent analysis of the anger proneness scale determined that there were two subscales—one that seemed to measure angry temperament ("I am a hotheaded person") and the other that seemed to measure angry reactions ("I feel infuriated when I do a good job and get a poor evaluation").

The Spielberger group has also developed the Anger Expression Scale that assesses the directionality of anger, that is, whether anger is typically directed outward toward other persons or to the environment (eight items), or inward toward the self by being suppressed (eight items). The format for the anger expression scale is to ask respondents how often they behave in a specific manner when they get angry. Responses include "Almost never," "Sometimes," "Often," or "Almost always." Items in the anger outward scale include "Slam doors," "Say nasty things," "Make sarcastic remarks to others," and "Argue with others." Items in the anger inward scale include "Withdraw from people," "Pout or sulk," "Boil inside," and "Harbor grudges." The outward expression of anger is used as a measure of aggression.

In another research program that was designed to create and evaluate a scale for the measurement of anger, Siegel (1985) developed a thirty-eight-item Multidimensional Anger Inventory. The dimensions included the frequency, duration, and magnitude of anger, the range of situations in which anger is experienced, the mode of anger expression (anger expressed inward or outward), and the extent of hostility in the individual's reaction and outlook. Each item is rated by respondents in terms of how descriptive they are—on a five-point scale ranging from completely undescriptive to completely descriptive.

Frequency of anger is assessed by such items as "I tend to get angry more frequently than most people." Duration of anger is assessed by such items as "When I get angry, I stay angry for hours." Magnitude of anger is assessed by such items as "People seem to get angrier than I do in similar situations" (an item that is reverse-scored since if that item is completely descriptive of the respondent it suggests a low level of magnitude). Range of situations in which anger is expressed is assessed by such items as "I get angry when people are unfair," "I get angry when I am delayed," and "I get angry when I have to work with incompetent people." Mode of anger expression is assessed by such items as "When I am angry with someone, I let that person know" (Anger outward), and "I harbor grudges that I don't tell anyone about" (anger inward). Hostility is assessed by such items as "Some of my friends have habits that annoy and bother me very much," "People can bother me just by being around," and "At times, I feel angry for no specific reason."

As is the case with all psychological scales, the development of these scales underwent the series of steps that have been described in Chapter 7. Following the final selection of scale items, the scales themselves were evaluated by determining the extent to which they yield scores that are in agreement with related scales (concurrent validity) and by determining whether groups of people who should differ from each other on these scales, at least theoretically, do in fact differ (predictive validity).

In the case of the Spielberger groups scales, for example, significant relationships between hostility and the risk of coronary artery disease among persons suspected of the disease have been found. In addition, hostility and anger have been assessed in large samples of healthy men who have then been followed for two decades or more to determine their risk of developing coronary artery disease in the future. Hostility and anger have been found to be remarkably stable traits with very high correlations between scores obtained as long as 4 years apart (also see Bergman & Magnusson, 1986). In these long-term studies, hostility and anger scores were found to be significantly related to the risk of developing coronary artery disease during the next decade and with the coronary artery disease death rate during the next two decades. In addition, hostility and anger scores are also associated with increased rates of developing a wide variety of other diseases as well (Williams, Barefoot, & Shekelle, 1985).

In one long-term study, Barefoot, Dahlstrom, and Williams (1983) followed a sample of 250 physicians who had completed the hostility and anger scale as part of a larger test battery 25 years earlier when they were in medical school. Their findings were quite extraordinary. Among the physicians who had scored below the median on the hostility and anger scale, 2.2 percent had died in the ensuing 25 years; among the physicians who had scored at or above the median, 13.4 percent had died. Williams and associates (1985) feel that the hostility and anger scale may measure a fundamental psychological characteristic and in their additional studies of the properties of the scale they have found that there are strong elements of the trait of cynicism contained within it.

Spielberger and his colleagues have also examined the relationships between scores on their anger scales and high blood pressure (hypertension). As will be seen below, hypertension is a common precursor of heart disease. The Spielberger group found that hypertensives score higher on anger intensity and anger proneness (particularly the anger reaction subscale) than do general medical patients with no history of hypertension. Other studies (see Spielberger et al., 1985) have shown that there are significant correlations between blood pressure and scores on the anger outward and anger inward scales.

The link between anger and hostility on the one hand, and coronary artery disease on the other hand may be found in the body's neurohormonal systems. The two sexes differ in hostility and anger, and it is thought that these differences may be due to the presence of testosterone secretions in the male and may account for the differential risk of coronary artery disease in the two sexes. In addition, anger and hostility produce epinephrine and norepinephrine secretions. The secretion of epinephrine is a basic arousal reaction of the body, while the secretion of norepinephrine induces a rise in both systolic and blood pressure as well as other cardiovascular responses. People with high Type A scores tend to experience greater arousals of these neurohormonal reactions than do people with low Type A scores (also see Siegman, Dembroski, & Ringel, 1987).

The role of stress in the maintenance of coronary disease can be seen in the work of Byrne, Whyte, and Butler (1981) who examined a cohort of 120 men and women who survived heart attacks. This group of patients, whose average age was 53, was originally identified and examined between 10 and 14 days following their admission into a coronary care unit, and all of them who could be located were examined again 8 months later. At the initial interview, the Illness Behavior Questionnaire (IBQ—see Chapter 9) was administered. Byrne and associates computed their own factor analysis of the questionnaire responses (see Byrne & Whyte, 1978) and found eight factors which they labeled somatic concern, psychosocial precipitants, affective disruption, affective inhibition, illness recognition, subjective tension, sick role acceptance, and trust in the doctor. Several of these factors were similar to the ones originally found by Pilowsky (1978c).

At the time of the followup interview, information was collected regarding health status since the heart attack. Of the original sample of 120 persons, information was obtained 8 months later regarding 102 persons (85 percent). Among these 102 persons were 20 who had had a recurrence of the heart disease, and 7 who died as a direct consequence of the heart attack, and whose death certificates and medical records were consulted. Of the eight aspects of the heart disease that were assessed at the time of the initial interview, one—psychosocial precipitants—was significantly related to recurrence of the disease, whether fatal or nonfatal, during the next 8 months. The six items on the psychosocial precipitants scale all referred to personal, social, and financial worries prior to the heart attack that, in the judgment of the patient, may have contributed to the attack. This finding is particularly persuasive since this study incorporated a prospective design in which patients' self-reports were analyzed in relationship to events that occurred later in their lives.

Somewhat similar findings were obtained in a larger study reported by Ruberman, Weinblatt, Goldberg, and Chaudhary (1984). Data came from a sample of 2320 persons with coronary heart disease interviewed between 2 and 3 months following the attack, and again 3 years later. Four psychosocial variables were assessed—level of stress, level of social isolation, Type A behavior pattern, and depression. It was hypothesized that stress or coping difficulties, social isolation and difficulties or unwillingness to communicate, Type A behavior pattern, and depression would be associated with increased risk of death.

Examination of the data revealed that high life stress and social isolation were significantly associated with risk of death following the heart attack, and that these relationships were particularly remarkable among patients with low educational levels. Significant relationships were not found in the case of Type A behavior or depression. High stress levels and social isolation have been found to increase the risk of coronary disease in a number of other studies as well (see, for example, Horowitz et al., 1979; Karasek et al., 1981; Medalie & Goldbourt, 1976; Thiel, Parker, & Bruce, 1973).

## PREVENTION OF HEART DISEASE

In the case of coronary disease, two important facts pertinent to preventive intervention have been established. First, persons who have elevated blood pressure, high serum cholesterol, or who smoke are at excess risk; and second, this excess risk is true most particularly in younger persons. Men and women between ages 35 and 44 are four times more likely to develop coronary disease if they have elevated blood pressure than if they do not. At ages 55 and above, however, there is virtually no excess risk of heart disease among people who are hypertensive. In addition, high serum cholesterol is associated with a sevenfold excess risk of coronary disease among persons below age 55; and, persons who smoke more than twenty cigarettes per day, when compared with nonsmokers, have a fourfold excess risk among persons under age 45.

Thus, the target population for community-based preventive intervention programs needs to be relatively young. Unfortunately, more than three-quarters of all deaths from coronary disease occur among persons above 65 years of age. Even though it would take many years to see the favorable results, there seems no question about the fact that a substantial number of premature deaths could be prevented if persons between ages 35 and 65 were to reduce their blood pressure and cholesterol levels and quit smoking.

In a recent review of major efforts to prevent coronary disease, Winkelstein and Marmot (1981) grouped these prevention programs into three categories based on the strategies they employed in their implementation. The first category involves screening of the population for evidence of risk factors, and then specifically targeting those individuals who are judged to be at high risk. The second category is aimed at entire communities and involves health education and community organization approaches. The third category, called the ecological model, takes the indirect approach of making changes in the community that might reduce risk. For example, a community might improve public transportation in order to reduce the stress of driving on crowded streets. Or, a community might reduce the air pollution level by requiring the reduction of emissions from a local electric generating plant.

Ecological models of coronary disease prevention programs are theoretically feasible, but in fact, have yet to be mounted in any practical sense. In addition, such programs are unusually complex to evaluate, in part because they require very long time frames for their impact to be felt. The time may come when ecological model programs will be reported, but, for the moment, only the high risk group model and the public health education model have been employed in the development of such preventive intervention programs.

One example of a preventive program that follows the high risk group model is the Chicago Coronary Prevention Evaluation Program (Stamler et al., 1980). This program sought to reduce the levels of high-risk factors in a sample of coronary prone men aged 40 to 59 by means of nonpharmacological methods. The project extended over a 15-year period (1958 to 1973) and involved more than 500 men who were judged to be at high risk but asymptomatic at the start of the study. The preventive intervention program consisted of visits to the program clinic for counseling with regard to diet, smoking cessation, and for supervision of antihypertensive drug therapy when that therapy was deemed necessary. During the first 6 months of the program, study participants visited the clinic monthly. Afterwards, they visited the clinic every 3 months.

About 65 percent of the men in the study remained full-time participants throughout the entire program. Average blood pressures for these men were reduced to normal levels during the course of the project period. Serum cholesterol levels were reduced by about 10 percent, and there was a modest reduction in the proportion of smokers from an initial level of 36.8 percent to 28.1 percent. Mortality rates from coronary disease in the sample of participating subjects were about 25 percent lower than in a sample of men matched for age and risk factor who were not in the study. This early study clearly demonstrated that lifestyle counseling could be effective in reducing the risk of coronary disease.

As a consequence of the success of the Chicago Coronary Prevention Evaluation Program, a much larger study was subsequently undertaken. This newer study, the Multiple Risk Factor Intervention Trial, was begun in 1973 and is based in twenty communities (Multiple Risk Factor Intervention Trial Group, 1978). An initial group of 370,000 men were examined, and from this group, a sample of nearly 13,000 men were identified who were asymptomatic but at high risk—again judged on the basis of their blood pressure, cholesterol levels, and smoking behavior.

The preventive intervention program began with ten group meetings that provided the participants with information regarding risk factors in coronary disease in a context that resulted in group building that was hoped would facilitate the necessary modifications in their health-related behaviors. Spouses were encouraged to attend these meetings as well. Behavior modification procedures were used to reduce smoking and cholesterol levels, and efforts at blood pressure reduction included both behavioral and drug procedures. The group meetings were followed by individual case conferences and other forms of maintenance as indicated. Annual physical examinations of study participants are undertaken as part of the evaluation procedure. This study is still in progress, and no final results have been reported.

Two important examples of preventive intervention programs for coronary disease using a combination of the high risk group and the public health education model have been reported. One of these is the Stanford Heart Disease Prevention Project based in northern California (Leventhal, Safer, Cleary, & Gutmann, 1980; Maccoby & Alexander, 1979; Maccoby & Farquhar, 1975; Maccoby, Farquhar, Wood, & Alexander, 1977; Meyer et al., 1980). Maccoby and his colleagues successfully used health education instructional and mass media techniques to help effect behavioral change in the areas of diet, exercise, and smoking—the three behavioral domains that have been implicated in the cause of coronary disease. It should be noted that their approach is dramatically different from the one used by Lynch (1977, 1985)—such is the complexity of heart disease. While Lynch emphasized the role of social relationships and social support in preventing and in treating coronary disease, Maccoby and his colleagues focused on diet, exercise, and smoking cessation.

Maccoby, a specialist in communication research, and Farquhar, a professor of medicine and specialist in the prevention of heart disease, were drawn to the study of the role of health education in the prevention of heart disease because of the very high incidence of the disorder, particularly in Westernized countries.

Because of the persuasive research linking faulty diet, lack of exercise, and smoking to increased risk of heart disease, these scientists launched an effort to reduce the prevalence of these risk-producing behavior patterns. These authors were very aware of the difficulties involved in attempting to change behavior. They were also aware that not all attempts at changing behavior by means of health education had been successful. They concluded from their review of the literature that "people who hold erroneous views on such matters as diet, drugs, or smoking would be more likely to be influenced by communications advocating positions not too different from their own" (p. 116). In addition, they concluded that they wanted to work at the community level, that is, that they should attempt to have a measurable impact on behavior in an entire community of persons at risk of developing heart disease, using mass media alone in their health education program.

Accordingly, the authors located three semirural communities in northern California. They performed an initial survey of random samples of persons aged 35 to 59, ascertaining the level of information and the nature of attitudes and behaviors with respect to diet, exercise, and smoking. They then conducted physical examinations in specially established clinics. The authors obtained a very high response rate—more than 80 percent of their randomly drawn samples were interviewed and participated in a physical examination.

One of the three communities served as a control. Four surveys of all study participants were conducted 1 year apart in the three communities, including the "no treatment" control community. A media compaign was conducted in the second community over the next 3 years. In the third community that same media campaign was supplemented by an intensive instructional program for selected members of the group determined to be at particularly high risk of developing heart disease.

The media campaign was designed and pretested by professional media experts not only to inform and motivate people but also to stimulate behavior changes that, it was hoped, would reduce the risk of heart disease. Because nearly 20 percent of the population in the three communities was Spanish-speaking, the entire media campaign was bilingual. The health education campaign included TV spot announcements and radio spot announcements and minidramas. Local newspapers carried specially prepared columns dealing with diet and with other pertinent health issues. Other printed items were prepared, including a basic information booklet, a cookbook, and a heart health calendar, and additional messages were displayed on local billboards.

The special additional intensive program in the third community was aimed at two-thirds of the highest 25 percent of the people at risk (as assessed with a number of scales that measure risk of heart disease). The remaining third of the high-risk population served as the control group for this special intensive program. Participants in the special program received instruction in groups of fifteen, or, if unable to attend group meetings, individually in their homes. Again, the emphasis of this special program was on effecting changes in diet, exercise, and smoking behaviors.

Insofar as information, attitudes, and behavior were concerned, people changed more in the two towns where the media program took place than in the control town. In addition, people in the high-risk group who received intensive instruction changed more than people who were only exposed to the general mass media information program.

Risk-reduction effects were found after 2 years in both communities where the health education program had been inaugurated. The level of risk of coronary disease decreased by 17 percent in those two communities. In contrast, the risk increased more than 6 percent in the control community. During the first year of the program, changes in behavior were seen most clearly in the community with the two-phase health education program. By the end of the second year, however, significant further decreases in risk had taken place in the community with the mass media health education program alone. That is, the mass media program plus intensive instruction had more rapid effects, but similar reductions in risk were achieved through mass media alone after one additional year. In comparison with the control community, the experimental communities showed significant reductions in smoking, blood pressure, saturated fat consumption, and plasma cholesterol, as well as in overall risk of coronary disease.

In another study evaluating a similar health education program designed to reduce the incidence of cardiovascular disease, a group in Finland (Klos & Rosenstock, 1982; McAlister, Puska, Salonen, Tuomilehto, & Koskela, 1982; Wagner, 1982) attempted to reduce smoking levels and reduce serum cholesterol and blood pressure by promoting diets lower in saturated fat and higher in vegetables and low-fat products. Finland, at the time of the study, had a history of unusually high rates of heart disease.

The 5-year program began in 1972 and used multiple procedures for attaining its objectives, including: (1) improved preventive services through identification of persons at high risk and provision of medical attention; (2) dissemination of information on health maintenance; (3) efforts to persuade people to change their behavior on the basis of this information; (4) competency building in the areas of self-control, environmental management, and social action; (5) social support building and community organizational development to facilitate social action; and (6) environmental change.

The initial effects of the program were studied by contrasting the experimental community with a neighboring county in which the experimental program did not exist. While no significant changes in smoking, serum cholesterol levels, or blood pressure were found in the control community during the 5-year period of the study, a number of significant changes were found in the experimental community, including reduced cholesterol level in men and reduced smoking and blood pressure in both men and women. In comparison with the control community, men in the experimental community had a 17 percent drop in the risk of heart disease, while women had a 12 percent drop in the risk of heart disease. In a more recent report from this group, Kottke and associates (1984) were able to show that paralleling this decline was a significantly reduced perceived risk of heart disease. That is, improvements in the subjective sense of health were found to follow reductions in objective risk of heart disease.

While there appear to be few prevention programs that focus on improving the ability to cope with anger and hostility, the results of the research reported earlier in this chapter linking these emotions with the increased risk of coronary artery disease, among other disorders, would suggest that another approach to prevention that should be evaluated is to help the general population or specific high-risk groups deal with anger and hostility (and perhaps cynicism) in less self-destructive ways. Rosenman (1985) has suggested that modifying angry and hostile behavior might be successful using approaches such as assertiveness training that change how people think about and react to experiences that may make them angry. Chesney (1985) has called attention to the fact that in our society, the expression of anger often has reinforcing payoffs, and thus it may be particularly difficult to persuade people to express their anger in more measured terms.

In one of the few studies in which efforts were made to help people control their anger, Moon and Eisler (1983) compared the effectiveness of three different strategies—cognitive stress inoculation, problem-solving training, and social skills training. Each of the three strategies was designed to modify cognitive mediating processes, that is, the way people thought about their angry feelings. All three experimental groups received the special training once a week for 5 weeks. In addition, a minimal treatment attention control group was established.

Cognitive stress inoculation was designed to help participants understand the nature of their responses to anger and practice the modification of their thoughts when angry, in order to reduce the stressfulness of their reactions. Problem-solving training helped participants identify the problems associated with their anger, generate a number of possible solutions to the problems, and implement and evaluate the best solutions. Social skills training used role playing and was designed to increase appropriate assertiveness and other behaviors when faced with anger-provoking situations. A total of ten college students, all of whom scored above the mean on an anger inventory, were assigned to each of the three experimental groups and to the minimal treatment control group. Dependent measures of anger were collected before and after the treatment programs and included behavioral measures of aggression, physiological measures of pulse and blood pressure, self-report measures of anger intensity and anger response style, and frequency of anger-provoking incidents per week as determined by anger diaries kept by all subjects.

Members of all three treatment groups improved significantly more than the minimal attention control group on the weekly number of anger-provoking incidents. The stress inoculation program was the weakest of the three intervention programs. Students in this program became less angry but also appeared to withdraw from anger-provoking situations without improving assertiveness. The other two treatment programs were more behavioral in their design, and as a consequence, participants in those programs not only became less angry but also increased their assertiveness and other forms of socially skilled behavior and their ability to interact competently with others (also see Nunes, Frank, & Kornfeld, 1987).

## REHABILITATION OF THE CORONARY DISEASE PATIENT

Paralleling studies of risk factors in the development of coronary heart disease have been a number of studies of psychosocial factors associated with the treatment of patients following heart attack (Debusk, 1980; Garrity, 1981; Gruen, 1975). Regarding patients' experiences in the intensive care unit (the first setting where heart attack patients are usually treated), the widely accepted view of the patient is of someone with initial high anxiety who then typically makes use of the defense called "denial," that is, the repudiation (either conscious or unconscious) of the meaning of an event in order to reduce fear or anxiety or some other unpleasant feeling associated with it. There is no evidence that the intensive coronary care unit in the hospital produces any significant distress by itself, and at the same time, there is evidence that the use of denial appears to reduce the risk of death among persons with coronary heart attacks (Gentry, Foster, & Haney, 1972; Hackett, Cassem, & Wishnie, 1968).

There is some evidence (see Gruen, 1975; Lenzner & Aronson, 1972; Rahe, Ward, & Hayes, 1979) that brief individual or group psychotherapy can have significant benefits during the early phase of hospital treatment. Among these benefits are increased responsivity, animation, and alertness; fewer days in the coronary care unit; and fewer symptoms of heart failure. Brief group therapy appears to provide an important measure of support that results in more successful rehabilitation. Equally effective in shortening the disability associated with coronary heart disease is early mobilization and early discharge (Garrity, 1981).

Gruen (1975) examined the effects of brief psychotherapy on the recovery process following a myocardial infarction in a sample of seventy patients admitted to a community hospital and randomly divided into an experimental and control group. Members of the control group received normal hospital care, while those in the experimental group received, in addition to normal hospital care, weekday 30-minute individual psychotherapy sessions during the hospitalization period that lasted an average of 23 days. Dependent measures of adjustment were collected during the hospitalization and 4 months later, and included several standardized self-report questionnaires, as well as such objective indices as number of days of hospitalization, number of days in intensive care, number of days on which the patient was attached to the heart monitor, evidence of angina and other pains based upon physician and nursing notes, presence of coronary arrhythmias, evidence of congestive heart failure, and a variety of medical and psychological reactions culled from physician and nursing notes.

The brief psychotherapy approach involved exploration, feedback, and positive reinforcement and was based on a number of assumptions regarding sources of therapeutic efficacy—interest in the patient, reassurance, search for positive coping mechanisms and other strengths, reflection of feelings, maintenance of feedback within tolerable limits, encouragement of autonomous coping activities, attempts at conflict resolution, and reinforcement of coping efforts.

On all measures that significantly differentiated control and experimental patients, those patients who participated in the brief psychotherapy experience scored better. Included in these significant differences were days in the hospital, days in intensive care, days on the heart monitor, presence of congestive heart failure, evidence of weakness and depression in nursing and physician notes, and scores on self-report measures of anxiety and sadness while hospitalized. At the time of the followup interview, experimental short-term therapy patients had significantly lower scores on anxiety and retarded activity than did control-group patients.

There is considerable evidence that providing detailed information about what medical care personnel are doing and why can be very reassuring (see Chapter 7). Early mobilization and exercise can be helpful in reducing the sense of depression and in increasing the sense of self-control. In a recent review of the literature on the effectiveness of information and emotional support in the care of coronary heart disease patients, Mumford, Schlesinger, and Glass (1982) found that these interventions reduced the length of hospitalization an average of 2 days, and at very little cost, certainly far less than the cost of an additional 2 days in the hospital.

Lambert and Lambert (1979) have described a three-stage reaction to coronary heart disease on the part of the patient as: (1) repudiation; (2) recognition; and (3) reconciliation. During the first stage, patients tend to deny their loss of health (Levine et al., 1987). During the second stage, patients are depressed, guilt-laden, and often angry. Their anger is directed at any likely target—family members as well as health service providers. During the third stage, patients make peace with their condition and learn to live with the realities of their postcoronary heart disease condition. Many of the problems that occur during the period of acute illness can be moderated by skillful support and education provided by health care personnel.

As the survival rate from first heart attacks has begun to increase, attention has been directed to the development of intervention programs with survivors that are designed to reduce the risk of recurrence of the disorder. The preliminary findings of one such study were recently reported by Thoresen, Friedman, Gill, and Ulmer (1982). This group, located in the San Francisco Bay area, recruited a sample of about 1000 post–heart attack patients in order to determine whether the incidence of recurrence of coronary heart disease and the extent of Type A behavior (Friedman & Rosenman, 1974) could be reduced over a 5-year period by means of a psychological treatment program based on a cognitive social learning model.

Two treatment conditions and a control group were formed. One treatment condition consisted of small groups (8 to 12 members) conducted by cardiologists, while the other treatment condition consisted of groups of the same size conducted by psychologists or psychiatrists. The groups met every 2 weeks for 2 months, monthly for the next 3 months, and every 2 months for the remainder of the first year of the project.

Patients in the cardiologist-led groups received advice and information from the group leader. Illustrated lectures regarding the pathology of coronary heart disease were presented, along with information regarding anxiety, depression, and fears associated with their experiences of illness. No attention was given to chronic stress or Type A behavior patterns, and no attempt was made to alter Type A behavior. Patients in the mental health professional-led groups received instruction and training in methods to alter Type A behaviors, particularly those associated with their persistent struggle to meet an excessive number of demands. The purpose of this group program was to encourage behavior change, with an emphasis on the family, community, and work environment.

Preliminary results of the project indicated a significantly reduced rate of recurrence of coronary heart disease and a reduction in Type A behavior in the behavior change group when contrasted with the cardiologist-led groups and the control group.

Psychosocial issues are paramount when a person with coronary heart disease returns home for convalescence and rehabilitation after a period of hospitalization. These issues are particularly important given the fact that a substantial proportion of these patients have the traits and behavior patterns of the Type A personality.

Rehabilitation responsibilities fall disproportionately on the shoulders of the spouse. Most wives of coronary patients find the period of convalescence stressful. Their husbands are frequently irritable, far more dependent than they ever were before in their adult lives, afraid, anxious, helpless, and depressed. In addition, their convalescing husbands are worried about their abilities to return to a normal sex life and to a normal work life. In both cases, happily, the majority of patients can resume near-normal functioning (Lindemann, 1981).

One particular type of stress that coronary disease patients appear to be unusually vigilant about is associated with the resumption of their sex lives. Under certain circumstances, sexual behavior can be very stressful, but recent research that has examined the incidence of heart attacks during sexual intercourse suggests that these deaths tend to occur only under unusual circumstances. Investigators in a Japanese study (cited in Hackett, 1986) analyzed the autopsy records of 5000 people who had died suddenly. Of these people, 34 had died during sexual intercourse, but 30 of them were with someone other than their spouse. Furthermore, the average age of the sexual partner was 18 years younger than the person who died, and virtually all of the deaths occurred to people who had blood alcohol levels in the intoxicated range.

## HYPERTENSION

Under ordinary circumstances, blood pressure is maintained by a complex regulatory mechanism that works on the principle of feedback to keep blood fluid volume and the space it fills in balance. Should the heart start pumping more blood into the blood stream as a result of exercise or physical or psychological stress, the blood vessels dilate in order to allow for that additional blood without unduly elevating blood pressure.

As the heart pumps blood through the arteries, it exerts pressure against the walls of these strong but elastic blood vessels. Two measures of blood pressure are typically calculated—the *systolic* blood pressure, when the blood is being forced ahead by the heart, and the *diastolic* blood pressure, that pressure exerted against the blood vessels between beats of the heart. Blood pressure is measured in terms of the equivalent pressure exerted by a column of mercury of a given height in millimeters (mmHg). Systolic blood pressure varies between 100 and 120 mmHg in young adults and between 120 and 140 in older adults.

Under abnormal conditions, such as when a disease is present that results in abnormal retention of water and salt, this complex feedback mechanism does not function properly and hypertension can occur. It is estimated that 10 to 15 percent of all cases of hypertension are the result of some disease process. These conditions can often be successfully treated by surgery or other medical methods. The remaining 85 to 90 percent are of unknown origin. Hypertension of unknown origin is often called primary, essential, or idiopathic hypertension (Shapiro & Goldstein, 1982).

It is currently estimated that 35 million people in the United States have high blood pressure and that an additional 25 million people have borderline hypertension. The total number of people with blood pressure above the optimal level represents about 25 percent of the American population.

Blood pressure generally increases with age and weight, and men typically have higher blood pressure than women of similar age. Blacks are usually found to have higher blood pressure than whites, and blood pressure is generally lower in people with a lower body mass index (a ratio of weight to height), or who are better educated and more affluent, or who do not have a history of hypertension in their families. Children of hypertensive parents have about twice the risk of high blood pressure as do children of parents without hypertension, although the reasons for this excess risk may be as much environmental as genetic.

These relationships are all relatively weak, however, and do not all hold across different cultures and different groups within the same culture. Blood pressure is fairly constant over time, however, and thus one can identify a high-risk group by locating children and adolescents with relatively high blood pressure (Herd & Weiss, 1984).

Insofar as psychological determinants of hypertension are concerned, there are a number of careful studies that support the hypothesis that precipitation or acceleration of hypertension takes place in a setting characterized by acute emotional trauma of great significance to the patient (Melamed, 1987; Shapiro, 1982b). In addition, a number of epidemiologic studies have shown that hypertension increases in populations exposed to severe and prolonged stress. Examples of such stresses would include persons living in economic deprivation, or working under unusually stressful conditions, such as air traffic controllers (Shapiro, 1982a).

Examining these psychological determinants clearly suggests that anger and hostility may be almost as predictive of hypertension as it is of coronary artery disease. Indeed, a number of studies and reviews have been published within the past 2 or 3 years that all testify to the important relationship of hypertension to these fundamental emotions (Cottington, Matthews, Talbott, & Kuller, 1986; Dimsdale et al., 1986; James et al., 1986; Mann, 1986; Manuck, Morrison, Bellack, & Polefrone, 1985; Schneider et al., 1986), and in retrospect, it may be that Alexander (1939) got one right when he postulated that the inability to express anger is associated with excess risk of hypertension.

Cottington and associates (1986) studied a random sample of about 350 male workers and found that in workers who suppress their anger, hypertension was more strongly associated with self-reports of an uncertain job future and a variety of sources of dissatisfaction with their jobs than among people who do not suppress their anger. Dimsdale and colleagues (1986) studied a sample of 572 men and women who participated in a blood pressure screening program at a government unemployment office and found that systolic blood pressure was significantly related to suppressed anger, particularly among white men. James and associates (1986) found in a sample of ninety borderline hypertensives whose blood pressure was automatically monitored and recorded, and who completed a number of self-report measures of emotional state during a 24-hour period, that emotional arousal significantly increased both systolic and diastolic blood pressure. Blood pressure was significantly higher when participants reported being angry or anxious than when they reported being happy.

Schneider and co-workers (1986) contrasted a group of thirty-three borderline hypertensives who all demonstrated high blood pressure in the laboratory but who differed in their blood pressure measurements recorded at home. The subgroup who demonstrated continuing high blood pressure at home scored significantly higher on measures of anger as well as measures of the tendency to suppress anger than did the group whose blood pressure tended to decrease when at home.

Hypertension is a risk factor for coronary disease, stroke, blindness, and kidney dysfunction, among other disorders (Rice & Kleinman, 1980). In addition, there is a remarkably linear relationship between diastolic blood pressure and life expectancy. Even persons with diastolic blood pressure at the high end of the range ordinarily considered normal (90 mmHg) need to lower it. This general finding is reinforced by the growing evidence that, even in the borderline range, careful use of drugs that reduce blood pressure can have very beneficial effects on life expectancy. Given the significance of high blood pressure for health, it is extraordinary to note that only about half of people with hypertension are aware of that fact.

Because such a small proportion of people with high blood pressure know about it, efforts are currently underway to make the assessment of blood pressure more easily available (Kasl, 1978). Reasonably accurate blood pressure measurement devices are increasingly found in supermarkets. Health screening programs that invariably include the measurement of blood pressure are becoming routine in most American communities. Dental offices are beginning to provide blood pressure assessments as part of their routine dental hygiene. Finally, a number of communities have begun quite effective neighborhood blood pressure screening programs (see, for example, Artz, Cooke, Meyers, & Stalgaitis, 1981).

There is consistent evidence that hypertension is far more prevalent in modern industrialized societies than in developing societies and that stress may be a causative factor in hypertension. Blood pressure has been found to increase among soldiers in chronic danger situations and among people who are the victims of natural disasters. These blood pressure increases appear to be greater among persons with family histories of hypertension (Shapiro & Goldstein, 1982).

Jenkins, Tuthill, Tannenbaum, and Kirby (1979) have examined the relationship of social environment to hypertension by correlating demographic, social, and economic data with mortality rates attributed to hypertension across the thirty-nine mental health catchment areas in Massachusetts. Mental health catchment areas are geographic subdivisions of each state that were identified at the time that the federal government was encouraging and supporting the development and staffing of comprehensive community mental health centers (Bloom, 1984). Of the 130 social indicators that Jenkins and co-workers examined, 79 were significantly correlated with hypertension death rates. Death rates were highest in catchment areas with low occupational status, low median education, widespread poverty, broken families, and substandard housing. Interestingly, while these social factors were also highly correlated with death rates from heart disease and homicide, they were not correlated with death rates from respiratory diseases and stroke. Thus from a social epidemiological point of view, different sets of diseases may be identifiable that could realistically be studied in terms of their specific relationships to social factors in the environment.

While studies such as this one do not demonstrate any cause and effect relationship, if results such as these were found in other geographic areas as well, it would be relatively easy to identify those geographic areas where the need for community hypertension control programs would be greatest. It would also be rather easy to pinpoint those persons who might be at highest risk. At the same time, however, it is important to acknowledge, as Jenkins and associates do, that the mechanisms by which community social characteristics become internalized are unknown and will require considerable research to be fully understood.

### Psychological Control of Hypertension

Most researchers believe that biological predisposing factors to hypertension must be present in order to precipitate clinical hypertension. Thus, the sequence of events leading to hypertension would be: (1) genetic or other biological predisposition to hyperactivity of the autonomic nervous system; plus (2) chronic or intense acute stress; leading to (3) intermittent rise in cardiac output and consequent blood pressure; which, in turn, leads to (4) structural changes in the blood vessels; and (5) diagnosable clinical hypertension.

Pharmaceutical treatment of clinical hypertension is clearly effective in lowering blood pressure levels enough to reduce the mortality and morbidity rate from cerebrovascular disease and hypertension heart failure (Veterans Administration Cooperative Study Group on Hypertensive Agents, 1970). Recent studies have shown that these illness and death rates can also be reduced in persons with blood pressure levels that are below clinical minimums but still above the optimal (Hypertension Detection and Follow-up Program Cooperative Group, 1979; Shapiro & Goldstein, 1982). Accordingly, the most common form of treatment for hypertension is pharmacological.

In spite of the clear effectiveness of antihypertensive medications, there are a number of persuasive reasons for the continued search for nonmedicinal solutions to the problem of hypertension. First, there is a growing reluctance to take any medication over a long period of time, since there are occasionally significant metabolic, hematologic, and psychiatric side effects (Shapiro & Jacob, 1983). Second, the controlled studies of antihypertensive medications indicate that a substantial number of persons in placebo control groups show blood pressure reductions. Third, nonmedicinal approaches to the control of hypertension need not be thought of as an alternative to medicinal approaches, but rather as a parallel approach to a multidimensional disorder.

Finally, as has been noted by Miller (1983), there is a particularly high level of adherence failure with medical regimens for hypertension (see Chapter 12) mainly because while hypertension has few symptoms, antihypertension drugs have many unpleasant side effects. As a consequence, there is a growing interest in nonpharmacological methods of controlling hypertension, that is, methods that stress psychosocial approaches. Among the methods that have been employed are those designed to encourage lifestyle changes, such as weight reduction, lowering salt intake, exercise, and improving stress-coping skills.

In addition, efforts to reduce blood pressure more directly have been studied using such techniques as biofeedback, hypnosis, meditation, and other forms of relaxation training (Gutmann & Meyer, 1981; Orton, Beiman, & Ciminero, 1982; Pinkerton, Hughes, & Wenrich, 1982; Seer, 1979; Shapiro, 1982b; Shapiro & Goldstein, 1982; Shapiro & Jacob, 1983; Southam, Agras, Taylor, & Kraemer, 1982; Taylor, 1980; Taylor, Farquhar, Nelson, & Agras, 1977). Relaxation programs generally appear to have a significant impact on reducing blood pressure, although in some studies, members of the group not participating in the relaxation program catch up with the experimental group members after a number of months. Thus, at worst, the relaxation programs appear to bring about a more rapid reduction in blood pressure than generally occurs with medication alone.

A representative example of an evaluation of a relaxation program for hypertensives can be found in the work of Irvine, Johnston, Jenner, and Marie (1986). These investigators, working in Toronto, divided a total of thirty-two hypertensives into two groups. One group served as a control and took part in a mild exercise program that was designed not to have any measurable effect on blood pressure, that is, to serve as a placebo, while the experimental group took part in ten 1-hour weekly individual treatment sessions that included educational information regarding stress and hypertension, followed by relaxation training, the use of biofeedback procedures, and the application of stress management techniques in daily life. Half of the patients in each group were taking antihypertensive drugs. Measures of blood pressure were obtained by nursing personnel who were blind to the patients' treatment groups.

In general, the experimental education and relaxation program was superior to the control procedure in reducing diastolic blood pressure at the conclusion of the program and in reducing both diastolic and systolic blood pressure at the 3-month followup examination. These differences were true among both the medicated as well as the unmedicated subgroups.

On the basis of the research reported thus far, the most effective methods of psychological intervention for hypertension combine various forms of relaxation training with medical treatment (Hatch et al., 1985; Orton, Beiman, & Ciminero, 1982). Virtually all forms of relaxation training have been studied, including progressive muscle relaxation, transcendental meditation, yoga, and autogenic training. The principal biofeedback techniques that have been studied have included procedures designed to assist relaxation by lowering muscular tension, as well as procedures designed to lower blood pressure directly. These various approaches have been studied individually and in various combinations.

Among the various relaxation approaches studied individually, passive forms of relaxation such as transcendental meditation appear to have smaller effects on blood pressure than active relaxation approaches such as progressive muscle relaxation (see, for example, Brauer et al., 1979; Hafner, 1982). Biofeedback procedures designed to lower blood pressure directly are about as effective as the average relaxation technique, and relaxation approaches used in combination with biofeedback do not appear to be more effective than either approach used individually. Within the last several years there have been a number of publications attesting to the fact that training hypertensives to raise their skin temperature by biofeedback procedures lowers blood pressure about as much as training hypertensives to reduce their blood pressure directly. Increases in skin temperature are associated with dilation of the blood vessels, which, in turn, results in reductions in blood pressure (Blanchard et al., 1984; Erbeck, Elfner, & Driggs, 1983).

According to Miller (1983; also see Seer, 1979), one of the most successful programs that has been developed to reduce hypertension is that of Patel, Marmot, and Terry (1981; also see Patel & North, 1975). This program combines a number of procedures designed to enhance relaxation, including rhythmic slow breathing, muscular relaxation, meditation, and biofeedback. In addition, the program includes educational components designed to help patients cope more successfully with everyday stresses. Substantial reductions in both systolic and diastolic blood pressure have been reported by this group, reductions that would have a significant effect on a considerable number of persons suffering from high blood pressure.

In his review of the Patel group's 6-week program, Seer (1979) noted that there were substantial reductions in blood pressure in the experimental group at the conclusion of the program as well as at the time of the 3-month followup examination, and that the reductions were significantly greater than in a control group who attended the same number of sessions but simply rested and relaxed on their own. In addition, Seer (1979) noted that the results were particularly convincing in that the investigators used an experimental design in which control subjects later underwent the full training procedure and as a result reduced their blood pressure by the same amount as the original experimental group.

Shapiro and Jacob (1983), in their review of nonpharmacologic approaches to the treatment of hypertension, conclude that psychosocial approaches, if instituted early enough, can delay and sometimes make unnecessary the use of medications for the treatment of high blood pressure. Most often, however, psychosocial approaches cannot substitute for medical approaches to the treatment of clinical hypertension. In spite of the continued importance of medication in the management of hypertension, however, Shapiro and Jacob suggest that

> all patients should be introduced to some type of psychological or behavioral therapy; for most of them, this approach will . . . consist of support and reassurance in the traditional sense. Specific patients can be taught behavioral techniques. If behavioral techniques aimed at stress reduction are chosen, the choice between different methods is guided more by the likelihood of patient acceptance than by the presumed efficacy of a certain technique. (p. 306)

A coordinated national educational program designed to create a more informed citizenry about hypertension has been underway since 1972. This program, called the National High Blood Pressure Education Program (NHBPEP), is administered by the National Heart, Lung, and Blood Institute of the National Institutes of Health; it consists of a coalition of a number of federal, national, state, and community agencies (Roccella, 1985; Roccella & Ward, 1984). Through education of the public, education of health professionals, technical assistance, and research support, the NHBPEP is working toward informing the public about the severity of hypertension, about its ease of detection, and about the effectiveness of its treatment.

In its most recent progress report, Roccella (1985), who serves as the coordinator of the NHBPEP, noted that progress is being made in preventing disease and premature death from hypertension, in bringing hypertension under long-term control, and in giving Americans a better understanding of the consequences of uncontrolled high blood pressure.

## SUMMARY

- There has been a remarkable decrease in the death rate attributable to heart disease in the United States, although it is not clear whether that decrease is due to a reduction in the number of heart attacks or to improvements in medical care.

- A number of risk factors associated with coronary disease are modifiable, including cigarette smoking, hypertension, and cholesterol levels. A substantial number of premature deaths from heart disease could be prevented if persons between the ages of 35 and 65 were to reduce their blood pressure and cholesterol levels and quit smoking.

- Several personality factors appear to make people at greater risk for heart disease. Included among these factors are social isolation, tension, and the so-called Type A personality, characterized by a sense of time urgency, high competitiveness and impatience, and quickness to anger.

- Of all aspects of the Type A personality that have been studied, greatest attention has been directed to the examination of anger, hostility, and aggression. These interrelated emotions and attitudinal sets are significantly associated with the risk of coronary artery disease and hypertension.

- Three prevention models have been identified in the case of heart disease—the high risk model, involving population screening and special programs for those found to be at high risk, the public health education model, involving health education programs for the entire community, and the ecological model, involving environmental change.

- Wherever heart disease preventive intervention programs have been installed, death rate has shown a subsequent reduction.
- Hypertension is a risk factor for heart disease, stroke, blindness, and kidney dysfunction. Life expectancy is powerfully linked to diastolic blood pressure.
- In the case of hypertension, perhaps the biggest problem is that only a minority of people with the condition are aware of it. Accordingly, efforts are underway to make the assessment of blood pressure more easily available.

# Psychosocial Aspects
# of Cancer and Asthma
# 11

## INTRODUCTION

In this chapter, psychosocial aspects of cancer and asthma will be reviewed. This is the last of four chapters that deal with psychosocial aspects of specific disorders, and at the end, a number of concluding comments that pertain to all four chapters will be made.

## CANCER

In contrast to normal cells, cancer cells are able to proliferate uncontrollably, to invade and overwhelm normal tissues, and to spread, or metastasize, to distant sites in the body. As a consequence of factors not yet understood, after cells become cancerous, their growth and location are no longer controlled by normal bodily inhibitory processes, and, as a consequence, they are able to begin an uninhibited spread and expansion that can overwhelm the body and lead to death.

Since 1940, cancer (actually, a group of diseases) has been the second leading cause of death in the United States, second only to coronary disease in the general population. In 1940, the death rate per 100,000 population was about 120. In 1980, the cancer death rate had increased to 186 per 100,000 (Levy & Moskowitz, 1982).

With the possible exception of AIDS, there is probably no disease more devastating and more dreaded than cancer. Hersh (1979) has noted that "cancer represents *the* abnormal condition of physical self that symbolizes both our tenuous hold on life and the fragile reality of our control" (p. 176). Almost every aspect of the patient's life is affected by the disease or by its treatment. Even if the treatment is successful, there is a lingering fear of its return, and the psychological impact of the disease, in terms of depression, anger, and anxiety, is well known (Redd & Andrykowski, 1982). Under these circumstances, it is understandable that social scientists should try to identify ways in which psychosocial interventions might play a useful role in the prevention or in the management of the disease.

The psychosocial literature on cancer divides itself into four domains. First, there are a series of studies that seek to identify psychosocial factors associated with excess risk of developing cancer. Second, there are reports of psychosocial factors associated with adjustment and prognosis. Third, since cancer treatments are frequently noxious, a number of studies have been reported regarding psychosocial factors and interventions that may reduce the negative responses to those noxious treatments.

Finally, a number of studies have dealt with the nature of the stresses on the family of a cancer patient and the role of the family in the management of those patients. Studies of families of cancer patients can, in turn, be divided into those that focus on adults as patients and those that focus on children as patients. Family studies were discussed in Chapter 3 as part of the more general discussion of family stress and its relationship to health.

### Psychosocial Risk Factors

According to Sklar and Anisman (1981), the hypothesis that psychosocial factors may play a role in enhancing the risk of cancer is not a new one. Such a hypothesis was advanced by Galen in the second century, and again in the seventeenth and eighteenth centuries by highly respected cancer specialists. Efforts to test this general hypothesis have appeared in empirical form on numerous occasions in the twentieth century (Barofsky, 1981).

Retrospective studies have sometimes found that stressful life events in general (Goodkin, Antoni, & Blaney, 1986; also see Chapter 3), and losses of emotional relationships in particular, have occurred much more frequently prior to the precipitation of cancer than they have in the same period of time in the case of matched healthy control groups of children as well as adults. Some forms of cancer appear at excess rates among persons who have undergone marital disruption, either through divorce or bereavement (Ernster, Sacks, Selvin, &

Petrakis, 1979). There is also some evidence that cancer rate is particularly high among persons who feel hopeless and unable to cope and who are unable to express negative emotions. As you will see, however, nearly all of these studies have such profound methodological problems that they are virtually impossible to accept with any confidence. In addition, as Fox (1983) has indicated, whether the subjects studied are human beings or animals, for virtually every study linking a psychosocial factor etiologically with cancer, other studies cast doubt on that relationship (see, for example, Justice, 1985).

Retrospective studies are far weaker methodologically than are prospective studies, since they are more subject to errors in distinguishing between causes and effects and in the reporting of past events. Greater confidence is expressed for the results of prospective studies. Thus, it is important to note that some prospective studies (see, for example, Greer & Morris, 1975; Thomas, 1976) have tended to support the hypothesis that psychological factors associated with stress are predictive of later cancer development.

Greer and Morris (1975) undertook a psychological examination of a group of 160 women who were suspected of having breast cancer and who were about to undergo a breast tumor biopsy. They contrasted the psychological test results in the group of 69 women who subsequently were found to have breast cancer and the group of 91 women whose tumors were found to be benign. Thus, the psychological study was undertaken without information about the results of the biopsy—which, in fact, did not take place until the next day.

The psychological assessment included measures of major stressful life events, psychiatric history, intelligence, the degree to which patients concealed or expressed their emotions, social adjustment, work satisfaction, and depression. The one major significant finding was that cancer patients differed from noncancer patients in the extent to which they engaged in either extreme suppression or extreme expression of emotions. While both types of emotional abnormalities were significantly different in the two groups of women, the difference in the case of emotional suppression was far greater. The cancer group showed much more frequent abnormalities in emotional expression—only 29 percent demonstrated apparently normal expression of emotions in contrast to 72.5 percent of the noncancer group.

Further questioning of the women in this study, along with their husbands, suggested that these abnormalities in emotional expression had been true for the entire adult lives of the women, and in many cases for their childhoods as well. While the authors were unable to speculate very fruitfully as to the basis of this association, they did suggest that it would be useful to examine the relationship of emotional expression as a psychological trait and hormonal and immunological response patterns.

One assumption in the Greer and Morris study, as in virtually all prospective studies of this type, is that patients cannot accurately predict the results of impending biopsies. If, as has recently been reported by Scherg (1987), it should turn out that patients can, in fact, predict significantly better than chance whether the biopsies that they are about to undergo will yield favorable or unfavorable results, studies of this kind would not be truly prospective, in the sense that the personality assessments really preceded the diagnosis. It would be useful to determine whether patients who are about to undergo diagnostic procedures for potential medical disorders can predict the outcome of these procedures at an accuracy level significantly better than chance, and whether such predictions are more accurate with life-threatening conditions than with more benign conditions.

A more recent study (Kneier & Temoshok, 1984) has also found that coping reactions that involved suppression or repression were unusually common among persons suffering from malignant melanomas, that is, skin cancers. These coping reactions were diagnosed when reported anxiety was significantly lower than physiologically measured anxiety in response to anxiety-provoking statements in an experimental procedure. In addition, a number of paper and pencil tests that assessed repressive coping styles were also administered to the participants.

A total of sixty people took part in this study. The group consisted of twenty persons with malignant skin cancer, twenty persons suffering from cardiovascular disease, and twenty disease-free controls. The three groups were matched on the basis of ethnic origin, gender, and age, and the skin cancer and cardiovascular patients were matched in terms of disease severity. All skin cancer patients had had their skin lesions removed at least 3 months previously, and there was no evidence that any of the lesions had spread.

Kneier and Temoshok found that repressive coping reactions were significantly greater in the malignant melanoma group than in both the cardiovascular group and the disease-free controls. In addition, the malignant melanoma group received higher repressive coping scores on the paper and pencil personality tests. Finally, examination of the relationship between degree of illness severity and extent of repressive coping reactions indicated that no significant relationships existed within either group of patients.

Given these findings, Kneier and Temoshok evaluated a number of possible explanations. Because there were no differences in repressive coping as a function of disease severity, it seemed unlikely that the malignant melanoma caused the repressive coping. The investigators argued that if the disease produced the repressive coping, the more severe disease should have produced more extreme repression. The authors also did not feel that the melanoma caused the repressive coping style, particularly since the prognosis seemed generally good for the melanoma patients.

Kneier and Temoshok proposed that their results could best be understood as the consequences of a repressive coping style having predated but not caused the malignant melanoma, that is, that melanoma patients may have a premorbid tendency toward a repressive coping style, and that perhaps their patients were melanoma-prone. The findings of this study are tentative, to be sure, but the study results certainly justify a replication with other samples of cancer patients in other settings.

Carolyn Bedell Thomas has been associated for many years with the Precursors Study, a broad spectrum longitudinal investigation of seventeen successive graduating classes of medical students (1948–1964) at Johns Hopkins Medical School. In this study, large amounts of data were collected when the study participants were healthy young medical students. Now, these participants are physicians nearing middle age, and for some years it has been possible to examine how early characteristics of these physicians are related to current assessments of health and illness. Patterns of characteristics unequivocally preceding the onset of disease and death are beginning to emerge from these studies.

In her 1976 study (also see Thomas, Duszynski, & Shaffer, 1979), Thomas found that when study participants who had developed malignant tumors were contrasted with healthy members of the same graduating classes, they did not differ in measures of depression, anxiety, and anger that had been collected many years earlier, but those physicians who later developed cancer did differ in that they earlier reported an unusual lack of closeness to their parents.

In another study, Shaffer, Duszynski, and Thomas (1982) found that study participants who subsequently developed cancers scored lower than those who did not on a measure of intellectual interests. This measure assesses level of interest in books, art, concerts, writing, acting, singing, and dancing. Thomas and associates suggest, not very persuasively, that this measure may be an index of stamina, that is, the ability to withstand disease, fatigue, or hardship, and that medical students who subsequently develop cancer demonstrate less stamina as students than do those students who did not later develop cancer.

In still another study with the same sample, Duszynski, Shaffer, and Thomas (1981) found that there were no differences between the cancer and noncancer groups in four childhood stressful life events—death of a parent, divorce of parents, death of a sibling, or birth of a younger sibling (also see Grossarth-Maticek, Bastiaans, & Kanazir, 1985; Grossarth-Maticek, Kanizir, Schmidt, & Vetter, 1985).

These findings need to be replicated in other samples because of two compelling reasons. First, since so many comparisons were made between healthy and ill subjects, some findings are going to emerge as statistically significant by chance. Second, few, if any, of the findings are based on tests of specific theoretically derived hypotheses. Because the Precursors Study is based on a sample of more than 1300 medical students, one way the principal investigators can replicate their findings is by analyzing their data as if they had conducted two or three independent studies.

That is, the overall samples of medical students with cancer and medical students without cancer could each be randomly divided in half or in thirds. The investigators could then try to determine if there were differences between one subgroup of students with cancer and one subgroup without; investigators could then evaluate the stability of whatever differences are found (such as, for example, level of intellectual interest) by seeing whether the differences also exist when the other subgroups of participants are compared. Since the two subgroups of students would have been created at random, the second or third statistical comparison would be an independent test of the hypothesis generated by the first statistical comparison. Under these circumstances, if the same statistically significant finding is obtained in the two or three different analyses, far greater credibility could be accorded to the finding.

The body of research attempting to identify psychological risk factors for cancer is still not thought of as persuasive; Sklar and Anisman (1981), following their review of the relationships of stress and cancer, have concluded that stress, because of its profound effects on physiological functioning, may influence the course of a malignancy, although it may not cause the disease.

Similarly conservative conclusions were arrived at by Morrison and Paffenbarger (1981) and by Fox (1983) in their reviews of research studies that have examined the role of social and psychological factors in the etiology of cancer. According to these reviewers, most of these studies have such severe methodological problems that they cannot be interpreted.

For example, Morrison and Paffenbarger examined the work of LeShan (1966) who contrasted the emotional life histories of 450 adult cancer patients and 150 matched controls. Hypotheses regarding presumed differences between the two groups were developed, tested, refined, and retested. A specific developmental pattern of inability to relate to others that had begun in childhood following some personal loss was found to characterize 72 percent of the cancer patients and only 10 percent of the control group.

Unfortunately, the method employed by LeShan was to develop a set of hypotheses on the data set, and then to test these same hypotheses on the same data set—a method that was sure to yield significant results. Morrison and Paffenbarger (1983) noted that "when a set of data has been used for exploratory analysis, replication on another set of data is needed for confirmatory analysis" (p. 138). In addition, these authors indicated other serious methodological flaws with the study, including failure to control for differences in recall of childhood events between the cancer and the control groups, failure to keep the judges blind to whether they were rating cancer or control subjects, and failure to control for chance findings. Thus, the results of the LeShan study cannot be viewed with any confidence.

Morrison and Paffenbarger concluded:

Investigators of biobehavior in the etiology of cancer have given insufficient attention to those epidemiologic principles which would establish a causal relation between behavioral characteristics and human cancers. . . . As a group, these studies have failed to meet essential epidemiologic criteria such as strong association, consistency, reproducibility, and specificity. (p. 155; also see Chapter 1)

In the case of links between psychosocial factors and etiology, Fox (1983) came to a similar cautionary conclusion:

One cannot trust any of the results . . . merely on the basis of reported findings. The experiments must be carefully reviewed and suspicion of possible bias and unreliability should lead one to put a finding aside, waiting, instead, for studies with rigorous design and replication. Rigorous design requires controlling for (by matching or statistical analysis) those variables that might affect the outcome, as well as proper sampling. My position is that the case is still open on the psychogenic etiology of cancer. . . . At best the present position must be tentative, if not outright speculative. (p. 25)

### Adjustment and Prognosis

In spite of the fact that many of the methodological problems inherent in establishing a cause-effect connection between psychosocial factors and cancer incidence hold true in the case of establishing a relationship between such factors and cancer prognosis, duration, or survival rate, there is reason to believe that psychosocial factors might be more strongly related to adjustment to cancer and to prognosis than to incidence (Fox, 1983).

In a study of coping with the threat of cancer, Hobfoll and Walfisch (1984) examined emotional distress, self-esteem, and level of social support in a sample of fifty-five Israeli women the day before they underwent a biopsy for suspected cancer. This sample of women was found not to have cancer and was drawn from a larger study. As might well be suspected, scores on the measures of emotional distress were very high. Measures of emotional distress were found to be significantly lower among women with higher levels of self-esteem and greater numbers of family and friends with whom they shared common interests.

Issues involved in coping with cancer have been examined in a number of studies. For example, Heinrich and Schag (1984) explored the nature and severity of psychosocial problems faced by cancer patients. These investigators developed the Cancer Inventory of Problem Situations, an instrument consisting of 131 items that are designed to identify cancer patients' day-to-day problems. Their initial evaluation of the instrument with a mixed sample of eighty-four cancer patients revealed that the disorder has a significant and extensive impact on psychosocial and physical functioning. Specifically, they found moderate to severe problems in the areas of personal and interpersonal functioning, activity management, work, and in the patients' involvement with the health care system.

More than half of the patients in the Heinrich and Schag study mentioned problems in the area of personal care, including sleeping, eating, changes in physical appearance, and physical and social activities. In addition, about the same proportion of patients mentioned problems in every aspect of medical care that was assessed. Insofar as interpersonal interactions were concerned, most patients mentioned difficulties in communication with their spouses, family, and friends, and in dating and sexuality. Finally, a majority of patients mentioned problems in the areas of employment and in their own intellectual abilities.

Depression, defensiveness, use of such defenses as denial, repression, and regression, and rigidity of beliefs all seem to be associated with an undesirable course of the disorder. Conversely, emotional resiliency, flexibility of beliefs, strong self-concept, and high social competency all seem to be associated with a more desirable course of the disease (Fox, 1983).

Taylor, Lichtman, and Wood (1984; also see Taylor, 1983) have examined adjustment to breast cancer as a function of attributional style and psychological control mechanisms. Attributional style refers to the ways in which people search for cause and meaning when facing a threatening situation. This search represents an effort to understand, predict, and control the threat. Four different attributional styles have been identified in the literature—attributing responsibility to the self, assigning responsibility to other people, attributing responsibility to some aspect of the physical environment, and attributing the threatening situation to chance.

In a sample of seventy-eight women with breast cancer, Taylor, Lichtman, and Wood (1984) found that virtually all patients engaged in some form of causal search to explain their disorder and that adjustment to breast cancer was significantly negatively correlated with the degree to which patients blamed others for their disorder. That is, blaming another person for one's disorder is associated with poorer coping.

Psychosocial factors associated with survival rate and length of life following diagnosis can be studied by following a group of patients prospectively on whom psychological assessments have been made in order to determine the extent to which any aspect of psychosocial functioning is associated with increased survival rate or life expectancy. Relatively few such studies have been reported, although there is some consistency in their results. In one such study, Derogatis, Abeloff, and Melisaratos (1979) found that short-term survivors and long-term survivors differed rather substantially on a number of psychological dimensions.

In their study, Derogatis, Abeloff, and Melisaratos assessed thirty-five women who were receiving treatment for metastatic breast cancer in the outpatient department of the Johns Hopkins Oncology Center in Baltimore. The psychological assessment took place at the time of their second visit to the clinic and included a variety of measures of psychosocial adjustment, attitudes and expectancies, psychological symptomatology, and the adequacy of the adjustment to illness. Survival data were determined a year later, and the thirty-five women were divided into two groups according to their survival 1 year after the baseline psychological evaluation. A total of twenty-two women were still alive and were grouped into a long-term survival group. The remaining thirteen women had all died within the year and were considered as short-term survivors.

Long-term survivors, when contrasted with short-term survivors, had demonstrated—at the time of their baseline psychological assessment 1 year earlier—significantly higher levels of anxiety, hostility, psychoticism, depression, and guilt. The survivors had been less well adjusted to their illnesses and had been expressing significantly more negative attitudes toward their illness and its treatment.

Derogatis, Abeloff, and Melisaratos (1979) summarize their findings as follows:

> Cancer patients whose coping styles facilitate external, conscious expression of negative emotions and psychological distress appear to survive longer; individuals whose coping styles involve suppression or denial of affect or psychological distress have a shorter length of survival. (p. 1507)

These findings were judged to be very similar to those obtained in earlier studies, in which cancer patients with short survival times were found to be unusually polite, apologetic, and acquiescent, and long-term survivors were found to be noisy, expressive, angry, and complaining.

### Psychosocial Factors in Cancer Treatment

It should not be surprising that persons with cancer undergo significant and long-lasting psychosocial as well as biological distress. A large proportion of such patients are understandably depressed and uneasy, and these feelings are not easily dissipated. Thus, it is particularly appropriate that psychologists are interested in determining the relationships of psychological factors to the course of the disease and in the development and evaluation of intervention programs designed to reduce these stresses that are a by-product of the disease (Wellisch, 1981).

Holland and Rowland (1981) have noted that two relatively new developments have brought greater attention to the role of psychosocial factors in cancer treatment. First, with improvements in the treatment of cancer, greater numbers of patients are being cured or are having longer disease-free periods. As a consequence, greater interest is being expressed regarding the quality of life of the patient during and following treatment. Second, psychiatrists, psychologists, and other mental health professionals have become increasingly interested in the mental health aspects of medical disorders and the medical care system.

Coping with Cancer.    In one of the early efforts to provide emotional assistance to cancer patients, Gordon, Freidenbergs, Diller, Hibbard, Wolf, Levine, Lipkins, Ezrachi, and Lucido (1980) initiated a psychosocial evaluation and rehabilitation intervention program for a group of 157 adult cancer patients; the investigators then evaluated the program by contrasting the group with a matched control group of 151 patients who received the initial evaluation and normal hospital care, but who did not participate in the experimental rehabilitation intervention program. These authors described their intervention program as follows:

> It was apparent that intervention would be most frequent during inpatient hospitalization, but previous work . . . had indicated that some problems do not emerge until posthospitalization. Thus, it was decided that the program would need to extend beyond the initial hospitalization period and be available to patients for 6 months. . . . It was also decided that three basic types of intervention would be employed. . . . The first type involved educating the patient about how to live with the disease effectively. . . . The second type of intervention, counseling, was focused on the patient's reactions to and feelings toward the disease. . . . The final category of intervention involved environmental manipulation, including consultations with other health care personnel . . . and formal service referrals to appropriate agencies. (pp. 745–746)

Services were provided by a team that included psychologists, social workers, and a psychiatric nurse, and each patient was served by one member of this team for the entire duration of the psychosocial intervention program. Dependent measures of adjustment were obtained at four points—at the time of hospital admission, hospital discharge, 3 months later, and 6 months later. These measures included problem-oriented structured clinical interviews and assessments of quality of life, perception of medical status, stressful life events, emotional status, locus of control, and psychiatric impairment.

One aspect of the research design justifies special mention. The investigators were very sensitive to the fact that it would be difficult to conduct the study if both control and experimental intervention program patients were identified at the same time, since it would inevitably mean that some patients sharing a hospital room or a hospital ward might be assigned to different groups. Accordingly, the investigators decided on a research strategy that involved the creation of two control groups in a multiple time series design. Specifically, patients admitted for the first 6-month period of the study were assigned to the first control group, patients admitted during the following 12 months were assigned to the experimental intervention group, and patients admitted during the following 6 months were assigned to the second control group. Which group a patient was assigned to, then, became a function of when the patient was admitted to the hospital.

Patients in all three groups were evaluated at four points in time, as stated earlier. Of course, the research design cannot deal satisfactorily with all methodological questions that could be raised, but it does deal with many of the most important questions. Thus, for example, comparison of data from the two control groups could determine whether there were any significant changes in the characteristics of patients admitted to the hospital or to outcome that could be due to changes in medical care that could be attributed to the existence of the experimental intervention program.

The average number of psychosocial problems decreased after discharge from the hospital for both the intervention and control groups, but judged severity of the problems was significantly less for the intervention group than for the control group at the time of hospital discharge. Patients in the intervention group generally showed a more rapid decline in anxiety, hostility, and depression than did patients in the control group, and, in addition, appeared to have a more realistic outlook, a higher frequency of returning to work, and a more active life following discharge. We have already seen that hospitalized patients who freely express their anxiety and hostility tend to outlive those who are more passive. Perhaps that relationship holds only if cancer patients are not well enough to be discharged. That is, if they can be discharged, successful coping is associated with reduced anxiety and hostility.

Worden and Weisman (1984) have recently reported on their efforts to lower emotional distress and improve coping skills in newly diagnosed cancer patients. By means of an initial screening procedure, they identified a group of fifty-nine patients who appeared to be at high risk for emotional distress and poor coping. These patients were provided one of two different four-session psychotherapeutic interventions. A second group of fifty-eight high-risk patients was identified who served as a no-psychotherapy control. All patients were seen every 2 months for followup interviews, and were assessed 2, 4, 6, and 12 months after the intervention program was concluded.

One of the psychotherapy programs was patient-centered and focused on specific problems the patient was currently facing and on ways such problems could be handled. The therapist's role was to help the patient identify and explore ways of solving the problems. The second psychotherapy program was more didactic and provided specific step-by-step approaches to problem solving. While the first therapy program focused on individual personal problems of the patient, the second program focused on common problems that most cancer patients encountered in coping with their illnesses.

The hypothesis that the level of emotional stress would be lower in the intervention group than in the control group was confirmed. While the initial level of emotional distress was the same in the intervention and control groups, the intervention groups had significantly lower emotional distress at each followup assessment. Intervention appeared to reduce levels of denial associated with the facts and implications of the illness and to increase realistic appraisal of the illness.

The second hypothesis, that intervention would strengthen the patient's ability to cope effectively with problems, was also confirmed. There were no significant differences in the number or types of different concerns expressed by patients in the intervention and control groups, but problems were better resolved by persons in the intervention groups. The patients in the two different intervention groups did not differ either in level of emotional distress or in coping skills. That is, both psychotherapeutic programs appeared to be equally successful in bringing about improved adjustment to the disease. Worden and Weisman (1984) concluded:

> Many newly diagnosed patients believe that change is impossible, despair will persist, effort is futile, and a better outcome is beyond hope. Their morale is low because personal control is enfeebled. Self-esteem has been compromised, because the original problems have been joined by feelings of weakness, helplessness, and discouragement. Our view is that change is possible, patients can be helped to take steps on their own behalf, problems can be reduced to manageable proportions, and psychosocial interventions are feasible and cost-effective. (p. 249)

A special problem for cancer patients lies in the fact that many pharmaceutical treatments produce aversive pretreatment reactions such as vomiting and nausea. Controlling these aversive reactions has been the subject of a good deal of research—a field that has recently been reviewed by Redd and Andrykowski (1982).

Medications are used to kill cancer cells. At the same time, however, healthy cells are also damaged, including cells in the bone marrow, the gastrointestinal tract, the reproductive system, and hair follicles. This toxic reaction to medications often includes nausea, vomiting, diarrhea, sterility, and hair loss. For many patients, the nausea and vomiting occur not only after treatment, but before treatment as well—a condition that is stressful and often humiliating. Reasons for pretreatment toxic reactions are not clear, but these reactions appear to be more severe among patients whose posttreatment nausea and vomiting are more severe and who are more anxious. It also seems clear that a conditioning process takes place, in which the nausea and vomiting are triggered on the basis of proximity to the treatment setting.

Four different methods of stimulus modification have been assessed in controlling pretreatment toxic symptoms—hypnosis, muscle training, biofeedback, and systematic desensitization. All seem effective and equally so in reducing the nausea and vomiting, a finding that seems remarkable to Redd and Andrykowski (1982) given the variety of people and cancers studied, the variation in the stage of the disease in each individual case, and the variety of medications that were employed in the treatment of the malignancies.

Redd has also examined the utility of contingency management approaches to reducing the symptoms of patients receiving intensive treatment for their malignancies (1982). Examination of the setting in which toxic reactions to treatment occurred indicated to Redd that inadvertent social reinforcement by hospital staff and family members for these various toxic reactions was taking place and that patients can make discriminations such that personnel directly associated with the treatment procedure become the stimulus for toxic reactions. Based upon this analysis, Redd modified the social reinforcement contingencies associated with the treatment procedure in the case of a 64-year-old terminal cancer patient; Redd was able to show a reduction in the frequency of toxic reactions with no change in the quality of medical and nursing care and in the nature of the patient's social interactions. Specifically, if the patient complained in the absence of any discernable problem, nursing staff were instructed to leave the room, to monitor the patient from outside the room, and to return only after the patient's complaints had stopped for a period of 2 minutes. Time periods without complaints associated with toxic reactions were rewarded with special attention on the part of nursing personnel. Again, there is a question about the justification of trying to reduce complaining, since, as we have already seen, patients who complain tend to outlive those who don't.

In addition to examining the effects of psychosocial intervention on the course of adjustment to cancer treatment, a number of social scientists have been interested in determining whether characteristics of patients or of the intervention programs are associated with increased survival rate or survival duration. In a recent study of the relationship of psychological factors to survival rate among a group of advanced, high-risk cancer patients, Cassileth, Lusk, Miller, Brown, and Miller (1985) did not find that social or psychological factors were related to survival rate. They assessed psychosocial factors that have been found to predict longevity in general populations or in cancer patients in general, and included measures of social support, life satisfaction, self-reported views of general health, sense of hopelessness and helplessness, and coping skills. These measures were unrelated either to survival rate or to how long it took for the disease to recur.

These authors acknowledge, however, that psychosocial factors might influence the original precipitation of the disorder and its course in less severe cases. Of course, one must also take into account the fact that their study was not an evaluation of an intervention program. But, in the case of advanced cancers, the authors have concluded that the "inherent biology of the disease alone determined the prognosis, overriding the potentially mitigating influence of psychosocial factors" (p. 1555).

Simonton, Matthews-Simonton, and Sparks (1980) have been assessing the effects of psychological intervention in the treatment of advanced cancer patients in terms of their survival rates, and have reported on their initial findings on their first group of 225 patients. Their intervention program consisted of an initial psychological evaluation, the results of which were shared with the patients, a 5 to 10 day period of individual and group psychotherapy, and additional 5-day therapy sessions every 3 months. Their therapeutic program included relaxation, assertiveness training, mental imagery used in the service of desensitization, goal setting, addressing fears, adding flexibility of thinking, expressing anger, and reconsidering early childhood decisions. Their intervention program is designed to accentuate the positive—to make positive expectancies more explicit, to provide information that will support positive beliefs, and to instruct patients in the use of motivation-enhancing coping mechanisms.

While these investigators did not have matched control groups who did not participate in their psychological intervention program, they did compare the duration of survival in their sample with diagnosis-specific figures reported nationally. Their findings indicated that times of survival in their groups were about twice as long as times of survival in groups matched for diagnosis reported in national studies.

BREAST CANCER.    A large number of studies have been reported regarding psychosocial factors in the management of breast cancer.

In an interesting series of studies, Leventhal, Nerenz, and Steele (1984) interviewed a number of patients undergoing chemotherapy for breast cancer or for lymphomas in order to learn about their expectations and beliefs concerning the disease and its treatment, and how these attitudes related to their self-report measures of distress. Chemotherapy in this group consisted of a sequence of cycles, each beginning with an injection of highly toxic anticancer drugs followed by several days of toxic oral medications, and then a period of 1 to 2 weeks without medications. The entire procedure was then repeated—often for as long as 1 year or more. Three symptoms—fatigue, weakness, and pain—were most clearly associated with distress, mainly because they resulted in very significant changes from the way patients generally felt.

Patients were undergoing chemotherapy for two different reasons. In one case, the chemotherapy was the principal treatment for the active disease. In the other case, the chemotherapy was ancillary to prior, presumably successful, surgical treatment. These two groups of patients had different psychological reactions to the chemotherapy. Patients for whom the chemotherapy was the principal treatment were made uneasy and fearful by the symptoms of fatigue, weakness, and pain, thinking that it meant that their disease was getting worse. Patients for whom the chemotherapy was an adjunct felt that the surgery had cured their cancers and that the chemotherapy was not needed.

In many cases, patients could monitor their own progress because they could palpate their own tumors and feel them getting smaller. Chemotherapy often resulted in a rapid disappearance of the tumors. This disappearance frequently made patients particularly distressed, because they were forced to undergo additional uncomfortable treatment for no apparent reason they could discern. Leventhal, Nerenz, and Steele (1984) noted that cancer patients often think of their illnesses by using an acute disease model. Thus, these patients were particularly distressed to have to continue their chemotherapy when they felt their disease had already been cured.

Wood, Taylor, and Lichtman (1985; also see Taylor, 1983; Taylor, Lichtman, & Wood, 1984) have studied the coping process of women undergoing treatment for breast cancer as it related to the phenomenon of social comparison. Comparisons with others are made for two reasons—self-evaluation and self-enhancement. Wood and her colleagues conducted detailed interviews with seventy-eight women with breast cancer and found that the overwhelming majority of these women engaged in what is called downward comparison, that is, comparison with people worse off than themselves. This kind of social comparison clearly serves the goal of enhancing the self, by seeing oneself as in better condition and as having a better prognosis than others with similar diagnoses undergoing similar treatments.

Meyerowitz (1980) has summarized the literature dealing with psychosocial correlates of breast cancer and its treatments and has noted that many physicians, even though aware of the psychologically traumatic nature of breast cancer and its treatment, are still loath to raise psychological issues with their breast cancer patients. This reluctance is often due to the fact that physicians, untrained in interviewing techniques, are unsure about how to deal with the responses they will receive.

The diagnosis and initiation of treatment of breast cancer understandably and often results in emotional distress, most commonly, depression, anxiety, anger, and fear of recurrence. This set of emotions typically lasts well beyond the physical recovery from the treatment. In addition, other studies have reported that women who have been surgically treated for breast cancer often experience such life pattern changes as insomnia, nightmares, loss of appetite, and difficulty in returning to usual household and employment responsibilities.

The surgical removal of the tumor, often requiring breast amputation, requires enormous physical and psychological adaptation, and there is considerable evidence that the sexual and intimate life of the woman and her partner is often seriously stressed. For these reasons, a number of writers have advocated that family therapy and sexual counseling be provided in order to enhance family adjustment (May, 1981). These interpersonal impairments tend to be relatively long-lasting, although about 85 percent of breast cancer patients report that by the time that 5 years have elapsed they have returned to their preoperative functioning and life quality (see, for example, Craig, Comstock, & Geiser, 1974; Taylor, 1984; Wellisch, Jamison, & Pasnau, 1978).

A rather large number of studies have been undertaken to determine which preoperative psychological characteristics are associated with the most satisfactory postoperative outcome following treatment for breast cancer. According to Meyerowitz (1980), these studies have such severe methodological problems that their results are not persuasive. The single most common methodological problem is that the assessment of psychological characteristics takes place after the diagnosis of breast cancer has been made or is suspected. Thus, the concerns about breast cancer, as described in the preceding discussion, have already begun to impact on the measures that are supposed to describe the pretreatment characteristics of the patients.

Another serious methodological problem is the failure to study appropriately selected comparison populations. It is quite likely, for example, that many of the factors associated with the quality of breast cancer treatment outcome are not specific to breast cancer, but are the same as might be found for many other medical or surgical procedures.

In spite of the problems inherent in after-the-fact identification of psychological correlates of treatment outcome, there are some tentative findings worthy of attempts at verification. Among the characteristics associated with the poorest outcome are a history of depression, suicidal tendencies, other physical illnesses and symptoms, the anticipation of little support from others, a sense of self-esteem based upon beauty and shapeliness, high neuroticism, and unrealistic preoperative expectations that the tumor would be benign.

Another factor that appears to be associated with breast cancer treatment outcome is the nature of the preparation of the patient prior to surgery. This preparation must involve the husband, and must include supportive and informative discussions with the surgeon. But, as has already been noted, surgeons are often not particularly comfortable conducting such discussions. Similarly, the nature of postsurgical medical and nursing care as well as postsurgical support and empathy from the husband are important in helping determine the quality of the outcome (Dunkel-Schetter, 1984; Freidenbergs, Gordon, Hibbard, & Diller, 1980; Worden & Weisman, 1980).

HELPING SPOUSES COPE.  A final aspect of cancer treatment that has important psychosocial implications concerns itself with the spouse of the cancer patient. Cancer has a very significant impact on spouses, and they are frequently as distressed or even more distressed than the patients. In a study designed to develop and evaluate a treatment program that involved patients and their spouses, Heinrich and Schag (1985) developed a group program that focused on stress and activity management. The program was designed to demonstrate improvement in three areas—cancer information, psychosocial adjustment, and daily activities. A total of twenty-six patients and their spouses participated in the 6-week-long program, and the participants were contrasted with matched couples for whom customary current available care was provided. Thus, it was possible to contrast patients as well as spouses in the treatment and control conditions. About two-thirds of the patients were male, and most were retired, middle-class, white, and high school graduates.

Dependent measures of treatment success included an assessment of knowledge about cancer, psychosocial adjustment to illness, quality of life, daily activity level, evaluation of current care, and psychological distress. Evaluations were conducted at the start and completion of the group program. Followup interviews were conducted by telephone 2 and 4 months after the conclusion of the program, but the severe effects of the illness prevented the collection of data from a sufficient number of study participants at the final followup interview.

The experimental treatment program was designed to educate patients and their spouses about cancer and its impact and teach skills that could be used to manage stress and daily problems and to increase physical and recreational activities. Knowledge about cancer was found to have significantly improved in both patients and spouses in the experimental group over that in the case of patients and spouses in the control group. In addition, patients generally exhibited greater increases in knowledge about cancer than did spouses.

In the area of psychosocial adjustment, patients in both experimental and control conditions exhibited significant improvement. Spouses in both experimental and control conditions exhibited improvement, as well, but the amount did not achieve statistical significance. Level of physical and recreational activity did not improve significantly for the patients in either group, but spouses in the experimental group were significantly more active at the time of the posttreatment evaluation.

Patients in the experimental group as well as their spouses also expressed greater satisfaction with the care that was received than did the control group study group members. With the exception of the activity management component of the program, independent assessments indicated that members of the experimental group reported more improvement than did members of the control group. At the time of the 2-month followup telephone interview, experimental group patients reported more frequent use of stress management techniques, which they also rated as being more helpful in coping with medically related stresses.

## ASTHMA

The symptoms of asthma (more properly called bronchial asthma) have been known since antiquity. The disorder had been identified at the time of Hippocrates (460–370 B.C.) and was already described in detail in the second century (Pinkerton, Hughes, & Wenrich, 1982; Rainwater & Alexander, 1982; Rosenblatt, 1976).

While there is still some difficulty in developing a clearly agreed-upon definition of asthma, its fundamental characteristic is a reversible airway obstruction that results in paroxysmal wheezing and labored breathing (commonly referred to as an asthma attack) that is due to some combination of smooth muscle spasm, tissue swelling, and excessive mucous secretion. Quite sophisticated diagnostic techniques are now available that have replaced the earlier unreliable diagnosis of asthma made simply on the basis of evidence of wheezing. Today the diagnosis is not made simply on the basis of symptoms. Rather, it is made on the basis of assessments of pulmonary physiology, blood counts, skin tests, and the detection of elevated levels of specific antibodies. Asthmatic attacks are intermittent, vary in severity from patient to patient and from episode to episode, and, in contrast to emphysema, are reversible, either following adequate treatment, or sometimes as a consequence of spontaneous recovery.

Creer (1982) has recently reviewed the empirical literature on asthma in the context of the early work of French and Alexander (1941). The problems with their psychosomatic approach can be clearly seen in this excerpt:

> French and Alexander . . . blended together existing psychological theories of asthma, primarily culled from the psychoanalytic literature, and data gathered from 27 asthmatic patients undergoing psychoanalysis. From such a base, they concluded that: (a) asthmatic patients are subject to a universal conflict between an infantile dependent attachment to their mother and other emotional attitudes (especially sexual-genital wishes) that are incompatible with and threaten such a dependent emotional attitude; (b) the asthma attack is somehow related to an inhibited suppressed cry by the patient for his mother; (c) the asthmatic patient has a unique personality; and (d) psychotherapy, particularly psychoanalysis, will alleviate the symptoms of asthma. It might seem easy to ignore the conclusions by French and Alexander, but it is impossible to do so. In respect to psychological factors and asthma, their work has easily had the greatest impact of anything written on the subject. The ideas expressed by French and Alexander have proven amazingly durable: Despite data to the contrary, they continued to be espoused by . . . "true believers". (Creer, 1982, p. 916)

In his critical review of the empirical literature on asthma, Creer has concluded that: (1) there is little evidence to suggest that children with asthma experience any unusual relationship with their mothers; (2) there is no evidence that asthma represents a repressed cry for one's mother; (3) in the reviews of the literature on personality factors and asthma, there are no persuasive data to support the contention that asthmatics have a unique set of personality characteristics; and (4) there is no evidence to suggest that traditional methods of psychotherapy alleviate asthma (also see Wittkower, 1974).

There is substantial evidence, however, that psychological factors are implicated in a significant proportion of asthma attacks. Fear and anxiety are common precipitants of asthma attacks among asthmatics, and there is evidence that such attacks can be induced by suggestion (Stein, 1982). Asthmatic attacks can be precipitated by a hypersensitivity, or enhanced reactivity, to a foreign substance that serves as an allergen. But there is considerable evidence from research studies with both animal and human subjects that psychosocial factors can play a role in potentiating or in moderating the effects of these allergens, generally by impacting on the immunologic system of the body. There is no evidence that a single specific neurological factor is involved in bronchial asthma, although many biological theories suggest that the hypothalamus may play a particularly important role in this process. The view of asthma as a single disorder that affects everyone alike is no longer held. Rather, asthma is now viewed as a complex and multifaceted disorder.

### Psychological Treatment of Asthma

Three psychological approaches have been used in the treatment of asthma: (1) psychotherapeutic treatment of conflicts that exist within the patient or within the family; (2) behavioral treatments such as systematic desensitization and relaxation; and (3) interventions designed to modify some cognitive aspect of the patient's asthma-related behavior, such as the process of concluding that an asthma attack is underway. Thus, the studies of psychosocial treatment approaches are as complex as the theories of how asthma develops (Alexander, 1981).

Relaxation, hypnosis, and contingency management approaches (De Piano & Salzberg, 1979; Moore, 1965; Pinkerton, Hughes, & Wenrich, 1982; Rainwater & Alexander, 1982; Yorkston et al., 1974) seem to have little clinically significant effect on respiratory functioning as such, but do provide important benefits in reducing much of the anxiety secondarily associated with the disorder. Psychotherapeutic approaches to dealing with the underlying conflicts that are presumably associated with the development and maintenance of asthma are without effect. Pinkerton, Hughes, and Wenrich (1982) summarize their evaluation of the psychological intervention literature in the case of asthma as follows:

> Psychological therapies do not prove effective as a cure for asthma. However, it is now believed that psychological difficulties can and do result from asthma. In this area, psychological treatment of anxiety and fear-related responses, which may precipitate an attack, or treatment of the maladaptive behavioral response patterns of the person having asthma or his family members, has proven quite successful. The treatment modalities of relaxation, desensitization, and biofeedback have shown success in reducing anxiety and fear-related responses which may exacerbate an attack. The operant conditioning therapies have proven quite successful in treating the maladaptive behavioral response patterns that maintain asthma-like behavior. (p. 244)

There is some evidence that family therapy can be a valuable adjunct to conventional medical treatment of asthma. Gustafsson, Kjellman, and Cederblad (1986) divided a group of eighteen children with severe, chronic bronchial asthma into two groups and provided family therapy to one of the groups in addition to the normal medical treatment all patients were receiving. Their family therapy, that lasted an average of about eight sessions, dealt with the role of the child's asthma symptoms in the family system and tried to enhance communication about the emotional impact of the child's asthma on family members.

Gustafsson and colleagues found that while the children who received conventional medical treatment showed no significant change in the symptoms of asthma, children in the family therapy group demonstrated significant improvement over a 3½-year followup period on a number of different measures of the severity of the disorder; these followup data were collected by a pediatric allergist who did not know whether or not specific children and their families were part of the family therapy group. The measures that improved significantly included general pediatric assessment, breathing volume and flow, days without functional impairment, and reduced use of drugs. Similar findings were reported in the case of adult asthmatics by Deter (1986).

In view of the fact that asthma is generally most successfully treated by medication, one important line of investigation by health psychologists concerns itself with understanding the factors that are associated with medical failure. This line of research has helped in the design of individualized medical treatment programs based upon the analysis of personality factors. For example, Kinsman, Dirks, and Jones (1982; see also Jones, Dirks, & Kinsman, 1980) have been examining the psychological factors that serve to perpetuate physical illness in general, and asthma in particular. They have coined the term *psychomaintenance* to refer to the psychological and behavioral factors that "maintain and increase both perceived severity and medical intractability of the illness once it has already developed" (1982, p. 435).

These investigators are interested in such issues as why certain patients continue to be dysfunctional despite having had medical treatment that is ordinarily effective, why certain patients appear to require an unusually intensive medical care regimen, and more generally, what patients do that contributes adversely to their response to medical treatment. One form of psychomaintenance that is of interest to this group is the failure to adhere to therapeutic regimens (see Chapter 12).

Kinsman, Dirks, and Jones make two important assumptions in their work that is designed to assess and identify personal styles that contribute to the failure of medical treatment. First, they believe that such behavior may have many different psychological origins; and second, they believe that an accurate diagnosis of the psychological bases of psychomaintenance is a prerequisite for the resolution of each specific case. Their model for assessing psychomaintenance is multidimensional and includes not only an analysis of the onset, type, and severity of the illness, but also an analysis of the patient's personality style, attitudes toward the illness and its treatment, subjective experience of the illness, and illness-related behavior. They write:

> From the standpoint of psychomaintenance, it is assumed that the patient brings to the illness a personal style that may either defeat, have no effect on, or facilitate medical management. Assessment of psychomaintenance potentials and these styles begins at the level of personality and then proceeds to explore the linkages among personality factors and the more illness-specific attitudes and symptom reports. The linkages between these levels reveal much about how the person is apt to regard asthma, experience it, and behave during its treatment. (pp. 441–442)

The assessment procedure that these authors have developed is based upon the Battery of Asthma Illness Behavior (BAIB). Three sets of psychological test instruments comprise the battery—a set of personality measures derived from a number of standardized objective personality measurement instruments; a set of attitude and opinion measures developed by the authors that tap the illness-pertinent dimensions of optimism, regard for medical staff, specific internal awareness of symptoms, external locus of control, and the sense of stigma; and, finally, the Asthma Symptom Checklist that assesses ten symptom categories commonly associated with asthma, such as panic and anxiety focused on asthma attacks, feelings of irritation, reduced energy level and fatigue, breathing difficulties, chest congestion, feelings of anger, and symptoms of rapid breathing, heart pounding, and panting.

On the basis of a sophisticated analysis of this test battery, the authors have been able to identify a number of what might be called "patient types," and for each type, they have identified a set of treatment recommendations that are designed to reduce psychomaintenance. For example, one patient type is the person with high panic and fear and excessive vigilance. Such patients exaggerate their distress, have severe but diffuse symptoms, are passive and withdrawn, but at the same time excessively dependent and anxious. Regarding their asthma, these patients are generally pessimistic, dissatisfied with the quality of their medical care, and tend to think of themselves as stigmatized and victimized by their illness. Regarding their specific symptoms, these patients have high levels of anxiety regarding their breathing difficulties, report frequent and severe hyperventilation, but are usually ineffective in self-management.

With patients of this type, for example, Kinsman, Dirks, and Jones (1982) believe that medical treatment should make a careful distinction between symptoms due to asthma and symptoms due to anxiety, should avoid overmedication, should educate the patient about the importance of compliance with the treatment program, should include training in relaxation techniques and other forms of enhanced self-control, and should include a course of psychotherapy designed to address the self-defeating ways of reacting to stress.

## CONCLUDING COMMENTS

In reviewing the nature of the assertions regarding psychosocial components of the five disorders discussed in this chapter and the three that preceded it, a striking number of similarities can be found. These similarities speak to a significant generic component to illness. These generic, that is, nonspecific, consequences of psychosocial factors on health and illness have not gone unrecognized in the health psychology literature. To put it another way, no matter what psychosocial characteristic is studied, patients with chronic pain, coronary disease, hypertension, cancer, and asthma are far more similar to each other than they are different from each other (Friedman & Booth-Kewley, 1987).

In commenting on prospective studies of psychosocial factors associated with cancer, for example, Sklar and Anisman (1981) found that the presence of unresolved psychological problems related to family relationships was associated not only with cancer, but also with the risk of psychiatric disorders such as depression and mania.

We have already discussed the longitudinal study of Johns Hopkins Medical School students. As part of that study, Betz and Thomas (1979) have examined the relationship of temperament to subsequent measures of health and illness. These investigators think of temperament as a dispositional tendency in the emotional sphere that is largely determined at birth and constant over the lifetime of the individual. Temperament is described in such terms as calm, irascible, sensitive, energetic, reflective, practical, and indifferent.

Three temperament types were identified by Betz and Thomas: (1) slow and solid; (2) rapid and facile; and (3) irregular and uneven, a typology that had been used by others as well in the study of temperament. Medical students who were thought of as slow and solid were those who thought about their problems in a very broad context, who were cautious in new situations, and who depended on their own resources. Those students who were thought of as rapid and facile were bright, clever, spontaneous, and articulate, and thought about their problems largely in terms of the immediate and the present. Finally, students who were irregular and uneven in temperament were moody, confused, sometimes overdemanding as well as underdemanding, and variable in terms of how much time they took in dealing with problems, either taking too much or too little time. Medical students could apparently be sorted out into one of these three temperament types with reasonable reliability.

In two studies, with two different samples of medical students, those who earlier were identified as of irregular and uneven temperament were found to be significantly more vulnerable to illness, but no differences in the relationships of temperament to illness were found as a function of any particular illness. That is, temperament was associated with the risk of illness in general rather than with the risk of any specific illness.

Cassileth Lusk, Strouse, Miller, Brown, Cross, and Tenaglia (1984) examined psychological adaptation among patients with chronic illnesses, including arthritis, diabetes, cancer, kidney disease, and dermatologic disorders. They found important relationships between measures of mental health and such variables as recency of diagnosis, declining physical status, and age, but no differences at all among the five chronic illnesses. Older patients generally reported better mental health than younger patients; patients whose disorders had been diagnosed within the previous 4 months generally reported poorer mental health than those whose disorder had been diagnosed less recently; mental health scores generally decreased with declining physical status.

Some years ago, Syme and Torfs (1978) reviewed the epidemiological research that had been reported on the topic of hypertension and were struck by the similarities in psychosocial factors that had been identified as associated with diseases of all types. They concluded that increased attention should be paid to understanding susceptibility to illness in general. Thus, we are seeing different investigators coming to one important conclusion, namely, that while it may be important to arrive at a specific diagnosis for some purposes, there may be other reasons for paying more attention to what might be called generalized susceptibility.

Regarding this hypothesized generalized susceptibility, a number of possibilities are worthy of investigation. It is possible, for example, that generalized susceptibility is psychosocial, while specific susceptibility is biological. It is also possible that biological factors play a predominant role in predisposing certain individuals to a specific disorder, but that psychosocial factors play the predominant role in determining whether the potential disorder is precipitated and what its course might be.

An editorial in the *New England Journal of Medicine* (Angell, 1985) has, however, called attention to the danger that in our consideration of how psychological factors play a role in the precipitation or perpetuation of specific illnesses, we may lose sight of the role of biology. The danger is that we can come to believe that illness is our fault. In that editorial, Angell wrote, "Our belief in disease as a direct reflection of mental state is largely folklore. Furthermore, the corollary view of sickness and death as a personal failure is a particularly unfortunate form of blaming the victim. At a time when patients are already burdened by disease, they should not be further burdened by having to accept responsibility for the outcome" (p. 1572).

While the position expressed in the editorial may not accurately reflect the existing psychosocial knowledge base related to health and illness ("Council condemns," 1985), the task is to give biology its proper due—not too little and not too much. The danger is that in our concern for the *psychology* of health, we will forget the *biology* of health. Psychologizing about health and illness is an activity that is particularly rampant in the case of poorly understood dreaded diseases, and the history of medicine includes a number of examples of such inappropriate psychologizing. When the tubercle bacillus was discovered, "the elaborate construct of the tuberculosis-prone personality evaporated" (Angell, 1985, p. 1571). A similar transformation took place in the theories of general paresis when the cause was discovered to be an earlier syphillitic infection of the central nervous system.

Today, there is much talk about a cancer-prone personality. Simonton and Simonton (1975; also see Applebaum, 1977), for example, believe that cancer patients are responsible for bringing about their cancer, that cancer serves some purpose for them, and that if their minds are capable of bringing it about, they are capable as well of getting rid of it. The danger in talking about the patient's will to live as being responsible for his or her recovery is that it leaves us little alternative than to blame those patients who fail to overcome their illnesses.

In these four chapters we have examined the rationale and effectiveness of psychological intervention programs in medical settings. If one considers psychological intervention to be the bottom line of health psychology, then it is important to realize that such intervention strategies have already been discussed in five separate contexts in this volume. First, we have seen the use of psychological interventions in three preventive contexts: (1) helping people cope with stress (Chapter 3); (2) helping people become more informed about health and illness and behave more competently when facing challenges to their well-being (Chapter 4); and (3) helping people learn about the counterproductive aspects of certain lifestyles and to change these lifestyles where possible (Chapters 5 and 6). Second, we have seen how psychologists think about intervention in the treatment context. Specifically, we have discussed ways in which psychologists go about reducing the anxiety and discomfort associated with medical care (Chapter 7), and now, we have seen how psychologists think about psychosocial components of a variety of illnesses and how psychological interventions can reduce the duration and discomfort of these illnesses, if not their incidence. In the next chapter, we will examine the important problem of adherence to medical care regimens and see how health psychologists have gone about increasing adherence (Chapter 12). Finally, in the last chapter we will examine the process of becoming a health professional, and, in passing, we will see how health psychologists have sought to make that process less stressful and more fulfilling.

These four chapters have presented an impressive number of studies that speak to the effectiveness of psychological interventions in the treatment of a wide variety of medical disorders. This demonstrated effectiveness is particularly noteworthy given that most medical settings do not provide optimal opportunities for these interventions to be fully integrated into the comprehensive treatment program.

Psychological interventions have a clear role to play in improving the ability to cope with a disease once it has been diagnosed. The disorders that seem to respond most dramatically to psychological interventions include heart disease, cancer, hypertension, and chronic pain. Less evidence of the effectiveness of psychological interventions is available in the case of asthma, although some positive consequences of psychological interventions have been reported.

Every form of intervention described in these chapters has been found to be effective for some disorder, and often, for many different disorders. Thus, for example, hypnosis may be effective in the case of skin disorders, headaches, asthma, and for the management of both acute and chronic pain; psychotherapeutic interventions have been found to assist in coping with heart disease and cancer; relaxation training programs have been found to assist patients in coping with chronic pain, headaches, cancer, and hypertension; and contingency management programs have been found to be effective with patients suffering from asthma, cancer, chronic pain, and hypertension. In addition, brief psychotherapy has been found to be effective in reducing the overutilization of medical care and secondary anxiety and in facilitating rehabilitation. The cost of brief psychotherapy appears to be more than offset by the savings in other medical care expenditures.

Behavior modification procedures appear to be very helpful in treating people with chronic pain for whom medical procedures have either failed or are considered inappropriate. Thus, in the area of chronic pain, focusing on the *what* of behavior appears to have greater payoff than focusing on the *why* of behavior, even though exploring why people develop chronic pain or why the pain persists may be inherently a more interesting and intellectually challenging task.

Psychological interventions are arguably more effective in treatment and rehabilitation than in prevention, although this conclusion may be due to the fact that the demonstration of effectiveness of preventive intervention is substantially more complex than the demonstration of treatment effectiveness. Psychological interventions make a difference far more quickly in the case of coping with illness than in inducing health-enhancing behavior and preventing illness.

The role of the psychologist as part of the treatment team in the medical setting is becoming increasingly well-established. Only the future will tell how that potential role gets played out, since its implementation is inevitably part of the two major debates that are taking place in the medical care system: (1) Will a biopsychosocial orientation to health and illness functionally replace the biomedical orientation that is still prevalent among health care providers; and (2) in the competition for the health dollar, will psychologists be able to establish a secure and unchallenged role in the health care delivery system.

## SUMMARY

- Evidence linking psychosocial factors as a causative agent for cancer is unconvincing, in part because all reported studies in this area have severe methodological weaknesses. Psychosocial factors do, however, appear to influence the course of cancer once it has been developed.

- There is some evidence that life expectancy among cancer patients is greater when patients express their negative emotions and distress, when they seem more hostile, depressed, and anxious, and when they do not spend a lot of time being polite, apologetic, and acquiescent.

- Psychological intervention programs play an effective role in helping patients cope with cancer and its treatment.

- Early psychosomatic theories of asthma that linked it to disturbances in the mother-child relationship and to excessive levels of dependency have not been shown to have any validity.

- Psychological factors appear to be clearly implicated in the precipitation of asthma attacks among asthmatics.

- Psychosocial treatment for asthma appears to play a significant supplementary role in the comprehensive medical treatment program, particularly if these treatment plans are tailored to the specific psychosocial needs of the patient.

- Risk factors for a variety of disorders appear to be quite similar to each other, and there is reason to believe that there is a general susceptibility factor. Accordingly, it may be that much more can be accomplished in both preventing disease as well as increasing recovery rate when diseases have already occurred by attending to general nonspecific factors than in the search for factors that place people at risk for some specific disease.

- Five specific disorders appear to be particularly responsive to psychological intervention procedures—heart disease, hypertension, cancer, asthma, and chronic pain. While these interventions rarely cure these disorders, they do serve to reduce anxiety, fear, and discomfort, to enhance coping skills, to potentiate the effectiveness of medication, and to reduce the duration of disability associated with these disorders.

- Provision of information constitutes an important form of psychological intervention when working with people with diagnosed physical illnesses. The information can be related to the illness itself as well as to ways of coping with the disorder.

- In general, multicomponent psychological intervention programs are more effective than single component programs, almost regardless of the illness in question.

- An important role of psychological intervention is in helping family members cope with illnesses in members of their families.

# Adherence to Medical Treatment Programs

# 12

## INTRODUCTION

Adherence to a treatment program refers to the extent to which patients follow the recommendations of their physicians or other health care providers; it can be thought of as a form of decision making (Janis, 1984a). Failure to adhere to preventively oriented programs that attempt to change lifestyles was discussed in Chapters 5 and 6. In this chapter, we will examine adherence to health care programs that deal with treatment of existing disorders, particularly failure to adhere to medication programs. It is this medicinal aspect of adherence that has been most actively investigated (see, for example, Dunbar & Agras, 1980), although other components of adherence, such as keeping appointments or following recommendations that do not involve medications, have also been studied.

In the early literature on adherence, the term *compliance* was more commonly used than adherence. DiMatteo and Friedman (1982) have made a persuasive case that the term *adherence* is far more satisfactory. Regarding the term *compliance* they write:

This term tends to reflect and perpetuate the image of patients as passive, submissive, and unable to make their own decisions. It creates ex-

pectations that providers of health care are all-knowing and all-power-
ful, and can decide what is best for the patient. The term tends to imply
an attitude held for a long time by the medical profession—that if recommendations are not followed, it is the fault of the patient. (p. 36; also
see Haynes, Taylor, & Sackett, 1979; Sackett & Haynes, 1976)

The term "adherence" leads investigators to focus on what people do,
while the term "compliance" focuses on who people are, mainly by looking for
characteristics of the so-called "compliant personality." Efforts to identify the
personality or demographic characteristics that uniquely distinguish the non-
complier have produced few significant findings, and Leventhal, Zimmerman,
and Gutmann (1984), among others, believe it is far more fruitful to think of
adherence as a complex process of self-regulation that occurs in a social context
and that involves patients in a health care provider system. Adherence, therefore, involves both internal as well as external determinants.

Kristeller and Rodin (1984) have suggested that it may not be possible to
agree on a single word to describe what is, in reality, a complex process. They
have suggested that the process be divided into three stages: (1) *compliance*—the
initial agreement to and following of a clinical prescription on the part of the
patient; (2) *adherence*—the continued following of a negotiated treatment plan
under supervision, in the face of conflicting demands; and (3) *maintenance*—the
incorporation into a general lifestyle of unsupervised health-related behavior.
This multiple-stage model underlines the active role of self-regulation that patients must often play in their own treatment and provides a useful framework
for analyzing failures to follow a treatment plan as well as interventions that can
increase adherence.

Failure to adhere to a medical care treatment program compromises the
full benefit of the treatment procedure, thus increasing morbidity and mortality
rates. Failure to adhere to a medical care treatment program also signals dissatisfaction with medical care, disrupts the patient's relationship with the health care
provider, and increases the overall cost of medical care. Indeed, cost-effectiveness analyses typically indicate that money spent to increase adherence to medical care programs is money well spent (Dunbar & Stunkard, 1979; Masur, 1981).

From a different point of view, adherence can be thought of within the
context of the legal concept of *informed consent* (Ley & Morris, 1984). Adherence
to medical treatment programs requires a sufficient level of understanding on
the part of the patient to be assured that the patient can make an informed
decision. From a legal point of view it is not enough for patients to adhere to a
medical treatment program simply because the health care provider tells them to
do so; they must also understand what is required of them and why and what the
risks are of adhering as well as of not adhering to the treatment program.

Differential adherence to a treatment program, such as to some particular drug, also throws into doubt evaluation studies of alternative forms of medical care. If the rate of adherence differs significantly in the case of two competing drug treatments, one can erroneously conclude that one treatment is

superior to the other, while, in fact, it may be only that the adherence rate is different.

In general, failure to adhere to a medical care treatment program can be due to lack of understanding of what the health care provider wants, unwillingness to adhere to the program, or inability to do so. These phenomena can be a consequence of psychological attributes of the patient, environmental or situational characteristics, characteristics of the treatment program, or of the nature of the relationship between the patient and the health care professional (Haynes, Taylor, & Sackett, 1979; Sackett & Haynes, 1976).

The health belief model (Becker, 1974; Becker & Maiman, 1975; Becker, Maiman, Kirscht, Haefner, & Drachman, 1977) was introduced in Chapter 5 as a framework for understanding adherence to treatment programs that are designed to reduce obesity. The model has been modified by Masur (1981) to facilitate the overall understanding of the problem of adherence to medical treatment programs. In this model, adherence is seen as a function of the interactions of four sets of variables: (1) preexisting general readiness to adhere to treatment program requirements; (2) factors that may modify that readiness in the specific instance; (3) conditions immediately antecedent to the specific adherence opportunity; and (4) consequences of adherence or failure to adhere to the specific treatment program.

The readiness variables, including general health-related motivations, including adherence-related motivations, form the cognitive base of adherence. The moderating factors include demographic characteristics of the patient, characteristics of the specific treatment program, and specific motivations regarding the current illness. Antecedent conditions include both internal components, such as symptoms of discomfort, and external components, such as reminders of adherence-promoting action. Finally, the consequences of adherence, or its failure, include such internal phenomena as relief of pain and such external phenomena as praise or decreased health-related expenditures.

In this chapter, we will first examine the various ways that adherence to medical care is assessed. Then, we will review the literature on the prevalence of the problem of failure to adhere to treatment programs. As you will see, there is a special problem regarding the failure to adhere to treatment programs for hypertension. The next three sections will review the research studies that have sought to understand nonadherence in terms of: (1) characteristics of the treatment program; (2) demographic characteristics of the patient; and (3) psychosocial characteristics of the patient and of the patient-physician relationship. Finally, the chapter will examine efforts that have been made to improve adherence rates.

## MEASUREMENT OF ADHERENCE

Definition and measurement of adherence tends to vary from study to study, in part because of differences in the nature of the treatment modality. Specific treatment programs lend themselves to specific ways of assessing adherence.

Clearly, however, studies that use different measurement procedures for assessing adherence are difficult to compare, and most investigators now believe that every effort should be made to develop standard procedures for the assessment of adherence (Gordis, 1979; Marston, 1970).

### Clinical Outcome

Five major strategies for assessing adherence are currently in use (Masek, 1982; Masur, 1981). First, adherence is often assessed by clinical outcome—the assumption being that if the patient takes the medication that is prescribed, the condition will improve. Thus, failure to improve is a measure of non-adherence. There are, of course, a number of serious problems with using improvement as a measure of treatment program adherence, and improvement is rarely used alone as a measure of adherence. First, certain medications may be relatively ineffective, with the result that adherence and improvement are unrelated. Second, improvement can occur as a consequence of factors having nothing to do with medication or with medical care, such as changes in diet or reductions in conflict at home or at work. Third, patients sometimes take several medications with varying degrees of adherence, making it quite impossible to know which medication, if any, might have been related to the clinical improvement.

### Patient Self-report

The second assessment of adherence is by patient self-report. That is, the investigator takes the position that if patients say that they have adhered to the treatment program, then they have. In some cases, self-reports are quite valid, but generally this is not the case. While patients who adhere to a treatment program rarely report that they do not adhere, the reverse is far more common. Thus, the difficulty is in distinguishing between people who say that they are adhering to a treatment program when they, in fact, are not, and those who say they are adhering to a treatment program who, in fact, are. There is some evidence, however (Dunbar & Stunkard, 1979), that while patients may not be valid reporters of their own past behavior regarding treatment programs adherence, they are fairly good predictors of their own future adherence rates. Thus, patients at risk of not adhering to a treatment program can often be identified in advance for special attention and intervention.

### Medication Measurement

Third, adherence is assessed by medication measurements, such as by tablet counts, bottle counts, or by checking prescription refills. On the one hand, medication that is still in the bottle has clearly not been taken by anyone. On the other hand, however, in using medication measurement as an index of adherence, one clearly has to assume that the medication that is no longer in the bottle has been taken by the patient and by no one else.

Most studies find a fair amount of agreement between medication measurement (which is easy, quick, and inexpensive) and chemical analyses (which tend to be difficult, slow, and expensive). In the case where the amount of medication taken is not absolutely crucial to treatment effectiveness, such as in the treatment of peptic ulcer, medication measurement may be quite adequate as an indicator of treatment program adherence. In other cases, however, where precise amounts of a particular medication must be taken, medication measurement may not be accurate enough.

### Medication Monitors

The fourth method of assessing adherence is by means of medication monitors—devices that measure when medications are removed from their containers. This form of adherence assessment is particularly valuable when medications need to be taken at some more or less regular interval, for example, one pill daily. In one such device, described by Masur (1981), pills are packaged in a stack, and alongside the stack is a strip of radiation-sensitive film. On the top of the stack (the end that would contain the pill that would be taken last) is a radiation-emitting chemical, such as a small uranium source, and a spring that keeps pressure on the stack. The longer the uranium source remains stationary, the darker is the mark it leaves on the strip of radiation-sensitive film. Thus, when the empty package is returned to the investigator, the film can be developed and examined. Removing the pills at regular intervals will produce a pattern of equally dark spots. Forgetting to take a pill for a long period of time will result in a very dark spot on the film. Taking several pills at once will result in an absence of spots.

In one study using the medication monitor, Moulding, Onstad, and Sbarbaro (1970; also see Moulding, 1979) found that 31 percent of a sample of 122 patients with tuberculosis took less than 70 percent of their medications for 1 month or more, thus presumably jeopardizing the effectiveness of the medication.

### Chemical Analysis

Finally, the fifth method for assessing adherence is by direct chemical analysis of urine or blood serum. In the case of urine or blood serum tests, direct measures of the presence of the medication can be undertaken. Alternatively, a detectable chemical compound called a *tracer,* that is not discriminable by the patient and that is inert insofar as the disorder is concerned, is added to the medication. We have already met the tracer in the section on methodological issues in the control of cigarette smoking in Chapter 6. Chemical tests or tracers are the most accurate method that is currently available for the assessment of medical treatment program adherence, and most studies of other methods of assessing adherence contrast those methods with the results of chemical tests.

Even so there are problems with chemical tracers. Besides being inconvenient, and, in the case of blood tests, invasive, not all medications can be traced or tested. Not all laboratory procedures are perfectly reliable. Some tracers are absorbed by the body too quickly, others too slowly. Many tests cannot distinguish between a medication taken regularly over a long period of time and one taken irregularly but just before the urine or blood sample is collected. Levels of tracers in the urine or blood serum are often influenced by changes in body metabolism, diet, or weight. Finally, some tests are extremely expensive or time-consuming.

In summary, methods for the assessment of treatment program adherence are imperfect, and when in error, tend to overestimate compliance. Direct observation of adherence is an ideal method but generally impractical except with drugs that are taken very infrequently, or in settings such as hospitals where the patient is under constant observation. In order to improve the validity of adherence assessment, multiple assessment procedures may be necessary, although such multiple assessments may be suitable only in experimental studies but impractical in clinical settings. The careful study of adherence to medical treatment procedures is nonetheless crucial and will require continued attention to how adherence is to be most usefully assessed.

## PREVALENCE OF ADHERENCE FAILURE

Becker and Maiman (1975), among others, suggest that failure to adhere to medical treatment is among the best documented but least understood health-related behaviors. It has been estimated that between one-third and one-half of patients fail to cooperate fully with their medical regimens (Marston, 1970; Masur, 1981; Sackett & Snow, 1979; Stone, 1979a), and that failure to cooperate is even greater when lifestyle changes are recommended than when it is merely a matter of taking medication (DiMatteo & Friedman, 1982).

In recent studies of adherence with treatment plans specifically involving medication (Haggerty & Roghman, 1972; Millis, 1975; Stamler, Schoenberger, Shekelle, & Stamler, 1974), only between one-quarter and one-half of patients were taking the drugs that were prescribed, and fewer were paying attention to how frequently and when to take medications and to restrictions on accompanying food intake. Health care professionals rarely ask about adherence and generally underestimate the extent to which patients fail to adhere to the treatment program they have prescribed (Charney, 1972). It has been estimated that the annual cost to the medical care system of nonadherence to prescribed medication regimens amounts to between $400 and $800 million (Food and Drug Administration, 1980). This cost comes about because failure to adhere to medical treatment programs or to directions regarding certain medications: (1) often is as bad as not taking the medications at all, with the result that additional costs for medications need to be incurred; (2) often results in the need for additional appointments with clinicians; and (3) sometimes results in the condition becoming more severe, thus requiring more extensive and expensive treatment.

Not only are adherence rates far lower than health care providers believe, but in studies that have examined the ability of health care providers to predict which patients will adhere to treatment programs and which will not, accuracy of predictions has been found to be low (see, for example, Mushlin & Appel, 1977; Paulson, Krause, & Iber, 1977).

### Adherence Failure in Hypertension

As was indicated in Chapter 10, hypertension constitutes a major public health problem, since it is a leading cause of heart disease, stroke, and kidney failure. Because hypertension is often asymptomatic, efforts to treat it medicinally are particularly prone to failure (Leventhal, Zimmerman, & Gutmann, 1984; SerVass & Weinberger, 1979). Shapiro (1982b) described the problem as one of "persuading the patient with hypertension, who ordinarily does not have any symptoms, to take medications perhaps for a lifetime, medications that may have side effects" (p. 229).

Cases of hypertension are commonly found in screening programs, that is, in programs that measure blood pressure in large numbers of people who, for example, work in the same setting or live in the same neighborhood. It has been estimated that about half of hypertensives who are detected in such screening program are lost to followup with a year (Kasl, 1978).

One interesting longitudinal study of factors associated with control of hypertension is taking place in the rural community of Edgecombe County, North Carolina (James et al., 1984; Wagner et al., 1984; Williams et al., 1985). This group has examined the prevalence of hypertension in a random sample of more than 2000 adults. A total of 539 men and women were found who had elevated blood pressure levels.

The sample of 539 men and women was categorized into seven groups as a function of awareness of hypertension, treatment history, and degree of control of their hypertension as a consequence of their treatment. The groups ranged from: (1) unaware of hypertension, with the last blood pressure reading more than 2 years ago; to (3) unaware of hypertension, with the last blood pressure check between 0 and 6 months ago; to (4) aware of hypertension but never treated; to (7) aware of hypertension, currently in treatment, and currently under control. In general, the progression from being unaware of hypertension to being aware of hypertension, in treatment, and under control was associated with increasing probability of being older, white, and female. In the case of women, this progression was further associated with higher family income and educational level. Among men, this progression was associated with higher levels of self-reported morbidity.

Since the overwhelming majority of hypertensive women were aware of their hypertension, these investigators concluded that the most serious clinical problem was to increase the proportion of hypertensive women who enter and remain in treatment. Other analyses contrasting the aware untreated hypertensive women with the aware treated hypertensive women revealed that those who were untreated had financial and transportation problems related to getting to medical treatment, higher levels of dissatisfaction with medical care, and less confidence in antihypertensive medication. In the case of men, nearly half were unaware of their hypertension. Hence, the pertinent issue was detection.

This group of investigators also examined factors associated with barriers to the use of medical care. In general, the entire sample made less use of medical care than was judged appropriate on the basis of their symptoms. Within the sample, however, hypertensive blacks found medical care to be less accessible, less satisfactory, and less affordable than hypertensive whites, and made less use of the medical care system.

When those hypertensives who adhered to a treatment program were contrasted with those who did not, these investigators found that the non-adherents were less well educated and had the least accurate understanding of their health. The relationship between social support (see Chapter 3) and adherence was also examined, and the investigators found that, in the case of women, lower adherence was associated with less social support from their husbands, their friends, and from people in their work settings. In the case of men, lower treatment adherence was associated with poorer social support in the work setting (also see Caplan et al., 1976; Harrison, Caplan, French, & Wellons, 1982).

In summary, the Edgecombe County studies have found that about one-quarter of randomly selected adults have elevated blood pressure and that many of them are unaware of their hypertension. Awareness and participation in antihypertensive treatment programs is significantly more common among women than men, among whites than blacks, and among older than younger persons. Among men, the problem is to increase their awareness of their own elevated blood pressures, a task that might best be accomplished by developing more systematic work-based screening programs. In the case of women, the problem is to increase their participation in appropriate treatment programs. Achieving this increase will apparently require changes in the organization and financing of medical care that will make medical care more accessible.

## TREATMENT CHARACTERISTICS AND ADHERENCE RATES

In an effort to understand variation in adherence rates, social scientists have examined them from three major points of view: (1) as a function of characteristics of the treatment program; (2) as a function of demographic characteristics of the patient; and (3) as a function of psychosocial characteristics of the patient or of the patient–health care provider relationship.

Complexity of the treatment program appears to be negatively related to adherence, that is, the more complex the treatment program, the less adherence can be expected. Complexity can be a matter of how many different medications are prescribed, or how difficult the schedule, dosage, sequence, or timing is for taking the medications. Adherence rates, particularly as assessed by accuracy in taking the right prescribed medications in the right dose at the right time, decrease dramatically with the number of drugs that are prescribed.

Drugs that produce adverse side effects have not been found to have lower adherence rates than those that have no such side effects, but severity of the disorder appears to be directly related to adherence. In most cases, persons with more severe disorders tend to have higher adherence rates.

It is easier to adhere to a medical care treatment program when it is of short duration and when it brings prompt and significant relief. In the case of chronic conditions, such as diabetes, that require long-term medication that has little obvious effect, adherence is far poorer.

Miller (1983) has theorized that this decrease in adherence rate is a function of the *gradient of reinforcement,* that is, the fact that immediate rewards are usually more effective than delayed rewards in modifying behavior. If a medical treatment program cannot be expected to yield virtually immediate results, it is far less likely to be followed than one that does yield results that can be quickly perceived. This factor is particularly important in understanding the failure to adhere to preventively oriented health regimens that may never yield persuasive observable results.

## DEMOGRAPHIC FACTORS AND ADHERENCE RATES

Some 2000 different variables have been examined in terms of their relationship with adherence rates (Haynes, 1976b). The relationship of demographic factors—such as age, gender, intelligence, education, social class, occupation, marital status, race, and religion—to adherence rates is relatively weak (Epstein & Masek, 1978; Kasl, 1975; Masur, 1981; Sackett & Haynes, 1976). What relationships are found tend to be complex rather than unidimensional. That is, adherence has been shown to be a function of the interaction of disease, gender, and age. Kasl (1975) has noted, for example, that older people tend to adhere more frequently to treatment programs for hypertension, while younger people tend to adhere more frequently to treatment programs for reducing excessive cholesterol levels. Similarly, in smoking cessation programs, it has been found that a husband's efforts to stop smoking will be enhanced somewhat if the wife disapproves of his smoking, but that a wife's efforts to stop smoking will not be enhanced if the husband disapproves of her smoking. There is some evidence, however, that when these demographic factors are combined with other variables such as the nature of the illness or of the treatment program, the obtained relationships may be stronger than the relationship of treatment or illness characteristics to adherence rate alone, and may thus contribute to our understanding of adherence.

In addition, awareness is increasing that health care requires complex resource expenditures and that resources of time, money, and energy are often in limited supply. Patients who cannot afford medications that are prescribed for them do not buy the medications. Patients without automobiles or without access to usable forms of mass transportation cannot get to distant medical care settings. Patients with other pressing problems, such as a sick child at home, find it difficult to tend to their own medical problems.

Demographic factors associated with differential adherence rates in the case of specific disorders have also been studied. For example, Greenwald, Becker, and Nevitt (1978), examining the behavior of clients in a cancer detection facility, found that delay or failure to visit a physician after being told that the possibility of cancer was present could be accounted for by occupational status and characteristics of recent contacts with the health care system. Specifically, those persons with relatively high occupational status and those persons with better relationships with health care providers—for example, those who listed the name of a family physician on the intake form, those who reported relatively recent visits to a physician, and those who were referred to the cancer detection program by a physician—tended to delay less.

In another study, Korsch, Fine, and Negrete (1978) found that a small set of demographic factors characterized families who did not adhere to post kidney-transplant immunosuppressive treatments required by their children. These factors included lower income, absent fathers, and communication difficulties within the family as well as with health care practitioners.

## PSYCHOSOCIAL FACTORS AND ADHERENCE RATES

A number of different psychosocial theories have been advanced to account for the failure to adhere to a medical treatment program. These theories locate the problem either in the patient or in the relationship between the clinician and the patient.

### Patient Characteristics

Four types of patient attributes have been hypothesized in the literature as being related to poor adherence rates: (1) personality characteristics; (2) psychodynamic attributes; (3) learning deficiencies; and (4) lack of information.

One group of studies has examined the relationships of personality characteristics of the patient to adherence rates. Two specific psychological attributes of the patient have been found to be related to level of adherence with health care treatment programs. First, there appears to be an optimum level of anxiety that results in high adherence rates. Anxiety levels that are too low or two high are significantly associated with adherence failure. Second, attitudes toward health and health care are associated with adherence rates. Patients who feel less vulnerable and less threatened by current or future illnesses, who are less concerned about their own health, who believe that modern medicine is not particularly efficacious, and who believe that medical costs are too high all have lower adherence rates. General personality traits, such as cooperativeness or dependence, have not been found to be meaningfully associated with level of adherence to medical care treatment programs (Stone, 1979).

Another group of theorists thinks of adherence failure in psycho-dynamic terms, that is, as behavior that signals some deeper problem, such as resistance, hostility to authority, fear of dependency, guilt, rage, the repetition compulsion, or the like (see, for example, Applebaum, 1977). A third group sees adherence failure as the result of intellectual limitations on the part of the patient that can be corrected by appropriate reinforcement contingencies or by changes in how pertinent information is provided (Epstein & Masek, 1978). Finally, a fourth group sees adherence failure as the result of a lack of information, that is, as a cognitive defect, correctable by the provision of the appropriate information (Leventhal, 1973). Most recent empirical research has focused on informational variables.

Numerous studies have examined the fund of information patients have about their illnesses and the relationship of that information base to subsequent adherence rates. People obtain health-related information from many sources besides their physicians. Even in the clinical setting, considerable information is made available to patients that does not require interaction with the physician. Waiting rooms contain innumerable pamphlets appropriate to the setting, and many medical facilities have books, films, audiotapes, and videotapes readily available on demand.

Thus, the question of whether adherence rates are related to how much and what patients know about their illnesses is a very pertinent one. Indeed, with physicians often so busy in their offices, health-related information may be increasingly provided in written form. Generally speaking, most studies have not found that there are powerful relationships between the fund of information a patient has and adherence to medical treatment programs. Subjective evaluation of that knowledge as it seems to apply to one's own condition seems to be more clearly related to adherence than does the fund of factual information. In addition, there is some evidence that knowledge about etiology is less influential than knowledge about the normal course of the disorder in determining subsequent adherence (Masur, 1981).

Because oral communication between the health care provider and the patient is often incomplete, incomprehensible, unsatisfying, forgotten, or ineffective, attention has recently been directed toward a greater understanding of supplementary written communication (Ley & Morris, 1984). Between one-third and one-half of all patients report feeling insufficiently informed about their illnesses, and about the same proportion appear to misunderstand or forget the information that is presented to them orally. Most patients appear to want written information about their treatment program, and there is evidence that such information often increases their knowledge and understanding, increases their adherence rates, and improves therapeutic outcome (Ley & Morris, 1984).

Critical examination of written information provided in medication inserts has shown that the language is often too difficult for its intended audience. Written instructions have been found to be unclear, excessively technical, and ambiguous, and to use terms that are inappropriate and incomprehensible. In addition, there are obvious problems when the patient is not fluent or literate in the language in which the information is written. Considerable effort is currently being made to improve the readability of package inserts, and Ley and Morris (1984) have noted that if efficient written information could reduce noncompliance by only 10 percent, somewhere between 40 and 80 million dollars in health care costs could be saved annually.

### Health Care Provider–Patient Interaction

Examining patient-provider interaction treats the issue of adherence as one requiring the study of the transactions of at least two people, rather than simply the study of the patient (Stone, 1979). These transactions can be thought of as a series of episodes to which both the patient and the health care provider bring habitual ways of interacting and in which both have goals. The interactional view assumes that the patient and the health care provider share a joint responsibility for a successful outcome.

Interactions have been thought of as having a number of different possible characteristics (Szasz & Hollender, 1956). The health care provider can be active, expecting the patient to be passive—somewhat analogous to the practice of veterinary medicine or to the relationship of a parent and an infant. The health care provider can offer guidance, expecting that the patient will cooperate—as in the stereotyped relationship of teacher and pupil or parent and adolescent child. Or, alternatively, the health care provider can create a collegial interaction in which the provider and the patient participate as two adults in a mutual fashion—with the result that the patient takes an active self-regulatory role in the treatment program.

The factor that appears to have the most powerful relationship to the likelihood of proper adherence to the medical care regimen is the quality of the relationship between the patient and the health care practitioner (Charney, 1972; DiMatteo, 1979, 1985; DiNicola & DiMatteo, 1984; Doyle & Ware, 1977; Kasl, 1975; Stone, 1979). Many writers believe that physicians have too little training in the development of their communication skills (Mechanic, 1976; Poole & Sanson-Fisher, 1979; Wertheimer, Bertman, Wheeler, & Siegal, 1985).

Duffy, Hamerman, and Cohen (1980) identified ten communication skills that were, in their opinion, central to the physician-patient relationship. They observed twenty interns and residents in sixty patient contacts and found a range from 27 percent to 97 percent in the number of clinic visits in which these communication skills were present. Five skills were present in 80 percent or more of clinic visits. In descending order of frequency, these were: (1) direct physical examination to areas relevant to the patient's illness (97 percent); (2) explaining the nature of prescribed medication and therapy (91 percent); (3) assessing patient compliance in a nonthreatening way (90 percent); (4) facilitating patient communication by listening and encouraging the patient to speak (83 percent); and (5) developing the history of the illness out of the patient's own words (82 percent).

The skills least commonly observed, in ascending order of frequency, were: (1) asking the patient what he or she understands about the illness (27 percent); (2) ascertaining the patient's emotional response to illness (35 percent); (3) inquiring about the patient's current social history (59 percent); (4) explaining to the patient the nature of the illness (62 percent); and (5) permitting the patient to ask questions (75 percent).

As can be noted from these findings, the biology of the disorders tended to be more adequately dealt with than the psychology and sociology of the disorders, and the physicians tended to be relatively unempathic. Duffy, Hamerman, and Cohen concluded that it was important to teach the communication skills that are underdeveloped and to create an environment that is conducive to learning these skills because internists need to be able to recognize and address the psychological and social factors contributing to medical illness and to recognize and be responsive to the emotional distress associated with illness.

There seems to be some uncertainty in the literature regarding whether adherence is better if the patient sees the same clinician at each appointment. In their review of the literature, Dunbar and Stunkard (1979) have concluded that adherence is improved when the patient has a consistent relationship with the same clinician (also see Becker, Drachman, & Kirscht, 1974; Kirscht & Rosenstock, 1979). Yet, according to Gordis and Markowitz (1971), well-controlled studies suggest that there is no significant relationship between adherence rates and the degree of continuity of the patient-clinician relationship. Doyle and Ware (1977), for example, found that physician conduct was far more important than continuity of care in its relationship to general satisfaction with health care. That is, a good relationship between the patient and the clinician can be established that can have a significant impact on adherence to the treatment program, even if the patient sees the clinician only once. The reaction to the specific clinical contact appears to be more important than any generalized attitudes toward health care or health care providers.

Two factors in that relationship are particularly important—the quality of information communication and the level of rapport. DiNicola and DiMatteo (1984) refer to these two factors as the instructional component and the affective component of the relationship. DiMatteo (1979) distinguishes between treating the disease—the technical and instrumental dimension—and treating the diseased person—the emotional and empathic dimension. Research studies have repeatedly documented the existence of severe communication problems between physicians and their patients (see, for example, Boyd, Covington, Stanaszek, & Coussons, 1974; Hall, Roter, & Rand, 1981; Masur, 1981; Svarstad, 1976; Waitzkin, 1984). In a study of sixty women of menopausal age, for example, Berkun (1986) reported that 90 percent of them complained that they were given insufficient information about menopause by their physicians, partly because their physicians varied enormously in their abilities to communicate with their patients.

Characteristics of the communication between physicians and their patients have been studied for a number of years (see Ley, 1977; Ley & Morris, 1984). Patients tend to remember remarkably little of what physicians say to them (often less than half of what is said), and clearly the health care provider needs to know how to communicate to patients in ways that are easy to understand, and needs to take the time to find out if the patient has understood what has been said. Not surprisingly, Svarstad (1976), among others, has found that adherence rates are significantly higher among patients who have a clear understanding of what they are being instructed to do than among patients whose understanding is inaccurate.

Adherence has also been found to be related to the extent to which patients feel good about how they have been treated, that is, by the nature of the relationship they feel they have with the health care professional. Korsch and Negrete (1972), for example, found that mothers of children requiring medical care were more likely to adhere to the prescribed medical care treatment program to the extent that they felt accepted, appreciated, and respected by the physician. While patients adhere to courses of action prescribed by their physicians because they recognize that physicians are usually more expert than they are, patients' levels of adherence are dramatically increased by a sense that the physician cares for them and values their responsible health-related behavior.

Unlike demographic factors and characteristics of the treatment program that cannot easily be changed, the nature of the physician-patient relationship can be modified. Thus, efforts to "humanize" that relationship offer very promising intervention leverage for increasing adherence rates. Stone (1979) has noted, however, that in spite of the emphasis being placed on teaching communication skills to health professionals both while they are students and as part of their continuing education, few of these efforts have examined their effects on the subsequent behavior of their patients (also see DiMatteo, 1979).

## IMPROVING ADHERENCE RATES

Three approaches have been explored in attempting to improve adherence rates to medical treatment programs. The first approach is the development of patient education programs and the assessment of whether such programs result in improved adherence-related behavior. The second approach is to make changes in the treatment program, including changes in the behavior of the health care practitioner in the hopes that such changes will enhance adherence rates. Finally, many programs have attempted to use behavior modification approaches with the patient in order to improve adherence rates directly rather than indirectly. The greatest number of studies are probably in this last category—deliberate efforts to modify directly the adherence-related behavior of the patient.

In each individual instance, failure to adhere to a medical treatment program may require a careful diagnosis before a successful remedy can be applied. Box 12–1 illustrates such a diagnostic procedure.

**Box 12–1**  *Psychological Intervention in the Case of Adherence Failure*

Solving adherence problems in a clinical setting usually requires a functional analysis of the antecedents and consequences of the nonadherent behavior. This case study will illustrate this process and the work of the health psychologist in the inpatient setting.

The case involved a 5-year-old girl, Beverly, who was admitted with undiagnosed leukemia. Following some period of hospitalization, she began to refuse not only her medications, but also physical examinations and food. She became abusive with hospital staff who found themselves avoiding her unless a medical procedure was to be performed. Following several observation sessions, it became apparent that Beverly's nonadherence was a function of several factors. First, she was attended to by her mother around the clock, and her mother virtually had assumed the role of primary nurse. Second, the cytotoxic drugs she was taking made her chronically nauseous and weak and caused her hair to fall out. Third, from the beginning of her hospital stay, she was in isolation due to lowered immunity, and visitors had to wear gowns, head caps, and masks when visiting her.

Several reinforcers were evaluated, with mother's attention being the most potent. Since there was a strong possibility that Beverly would die, we were reluctant to make mother's attention contingent on taking her medication regularly, letting her doctor examine her, and consuming an adequate number of calories per day. However, a point system and attempts to establish hospital staff as social reinforcers failed.

After explaining our analysis to Beverly's mother, she agreed to withdraw her attention for brief intervals when Beverly failed to meet the behavioral criteria established. The implementation of this program initially resulted in severe tantrums from Beverly. But with continued support and guidance, Beverly's mother was able to follow through and a significant increase in adherence with the three desired behaviors (taking medication, letting the doctor examine her, and eating) resulted. Also, attempts to "normalize" Beverly's hospital environment were implemented by allowing visitors to enter her room without scrubbing and dressing as long as they remained a certain distance from her, and by providing special treats not previously on her menu that she had enjoyed at home.

Beverly was finally discharged after 4 months, with her leukemia in remission.

(Adapted from Masek, 1982 with permission.)

### Patient Education

As already indicated, education, in terms of the presentation of facts regarding some particular illness, has relatively little impact on adherence rates (Haynes, 1976a; Neufeld, 1976; see also Chapter 4). In one such study (Sackett et al., 1975), a patient education program with a sample of 230 hypertensive steelworkers improved their understanding of hypertension but did not improve their adherence to the medical treatment program.

Far less attention has been directed in the research literature, however, to the use of educational procedures designed to influence attitudes and beliefs related to adherence, or to enhancing comprehension of the information that is being transmitted to the patient. These areas offer considerable promise. Furthermore, patient education is increasingly becoming part of the responsibility of pharmacists, nurses, physical therapists, medical social workers, and physician assistants, but few studies have yet been reported regarding their effectiveness in increasing adherence rates.

What is clear is that great amounts of hurriedly delivered, excessively technical information delivered to the patient in a flurry by the busy physician is hardly the way to assure an adequate degree of adherence. Accordingly, it may be appropriate to be very deliberate about bringing consumer health education skills (see Chapter 4) to these health care providers by some form of staff development or in-service education.

### Treatment Program Modification

A number of creative approaches toward increasing adherence rates by modifying certain aspects of the treatment program have been reported. These approaches attempt, in general terms, to tailor the treatment program to the already-existing habitual behaviors of the patient, such as by linking pill-taking with nighttime toothbrushing, checking the eating habits of patients before assigning medications to be taken with meals, or asking whether the patient might prefer liquid medication rather than pills.

In one such study, Haynes and associates (1976) found that adherence could be substantially improved by teaching hypertensives to measure and chart their own blood pressures, chart their pill-taking behavior, and tailor their pill-taking to their daily habits. While adherence rates in a control group were unchanged over a 6-month time period, adherence increased more than 21 percent in the experimental group where these modifications in the treatment program were made. In addition, blood pressure fell in 85 percent of the members of the experimental group as compared with a drop in 56 percent of the control group.

One particularly interesting approach to increasing adherence rates is by innovative packaging of medications. The remarkable packaging of oral contraceptives that, in effect, has built-in reminders to take the medication, is a case in point. Innovative packaging of this kind undoubtedly increases the costs of producing medications and thus, potentially at least, reduces the profits associated with these sales (Masur, 1981). But the sales of antibiotics, in which dosage also needs to be carefully followed, are surely sufficient to justify similar dose-reminder packaging.

### Direct Modification of Patient Behavior

Behavior modification approaches to increasing adherence rates have a special appeal to psychologists, who have developed a variety of remarkably effective strategies for modifying behavior (Benfari, Eaker, & Stoll, 1981; Epstein & Cluss, 1982; Zifferblatt, 1975). Two approaches have been followed in the behavioral modification of adherence-related behavior: (1) manipulation of antecedent events, that is, events that precede the desired behavior; and (2) manipulation of consequent events, that is, events that occur after the desired behavior.

ANTECEDENT MANIPULATION. Manipulation of events that precede the desired behavior involves giving patients reminders to adhere to the treatment program. For example, Azrin and Powell (1969) developed a portable timing device and medication dispenser that could be set to generate a tone at specified intervals (depending on when the medication was to be taken). The tone could be turned off only by activating a knob that would, at the same time, eject a tablet into the user's hand. In an analysis of the timing device, Azrin and Powell found that substantially fewer pills were missed by patients using the device than by those employing the more customary method of relying on one's wristwatch. Current developments in miniaturization of computer chips have made it possible to build such cueing devices into watches by the provision of multiple alarms that sound at fixed times each day. Other even less costly forms of antecedent manipulation include sending out post-card reminders or using telephone reminders to encourage adherence to office appointments, and using posted notices, calendars, and medication charts to encourage adherence to medication programs.

Encouraging patients to continue medical treatment is a problem of the greatest importance to most clinicians. According to Rosenstock and Kirscht (1979), the likelihood of prematurely abandoning a treatment program is related to social isolation, negative attitudes and behavior on the part of the health service provider, low motivation on the part of the patient, inaccessibility of treatment, low socioeconomic status, and social instability. It should be noted that while some of these factors have to do with characteristics of the client, others have to do with characteristics of the medical care system. In fact, Rosenstock and Kirscht suggest that relatively simple changes in the ways in which services are organized and delivered can dramatically reduce the dropout rate. Modification of antecedent conditions, such as by reminding patients of appointments, increasing the ease of accessibility throughout the medical care system, and developing more personalized, convenient care have all been shown to be effective in increasing adherence to the treatment program.

For example, SerVass and Weinberger (1979) described a referral method that appeared to improve adherence rates in a sample of governmental employees in Indiana who were detected as hypertensives in a screening program. The traditional referral method (that was used in the case of those employees randomly assigned to the control group) was to inform them that their blood pressure was elevated, that this fact might represent a health problem, and that they should consult their physician for further evaluation and information. These employees were given a referral form and an educational brochure about hypertension. Part of the referral form was to be returned to the investigators by the physician. This part of the form made it possible for the physician to record the measurement of blood pressure obtained in the office and, at the same time, to confirm that the employee had complied with the referral.

In contrast, hypertensives randomly assigned to the experimental group were referred to their physicians by a different method. First, in addition to receiving an educational brochure and a referral form, this group viewed a short videotape presentation designed to describe the problem of uncontrolled hypertension and the methods available for its treatment, and to encourage them to visit their physicians. In addition, each hypertensive in the experimental group was interviewed briefly by a health counselor who offered to answer questions and to make an appointment with the individual's personal physician. A list of physicians who were willing to accept new patients was provided. Finally, if the referral cards were not returned to the investigators within 6 weeks, a telephone call was made to the individuals to determine if they had sought medical care and to encourage the need to do so, if they had not.

More than 6,000 employees out of a total of nearly 13,000 were screened, of whom 546 were found to have elevated blood pressure. Only about 60 percent of these employees knew about their hypertension, but all were randomly assigned to either the standard referral program or what the authors called the "motivated" referral program. Striking differences were found in the proportion of referral cards returned to the investigators—nearly 79 percent in the case of the motivated referral program participants versus only 29 percent in the case of the standard referral program participants. Interestingly, compliance with either the standard or the motivated referral procedure was no different in the case of those persons who previously knew about their hypertension (also see Haynes et al., 1976; Sackett et al., 1975; Shapiro, 1982b).

CONSEQUENCE MANIPULATION. Manipulation of the consequences of adherence-related behavior, that is, events that take place after the desired behavior, is assisted by reinforcing such behavior through some program of reward and punishment. A number of studies have shown that it is relatively easy and inexpensive to increase adherence by monetary rewards, or by providing alternatives to the patient in which adherence is clearly the more desirable—for example, giving chronic alcoholics the choice of taking Antabuse in the presence of a probation officer for a 1-year period of time, or going to jail for 90 days. In this study, Haynes (1973) found that virtually all of the alcoholics (138 out of 141) chose the Antabuse treatment rather than jail, and that at the end of the year, 66 were still receiving the medication, 49 had left town, 17 had been returned to jail, 3 were hospitalized, and 3 were lost to the study. In the case of the alcoholics who remained in town (including those who broke probation), a search of their records indicated that they had had an average of 3.8 arrests during the year preceding Antabuse treatment, and only 0.3 arrests during the year on treatment—a reduction of more than 90 percent.

Most programs involving monetary reward require an initial deposit on the part of the patient with the understanding that the deposit will be returned at the end of treatment if there has been complete adherence to the treatment program, and that some proportion of the deposit will be lost in the event that there is a failure of adherence (for example, see Bigelow, Strickler, Liebson, & Griffiths, 1976; Epstein & Masek, 1978).

Magrab and Papadopoulou (1977) described the use of a token economy system to help children who were suffering from renal failure and who were undergoing hemodialysis maintain their dietary compliance. Fairly severe dietary restrictions are necessary for persons who suffer from kidney failure because of the dangers of fluid overload and subsequent congestive heart failure, hypertension, and bone disease, among other conditions. Under these circumstances, any approach that encourages increased dietary compliance increases both the quality and the duration of life (also see Manley & Sweeney, 1986).

The method used by Magrab and Papadopoulou involved the assessment of dependent measures of dietary compliance—weight, potassium levels, and blood urea nitrogen levels. Points were provided that could be converted into money or desired gifts if the patients maintained measures within normal limits. Four adolescents, ages 11 to 18, who underwent kidney dialysis two or three times every week, were included in the study. Three of the four children had had chronic problems of dietary compliance failure. The children were allowed to select their own gifts. Analysis of the dependent measures during and after the treatment phase indicated that the token economy program was very successful. Weight gain was reduced by 45 percent, and potassium and blood urea nitrogen levels were maintained within normal limits.

Another form of consequence manipulation is to provide feedback to patients based on chemical analyses that indicate their degree of adherence to some medication program (see, for example, Gundert-Remy, Remy, & Weber, 1976). Most of these approaches find that adherence rate increases with the number of feedback reports. This feedback procedure is most useful in the case of medications that need to be taken over long periods of time, for example, dilantin in the case of seizure disorders, or medications for hypertension or cardiac difficulties.

Improving adherence rates requires a multidimensional approach on the part of the health care professional. First, it requires the recognition and acceptance of the fact that characteristics of the professional may play a role in lowered adherence. Second, it requires mutual participation by the physician and the patient in an interdependent problem-solving process. This process requires skillful problem presentation by the patient and analytic diagnostic interviewing by the health care professional. Furthermore, a collaborative approach to the development of a remedial plan that is sensitive to the patient's predicament and that both the physician and the patient fully understand as well as shared responsibility for monitoring adherence are essential components of this type of adherence-improvement program.

## CONCLUDING COMMENTS

At first glance, it would seem absurd that a person who has gone to the trouble of visiting a health care provider because of some physical or psychological symptoms and who has then received some advice regarding a recommended course of action that would presumably reduce or remove those symptoms would ignore the advice. As this chapter has noted, adherence to a medical treatment program is a complex interpersonal act, far more complex than one would think initially. Perhaps every patient needs to be thought of as significantly at risk of not adhering to a medical treatment program.

Yet, more thoughtful examination of the problem of nonadherence reveals it to be a reflection of the ambivalent relationship between the health care system and its clients. Health service providers frequently fail to do what they know to be necessary to assure optimal adherence to their prescribed treatment programs. Patients frequently fail to adhere to the treatment program they have expended energy and money to obtain.

Janis (1984a) has built a model of personal decision making that is useful in understanding medical treatment program adherence around the concept of decisional conflict. Janis thinks of decisional conflict as due to simultaneous opposing tendencies within an individual to accept and to reject a given course of action, or, what is frequently but somewhat loosely called ambivalence. At some level, patients appear to weigh the alternatives when faced with a recommended treatment program. If a decision to adhere to a recommended treatment program cannot be made easily, from a psychological point of view, a patient may fail to adhere to the recommendation as a way of reducing the anxiety generated by the need to choose. That is, it may often be easier not to adhere to a treatment program than to choose to adhere to it.

Looking more closely at the decisional conflict involved in treatment program adherence, Janis (1984a) has distinguished five coping patterns: (1) unconflicted nonadherence, generally due to complacency or to denial of danger; (2) unconflicted adherence, that is, prompt agreement to do whatever the

health care provider suggests, without consideration of the possible consequences; (3) defensive avoidance (or what might be called conflicted nonadherence), based on high anxiety, denial of ominous symptoms, wishful ra-
tionalization, and procrastination; (4) hypervigilance, associated with
overwhelming conflict, distraught panic, and impulsive vacillation and decision
making; and (5) vigilance, characterized by the careful search for pertinent
information and deliberate and effective problem solving.

The first four coping patterns are, according to this analysis, generally
irrational and maladaptive, while the fifth pattern is generally rational and adaptive except when danger is imminent and an adherence-related decision must be
made quickly. Janis believes that a rational weighing of costs and benefits of the
various decision possibilities will occur when the patient adopts the vigilant coping style. Accordingly, much of his applied research has been concerned with
encouraging the development of that style of decision making on the part of
patients in the medical care system.

Under some circumstances, nonadherence can be relatively unimpor-
tant. For example, adherence is important to the extent that a treatment of
proven effectiveness is prescribed. If a given treatment has only limited effectiveness, adherence is clearly less of an issue. That is, adherence to an imperfect
treatment will inevitably yield imperfect results. For example, Janis (1984a) has
examined the consequences of adherence failure as a function of the adequacy
of the recommended treatment. Clearly, when the recommended treatment is
adequate, adherence failure will result in treatment failure. On the other hand,
when the recommended treatment is inadequate (whether because of misdiag-
nosis, mistreatment, or the lack of effective treatment), adherence may be
harmful. Under those circumstances, failure to adhere to the poorly developed
treatment program can result in limited treatment success (perhaps due to spontaneous recovery) without endangering the patient.

Furthermore, even in the case of clearly effective medications, the relationship between adherence rate and treatment outcome is uncertain. For example, with some medications, nearly complete treatment effectiveness may be
obtained when adherence rate is as low as 25 percent, while in other cases,
optimum treatment effectiveness requires virtually perfect adherence (Sackett &
Snow, 1979).

In examining the patient-clinician interaction, we have seen that some
directives meet health care providers' needs more than patients' needs. In this
circumstance, nonadherence may, in fact, be desirable. Nonadherence may be
appropriate, for example, when patients have the impression that the health
care provider does not fully understand the issue that is of concern to them.
Indeed, it should not be forgotten that patients have the right to disregard their
physicians' recommendations.

What is perhaps the most interesting aspect of the research on improving adherence rates is the mismatch between what are judged to be the most
likely ways of improving those rates and the character of reported research.
There is virtually unanimous agreement, for example, that modifying the behav-

ior of the health care provider in order to modify the nature of the patient-clinician interaction has the best chance of improving adherence rates (Kasl, 1975; Masek, 1982; Masur, 1981). In spite of this agreement, however, almost no well-controlled studies attempting to modify clinician-patient interactions have been reported. This scarcity of research may reflect the lack of interest health care providers have for changing their behavior. In the context of this chapter, we may well realize that there can be nonadherence on the part of the clinician as well as nonadherence on the part of the patient (Gordis, 1979, pp. 42–45).

The other intervention that virtually all investigators agree about is medication packaging. There seems to be little question but that innovative packaging can significantly increase adherence rates. Yet, again, little research is being reported. As suggested in the chapter, there may be economic reasons for the lack of applied research in this area. In fact, economic considerations may play a far more important role in ultimately improving adherence rates than is currently believed. With the growing number of physicians and the growing cost of medical care (see Chapter 2), increased competition and increased need to reduce costs wherever possible may turn out to have unanticipated influence on health service provider behavior. Health care providers may soon become far more sensitive to the importance of having patients be "satisfied customers" and to how characteristics of their own behavior reduce patient satisfaction. At the same time, while the exact cost is not precisely known, nonadherence to medical treatment programs is certainly costly and needs to be reduced if only to reduce the cost of medical care.

Failure to adhere to medical treatment programs continues in spite of a growing interest in its prevention. As this chapter suggests, the likelihood of being able to identify the so-called noncompliant personality is remote, although the hope is persistent. According to Epstein and Cluss (1982), for example, it is appropriate to think of adherence as a habit, and to look to the psychological literature on habit formation to get clues as to how to proceed. In this text, we have seen the concern with our inability to establish habits, such as adherence, as well as with our inability to extinguish habits, such as smoking. Perhaps, as Epstein and Cluss half-jokingly suggest, we need to add nicotine to antihypertensive medication in order to make antihypertensive medication habit-forming.

It is also somewhat discouraging, from an ideological point of view, to realize that one of the best motivators for adherence to medical treatment programs is financial. If you pay patients, they seem far more willing to adhere to medical treatment programs than if they receive no monetary reward.

## SUMMARY

- The concept of adherence, as applied to medical treatment programs, is a complex one, and includes compliance, which is a patient characteristic, along with characteristics of the patient-physician interaction, such as the level of understanding the patient has for the treatment program being prescribed.

- It is generally believed that between one-third and one-half of patients fail to adhere completely to a medical treatment program. In addition, evidence from a variety of studies suggests that health care providers cannot predict which patients will adhere to a treatment program and which will not.

- Adherence is thought of as a function of preexisting readiness to adhere to a treatment program, special factors that may modify that readiness, and the reinforcement consequences of adherence or failure to adhere to specific treatment programs.

- Under some conditions, failure to adhere to a medical treatment program can compromise the treatment program, increase the duration of morbidity, increase the mortality rate and the cost of medical care, and can make it impossible to conduct adequate evaluation studies of various medications.

- Self-report measures of adherence rate present problems of validity. While it is rare that persons who adhere to a treatment program report that they do not adhere, the reverse is frequently true.

- Creative measurement procedures have been developed for assessing adherence rates that do not rely on self-report. Among these procedures are ones that measure how much medication remains to be taken, chemical analyses of the person in order to assess how much medication has been ingested, and medication monitors that actually assess when a medication has been removed from the container.

- Adherence rates are particularly low when the treatment program is complex and long-lasting and when medications produce undesirable side effects.

- Adherence rates are low when patients cannot afford to purchase medications that are prescribed for them and when patients do not have adequate access to pharmacies, or have other reality constraints that prevent them from obtaining the medications.

- Adherence rates are low when patients do not understand what physicians have told them, when their anxiety levels are either too low or too high, and among patients who do not believe that medical care is particularly effective and who believe that medical care costs are too high.

- Adherence rate is low when the relationship between the patient and the physician is poor. Such relationship problems are usually related to the fact that the physician is not sufficiently trained in how to establish rapport and develop productive relationships with patients.

- Three approaches have been used in order to improve adherence rates: the development of patient education programs, changing certain aspects of the medical treatment program, and using behavior modification approaches.

# A Psychological Portrait
# of Health Care Providers
# 13

## INTRODUCTION

It is important to understand the world through the eyes of health service providers. First, each of us, if our lives take a normal course, will have a number of very significant interactions with health care professionals, and at key points, our lives will be in their hands. Our own competence in dealing with health care professionals will depend, in part, on our understanding of the nature of their work and of how they cope with their work pressures. Second, for those of you who intend to become health care professionals, it is particularly appropriate to learn about how that choice will likely affect your lives. Finally, for those of you who may work with health care professionals, your ability to work successfully with them will depend, in part, on your understanding of the forces that are making them what they are.

Because of the unusually important role that society has assigned to the physician, most of the psychosocial research on health care professionals concerns itself with physicians. A far smaller body of research exists about the professional and personal lives of nurses, and almost none at all about other health care providers, such as medical social workers, medical technicians, and health psychologists. What seems clear at the outset is that choosing to spend one's professional life working closely with people who are ill presents its own particular stresses and challenges. No task in health psychology is more important than learning more about those stresses and seeking to reduce them when they appear to be counterproductive.

## THE PROCESS OF MEDICAL EDUCATION

Stresses associated with medical education and a medical career start early and continue throughout the professional lifetime. The general approach that investigators have taken in the study of the process of medical education includes: (1) examining medical student personality characteristics and their changes, both as predictors of academic achievement (see, for example, Parlow & Rothman, 1974), and as a way of monitoring the impact of the medical educational experience; and (2) examining the medical school as a stress-inducing environment that may negatively impact on academic and professional achievement (Rosenbaum, 1976).

Studies of the nature of medical education and its impact on medical students have been conducted throughout the entire process of medical education—during medical school, during the internship, and during the residency program. A number of recent studies have been concerned with gender differences in the stressfulness of medical education and medical practice.

### Choosing a Medical Career

Dedication to a career in medicine comes relatively early in the lives of young people. Nearly half of all medical students choose to enter a medical career before graduating from high school, and more than three-quarters of medical students decide on a medical career before completing 2 years of undergraduate college education (Czinkota & Johnston, 1983).

It has been hypothesized that the choice of a medical career, as other occupational choices, depends partly on childhood experience. Two aspects of these experiences—identification and reparation—were identified in a study of first-year medical and law students at McGill University in Montreal, conducted by Paris and Frank (1983). They found that choice of a medical career, whether on the part of males or females, was significantly related to the fact that the father was also a physician. Among medical and law students whose fathers were not physicians, Paris and Frank also found that medical students more frequently reported a history of illness in their families than did law students, and that law students more frequently reported a history of exposure to an event requiring the services of an attorney than did medical students.

There is no doubt that premedical undergraduates are dramatically different from other college undergraduates. Sade, Fleming, and Ross (1984) surveyed a large sample of faculty members at thirteen South Carolina undergraduate colleges regarding their perceptions of premedical and nonpremedical undergraduates, and found many significant differences in those perceptions. In comparison with nonpremedical undergraduates, premedical undergraduates were thought to be significantly more competitive, cynical, academically overspecialized, narrow in their interests, and overachieving, at the same time that they were viewed as highly motivated, self-disciplined, goal-oriented, and proud of their career choice.

In a study of premedical and nonpremedical undergraduates at Yale, Hackman and associates (1979) found that no undergraduate student had a more negative stereotype than the premedical student. Premedical students were thought of as excessively hard-working, competitive, grade-conscious, narrow in their interests, less sociable than other students, and more interested in money and prestige (also see Conrad, 1986). What is even more important, premedical students hold the same view of themselves as other students do of them. While premedical students, in describing what they consider to be important in a career, gave significantly greater importance than nonpremedical students to being helpful to others, working with people, and having the opportunity to make an important contribution to society, they also differ significantly in identifying other important career characteristics such as security and prestige (also see Czinkota & Johnson, 1983).

Unquestionably, part of the competitiveness and narrowness on the part of the premedical student is due to the demands made by medical schools in their selection of which medical students to admit. Medical school faculty are not of one mind about what constitutes the best undergraduate preparation for medical school (see, for example, American Medical Association, 1982; Creditor & Creditor, 1982; Jones & Thomae-Forgues, 1984; Lewis, 1984; Weingartner, 1980; Yens & Stimmel, 1982; and Zeleznik, Hojat, & Veloski, 1983), but what is clear is that few career objectives are more competitive than a medical career.

The statistics of applications to medical school give a vivid portrayal of that competitiveness. In 1985, there were about 33,000 applications filed for admission into the 127 accredited medical schools in the United States. Each applicant applied to an average of nine medical schools, and only about half of these applicants were admitted anywhere (Crowley, Etzel, & Petersen, 1986; Association of American Medical Colleges, 1985; American Medical Association, 1985). Once admitted, there is very little attrition. During the 1984–1985 academic year, fewer than 3 percent of enrolled medical students withdrew or were dismissed from their medical training.

As a consequence of the fact that not all qualified applicants can be admitted to medical schools, and in spite of the fact that there is already a surplus of physicians, a thriving so-called "offshore" medical school enterprise has begun that is causing considerable consternation among medical school faculty in the United States. Offshore medical schools are located outside of the United States (mainly in Mexico and in the Caribbean), hold foreign charters, maintain corporate offices in the United States, and have student bodies com-

posed largely of U.S. citizens. They are profit-making organizations whose existence depends on: (1) large numbers of American citizens who seek to enter the
medical profession; (2) subsidies provided by various public and private agencies
in the United States; (3) the willingness of a significant number of faculty members from U.S. medical schools to serve as visiting professors in return for paid
vacations for themselves and their families; and (4) the willingness of hospitals in
the United States to provide clinical experience for these students, since adequate clinical facilities do not exist in these offshore facilities.

If any of these conditions were to change, it is generally believed that
those who operate these institutions would probably need to turn to other
sources of income (Swanson, 1985). According to a recent report of the U.S.
General Accounting Office (1981), none of the offshore schools provides a medical education that is comparable in quality to that found in American medical
schools.

Most Americans discovered the existence of offshore medical schools in
1983 at the time of the American invasion of the island of Grenada in the
Caribbean. One of the justifications of the invasion was the large number of
American students at St. George's Medical School who were thought to be in
some personal jeopardy as a result of the unstable political situation in Grenada.

It is often thought that American students who attend these offshore
medical schools are qualified applicants to American medical schools who have
been denied admission simply because the number of available places is smaller
than the number of qualified applicants. In fact, more than half of American
medical students at these offshore medical schools have never applied to American medical schools (Swanson, 1985). If we assume that virtually all U.S. citizens
would prefer to attend an accredited medical school in the United States rather
than an offshore medical school, then there is reason to be concerned about the
general quality of those students who do not even apply to U.S. medical schools.

A growing problem with offshore medical schools is that it is becoming
very difficult for their graduates to obtain internships and residency placements
in U.S. hospitals. In a survey of United States hospitals conducted in January of
1985, only 166 out of a total of 5800 hospitals (less than 3 percent) sponsored
clinical training for students from foreign medical schools (Signer & Crowley,
1986). According to a recent report regarding medical students trained abroad,
Stimmel and Graettinger (1984) noted that "the majority of foreign medical-
school graduates, even those who are U.S. citizens, cannot expect to obtain a
residency" (p. 234). Medical school graduates who cannot obtain residency training are in considerable difficulty, because all but fourteen states require residency training in order to obtain licensure. Yet these graduates have few alternatives
open to them. They can reapply for residencies, but there is no reason to believe
that they will be more successful on their second application. Alternatively, they
could enter the general practice of medicine in one of the states not requiring
the completion of residency training, but, according to Stimmel and Graettinger,
while this decision would "undoubtedly result in additional primary-care physi-

cians, it would do so at the risk of providing less than optimal medical care—a solution neither physician nor patient would find attractive" (p. 234).

The demand for entrance to medical school may be abating, perhaps due to the growing realization that there is a surplus of physicians in the United States. That surplus is estimated to be as high as 50,000 physicians (Czinkota & Johnston, 1983; Iglehart, 1986c), and appears to be increasing rapidly as attention is turning to medical cost containment. The most recent information regarding supply and demand of physician services (Levey, 1986) predicts that in the year 2000 there will be 643,000 practicing physicians available in the United States, but a need for only 498,000—a surplus of 145,000, and a tripling of the estimated number of surplus physicians today.

## MEDICAL EDUCATION IN A DEVELOPMENTAL CONTEXT

Interest in medical student personality dimensions has led to the conceptualization of medical education as a series of developmental challenges to the student. Gaensbauer and Mizner (1980) have examined each of the phases of medical school in terms of the developmental and adaptive tasks that are presented to the student. Their data come from their experiences providing psychiatric consultation to medical students, and while their findings might not have been dramatically different had they chosen to study graduate education in another profession, their findings are important in their own right (also see Pfeiffer, 1983).

The first year of medical school, in their experience, presents three sets of stresses: (1) intellectual demands related to the complexity and amount of the material to be mastered; (2) extraordinary competition among students; and (3) severe disruption of social and personal relationships related to the transition to medical school.

The adaptive tasks associated with these stresses are to develop the ability to tolerate uncertainty about the intellectual material without becoming unduly anxious, to achieve a level of performance that is appropriate to one's ability, and to establish a set of satisfying socially supportive relationships while avoiding regressive or impulsive behavior (also see Grover & Smith, 1981).

The second year of medical school presents the challenge of the personal commitment to the profession of medicine. This challenge crisis is typically associated with the beginning of a period of intense exposure to clinical medicine, to illness, to fear, and to suffering. The adaptive task, according to Gaensbauer and Mizner, is to "begin to develop some sense of detachment about the study of disease without losing sight of its human implications" (p. 64).

The third year of medical school is the time when medical students establish their identity as physicians. This process comes about through the total immersion in clinical work including its most sobering aspects—decisions that bear on life and on death, acceptance of one's own helplessness in the face of those medical situations that have an unavoidable negative outcome, and an extraordinary increase in level of responsibility for the welfare of others. With this increase in responsibility comes the risk that mistakes will be made for which blame and guilt will have to be assigned (Mizrahi, 1984).

Impending completion of medical education serves as the greatest source of stress to the fourth-year medical student, according to Gaensbauer and Mizner (1980). With the end of the medical school approaching, many students suffer a revival of anxiety regarding their own competence and ability to perform satisfactorily as fully trained physicians. There seems little question that medical school has a profound effect upon the values and attitudes of medical students, and that many medical school faculty are concerned about the specific nature of this effect.

Perhaps the most discouraging assertion about the effects of medical school was made by Eron (1958). He concluded from his research that medical students tended to increase in cynicism and decrease in humanitarianism during their medical school experience. This set of findings has been replicated by others on a number of occasions (see, for example, Kopelman, 1983), and there is little reason to believe that studies that might be conducted today would yield significantly different results. We have already seen, however, that premedical students as undergraduates are sometimes described in the same terms—cynical and low in compassion. Physicians are being trained today to be more head than heart, and more concerned about their patients' physiology than their psychology, and some but not all of them are not particularly happy about it.

One approach to changing this reality is to change the nature of the medical school curriculum by adding courses that are designed to draw medical student's attention to emotional and family problems of patients as well as to their physical problems, and to prevention and rehabilitation of disease as well as to acute treatment. Evaluation studies generally show that these courses have no lasting effect on the attitudes and values of medical students, however, and at best slow down rather than stop or reverse the increase in cynicism and the decrease in human compassion noted among medical school students.

According to Rezler (1974), the only hope for producing a new breed of physician who will think of patients not only in terms of their biology, but also in terms of their psychology and sociology, is to change the criteria that are used for medical student recruitment. Selecting medical students solely on the basis of their academic or intellectual qualifications runs the risk of selecting students who hold attitudes that are contrary to the ones, such as compassion and humanitarianism, that medical schools are increasingly finding desirable.

### Sources of Stress among Medical Students

A useful introduction to the world of the medical student can be found in the description of medical education prepared by Awbrey (1985) as he reflected on his experiences in medical school several years after graduation. In addition to describing the problems associated with being "lectured to death," with a curriculum that was unnecessarily fragmented, faculty members who varied in competence and effectiveness, unsatisfying clinical clerkships during medical school, and the anxieties associated with meeting the costs of medical education (also see Shea & Fullilove, 1985), Awbrey specifically commented on the stressful nature of medical education. He wrote:

> After completion of a premedical curriculum, progressively more responsibility is delegated to the future physician throughout medical school and residency education. Greater authority also produces greater responsibility, and greater responsibility produces greater stress . . . manifest as feelings of unhappiness, depression, anxiety, and dissatisfaction with performance. (p. 101)

Awbrey's autobiographical description of the stresses of medical education is not atypical. Edwards and Zimet (1976; also see Rosenberg, 1971) surveyed medical students in all 4 years of training at the University of Colorado School of Medicine in order to identify their greatest areas of concern and found that the most important problems, in order of severity, were lack of time for recreation and socialization, being unable to learn everything that needs to be known, preparing for and taking examinations, fear of making a mistake, feeling dehumanized and lonely, lack of money, and uncertainty about choice of a profession (see Fishman & Zimet, 1972; Held & Zimet, 1975; Kritzer & Zimet, 1967; Zimet, 1975). Furthermore, many of these problems tended to become more severe over time.

In a more recent study of perceived stress among medical, law, and academic graduate students at the University of Arizona, Heins, Fahey, and Leiden (1984) obtained similar findings regarding medical students. Major sources of stress, in order of severity, were: (1) insufficient time for study and recreation; (2) inability to understand and master the academic material; (3) worry about money; and (4) feeling anonymous, dehumanized, or devalued in class.

Medical school students worked a significantly greater number of hours per week than either of the other two student groups and had less time for sleep, household chores, and socialization with friends. Similar findings regarding stress in medical school were obtained by Clark and Rieker (1986; also see Cartwright, 1982; Pearce & Sheldon, 1984; Wolf & Kissling, 1984).

Linn and Zeppa (1984) compared perceived stress before and after a 12-week-long surgical clerkship during the third year of medical school in a sample of students at the University of Miami School of Medicine. As was noted earlier, the third year, in most medical schools, is characterized by intense clinical activity and provides the occasion where medical students for the first time take clinical responsibility for patients, often including the need to deal with life-and-death issues. As should not be surprising, the third year is perhaps the most stressful period in medical school.

At the start of the third year of medical school, reported sources of stress were very similar to those already identified—in order of importance, a self-imposed need to do well in medical school, an overwhelming amount of material to master, and lack of time for all forms of self-interest including friends, family, and study. Linn and Zeppa (1984) found that the level of unfavorably perceived stress during the clerkship was significantly associated with poor final grades on the clerkship and low levels of self-esteem and internal locus of control. They concluded that "educators need to develop ways of helping students cope with stress so that learning can be facilitated, and, more importantly, so that stresses of practice might be handled more successfully" (p. 12).

THE FEMALE MEDICAL STUDENT.  The number of women in medical school has increased dramatically in the past two decades. In 1970, fewer than 10 percent of medical students were women. As of 1985, the proportion had increased to more than 30 percent (Association of American Medical Colleges, 1985; Clark & Rieker, 1986; Crowley, Etzel, & Petersen, 1986; Eisenberg, 1983). With this increase has come an increased interest in gender differences in reported stress. Edwards and Zimet (1976) found that women medical students reported significantly more concern than men in the areas of loneliness, feeling out of place in medical school, and feeling that they would not be able to achieve their academic goals.

Lloyd and Gartrell (1981), who examined gender differences in first-year medical student mental health at the University of Texas Medical School at Houston, found that while there were no significant gender differences at the start of the year, by midyear women students had developed more symptoms of depression and anxiety and reported less life satisfaction. By the end of the first year of medical school, gender differences were smaller than was the case at midyear, but similar in direction.

Clark and Rieker (1986), who studied medical and law students at the University of North Carolina, similarly found that women reported significantly more stress then men, due to disturbances in interpersonal relationships, sexism, and insufficient time. Gaensbauer and Mizner (1980), in their study of female medical school students noted the special set of conflicts that often exists for the woman in medical school. Women often have unusual difficulties in achieving a proper balance between their personal and professional lives, between their role as physicians and their identity as women, and between their need to be assertive and forceful, on the one hand, while being nurturing on the other hand (also see Bergquist et al., 1985).

ENHANCING MEDICAL STUDENT WELL-BEING.  There is some evidence (Vaillant, Sobowale, & McArthur, 1972) that some of the emotional difficulties exhibited by physicians actually predate their entrance into medical school, that is, that the stress of a medical education and medical practice add problems to those that are already present. At the same time, however, it is clear that the medical school experience itself can involve excessive levels of stress that are independent of pre-medical school experiences or personal characteristics.

The stress associated with the role of medical student has not gone unrecognized, and a number of efforts to help medical students cope with the stresses of a medical education have recently been reported (Huebner, Royer, & Moore, 1981; Kelly, Bradlyn, Dubbert, & St. Lawrence, 1982). Brown and Barnett (1984) surveyed faculty members at twelve randomly selected medical schools regarding their interactions with medical students who are experiencing personal problems, and found that the average faculty member reported spending about 1 hour a week, usually with one student, discussing problems of at least moderate concern that might or might not be related to medical school experiences. Problems most commonly reported by students included career reconsideration, unsatisfying interactions with faculty members, interpersonal problems, and financial concerns. Faculty members who responded to the survey generally felt that it was important to listen and to be responsive to student's personal problems, although they did not think that they were as helpful as they could have been (also see Hilberman et al., 1975; Weinstein, 1983).

One strategy that is used at an increasing number of medical schools is the student self-help group, where students at all levels of education can come together voluntarily to discuss personal as well as general concerns. One such group program, established at the Albert Einstein College of Medicine in 1977, was recently described by Goetzel and colleagues (1984). At the time of their report, seven self-help groups, involving about 100 students and 14 faculty members, were being conducted. A total of 26 students completed questionnaires regarding their experiences with the self-help group program.

As for motivating factors that resulted in students deciding to participate in the self-help experience, the most common ones were the desire to make new friends (in a social affiliation rather than in a romantic sense) and to discuss personal concerns in a nonthreatening environment. Students evaluated their group experiences as relatively meaningful, and as successful in reducing their sense of social isolation and inability to solve personal problems. Most students specifically noted that the opportunity to get together with faculty members in the self-help group setting was a particularly important benefit of the experience.

Some attention has been directed to the problem of suicide among medical students. The suicide rate among male medical students is similar to that among age-matched males not in medical school. In the case of female medical students, however, their rate is similar to that of male medical students, but three times greater than age-matched women not in medical school. Pepitone-Arreola-Rockwell, Rockwell, and Core (1981), who obtained these results from a survey of deans of student affairs in U.S. medical schools, proposed three preventive intervention strategies in order to reduce the suicide rate among medical students. First, greater attention should be directed toward identifying and meeting the mental health needs of medical students. Second, suicide-proneness can be assessed with enough accuracy to justify long-range prevention efforts. Third, since students at the end of their first year and at the beginning of their second year in medical school appear to be unusually vulnerable to suicide, special attention needs to be directed to this group. Among the strategies that might be particularly helpful would be efforts to reduce the resistance to helpseeking, provide cognitively oriented health education, and assign a personal, mature, clinical "big brother" or "big sister" who could serve as a role model to each student nearing the end of the first year of training (also see Borenstein & Cook, 1982).

### The Medical Internship and Residency

Paralleling the growing awareness of the psychosocial concerns of the medical student has been an increasing awareness of the medical internship and residency as a particular source of stress and discomfort. The internship year is the bridge between the student role and that of the fully qualified medical professional. Typically, additional skills are acquired during the internship year, but at the cost of great personal stress. As to the nature of these stresses, Siegel and Connelly (1978) noted that interns usually receive little emotional support in the course of their work, and often their goal becomes mere survival, that is, making it through the day, getting more sleep, and just doing what needs to be done to carry out their medical responsibilities. While the goals of most medical training programs include teaching physicians to treat the whole person, to recognize that physical symptoms may reflect problems in the individual's life, and to work preventively, many internships and residencies fail to apply this same principle to their trainees.

McCue (1985) notes that for the first time in their own careers, house officers (the generic term for interns and residents) must assume responsibility for difficult and emotionally charged problems involving such issues as sexuality, disability, and death. Mature behavior is now demanded of residents, after years of maturational delay due to their intense commitment to medical education. In addition, new responsibilities of marriage and parenthood may be encountered, financial pressures from accumulated debts may intensify, and medical school friendships and emotional supports are lost and must be replaced. Finally, fears of inadequate performance as a physician during residency may cause residents to ignore their personal development as they concentrate single-mindedly on their professional development (also see Uliana, Hubbell, Wyle, & Gordon, 1984).

A particularly compelling study of the stresses and coping mechanisms of interns was reported by Adler, Werner, and Korsch (1980; also see Werner, Adler, Robinson, & Korsch, 1979) based upon data collected from four consecutive groups of pediatric interns in a 1-year-long training program at the Childrens Hospital of Los Angeles. About twenty-five interns were involved in the program every year, and virtually all of them participated in the study. A seventy-five-item questionnaire was administered at the start and end of each year, and in 2 of the 4 years, an additional questionnaire administration took place midyear. About one-third of the interns were women, and about half of the interns were married. No differences in reported stress or coping processes were found, however, as a function of gender or marital status.

The questionnaire assessed eight different aspects of the internship experience: (1) attitudes toward patients; (2) confidence that the interns felt in their abilities; (3) amount of perceived stress; (4) extent of help seeking for purposes of coping with stress; (5) attitudes toward colleagues; (6) extent to which interns felt they were learning; (7) perceived quality of life outside of the hospital; and (8) general feelings about the internship.

Questionnaires were modified from time to time during the 4 years of data collection, and certain additional questions were asked on occasion. A performance rating was obtained for each participating intern from the physicians in charge of the training program.

The data from each group of interns were analyzed separately, as if there were four different studies based on four different cohorts of interns. One of the strengths of this approach to data analysis is that it is as if there are four independent tests of the hypotheses explored in this research project. The most important analyses undertook to examine the changes in questionnaire scores from the beginning to the end of the internship year. While perceived self-confidence increased from the beginning to the end of each of the 4 years, and while the need for external help seemed to diminish from the beginning to the end of each of the 4 years, these changes seemed to be achieved at substantial personal cost. For two of the four cohorts of interns, attitudes toward patients and attitudes toward colleagues became less positive. Reported quality of life dropped significantly and consistently during the year, as did the general evaluation of the internship as a learning experience.

In their efforts to interpret the pedagogical significance of these "disappointing" (to use the authors' word) findings, Adler, Werner, and Korsch noted that much could be done to reduce the unnecessary stresses that interns face and at the same time to increase the sense of excitement that should characterize the internship and make it an even better learning experience.

The level of stress under which interns and residents function is so frequently excessive that Small (1981) has coined the term "house officer stress syndrome" to describe the phenomenon. According to Small, the syndrome includes episodic cognitive impairment, chronic anger, pervasive cynicism, and family discord. In severe cases, the syndrome includes major depression, suicidal ideation, and substance abuse. Small noted that between 1 to 2 percent of physicians abuse narcotics—a rate five times greater than nonphysicians in the same general age group—and that 20 percent of physician suicides are accompanied by drug abuse and 40 percent are associated with alcohol abuse (also see Alexander, Monk, & Jonas, 1985; Asken & Raham, 1983; Frey, Demick, & Bibace, 1981; Herzog, Wyshak, & Stern, 1984; Nelson & Henry, 1978).

Among married residents, half or more reported the following problems (in decreasing order of frequency): lack of time to see friends, inability to help with housework, lack of meaningful role for spouse, and spouse complaints about long working hours, particularly on weekends. More than 30 percent of the married residents also reported often being too tired for sex, and a series of complaints by the spouse—loneliness, competitiveness, too great a proportion of the responsibility for child rearing, and the need for the resident to spend nights away from home. Overall, the principal problems identified by residents and their spouses concerned themselves with insufficient time, inability to study enough, and problems related to self-confidence. There is a general tendency for these problems to diminish with time in the residency program.

Among practicing physicians there seems to be a love-hate relationship with the internship as viewed retrospectively. In a quite remarkable exchange of letters that took place in 1981, Norman Cousins, whose 1979 book, "Anatomy of an Illness" attracted worldwide attention because of its criticisms of the practice of medicine, and who subsequently joined the staff of the Program in Medicine, Law, and Human Values of the UCLA School of Medicine, published a letter in the Journal of the American Medical Association expressing criticism of the medical internship—that "ordeal . . . that put[s] medical school students through a human meat grinder before they can qualify as full-fledged physicians" (1981a, p. 377).

Cousins noted that he had spoken with medical students and physicians in medical schools and hospitals throughout the country and that he found little support for the practices he found virtually everywhere that he likened to a kind of hazing. He was referring mainly to the practice of overworking interns far past the point where they could provide good medical care. In Cousin's words, "the custom of overworking interns has long since outlived its usefulness. It doesn't lead to the making of better physicians. It is inconsistent with the public interest. It is not really worthy of the tradition of medicine" (1981a, p. 377).

In publishing a sample of replies to Cousins' letter, the editors of the Journal of the American Medical Association noted that they had received "an avalanche" of thoughtful commentary. Cousins was given the opportunity to read the letters and to comment on them. He noted (1981b) that the letters ran about 60 percent opposed to his point of view and 40 percent in favor, and that the content of the comments favorable to current internship practices could be grouped into four categories: (1) the internship was a rite of passage; (2) the internship conditioned the medical student to the realities of medical practice; (3) the institution of the internship had to be continued because hospitals need low-cost labor such as performed by interns; and (4) there is no persuasive evidence that interns' going without sleep is dangerous to the health of patients. On the positive side, two types of responses were discerned by Cousins: (1) the internship should be changed because it is poor pedagogy, has no planned curriculum, and may, purely by chance, not provide a number of important experiences that are judged necessary in the preparation of a physician; and (2) reforms are already being made in many internships in the direction proposed by Cousins and others.

PSYCHOSOCIAL SUPPORT IN RESIDENCY TRAINING.   Berg and Garrard (1980a, 1980b) examined the nature of psychosocial support available to medical residents by means of a national survey of nearly 500 residency training programs in the specialties of family practice, obstetrics and gynecology, pediatrics, psychiatry, internal medicine, and surgery. Ten different types of support were identified—support groups, allowing part-time residencies, professional counseling, child care services, formal "gripe" sessions, seminars dealing with medical issues such as the dying patient or euthanasia, seminars dealing with personal issues, such as drug abuse, or balancing of professional and private life, paid sick leave, planned social activities, and provision of financial advisors—and residency program directors were asked to check all types of support that were available to their residents.

Two findings in this survey are particularly noteworthy. First, support from medical school faculty members is more readily available for professionally related issues than for personal or family-related issues. Second, residency programs in psychiatry and in family practice are more likely to provide these ten types of support than residency programs in the other specialties. In the case of seven of the ten support types, the differences are statistically significant (also see Mazie, 1985; Pearce & Sheldon, 1984).

ENHANCING WELL-BEING AMONG INTERNS AND RESIDENTS.   Interest in the use of support groups for enhancing the well-being of interns and residents has been expressed almost as often as in the case of medical students. Siegel and Donnelly (1978) described the use of such a support group mechanism in the case of pediatric interns at the Boston City Hospital. This group was established early in the year and met weekly for 10 weeks to discuss the stresses of the internship. The group was designed to help interns get to know one another outside of their usual work setting and to provide them an opportunity to share their thoughts and feelings about their internship experiences and their relationship to their personal and professional development. The group appeared to be particularly useful in providing a forum for the discussion of personal versus professional role conflicts.

During the first few sessions, interns discussed work stress, responsibility for decision making, sleep loss, their anxiety and sense of being overwhelmed. Later, discussions turned to such topics as why the interns had chosen the career of medicine, the fragility of life, differences between caring for children and caring for adults, the interns' lack of self-confidence and fear of admitting that they did not know something, and their anger and sense of helplessness in the face of what they felt was a lack of support from the hospital staff (also see Pfifferling, 1983; Strahilevitz et al., 1982; Ziegler, Kanas, Strull, & Bennet, 1984).

CHANGES IN DECISION-MAKING PRACTICES.   There seems little question that internship and residency training experiences modify many important attitudes. One of the attitudes that is of interest to social scientists who study health care providers is leadership style, specifically willingness to share authority for decision making.

It is hard to imagine a profession with greater power, from a societal point of view, than the profession of medicine. Indeed, there is evidence that interest in power, in the sense of influencing others, is often part of the cluster of personality traits that characterizes young people who are interested in medical careers. Physicians are fully prepared, even prior to completing their medical training, to make what have been called *substitute judgments* for their patients (Bloom & Asher, 1982), that is, to tell patients exactly what they should do largely without regard to what they might want to do. Freidson (1970) has suggested that this sense of social power may be just as important to a profession as its special set of skills. The ability to assign the sick role is, after all, a very powerful one in any society, for it confirms the right of an individual not to meet his or her normal role expectations. Freidson has noted that this exercise of power is also seen in the activities of physicians to control the acquisition, dissemination, and application of medically relevant information (also see Waitzkin and Waterman, 1974).

The ways in which experiences during the medical or surgical residency can modify attitudes toward shared decision making can be seen in the work of Eisenberg, Kitz, and Webber (1983; also see McCue, Magrinat, Hansen, & Bailey, 1986). These investigators examined those attitudes in a sample of medical and surgical residents at the beginning of their first year of residency and again at the end of their third year of residency using a scale that assessed four aspects of shared decision making: (1) confidence in the capacity of subordinates to make reasonable decisions; (2) willingness to share goals and information with subordinates; (3) willingness to involve subordinates in the decision-making process; and (4) ability of subordinates to accept responsibility for their own decisions independently of the possibility of reward or punishment. Scores at one end of each scale were thought of as indicating an authoritarian attitude toward shared decision making, while scores at the other end of each scale were thought of as indicating a participatory attitude.

Interestingly, this same scale had previously been used with a large sample of business people, and thus the scores of the medical and surgical residents could not only be compared with each other at two points in time during the residency period, but could also be contrasted with the scores of persons in business. In addition, some of the most interesting findings are those that demonstrate the differences between the practice of general medicine and the practice of surgery.

Regarding confidence in the capacity of subordinates to make reasonable decisions, scores of the residents at the start of their first year were substantially more participatory than those of the business persons, with medical and surgical residents having very similar scores. People in business were far more authoritarian than either medical or surgical residents, in that they had less confidence in the ability of subordinates. By the end of the third year of residency, however, medical residents continued to be participatory in their attitudes, while surgical residents had become more authoritarian—about as authoritarian as the business persons had been.

Regarding the willingness to share goals and information with subordinates, scores of first-year residents were very similar to those of the business persons, and did not differ significantly from each other. At the end of the third year, however, while scores of the medical residents had not changed, those of the surgical residents had become significantly more authoritarian.

In the case of willingness to involve subordinates in decision making, initial scores of residents were not notably different from those of people in business, but by the end of the third year, surgical residents had become more authoritarian in their attitudes. An identical result was found regarding confidence in the ability of subordinates to accept responsibility for their own decisions. Thus, in general, surgical residents became more authoritarian over time, while medical residents remained less authoritarian and not dramatically different from the comparison group of business people in their attitudes toward shared decision making.

These findings are consistent with other studies that have identified differences in the social structure of medical and surgical wards. On medical wards, it has been found that decisions are usually made by consensus among all physicians at all levels of training, while on surgical wards a far more bureaucratic structure exists in which decisions are made by the chief resident that are then handed down to subordinate residents. Each decision-making strategy has its advantages and disadvantages. Thus, the authoritarian mode has advantages when there is pressure of time and when predictability is essential, and it may be unusually appropriate for surgical wards. On the other hand, the authoritarian mode is completely dependent on the wisdom of the designated leader and can be detrimental to learning and morale of subordinates.

### Stress among Practicing Physicians

A measure of the personal cost of a medical career can be seen in the analyses of health-related statistics of physicians. A century ago, Ogle (1886) noted that physicians have higher death rates from a very wide variety of causes, including suicide, than members of other professions. Ogle put his conclusions in perfect nineteenth-century English:

> The ancient belief, which for ages was accepted by the general public and was supported by the theses of learned writers, that the life of a medical man was as a rule longer and freer from disease than that of an ordinary individual, inasmuch as, when in health, he guided his steps by the laws of hygiene, and when in sickness had the advantage of the best advice . . . received its death-blow as soon as the pitiless test of statistical inquiry was applied to the subject. (p. 235)

Mumford (1983) summarized the more recent literature by noting that "cynicism, alcoholism, addiction, divorce, and suicide are prevalent to excess among physicians" (p. 436). Pearson (1982) said it even more succinctly: "Being a doctor may be dangerous to your health" (p. 194). Physicians and dentists are more prone to die of coronary heart disease than the average person (Djerassi, 1971; King, 1970). Suicide is more prevalent among physicians, dentists, pharmacists, and medical students than the general population (Craig & Pitts, 1968; Everson & Fraumeni, 1975; King, 1970; Rose & Rosow, 1973; Steppacher & Mausner, 1974). Burnout is unusually common among health care professionals.

Specific illnesses are unusually common among certain groups of physicians, a pattern that strongly suggests environmental causes of these diseases. For example, anesthesiologists develop malignancies that are associated with the use of some anesthetics. Radiologists are particularly vulnerable to diseases associated with radiation. Many physicians and nurses contract a variety of infectious diseases from the hospital environment or from their patients (Cartwright, 1982; Maslach, 1976).

There is considerable evidence that physicians who are in more stressful specialties are at greater risk for the development of stress-related illnesses. Russek (1960, 1962) was able to show that independent judges rated dermatology as minimally stressful and general practice as maximally stressful. While the risk of coronary heart disease increased with age in both groups of physicians, contrasting these two groups of physicians indicated that in the age group between 40 and 69, general practitioners were three times more likely than dermatologists to have heart disease.

King (1970) surveyed mortality rates among physicians and other professional groups in a number of different countries as reported in official statistics for the first half of the twentieth century. In order to interpret the findings regarding excess rates of morbidity or mortality among physicians, King has suggested that three factors need to be taken into consideration—the physician's background, the environment within which the physician works, and the physician's behavior patterns. Using this general interpretive model, King (1970) hypothesized that the excess rates of mortality from heart disease, cerebrovascular accidents, and suicide among physicians seem to be a reflection of their materialistic outlook on life, and the extreme mental and physical strain under which they often function. In addition, King suggested that the high mortality among physicians may also reflect their negative attitudes and behaviors regarding health and medical care for themselves, as evidenced in their delays in seeking medical treatment.

As for the rate of suicide among physicians, studies that have been undertaken to examine this variable are somewhat out of date and do not all come to the same conclusions. In addition, choice of medical specialty is certainly not random, and physicians who have emotional problems may be disproportionately drawn to specific medical specialties. Thus, an excess risk of suicide may precede entrance into a medical specialty group. By that same line of reasoning, physicians who are themselves physically ill may be attracted to certain less stressful or demanding medical specialties.

Ross (1971) evaluated the twentieth-century international literature and concluded that: (1) suicide among physicians is high, particularly among female physicians; (2) among physicians who commit suicide, there is a high incidence of psychiatric illness, alcoholism, and drug abuse; and (3) a number of demographic factors are meaningfully associated with the risk of suicide. Among these factors are age (physicians commit suicide at much younger ages than the general population of suicides), and specialty group (suicide is most frequent among psychiatrists, and least frequent among pediatricians, dermatologists, surgeons, and pathologists). Ross suggests that the suicide rate is lowest among those specialty groups that have intermittent and generally less intense emotional relationships with their patients.

Rose and Rosow (1973) surveyed death certificates in California over a 3-year period of time and found that the rate of suicide was twice as high for physicians as for the general population. Among persons age 45 to 54, for example, the suicide rate of physicians was 119 per 100,000 per year as compared with a rate of 44 per 100,000 per year among the general population in the same age group. Not only was the rate of suicide excessive among physicians, but when the entire sample was grouped according to occupational category, of the resulting twenty-one groups, three of the four highest suicide rates occurred among health service providers—pharmacists, dentists, and physicians.

In examining their data more closely, Rose and Rosow found that half of the physician suicides occurred during the most productive phase of the typical physician's life—between ages 35 and 54. In the case of marital status, while in the general population the ratio of suicide rate among divorced to married persons is about 3:1, the ratio among divorced to married physicians is 13:1. In contrast to the findings in the literature reviewed by King (1970) and by Ross (1973), however, Rose and Rosow did not find meaningful differences in the suicide rate as a function of medical specialty. Rose and Rosow concluded, however, that "suicide is a general problem of major proportions for physicians and health care workers, who, ironically, have dedicated their lives to caring for others" (p. 803).

Vaillant, Sobowale, and McArthur (1972) studied a sample of forty-six physicians over a 30-year time period starting with their sophomore year in college and contrasted their health over this period of time with a matched sample of nonphysicians. In comparison with the nonphysicians, the physicians more often had bad marriages or were divorced, were regular users of tranquilizers or abusers of alcohol or other drugs, and more of them had been seen in ten or more visits by a psychiatrist or were hospitalized with a psychiatric disorder.

In analyzing the nature of the inevitable stresses under which physicians function, McCue has suggested that they can be divided into three categories: (1) working with intensely emotional aspects of life, such as suffering, fear, sexuality, and death; (2) inadequate training for many fundamental professional tasks, such as handling of problem patients; and (3) unrealistic demands of patients for certainty when the field is characterized by inadequate medical knowledge. Complicating the stresses that physicians face is the need to adapt to the rapid changes that are taking place in the ways in which they have become accustomed to practicing medicine (Burnum, 1984; also see Chapter 2).

Most physicians have never experienced a life-threatening illness and tend to underprescribe palliative drugs, that is, drugs that serve to reduce suffering. Furthermore, many of the procedures that are now part of medical diagnosis and treatment induce pain, fear, and discomfort. The physician is required to probe into areas of the body that are private and hidden from nearly all other people. This reality sets up complex feelings in both the patient and the physician, feelings that never entirely disappear. Failure to keep patients alive, in spite of all efforts, remains a source of stress for most physicians throughout their professional lives. The demands of medical practice not uncommonly result in physicians' emotional withdrawal from their families, in social isolation, and in the denial of professional problems. Special problems exist in the case of physicians who have medical school appointments since they must not only meet the professional demands of a clinical practice but also of an academic life (Bland & Schmitz, 1986; Linn, Yager, Cope, & Leake, 1985).

WOMEN PHYSICIANS.    The past decade has seen a substantial increase in the proportion of female medical students and practicing physicians, but the proportion of women in medicine is not random across the medical specialties. In the case of medical residents regardless of specialty, for example, the proportion of women averages 19.2 percent, but ranges from 1.9 percent in urology to 41.5 percent in pediatrics. In general, it appears as if occupational role is more important than gender in determining morbidity and mortality experiences among physicians. Eisenberg (1983), writing about women as physicians, remarked that "optimists have contended that women will change medicine for the better; pessimists have had reason for concern that medicine will change women for the worse" (p. 538). If differences in gender-specific suicide rates are considered, the pessimists seem to have made the more accurate prediction.

In addition to having to cope with the professional role, women physicians have special problems in combining professional and nonprofessional life roles, as do other groups of professional women. While many male physicians select wives who assume virtual total responsibility for the household and for child rearing, women would not likely find such an arrangement satisfactory, even if a house-husband could be found. In this context, the changes that are taking place in the nature of medical practice (see Chapter 2) may very well be finding a very receptive medical audience (Eisenberg, 1983).

THE IMPAIRED PHYSICIAN.    An impaired physician is one who is unable to practice medicine adequately because of physical or mental illness, including alcoholism or drug dependence (Council on Mental Health, 1973). Alcoholism and drug dependence are singled out in this definition because the greatest health-related problems faced by physicians are the problems of drug and alcohol abuse—problems that are substantially more common among physicians than among other adults of comparable age (Modlin & Montes, 1964; Newsom, 1977). It is generally believed that these problems are a consequence of two factors—high stress and easy availability of drugs.

These problems are of sufficient importance so that programs for impaired physicians are now being established by state medical societies and suggestions for individual components of such programs are appearing in the literature (Bittker, 1976; Cloutier, 1982; Pearce & Sheldon, 1984; Spears, 1981). Interest in the problems of impaired psychologists is growing, and the American Psychological Association is currently surveying state psychological associations to develop a beginning understanding of the magnitude of the problem (Laliotis & Grayson, 1985).

McAuliffe and colleagues (1986) reported that in their survey of 700 medical students and practicing physicians, nearly 60 percent of physicians and 80 percent of medical students reported having used psychoactive drugs (marijuana, cocaine, tranquilizers, and opiates) at some time in their lives, with one-third of physicians and more than 40 percent of medical students reporting use of these drugs within the last year. About 4 percent of respondents (eleven physicians and twenty medical students) reported themselves as being drug dependent. Rates of drug use varied by professional specialty and were highest among psychiatrists and lowest among obstetricians and gynecologists.

McAuliffe and associates reviewed the available evidence and concluded that the recreational use of drugs has greatly increased in the past several decades among both physicians and medical students and will continue to grow unless something is done to retard that growth.

In 1972, the American Medical Association approved a statement on the impaired physician that had been prepared by its Council on Mental Health. In that statement it was asserted that physicians have the ethical responsibility to take cognizance of the inability of a colleague to practice medicine by reason of physical or mental illness, and in those situations where the impaired physician is unable or unwilling to seek help, to take the initiative to advise the physician to obtain treatment or curtail his or her practice. The Council noted that often "the physician-patient denies he is ill, lacks insight into his problem, avoids medical assistance, and minimizes his problem outright" (p. 687), and that "peer referral for help usually reveals an entrenched 'conspiracy of silence'" (p. 687).

Regarding the procedure to be followed when a physician suspects that a colleague is impaired, the AMA Council on Mental Health recommended that if the individual physician cannot be persuaded to seek help, the problem should be referred to the medical staff of the hospital. If that avenue is not feasible, a specially designated committee of the state or county medical society should be consulted, and if the medical society is unable or unwilling to act, the matter should be referred to the appropriate licensing body in the state.

Pearson (1982), a psychiatrist, recently reviewed his experiences treating about 250 impaired physicians over the previous 36 years in his practice at the

Institute of Pennsylvania Hospital (also see Johnson and Connelly, 1981; Smith & Steindler, 1982). Pearson commented that the most prominent early sign of emotional disturbance was the physicians' hurried existence. With increasing impairment, their everyday lives became progressively more chaotic, particularly in such areas as keeping office hours and appointments, maintaining regular sleeping and eating habits, and accepting family responsibilities.

In a recent psychometric analysis of thirty-eight impaired physicians who had been admitted to a private psychiatric hospital in North Carolina over a number of years, Dorr (1981) reported on their personality characteristics as assessed by means of the Minnesota Multiphasic Personality Inventory. These physicians averaged 43 years old and were hospitalized an average of about 2 months. Most were married, and they came from a variety of medical specialty groups.

On the MMPI, this sample of impaired physicians demonstrated considerable emotional distress in general and very high depression scores in particular. In comparison with the MMPI scores obtained from a comparison group of nonhospitalized physicians, the hospitalized impaired physicians had significantly higher scores on every pathological scale.

There seems little doubt of the growing willingness on the part of the medical profession to identify certain of its members as impaired and to try to provide help to these physicians. As a matter of fact, most state medical societies have active impaired physician committees. The hospital represents the most likely setting for identifying the impaired physician because of the semipublic nature of medical practice there. Threatened revocation of hospital privileges can be a serious problem for physicians, since obtaining and maintaining hospital privileges is usually necessary for physicians to earn their livelihood. Thus, one question that patients could well ask when selecting a physician is where they hospitalize their patients who need hospitalization. A physician who does not have hospital privileges may very well be an impaired physician.

The "Hateful" Patient.   As for the responsibilities of patient care, stress is particularly intense in the case of caring for patients that kindle aversion or malice in the physician. Such patients are often referred to as "hateful" (Winnicott, 1949), or, in more antiseptic language, as "frequent consulters" (Robinson & Granfield, 1986). Whatever they are called, they are often dreaded, and while patients of this type are not common, they can generate intense emotional conflict in the physician.

Groves (1978) examined the brief literature on these difficult patients and the physician's reactions to them, and then identified with considerable sensitivity, four types of patients who seem to bring out the worst in the health care provider—the *dependent clinger,* the *entitled demander,* the *manipulative help-rejecter,* and the *self-destructive denier.* These patients often have psychiatric disorders that complicate their physical difficulties as well as their relationships with their physician (Goodwin, Goodwin, & Kellner, 1979).

The dependent clinger is initially exceedingly grateful to the physician for whatever service has been provided, which frequently triggers feelings of omnipotence on the part of the physician. Soon, however, as the dependency on the part of the patient increases in intensity and irrationality, the patient becomes the "unplanned, unwanted, unlovable child" and the physician the "inexhaustible mother" (p. 885). According to Groves, "the clinger must be told as early in the relationship as possible, and as tactfully and firmly as possible, that the physician has not only human limits to knowledge and skill but also limitations to time and stamina" (p. 885).

The entitled demander, while just as dependent as the clinger, uses intimidation, devaluation, and guilt-induction to "place the doctor in the role of the inexhaustible supply depot" (p. 885). The physician often does not recognize this behavior for what it is—hostile on the surface, to be sure, but frightened and fearful underneath. Groves suggests that the physician should never contradict or deny the patient's entitlement to good medical care, but should try to redirect the entitlement in a more useful direction.

Manipulative help-rejecters also seem to have an insatiable need for emotional support, but act as if no treatment can possibly help them. As the physician tries harder to be helpful, the patient counters with triumphant reports of yet another medical failure. Symptoms that are diminished in intensity are quickly replaced by new symptoms. In many cases the rejection of help covers a severe depression, but referral for psychiatric help is rarely easy or successful.

Self-destructive deniers have given up hope of ever having their needs met and appear to derive pleasure from their self-destructiveness and their chronic thwarting of medical efforts on their behalf. Often their self-destructiveness results in their death. Accordingly, Groves suggests that these patients be thought of as terminally ill, and that the physician have the same objective in their care as with any other terminally ill patient—to help them live as long and as comfortably as possible.

These four types of patients all have enormous dependency needs and require extraordinary skill and patience on the part of the physician for their clinical management. They somehow bring out the best and the worst in the physician. Groves notes, by way of summary, that "dependent *clingers* evoke aversion. Entitled *demanders* evoke fear and then counterattack. Manipulative *help-rejecters* evoke guilt and feelings of inadequacy. Self-destructive *deniers* . . . evoke all these negative feelings, as well as malice and, at times, the secret wish that the patient will 'die and get it over with'" (p. 887).

## THE PROCESS OF NURSING EDUCATION

In contrast to medical education, in which a single general model prevails, nursing education has traditionally taken place in three different modes. Diploma-granting programs, usually based in general hospitals, require prior high school graduation, and are typically 2 years in length. These programs provide preparation for taking the examination to become a registered nurse. Associate-degree programs are typically based in community colleges and combine nursing education with the 2-year associate degree representing the completion of 2 years of university work. Baccalaureate programs are university-based and combine a 4-year university education (with a bachelor's degree) with preparation for the examination for the status of registered nurse. Most colleges and universities award very little academic credit to registered nurses who have graduated from diploma programs and want to work toward college degrees. These 2-year diploma programs have been gradually replaced by associate degree and baccalaureate programs over the past 25 years, as part of a general upgrading and professionalization of nursing. There are relatively few significant differences among senior nursing students in these three nursing programs in the areas of intellectual level, leadership qualities, attitudes toward research, and future aspirations (Meleis & Farrell, 1974).

Socialization into the profession of nursing begins in nursing school and continues for some period of time after the graduate begins work as a nursing professional (Brown, Swift, & Oberman, 1974; McCain, 1985). Nursing students have a particular set of problems in their professional development that are virtually nonexistent among medical students, namely, their frequent low self-esteem, poor self-image, and belief in external locus of control. The position of the nurse in the world of the health service provider is, to use the phrase of Fagin and Diers (1983), the "classic underdog, struggling to be heard, approved, and recognized" (p. 116). Nurses typically function in the traditional role of "handmaiden," in settings that are generally dominated by the more powerful physician. Kalisch (1975), herself a nurse, writing about her experiences as a medical patient, noted that Aesculapius (see Chapter 1), "the god of medicine in ancient Roman mythology, is alive and well today and working in medical care delivery settings, U.S.A." (p. 22).

Henderson (1964), describing the early history of nursing, has noted that

> with the passage of the nurse registration act in England and the state nurse practice acts in the United States around the turn of the century, it became necessary to describe nursing in such a way as to protect the public and the nurse. The definitions at this time were necessarily concerned with what the nurse was legally empowered to do and, as most nurses were then working as private practitioners in homes and hospitals, most of the legal definitions implied that the nurse operated under the supervision of a physician. They failed to identify that aspect of her work that was independent or self-directed. The idea of the nurse as merely the physician's assistant, however, has never been satisfying to the occupation as a whole or to many of its individual members. (p. 62)

Henderson views the nurse as an independent practitioner of basic nursing care, a role not to be confused with diagnosis or treatment of disease, which she sees as the physician's realm. Since her views would probably be endorsed by the majority of nursing practitioners, they are worth quoting: "I see nursing as primarily complementing the patient by supplying what he needs in knowledge, will, or strength to perform his daily activities and also to carry out the treatment prescribed for him by the physician" (p. 66).

One of the increasingly recognized roles of the nurse is that of serving as a mediator in the physician-patient relationship. In this capacity, the nurse can help the patient and the family deal successfully with problems they may be experiencing in their relationship with the physician and can help the physician understand the patient's motivations and ways of dealing with the anxiety associated with the illness (also see Henderson, 1964; Jones, 1982). In order to be comfortable in the new role of mediator, the nurse must have a satisfactory level of internal locus of control, and Dufault (1985) has recently demonstrated that it is possible to influence the sense of control among student nurses in the direction of greater internality by means of an experimental seminar that gives the student the opportunity to explore the future of the professional nurse's role in the health service delivery system.

A recent study of the attitudes toward patient rights on the part of nurses and medical students at the beginning and at the end of their university training (Kurtzman, Block, & Steiner-Freud, 1985) illustrates the need for this facilitative role of the nurse. In this study, an assessment of attitudes toward the rights of hospitalized patients was undertaken, and the investigators found that while first-year students in nursing and medicine had approximately the same attitude scores, fourth-year students differed in their attitudes. In the case of medical students, attitudes toward the rights of hospitalized patients became less supportive with time, while in the case of nursing students, attitudes toward these rights became significantly more supportive with time.

Hammer and Tufts (1985) attribute the problem of low self-esteem among nurses to another factor—the authoritarian behavior of nursing educators. Nursing students can be made to feel inferior not only to physicians but to senior nurses as well, with serious and long-lasting impairment of their level of self-esteem. Further complicating the self-image of members of the nursing profession are long-standing issues about the profession itself. Is nursing an independent profession, or does it exist primarily to carry out the directives of members of the medical profession? How can nurses be professionals if they need only 2 years of postsecondary school education to qualify as fully trained practitioners?

Insofar as nursing educators are concerned, Hammer and Tufts urge them to deal with nursing students in ways that are affirming and supportive, such as by showing unconditional acceptance and belief in the abilities and potential of each nursing student, providing opportunities for nursing students to have successful clinical experiences, and avoiding being overly critical as well as avoiding the constant threat that the nursing student might not succeed (also see Cohen, 1981; Lampkin, Cannon, & Fairchild, 1985).

### Sources of Stress among Nursing Students

In an interesting study of motives for entering nursing school, Morris and Grassi-Russo (1979) surveyed fifty-four 2-year diploma school of nursing students who had been admitted but not yet started nursing school. The students ranged in age from 17 to 32, with a mean age of 20. The students were presented a list of ten items that were thought to include all of the major motivating factors in entering the nursing profession, and were asked to rank them twice—once in terms of their own motives, and again in terms of what they judged to be the motives of most people entering nursing school.

Motives for self and others were fairly highly correlated. Highest on both lists were "helping people" and "interest in science and medicine." Lowest on both lists was "having nurses in the family." Most students rated themselves as more altruistic and humanistic and as less material in their motives than other beginning nursing students. Students ranked "financial reward" as lower for themselves than for others as a motivating factor in entering nursing school, and ranked "improvement of health care" as higher for themselves than for others. In addition, they ranked "professional status" as more important for others than for themselves, and ranked "close relationships with people" as more important for themselves than for others. These discrepancies between ratings of self and rating of others suggested to Morris and Grassi-Russo that students entered nursing school thinking of themselves as different from others in their entrance class, and that this perceived difference could serve as an important source of tension.

Nursing students share with medical students a high level of initial self-doubt about their clinical effectiveness. In the case of the nurse, many of whom begin their training right out of high school, their self-doubts are in part a reflection of their chronological age. That is, student nurses are often actively struggling with issues related to their own psychosexual development at the same time that they are trying to master a set of clinical skills that demand the highest level of effort (Donnelly, 1981).

Under these circumstances, developing an understanding of how nursing students cope with clinical performance-related anxiety can be very important in developing strategies for controlling stress. Manderino and Yonkman (1985) have described the process of stress inoculation by which they help students cope with performance-related anxiety. Stress inoculation is a cognitively oriented coping skills program that is designed to help students manage future stressful situations. The program is divided into three phases—information, skills acquisition, and application.

Students are taught how to cope with the major anxiety-provoking thinking patterns to which they are vulnerable: (1) catastrophizing, that is, converting every criticism into a complete disaster; (2) overgeneralizing, that is, concluding that any inadequate performance means that the performance will always be inadequate; (3) dichotomous thinking, that is, thinking in the extremes of perfection or hopelessness; and (4) shoulds, that is, assigning unreasonable demands upon oneself or others.

In addition, students are taught how to generate positive coping statements and how to relax. Finally, students are given opportunities to practice these coping skills under simulated stressful conditions. Similar stress management programs have been reported with students in practical nursing programs (Wernick, 1984; also see Davidhizar & McBride, 1985).

## CONCLUDING COMMENTS

The life of the health care provider is enormously stressful, even though it is a fulfilling one. A medical or nursing education has a profound impact on students. Stress begins early—certainly, in the case of the physician, as early as the high school years, when most of them make a decision to become physicians. There is stress, perhaps increasing stress, at every step of the way, and it is easy, after reading the literature, to conclude that not enough attention is focused on the counterproductive aspects of that stress on the part of medical school, nursing school, and hospital administrators.

Indeed, one of the reasons why the health maintenance organization and other forms of organized health service delivery may be gaining in popularity is because the professional and personal life of the health service provider may be far more pleasant, predictable, and orderly than is the case when health services are provided in solo or group practice on a fee-for-service basis.

Some of the tension associated with training and practice in the health service delivery system is undoubtedly irreducible. The struggle to keep human beings alive and healthy is, after all, one that is ultimately lost. But an increasing number of faculty members in both medical and nursing schools appear to be concerned about reducing those sources of tension that can be reduced and about introducing an increased amount of compassion and civility into both the academic and clinical components of the medical and nursing curriculum.

Reported analyses of the nature of these stresses suggests that each step in the medical and nursing practice career has an identifiable set of challenges, and that a unique set of interventions can be designed for each of these steps to reduce the intensity of some stresses, eliminate others, and improve coping skills in dealing with those stresses that remain.

At the same time, however, it would be well to remember that physicians have some characteristics that are not always admired, and that some of these characteristics predate their entrance into medical school and the profession of medicine. There is no question that, as a class, physicians are seen as excessively interested in money and prestige, and that they are viewed as cynical and not particularly compassionate. That is, there is some reason to believe that the profession of medicine attracts a particular type of young person, a type who is not altogether admired, or who is grudgingly admired.

Since the profession of medicine is undergoing a major transformation, there may be a change in the kind of young person who will be drawn to the practice of that profession in the future. The current and growing surplus of physicians will likely reduce the rate of change, but if physicians increasingly find themselves working in salaried positions, with greater demands for interdependence with colleagues, and in a setting where they perform their skills in a more public arena, a different type of person might be drawn to the profession.

The literature on the psychology of the health care provider is overly influenced by studies of physicians. There is a far smaller literature about members of the nursing profession, and even less about other lower-level health care providers who make up the bulk of the millions of people who work in hospitals. The amount of literature seems to be in direct proportion to the power of the group being studied and in inverse proportion to their numbers. Yet, in medical care settings, on a day-to-day basis, the importance of nursing personnel cannot be overestimated. The lack of an adequate empirical literature on nursing personnel, as well as on such other health care providers as pharmacists, dentists, optometrists, chiropractors, and health psychologists, among others, creates a special research agenda for the future.

The extraordinary contribution of health care professionals to all our lives is directly apparent in our discussion of health and illness in the United States, and it will be fascinating to observe and to become part of the changing nature of health service delivery. We are likely to be the last generation of Americans who will receive our health care from fee-for-service physicians, and both their world and ours have begun a dramatic transformation.

All this speaks to a special urgency about the field of health psychology. Working side by side with other health service providers, health psychologists will likely play an increasingly significant role in every theme that has been examined in this volume—in consumer health education, in stress reduction and stress management, in reducing the prevalence of self-destructive lifestyles, in making the medical care system more responsive to the psychosocial needs of its patients, in helping in the prevention and treatment of many illnesses that are currently not under control, and in helping humanize the educational system that creates health professionals.

## SUMMARY

- Physicians and nurses differ in important respects from other people, and it is important to know what the day-to-day lives of these health service providers are like and what their experiences are in becoming health care professionals.

- A surplus of physicians already exists and threatens to increase in the coming years. Only about half of applicants to medical school are ever admitted, and in spite of this surplus, a thriving offshore medical school system exists that offers what is generally considered to be an inferior medical education to U.S. students, most of whom never apply to medical schools in the United States.

- Medical students bring a certain set of personality characteristics with them to medical school, and these characteristics are not entirely flattering either to medical students themselves or to their fellow university students.

- The process of becoming a physician is significantly and increasingly stressful throughout virtually the entire medical career, starting with high school, when most young men and women who ultimately become physicians make that career choice, continuing through every aspect of medical training, and into medical practice.

- The most commonly identified stresses during the period of medical education and training are lack of time to study and to develop fulfilling personal lives, a sense of being overwhelmed by the material that needs to be mastered, fear of making mistakes that could cause unnecessary pain or even death to patients, loneliness and a feeling of dehumanization, financial worries, and uncertainty about career choice. These stresses are chronic and often leave medical students physically and sometimes emotionally exhausted.

- A dramatic increase in the number and proportion of women entering a medical career has taken place in the last two decades. As a consequence, growing attention is being paid to the special problems faced by women who wish to enter a career historically dominated by men and who hope to combine a medical career with having their own families.

- Some, but not all, medical schools and hospitals are beginning to recognize the importance of providing help to medical students and to interns and residents whose level of stress is becoming unmanageable. Most of these intervention programs are effective in achieving their objectives.

- The period of internship and residency training is fraught with enormous responsibilities associated with issues of appropriate clinical management. Interns and residents tend to work so many hours each week as to lose their effectiveness and ability to learn, and often report excess levels of depression, marital disruption, drug abuse, cognitive impairment, and suicidal thought.

- A special problem exists for physicians in dealing with patients whose needs appear to be insatiable and who present problems that make them very difficult to like and to deal with sympathetically.

- Medical education and training goes through a series of recognizable and fairly consistent steps, each of which brings its own stresses and challenges. It is generally believed that one of the by-products of these educational experiences is that medical students, who bring with them into medical school a certain level of cynicism, leave their training even more cynical and less compassionate than they were when they started their training.

- There is substantial evidence that the practice of medicine puts many physicians at excess risk of premature mortality and morbidity, of suicide, of psychiatric depression, and of alcohol and other forms of drug abuse.

- Growing public and professional recognition of the existence of the impaired physician is occurring, along with growing attention to the need to provide therapeutic and rehabilitative help for those physicians who become emotionally disabled.

- Training and practice in the profession of nursing also brings with it a number of significant stresses. A number of these stresses are unique to the nursing profession and include a chronically low level of self-esteem and a chronic need to describe their work responsibilities in ways that allow them an acceptable level of autonomy.

- A number of efforts to provide support to nursing students during their period of training have been reported. These preventive intervention programs have generally been found to be very helpful in assisting nursing students to cope with the stresses associated with their academic and clinical training.

# Glossary

**Acute illness**  An illness, usually biological in nature, and usually reversible, that occurs over a relatively short period of time and that appears to be the result of some infectious process.

**Acute pain**  Pain of short duration that serves to alert a person that something is wrong with the body and that something needs to be done to correct the situation.

**Aesculapius**  The ancient Greek physician whose name is now associated with the belief that health is a state and can often be regained by the efforts of the physician.

**Alarm reaction**  The first stage in the general adaptation syndrome as described by Selye, in which the body becomes alerted to an externally caused stress.

**American Psychological Association**  A national organization of psychologists to which most applied and academic psychologists belong; the APA has a Division of Health Psychology to which most health psychologists belong.

**Anorexia nervosa**  An eating disorder characterized by an unwillingness or inability to eat.

**Anthrax**  A sometimes fatal acute bacterial disease of the skin that can spread to the lymph nodes and bloodstream, transmitted by contaminated animal hair or skin.

**At-risk group**  A group, usually identified on the basis of some demographic characteristic, that is statistically at excess risk of developing some particular disease or illness.

**Attributable risk**  The proportion of all persons with a particular disease that can be attributed to exposure to a presumed causative agent.

**Autonomic nervous system**  That portion of the nervous system that automatically controls the glands and the smooth muscles of the heart, the blood vessels, the stomach lining, and the intestines.

**Autonomy**  The extent to which an individual is able to maintain an adequate lifestyle without assistance.

**Bacteriology**  The science that deals with bacteria, one-celled organisms that frequently transmit disease.

**Balneology**    The practice of using healing waters and other naturally occurring substances for therapeutic purposes.

**Behavioral health**    The field of psychology that focuses on psychological factors in health maintenance and in the prevention of illness.

**Behavioral medicine**    An interdisciplinary field that integrates behavioral and biomedical science, knowledge, and techniques and applies this knowledge base to prevention, diagnosis, treatment, and rehabilitation.

**Benign pain**    Pain that is not associated with a malignant disease such as cancer.

**Beriberi**    A nutritional disease due to lack of vitamin $B_1$ in the diet, characterized by weakness, paralysis, anemia, and wasting away.

**Biofeedback**    A procedure that provides individuals with immediate information regarding physiological processes of which they are ordinarily unaware, so that they can learn to control those processes in order to reduce anxiety or pain.

**Biogenic pain**    Chronic pain that appears to be explainable on the basis of physical abnormalities, and thus, thought of as primarily due to organic characteristics of the body.

**Biopsychosocial theory**    The belief that all illness is the result of the complex interaction of biological, psychological, and sociological factors.

**Birth rate**    Number of live births divided by the total population, usually expressed as so many births per 1000 population.

**Bronchial asthma**    A reversible airway obstruction that results in paroxysmal wheezing and labored breathing due to some combination of smooth muscle spasm, tissue swelling, and excessive mucous secretion.

**Cancer**    A group of illnesses in which abnormal cells are formed that are able to proliferate, invade, and overwhelm normal tissues, and to spread to distant sites in the body.

**Case-control study**    Any study design in which groups of people who differ in some aspect of their current status are contrasted in terms of prior experiences or history.

**Causalgia**    Chronic severe burning pain that frequently occurs after a bullet wound or other tearing wound.

**Cervical cytology**    Examination of cells in the cervix of the uterus for the purpose of disease or prodromal disease detection.

**Cholera**    An acute intestinal disease transmitted by contaminated water, and food, and by flies, endemic in parts of Asia. Fatality rate can vary from 15 percent to as high as 75 percent.

**Chronic illness**    An illness that can be predominantly physical or psychological that is usually long-lasting and irreversible.

**Chronic pain**    Persistent pain lasting 6 months or longer that no longer serves an alerting function, but that rather is a disorder in and of itself.

**Clinical health psychology**    The field of psychology that concerns itself with ways in which psychological knowledge can be applied to the prevention and treatment of all forms of mental and physical disorders.

**Clinical neuropsychology**    The specialized field of psychology that studies the relationships between neurological and psychological factors in health and illness.

**Coinsurance**    That proportion of medical costs that must be paid by the insurance holder after the deductible cost has been paid—often 20 percent of medical bills over the annual deductible amount.

**Cohort study**    Any study design in which groups of people who differ in some aspect of their histories are contrasted, generally in terms of subsequent outcome variables.

**Community mental health**    The field of inquiry devoted to the study of mental health and mental illness as a community phenomenon, and to ways of preventing and treating mental disability through community intervention.

**Community psychology**    A branch of psychology that examines how community characteristics play a role in human welfare, and in how changing such characteristics can result in increased qulaity of life.

**Compensative existence**    The condition of people who live in a manner that trades thriving vitality for security and who would rather tolerate something being wrong with themselves than take a chance on dealing with it forthrightly.

**Consumer health education**  Educational efforts targeted to consumers of health services that are designed to make them less vulnerable to disease and more competent in the selection and evaluation of health services.

**Contextual thinking**  The belief that all phenomena are caused by multiple reasons.

**Contingency management**  Any systematic procedure that uses the basic principles of learning theory in order to modify behavior.

**Cost-effectiveness**  A measure of the benefits of some therapeutic or preventive program that takes into account its cost as well as its outcome.

**Decompensative existence**  The condition of people who are ill, and who must trade off a significant decrease of life quality and vitality in return for remaining alive.

**Deductibles**  Initial costs of medical care that must be paid by the insurance holder each year before payments will be made by the health insurance policy.

**Demography**  The scientific study and analysis of vital statistics, such as gender, age, births, deaths, illnesses, and so forth, for the purposes of developing an improved understanding of human behavior, including health-related behavior.

**Denial**  The conscious or unconscious repudiation of the meaning of an event in order to reduce fear or anxiety or some other unpleasant feeling associated with the event.

**Detoxification**  Elimination of undesired substances, including medications, from the body, usually by a process of reducing the intake of the substance over an extended period of time.

**Diagnostic related groups**  A classification system for patients covered by medicare that determines the amount of money that will be paid to hospitals for their care.

**Diastolic blood pressure**  A measure of blood pressure taken between beats of the heart.

**Diphtheria**  An acute infectious disease of the tonsils, larynx, and nose, characterized by sore throat, fever, and difficulty breathing.

**Disease prevention**  Any activity designed to prevent specified diseases from occurring.

**Endocrinologist**  A specialist in the study of the bodily glands that produce internal secretions that are carried by the blood or lymph and that regulate certain bodily functions.

**Endorphin**  An opiate-like substance produced naturally by the body itself that serves to reduce pain and produce euphoria.

**Epidemiological catchment area**  Geographic areas in the United States, of city or county size, that form the basis for selection of subjects for longitudinal studies of mental disorders.

**Epidemiology**  The study of the distribution and determinants of disease.

**Factorial structure**  An important statistical attribute of a measurement scale that identifies the various domains that are tapped by the scale.

**Family life education**  A type of health education program identified by its target group—the family.

**Fertility rate**  Number of live births divided by the population of women of childbearing age, usually 15 to 44, expressed as so many births per 1000 population of women of childbearing age.

**Fetal death ratio**  The number of babies born dead as a ratio to the number born alive, usually presented as fetal deaths per 1000 live births.

**Formistic thinking**  Either-or thinking, that is, using the assumption that either A or B is true, and that the establishment of validity depends on determining which.

**Functional adequacy**  The extent to which individuals are capable of fulfilling the requirements of a social role appropriate to their age and sex.

**Functional existence**  The condition of people who are thriving and living full rich lives by insisting on being the best that they can be.

**General adaptation syndrome**  The three-step syndrome described by Hans Selye explaining how the body reacts to external stress, in ways that may result in stress-related illness.

**Geneticist**  A specialist in the field of biology who deals with heredity and its effects on structure or behavior of an organism.

**Germ theory**  A theory of disease origin that held that every disease was caused by a specific germ.

**Goiter** A nutritional disorder due to deficiency of iodine in the diet that results in an enlarged thyroid gland and resultant swelling in the front of the throat.

**Health behavior** Activities undertaken by individuals who believe themselves to be healthy for the purpose of preventing or detecting disease.

**Health care provider** Any one of a number of health professionals, including physicians, nurses, psychologists, or medical technicians, who provide direct health care services to persons who are ill.

**Health care psychology** The field of psychology that is concerned about the delivery of health care services.

**Health field** A framework for considering health and illness that includes four components—human biology, the environment, lifestyle, and health care organization.

**Health maintenance organization** An organized system of health care that provides comprehensive medical services for enrolled members for a fixed, prepaid annual fee through a single organization and payment mechanism.

**Health perception** Attitudes a person has about the quality of his or her own health.

**Health promotion** Any activity designed to reduce vulnerability to disease in general or to enhance health.

**Health service provider** A person in a medical care system who provides direct health-related services to a client or patient population.

**Homeostasis** The fundamental principle of physiology that describes the mechanisms that keep the internal environment of the body constant so that all cells are able to function optimally.

**Hygeia** The symbol, from ancient Greece, of the view that health means living according to reason, and hence, that health is a process.

**Hypertension** High blood pressure.

**Hypochondriasis** A conviction that a disease is present, and a persistent preoccupation with physical health, out of proportion to any existing justification.

**Illness behavior** The manner in which persons monitor their bodies, define and interpret their symptoms, take remedial actions, and use the health care system.

**Illness** A group of symptoms or a condition that underlies these symptoms.

**Immunization** The process whereby a person is made immune to an infectious disease by the inoculation of a substance related to the disease that causes the body to produce antibodies that successfully combat the disease process.

**In-service training** Educational programs for health professionals who are currently employed designed to keep them up-to-date on new developments in their field; also called continuing education or staff development.

**Infant mortality rate** Deaths to babies born alive that occur prior to one year of age, usually reported as deaths per 1000 live births.

**Infectious disease** A disease that is caused by a germ that can be transmitted from person to person.

**Informed consent** Consent for some medical procedure given by a patient or a patient's family, after being fully informed about the advantages, disadvantages, and dangers of the proposed procedure.

**Kwashiorkor** A nutritional disease of children and young adults due to lack of protein in the diet.

**Lifestyle** In the context of health psychology, refers to any behavior, such as smoking, alcohol abuse, lack of exercise, or poor nutrition, that has negative consequences for health and life quality.

**Malaria** An intermittent and recurrent infectious disease transmitted by the bite of an infected anopheles mosquito, characterized by severe chills and fever.

**Malignant pain** Pain associated with a malignant disease, particularly, cancer.

**Malingering** Lying about the existence of symptoms or about their intensity in order to achieve some objective, such as to get out of responsibility, to obtain financial compensation, to evade prosecution, or to obtain drugs.

**Mantra** A set of sounds used in transcendental medication that is thought to help increase the awareness of thoughts prior to their fully developed form.

**Maternal mortality rate** Deaths to mothers arising from complications of pregnancy, childbirth, or the period immediately after childbirth, reported as a rate per 100,000 live births.

**Mechanistic thinking** Single cause-single effect thinking, based upon the assumption that every effect has a single cause and that the effect is fully explained when that single cause is determined.

**Medical care system**    The aggregate of services available in a community for preventing and treating medical illness.

**Medical psychology**    The study of psychological factors related to any aspects of physical health, illness, and its treatment, at the individual, group, and systems level.

**Mental health education**    The process of providing mental-health related information to the public in order to facilitate behavior change that results in improved mental health practices.

**Mental health**    Health as assessed by the adequacy of psychological functioning.

**Miasma theory**    A theory of disease origin that held that soil polluted with waste products gave off a poisonous gaseous substance (miasma) that caused disease.

**Morbidity**    Illness, usually calculated as a rate so that the probability of illness from a particular cause can be calculated in a specified population.

**Mortality**    Death, usually calculated so that the number of deaths can be expressed as a ratio to births or as a probability rate in a specified population.

**Neonatal death rate**    Deaths to babies born alive that occur prior to 28 days of age, usually reported as deaths per 1000 live births.

**Neurotransmitter**    Naturally produced substances in the body that play a role in facilitating or impeding the transmission of impulses in the central nervous system.

**Nutritional disease**    A disease that is caused by faulty nutrition, either due to a lack of an essential dietary component or because of insufficient or excessive dietary intake.

**Nutritionist**    A specialist in the study of nutrition, the processes by which an organism takes in and assimilates food for promoting growth and replacing worn or injured tissues.

**Organistic thinking**    Thinking that assumes that everything is connected to everything else, that illnesses, for example, occur because of complex interactions of different environmental and personal characteristics.

**Pain behavior**    Observable behavior that is associated with self-reports of pain, and hence, useful as dependent measures of interest on the part of scientists who study pain.

**Pain sensitivity range**    The range of tolerable pain, thus the difference between pain tolerance and pain threshold.

**Pain threshold**    The point at which an individual first perceives stimulation to be painful.

**Pain tolerance**    The point at which an individual is not willing to accept painful stimulation of a higher magnitude or to continue to endure painful stimulation at a given level of intensity.

**Parasympathetic nervous system**    That portion of the autonomic nervous system that is dominant during periods of relaxation and recuperation.

**Patient education**    Consumer health education programs targeted at patients in the medical care system.

**Pellagra**    A nutritional disease endemic in many parts of the world due to lack of nicotinic acid (niacin) in the diet, characterized by gastric disturbances, skin eruptions, and psychiatric symptoms.

**Phantom limb pain**    Pain, sometimes of great severity, that appears to originate in a limb that has been amputated, that is, in a "phantom limb."

**Physical health**    Health as assessed by the presence or absence of biological abnormalities.

**Pierre the Pelican**    The name given to the series of health education newsletters prepared for first-time mothers in the state of Louisiana.

**Placebo**    A medication or procedure that has a therapeutic effect in and of itself, without regard to its pharmacology or specific properties.

**Plague**    A highly fatal infectious disease, of a number of different varieties, characterized by fever, shock, delirium, hemorrhaging, and coma.

**Polio**    An acute viral disease that destroys nerve cells in the spinal cord or brain stem and usually leaves the victim paralyzed.

**Postnatal**    The period of time after birth, usually considered in the context of health-related aspects of the newborn child or of the new mother.

**Premature death**    Deaths that occur before the age of 70, and that result in an unusually large number of years of life lost, hence, a measure that has important implications for judging the quality of a health care delivery system.

**Prenatal**  The time before birth, usually considered in the context of health-related aspects of the pregnant woman or of the fetus.

**Prevention**  Activities that are designed to prevent illnesses from occurring, either by means of disease-specific procedures or by general approaches to health promotion.

**Prognosis**  A measure of anticipated changes in level of health in the future.

**Prospective payment system**  A system for the reimbursement of hospital bills for patients covered by Medicare, in which a flat fee is paid for the treatment of each patient as a function of his or her diagnosis.

**Prospective study**  An epidemiological study design in which groups of people who differ in their levels of exposure to a presumed causative agent are followed in time to determine if there are subsequent differences in disease rates.

**Psychobiology**  The term coined by Adolf Meyer to represent the view that mental disorder results from the interaction of biological and psychological factors.

**Psychogenic pain**  Chronic pain that appears in the apparent absence of physical findings to account for it, and thus thought to be of psychological origin.

**Psychosomatic disorders**  Physical disorders that are thought to be caused by psychological conflict or to be associated with certain specific personality characteristics.

**Psychosomatic medicine**  The branch of medicine that concentrates on the study and treatment of a small set of physical disorders that are believed to be primarily of psychological origin.

**Public assistance**  Support services and payments provided from tax revenues to people in need to pay for living expenses such as food, rent or medical costs—often called "welfare" payments.

**Public health**  A field that concerns itself with the health of a collectivity and that concentrates on improving levels of health by preventing disease wherever possible.

**Rabies**  A rare but highly fatal acute encephalitis resulting from the bite of a rabid animal.

**Reductionism**  The philosophic view that complex phenomena are ultimately derived from a single primary principle.

**Relative risk**  The risk of developing a particular disease among a group of people exposed to a presumed causative agent divided by the risk of developing that same disease among an unexposed group.

**Reliability**  The extent to which a measurement procedure gives similar results when it is employed on several different occasions or by different examiners or test administrators.

**Retrospective study**  An epidemiological study design in which groups of people who differ in their current disease state are examined to determine if there were differences in their disease-related histories.

**Rickets**  A nutritional disease, primarily of children, caused by lack of vitamin D, sunlight, or calcium salts in the diet resulting in softening and bending of the bones.

**Rubella**  A mild infectious disease characterized by a rash and enlargement of lymph nodes, and particularly hazardous to women who acquire the disease during pregnancy.

**Sanitation movement**  The nineteenth-century movement to reduce disease incidence by improving the state of environmental sanitation.

**Secondary gain**  The secondary benefits of illness that occur as a consequence of increased support or attention, or of reductions in responsibilities that must be carried out.

**Scurvy**  A nutritional disease due to lack of vitamin C in the body, characterized by weakness, anemia, spongy gums, and bleeding from the mucous membranes.

**Self-help movement**  A rapidly growing movement in the United States whereby groups of people who have some particular disorder band together for purposes of mutual assistance.

**Set-point weight**  The weight of any particular person that represents his or her "normal" weight, to which that person will return after terminating any effort to lose or gain weight.

**Sexually transmitted diseases**  Any infectious disease transmitted by sexual contact.

**Sick role behavior**  Activities undertaken by those who consider themselves ill for the purpose of getting well.

**Smallpox**  An acute infectious virus disease characterized by fever, vomiting, and pustular eruptions that often leave pitted scars or pockmarks.

**Social health**  Health as assessed by the quality of social relationships.

**Social insurance**  Financial benefits that are

available to a population as a matter of right, and that are usually funded by tax revenues.

**Social support system**  A group of people and agencies that interdependently provide support to a person, usually at times of stress; also called a social network.

**Stage of exhaustion**  The third stage in Selye's general adaption syndrome, in which the body becomes exhausted from defending itself again external stress; this exhaustion can result in illness.

**Stage of resistance**  The second stage in Selye's general adaptation syndrome, in which the body actively defends itself against an external stress.

**Strain**  The body's internal responses to external stress-related demands.

**Stress management**  Techniques that can be taught to people to help them cope with chronic stress.

**Stress**  An external demand on the body that may produce internal physiological or psychological disturbances if it is not promptly and satisfactorily met.

**Stressful life event**  An event that has the power to cause internal strain in a person that may increase that person's vulnerability to illness.

**Subjective expected utility**  A theory of rational decision making, in which people are thought to weigh the pros and cons of all available alternatives in terms of probabilities and consequences, and then choose the alternative with the greatest weight.

**Sympathetic nervous system**  That portion of the autonomic nervous system that is dominant during times of stress.

**Syndrome**  A group of symptoms that frequently occur together, thus constituting the characteristics of some particular disease or disorder.

**Systems approach**  An explanatory approach that assumes that every element in a system is connected with every other element, and that therefore, a phenomenon can be understood only in terms of interdependencies among system components.

**Systolic blood pressure**  A measure of blood pressure taken when the blood is being forced ahead by the heart.

**Tetanus**  An acute infectious disease transmitted through the skin, usually by wounds, characterized by muscle rigidity often near the site of the wound.

**Treatment**  Activities designed to shorten the duration of an illness that is already present.

**Tuberculosis**  A chronic bacterial disease, known throughout most of the world, caused by the tubercle bacillus, and transmitted by direct contact; incidence and mortality rate appear to be decreasing.

**Typhoid fever**  A systemic widespread infectious disease, transmitted by contact with a carrier, that is characterized by fever, malaise, and anorexia. Fatality rate can be as high as 10 percent.

**Typhus**  An acute infectious disease caused by a rickettsia transmitted to people by the bite of fleas or lice, and characterized by fever, weakness, and the eruption of red spots on the skin.

**Validity**  The extent to which a scale truly measures the concept or dimension that it is intended to measure.

**Virologist**  A specialist in the study of viruses—microorganisms that cause various diseases, such as smallpox.

**Wellness**  A concept of health that includes psychosocial as well as physical health, and includes not only the absence of disease but also the presence of pleasure and high life-quality among its defining characteristics.

**Yellow fever**  An acute infectious disease, transmitted mainly by mosquitoes, that is found in Africa and South America, and is characterized by fever, nausea, backache, prostration, and vomiting; fatality rate averages about 5 percent.

# References

AAKSTER, C. W. (1974). Psycho-social stress and health disturbances. *Social Science and Medicine, 8*, 77–90.

ABRAHAMS, R. B., & PATTERSON, R. D. (1978–1979). Psychological distress among the community elderly: Prevalence, characteristics and implications for service. *International Journal of Aging and Human Development, 9*, 1–18.

ABRAMSON, L. Y., SELIGMAN, M.E.P., & TEASDALE, J. D. (1978). Learned helplessness in humans: Critique and reformulation. *Journal of Abnormal Psychology, 87*, 49–74.

ADAMS, P. R., & ADAMS, G. R. (1984). Mount Saint Helen's ashfall: Evidence for a disaster stress reaction. *American Psychologist, 39*, 252–260.

ADAY, L. A., & ANDERSEN, R. (1974). A framework for the study of access to medical care. *Health Services Research, 9*, 208–220.

ADDISON, W. (1951). *English spas.* London: B. T. Batsford.

ADER, R. (1981). Behavioral influences on immune responses. In S. M. Weiss, J. A. Herd, & B. H. Fox (Eds.), *Perspectives on behavioral medicine: Proceedings of the Academy of Behavioral Medicine Research Conference, Snowbird, Utah, June 3–6, 1979* (pp. 163–182). New York: Academic Press.

ADER, R., & COHEN, N. (1984). Behavior and the immune system. In W. D. Gentry (Ed.), *Handbook of behavioral medicine* (pp. 117–173). New York: Guilford Press.

ADLER, R., WERNER, E. R., & KORSCH, B. (1980). Systematic study of four years of internship. *Pediatrics, 66,* 1000–1008.

AGNEW, D. C., & MERSKEY, H. (1976). Words of chronic pain. *Pain, 2,* 73–81.

AGRAS, W. S. (1982). Behavioral medicine in the 1980s: Nonrandom connections. *Journal of Consulting and Clinical Psychology, 50,* 797–803.

AGRAS, W. S. (1984). The behavioral treatment of somatic disorders. In W. D. Gentry (Ed.), *Handbook of behavioral medicine* (pp. 479–530). New York: Guilford Press.

AHMED, P. I., KOLKER, A., & COELHO, G. V. (1979). Toward a new definition of health: An overview. In P. I. Ahmed, & G. V. Coelho (Eds.), *Toward a new definition of health: Psychosocial dimensions* (pp. 7–22). New York: Plenum.

AJZEN, I., & FISHBEIN, M. (1977). Attitude-behavior relations: A theoretical analysis and review of empirical research. *Psychological Bulletin, 84,* 888–918.

ALBEE, G. W. (1979). Primary prevention. *Canada's Mental Health, 27,* 5–9.

ALBEE, G. W. (1985). The answer is prevention. *Psychology Today,* February, 60–64.

ALBINO, J. E. (1983). Health psychology and primary prevention: Natural allies. In R. D. Felner, L. A. Jason, J. N. Moritsugu, & S. S. Farber (Eds.), *Preventive psychology: Theory, research and practice* (pp. 221–233). New York: Pergamon Press.

Alcohol-associated premature mortality—United States, 1980. (1985). *Morbidity and Mortality Weekly Report, 34,* 493–494.

ALDERMAN, M. H. (1984). Worksite treatment of hypertension. In J. D. Matarazzo, S. M. Weiss, J. A. Herd, N. E. Miller, & S. M. Weiss (Eds.), *Behavioral health: A handbook of health enhancement and disease prevention* (pp. 862–869). New York: Wiley.

ALEXANDER, A. B. (1981). Behavioral approaches in the treatment of bronchial asthma. In C. K. Prokop & L. A. Bradley (Eds.), *Medical psychology: Contributions to behavioral medicine* (pp. 373–394). New York: Academic Press.

ALEXANDER, D., MONK, J. S., & JONAS, A. P. (1985). Occupational stress, personal strain, and coping among residents and faculty members. *Journal of Medical Education, 60,* 830–839.

ALEXANDER, F. (1939). Emotional factors in essential hypertension: Presentation of a tentative hypothesis. *Psychosomatic Medicine, 1,* 173–179.

ALEXANDER, F. G., & SELESNICK, S. T. (1966). *The history of psychiatry.* New York: New American Library.

ALFORD, G. S., BLANCHARD, E. B., & BUCKLEY, T. M. (1972). Treatment of hysterical vomiting by modification of social contingencies: A case study. *Journal of Behavior Therapy and Experimental Psychiatry, 3,* 209–212.

ALTMAN, D. G., FLORA, J. A., FORTMANN, S. P., & FARQUHAR, J. W. (1987). The cost effectiveness of three smoking cessation programs. *American Journal of Public Health, 77,* 162–165.

AMERICAN MEDICAL ASSOCIATION.   (1982). Future directions for medical education. *Journal of the American Medical Association, 248,* 3225–3239.

AMERICAN MEDICAL ASSOCIATION.   (1985). 85th annual report on medical education in the United States: Executive summary. *Journal of the American Medical Association, 254,* 1553–1554.

AMERICAN PSYCHIATRIC ASSOCIATION   (1980). *Diagnostic and statistical manual of mental disorders* (3rd ed.). Washington, DC: American Psychiatric Association.

AMERICAN PSYCHOLOGICAL ASSOCIATION.   (1976). Task force on health research. Contributions of psychology to health research: Patterns, problems, and potentials. *American Psychologist, 31,* 263–274.

AMORY, C.   (1948). *The last resorts.* New York: Harper.

ANDERSEN, M. S.   (1985). Hypnotizability as a factor in the hypnotic treatment of obesity. *International Journal of Clinical and Experimental Hypnosis, 33,* 150–159.

ANDERSEN, R. M., GIACHELLO, A. L., & ADAY, L. A.   (1986). Access of Hispanics to health care and cuts in services: A state-of-the-art overview. *Public Health Reports, 101,* 238–252.

ANDERSON, J. P.   (1982). Relaxation training and relaxation-related procedures. In D. M. Doleys, R. L. Meredith, & A. R. Ciminero (Eds.), *Behavioral medicine: Assessment and treatment strategies* (pp. 69–81). New York: Plenum.

ANDERSON, K. O., BRADLEY, L. A., YOUNG, L. D., McDANIEL, L. K., & WISE, C. M.   (1985). Rheumatoid arthritis: Review of psychological factors related to etiology, effects, and treatment. *Psychological Bulletin, 98,* 358–387.

ANDRASIK, F., BLANCHARD, E. B., ARENA, J. G., TEDERS, S. J., TEEVAN, R. C., & RODICHOK, L. D.   (1982). Psychological functioning in headache sufferers. *Psychosomatic Medicine, 44,* 171–182.

ANDRASIK, F., COLEMAN, D., & EPSTEIN, L. H.   (1982). Biofeedback: Clinical and research considerations. In D. M. Doleys, R. L. Meredith, & A. R. Ciminero (Eds.), *Behavioral medicine: Assessment and treatment strategies* (pp. 83–116). New York: Plenum.

ANDREWS, G., TENNANT, C., HEWSON, D. M., & VAILLANT, G. E.   (1978). Life event stress, social support, coping style, and risk of psychological impairment. *Journal of Nervous and Mental Disorders, 166,* 307–316.

ANDREWS, J. L., JR.   (1983). Reducing smoking in the hospital: An effective model program. *Chest, 84,* 206–209.

ANGELL, M.   (1985). Disease as a reflection of the psyche. *New England Journal of Medicine, 312,* 1570–1572.

ANNAS, G. J.   (1983). Nuclear power: Psychology and statistics. *American Journal of Public Health, 73,* 1327–1328.

ANTONOVSKY, A., & HARTMAN, H.   (1974). Delay in the detection of cancer. *Health Education Monographs, 2,* 98–128.

APPLEBAUM, S. A.   (1977). The refusal to take one's medicine. *Bulletin of the Menninger Clinic, 41,* 511–521.

ARNETZ, B. B., & FJELLNER, B.   (1986). Psychological predictors of neuroendocrine responses to mental stress. *Journal of Psychosomatic Research, 30,* 297–305.

ARONOWITZ, E., & BROMBERG, E. M. (EDS.).   (1984). *Mental health and long-term physical illness.* Canton, MA: Prodist.

ARONSON, M. K., LEVIN, G., & LIPKOWITZ, R.   (1984). A community-based family/patient group program for Alzheimer's disease. *The Gerontologist, 24,* 339–342.

ARTHUR, R. J.   (1982). Life stress and disease: An appraisal of the concept. In L. J. West & M. Stein (Eds.), *Critical issues in behavioral medicine* (pp. 3–17). Philadelphia: J. B. Lippencott.

ARTZ, L., COOKE, C. J., MEYERS, A., & STALGAITIS, S.   (1981). Community change agents and health interventions: Hypertension screening. *American Journal of Community Psychology, 9,* 361–370.

ASKEN, M. J.   (1979). Medical psychology: Toward definition, clarification, and organization. *Professional Psychology, 10,* 66–73.

ASKEN, M. J., & RAHAM, D. C.   (1983). Resident performance and sleep deprivation: A review. *Journal of Medical Education, 58,* 382–388.

ASSOCIATION OF AMERICAN MEDICAL COLLEGES.   (1985). Annual meeting and annual report, 1984. *Journal of Medical Education, 60,* 232–277.

AWBREY, B. J.   (1985). Reflections on medical education: Concerns of the student. *Journal of Medical Education, 60,* 98–105.

AZRIN, N. H., & POWELL, J.   (1969). Behavioral engineering: The use of response priming to improve prescribed self-medication. *Journal of Applied Behavior Analysis, 2,* 39–42.

BADAWI, K., WALLACE, R. K., ORME-JOHNSON, D., & ROUZERE, A. M.   (1984). Electrophysiologic characteristics of respiratory suspension periods occurring during the practice of the transcendental meditation program. *Psychosomatic Medicine, 46,* 267–276.

BAKER, M. D., MOORE, S. E., & WISE, P. H.   (1986). The impact of 'bottle bill' legislation on the incidence of lacerations in childhood. *American Journal of Public Health, 76,* 1243–1244.

BAKER, S. P.   (1981). Childhood injuries: The community approach to prevention. *Journal of Public Health Policy, 2,* 235–246.

BANDURA, A.   (1977). Self-efficacy: Toward a unifying theory of behavioral change. *Psychological Review, 84,* 191–215.

BANDURA, A.   (1982). Self-efficacy mechanism in human agency. *American Psychologist, 37,* 122–147.

BANNERMAN, R. H., BURTON, J., & WEN-CHIEH, C. (EDS.).   (1983). *Traditional medicine and health care coverage: A reader for health administrators and practitioners.* Geneva: World Health Organization.

BARBARIN, O. A., & CHESLER, M.   (1986). The medical context of parental coping with childhood cancer. *American Journal of Community Psychology, 14,* 221–235.

BARBARIN, O. A., HUGHES, D., & CHESLER, M. A.   (1985). Stress, coping, and marital functioning among parents of children with cancer. *Journal of Marriage and the Family, 47,* 473–480.

BAREFOOT, J. C., DAHLSTROM, W. G., & WILLIAMS, R. B. (1983). Hostility, CHD incidence, and total mortality: A 25-year follow-up study of 255 physicians. *Psychosomatic Medicine, 45,* 59–63.

BAROFSKY, I. (1981). Issues and approaches to the psychosocial assessment of the cancer patient. In C. K. Prokop & L. A. Bradley (Eds.), *Medical psychology: Contributions to behavioral medicine* (pp. 55–65). New York: Academic Press.

BARR, J. K. (1983). Physicians' views of patients in prepaid group practice: Reasons for visits to HMOs. *Journal of Health and Social Behavior, 24,* 244–255.

BARRERA, M., & AINLAY, S. L. (1983). The structure of social support: A conceptual and empirical analysis. *Journal of Community Psychology, 11,* 133–143.

BARRERA, M., SANDLER, I. N., & RAMSAY, T. B. (1981). Preliminary development of a scale of social support: Studies on college students. *American Journal of Community Psychology, 9,* 435–447.

BARTLETT, E. E. (1981). The contribution of school health education to community health promotion: What can we reasonably expect? *American Journal of Public Health, 71,* 1384–1391.

BARTROP, R. W., LOCKHURST, E., LAZARUS, L., KOLOH, L. G., & PENNY, R. (1977). Depressed lymphocyte function after bereavement. *Lancet, 1,* 834–836.

BARUCH, G. (1981). Moral tales: Parents' stories of encounters with the health professions. *Sociology of Health and Illness, 3,* 275–295.

BATCHELOR, W. F. (1984). AIDS: A public health and psychological emergency. *American Psychologist, 39,* 1279–1284.

BAUM, A., FLEMING, R., & SINGER, J. E. (1982). Stress at Three Mile Island: Applying psychological impact analysis. In L. Bickman (Ed.), *Applied social psychology annual, Vol. 3* (pp. 217–248). Beverly Hills, CA: Sage.

BAUM, A., SINGER, J. E., & BAUM, C. S. (1981). Stress and the environment. *Journal of Social Issues, 37,* 4–35.

BEALS, R. K., & HICKMAN, N. W. (1972). Industrial injuries of back and extremities: Comprehensive evaluation—an aid in prognosis and treatment. *Journal of Bone and Joint Surgery, 54,* 93–111.

BECK, A. T. (1963). Thinking and depression: Idiosyncratic content and cognitive distortions. *Archives of General Psychiatry, 9,* 324–333.

BECK, E. M. (ED.). (1968). *Bartlett's familiar quotations* (14th ed.). Boston, MA: Little, Brown.

BECKER, M. H. (ED.). (1974). The health belief model and personal health behavior. *Health Education Monographs, 2,* 324–473.

BECKER, M. H., DRACHMAN, R. H., & KIRSCHT, J. P. (1974). A field experiment to evaluate various outcomes of continuity of physician care. *American Journal of Public Health, 64,* 1062–1070.

BECKER, M. H., & MAIMAN, L. A. (1975). Sociobehavioral determinants of compliance with health and medical care recommendations. *Medical Care, 13,* 10–24.

BECKER, M. H., MAIMAN, L. A., KIRSCHT, J. P., HAEFNER, D. P., & DRACHMAN, R. H. (1977). The health belief model and prediction of dietary compliance: A field experiment. *Journal of Health and Social Behavior, 18,* 348–366.

BEECHER, H. K. (1956). Relationship of significance of wound to pain experienced. *Journal of the American Medical Association, 161,* 1609–1613.

BEECHER, H. K. (1968). The measurement of pain in man: A re-inspection of the work of the Harvard group. In A. Soulairac, J. Cahn, & J. Charpentier (Eds.), *Pain: Proceedings of the international symposium on pain organized by the laboratory of psychophysiology, faculty of sciences, Paris, April 11–13, 1967* (pp. 201–213). New York: Academic Press.

Behavioral risk factor prevalence surveys—United States, first quarter, 1982. (1983). *Morbidity and Mortality Weekly Report, 32,* 141–143.

BELLACK, A. S., & WILLIAMSON, D. A. (1982). Obesity and anorexia nervosa. In D. M. Doleys, R. L. Meredith, & A. R. Ciminero (Eds.), *Behavioral medicine: Assessment and treatment strategies* (pp. 295–316). New York: Plenum.

BENATAR, S. R. (1986). Medicine and health care in South Africa. *New England Journal of Medicine, 315,* 527–532.

BENFARI, R. C., EAKER, E., & STOLL, J. G. (1981). Behavioral interventions and compliance to treatment regimes. *Annual Review of Public Health, 2,* 431–471.

BENFARI, R. C., OCKENE, J. K., & McINTYRE, K. M. (1982). Control of cigarette smoking from a psychological perspective. *Annual Review of Public Health, 3,* 101–128.

BENOWITZ, N. L., JACOB, P., KOZLOWSKI, L. T., & YU, L. (1986). Influence of smoking fewer cigarettes on exposure to tar, nicotine, and carbon monoxide. *New England Journal of Medicine, 315,* 1310–1313.

BERG, J. K., & GARRARD, J. (1980a). Psychosocial support in residency training programs. *Journal of Medical Education, 55,* 851–857.

BERG, J. K., & GARRARD, J. (1980b). Psychosocial support of residents in family practice programs. *Journal of Family Practice, 11,* 915–920.

BERGER, B. G., & OWEN, D. R. (1983). Mood alteration with swimming—Swimmers really do "feel better." *Psychosomatic Medicine, 45,* 425–433.

BERGMAN, L. R., & MAGNUSSON, D. (1986). Type A behavior: A longitudinal study from childhood to adulthood. *Psychosomatic Medicine, 48,* 134–142.

BERGQUIST, S. R., DUCHAC, B. W., SCHALIN, V. A., ZASTROW, J. F., BARR, V. L., & BOROWIECKI, T. (1985). Perceptions of freshman medical students of gender differences in medical specialty choice. *Journal of Medical Education, 60,* 379–383.

BERKOWITZ, R., EBERLEIN-FRIES, R., KUIPERS, L., & LEFF, J. (1984). Educating relatives about schizophrenia. *Schizophrenia Bulletin, 10,* 418–429.

BERKUN, C. S. (1986). In behalf of women over 40: Understanding the importance of the menopause. *Social Work, 31,* 378–384.

BERNI, R., & FORDYCE, W. E. (1977). *Behavior modification and the nursing process* (2nd ed.). St. Louis, MO: C. V. Mosby.

BERRY, R. E., BOLAND, J. P., SMART, C. N., & KANAK, J. R. (1977). *The economic cost of alcohol abuse, 1975.* Bethesda, MD: National Institute of Alcohol Abuse and Alcoholism.

BETZ, B. J., & THOMAS, C. B. (1979). Individual temperament as a predictor of health or premature disease. *Johns Hopkins Medical Journal, 144,* 81–89.

BIELIAUSKAS, L. A. (1982). *Stress and its relationship to health and illness.* Boulder, CO: Westview Press.

BIGELOW, G., STRICKLER, D., LIEBSON, I., & GRIFFITHS, R. (1976). Maintaining disulfiram ingestion among outpatient alcoholics: A security-deposit contingency contracting procedure. *Behavior Research and Therapy, 14,* 378–381.

BIRENBAUM, A. (1981). *Health care and society.* Montclair, NJ: Allanheld, Osmun & Co.

BISTLINE, J. L., & FRIEDEN, F. P. (1984). Anger control: A case study of a stress inoculation treatment for a chronic aggressive patient. *Cognitive Therapy and Research, 8,* 551–556.

BITTKER, T. E. (1976). Reaching out to the depressed physician. *Journal of the American Medical Association, 236,* 1713–1716.

BLACK, R. G. (1975). The chronic pain syndrome. *Surgical Clinics of North America, 55,* 999–1011.

BLACK, R. G., & CHAPMAN, C. R. (1976). SAD index for clinical assessment of pain. In J. J. Bonica & D. Albe-Fessard (Eds.), *Advances in pain research and therapy: Vol. 1* (pp. 301–305). New York: Raven Press.

BLANCHARD, E. B. (1982). Behavior medicine: Past, present, and future. *Journal of Consulting and Clinical Psychology, 50,* 795–796.

BLANCHARD, E. B., & ANDRASIK, F. (1982). Psychological assessment and treatment of headache: Recent developments and emerging issues. *Journal of Consulting and Clinical Psychology, 50,* 859–879.

BLANCHARD, E. B., ANDRASIK, F., APPELBAUM, K. A., EVANS, D. D., MYERS, P., & BARRON, K. D. (1986). Three studies of the psychologic changes in chronic headache patients associated with biofeedback and relaxation therapies. *Psychosomatic Medicine, 48,* 73–83.

BLANCHARD, E. B., JACCARD, J., ANDRASIK, F., GUARNIERI, P., & JURISH, S. E. (1985). Reduction in headache patients' medical expenses associated with biofeedback and relaxation treatments. *Biofeedback and Self-Regulation, 10,* 63–68.

BLANCHARD, E. B., MCCOY, G. C., ANDRASIK, F., ACERRA, M., PALLMEYER, T. P., GERARDI, R., HALPERN, M., & MUSSO, A. (1984). Preliminary results from a controlled evaluation of thermal biofeedback as a treatment for essential hypertension. *Biofeedback and Self-Regulation, 9,* 471–495.

BLAND, C. J., & SCHMITZ, C. C. (1986). Characteristics of the successful researcher and implications for faculty development. *Journal of Medical Education, 61*, 22–31.

BLENDON, R. J., & ALTMAN, D. E. (1984). Public attitudes about health-care costs: A lesson in national schizophrenia. *New England Journal of Medicine, 311*, 613–616.

BLOOM, B. L. (1984). *Community mental health: A general introduction* (2nd ed.). Monterey, CA: Brooks/Cole.

BLOOM, B. L., & ASHER, S. J. (1982). Patient rights and patient advocacy: A historical and conceptual appreciation. In B. L. Bloom and S. J. Asher (Eds.), *Psychiatric patient rights and patient advocacy: Issues and evidence* (pp. 19–56). New York: Human Sciences Press.

BLOOM, B. S., KNORR, R. S., & EVANS, A. E. (1985). The epidemiology of disease expenses: The costs of caring for children with cancer. *Journal of the American Medical Association, 253*, 2393–2397.

BLUME, S. B. (1986). Women and alcohol: A review. *Journal of the American Medical Association, 256*, 1467–1470.

BOHMAN, M. (1978). Some genetic aspects of alcoholism and criminality. *Archives of General Psychiatry, 35*, 269–276.

BOHMAN, M., SIGVARDSSON, S., & CLONINGER, C. R. (1981). Maternal inheritance of alcohol abuse: Cross-fostering analysis of adopted women. *Archives of General Psychiatry, 38*, 965–969.

BONICA, J. J. (1976). Organization and function of a multidisciplinary pain clinic. In M. Weisenberg, & B. Tursky (Eds.), *Pain: New perspectives in therapy and research* (pp. 11–20). New York: Plenum.

BOOTH-KEWLEY, S., & FRIEDMAN, H. S. (1987). Psychological predictors of heart disease: A quantitative review. *Psychological Bulletin, 101*, 343–362.

BORENSTEIN, D. B., & COOK, K. (1982). Impairment prevention in the training years: A new mental health program at UCLA. *Journal of the American Medical Association, 247*, 2700–2703.

BORKOVEC, T. D. (1982). Insomnia. *Journal of Consulting and Clinical Psychology, 50*, 880–895.

BORKOVEC, T. D., GRAYSON, J. B., O'BRIEN, G. T., & WEERTS, T. C. (1979). Relaxation treatment of pseudoinsomnia and idiopathic insomnia: An electroencephalographic evaluation. *Journal of Applied Behavior Analysis, 12*, 37–54.

BORYSENKO, M., & BORYSENKO, J. (1982). Stress, behavior, and immunity: Animal models and mediating mechanisms. *General Hospital Psychiatry, 4*, 59–67.

BOURNE, L. E., & EKSTRAND, B. R. (1985). *Psychology: Its principles and meanings* (5th ed.). New York: Holt, Rinehart and Winston.

BOYCE, W. T., JENSEN, E. W., CASSEL, J. C., COLLIER, A. M., SMITH, A. H., & RAMEY, C. T. (1977). Influence of life events and family routines on childhood respiratory tract illness. *Pediatrics, 60*, 609–615.

BOYD, J. R., COVINGTON, T. R., STANASZEK, W. F., & COUSSONS, R. T.  (1974). Drug-defaulting: II—Analysis of noncompliance patterns. *American Journal of Hospital Pharmacy, 31,* 485–491.

BOYD, J. S., & MOSCICKI, E. K.  (1986). Firearms and youth suicide. *American Journal of Public Health, 76,* 1240–1242.

BRADLEY, L. A.  (1983). Coping with chronic pain. In T. G. Burish & L. A. Bradley (Eds.), *Coping with chronic disease: Research and applications* (pp. 339–379). New York: Academic Press.

BRADLEY, L. A., & PROKOP, C. K.  (1981). The relationship between medical psychology and behavioral medicine. In C. K. Prokop & L. A. Bradley (Eds.), *Medical psychology: Contributions to behavioral medicine* (pp. 1–4). New York: Academic Press.

BRADLEY, L. A., PROKOP, C. K., GENTRY, W. D., VAN DER HEIDE, L. H., & PRIETO, E. J.  (1981). Assessment of chronic pain. In C. K. Prokop & L. A. Bradley (Eds.), *Medical psychology: Contributions to behavioral medicine* (pp. 91–117). New York: Academic Press.

BRANDT, E. N.  (1984). Infant mortality—A progress report. *Public Health Reports, 99,* 284–288.

BRAUER, A. P., HORLICK, L., NELSON, E., FARQUHAR, J. W., & AGRAS, W. S.  (1979). Relaxation therapy for essential hypertension: A Veterans Administration outpatient study. *Journal of Behavioral Medicine, 2,* 21–29.

BRAWLEY, E. A., & MARTINEZ-BRAWLEY, E. E.  (1984). Using community news media to broaden mental health center prevention efforts. *American Journal of Orthopsychiatry, 54,* 318–321.

BRAY, G. A.  (1984). The role of weight control in health promotion and disease prevention. In J. D. Matarazzo, S. M. Weiss, J. A. Herd, N. E. Miller, & S. M. Weiss (Eds.), *Behavioral health: A handbook of health enhancement and disease prevention* (pp. 632–656). New York: Wiley.

BRENA, S. F. (ED.).  (1978). *Chronic pain: America's hidden epidemic.* New York: Atheneum/SMI.

BRESLOW, L.  (1982). Control of cigarette smoking from a public policy perspective. *Annual Review of Public Health, 3,* 129–151.

BRESLOW, L., FIELDING, J. E., & LAVE, L. B. (EDS.).  (1980). *Annual Review of Public Health, 1,* 1–411.

BROOKS, G. R., & RICHARDSON, F. C.  (1980). Emotional skills training: A treatment program for duodenal ulcer. *Behavior Therapy, 11,* 198–207.

BROSKOWSKI, A.  (1981). The health–mental health connection: An introduction. In A. Broskowski, E. Marks, & S. H. Budman (Eds.), *Linking health and mental health* (pp. 13–25). Beverly Hills, CA: Sage.

BROWN, E. R.  (1983). Medicare and medicaid: The process, value, and limits of health care reforms. *Journal of Public Health Policy, 4,* 335–366.

BROWN, J. C., & BARNETT, J. M.  (1984). Response of faculty members to medical students' personal problems. *Journal of Medical Education, 59,* 180–187.

BROWN, J. S., SWIFT, Y. B., & OBERMAN, M. L.  (1974). Baccalaureate students' images of nursing: A replication. *Nursing Research, 23,* 53–59.

BROWNELL, K. D.  (1982). Obesity: Understanding and treating a serious, prevalent, and refractory disorder. *Journal of Consulting and Clinical Psychology, 50,* 820–840.

BROWNELL, K. D., COHEN, R. Y., STUNKARD, A. J., FELIX, M. R. J., & COOLEY, N. B.  (1984). Weight loss competitions at the work site: Impact on weight, morale and cost-effectiveness. *American Journal of Public Health, 74,* 1283–1285.

BROWNELL, K. D., MARLATT, G. A., LICHTENSTEIN, E., & WILSON, G. T.  (1986). Understanding and preventing relapse. *American Psychologist, 41,* 765–782.

BROWNELL, K. D., & STUNKARD, A. J.  (1981). Couples training, pharmacotherapy, and behavior therapy in the treatment of obesity. *Archives of General Psychiatry, 38,* 1224–1229.

BROWNELL, K. D., STUNKARD, A. J., & McKEON, P. E.  (1985). Weight reduction at the work site: A promise partially fulfilled. *American Journal of Psychiatry, 142,* 47–51.

BRUNER, G. G.  (1984). Rational-emotive education for parent study groups. *Individual Psychology, 40,* 228–231.

BRUNSWICK, A. F., & MESSERI, P.  (1986). Drugs, lifestyle, and health: A longitudinal study of urban black youth. *American Journal of Public Health, 76,* 52–57.

BRYANT, J. H.  (1984). Health services, health manpower, and universities in relation to health for all: An historical and future perspective. *American Journal of Public Health, 74,* 714–719.

BUDZYNSKI, T. H., & STOYVA, J. M.  (1969). An instrument for producing deep muscle relaxation by means of analog information feedback. *Journal of Applied Behavior Analysis, 2,* 231–237.

BUMPERS, D.  (1984). Securing the blessings of liberty for posterity: Preventive health care for children. *American Psychologist, 39,* 896–900.

BURCHFIELD, S. R.  (1979). The stress response: A new perspective. *Psychosomatic Medicine, 41,* 661–672.

BURDEN, D. S., & KLERMAN, L. V.  (1984). Teenage parenthood: Factors that lessen economic dependence. *Social Work, 29,* 11–16.

BURKE, R. J., & WEIR, T.  (1977). Marital helping relationships: The moderators between stress and well-being. *Journal of Psychology, 95,* 121–130.

BURNS, B. J., & BURKE, J. D.  (1985). Improving mental health practices in primary care: Findings from recent research. *Public Health Reports, 100,* 294–300.

BARNUM, J. F.  (1984). The unfortunate case of Dr. Z: How to succeed in medical practice in 1984. *New England Journal of Medicine, 310,* 729–730.

BYRNE, D. G., & WHYTE, H. M.  (1978). Dimensions of illness behaviour in survivors of myocardial infarction. *Journal of Psychosomatic Research, 22,* 485–491.

BYRNE, D. G., WHYTE, H. M., & BUTLER, K. L.   (1981). Illness behaviour and outcome following survived myocardial infarction: A prospective study. *Journal of Psychosomatic Research, 25,* 97–107.

CAIRNS, D., THOMAS, L., MOONEY, V., & PACE, J. B.   (1976). A comprehensive treatment approach to chronic low back pain. *Pain, 2,* 301–308.

CALNAN, M. W., & MOSS, S.   (1984). The health belief model and compliance with education given at a class in breast self-examination. *Journal of Health and Social Behavior, 25,* 198–210.

CANNON, J. T., LIEBESKIND, J. C., & FRENK, H.   (1978). Neural and neurochemical mechanisms of pain inhibition. In R. A. Sternbach (Ed.), *The psychology of pain* (pp. 27–47). New York: Raven Press.

CANNON, W. B.   (1932). *The wisdom of the body.* New York: Norton.

CAPLAN, R. D., ROBINSON, E.A.R., FRENCH, J.R.P., CALDWELL, J. R., & SHINN, M.   (1976). *Adhering to medical regimens: Pilot experiments in patient education and social support.* Ann Arbor, MI: Research Center for Group Dynamics, Institute for Social Research, University of Michigan.

CARLAW, R. W., & DiANGELIS, N. M.   (1982). Promoting health and preventing disease—Some thoughts for HMOs. *Health Education Quarterly, 9,* 81–94.

CARRINGTON, P.   (1982). Meditation techniques in clinical practice. In L. E. Abt & I. R. Stuart (Eds.), *The newer therapies: A sourcebook* (pp. 60–78). New York: Van Nostrand Reinhold.

CARTOOF, V. G., & KLERMAN, L. V.   (1986). Parental consent for abortion: Impact of the Massachusetts law. *American Journal of Public Health, 76,* 397–400.

CARTWRIGHT, L. K.   (1982). Sources and effects of stress in health careers. In G. C. Stone, F. Cohen, N. E. Adler (Eds.), *Health psychology: A handbook* (pp. 419–445). San Francisco, CA: Jossey-Bass.

CASAS, A., & VARGAS, H.   (1980). The health system in Costa Rica: Toward a national health service. *Journal of Public Health Policy, 1,* 258–279.

CASE, R. B., HELLER, S. S., CASE, N. B., MOSS, A. J., AND THE MULTICENTER POST-INFARCTION RESEARCH GROUP.   (1985). Type A behavior and survival after acute myocardial infarction. *New England Journal of Medicine, 312,* 737–741.

CASSEL, J.   (1974a). Psychosocial processes and "stress": Theoretical formulation. *International Journal of Health Services, 4,* 471–482.

CASSEL, J.   (1974b). An epidemiological perspective of psychosocial factors in disease etiology. *American Journal of Public Health, 64,* 1040–1043.

CASSILETH, B. R., LUSK, E. J., MILLER, D. S., BROWN, L. L., & MILLER, C.   (1985). Psychosocial correlates of survival in advanced malignant disease? *New England Journal of Medicine, 312,* 1551–1555.

CASSILETH, B. R., LUSK, E. J., STROUSE, T. B., & BODENHEIMER, B. J.   (1984). Contemporary unorthodox treatments in cancer medicine. *Annals of Internal Medicine, 101,* 105–112.

CASSILETH, B. R., LUSK, E. J., STROUSE, T. B., MILLER, D. S., BROWN, L. L., CROSS, P. A., & TENAGLIA, A. N.   (1984). Psychosocial status in chronic illness: A comparative analysis of six diagnostic groups. *New England Journal of Medicine, 311,* 506–511.

Center established for health communication. (1986, Feb.). *Harvard School of Public Health Health Sciences Report,* p. 9.

CHAMBERLIN, R. W. (1984). Strategies for disease prevention and health promotion in maternal and child health: The "ecologic" versus the "high risk" approach. *Journal of Public Health Policy, 5,* 185–197.

CHAPMAN, C. R. (1976). Measurement of pain: Problems and issues. In J. J. Bonica & D. Albe-Fessard (Eds.), *Advances in pain research and therapy: Vol. 1* (pp. 345–353). New York: Raven Press.

CHARLESWORTH, E. A., WILLIAMS, B. J., & BAER, P. E. (1984). Stress management at the worksite for hypertension: Compliance, cost-benefit, health care and hypertension-related variables. *Psychosomatic Medicine, 46,* 387–397.

CHARNEY, E. (1972). Patient-doctor communication: Implications for the clinician. *Pediatric Clinics of North America, 19,* 263–279.

CHASNOFF, I. J., BURNS, W. J., SCHNOLL, S. H., & BURNS, K. A. (1985). Cocaine use in pregnancy. *New England Journal of Medicine, 313,* 666–669.

CHESNEY, M. A. (1985). Anger and hostility: Future implications for behavioral medicine. In M. A. Chesney & R. H. Rosenman (Eds.), *Anger and hostility in cardiovascular and behavioral disorders* (pp. 277–290). Washington, DC: Hemisphere.

CHRISTIDIS, D., INCE, L. P., ZARETSKY, H. H., & PITCHFORD, L. J. (1986). A cross-modality approach for treatment of chronic pain: A preliminary report. *Psychosomatic Medicine, 48,* 224–228.

CLARK, E. J., & RIEKER, P. P. (1986). Gender differences in relationships and stress of medical and law students. *Journal of Medical Education, 61,* 32–40.

CLEARY, P. J. (1980). A checklist for life event research. *Journal of Psychometric Research, 24,* 199–207.

CLENDENING, L. (1942). *Source book of medical history.* New York: Dover Publications.

CLONINGER, C. R., BOHMAN, M., & SIGVARDSSON, S. (1981). Inheritance of alcohol abuse: Cross-fostering analysis of adopted men. *Archives of General Psychiatry, 38,* 861–868.

CLOUTIER, C. (1982). An analysis of formal controls on impaired physicians. *Psychiatric Annals, 12,* 225, 229, 233, 236–237.

COATES, T. J., TEMOSHOK, L., & MANDEL, J. (1984). Psychosocial research is essential to understanding and treating AIDS. *American Psychologist, 39,* 1309–1314.

COBB, S. (1974). A model for life events and their consequences. In B. S. Dohrenwend & B. P. Dohrenwend (Eds.), *Stressful life events: Their nature and effects* (pp. 151–156). New York: Wiley & Sons.

COBB, S. (1976). Social support as a moderator of life stress. *Psychomatic Medicine, 38,* 300–314.

CODDINGTON, R. D. (1972a). The significance of life events as etiologic factors in the diseases of children. I.—A survey of professional workers. *Journal of Psychosomatic Research, 16,* 7–18.

CODDINGTON, R. D. (1972b). The significance of life events as etiologic factors in the diseases of children. II.—A study of a normal population. *Journal of Psychosomatic Research, 16,* 205–213.

COHEN, F. (1979). Personality, stress, and the development of physical illness. In G. C. Stone, F. Cohen, & N. E. Adler (Eds.), *Health psychology: A handbook* (pp. 77–111). San Francisco, CA: Jossey-Bass.

COHEN, F. (1984). Coping. In J. D. Matarazzo, S. M. Weiss, J. A. Herd, N. E. Miller, & S. M. Weiss (Eds.), *Behavioral health: A handbook of health enhancement and disease prevention* (pp. 261–274). New York: Wiley.

COHEN, F., & LAZARUS, R. S. (1979). Coping with the stresses of illness. In G. C. Stone, F. Cohen, N. E. Adler (Eds.), *Health psychology: A handbook* (pp. 217–254). San Francisco, CA: Jossey-Bass.

COHEN, H. A. (1981). *The nurse's quest for professional identity.* Menlo Park, CA: Addison-Wesley.

COHEN, S. (1984). The chronic intractable benign pain syndrome. *Drug Abuse & Alcoholism Newsletter, 13,* No. 4.

COHEN, S. (1985a). Twenty questions frequently asked by students: Part I. *Drug Abuse & Alcoholism Newsletter, 14,* No. 3.

COHEN, S. (1985b). Twenty questions frequently asked by students: Part II. *Drug Abuse & Alcoholism Newsletter, 14,* No. 4.

COHEN, S. (1986a). Marijuana research: Selected recent findings. *Drug Abuse & Alcoholism Newsletter, 15,* No. 1.

COHEN, S. (1986b). Just say no. *Drug Abuse & Alcoholism Newsletter, 15,* No. 3.

COHEN, S. (1986c). Withdrawal. *Drug Abuse & Alcoholism Newsletter, 15,* No. 8.

COHEN, S. (1986d). Controversies involving urine testing. *Drug Abuse & Alcoholism Newsletter, 15,* No. 5.

COHEN, S. (1986e). The implications of crack. *Drug Abuse & Alcoholism Newsletter, 15,* No. 6.

COHEN, S. (1986f). Intoxication. *Drug Abuse & Alcoholism Newsletter, 15,* No. 7.

COHEN, S. (1986g). A treatment of alcoholism—Soviet style. *Drug Abuse & Alcoholism Newsletter, 15,* No. 4.

COHEN, S., KAMARCK, T., & MERMELSTEIN, R. (1983). A global measure of perceived stress. *Journal of Health and Social Behavior, 24,* 385–396.

COLLINS, D. L., BAUM, A., & SINGER, J. E. (1983). Coping with chronic stress at Three Mile Island: Psychological and biochemical evidence. *Health Psychology, 2,* 149–166.

COMMITTEE ON INTERSTATE AND FOREIGN COMMERCE, U.S. HOUSE OF REPRESENTATIVES (1978). *Surgical performance: Necessity and quality.* 95th Congress, 2d Session. Committee Print 95–71. Washington, DC: U.S. Government Printing Office.

CONRAD, P. (1986). The myth of cut-throats among premedical students: On the role of stereotypes in justifying failure and success. *Journal of Health and Social Behavior, 27,* 150–160.

COOKE, D. J., & GREENE, J. G.   (1981). Types of life events in relation to symptoms at the climacterium. *Journal of Psychosomatic Research, 25,* 5–11.

COOPER, K. H.   (1968). *Aerobics.* New York: Bantam Books.

COOPER. M. J., & AYGEN, M. M.   (1979). A relaxation technique in the management of hypercholesterolemia. *Journal of Human Stress, 5,* 24–27.

COPE, Z. (1958). *Florence Nightingale and the doctors.* Philadelphia, PA: Lippincott.

CORLEY, M. J., & ZLUTNICK, S.   (1981). A model for inpatient liaison-consultation with chronic pain patients. In J. M. Ferguson & C. B. Taylor (Eds.), *The comprehensive handbook of behavioral medicine: Vol. 2—Syndromes & special areas* (pp. 191–206). New York: SP Medical & Scientific Books.

COSTA, L.   (1983). Clinical neuropsychology: A discipline in evolution. *Journal of Clinical Neuropsychology, 5,* 1–11.

COSTA, P. T., & McCRAE, R. R.   (1985). Hypochondriasis, neuroticism, and aging: When are somatic complaints unfounded? *American Psychologist, 40,* 19–28.

COSTILO, L. B.   (1985). Antitrust enforcement in health care: Ten years after the AMA suit. *New England Journal of Medicine, 313,* 901–904.

COTTINGTON, E. M., MATTHEWS, K. A., TALBOTT, E., & KULLER, L. H.   (1986). Occupational stress, suppressed anger, and hypertension. *Psychosomatic Medicine, 48,* 249–260.

Council condemns journal editorial.   (1985, Oct.). *APA Monitor,* p. 6.

COUNCIL ON MENTAL HEALTH   (1973). The sick physician: Impairment by psychiatric disorders, including alcoholism and drug dependence. *Journal of the American Medical Association, 223,* 684–687.

COUSINS, N.   (1979). *Anatomy of an illness.* New York: Norton.

COUSINS, N.   (1981a). Internship: Preparation or hazing? *Journal of the American Medical Association, 245,* 377.

COUSINS, N.   (1981b). Norman Cousins responds. *Journal of the American Medical Association, 246,* 2144.

CRAIG, A. G., & PITTS, F. N.   (1968). Suicide by physicians. *Diseases of the Nervous System, 29,* 763–772.

CRAIG, K. D.   (1978). Social modeling influences on pain. In R. A. Sternbach (Ed.), *The psychology of pain* (pp. 73–109). New York: Raven Press.

CRAIG, T. J., COMSTOCK, G. W., & GEISER, P. B.   (1974). The quality of survival in breast cancer: A case-control comparison. *Cancer, 33,* 1451–1457.

CREDITOR, U. K., & CREDITOR, M. C.   (1982). Curriculum choices of premedical students. *Journal of Medical Education, 57,* 436–441.

CREER, T. L.   (1982). Asthma. *Journal of Consulting and Clinical Psychology, 50,* 912–921.

CRISP, A. H., QUEENAN, M., & D'SOUZA, M. F.   (1984). Myocardial infarction and the emotional climate. *The Lancet,* March 17, 616–619.

CRITCHLOW, B. (1986). The powers of John Barleycorn: Beliefs about the effects of alcohol on social behavior. *American Psychologist, 41,* 751–764.

CROCKETT, D. J., PRKACHIN, K. M., CRAIG, K. D., & GREENSTEIN, H. (1986). Social influences on factored dimensions of the McGill pain questionnaire. *Journal of Psychosomatic Research, 30,* 461–469.

CROWLEY, A. E., ETZEL, S. I., & PETERSEN, E. S. (1986). Undergraduate medical education. *Journal of the American Medical Association, 256,* 1557–1564.

CUDABACK, D., DARDEN, C., NELSON, P., O'BRIEN, S., PINSKY, D., & WIGGINS, E. (1985). Becoming successful parents: Can age-paced newsletters help? *Family Relations, 34,* 271–275.

CUMMINGS, N. A. (1977a). The anatomy of psychotherapy under national health insurance. *American Psychologist, 32,* 711–718.

CUMMINGS, N. A. (1977b). Prolonged (ideal) versus short-term (realistic) psychotherapy. *Professional Psychology, 8,* 491–501.

CUMMINGS, N. A. (1986). The dismantling of our health system: Strategies for the survival of psychological practice. *American Psychologist, 41,* 426–431.

CUMMINGS, N. A., & FOLLETTE, W. T. (1968). Psychiatric services and medical utilization in a prepaid health plan setting: Part II. *Medical Care, 6,* 31–41.

CUSHNER, I. M. (1981). Maternal behavior and perinatal risks: Alcohol, smoking, and drugs. *Annual Review of Public Health, 2,* 201–218.

CZINKOTA, M. R., & JOHNSTON, W. J. (1983). Choosing a career and specialty: When do students decide? *Health Care Management Review, 8,* 43–51.

DAKOF, G. A., & MENDELSOHN, G. A. (1986). Parkinson's disease: The psychological aspects of a chronic illness. *Psychological Bulletin, 99,* 375–387.

DALY, E. J., DONN, P. A., GALLIHER, M. J., & ZIMMERMAN, J. S. (1983). Biofeedback applications to migraine and tension headaches: A double-blinded outcome study. *Biofeedback and Self-Regulation, 8,* 135–152.

DALZELL-WARD, A. J. (1976). The new frontier of preventive medicine. *Public Health London, 90,* 101–109.

DANS, P. E., WEINER, J. P., & OTTER, S. E. (1985). Peer review organizations: Promises and potential pitfalls. *New England Journal of Medicine, 313,* 1131–1137.

DAVID, H. P. (1986). Population, development, and reproductive behavior: Perspectives for population and health psychology, *American Psychologist, 41,* 309–312.

DAVID, H. P. & MATEJCEK, Z. (1982). Children born to women denied abortion: An update. *Family Planning Perspectives, 13,* 32–34.

DAVIDHIZAR, R. E., & McBRIDE, A. (1985). How nursing students explain their success and failure in clinical experiences. *Journal of Nursing Education, 24,* 284–290.

DE ANDRADE, J. R. (1978). Common painful experiences: Low-back pain. In S. F. Brena (Ed.), *Chronic pain: America's hidden epidemic* (pp. 166–174). New York: Atheneum/SMI.

DEBUSK, R. F. (1980). Cardiac rehabilitation: Current status and future prospects. In J. M. Ferguson & C. B. Taylor (Eds.), *The comprehensive handbook of behavioral medicine: Vol. 1—Systems interventions* (pp. 89–100). New York: SP Medical & Scientific Books.

DeFrank, R. S., Jenkins, C. D., & Rose, R. M.   (1987). A longitudinal investigation of the relationships among alcohol consumption, psychosocial factors, and blood pressure. *Psychosomatic Medicine, 49,* 236–249.

DeLeon, P. H., Uyeda, M. K., & Welch, B. L.   (1985). Psychology and HMOs: New partnership or new adversary? *American Psychologist, 40,* 1122–1124.

Deodhar, N. S.   (1982). Primary health care in India. *Journal of Public Health Policy, 3,* 76–99.

De Piano, F. A., & Salzberg, H. C.   (1979). Clinical applications of hypnosis to three psychosomatic disorders. *Psychological Bulletin, 86,* 1223–1235.

Depue, R. A., & Monroe, S. M.   (1986). Conceptualization and measurement of human disorder in life stress research: The problem of chronic disturbance. *Psychological Bulletin, 99,* 36–51.

Depue, R. A., Monroe, S. M., & Shackman, S. L.   (1979). The psychobiology of human disease: Implications for conceptualizing the depressive disorders. In R. A. Depue (Ed.), *The psychobiology of the depressive disorders: Implications for the effects of stress* (pp. 3–20). New York: Academic Press.

Derogatis, L. R.   (1986). The psychosocial adjustment to illness scale (PAIS). *Journal of Psychosomatic Research, 30,* 77–91.

Derogatis, L. R., Abeloff, M. D., & Melisaratos, N.   (1979). Psychological coping mechanisms and survival time in metastatic breast cancer. *Journal of the American Medical Association, 242,* 1504–1508.

Deter, H. C.   (1986). Cost-benefit analysis of psychosomatic therapy in asthma. *Journal of Psychosomatic Research, 30,* 173–182.

Deykin, E. Y., Levy, J. C., & Wells, V.   (1987). Adolescent depression, alcohol and drug abuse. *American Journal of Public Health, 77,* 178–182.

Dillbeck, M. C.   (1977). The effect of the transcendental meditation technique on anxiety level. *Journal of Clinical Psychology, 33,* 1076–1078.

DiMatteo, M. R.   (1979). A social-psychological analysis of physician-patient rapport: Toward a science of the art of medicine. *Journal of Social Issues, 35,* 12–33.

DiMatteo, M. R.   (1985). Physician-patient communications: Promoting a positive health care setting. In J. C. Rosen & L. J. Solomon (Eds.), *Prevention in health psychology* (pp. 328–365). Hanover, NH: University Press of New England.

DiMatteo, M. R., & Friedman, H. S. (Eds.).   (1979). Interpersonal relations in health care. *Journal of Social Issues, 35,* 1–208.

DiMatteo, M. R., & Friedman, H. S.   (1982). *Social psychology and medicine.* Cambridge, MA: Oelgeschlager, Gunn & Hain.

Dimsdale, J. E., Hackett, T. P., Hutter, A. M., Block, P. C., Catanzano, D. M., & White, P. J.   (1979). Type A behavior and angiographic findings. *Journal of Psychosomatic Research, 23,* 273–276.

Dimsdale, J. E., Pierce, C., Schoenfeld, D., Brown, A., Zusman, R., &

GRAHAM, R.   (1986). Suppressed anger and blood pressure: The effects of race, sex, social class, obesity, and age. *Psychosomatic Medicine, 48,* 430–435.

DiNICOLA, D. D., & DiMATTEO, M. R.   (1984). Practitioners, patients, and compliance with medical regimens: A social psychological perspective. In A. Baum, S. E. Taylor, & J. E. Singer (Eds.), *Handbook of psychology and health: Vol. 4—Social psychological aspects of health* (pp. 55–84). Hillsdale, NJ: Lawrence Erlbaum Associates.

DISHMAN, R. K., & GETTMAN, L. R.   (1980). Psychobiologic influences on exercise adherence. *Journal of Sport Psychology, 2,* 295–310.

DJERASSI, E.   (1971). Some problems of occupational diseases of dentists. *International Dental Journal, 21,* 252–269.

DOBSON, C. B.   (1983). *Stress: The hidden adversary.* Ridgewood, NJ: Bogden & Son.

DOHERTY, W. J.   (1985). Family interventions in health care. *Family Relations, 34,* 129–137.

DOHERTY, W. J., & McCUBBIN, H. I.   (1985). Families and health care: An emerging arena of theory, research, and clinical intervention. *Family Relations, 34,* 5–11.

DOHRENWEND, B. P.   (1979). Stressful life events and psychopathology: Some issues of theory and method. In J. E. Barrett, R. M. Rose, & G. L. Klerman (Eds.), *Stress and mental disorder* (pp. 1–15). New York: Raven Press.

DOHRENWEND, B. S.   (1978). Social stress and community psychology. *American Journal of Community Psychology, 6,* 1–14.

DOHRENWEND, B. S., & DOHRENWEND, B. P.   (1974). *Stressful life events: Their nature and effects.* New York: Wiley & Sons.

DOHRENWEND, B. S., DOHRENWEND, B. P., DODSON, M., & SHROUT, P. E.   (1984). Symptoms, hassles, social supports and life events: Problem of confounded measures. *Journal of Abnormal Psychology, 93,* 222–230.

DOLCE, J. J., & RACZYNSKI, J. M.   (1985). Neuromuscular activity and electromyography in painful backs: Psychological and biomechanical models in assessment and treatment. *Psychological Bulletin, 97,* 502–520.

DOMASH, L. H.   (1977). Introduction. In D. W. Orme-Johnson & J. T. Farrow (Eds.), *Scientific research on the transcendental meditation program: Collected papers, volume 1* (pp. 13–31). Weggis, Switzerland: Maharishi European Research University Press.

DONALDSON, M. S., NICKLASON, J. A., & OTT, J. E.   (1985). Needs-based health promotion program services as HMO marketing tool. *Public Health Reports, 100,* 270–277.

DONNELLY, J. A.   (1981). Stress and the adolescent nurse. *Australian Nurses' Journal, 11,* 37–38.

DORR, D.   (1981). MMPI profiles of emotionally impaired physicians. *Journal of Clinical Psychology, 37,* 451–455.

DOUGHERTY, A. M., & DECK, M. D.   (1984). Helping teachers to help children cope with stress. *Humanistic Education and Development, 23,* 36–45.

DOYLE, B. J., & WARE, J. E.   (1977). Physician conduct and other factors that affect consumer satisfaction with medical care. *Journal of Medical Education, 52,* 793–801.

DUBOS, R. J. (1950). *Louis Pasteur: Free lance of science.* Boston, MA: Little, Brown and Co.

DUBOS, R. (1959). *Mirage of health: Utopias, progress, and biological change.* New York: Harper.

DUBUISSON, D., & MELZACK, R. (1976). Classification of clinical pain descriptions by multiple group discriminant analysis. *Experimental Neurology, 51,* 480–487.

DUFAULT, M. A. (1985). Changing the locus of control of registered nurse students with a futuristic-oriented course. *Journal of Nursing Education, 24,* 314–320.

DUFFY, D. L., HAMERMAN, D., & COHEN, M. A. (1980). Communication skills of house officers: A study in a medical clinic. *Annals of Internal Medicine, 93,* 354–357.

DUNBAR, F. (1954). *Emotions and bodily changes.* New York: Columbia University Press.

DUNBAR, J. M., & AGRAS, W. S. (1980). Compliance with medical instructions. In J. M. Ferguson & C. B. Taylor (Eds.), *The comprehensive handbook of behavioral medicine: Vol. 3—Extended applications & issues* (pp. 115–145). New York: SP Medical & Scientific Books.

DUNBAR, J. M., & STUNKARD, A. J. (1979). Adherence to diet and drug regimen. In R. Levy, B. Rifkind, B. Dennis, & N. Ernst (Eds.), *Nutrition, lipids, and coronary heart disease* (pp. 391–423). New York: Raven Press.

DUNKEL-SCHETTER, C. (1984). Social support and cancer: Findings based on patient interviews and their implications. *Journal of Social Issues, 40* (4), 77–98.

DURELL, J., & BUKOSKI, W. (1984). Preventing substance abuse: The state of the art. *Public Health Reports, 99,* 23–31.

DUSZYNSKI, K. R., SHAFFER, J. W., & THOMAS, C. B. (1981). Neoplasm and traumatic events in childhood: Are they related? *Archives of General Psychiatry, 38,* 327–331.

EASTWOOD, M. R. (1975). *The relation between physical and mental illness.* Toronto: University of Toronto Press.

EDWARDS, M. T., & ZIMET, C. N. (1976). Problems and concerns among medical students. *Journal of Medical Education, 51,* 619–625.

EGBERT, L. D., BATTIT, G. E., WELCH, C. E., & BARTLETT, M. K. (1964). Reduction of postoperative pain by encouragement and instruction of patients. *New England Journal of Medicine, 270,* 825–827.

EISENBERG, C. (1983). Women as physicians. *Journal of Medical Education, 58,* 534–541.

EISENBERG, J. M., KITZ, D. S., & WEBBER, R. A. (1983). Development of attitudes about sharing decision-making: A comparison of medical and surgical residents. *Journal of Health and Social Behavior, 24,* 85–90.

EISENBERG, J. M., & WILLIAMS, S. V. (1981). Cost containment and changing physicians' practice behavior: Can the fox learn to guard the chicken coop? *Journal of the American Medical Association, 246,* 2195–2201.

EKERDT, D. J., BADEN, L., BOSSÉ, R., & DIBBS, E. (1983). The effect of retirement on physical health. *American Journal of Public Health, 73,* 779–783.

ELLIOT, R. S., & BUELL, J. C. (1981). Environmental and behavioral influences in the major cardiovascular disorders. In S. M. Weiss, J. A. Herd, & B. H. Fox (Eds.), *Perspectives on behavioral medicine: Proceedings of the Academy of Behavioral Medicine Research Conference, Snowbird, Utah, June 3–6, 1979* (pp. 25–39). New York: Academic Press.

ELLIOTT, G. R., & EISDORFER, C. (EDS.). (1982). *Stress and human health.* New York: Springer Publishing Co.

ELLIS, A. (1970). *The essence of rational psychotherapy: A comprehensive approach to treatment.* New York: Institute for Rational Living.

ELLIS, A. (1977). Rational emotive therapy: Research data that support the clinical and personality hypothesis of R.E.T. and other modes of cognitive behavior therapy. *Counseling Psychologist, 7,* 2–42.

ENGEL, G. L. (1959). "Psychogenic" pain and the pain-prone patient. *American Journal of Medicine, 26,* 899–918.

ENGEL, G. L. (1980). The clinical application of the biopsychosocial model. *American Journal of Psychiatry, 137,* 535–544.

ENGSTROM, D. (1984). A psychological perspective of prevention in alcoholism. In J. D. Matarazzo, S. M. Weiss, J. A. Herd, N. E. Miller, & S. M. Weiss (Eds.), *Behavioral health: A handbook of health enhancement and disease prevention* (pp. 1047–1060). New York: Wiley.

ENOS, D. D., & SULTAN, P. (1977). *The sociology of health care: Social, economic, and political perspectives.* New York: Prager.

EPSTEIN, L. H., BECK, S., FIGUEROA, J., FARKAS, G., KAZDIN, A. E., DANEMAN, D., & BECKER, D. (1981). The effects of targeting improvements in urine glucose on metabolic control in children with insulin dependent diabetes. *Journal of Applied Behavior Analysis, 14,* 365–375.

EPSTEIN, L. H., & CLUSS, P. A. (1982). A behavioral medicine perspective on adherence to long-term medical regimens. *Journal of Consulting and Clinical Psychology, 50,* 950–971.

EPSTEIN, L. H., & MASEK, B. J. (1978). Behavioral control of medicine compliance. *Journal of Applied Behavior Analysis, 11,* 1–9.

EPSTEIN, L. H., & WING, R. R. (1980). Behavioral approaches to exercise habits and athletic performance. In J. M. Ferguson & C. B. Taylor (Eds.), *The comprehensive handbook of behavioral medicine: Vol. 1—Systems interventions* (pp. 125–137). New York: SP Medical & Scientific Books.

EPSTEIN, L. H., & WING, R. R. (1987). Behavioral treatment of childhood obesity. *Psychological Bulletin, 101,* 331–342.

ERBECK, J. R., ELFNER, L. F., & DRIGGS, D. F. (1983). Reduction of blood pressure by indirect biofeedback. *Biofeedback and Self-Regulation, 8,* 63–72.

ERNSTER, V. L., SACKS, S. T., SELVIN, S., & PETRAKIS, N. L.   (1979). Cancer incidence by marital status: U.S. third national cancer survey. *Journal of the National Cancer Institute, 63,* 567–578.

ERON, L. D.   (1958). The effect of medical education on attitudes: A follow-up study. *Journal of Medical Education, 33,* 25–33.

ERSHOFF, D. H., AARONSON, N. K., DANAHER, B. G., & WASSERMAN, F. W. (1983). Behavioral, health, and cost outcomes of an HMO-based prenatal health education program. *Public Health Reports, 98,* 536–547.

EVANS, A. S.   (1978). Causation and disease: A chronological journey. *American Journal of Epidemiology, 108,* 249–258.

EVANS, B.   (1968). *Dictionary of quotations.* New York: Avenel Books.

EVANS, R. I.   (1985). Psychologists in health promotion research: General concerns and adolescent smoking prevention. In J. C. Rosen & L. J. Solomon (Eds.), *Prevention in health psychology* (pp. 18–33). Hanover, NH: University Press of New England.

EVANS, R. I., HILL, R. C., RAINES, B. E., & HENDERSON, A. H.   (1981). Current behavioral, social, and educational programs in control of smoking: A selective, critical review. In S. M. Weiss, J. A. Herd, & B. H. Fox, (Eds.), *Perspectives on behavioral medicine: Proceedings of the Academy of Behavioral Medicine Research Conference, Snowbird, Utah, June 3–6, 1979* (pp. 261–284). New York: Academic Press.

EVANS, R. I., SMITH, C. K., & RAINES, B. E.   (1984). Deterring cigarette smoking in adolescents: A psychosocial-behavioral analysis of an intervention strategy. In A. Baum, S. E. Taylor, & J. E. Singer (Eds.), *Handbook of psychology and health: Vol. 4—social psychological aspects of health* (pp. 301–318). Hillsdale, NJ: Lawrence Erlbaum Associates.

EVERSON, R. B., & FRAUMENI, J. F.   (1975). Mortality among medical students and young physicians. *Journal of Medical Education, 50,* 809–811.

EYLES, J., & WOODS, K. J.   (1983). *The social geography of medicine and health.* London: Croom Helm.

FAGIN, C., & DIERS, D.   (1983). Nursing as metaphor. *New England Journal of Medicine, 309,* 116–117.

FARBER, A. S.   (1976). The Peckham experiment revisited: Cultivating health. *Health and Social Work, 1,* 28–38.

FARROW, J. T., & HEBERT, J. R.   (1982). Breath suspension during the transcendental meditation technique. *Psychosomatic Medicine, 44,* 133–153.

FERGUSON, J.   (1981). The behavioral treatment of anorexia nervosa. In J. M. Ferguson & C. B. Taylor (Eds.), *The comprehensive handbook of behavioral medicine: Vol. 2—Syndromes & special areas* (pp. 129–143). New York: SP Medical & Scientific Books.

FIELDING, J. E.   (1984). Evaluation of worksite health promotion: Some unresolved issues and opportunities. *Corporate Commentary, 1,* 9–15.

FISHER, E. B., DELAMATER, A. M., BERTELSON, A. D., & KIRKLEY, B. G.

(1982). Psychological factors in diabetes and its treatment. *Journal of Consulting and Clinical Psychology, 50,* 993–1003.

FISHMAN, D. B., & ZIMET, C. N. (1972). Specialty choice and beliefs about specialties among freshman medical students. *Journal of Medical Education, 47,* 524–533.

FLAY, B. R. (1987). Mass media and smoking cessation: A critical review. *American Journal of Public Health, 77,* 153–160.

FLICK, L. H. (1986). Paths to adolescent parenthood: Implications for prevention. *Public Health Reports, 101,* 132–147.

FOLEN, R. (1985). Interview with Representative Cecil Heftel. *American Psychologist, 40,* 1131–1136.

FOLKINS, C. H., LAWSON, K. D., OPTON, E. M., & LAZARUS, R. S. (1968). Desensitization and the experimental reduction of threat. *Journal of Abnormal Psychology, 73,* 100–113.

FOLKMAN, S., LAZARUS, R. S., GRUEN, R. J., & DELONGIS, A. (1986). Appraisal, coping, health status, and psychological symptoms. *Journal of Personality and Social Psychology, 50,* 571–579.

FOLLETTE, W. T., & CUMMINGS, N. A. (1967). Psychiatric services and medical utilization in a prepaid health plan setting. *Medical Care, 5,* 25–35.

FOOD AND DRUG ADMINISTRATION (1980). Prescription drug products: Patient package insert requirements. *Federal Register, 45,* 60754–60780.

FORD, M. J. (1986). The irritable bowel syndrome. *Journal of Psychosomatic Research, 30,* 399–410.

FORD, M. R. (1982). Biofeedback treatment for headaches, Raynaud's disease, essential hypertension, and irritable bowel syndrome: A review of the long-term follow-up literature. *Biofeedback and Self-Regulation, 7,* 521–536.

FORDYCE, W. E. (1976). *Behavioral methods for chronic pain and illness.* St. Louis, MO: C. V. Mosby.

FORDYCE, W. E. (1978). Learning processes in pain. In R. A. Sternbach (Ed.), *The psychology of pain* (pp. 49–72). New York: Raven Press.

FORDYCE, W. E. (1985). Back pain, compensation, and public policy. In J. C. Rosen & L. J. Solomon (Eds.), *Prevention in health psychology* (pp. 390–400). Hanover, NH: University Press of New England.

FORDYCE, W. E., & STEGER, J. C. (1979). Chronic pain. In O. F. Pomerleau & J. P. Brady (Eds.), *Behavioral medicine: Theory and practice* (pp. 125–153). Baltimore, MD: Williams & Wilkins.

FOX, B. H. (1983). Current theory of psychogenic effects on cancer incidence and prognosis. *Journal of Psychosocial Oncology, 1,* 17–31.

FOXX, R. M., & BROWN, R. A. (1979). Nicotine fading and self-monitoring for cigarette abstinence or controlled smoking. *Journal of Applied Behavior Analysis, 12,* 111–125.

FRANCE, R. D., HOUPT, J. L., SKOTT, A. M., KRISHNAN, K.R.R., & VARIA,

I. M. (1986). Depression as a psychopathological disorder in chronic low back pain patients. *Journal of Psychosomatic Research, 30,* 127–133.

FRANCES, R. J., & FRANKLIN, J. E. (1986). Primary prevention of alcohol and substance abuse. In J. T. Barter & S. W. Talbott (Eds.), *Primary prevention in psychiatry: State of the art* (pp. 119–141). Washington, DC: American Psychiatric Press.

FRANK, J. D. (1982). Biofeedback and the placebo effect. *Biofeedback and Self-Regulation, 7,* 449–460.

FREEMAN, C., CALSYN, D., & LOUKS, J. (1976). The use of the Minnesota Multiphasic Personality Inventory with low back pain patients. *Journal of Clinical Psychology, 32,* 294–298.

FREIDENBERGS, I., GORDON, W., HIBBARD, M. R., & DILLER, L. (1980). Assessment and treatment of psychosocial problems of the cancer patient: A case study. *Cancer Nursing, 3,* 111–119.

FREIDSON, E. (1970). *The profession of medicine: A study of the sociology of applied knowledge.* New York: Dodd, Mead.

FRENCH, T. M., & ALEXANDER, F. (1941). Psychogenic factors in bronchial asthma. *Psychosomatic Medicine Monographs,* No. 4.

FREY, J., DEMICK, J., & BIBACE, R. (1981). Variations in physicians' feelings of control during a family practice residency. *Journal of Medical Education, 56,* 50–56.

FRIEDMAN, G. D., DALES, L. G., & URY, H. K. (1979). Mortality in middle-aged smokers and nonsmokers. *New England Journal of Medicine, 300,* 213–217.

FRIEDMAN, H. S., & BOOTH-KEWLEY, S. (1987). The "disease-prone personality." *American Psychologist, 42,* 539–555.

FRIEDMAN, H. S., & DeMATTEO, M. R. (1979). Health care as an interpersonal process. *Journal of Social Issues, 35,* 1–11.

FRIEDMAN, M., & ROSENMAN, R. H. (1974). *Type A behavior and your heart.* Greenwich, CT: Fawcett.

FUNG, E. H., & LAZAR, B. S. (1983). Hypnosis as an adjunct in the treatment of von Willebrand's disease. *International Journal of Clinical and Experimental Hypnosis, 31,* 256–265.

GAENSBAUER, T. J., & MIZNER, G. L. (1980). Developmental stresses in medical education. *Psychiatry, 43,* 60–70.

GALLIN, R. S. (1980). Life difficulties, coping, and the use of medical services. *Culture, Medicine, and Psychiatry, 4,* 249–269.

Gallup survey finds that Americans are 'grossly misinformed' on birth control. (1985). *The Nation's Health,* April.

GARFIELD, S. L. (ED.). (1982). Behavioral medicine. *Journal of Consulting and Clinical Psychology, 50,* 793–1053.

GARRITY, T. F. (1981). Behavioral adjustment after myocardial infarction: A selective review of recent descriptive, correlational, and intervention research. In S. M. Weiss, J. A. Herd, & B. H. Fox, (Eds.), *Perspectives on behavioral medicine: Proceedings of the Academy of Behavioral Medicine Research*

*Conference, Snowbird, Utah, June 3–6, 1979* (pp. 67–87). New York: Academic Press.

GARRITY, T. F., WILSON, J. F., & HAFFERTY, F. W.   (1984). Improved medical care for the elderly: Intervening in medical education. *Journal of Community Psychology, 12,* 369–378.

GARTNER, A., & RIESSMAN, F.   (1984). *The self-help revolution.* New York: Human Sciences Press.

GATCHEL, R. J., & BAUM, A.   (1983). *An introduction to health psychology.* New York: Addison-Wesley.

GENTRY, W. D. (ED.).   (1984). *Handbook of behavioral medicine.* New York: Guilford Press.

GENTRY, W. D., FOSTER, S., & HANEY, T.   (1972). Denial as a determinant of anxiety and perceived health status in the coronary care unit. *Psychosomatic Medicine, 34,* 39–44.

GENTRY, W. D., STREET, W. J., MASUR, F. T., & ASKEN, M. J.   (1981). Training in medical psychology: A survey of graduate and internship training programs. *Professional Psychology, 12,* 224–228.

GENUTH, S. M., VERTES, V., & HAZELTON, I.   (1978). Supplemented fasting in the treatment of obesity. In G. A. Bray (Ed.), *Recent advances in obesity research: Vol. 2* (pp. 370–378). London: Newman.

GIBSON, R. M., LEVIT, K. R., LAZENBY, H., & WALDO, D. R.   (1984). National health expenditures, 1983. *Health Care Financing Review, 6,* (No. 2), 1–15.

GILL, J. S., ZEZULKA, A. V., SHIPLEY, M. J., GILL, S. K., & BEEVERS, D. G. (1986). Stroke and alcohol consumption. *New England Journal of Medicine, 315,* 1041–1046.

GIRDANO, D., & EVERLY, G.   (1979). *Controlling stress and tension: A holistic approach.* Englewood Cliffs, NJ: Prentice-Hall.

GOCHMAN, D. S.   (1982). Labels, systems and motives: Some perspectives for future research and programs. *Health Education Quarterly, 9,* 263–270.

GOETZ, A., & BERNSTEIN, J.   (1984). Computer developments in health risk management. *Corporate Commentary, 1,* 26–33.

GOETZEL, R. Z., CROEN, L. G., SHELOV, S., BOUFFORD, J. I., & LEVIN, G. (1984). Evaluating self-help support groups for medical students. *Journal of Medical Education, 59,* 331–340.

GOLDBERG, I. D., KRANTZ, G., & LOCKE, B. Z.   (1970). Effect of a short-term outpatient psychiatric therapy benefit on the utilization of medical services in a prepaid group practice medical program. *Medical Care, 8,* 419–428.

GOLDSMITH, M. F.   (1986). Worksite wellness programs: Latest wrinkle to smooth health care costs. *Journal of the American Medical Association, 256,* 1089–1091, 1095.

GOLDSTEIN, M. J.   (1973). Individual differences in response to stress. *American Journal of Community Psychology, 1,* 113–137.

GOLDSTON, S. E.   (1968). Mental health education in a community mental health center. *American Journal of Public Health, 58,* 693–699.

GOODKIN, K., ANTONI, M. H., & BLANEY, P. H. (1986). Stress and hopelessness in the promotion of cervical intraepithelial neoplasia to invasive squamous cell carcinoma of the cervix. *Journal of Psychosomatic Research, 30,* 67–76.

GOODSTADT, M. S., SHEPPARD, M. A., & CHAN, G. C. (1982). An evaluation of two school-based alcohol education programs. *Journal of Studies on Alcohol, 43,* 352–369.

GOODWIN, J. M., GOODWIN, J. S., & KELLNER, R. (1979). Psychiatric symptoms in disliked medical patients. *Journal of the American Medical Association, 241,* 1117–1120.

GOODWIN, J. S., GOODWIN, J. M., & VOGEL, A. V. (1979). Knowledge and use of placebos by house officers and nurses. *Annals of Internal Medicine, 91,* 106–110.

GOODWIN, R. G. (1972). The family life educator as change agent: A participant in problems and solutions. *Family Coordinator, 21,* 303–312.

GORDIS, L. (1979). Conceptual and methodologic problems in measuring patient compliance. In R. B. Haynes, D. W. Taylor, & D. L. Sackett (Eds.), *Compliance in health care* (pp. 23–45). Baltimore, MD: Johns Hopkins University Press.

GORDIS, M. D., & MARKOWITZ, M. (1971). Evaluation of the effectiveness of comprehensive and continuous pediatric care. *Pediatrics, 48,* 766–776.

GORDON, W. A., FREIDENBERGS, I., DILLER, L., HIBBARD, M., WOLF, C., LEVINE, L., LIPKINS, R., EZRACHI, O., & LUCIDO, D. (1980). Efficacy of psychosocial intervention with cancer patients. *Journal of Consulting and Clinical Psychology, 48,* 743–759.

GOTTLIEB, H., STRITE, L. C., KOLLER, R., MADORSKY, A., HOCKERSMITH, V., KLEEMAN, M., & WAGNER, J. (1977). Comprehensive rehabilitation of patients having chronic low back pain. *Archives of Physical Medicine and Rehabilitation, 58,* 101–108.

GRAHAM, D. T., LUNDY, R. M., BENJAMIN, L. S., KABLER, J. D., LEWIS, W. C., KUNISH, N. O., & GRAHAM, F. K. (1962). Specific attitudes in initial interviews with patients having different "psychosomatic" diseases. *Psychosomatic Medicine, 24,* 257–266.

GRAY, N, & DAUBE, M. (Eds.). (1980). *Guidelines for smoking control, UICC Technical Report Series: Vol. 52.* Geneva, Switzerland: International Union Against Cancer.

GREEN, E., GREEN, A., & WALTERS, D. (1970). Voluntary control of internal states: Psychological and physiological. *Journal of Transpersonal Psychology, 1,* 1–26.

GREENBERG, B. G., HARRIS, M. E., MACKINNON, E. F., & CHIPMAN, S. S. (1953). A method for evaluating the effectiveness of health education literature. *American Journal of Public Health and the Nation's Health, 45* 1147–1155.

GREENBERG, M. (1983). Environmental toxicology in the United States. In

McGlashan, N. D., & Blunden, J. R. (Eds.), *Geographical aspects of health* (pp. 157–174). London: Academic Press.

GREENLEY, J. R., & SCHOENHERR, R. A. (1981). Organization effects on client satisfaction with humaneness of service. *Journal of Health and Social Behavior, 22,* 2–18.

GREENWALD, H. P., BECKER, S. W., & NEVITT, M. C. (1978). Delay and noncompliance in cancer detection: A behavioral perspective for health planners. *Milbank Memorial Fund Quarterly, 56,* 212-230.

GREER, S., & MORRIS, T. (1975). Psychological attributes of women who develop breast cancer: A controlled study. *Journal of Psychosomatic Research, 19,* 147–153.

GROSS, A. R. (1986). The effect of coping strategies on the relief of pain following surgical intervention for lower back pain. *Psychosomatic Medicine, 48,* 225–241.

GROSSARTH-MATICEK, R., BASTIAANS, J., & KANAZIR, D. T. (1985). Psychosocial factors as strong predictors of mortality from cancer, ischaemic heart disease and stroke: The Yugoslav prospective study. *Journal of Psychosomatic Research, 29,* 167–176.

GROSSARTH-MATICEK, R., KANAZIR, D. T., SCHMIDT, P., & VETTER, H. (1985). Psychosocial and organic variables as predictors of lung cancer, cardiac infarct and apoplexy: Some differential predictors. *Personality and Individual Differences, 6,* 313–321.

GROVER, P. L., & SMITH, D. U. (1981). Academic anxiety, locus of control, and achievement in medical school. *Journal of Medical Education, 56,* 727–736.

GROVES, J. E. (1978). Taking care of the hateful patient. *New England Journal of Medicine, 298,* 883–887.

GRUEN, W. (1975). Effects of brief psychotherapy during the hospitalization period on the recovery process in heart attacks. *Journal of Consulting and Clinical Psychology, 43,* 223–232.

GRUENBERG, E. M. (1977). The failures of success. *Milbank Memorial Fund Quarterly/Health and Society, 55,* 3–24.

GRUNDY, S. M., BILHEIMER, D., BLACKBURN, H., BROWN, W. V., KWITEROVICH, P. O., MATTSON, F., SCHONFELD, G., & WEIDMAN, W. H. (1982). Rationale of the diet-heart statement of the American Heart Association: Report of Nutrition Committee. *Circulation, 65,* 839A–851A.

GRZESIAK, R. C. (1981). Rehabilitation psychology, medical psychology, health psychology, and behavioral medicine. *Professional Psychology, 12,* 411–413.

GUCK, T. P. (1984). Stress management for chronic pain patients. *Journal of Orthopedic and Sports Physical Therapy, 6,* 5–7.

GUNDERT-REMY, U., REMY, C., & WEBER, E. (1976). Serum digoxin levels in patients of a general practice in Germany. *European Journal of Clinical Pharmacology, 10,* 97–100.

GUSTAFSSON, P. A., KJELLMAN, N.-I. M., & CEDERBLAD, M. (1986). Family therapy in the treatment of severe childhood asthma. *Journal of Psychosomatic Research, 30,* 369–374.

GUTMANN, M. C., & MEYER, D. L. (1981). Social sciences in hypertension control. *Family & Community Health, 4,* 63–72.

GUYTON, A. C. (1982). *Human physiology and mechanisms of disease* (3rd ed.). Philadelphia, PA: W. B. Saunders.

HACKETT, T. (1986). Men and sex after a heart attack. *Harvard Medical School Health Letter, 11*(5), 5–6.

HACKETT, T. P., CASSEM, N. H., & WISHNIE, H. A. (1968). The coronary-care unit: An appraisal of its psychologic hazards. *New England Journal of Medicine, 279,* 1365–1370.

HACKMAN, J. D., LOW-BEER, J. R., WUGMEISTER, S., WILHELM, R. C., & ROSENBAUM, J. E. (1979). The premed stereotype. *Journal of Medical Education, 54,* 308–313.

HAFNER, R. J. (1982). Psychological treatment of essential hypertension: A controlled comparison of meditation and meditation plus biofeedback. *Biofeedback and Self-Regulation, 7,* 305–316.

HAGEN, R. L. (1981). Behavioral treatment of obesity: Progress but not panacea. In J. M. Ferguson & C. B. Taylor (Eds.), *The comprehensive handbook of behavioral medicine: Vol. 2—Syndromes & special areas* (pp. 67–94). New York: SP Medical & Scientific Books.

HAGGERTY, R. J., & ROGHMAN, K. S. (1972). Non-compliance and self-medication. *Pediatric Clinics of North America, 19,* 101–115.

HALL, J. A., ROTER, D. L., & RAND, C. S. (1981). Communication of affect between patient and physician. *Journal of Health and Social Behavior, 22,* 18–30.

HAMBURG, D. A., ELLIOTT, G. R., & PARRON, D. L. (EDS.). (1982). *Health and behavior: Frontiers of research in the biobehavioral sciences.* Washington, DC: National Academy Press.

HAMMER, R. M., & TUFTS, M. A. (1985). Nursing's self-image—Nursing education's responsibility. *Journal of Nursing Education, 24,* 280–283.

HANKIN, J., & OKTAY, J. S. (1979). *Mental disorder and primary medical care: An analytical review of the literature.* DHEW Pub. No. (ADM) 78-661. Washington, DC: U.S. Government Printing Office.

HARRISON, R. V., CAPLAN, R. D., FRENCH, J.R.P., & WELLONS, R. V. (1982). Combining field experiments with longitudinal surveys: Social research on patient adherence. In L. Bickman (Ed.), *Applied social psychology annual: Vol. 3* (pp. 119–150). Beverly Hills, CA: Sage.

HART, N. (1985). *The sociology of health and medicine.* Lancashire: Causeway Press Ltd.

HARTSOUGH, D. M., & SAVITSKY, J. C. (1984). Three Mile Island: Psychology and environmental policy at a crossroads. *American Psychologist, 39,* 1113–1122.

HASKELL, W. L. (1985). Exercise programs for health promotion. In J. C.

Rosen & L. J. Solomon (Eds.), *Prevention in health psychology* (pp. 111–129). Hanover, NH: University Press of New England.

HATCH, J. P., KLATT, K. D., SUPIK, J. D., RIOS, N., FISHER, J. G., BAUER, R. L., & SHIMOTSU, G. W. (1985). Combined behavioral and pharmacological treatment of essential hypertension. *Biofeedback and Self-Regulation, 10,* 119–138.

HATCH, J. P., & RILEY, P. (1985). Growth and development of biofeedback: A bibliographic analysis. *Biofeedback and Self-Regulation, 10,* 289–299.

HAUG, M. R., & LAVIN, B. (1981). Practitioner or patient—Who's in charge? *Journal of Health and Social Behavior, 22,* 212–229.

HAUSER, S. T., JACOBSON, A. M., WERTLIEB, D., BRINK, S., & WENTWORTH, S. (1985). The contribution of family environment to perceived competence and illness adjustment in diabetic and acutely ill adolescents. *Family Relations, 34,* 99–108.

HAVAS, S., & WALKER, B. (1986). Massachusetts' approach to the prevention of heart disease, cancer, and stroke. *Public Health Reports, 101,* 29–39.

HAVIK, O. E. (1981). Psychological intervention in physical illness: A review of outcome research concerning patient information and education. In B. Christiansen (Ed.), *Does psychology return its costs?* (pp. 170–206). Research in Clinical Psychology, Report No. 2. Oslo, Norway: Norwegian Council for the Sciences and Humanities.

HAWORTH, S. (1683). *A description of the duke's bagnio, and of the mineral bath and new spaw thereunto belonging with an account of the use of sweating, rubbing, bathing, and the medicinal vertues of the spaw.* London: Prince's Arms, St. Paul's Churchyard.

HAYNES, R. B. (1976a). Strategies for improving compliance: A methodologic analysis and review. In D. L. Sackett & R. B. Haynes (Eds.), *Compliance with therapeutic regimens* (pp. 69–82). Baltimore, MD: Johns Hopkins University Press.

HAYNES, R. B. (1976b). A critical review of the 'determinants' of patient compliance with therapeutic regiments. In D. L. Sackett & R. B. Haynes (Eds.), *Compliance with therapeutic regimens* (pp. 26–39). Baltimore, MD: Johns Hopkins University Press.

HAYNES, R. B., SACKETT, D. L., GIBSON, E. S., TAYLOR, D. W., HACKETT, B. C., ROBERTS, R. S., & JOHNSON, A. L. (1976). Improvement of medication compliance in uncontrolled hypertension. *Lancet, 1,* 1265–1268.

HAYNES, R. B., TAYLOR, D. W., & SACKETT, D. L. (EDS.). (1979). *Compliance in health care.* Baltimore, MD: Johns Hopkins University Press.

HAYNES, S. N. (1973). Contingency management in a municipally administered antabuse program for alcoholics. *Journal of Behavior Therapy and Experimental Psychiatry, 4,* 31–32.

HEALEY, J. M. (1986). Reducing the destructive impact of alcohol: The search for acceptable strategies continues. *American Journal of Public Health, 76,* 749–750.

HEINRICH, R. L., & SCHAG, C. C.  (1984). Living with cancer: The cancer inventory of problem situations. *Journal of Clinical Psychology, 40,* 972–980.

HEINRICH, R. L., & SCHAG, C. C.  (1985). Stress and activity management: Group treatment for cancer patients and spouses. *Journal of Consulting and Clinical Psychology, 53,* 439–446.

HEINS, M., FAHEY, S. N., & LEIDEN, L. I.  (1984). Perceived stress in medical, law, and graduate students. *Journal of Medical Education, 59,* 169–179.

HELD, M. L., & ZIMET, C. N.  (1975). A longitudinal study of medical specialty choice and certainty level. *Journal of Medical Education, 50,* 1044–1051.

HEMISTRA, N. W.  (1973). The effects of smoking on mood change. In W. L. Dunn (Ed.), *Smoking behavior: Motives and incentives* (pp. 197–207). Washington, DC: Winston.

HENDERSON, V.  (1964). The nature of nursing. *American Journal of Nursing, 64,* 62–68.

HENNON, C. B., & PETERSON, B. H.  (1981). An evaluation of a family life education delivery system for young families. *Family Relations, 30,* 387–394.

HERD, J. A.  (1984). Cardiovascular disease and hypertension. In W. D. Gentry (Ed.), *Handbook of behavioral medicine* (pp. 222–281). New York: Guilford Press.

HERD, J. A., & WEISS, S. M.  (1984). Overview of hypertension: Its treatment and prevention. In J. D. Matarazzo, S. M. Weiss, J. A. Herd, N. E. Miller, & S. M. Weiss (Eds.), *Behavioral health: A handbook of health enhancement and disease prevention* (pp. 789–805). New York: Wiley.

HERSEY, J. C., KLIBANOFF, L. S., LAM, D. J., & TAYLOR, R. L.  (1984). Promoting social support: The impact of California's "Friends Can Be Good Medicine" campaign. *Health Education Quarterly, 11,* 293–311.

HERSH, S. P.  (1979). Views on the psychosocial dimensions of cancer and cancer treatment. In P. I. Ahmed, & G. V. Coelho (Eds.), *Toward a new definition of health: Psychosocial dimensions* (pp. 175–190). New York: Plenum.

HERZOG, D. B., WYSHAK, G., & STERN, T. A.  (1984). Patient-generated dysphoria in house officers. *Journal of Medical Education, 59,* 869–874.

HETHERINGTON, R. W., & CALDERONE, G. E.  (1985). Prevention and health policy: A view from the social sciences. *Public Health Reports, 100,* 507–514.

HIEBERT, B. A.  (1983). A framework for planning stress control interventions. *Canadian Counsellor, 17,* 51–61.

HILBERMAN, E., KONANC, J., PEREZ-REYES, M., HUNTER, R., SCAGNELLI, J., & SANDERS, S.  (1975). Support groups for women in medical school: A first-year program. *Journal of Medical Education, 50,* 867–875.

HILGARD, E. R.  (1968). *The experience of hypnosis.* New York: Harcourt, Brace & World.

HILGARD, E. R.  (1971). Hypnotic phrenomena: The struggle for scientific acceptance. *American Scientist, 59,* 567–577.

HILGARD, E. R.  (1978). Hypnosis and pain. In R. A. Sternbach (Ed.), *The psychology of pain* (pp. 219–240). New York: Raven Press.

HIMMELSTEIN, D. U., LANG, S., & WOOLHANDLER, S. (1984). The Yugoslav health system: Public ownership and local control. *Journal of Public Health Policy, 3,* 423–431.

HINGSON, R., ZUCKERMAN, B., AMARO, H., FRANK, D. A., KAYNE, H., SORENSON, J. R., MITCHELL, J., PARKER, S., MORELOCK, S., & TIMPERI, R. (1986). Maternal marijuana use and neonatal outcome: Uncertainty posed by self-reports. *American Journal of Public Health, 76,* 667–669.

HINKLE, L. E. (1974). The effect of exposure to cultural change, social change, and changes in interpersonal relationships on health. In B. S. Dohrenwend & B. P. Dohrenwend (Eds.), *Stressful life events: Their nature and effects* (pp. 9–44). New York: Wiley.

HIRSCH, J. (1982). The psychobiology of obesity. In L. J. West & M. Stein (Eds.), *Critical issues in behavioral medicine* (pp. 183–192). Philadelphia: J. B. Lippencott.

HJELLE, L. A. (1974). Transcendental meditation and psychological health. *Perceptual and Motor Skills, 39,* 623–628.

HOBFOLL, S. E., & WALFISCH, S. (1984). Coping with a threat to life: A longitudinal study of self-concept, social support, and psychological distress. *American Journal of Community Psychology, 12,* 87–100.

HOBFOLL, S. E., & WALFISCH, S. (1986). Stressful events, mastery, and depression: An evaluation of crisis theory. *Journal of Community Psychology, 14,* 183–195.

HOCHBAUM, G. M. (1979). Behavior and education. In R. Levy, B. Rifkind, B. Dennis, & N. Ernst (Eds.), *Nutrition, lipids, and coronary heart disease* (pp. 365–390). New York: Raven Press.

HOLDEN, C. (1979). Pain, dying, and the health care system. *Science, 203,* 984–985.

HOLDER, H. D., & BLOSE, J. O. (1986). Alcoholism treatment and total health care utilization and costs: A four-year longitudinal analysis of federal employees. *Journal of the American Medical Association, 256,* 1456–1460.

HOLLAND, J. C., & ROWLAND, J. H. (1981). Psychiatric, psychosocial, and behavioral interventions in the treatment of cancer: An historical review. In S. M. Weiss, J. A. Herd, & B. H. Fox, (Eds.), *Perspectives on behavioral medicine: Proceedings of the Academy of Behavioral Medicine Research Conference, Snowbird, Utah, June 3–6, 1979* (pp. 235–259). New York: Academic Press.

HOLMES, T. H. (1979). Development and application of a quantitative measure of life change magnitude. In J. E. Barrett, R. M. Rose, & G. L. Klerman, (Eds.), *Stress and mental disorder* (pp. 37–53). New York: Raven Press.

HOLMES, T. H., & MASUDA, M. (1974). Life change and illness susceptibility. In B. S. Dohrenwend & B. P. Dohrenwend (Eds.), *Stressful life events: Their nature and effects* (pp. 45–72). New York: Wiley & Sons.

HOLMES, T. H., & RAHE, R. H. (1967). The social readjustment rating scale. *Journal of Psychosomatic Research, 11,* 213–218.

HOLROYD, K. A., PENZIEN, D. B., HURSEY, K. G., TOBIN, D. L., ROGERS, L.,

HOLM, J. E., MARCILLE, P. J., HALL, J. R., & CHILA, A. G. (1984). Change mechanisms in EMG biofeedback training: Cognitive changes underlying improvements in tension headache. *Journal of Consulting and Clinical Psychology, 52,* 1039–1053.

Homicide among young black males—United States, 1970–1982. (1985). *Morbidity and Mortality Weekly Report, 34,* 629–633.

HOROWITZ, M., SCHAEFER, C., HIROTO, D., WILNER, N., & LEVIN, B. (1977). Life event questionnaires for measuring presumptive stress. *Psychosomatic Medicine, 39,* 413–431.

HOROWITZ, M. J., BENFARI, R., HULLEY, S., BLAIR, S., ALVAREZ, W., BORHANI, N., REYNOLDS, A.-M., & SIMON, N. (1979). Life events, risk factors, and coronary disease. *Psychosomatics, 20,* 586–587, 591–592.

HOSSENLOPP, C. M., LEIBER, L., & MO, B. (1976). Psychological factors in the effectiveness of acupuncture for chronic pain. In J. J. Bonica & D. Albe-Fessard (Eds.), *Advances in pain research and therapy: Vol. 1* (pp. 803–809). New York: Raven Press.

HOUSE, J. S., STRECHER, V., METZNER, H. L., & ROBBINS, C. A. (1986). Occupational stress and health among men and women in the Tecumseh community health study. *Journal of Health and Social Behavior, 27,* 62–75.

HOUTS, P. S., HU, T. W., HENDERSON, R. A., CLEARY, P. D., & TOKUHATA, G. (1984). Utilization of medical care following the Three Mile Island crisis. *American Journal of Public Health, 74,* 140–142.

HUEBNER, L. A., ROYER, J. A., & MOORE, J. (1981). The assessment and remediation of dysfunctional stress in medical school. *Journal of Medical Education, 56,* 547–558.

HUGHES, J. R., CASAL, D. C., & LEON, A. S. (1986). Psychological effects of exercise: A randomized cross-over trial. *Journal of Psychosomatic Research, 30,* 355–360.

HULL, J. G., & BOND, C. F. (1986). Social and behavioral consequences of alcohol consumption and expectancy: A meta-analysis. *Psychological Bulletin, 99,* 347–360.

HUMBLE, C. G., SAMET, J. M., & PATHAK, D. R. (1987). Marriage to a smoker and lung cancer risk. *American Journal of Public Health, 77,* 598–602.

HUMPHREY, L. L., APPLE, R. F., & KIRSCHENBAUM, D. S. (1986). Differentiating bulimic-anorexic from normal families using interpersonal and behavioral observational systems. *Journal of Consulting and Clinical Psychology, 54,* 190–195.

HUNTER, M., PHILIPS, C., & RACHMAN, S. (1979). Memory for pain. *Pain, 6,* 35–46.

HYMAN, H. H. (1986). Are public hospitals in New York City inferior to voluntary nonprofit hospitals? A study of JCAH hospital surveys. *American Journal of Public Health, 76,* 18–22.

HYMOVICH, D. P. (1976). A framework for measuring outcomes of intervention with the chronically ill child and his family. In G. D. Grave & I. B. Pless

(Eds.), *Chronic childhood illness: Assessment of outcome* (pp. 91–93). DHEW Pub. No. (NIH) 76-877. Washington, DC: U.S. Government Printing Office.

HYPERTENSION DETECTION AND FOLLOW-UP PROGRAM COOPERATIVE GROUP. (1979). Five-year findings of the Hypertension Detection and Follow-up Program: I—Reduction in mortality of persons with high blood pressure, including mild hypertension. *Journal of the American Medical Association, 242,* 2562–2571.

IASP SUBCOMMITTEE ON TAXONOMY (1979). Pain terms: A list with definitions and notes on usage. *Pain, 6,* 249–252.

IGLEHART, J. K. (1985a). Medicare turns to HMOs. *New England Journal of Medicine, 312,* 132–136.

IGLEHART, J. K. (1985b). The Veterans Administration medical care system faces an uncertain future. *New England Journal of Medicine, 313,* 1168–1172.

IGLEHART, J. K. (1986a). Canada's health care system (First of three parts). *New England Journal of Medicine, 315,* 202–208.

IGLEHART, J. K. (1986b). Canada's health care system (Second of three parts). *New England Journal of Medicine, 315,* 778–784.

IGLEHART, J. K. (1986c). Canada's health care system (Third of three parts). *New England Journal of Medicine, 315,* 1623–1628.

IGLEHART, J. K. (1987). The political contest over health care resumes. *New England Journal of Medicine, 316,* 639–644.

ILLICH, I. (1976). *Medical nemesis: The expropriation of health.* New York: Random House.

INSTITUTE OF MEDICINE (1980). *Alcoholism, alcohol abuse, and related problems: Opportunities for research.* Washington, DC: National Academy of Science.

IRVINE, M. J., JOHNSTON, D. W., JENNER, D. A., & MARIE, G. V. (1986). Relaxation and stress management in the treatment of essential hypertension. *Journal of Psychosomatic Research, 30,* 437–450.

IVERSON, D. C., FIELDING, J. E., CROW, R. S., & CHRISTENSON, G. M. (1985). The promotion of physical activity in the United States population: The status of programs in medical, worksite, community, and school settings. *Public Health Reports, 100,* 212–224.

JACOB, R. G., & CHESNEY, M. A. (1984). Stress management for cardiovascular reactivity. *Behavioral Medicine Update, 6,* 23–27.

JACOBSON, E. (1929). *Progressive relaxation.* Chicago, IL: University of Chicago Press.

JACOBSON, E. (1970). *Modern treatment of tense patients.* Springfield, IL: Charles C. Thomas.

JACOBSON, E. (1977). The origins and development of progressive relaxation. *Journal of Behavior Therapy and Experimental Psychiatry, 8,* 119–123.

JAMES, G. D., YEE, L. S., HARSHFIELD, G. A., BLANK, S. G., & PICKERING, T. G. (1986). The influence of happiness, anger, and anxiety on the blood pressure of borderline hypertensives. *Psychosomatic Medicine, 48,* 502–508.

JAMES, S. A., WAGNER, E. H., STROGATZ, D. S., BERESFORD, S.A.A., KLEINBAUM, D. G., WILLIAMS, C. A., CUTCHIN, L. M., & IBRAHIM, M. A. (1984). The Edgecombe County (NC) high blood pressure control program: II—Barriers to the use of medical care among hypertensives. *American Journal of Public Health, 74,* 468–472.

JAMNER, L. D., & SCHWARTZ, G. E. (1986). Self-deception predicts self-report and endurance of pain. *Psychosomatic Medicine, 48,* 211–223.

JANIS, I. L. (1958). *Psychological stress: Psychoanalytic and behavioral studies of surgical patients.* New York: Wiley.

JANIS, I. L. (1984a). Improving adherence to medical recommendations: Prescriptive hypotheses derived from recent research in social psychology. In A. Baum, S. E. Taylor, & J. E. Singer (Eds.), *Handbook of psychology and health: Vol. 4—Social psychological aspects of health* (pp. 113–148). Hillsdale, NJ: Lawrence Erlbaum Associates.

JANIS, I. L. (1984b). The patient as decision maker. In W. D. Gentry (Ed.), *Handbook of behavioral medicine* (pp. 326–368). New York: Guilford Press.

JASON, L. A., GRUDER, C. L., MARTINO, S., FLAY, B. R., WARNECKE, R., & THOMAS, N. (1987). Work site group meetings and the effectiveness of a televised smoking cessation intervention. *American Journal of Community Psychology, 15,* 57–72.

JASON, L. A., & ZOLIK, E. S. (1980). Follow-up data on two dog-litter reduction interventions. *American Journal of Community Psychology, 8,* 737–741.

JASON, L. A., ZOLIK, E. S., & MATESE, F. J. (1979). Prompting dog owners to pick up dog droppings. *American Journal of Community Psychology, 7,* 339–351.

JEFFREY, D. B., & LEMNITZER, N. (1981). Diet, exercise, obesity, and related health problems: A macroenvironmental analysis. In J. M. Ferguson & C. B. Taylor (Eds.), *The comprehensive handbook of behavioral medicine: Vol. 2—Syndromes & special areas* (pp. 47–66). New York: SP Medical & Scientific Books.

JEFFREY, T. B., JEFFREY, L. K., GREULING, J. W., & GENTRY, W. R. (1985). Evaluation of a brief group treatment package including hypnotic induction for maintenance of smoking cessation: A brief communication. *International Journal of Clinical and Experimental Hypnosis, 33,* 95–98.

JEMMOTT, J. B., BORYSENKO, J. Z., BORYSENKO, M., McCLELLAND, D. C., CHAPMAN, R., MEYER, D., & BENSON, H. (1983). Academic stress, power motivation, and decrease in salivary secretory immunoglobulin A secretion rate. *Lancet, 1,* 1400–1402.

JEMMOTT, J. B., & LOCKE, S. E. (1984). Psychosocial factors, immunologic mediation, and human susceptibility to infectious disease: How much do we know? *Psychological Bulletin, 95,* 78–108.

JENCKS, S. F., & DOBSON, A. (1985). Strategies for reforming medicare's physician payments: Physician diagnosis-related groups and other approaches. *New England Journal of Medicine, 312,* 1492–1499.

JENKINS, C. D.   (1972). Social and epidemiologic factors in psychosomatic disease. *Psychosomatic Annals, 2,* 8–21.

JENKINS, C. D.   (1981). Behavioral factors in the etiology and pathogenesis of cardiovascular diseases: Sudden death, hypertension, and myocardial infarction. In S. M. Weiss, J. A. Herd, & B. H. Fox (Eds.), *Perspectives on behavioral medicine: Proceedings of the Academy of Behavioral Medicine Research Conference, Snowbird, Utah, June 3–6, 1979* (pp. 41–54). New York: Academic Press.

JENKINS, C. D., ROSENMAN, R. H., & FRIEDMAN, M.   (1967). Development of an objective psychological test for determination of the coronary-prone behavior pattern in employed men. *Journal of Chronic Diseases, 20,* 371–379.

JENKINS, C. D., ROSENMAN, R. H., & ZYZANSKI, S. J.   (1974). Prediction of clinical coronary heart disease by a test for the coronary-prone behavior pattern. *New England Journal of Medicine, 290,* 1271–1275.

JENKINS, C. D., TUTHILL, R. W., TANNENBAUM, S. I., & KIRBY, C.   (1979). Social stressors and excess mortality from hypertensive diseases. *Journal of Human Stress, 5,* 29–40.

JENKINS, C. D., ZYZANSKI, S. J., & ROSENMAN, R. H.   (1971). Progress toward validation of a computer-scored test for the Type A coronary-prone behavior pattern. *Psychosomatic Medicine, 33,* 193–202.

JESSOR, R.   (1982). Critical issues in research on adolescent health promotion. In T. J. Coates, A. C. Petersen, & C. L. Perry (Eds.), *Promoting adolescent health: A dialog on research and practice* (pp. 447–465). New York: Academic Press.

JESSOR, R.   (1984). Adolescent development and behavioral health. In J. D. Matarazzo, S. M. Weiss, J. A. Herd, N. E. Miller, & S. M. Weiss (Eds.), *Behavioral health: A handbook of health enhancement and disease prevention* (pp. 69–90). New York: Wiley.

JESSOR, R., & JESSOR, S. L.   (1977). *Problem behavior and psychosocial development: A longitudinal study of youth.* New York: Academic Press.

JETTE, A. M.   (1980). Health status indicators: Their utility in chronic-disease evaluation research. *Journal of Chronic Diseases, 33,* 567–579.

JOHNSON, J. E.   (1984). Psychological interventions and coping with surgery. In A. Baum, S. E. Taylor, & J. E. Singer (Eds.), *Handbook of psychology and health: Vol. 4—Social psychological aspects of health* (pp. 167–187). Hillsdale, NJ: Lawrence Erlbaum Associates.

JOHNSON, J. E., KIRCHHOFF, K. T., & ENDRESS, M. P.   (1975). Altering children's distress behavior during orthopedic cast removal. *Nursing Research, 24,* 404–410.

JOHNSON, J. E., & LEVENTHAL, H.   (1974). Effects of accurate expectations and behavioral instructions on reactions during a noxious medical examination. *Journal of Personality and Social Psychology, 29,* 710–718.

JOHNSON, J. E., & RICE, V. H. (1974). Sensory and distress components of pain: Implications for the study of clinical pain. *Nursing Research, 23,* 203–209.

JOHNSON, R. P., & CONNELLY, J. C. (1981). Addicted physicians: A closer look. *Journal of the American Medical Association, 245,* 253–257.

JOHNSTON, L. D., O'MALLEY, P. M., & BACHMAN, J. G. (1984). *Drugs and American high school students, 1975–1983: Highlights.* DHHS Pub. No. (ADM) 84-1317. Washington, DC: U.S. Government Printing Office.

JONES, E. F., FORREST, J. D., GOLDMAN, N., HENSHAW, S. K., LINCOLN, R., ROSOFF, J. I., WESTOFF, C. F., & WULF, D. (1985). Teenage pregnancy in developed countries: Determinants and policy implications. *Family Planning Perspectives, 17,* 53–63.

JONES, E. W. (1982). Advocacy—A tool for radical nursing curriculum planners. *Journal of Nursing Education, 21,* 40–45.

JONES, K., & VISCHI, T. (1979). Impact of alcohol, drug abuse, and mental health treatment on medical care utilization: A review of the research literature. *Medical Care, 17 (Supplement),* ii–82.

JONES, N. F., DIRKS, J. F., & KINSMAN, R. A. (1980). Assessment in the psycho-maintenance of chronic physical illness. *Journal of Psychiatric Treatment and Evaluation, 2,* 303–312.

JONES, R. F., & THOMAE-FORGUES, M. (1984). Validity of the MCAT in predicting performance in the first two years of medical school. *Journal of Medical Education, 59,* 455–464.

JORDEN, E. (1669). *A discourse of natural bathes, and mineral waters.* London: Thomas Salmon.

JOSEPH, J. G., EMMONS, C.-A., KESSLER, R. C., WORTMAN, C. B., O'BRIEN, K., HOCKER, W. T., & SCHAEFER, C. (1984). Coping with the threat of AIDS: An approach to psychosocial assessment. *American Psychologist, 39,* 1297–1302.

JUSTICE, A. (1985). Review of the effects of stress on cancer in laboratory animals: Importance of time of stress application and type of tumor. *Psychological Bulletin, 98,* 108–138.

KAHN, H. S., & ORRIS, P. (1982). The emerging role of salaried physicians: An organizational proposal. *Journal of Public Health Policy, 3,* 284–292.

KALISCH, B. J. (1975). Of half gods and mortals: Aesculapian authority. *Nursing Outlook, 23,* 22–28.

KANDEL, D. B., & LOGAN, J. A. (1984). Patterns of drug use from adolescence to young adulthood: I.—Periods of risk for initiation, continued use, and discontinuation. *American Journal of Public Health, 74,* 660–666.

KANE, R. A., & KANE, R. L. (1985). The feasibility of universal long-term-care benefits: Ideas from Canada. *New England Journal of Medicine, 312,* 1357–1364.

KANNEL, W. B., & GORDON, T. (EDS.). (1970). *The Framingham study: An epidemiological investigation of cardiovascular disease.* Washington, DC: U.S. Government Printing Office.

KAPLAN, R. M. (1984). The connection between clinical health promotion and health status: A critical overview. *American Psychologist, 39,* 755–765.

KAPRIO, J., KOSKENVUO, M., & RITA, H. (1987). Mortality after bereavement: A prospective study of 95,647 widowed persons. *American Journal of Public Health, 77,* 283–287.

KARASEK, R., BAKER, D., MARXER, F., AHLBOM, A., & THEORELL, T. (1981). Job decision latitude, job demands, and cardiovascular disease: A prospective study of Swedish men. *American Journal of Public Health, 71,* 694–705.

KASL, S. V. (1975). Issues in patient adherence to health care regimens. *Journal of Human Stress, 1,* 5–17, 48.

KASL, S. (1978). A social-psychological perspective on successful community control of high blood pressure: A review. *Journal of Behavioral Medicine, 1,* 347–381.

KASL, S. V., EVANS, A. S., & NIEDERMAN, J. C. (1979). Psychosocial risk factors in the development of infectious mononucleosis. *Psychosomatic Medicine, 41,* 445–466.

KEEFE, F. J. (1982). Behavioral assessment and treatment of chronic pain: Current status and future directions. *Journal of Consulting and Clinical Psychology, 50,* 896–911.

KEEFE, F. J., CRISSON, J. E., MALTBIE, A., BRADLEY, L., & GIL, K. M. (1986). Illness behavior as a predictor of pain and overt behavior patterns in chronic low back pain patients. *Journal of Psychosomatic Research, 30,* 543–551.

KEEFE, F. J., SURWIT, R. S., & PILON, R. N. (1979). A 1-year follow-up of Raynaud's patients treated with behavioral therapy techniques. *Journal of Behavioral Medicine, 2,* 385–391.

Keeping up with cholesterol. (1985). *Harvard Medical School Health Letter, June.* Boston, MA: Harvard University Press.

KEESEY, R. E. (1980). A set-point analysis of the regulation of body weight. In A. J. Stunkard (Ed.), *Obesity* (pp. 144–165). Philadelphia, PA: Saunders.

KELLY, J. A., BRADLYN, A. S., DUBBERT, P. M., & ST. LAWRENCE, J. S. (1982). Stress management training in medical school. *Journal of Medical Education, 57,* 91–99.

KELMAN, H. R. (1980). Health care of old people in Scotland: Lessons for the United States. *Journal of Public Health Policy, 1,* 177–186.

KELSEY, J. L., & OSTFELD, A. M. (1975). Demographic characteristics of persons with acute herniated lumbar intervertebral disc. *Journal of Chronic Diseases, 28,* 37–50.

KENDALL, P. C., & WATSON, D. (1981). Psychological preparation for stressful medical procedures. In C. K. Prokop & L. A. Bradley (Eds.), *Medical psychology: Contributions to behavioral medicine* (pp. 197–221). New York: Academic Press.

KENTALA, E. (1972). Physical fitness and feasibility of physical rehabilitation after myocardial infarction in men of working age. *Annals of Clinical Research (Supplement 9), 4,* 1–84.

KEPES, E. R., CHEN, M., & SCHAPIRA, M.   (1976). A critical evaluation of acupuncture in the treatment of chronic pain. In J. J. Bonica & D. Albe-Fessard (Eds.), *Advances in pain research and therapy: Vol. 1* (pp. 817–822). New York: Raven Press.

KESSLER, L. G., BURNS, B. J., SHAPIRO, S., TISCHLER, G. L., GEORGE, L. K., HOUGH, R. L., BODISON, D., & MILLER, R. H.   (1987). Psychiatric diagnoses of medical service users: Evidence from the epidemiologic catchment area program. *American Journal of Public Health, 77,* 18–24.

KETTERER, R. F.   (1981). *Consultation and education in mental health: Problems and prospects.* Beverly Hills, CA: Sage Publications.

KEWMAN, D. G., & ROBERTS, A. H.   (1983). An alternative perspective on biofeedback efficacy studies: A reply to Steiner and Dince. *Biofeedback and Self-Regulation, 8,* 487–497.

KEYS, A., BROZEK, J., HENSCHEL, A., MICKELSON, O., & TAYLOR, H. L.   (1950). *The biology of human starvation.* Minneapolis, MN: University of Minnesota Press.

KIECOLT-GLASER, J. K., FISHER, L. D., OGROCKI, P., STOUT, J. C., SPEICHER, C. E., & GLASER, R.   (1987). Marital quality, marital disruption, and immune function. *Psychosomatic Medicine, 49,* 13–34.

KIECOLT-GLASER, J. K., GARNER, W., SPEICHER, C., PENN, G. M., HOLLIDAY, J., & GLASER, R.   (1984). Psychosocial modifiers of immunocompetence in medical students. *Psychosomatic Medicine, 46,* 7–14.

KIECOLT-GLASER, J. K., RICKER, D., GEORGE, J., MESSICK, G., SPEICHER, C. E., GARNER, W., & GLASER, R.   (1984). Urinary cortisol levels, cellular immunocompetency, and loneliness in psychiatric patients. *Psychosomatic Medicine, 46,* 15–23.

KIECOLT-GLASER, J. K., SPEICHER, C. E., HOLLIDAY, J. E., & GLASER, R.   (1984). Stress and the transformation of lymphocytes by Epstein-Barr virus. *Journal of Behavioral Medicine, 7,* 1–12.

KING, H.   (1970). Health in the medical and other learned professions. *Journal of Chronic Diseases, 23,* 257–281.

KINNAIRD, J.   (1981). The British national health service: Retrospect and prospect. *Journal of Public Health Policy, 2,* 382–412.

KINSMAN, R. A., DIRKS, J. F., & JONES, N. F.   (1982). Psychomaintenance of chronic physical illness: Clinical assessment of personal styles affecting medical management. In T. Millon, C. Green, & R. Meagher (Eds.), *Handbook of clinical health psychology* (pp. 435–466). New York: Plenum.

KIRMIL-GRAY, K., EAGLESTON, J. R., THORESEN, C. E., & ZARCONE, V. P.   (1985). Brief consultation and stress management treatments for drug-dependent insomnia: Effects on sleep quality, self-efficacy, and daytime stress. *Journal of Behavioral Medicine, 8,* 79–99.

KIRSCHT, J. P.   (1983). Preventive health behavior: A review of research and issues. *Health Psychology, 2,* 277–301.

KIRSCHT, J. P., & ROSENSTOCK, I. M.   (1979). Patients' problems in following recommendations of health experts. In G. C. Stone, F. Cohen, & N. E. Adler (Eds.), *Health psychology: A handbook* (pp. 189–215). San Francisco, CA: Jossey-Bass.

KLEINMAN, J. C. (1986). Underreporting of infant deaths: Then and now. *American Journal of Public Health, 76,* 365–366.

KLOS, D. M., & ROSENSTOCK, I. M. (1982). Some lessons from the North Karelia project. *American Journal of Public Health, 72,* 53–54.

KNEIER, A. W., & TEMOSHOK, L. (1984). Repressive coping reactions in patients with malignant melanoma as compared to cardiovascular disease patients. *Journal of Psychosomatic Research, 28,* 145–155.

KOBASA, S. C. (1979). Personality and resistance to illness. *American Journal of Community Psychology, 7,* 413–423.

KOCH, A. (1985). "If only it could be me": The families of pediatric cancer patients. *Family Relations, 34,* 63–70.

KOLATA, G. (1985). Why do people get fat? *Science, 227,* 1327–1328.

KOOKEN, R. A., & HAYSLIP, B. (1984). The use of stress inoculation in the treatment of test anxiety in older students. *Educational Gerontology, 10,* 39–58.

KOOP, C. E., & LUOTO, J. (1982). "The health consequences of smoking: Cancer": Overview of a report of the Surgeon General. *Public Health Reports, 97,* 318–324.

KOOS, E. (1954). *The health of Regionville.* New York: Columbia University Press.

KOPELMAN, L. (1983). Cynicism among medical students. *Journal of the American Medical Association, 250,* 2006–2010.

KORSCH, B. M., FINE, R. N., & NEGRETE, V. F. (1978). Non-compliance in children with renal transplants. *Pediatrics, 61,* 872–876.

KORSCH, B. M., & NEGRETE, V. F. (1972). Doctor-patient communication. *Scientific American, 227,* 66–74.

KOTTKE, T. E., PUSKA, P., SALONEN, J. T., TUOMILEHTO, J., & NISSINEN, A. (1984). Changes in perceived heart disease risk and health during a community-based heart disease prevention program: The North Karelia project. *American Journal of Public Health, 74,* 1404–1405.

KRANTZ, D. S., & GLASS, D. C. (1984). Personality, behavior patterns, and physical illness: Conceptual and methodological issues. In W. D. Gentry (Ed.), *Handbook of behavioral medicine* (pp. 38–86). New York: Guilford Press.

KRANTZ, D. S., GRUNBERG, N. E., & BAUM, A. (1985). Health psychology. *Annual Review of Psychology, 36,* 349–383.

KRANTZ, D. S., & MANUCK, S. B. (1984). Acute psychophysiologic reactivity and risk of cardiovascular disease: A review and methodologic critique. *Psychological Bulletin, 96,* 435–464.

KRANTZ, D. S., SCHAEFFER, M. A., DAVIA, J. E., DEMBROSKI, T. M., MAC-DOUGALL, J. M., & SHAFFER, R. T. (1981). Extent of coronary atherosclerosis, Type A behavior, and cardiovascular response to social interaction. *Psychophysiology, 18,* 654–664.

KRAUS, M. L., GOTTLIEB, L. D., HORWITZ, R. I., & ANSCHER, M. (1985). Randomized clinical trial of atenolol in patients with alcohol withdrawal. *New England Journal of Medicine, 313,* 905–909.

KREPS, G. L., RUBEN, B. D., BAKER, M. W., & ROSENTHAL, S. R. (1987). Survey of public knowledge about digestive health and diseases: Implications for health education. *Public Health Reports, 102,* 270–277.

KRISTELLER, J. L., & RODIN, J. (1984). A three-stage model of treatment continuity: Compliance, adherence, and maintenance. In A. Baum, S. E. Taylor, & J. E. Singer (Eds.), *Handbook of psychology and health: Vol. 4—Social psychological aspects of health* (pp. 85–112). Hillsdale, NJ: Lawrence Erlbaum Associates.

KRITZER, H., & ZIMET, C. N. (1967). A retrospective view of medical specialty choice. *Journal of Medical Education, 42,* 47–53.

KURTZMAN, C., BLOCK, D. E., & STEINER-FREUD, Y. (1985). Nursing and medical students' attitudes toward the rights of hospitalized patients. *Journal of Nursing Education, 24,* 237–241.

LACROIX, A. Z., MEAD, L. A., LIANG, K.-Y., THOMAS, C. B., & PEARSON, T. A. (1986). Coffee consumption and the incidence of coronary heart disease. *New England Journal of Medicine, 315,* 977–982.

LALIOTIS, D. A., & GRAYSON, J. H. (1985). Psychologist heal thyself: What is available for the impaired psychologist? *American Psychologist, 40,* 84–96.

LALONDE, M. (1974). *A new perspective on the health of Canadians.* Ottawa: Canadian Government Printing Office.

LAMBERT, V. A., & LAMBERT, C. E. (1979). *The impact of physical illness.* Englewood Cliffs, NJ: Prentice-Hall.

LAMPKIN, N., CANNON, T. M., & FAIRCHILD, S. L. (1985). Crisis intervention: When the client is a nursing student. *Journal of Nursing Education, 24,* 148–150.

LANGER, E. J., JANIS, I. L., & WOLFER, J. A. (1975). Reduction of psychological stress in surgical patients. *Journal of Experimental Social Psychology, 11,* 155–165.

LAROCCO, J. M., HOUSE, J. S., & FRENCH, J.R.P. (1980). Social support, occupational stress, and health. *Journal of Health and Social Behavior, 21,* 202–218.

LATIMER, E. A., & LAVE, L. B. (1987). Initial effects of the New York state auto safety belt law. *American Journal of Public Health, 77,* 183–186.

LAZARUS, R. S. (1966). *Psychological stress and the coping process.* New York: McGraw-Hill.

LAZARUS, R. S. (1984). Puzzles in the study of daily hassles. *Journal of Behavioral Medicine, 7,* 375–389.

LEAVITT, F., GARRON, D. C., D'ANGELO, C. M., & MCNEILL, T. W. (1979). Low back pain in patients with and without demonstrable organic disease. *Pain, 6,* 191–200.

LeBaron, S., & Zeltzer, L. K. (1984). Research on hypnosis in hemophilia—Preliminary success and problems: A brief communication. *International Journal of Clinical and Experimental Hypnosis, 32,* 290–295.

Lenzner, A. S., & Aronson, A. L. (1972). Psychiatric vignettes from a coronary care unit. *Psychosomatics, 13,* 179–184.

Lerner, J. R. (1985). Stress management and weight control. *Journal of College Student Personnel, 26,* 86–87.

LeShan, L. (1964). The world of the patient in severe pain of long duration. *Journal of Chronic Diseases, 17,* 119–126.

LeShan, L. (1966). An emotional life-history pattern associated with neoplastic disease. *Annals of the New York Academy of Sciences, 125,* 780–793.

Lester, D., Leitner, L. A., & Posner, I. (1985). A note on locus of control and stress in police officers. *Journal of Community Psychology, 13,* 77–79.

Leventhal, H. (1973). Changing attitudes and habits to reduce risk factors in chronic disease. *American Journal of Cardiology, 31,* 571–580.

Leventhal, H., Nerenz, D. R., & Steele, D. J. (1984). Illness representations and coping with health threats. In A. Baum, S. E. Taylor, & J. E. Singer (Eds.), *Handbook of psychology and health: Vol. 4—Social psychological aspects of health* (pp. 219–252). Hillsdale, NJ: Lawrence Erlbaum Associates.

Leventhal, H., Safer, M. A., Cleary, P. D., & Gutmann, M. (1980). Cardiovascular risk modification by community-based programs for life-style change: Comments on the Stanford study. *Journal of Consulting and Clinical Psychology, 48,* 150–158.

Leventhal, H., Zimmerman, R., & Gutmann, M. (1984). Compliance: A self-regulation perspective. In W. D. Gentry (Ed.), *Handbook of behavioral medicine* (pp. 369–436). New York: Guilford Press.

Levey, G. S. (1986). Organizing to begin physician manpower planning. *New England Journal of Medicine, 315,* 1344–1347.

Levin, B. L., Glasser, J. H., & Roberts, R. E. (1984). Changing patterns in mental health service coverage within health maintenance organizations. *American Journal of Public Health, 74,* 453–458.

Levine, J., Warrenburg, S., Kerns, R., Schwartz, G., Delaney, R., Fontana, A., Gradman, A., Smith, S., Allen, S., & Cascione, R. (1987). The role of denial in recovery from coronary heart disease. *Psychosomatic Medicine, 49,* 109–117.

Levine, J. D., Gordon, N. C., & Fields, H. L. (1978). The mechanism of placebo analgesia. *Lancet, 2,* 654–657.

Levine, S., Scotch, N. A., & Vlasak, G. J. (1969). Unravelling technology and culture in public health. *American Journal of Public Health, 59,* 237–244.

Levy, R. I. (1981). The decline in cardiovascular disease mortality. *Annual Review of Public Health, 2,* 49–70.

Levy, R. I., & Moskowitz, J. (1982). Cardiovascular research: Decades of progress, a decade of promise. *Science, 217,* 121–129.

Levy, S. M. (1985). Emotional response to disease and its treatment. In J. C.

Rosen & L. J. Solomon (Eds.), *Prevention in health psychology* (pp. 299–310). Hanover, NH: University Press of New England.

LEWIS, G. L. (1984). Academic origins of medical school applicants and entrants, 1980–1982. *Journal of Medical Education, 59,* 825–828.

LEY, P. (1977). Psychological studies of doctor-patient communication. In S. Rachman (Ed.), *Contributions to medical psychology: Vol. 1* (pp. 9–42). New York: Pergamon Press.

LEY, P., & MORRIS, L. A. (1984). Psychological aspects of written information for patients. In S. Rachman (Ed.), *Contributions to medical psychology: Vol. 3* (pp. 117–149). New York: Pergamon Press.

LICHTENBERG, P. A., SWENSEN, C. H., & SKEHAN, M. W. (1986). Further investigation of the role of personality, lifestyle and arthritic severity in predicting pain. *Journal of Psychosomatic Research, 30,* 327–337.

LICHTENSTEIN, E. (1982). The smoking problem: A behavioral perspective. *Journal of Consulting and Clinical Psychology, 50,* 804–819.

LIGHT, D. W., LIEBFRIED, S., & TENNSTEDT, F. (1986). Social medicine vs professional dominance: The German experience. *American Journal of Public Health, 76,* 78–83.

LIN, N., SIMEONE, R. S., ENSEL, W. M., & KUO, W. (1979). Social support, stressful life events, and illness: A model and an empirical test. *Journal of Health and Social Behavior, 20,* 108–119.

LINDEMANN, J. E. (1981). *Psychological and behavioral aspects of physical disability: A manual for health practitioners.* New York: Plenum.

LINN, B. S., & ZEPPA, R. (1984). Stress in junior medical students: Relationship to personality and performance. *Journal of Medical Education, 59,* 7–12.

LINN, L. S., YAGER, J., COPE, D., & LEAKE, B. (1985). Health status, job satisfaction, job stress, and life satisfaction among academic and clinical faculty. *Journal of the American Medical Association, 254,* 2775–2782.

LINN, M. W., SANDIFER, R., & STEIN, S. (1985). Effects of unemployment on mental and physical health. *American Journal of Public Health, 75,* 502–506.

LIPID RESEARCH CLINICS PROGRAM (1984a). The lipid research clinics coronary primary prevention trial results: I.—Reduction in incidence of coronary heart disease. *Journal of the American Medical Association, 251,* 351–364.

LIPID RESEARCH CLINICS PROGRAM (1984b). The lipid research clinics coronary primary prevention trial results: II.—The relationship of reduction in incidence of coronary heart disease to cholesterol lowering. *Journal of the American Medical Association, 251,* 365–374.

LIPOWSKI, Z. J. (1976). Psychosomatic medicine: An overview. In O. Hill (Ed.), *Modern trends in psychosomatic medicine: Vol. 3* (pp. 1–20). London: Butterworths.

LIPSCOMB, J. (1982). Value preferences for health: Meaning, measurement, and use in program evaluation. In R. L. Kane & R. A. Kane (Eds.), *Values and long-term care.* Lexington, MA: D. C. Heath.

LLOYD, C., & GARTRELL, N. K. (1981). Sex differences in medical student mental health. *American Journal of Psychiatry, 138,* 1346–1351.

LOCKE, B. Z., & SLABY, A. E.   (1982). Preface. In D. Mechanic (Ed.), *Symptoms, illness behavior, and help-seeking* (pp. xi–xv). New York: Prodist.

LOCKE, S. E.   (1982). Stress, adaptation, and immunity: Studies in humans. *General Hospital Psychiatry, 4,* 49–58.

LOGAN, M. H., & HUNT, E. E.   (1976). Concepts of health and illness in highland Guatemala: Their implications for improvement in health care. In O. Hill (Ed.), *Modern trends in psychosomatic medicine: Vol. 3* (pp. 457–470). London: Butterworths.

LONG, B. C.   (1984). Aerobic conditioning and stress inoculation: A comparison of stress-management interventions. *Cognitive Therapy and Research, 8,* 517–541.

LORBER, J.   (1975). Good patients and problem patients: Conformity and deviance in a general hospital. *Journal of Health and Social Behavior, 16,* 213–225.

LOWENTHAL, M. F., & HAVEN, C.   (1968). Interaction and adaptation: Intimacy as a critical variable. *American Sociological Review, 33,* 20–30.

LOWMAN, C.   (1982). FAS researchers studying increased public knowledge. *NIAAA Information and Feature Service,* August 30, 1982.

LUGINBUHL, W. H., FORSYTH, B. R., HIRSCH, G. B., & GOODMAN, M. R.   (1981). Prevention and rehabilitation as a means of cost containment: The example of myocardial infarction. *Journal of Public Health Policy, 2,* 103–115.

LUTHE, W.   (1963). Autogenic training: Method, research and application in medicine. *American Journal of Psychotherapy, 17,* 174–195.

LUTHE, W. (ED.).   (1969). *Autogenic therapy.* New York: Grune & Stratton.

LYNCH, J. J.   (1977). *The broken heart: The medical consequences of loneliness.* New York: Basic Books.

LYNCH, J. J.   (1985). *The language of the heart: The body's response to human dialogue.* New York: Basic Books.

MACCOBY, N., & ALEXANDER, J.   (1979). Reducing heart disease risk using the mass media: Comparing the effects on three communities. In R. F. Muñoz, L. R. Snowden, & J. G. Kelly (Eds.), *Social and psychological research in community settings* (pp. 69–100). San Francisco: Jossey-Bass.

MACCOBY, N. & FARQUHAR, J. W.   (1975). Communication for health: Unselling heart disease. *Journal of Communication, 25,* 114–126.

MACCOBY, N., FARQUHAR, J. W., WOOD, P. D., & ALEXANDER, J.   (1977). Reducing the risk of cardiovascular disease: Effects of a community based campaign on knowledge and behavior. *Journal of Community Health, 3,* 100–114.

MACGREGOR, R. R.   (1986). Alcohol and immune defense. *Journal of the American Medical Association, 256,* 1474–1479.

MACMAHON, B., & PUGH, T. F.   (1970). *Epidemiology: Principles and methods.* Boston, MA: Little, Brown.

MAGRAB, P. R., & PAPADOPOULOU, Z. L.   (1977). The effect of a token economy on dietary compliance for children on hemodialysis. *Journal of Applied Behavior Analysis, 10,* 573–578.

MAIER, S. F., & LAUDENSLAGER, M.    (1985). Stress and health: Exploring the links. *Psychology Today, 19,* 44–49.

MAIER, S. F., & SELIGMAN, M.E.P.    (1976). Learned helplessness: Theory and evidence. *Journal of Experimental Psychology: General, 105,* 3–46.

MALMO, R. B.    (1986). Obituary: Hans Hugo Selye (1907–1982). *American Psychologist, 41,* 92–93.

MALONEY, S. K., & HERSEY, J. C.    (1984). Getting messages on the air: Findings from the 1982 alcohol abuse prevention campaign. *Health Education Quarterly, 11,* 273–292.

MANDERINO, M. A., & YONKMAN, C. A.    (1985). Stress inoculation: A method of helping students cope with anxiety related to clinical performance. *Journal of Nursing Education, 24,* 115–118.

MANLEY, M., & SWEENEY, J.    (1986). Assessment of compliance in hemodialysis adaptation. *Journal of Psychosomatic Research, 30,* 153–161.

MANN, A. H.    (1986). The psychological aspects of essential hypertension. *Journal of Psychosomatic Research, 30,* 527–541.

MANNING, W. G., LEIBOWITZ, A., GOLDBERG, G. A., ROGERS, W. H., & NEWHOUSE, J. P.    (1984). A controlled trial of the effect of a prepaid group practice on use of services. *New England Journal of Medicine, 310,* 1505–1510.

MANUCK, S. B., MORRISON, R. L., BELLACK, A. S., & POLEFRONE, J. M.    (1985). Behavioral factors in hypertension: Cardiovascular responsivity, anger, and social competence. In M. A. Chesney & R. H. Rosenman (Eds.), *Anger and hostility in cardiovascular and behavioral disorders* (pp. 149–172). Washington, DC: Hemisphere.

MARBACH, J. J., & LIPTON, J. A.    (1978). Aspects of illness behavior in patients with facial pain. *Journal of the American Dental Association, 96,* 630–638.

MARCINIAK, D.    (1984). A stress management training program for low income women. *Women & Therapy, 3,* 163–168.

MARCUS, A. C., & SIEGEL, J. M.    (1982). Sex differences in the use of physician services: A preliminary test of the fixed role hypothesis. *Journal of Health and Social Behavior, 23,* 186–197.

MARKIDES, K. S., & COREIL, J.    (1986). The health of Hispanics in the southwestern United States: An epidemiologic paradox. *Public Health Reports, 101,* 253–265.

MARSHALL, C. L.    (1977). *Toward an educated health consumer: Mass communication and quality in medical care.* U.S. Public Health Service Pub. No. (NIH) 77-881. Washington, DC: U.S. Government Printing Office.

MARSTON, M.–'V.    (1970). Compliance with medical regimens: A review of the literature. *Nursing Research, 19,* 312–323.

MARTIN, J. E., & DUBBERT, P. M.    (1982). Exercise applications and promotion in behavioral medicine: Current status and future directions. *Journal of Consulting and Clinical Psychology, 50,* 1004–1017.

MARTIN, J. L., & VANCE, C. S.    (1984). Behavioral and psychosocial factors in

AIDS: Methodological and substantive issues. *American Psychologist, 39,* 1303–1308.

MASEK, B. J.   (1982). Compliance and medicine. In D. M. Doleys, R. L. Meredith, & A. R. Ciminero (Eds.), *Behavioral medicine: Assessment and treatment strategies* (pp. 527–545). New York: Plenum.

MASLACH, C.   (1976). Burned out. *Human Behavior, 5*(9), 16–22.

MASLACH, G., & KERR, G. B.   (1983). Tailoring sex-education programs to adolescents—A strategy for the primary prevention of unwanted adolescent pregnancies. *Adolescence, 18,* 449–456.

MASTERS, J. C., CERRETO, M. C., & MENDLOWITZ, D. R.   (1983). The role of the family in coping with childhood chronic illness. In T. G. Burish & L. A. Bradley (Eds.), *Coping with chronic disease: Research and applications* (pp. 381–407). New York: Academic Press.

MASUR, F. T.   (1981). Adherence to health care regimens. In C. K. Prokop & L. A. Bradley (Eds.), *Medical psychology: Contributions to behavioral medicine* (pp. 441–470). New York: Academic Press.

MATARAZZO, J. D.   (1980). Behavioral health and behavioral medicine: Frontiers for a new health psychology. *American Psychologist, 35,* 807–817.

MATARAZZO, J. D.   (1982). Behavioral health's challenge to academic, scientific, and professional psychology. *American Psychologist, 37,* 1–14.

MATTHEWS, K. A., & AVIS, N. E.   (1982). Psychologists in schools of public health: Current status, future prospects, and implications for other health settings. *American Psychologist, 37,* 949–954.

MATTSON, M. E., POLLACK, E. S., & CULLEN, J. W.   (1987). What are the odds that smoking will kill you? *American Journal of Public Health, 77,* 425–431.

MATTSSON, A.   (1977). Long-term physical illness in childhood: A challenge to psychosocial adaptation. In R. H. Moos (Ed.), *Coping with physical illness* (pp. 183–199). New York: Plenum.

MAY, H. J.   (1981). Integration of sexual counseling and family therapy with surgical treatment of breast cancer. *Family Relations, 30,* 291–295.

MAYER, T. R., & MAYER, G. G.   (1985). HMOs: Origins and development. *New England Journal of Medicine, 312,* 590–594.

MAZIE, B.   (1985). Job stress, psychological health, and social support of family practice residents. *Journal of Medical Education, 60,* 935–941.

McALISTER, A., PUSKA, P., KOSKELA, K., PALLONEN, U., & MACCOBY, N.   (1980). Mass communication and community organization for public health education. *American Psychologist, 35,* 375–379.

McALISTER, A., PUSKA, P., SALONEN, J. T., TUOMELEHTO, J., & KOSKELA, K.   (1982). Theory and action for health promotion: Illustrations from the North Karelia project. *American Journal of Public Health, 72,* 43–50.

McAULIFFE, W. E., ROHMAN, M., SANTANGELO, S., FELDMAN, B., MAGNUSON, E., SOBOL, A., & WEISSMAN, J.   (1986). Psychoactive drug use among practicing physicians and medical students. *New England Journal of Medicine, 315,* 805–810.

McCain, N. L. (1985). A test of Cohen's developmental model for professional socialization with baccalaureate nursing students. *Journal of Nursing Education, 24,* 180–186.

McClelland, D. C., Alexander, C., & Marks, E. (1982). The need for power, stress, immune function, and illness among male prisoners. *Journal of Abnormal Psychology, 91,* 61–70.

McCreary, C., Turner, J., & Dawson, E. (1981). Principal dimensions of the pain experience and psychological disturbance in chronic low back pain patients. *Pain, 11,* 85–92.

McCubbin, H. I., McCubbin, M. A., Patterson, J. M., Cauble, A. E., Wilson, L. R., & Warwick, W. (1983). CHIP—coping health inventory for parents: An assessment of parental coping patterns in the care of the chronically ill child. *Journal of Marriage and the Family, 45,* 359–370.

McCue, J. D. (1982). The effects of stress on physicians and their medical practice. *New England Journal of Medicine, 306,* 458–463.

McCue, J. D. (1985). The distress of internship: Causes and prevention. *New England Journal of Medicine, 312,* 449–452.

McCue, J. D., Magrinat, G., Hansen, C. J., & Bailey, R. S. (1986). Residents' leadership styles and effectiveness as perceived by nurses. *Journal of Medical Education, 61,* 53–58.

McGlashan, N. D., & Blunden, J. R. (Eds.). (1983). *Geographical aspects of health.* London: Academic Press.

McGlashan, T. H., Evans, F. J., & Orne, M. T. (1969). The nature of hypnotic analgesia and placebo response to experimental pain. *Psychosomatic Medicine, 31,* 227–246.

McGrady, A. V., Bernal, G.A.A., Fine, T., & Woerner, M. P. (1985). Post traumatic head and neck pain, a multimodal treatment approach. *Journal of Holistic Medicine, 5,* 130–138.

McKeown, T. (1976). *The role of medicine: Dream, mirage, or nemesis?* London: Nuffield Provincial Hospitals Trust.

McKinlay, J. (1972). Some approaches and problems in the study of the use of services—An overview. *Journal of Health and Social Behavior, 13,* 115–152.

McLeroy, K. R., Green, L. W., Mullen, K. D., & Foshee, V. (1984). Assessing the effects of health promotion in worksites: A review of the stress program evaluations. *Health Education Quarterly, 11,* 379–401.

McPheeters, H. L. (1976). Primary prevention and health promotion in mental health. *Preventive Medicine, 5,* 187–198.

Mechanic, D. (1962). The concept of illness behavior. *Journal of Chronic Diseases, 15,* 189–194.

Mechanic, D. (1966). Response factors in illness: The study of illness behavior. *Social Psychiatry, 1,* 11–20.

Mechanic, D. (Ed.). (1976). *The growth of bureaucratic medicine.* New York: Wiley & Sons.

MECHANIC, D. (1978). *Medical sociology: A comprehensive text* (2nd ed.). New York: Free Press.

MECHANIC, D. (1982). The epidemiology of illness behavior and its relationship to physical and psychological distress. In D. Mechanic (Ed.), *Symptoms, illness behavior, and help-seeking* (pp. 1–24). New York: Prodist.

MECKLENBURG, M. E., & THOMPSON, P. G. (1983). The adolescent family life program as a prevention measure. *Public Health Reports, 98,* 21–29.

MEDALIE, J. H., & GOLDBOURT, U. (1976). Angina pectoris among 10,000 men: II. Psychosocial and other risk factors as evidenced by a multivariate analysis of a five year incidence study. *American Journal of Medicine, 60,* 910–921.

MEICHENBAUM, D. (1977). *Cognitive behavior modification.* New York: Plenum Press.

MELAMED, B. G., MEYER, R., GEE, C., & SOULE, L. (1976). The influence of time and type of preparation on children's adjustment to hospitalization. *Journal of Pediatric Psychology, 1,* 31–37.

MELAMED, B. G., & SIEGEL, L. J. (1975). Reduction of anxiety in children facing hospitalization and surgery by use of filmed modeling. *Journal of Consulting and Clinical Psychology, 43,* 511–521.

MELAMED, S. (1987). Emotional reactivity and elevated blood pressure. *Psychosomatic Medicine, 49,* 217–225.

MELEIS, A. I., & FARRELL, K. M. (1974). Operation concern: A study of senior nursing students in three nursing programs. *Nursing Research, 23,* 461–468.

MELZACK, R. (1973). *The puzzle of pain.* New York: Basic Books.

MELZACK, R. (1975a). The McGill pain questionnaire: Major properties and scoring methods. *Pain, 1,* 277–299.

MELZACK, R. (1975b). The promise of biofeedback: Don't hold the party yet. *Psychology Today, 9,* 18–22.

MELZACK, R., & DENNIS, S. G. (1978). Neurophysiological foundations of pain. In R. A. Sternbach (Ed.), *The psychology of pain* (pp. 1–26). New York: Raven Press.

MELZACK, R., & PERRY, C. (1975). Self-regulation of pain: The use of alpha-feedback and hypnotic training for the control of pain. *Experimental Neurology, 46,* 452–469.

MELZACK, R., & TORGERSON, W. S. (1971). On the language of pain. *Anesthesiology, 34,* 50–59.

MELZACK, R., & WALL, P. D. (1965). Pain mechanisms: A new theory. *Science, 150,* 971–979.

MELZACK, R., & WALL, P. D. (1983). *The challenge of pain.* New York: Basic Books.

MERSKEY, H. (1978). Pain and personality. In R. A. Sternbach (Ed.), *The psychology of pain* (pp. 111–127). New York: Raven Press.

MEYER, A. (1919/1948). The life chart. In A. Lief (Ed.), *The commonsense psychiatry of Dr. Adolf Meyer* (pp. 418–422). New York: McGraw-Hill.

MEYER, A. J., NASH, J. D., MCALISTER, A. L., MACCOBY, N., & FARQUHAR, J. W. (1980). Skills training in a cardiovascular health education campaign. *Journal of Consulting and Clinical Psychology, 48,* 129–142.

MEYEROWITZ, B. E. (1980). Psychosocial correlates of breast cancer and its treatments. *Psychological Bulletin, 87,* 108–131.

MEYERS, S. M. (1981). Growth in health maintenance organizations. In *Health: United States, 1981* (pp. 75–80). DHHS Pub. No. (PHS) 82-1232. Washington, DC: U.S. Government Printing Office.

MIDANIK, L. T., POLEN, M. R., HUNKELER, E. M., TEKAWA, I. S., & SOGHIKIAN, K. (1985). Methodologic issues in evaluating stop smoking programs. *American Journal of Public Health, 75,* 634–638.

MIDER, P. A. (1984). Failures in alcoholism and drug dependence prevention and learning from the past. *American Psychologist, 39,* 183–184.

MILLAR, W. J., & STEPHENS, T. (1987). The prevalence of overweight and obesity in Britain, Canada, and United States. *American Journal of Public Health, 77,* 38–41.

MILLER, G. H., & GERSTEIN, D. R. (1983). The life expectancy of nonsmoking men and women. *Public Health Reports, 98,* 343–349.

MILLER, H. L., FOWLER, R. D., & BRIDGERS, W. F. (1982). The public health psychologist: An ounce of prevention is not enough. *American Psychologist, 37,* 945–948.

MILLER, J. D., & CISIN, I. H. (1983). *Highlights from the National Survey on Drug Abuse: 1982.* DHHS Pub. No. (ADM) 83-1277. Washington, DC: U.S. Government Printing Office.

MILLER, L. S., & CROSS, H. J. (1985). Hypnotic susceptibility, hypnosis, and EMG biofeedback in the reduction of frontalis muscle tension. *International Journal of Clinical and Experimental Hypnosis, 33,* 258–272.

MILLER, N. E. (1978). Biofeedback and visceral learning. *Annual Review of Psychology, 29,* 373–404.

MILLER, N. E. (1980). A perspective on the effects of stress and coping on disease and health. In S. Levine & H. Ursin (Eds.), *Coping and health* (pp. 323–353). New York: Plenum.

MILLER, N. E. (1983). Behavioral medicine: Symbiosis between laboratory and clinic. *Annual Review of Psychology, 34,* 1–31.

MILLER, N. E. (1985). Some professional and scientific problems and opportunities for biofeedback. *Biofeedback and Self-Regulation, 10,* 3–24.

MILLER, W. R., & HESTER, R. K. (1986). Inpatient alcoholism treatment: Who benefits? *American Psychologist, 41,* 794–805.

MILLIS, J. (1975). *Pharmacists for the future: The report of the study commission on pharmacy.* Ann Arbor, MI: Health Administration Press.

MILLON, T. (1982). On the nature of clinical health psychology. In T. Millon, C. Green, & R. Meagher (Eds.), *Handbook of clinical health psychology* (pp. 1–25). New York: Plenum.

MILLON, T., GREEN, C. J., & MEAGHER, R. B. (1979). The MBHI: A new inventory for the psychodiagnostician in medical settings. *Professional Psychology, 10,* 529–539.

MILLON, T., GREEN, C. J., & MEAGHER, R. B. (1982). A new psychodiagnostic tool for clients in rehabilitation settings: The MBHI. *Rehabilitation Psychology, 27,* 23–35.

MIROTZNIK, J., SPEEDLING, E., STEIN, R., & BRONZ, C. (1985). Cardiovascular fitness program: Factors associated with participation and adherence. *Public Health Reports, 100,* 13–18.

MIZRAHI, T. (1984). Managing medical mistakes: Ideology, insularity and accountability among internists-in-training. *Social Science and Medicine, 19,* 135–146.

MODLIN, H. C., & MONTES, A. (1964). Narcotics addiction in physicians. *American Journal of Psychiatry, 121,* 358–369.

MOLUMPHY, S. D., & SPORAKOWSKI, M. J. (1984). The family stress of hemodialysis. *Family Relations, 33,* 33–39.

MONROE, S. M. (1983a). Major and minor life events as predictors of psychological distress: Further issues and findings. *Journal of Behavioral Medicine, 6,* 189–205.

MONROE, S. M. (1983b). Social support and disorder: Toward an untangling of cause and effect. *American Journal of Community Psychology, 11,* 81–97.

MONTGOMERY, R.J.V., GONYEA, J. G., & HOOYMAN, N. R. (1985). Caregiving and the experience of subjective and objective burden. *Family Relations, 34,* 19–26.

MOON, J. R., & EISLER, R. M. (1983). Anger control: An experimental comparison of three behavioral treatments. *Behavior Therapy, 14,* 493–505.

MOORE, N. (1965). Behaviour therapy in bronchial asthma: A controlled study. *Journal of Psychosomatic Research, 9,* 257–276.

MORGAN, W. M., & CURRAN, J. W. (1986). Acquired immunodeficiency syndrome: Current and future trends. *Public Health Reports, 101.* 459–465.

MORRIS, P. B., & GRASSI-RUSSO, N. (1979). Motives of beginning students for choosing nursing school. *Journal of Nursing Education, 18,* 34–40.

MORRISON, D. M. (1985). Adolescent contraceptive behavior: A review. *Psychological Bulletin, 98,* 538–568.

MORRISON, F. R., & PAFFENBARGER, R. A. (1981). Epidemiological aspects of biobehavior in the etiology of cancer: A critical review. In S. M. Weiss, J. A. Herd, & B. H. Fox (Eds.), *Perspectives on behavioral medicine: Proceedings of the Academy of Behavioral Medicine Research Conference, Snowbird, Utah, June 3–6, 1979* (pp. 135–161). New York: Academic Press.

MOSHER, J. F. (1982). Federal tax law and public health policy: The case of alcohol-related tax expenditures. *Journal of Public Health Policy, 3,* 260–283.

MOSHER, J. F. (1983a). Tax-deductible alcohol: An issue of public health policy and prevention strategy. *Journal of Health Politics, Policy and Law, 7,* 855–888.

MOSHER, J. F.   (1983b). Server intervention: A new approach for preventing drinking driving. *Accident Analysis & Prevention, 15,* 483–497.

MOSHER, J. F., & WALLACK, L. M.   (1981). Government regulation of alcohol advertising: Protecting industry profits versus promoting the public health. *Journal of Public Health Policy, 2,* 333–353.

MOULDING, T. S.   (1979). The unrealized potential of the medication monitor. *Clinical Pharmacology and Therapeutics, 25,* 131–136.

MOULDING, T., ONSTAD, G. D., & SBARBARO, J. A.   (1970). Supervision of outpatient drug therapy with the medication monitor. *Annals of Internal Medicine, 73,* 559–564.

MULTIPLE RISK FACTOR INTERVENTION TRIAL GROUP.   (1978). The multiple risk factor intervention trial. *Annals of the New York Academy of Science, 304,* 293–308.

MUMFORD, E.   (1983). Stress in the medical career. *Journal of Medical Education, 58,* 436–437.

MUMFORD, E., SCHLESINGER, H. J., & GLASS, G. V.   (1982). The effects of psychological intervention on recovery from surgery and heart attacks: An analysis of the literature. *American Journal of Public Health, 72,* 141–151.

MUÑOZ, R. F., GLISH, M., SOO-HOO, T., & ROBERTSON, J.   (1982). The San Francisco mood-survey project: Preliminary work toward the prevention of depression. *American Journal of Community Psychology, 10,* 317–329.

MURPHY, J. K., SPERR, E. V., & SPERR, S. J.   (1986). Chronic pain: An investigation of assessment instruments. *Journal of Psychosomatic Research, 30,* 289–296.

MURRELL, S. A., & NORRIS, F. H.   (1984). Resources, life events, and changes in positive affect and depression in older adults. *American Journal of Community Psychology, 12,* 445–464.

MURRELL, S. A., NORRIS, F. H., & HUTCHINS, G. L.   (1984). Distribution and desirability of life events in older adults: Population and policy implications. *Journal of Community Psychology, 12,* 301–311.

MUSHLIN, A. I., & APPEL, F. A.   (1977). Diagnosing potential noncompliance: Physicians' ability in a behavioral dimension of medical care. *Archives of Internal Medicine, 137,* 318–321.

NADITCH, M.   (1984a). Computer assisted worksite health promotion: The fit between workers and programs. *Corporate Commentary, 1,* 40–48.

NADITCH, M. P.   (1984b). The STAYWELL program. In J. D. Matarazzo, S. M. Weiss, J. A. Herd, N. E. Miller, & S. M. Weiss (Eds.), *Behavioral health: A handbook of health enhancement and disease prevention* (pp. 1071–1078). New York: Wiley.

NATHAN, P. E.   (1983). Failures in prevention: Why we can't prevent the devastating effect of alcoholism and drug abuse. *American Psychologist, 38,* 459–467.

NATHAN, P. E.   (1984a). The worksite as a setting for health promotion and positive lifestyle change. In J. D. Matarazzo, S. M. Weiss, J. A. Herd, N. E.

Miller, & S. M. Weiss (Eds.), *Behavioral health: A handbook of health enhancement and disease prevention* (pp. 1061–1063). New York: Wiley.

NATHAN, P. E.   (1984b). Johnson & Johnson's live for life: A comprehensive positive lifestyle change program. In J. D. Matarazzo, S. M. Weiss, J. A. Herd, N. E. Miller, & S. M. Weiss (Eds.), *Behavioral health: A handbook of health enhancement and disease prevention* (pp. 1064–1070). New York: Wiley.

NATIONAL CANCER INSTITUTE.   (1986). *Smoking, tobacco, and cancer program: 1985 report.* NIH Pub. No. 86-2687. Washington, DC: U.S. Government Printing Office.

NATIONAL CENTER FOR HEALTH STATISTICS.   (1983a). *Health, United States, 1983.* DHHS Pub. No. (PHS) 84-1232. Washington, DC: U.S. Government Printing Office.

NATIONAL CENTER FOR HEALTH STATISTICS.   (1983b). Americans assess their health: United States, 1978. *Vital and Health Statistics,* Series 10, No. 142. DHHS Pub. No. (PHS) 83-1570. Washington, DC: U.S. Government Printing Office.

NATIONAL CENTER FOR HEALTH STATISTICS.   (1983c). Physician visits: Volume and interval since last visit, United States, 1980. *Vital and Health Statistics,* Series 10, No. 144. DHHS Pub. No. (PHS) 83-1572. Washington, DC: U.S. Government Printing Office.

NATIONAL CENTER FOR HEALTH STATISTICS.   (1983d). Comparison of health expenditures in France and the United States, 1950–1978. *Vital and Health Statistics,* Series 3, No. 21. DHHS Pub. No. (PHS) 83-1045. Washington, DC: U.S. Government Printing Office.

NATIONAL CENTER FOR HEALTH STATISTICS.   (1983e). Disability days: United States, 1980. *Vital and Health Statistics,* Series 10, No. 143. DHHS Pub. No. (PHS) 83-1571. Washington, DC: U.S. Government Printing Office.

NATIONAL CENTER FOR HEALTH STATISTICS.   (1983f). Americans needing help to function at home. *Advance Data from Vital and Health Statistics,* No. 92. DHHS Pub. No. (PHS) 83-1250. Washington, DC: U.S. Government Printing Office.

NATIONAL CENTER FOR HEALTH STATISTICS.   (1983g). Drugs most frequently used in office practice: National ambulatory medical care survey, 1981. *Advance Data from Vital and Health Statistics.* No. 89. DHHS Pub. No. (PHS) 83-1250. Washington, DC: U.S. Government Printing Office.

NATIONAL CENTER FOR HEALTH STATISTICS.   (1984a). *Health, United States, 1984.* DHHS Pub. No. (PHS) 85-1232. Washington, DC: U.S. Government Printing Office.

NATIONAL CENTER FOR HEALTH STATISTICS.   (1984b). The management of new pain in office-based ambulatory care: National ambulatory medical care survey, 1980 and 1981. *Advance Data from Vital and Health Statistics,* No. 97. DHHS Pub. No. (PHS) 84-1250. Washington, DC: U.S. Government Printing Office.

NATIONAL CENTER FOR HEALTH STATISTICS.   (1984c). Use of contraception in the United States, 1982. *Advance Data from Vital and Health Statistics*. No. 102. DHHS Pub. No. (PHS) 85-1250. Washington, DC: U.S. Government Printing Office.

NATIONAL CENTER FOR HEALTH STATISTICS. (1985a). Provisional data from the health promotion and disease prevention supplement to the national health interview survey: United States, January–March 1985. *Advance Data from Vital and Health Statistics*. No. 113. DHHS Pub. No. (PHS) 86-1250. Washington, DC: U.S. Government Printing Office.

NATIONAL CENTER FOR HEALTH STATISTICS. (1985b). Annual summary of births, marriages, divorces, and deaths. United States, 1984. *Monthly Vital Statistics Report, 33*, No. 13, DHHS Pub. No. (PHS) 85-1120. Hyattsville, MD: Public Health Service.

NATIONAL CENTER FOR HEALTH STATISTICS. (1985c). Persons injured and disability days due to injuries: United States, 1980–1981. *Vital and Health Statistics,* Series 10, No. 149. DHHS Pub. No. (PHS) 85-1577. Washington, DC: U.S. Government Printing Office.

NATIONAL CENTER FOR HEALTH STATISTICS. (1985d). Utilization of short-stay hospitals: United States, 1983 annual summary. *Vital and Health Statistics,* Series 13, No. 83. DHHS Pub. No. (PHS) 85-1744. Washington, DC: U.S. Government Printing Office.

NATIONAL CENTER FOR HEALTH STATISTICS. (1985e). Health characteristics according to family and personal income: United States. *Vital and Health Statistics,* Series 10, No. 147. DHHS Pub. No. (PHS) 85-1575. Washington, DC: U.S. Government Printing Office.

NATIONAL CENTER FOR HEALTH STATISTICS. (1985f). *Charting the nation's health: Trends since 1960*. DHHS Pub. No. (PHS) 85-1251. Washington, DC: U.S. Government Printing Office.

NATIONAL CENTER FOR HEALTH STATISTICS. (1985g). *Health: United States, 1985*. DHHS Pub. No. (PHS) 86-1232. Washington, DC: U.S. Government Printing Office.

NATIONAL CENTER FOR HEALTH STATISTICS. (1985h). Office-based ambulatory care for patients 75 years old and over: National ambulatory medical care survey, 1980 and 1981. *Advance Data from Vital and Health Statistics*. No. 110, DHHS Pub. No. (PHS) 85-1250. Washington, DC: U.S. Government Printing Office.

NATIONAL CENTER FOR HEALTH STATISTICS. (1985i). Wanted and unwanted childbearing: United States, 1973–82. *Advance Data from Vital and Health Statistics*. No. 108. DHHS Pub. No. (PHS) 85-1250. Washington, DC: U.S. Government Printing Office.

NATIONAL CENTER FOR HEALTH STATISTICS. (1985j). Marriage and first intercourse, marital dissolution, and remarriage: United States, 1982. *Advance Data from Vital and Health Statistics*. No. 107. DHHS Pub. No. (PHS) 85-1250. Washington, DC: U.S. Government Printing Office.

NATIONAL CENTER FOR HEALTH STATISTICS. (1986a). Perinatal mortality in the United States: 1950–1981. *Monthly Vital Statistics Report, 34*(12) *Supp.* DHHS Pub. No. (PHS) 86-1120. Washington, DC: U.S. Government Printing Office.

NATIONAL CENTER FOR HEALTH STATISTICS.  (1986b). Aging in the eighties: Preliminary data from the supplement on aging to the National Health Interview Survey, United States, January–June 1984. *Advance Data from Vital and Health Statistics,* No. 115. May 1, 1986. DHHS Publ. No. (PHS) 86-1250. Washington, DC: U.S. Government Printing Office.

NATIONAL CENTER FOR HEALTH STATISTICS.  (1986c). Advance report of final natality statistics, 1984. *Monthly Vital Statistics Report, 34*(4) *Supp.* DHHS Pub. No. (PHS) 86-1120. Washington, DC: U.S. Government Printing Office.

NATIONAL CENTER FOR HEALTH STATISTICS.  (1986d). Advance report of final mortality statistics, 1984. *Monthly Vital Statistics Report, 35*(6) *Supp.*(2). DHHS Pub. No. (PHS) 86-1120. Washington, DC: U.S. Government Printing Office.

NATIONAL CENTER FOR HEALTH STATISTICS.  (1986e). 1985 summary: National hospital discharge survey. *Advance Data from Vital and Health Statistics.* No. 127. DHHS Pub. No (PHS) 86-1250. Washington, DC: U.S. Government Printing Office.

NATIONAL CENTER FOR HEALTH STATISTICS.  (1986f). Trends in smoking, alcohol consumption, and other health practices among U.S. adults, 1977 and 1983. *Advance Data from Vital and Health Statistics.* No. 118. DHHS Pub. No. (PHS) 86-1250. Washington, DC: U.S. Government Printing Office.

NATIONAL CENTER FOR HEALTH STATISTICS.  (1986g). The management of chronic pain in office-based ambulatory care: National ambulatory medical care survey. *Advance Data from Vital and Health Statistics.* No. 123. DHHS Pub. No. (PHS) 86-1250. Washington, DC: U.S. Government Printing Office.

NATIONAL CENTER FOR HEALTH STATISTICS.  (1987). 1985 summary: National ambulatory medical care survey. *Advance Data from Vital and Health Statistics.* No. 128. DHHS Pub. No. (PHS) 87-1250. Washington, DC: U.S. Government Printing Office.

NATIONAL INSTITUTE OF DRUG ABUSE.  (1985). *Epidemiology of heroin: 1964–1984.* Washington, DC: U.S. Government Printing Office.

NATIONAL INSTITUTES OF HEALTH  (1984). *Consensus development conference statement: Lowering blood cholesterol to prevent heart disease.* December 10–12, 1984. Washington, DC: National Heart, Lung, and Blood Institute.

NATIONAL SAFETY COUNCIL  (1982). *Accident facts.* Chicago, IL: National Safety Council.

NELSON, D. W., & COHEN, L. H.  (1983). Locus of control and control perceptions and the relationship between life stress and psychological disorder. *American Journal of Community Psychology, 11,* 705–722.

NELSON, E. G., & HENRY, W. F.   (1978). Psychosocial factors seen as problems by family practice residents and their spouses. *Journal of Family Practice, 6,* 581–589.

NESBITT, P. D.   (1973). Smoking, physiological arousal, and emotional response. *Journal of Personality and Social Psychology, 25,* 127–145.

NEUFELD, V. R.   (1976). Patient education: A critique. In D. L. Sackett & R. B. Haynes (Eds.), *Compliance with therapeutic regimens* (pp. 83–92). Baltimore, MD: Johns Hopkins University Press.

NEW DEFINITIONS: REPORT OF THE 1972–1973 JOINT COMMITTEE ON HEALTH EDUCATION TERMINOLOGY.   (1974). *Journal of School Health, 44,* 33–35.

NEWCOMB, M. D., MADDAHIAN, E., & BENTLER, P. M.   (1986). Risk factors for drug use among adolescents: Concurrent and longitudinal analyses. *American Journal of Public Health, 76,* 525–531.

NEWMAN, R. I., SERES, J. L., YOSPE, L. P., & GARLINGTON, B.   (1978). Multidisciplinary treatment of chronic pain: Long-term follow-up of low-back pain patients. *Pain, 4,* 283–292.

NEWSOM, J. A.   (1977). Help for the alcoholic physician in California. *Alcoholism: Clinical and Experimental Research, 1*(2), 135–137.

NORBECK, J. S.   (1981). Social support: A model for clinical research and application. *Advances in Nursing Science, 3,* 43–59.

NORBECK, J. S., LINDSEY, A. M., & CARRIERI, V. L.   (1981). The development of an instrument to measure social support. *Nursing Research, 30,* 264–269.

NORBECK, J. S., & TILDEN, V. P.   (1983). Life stress, social support, and emotional disequilibrium in complications of pregnancy: A prospective multivariate study. *Journal of Health and Social Behavior, 24,* 30–46.

NOUWEN, A., & SOLINGER, J.   (1979). The effectiveness of EMG biofeedback training in low back pain. *Biofeedback and Self-Regulation, 4,* 103–111.

NUNES, E. V., FRANK, K. A., & KORNFELD, D. S.   (1987). Psychologic treatment for the Type A behavior pattern and for coronary heart disease: A meta-analysis of the literature. *Psychosomatic Medicine, 48,* 159–173.

OCKENE, J. K., NUTTALL, R., BENFARI, R. C., HURWITZ, I., & OCKENE, I. S.   (1981). A psychosocial model of smoking cessation and maintenance of cessation. *Preventive Medicine, 10,* 623–637.

O'CONNOR, W. A., & AHMED, P. I.   (1979). Psychosocial dimensions of drug abuse. In P. I. Ahmed & G. V. Coelho (Eds.), *Toward a new definition of health: Psychosocial dimensions* (pp. 159–173). New York: Plenum.

OFFICE OF TECHNOLOGY ASSESSMENT.   (1985). *Smoking-related deaths and financial costs.* Health Program Staff memo, Sept., 1985.

OGLE, W.   (1886). Statistics of mortality in the medical profession. *Medico-Chirurgical Transactions, 69,* 217–237.

OLBRISCH, M. E.   (1977). Psychotherapeutic interventions in physical health: Effectiveness and economic efficiency. *American Psychologist, 32,* 761–777.

OLBRISCH, M. E., WEISS, S. M., STONE, G. C., & SCHWARTZ, G. E.   (1985). Report of the national working conference on education and training in health psychology. *American Psychologist, 40,* 1038–1041.

OLDRIDGE, N. B.   (1984). Adherence to adult exercise fitness programs. In J. D. Matarazzo, S. M. Weiss, J. A. Herd, N. E. Miller, & S. M. Weiss (Eds.), *Behavioral health: A handbook of health enhancement and disease prevention* (pp. 467–487). New York: Wiley.

OLSON, K. R., & SCHELLENBERG, R. P.   (1986). Farm stressors. *American Journal of Community Psychology, 14,* 555–569.

ORNE, M. T.   (1976). Mechanisms of hypnotic pain control. In J. J. Bonica & D. Albe-Fessard (Eds.), *Advances in pain research and therapy: Vol. 1* (pp. 717–726). New York: Raven Press.

ORTON, I. K., BEIMAN, I., & CIMINERO, A. R.   (1982). The behavioral assessment and treatment of essential hypertension. In D. M. Doleys, R. L. Meredith, & A. R. Ciminero (Eds.), *Behavioral medicine: Assessment and treatment strategies* (pp. 175–198). New York: Plenum.

OSTER, G., & EPSTEIN, A. M.   (1986). Primary prevention and coronary heart disease: The economic benefits of lowering serum cholesterol. *American Journal of Public Health, 76,* 647–656.

OSTER, G., HUSE, D. M., DELEA, T. E., & COLDITZ, G. A.   (1986). Cost-effectiveness of nicotine gum as an adjunct to physician's advice against cigarette smoking. *Journal of the American Medical Association, 256,* 1315–1318.

PANEL ON THE GENERAL PROFESSIONAL EDUCATION OF THE PHYSICIAN AND COLLEGE PREPARATION FOR MEDICINE.   (1984). *Physicians for the twenty-first century.* Washington, DC: Association of American Medical Colleges.

PARIS, J., & FRANK, H.   (1983). Psychological determinants of a medical career. *Canadian Journal of Psychiatry, 28,* 354–357.

PARKES, C. M.   (1981). Evaluation of a bereavement service. *Journal of Preventive Psychiatry, 1,* 179–188.

PARLOW, J., & ROTHMAN, A. I.   (1974). ATSIM: A scale to measure attitudes toward psychosocial factors in health care. *Journal of Medical Education, 49,* 385–387.

PARSONS, T.   (1958). Definitions of health and illness in the light of American values and social structure. In E. G. Jaco (Ed.), *Patients, physicians and illness* (pp. 165–187). New York: Free Press.

PATEL, C. H., MARMOT, M. G., & TERRY, D. J.   (1981). Controlled trial of biofeedback-aided behavioral methods in reducing mild hypertension. *British Medical Journal, 282,* 2005–2008.

PATEL, C. H., & NORTH, W.R.S.   (1975). Randomised controlled trial of yoga and biofeedback in management of hypertension. *Lancet, 2,* 93–95.

PATTERSON, J. M.   (1985). Critical factors affecting family compliance with home treatment for children with cystic fibrosis. *Family Relations, 34,* 79–89.

PAULSON, S. M., KRAUSE, S., & IBER, F. L.   (1977). Development and evaluation of a compliance test for patients taking disulfiram. *Johns Hopkins Medical Journal, 141,* 119–125.

PEARCE, T. L., & SHELDON, G. F.   (1984). Subgroup report on personal management skills. *Journal of Medical Education, 59,* 173–176.

PEARLIN, L. I. (1983). Role strains and personal stress. In H. B. Kaplan (Ed.), *Psychosocial stress: Trends in theory and research* (pp. 3–32). New York: Academic Press.

PEARSON, M. M. (1982). Psychiatric treatment of 250 physicians. *Psychiatric Annals, 12,* 194–206.

PECHACEK, T. F., & McALISTER, A. L. (1980). Strategies for the modification of smoking behavior: Treatment and prevention. In J. M. Ferguson & C. B. Taylor (Eds.), *The comprehensive handbook of behavioral medicine: Vol. 3. Extended applications & issues* (pp. 257–298). New York: SP Medical & Scientific Books.

PECK, C. L., & KRAFT, G. H. (1977). Electromyographic biofeedback for pain related to muscle tension. *Archives of Surgery, 112,* 889–895.

PENNEBAKER, J. W. (1982). *The psychology of physical symptoms.* New York: Springer-Verlag.

PEPITONE-ARREOLA-ROCKWELL, F., ROCKWELL, D., & CORE, N. (1981). Fifty-two medical student suicides. *American Journal of Psychiatry, 138,* 198–201.

PERLOFF, J. D., LeBAILLY, S. A., KLETKE, P. R., BUDETTI, P. P., & CONNELLY, J. P. (1984). Premature death in the United States: Years of life lost and health priorities. *Journal of Public Health Policy, 5,* 167–184.

PERRY, C. L., & JESSOR, R. (1985). The concept of health promotion and the prevention of adolescent drug abuse. *Health Education Quarterly, 12,* 169–184.

PETERSDORF, R. G., & FEINSTEIN, A. R. (1981). An informal appraisal of the current status of 'medical sociology'. *Journal of the American Medical Association, 245,* 943–950.

PFEIFFER, R. J. (1983). Early-adult development in the medical student. *Mayo Clinic Proceedings, 58,* 127–134.

PFIFFERLING, J. H. (1983). Coping with residency distress. *Resident & Staff Physician, 29,* 105–111.

PIGG, R. M. (1982). A national study on professional preparation in patient education. *American Journal of Public Health, 72,* 180–182.

PILOWSKY, I. (1978a). Psychodynamic aspects of the pain experience. In R. A. Sternbach (Ed.), *The psychology of pain* (pp. 203–217). New York: Raven Press.

PILOWSKY, I. (1978b). Pain as abnormal illness behaviour. *Journal of Human Stress, 4,* 22–27.

PILOWSKY, I. (1978c). A general classification of abnormal illness behaviours. *British Journal of Medical Psychology, 51,* 131–137.

PILOWSKY, I., CHAPMAN, C. R., & BONICA, J. J. (1977). Pain, depression, and illness behavior in a pain clinic population. *Pain, 4,* 183–192.

PILOWSKY, I., & SPENCE, N. D. (1975). Patterns of illness behaviour in patients with intractable pain. *Journal of Psychosomatic Research, 19,* 279–287.

PILOWSKY, I., & SPENCE, N. D. (1976a). Pain and illness behaviour: A comparative study. *Journal of Psychosomatic Research, 20,* 131–134.

PILOWSKY, I., & SPENCE, N. D. (1976b). Is illness behaviour related to chronicity in patients with intractable pain? *Pain, 2,* 167–173.

PILOWSKY, I., & SPENCE, N. D. (1976c). Illness behaviour syndromes associated with intractable pain. *Pain, 2,* 61–71.

PINKERTON, S. S., HUGHES, H., & WENRICH, W. W. (1982). *Behavioral medicine: Clinical applications.* New York: Wiley & Sons.

POMERLEAU, O. F. (1979). Behavioral medicine: The contribution of the experimental analysis of behavior to medical care. *American Psychologist, 34,* 654–663.

POMERLEAU, O. F. (1982). A discourse on behavioral medicine: Current status and future trends. *Journal of Consulting and Clinical Psychology, 50,* 1030–1039.

POMERLEAU, O. F., & BRADY, J. P. (1979). Introduction: The scope and promise of behavioral medicine. In O. F. Pomerleau & J. P. Brady (Eds.), *Behavioral medicine: Theory and practice* (pp. xi–xxvi). Baltimore, MD: Williams & Wilkins.

POOLE, A. D., & SANSON-FISHER, R. W. (1979). Understanding the patient: A neglected aspect of medical education. *Social Science and Medicine, 13A,* 37–43.

PRATT, C. C., SCHMALL, V. L., WRIGHT, S., & CLELAND, M. (1985). Burden and coping strategies of caregivers to Alzheimer's patients. *Family Relations, 34,* 27–33.

PRESIDENT'S COMMITTEE ON HEALTH EDUCATION (1973). *Report.* New York: Author.

PRICE, K. P. (1974). The application of behavior therapy to the treatment of psychosomatic disorders: Retrospect and prospect. *Psychotherapy: Theory, Research, and Practice, 11,* 138–155.

PUSKA, P., MCALISTER, A., NIEMENSIVU, H., PIHA, T., WIIO, J., & KOSKELA, K. (1987). A television format for national health promotion: Finland's "keys to health." *Public Health Reports, 102,* 263–269.

PYLE, G. F. (1983). Three decades of medical geography in the United States. In McGlashan, N. D., & Blunden, J. R. (Eds.), *Geographical aspects of health* (pp. 81–101). London: Academic Press.

QUALLS, P. J., & SHEEHAN, P. W. (1981). Electromyography biofeedback as a relaxation technique: A critical appraisal and reassessment. *Psychological Bulletin, 90,* 21–42.

QUAYLE, D. (1983). American productivity: The devastating effect of alcoholism and drug abuse. *American Psychologist, 38,* 454–458.

QUILL, T. E., LIPKIN, M., & LAMB, G. S. (1984). Health-care seeking by men in their spouse's pregnancy. *Psychosomatic Medicine, 46,* 277–283.

RABKIN, J. G. (1980). Stressful life events and schizophrenia: A review of the research literature. *Psychological Bulletin, 87,* 408–425.

RAHE, R. H. (1974). The pathway between subjects' recent life changes and their near-future illness reports: Representative results and methodological issues. In B. S. Dohrenwend & B. P. Dohrenwend (Eds.), *Stressful life events: Their nature and effects* (pp. 73–86). New York: Wiley & Sons.

RAHE, R. H. (1979). Life change events and mental illness: An overview. *Journal of Human Stress, 5,* 2–10.

RAHE, R. H., WARD, H. W., & HAYES, V. (1979). Brief group therapy in myocardial infarction rehabilitation: Three- to four-year follow-up of a controlled trial. *Psychosomatic Medicine, 41,* 229–242.

RAINWATER, N., & ALEXANDER, A. B. (1982). Respiratory disorders: Asthma. In D. M. Doleys, R. L. Meredith, & A. R. Ciminero (Eds.), *Behavioral medicine: Assessment and treatment strategies.* (pp. 435–446). New York: Plenum.

RAMESH, A. (1983). Developments in medical geography in India. In McGlashan, N. D., & Blunden, J. R. (Eds.), *Geographical aspects of health* (pp. 119–136). London: Academic Press.

RAPHAEL, B. (1977). Preventive intervention with the recently bereaved. *Archives of General Psychiatry, 34,* 1450–1454.

RAPHAEL, B. (1978). Mourning and the prevention of melancholia. *British Journal of Medical Psychology, 51,* 303–310.

RASKIND, R., & GLOVER, M. B. (1975). Profile of a low back derelict. *Journal of Occupational Medicine, 17,* 258–259.

REDD, W. H. (1982). Behavioural analysis and control of psychosomatic symptoms of patients receiving intensive cancer treatment. *British Journal of Clinical Psychology, 21,* 351–358.

REDD, W. H., & ANDRYKOWSKI, M. A. (1982). Behavioral intervention in cancer treatment: Controlling aversion reactions to chemotherapy. *Journal of Consulting and Clinical Psychology, 50,* 1018–1029.

REGIER, D. A., SHAPIRO, S., KESSLER, L. G., & TAUBE, C. A. (1984). Epidemiology and health service resource allocation policy for alcohol, drug abuse, and mental disorders. *Public Health Reports, 99,* 483–492.

REISINE, S. T. (1985). Dental health and public policy: The social impact of dental disease. *American Journal of Public Health, 75,* 27–30.

RESNICK, M. D. (1984). Studying adolescent mothers' decision making about adoption and parenting. *Social Work, 29,* 5–10.

REYNOLDS, R. A., & ABRAM, J. B. (EDS.). (1983). *Socioeconomic characteristics of medical practice 1983.* Chicago, IL: American Medical Association.

REYNOLDS S. B. (1984). Biofeedback, relaxation training, and music: Homeostasis for coping with stress. *Biofeedback and Self-Regulation, 9,* 169–179.

REZLER, A. G. (1974). Attitude changes during medical school: A review of the literature. *Journal of Medical Education, 49,* 1023–1030.

RICE, D. P., & KLEINMAN, J. C. (1980). National health data for policy and planning. *Health Policy Education, 1,* 129–141.

RICHARDSON, W. C. (1970). Measuring the urban poor's use of physicians' services in response to illness episodes. *Medical Care, 8,* 132–142.

RICKLES, W. H., ONODA, L., & DOYLE, C. C. (1982). Task force study section report: Biofeedback as an adjunct to psychotherapy. *Biofeedback and Self-Regulation, 7,* 1–33.

RILEY, V. (1981). Psychoneuroendocrine influences on immunocompetence and neoplasia. *Science, 212,* 1100–1109.

ROBBINS, A. (1984). Creating a progressive health agenda: 1983 Presidential address. *American Journal of Public Health, 74,* 775–779.

ROBERTS, A. H. (1981). The behavioral treatment of pain. In J. M. Ferguson & C. B. Taylor (Eds.), *The comprehensive handbook of behavioral medicine: Vol. 2—Syndromes & special areas* (pp. 171–189). New York: SP Medical & Scientific Books.

ROBERTS, N., BENNETT, S., & SMITH, R. (1986). Psychological factors associated with disability in arthritis. *Journal of Psychosomatic Research, 30,* 223–231.

ROBINSON, J. O., & GRANFIELD, A. J. (1986). The frequent consulter in primary medical care. *Journal of Psychosomatic Research, 30,* 589–600.

ROCCELLA, E. J. (1985). Meeting the 1990 hypertension objectives for the nation—A progress report. *Public Health Reports, 100,* 652–656.

ROCCELLA, E. J., & WARD, G. W. (1984). The national high blood pressure education program: A description of its utility as a generic program model. *Health Education Quarterly, 11,* 225–242.

ROE, B. B. (1985). Rational remuneration. *New England Journal of Medicine, 313,* 1286–1289.

ROEMER, M. I. (1980a). Private health insurance in a national health program: The U.S. experience. *Journal of Public Health Policy, 1,* 166–176.

ROEMER, M. I. (1980b). A world perspective on health care in the twentieth century. *Journal of Public Health Policy, 1,* 370–378.

ROEMER, M. I. (1984). The value of medical care for health promotion. *American Journal of Public Health, 74,* 243–248.

ROEMER, M. I. (1985). I. S. Falk, the committee on the costs of medical care, and the drive for national health insurance. *American Journal of Public Health, 75,* 841–848.

ROGERS, M. P., DUBEY, D., & REICH, P. (1979). The influence of the psyche and the brain on immunity and disease susceptibility: A critical review. *Psychosomatic Medicine, 41,* 147–164.

ROGERS, J., VACHON, M.L.S., LYALL, W. A., SHELDON, A., & FREEMAN, S.J.J. (1980). A self-help program for widows as an independent community service. *Hospital & Community Psychiatry, 31,* 844–847.

ROMANO, J. M., & TURNER, J. A. (1985). Chronic pain and depression: Does the evidence support a relationship? *Psychological Bulletin, 97,* 18–34.

ROSE, K. D., & ROSOW, I. (1973). Physicians who kill themselves. *Archives of General Psychiatry, 29,* 800–805.

ROSEN, J. C., & WIENS, A. N. (1979). Changes in medical problems and use of medical services following psychological intervention; *American Psychologist, 34,* 420–431.

ROSEN, R. H. (1984). Worksite health promotion: Fact or fantasy. *Corporate Commentary, 1,* 1–8.

ROSENBAUM, L. (1983). Biofeedback-assisted stress management for insulin-treated diabetes mellitus. *Biofeedback and Self-Regulation, 8,* 519–532.

ROSENBAUM, R. (1976). Stress in medical education. *Journal of Medical Education, 51,* 205.

ROSENBERG, P. P. (1971). Students' perceptions and concerns during their first year in medical school. *Journal of Medical Education, 46,* 211–218.

ROSENBLATT, M. B. (1976). History of bronchial asthma. In E. B. Weiss & M. S. Segal (Eds.), *Bronchial asthma: Mechanisms and therapeutics* (pp. 5–17). Boston, MA: Little, Brown.

ROSENMAN, R. H. (1985). Health consequences of anger and implications for treatment. In M. A. Chesney & R. H. Rosenman (Eds.), *Anger and hostility in cardiovascular and behavioral disorders* (pp. 103–125). Washington, DC: Hemisphere.

ROSENMAN, R. H., BRAND, R. J., SHOLTZ, R. I., & FRIEDMAN, M. (1976). Multivariate prediction of coronary heart disease during 8.5 year follow-up in the Western Collaborative Group Study. *American Journal of Cardiology, 37,* 902–910.

ROSENMAN, R. H., FRIEDMAN, M., STRAUS, R., WURM, M., JENKINS, C. D., & MESSINGER, H. B. (1966). Coronary heart disease in the Western collaborative group study. *Journal of the American Medical Association, 195,* 130–136.

ROSENMAN, R. H., FRIEDMAN, M., STRAUS, R., WURM, M., KOSITCHEK, R., HAHN, W., & WERTHESSEN, N. T. (1964). A predictive study of coronary heart disease: The Western collaborative group study. *Journal of the American Medical Association, 189,* 103–110.

ROSENSTOCK, I. M., & KIRSCHT, J. P. (1979). Why people seek health care. In G. C. Stone, F. Cohen, & N. E. Adler (Eds.), *Health psychology: A handbook* (pp. 161–188). San Francisco, CA: Jossey-Bass.

ROSS, C. E., & DUFF, R. S. (1982). Returning to the doctor: The effect of client characteristics, type of practice, and experiences with care. *Journal of Health and Social Behavior, 23,* 119–131.

ROSS, C. E., MIROWSKY, J., & DUFF, R. S. (1982). Physician status characteristics and client satisfaction in two types of medical practice. *Journal of Health and Social Behavior, 23,* 317–329.

ROSS, C. E., WHEATON, B., & DUFF, R. S. (1981). Client satisfaction and the organization of medical practice: Why time counts. *Journal of Health and Social Behavior, 22,* 243–255.

ROSS, M. (1971). Suicide among physicians. *Psychiatry in Medicine, 2,* 189–198.

ROTH, S., & COHEN, L. J. (1986). Approach, avoidance, and coping with stress. *American Psychologist, 41,* 813–819.

ROTTER, J. B. (1966). Generalized expectancies for internal versus external control of reinforcement. *Psychological Monographs, 80,* No. 609.

ROUECHÉ, B. (1984). Annals of medicine: A contemporary touch. *The New Yorker,* August 13, 1984, 76–85.

ROWLAND, K. F. (1977). Environmental events predicting death for the elderly. *Psychological Bulletin, 84,* 349–372.

ROWLAND, L. (1975). Personal communication, December 1, 1975.

ROYBAL, E. R. (1984). Federal involvement in mental health care for the aged: Past and future directions. *American Psychologist, 39,* 163–166.

RUBERMAN, W., WEINBLATT, E., GOLDBERG, J. D., & CHAUDHARY, B. S. (1984). Psychosocial influences on mortality after myocardial infarction. *New England Journal of Medicine, 311,* 552–559.

RUDERMAN, A. J. (1986). Dietary restraint: A theoretical and empirical review. *Psychological Bulletin, 99,* 247–262.

RUDERMAN, F. A. (1981). What is medical sociology? *Journal of the American Medical Association, 245,* 927–929.

RUNYAN, C. W., & EARP, J.A.L. (1985). Epidemiologic evidence and motor vehicle policy making. *American Journal of Public Health, 75,* 354–357.

RUSSEK, H. I. (1960). Emotional stress and coronary heart disease in American physicians. *American Journal of the Medical Sciences, 240,* 711–721.

RUSSEK, H. I. (1962). Emotional stress and coronary heart disease in American physicians, dentists, and lawyers. *American Journal of the Medical Sciences, 243,* 716–725.

RUSSELL, M.A.H., WILSON, C., TAYLOR, C., & BAKER, C. D. (1979). Effect of general practitioners' advice against smoking. *British Medical Journal, 2*(6184), 231–235.

SACKETT, D. L., & HAYNES, R. B. (EDS.). (1976). *Compliance with therapeutic regimens.* Baltimore, MD: Johns Hopkins University Press.

SACKETT, D. L., HAYNES, R. B., GIBSON, E. S., HACKETT, B. C., TAYLOR, D. W., ROBERTS, R. S., & JOHNSON, A. L. (1975). Randomized clinical trial of strategies for improving medication compliance in primary hypertension. *Lancet, 1,* 1205–1207.

SACKETT, D. L., & SNOW, J. C. (1979). The magnitude of compliance and noncompliance. In R. B. Haynes, D. W. Taylor, & D. L. Sackett (Eds.), *Compliance in health care* (pp. 11–22). Baltimore, MD: Johns Hopkins University Press.

SADE, R. M., FLEMING, G. A., & ROSS, G. R. (1984). A survey on the "premedical syndrome." *Journal of Medical Education, 59,* 386–391.

SANDERS, B. S. (1964). Measuring community health levels. *American Journal of Public Health, 54,* 1063–1070.

SARASON, I. G. (1980). Life stress, self-preoccupation and social supports. In I. G. Sarason & C. D. Spielberger (Eds.), *Stress and anxiety,* Vol. 7 (pp. 73–92). Washington, DC: Hemisphere.

SARASON, S. B. (1972). *The creation of settings and the future societies.* San Francisco, CA: Jossey-Bass.

SARGENT, J. D., GREEN, E. E., & WALTERS, E. D. (1973). Preliminary report on the use of autogenic feedback training in the treatment of migraine and tension headaches. *Psychosomatic Medicine, 35,* 129–135.

SCHAPS, E., MOSKOWITZ, J., MALVIN, J., & SCHAEFFER, G.  (1984). *The Napa drug abuse prevention project: Research findings.* DHHS Pub. No. (ADM) 84-1339, Washington, DC: U.S. Government Printing Office.

SCHERG, H.  (1987). Psychosocial factors and disease bias in breast cancer patients. *Psychosomatic Medicine, 49,* 302–312.

SCHERWITZ, L., GRAHAM, L. E., GRANDITS, G., BUEHLER, J., & BILLINGS, J.  (1986). Self-involvement and coronary heart disease incidence in the multiple risk factor intervention trial. *Psychosomatic Medicine, 48,* 187–199.

SCHERWITZ, L., MCKELVAIN, R., LAMAN, C., PATTERSON, J., DUTTON, L., YUSIM, S., LESTER, J., KRAFT, I., ROCHELLE, D., & LEACHMAN, R.  (1983). Type A behavior, self-involvement, and coronary atherosclerosis. *Psychosomatic Medicine, 45,* 47–57.

SCHILLING, R. F., GILCHRIST, L. D., & SCHINKE, S. P.  (1985). Smoking in the workplace: Review of critical issues. *Public Health Reports, 100,* 473–479.

SCHINKE, S. P., GILCHRIST, L. D., & SMALL, R. W.  (1979). Preventing unwanted adolescent pregnancy: A cognitive-behavioral approach. *American Journal of Orthopsychiatry, 49,* 81–88.

SCHINKE, S. P., GILCHRIST, L. D., & SNOW, W. H.  (1985). Skills intervention to prevent cigarette smoking among adolescents. *American Journal of Public Health, 75,* 665–667.

SCHLESINGER, H. J., MUMFORD, E., & GLASS, G. V.  (1980). Mental health services and medical utilization. In G. Vandenbos (Ed.), *Psychotherapy: From practice to research to policy* (pp. 71–102). Beverly Hills, CA: Sage.

SCHLESINGER, M., & DORWART, R.  (1984). Ownership and mental-health services: A reappraisal of the shift toward privately owned facilities. *New England Journal of Medicine, 311,* 959–965.

SCHMIDT, F. N., CARNEY, P., & FITZSIMMONS, G.  (1986). An empirical assessment of the migraine personality type. *Journal of Psychosomatic Research, 30,* 189–197.

SCHNEIDER, R. H., EGAN, B. N., JOHNSON, E. H., DROBNY, H., & JULIUS, S.  (1986). Anger and anxiety in borderline hypertension. *Psychosomatic Medicine, 48,* 242–248.

SCHOFIELD, W.  (1969). The role of psychology in the delivery of health services. *American Psychologist, 24,* 565–584.

SCHULTZ, J. H., & LUTHE, W.  (1959). *Autogenic training: A psychophysiological approach in psychotherapy.* New York: Grune & Stratton.

SCHWARTZ, A. E.  (1985). Bitter pill. *The New Republic,* February 18, 1985.

SCHWARTZ, G. E.  (1982). Testing the biopsychosocial model: The ultimate challenge facing behavioral medicine. *Journal of Consulting and Clinical Psychology, 50,* 1040–1053.

SCHWARTZ, G. E., & WEISS, S. M.  (1978a). Yale conference on behavioral medicine: A proposed definition and statement of goals. *Journal of Behavioral Medicine, 1,* 3–12.

SCHWARTZ, G. E., & WEISS, S. M.    (1978b). Behavioral medicine revisited: An amended definition. *Journal of Behavioral Medicine, 1,* 249–251.

SCITOVSKY, A. A., & RICE, D. P.    (1987). Estimates of the direct and indirect costs of acquired immunodeficiency syndrome in the United States, 1985, 1986, and 1991. *Public Health Reports, 101,* 5–20.

SCLAFANI, A.    (1980). Dietary obesity. In A. J. Stunkard (Ed.), *Obesity* (pp. 166–181). Philadelphia, PA: Saunders.

SEEMAN, M., & SEEMAN, T. E.    (1983). Health behavior and personal autonomy: A longitudinal study of the sense of control in illness. *Journal of Health and Social Behavior, 24,* 144–160.

SEER, P.    (1979). Psychological control of essential hypertension: Review of the literature and methodological critique. *Psychological Bulletin, 86,* 1015–1043.

SEIDELL, J. C., DE GROOT, L.C.P.G.M., VAN SONSBEEK, J.L.A., DEURENBERG, P., & HAUTVAST, J.G.A. J.    (1986) Associations of moderate and severe overweight with self-reported illness and medical care in Dutch adults. *American Journal of Public Health, 76,* 264–269.

SELYE, H.    (1974). *Stress without distress.* Philadelphia: Lippincott.

SELYE, H.    (1976). *The stress of life* (rev. ed.). New York: McGraw-Hill.

SELZER, M. L., & VINOKUR, A.    (1974). Life events, subjective stress and traffic accidents. *American Journal of Psychiatry, 131,* 903–906.

SEPKOVIC, D. W., & HALEY, N. J.    (1985). Biomedical applications of cotinine quantitation in smoking related research. *American Journal of Public Health, 75,* 663–665.

SERES, J. L., & NEWMAN, R. I.    (1976). Results of treatment of chronic low-back pain at the Portland Pain Center. *Journal of Neurosurgery, 45,* 32–36.

SERVAAS, B., & WEINBERGER, M. H.    (1979). The use of multi-media motivation in enhancing compliance of hypertensives discovered at a screening operation. *American Journal of Public Health, 69,* 382–384.

SHAFFER, J. W., DUSZYNSKI, K. R., & THOMAS, C. B.    (1982). Youthful habits of work and recreation and later cancer among physicians. *Journal of Clinical Psychology, 38,* 893–900.

SHAFII, M., LAVELY, R., & JAFFE, R.    (1974). Meditation and marijuana. *American Journal of Psychiatry, 131,* 60–63.

SHAFII, M., LAVELY, R., & JAFFE, R.    (1975). Meditation and the prevention of alcohol abuse. *American Journal of Psychiatry, 132,* 942–945.

SHANK, J.    (1983). Self-nurturance through leisure: An issue in the counseling of dual career women. *Women & Therapy, 2,* 63–68.

SHAPIRO, A. P.    (1982a). Stress and hypertension. In H. R. Brunner & H. Gavras (Eds.), *Clinical hypertension and hypotension* (pp. 367–386). New York: Marcel Dekker.

SHAPIRO, A. P.    (1982b). Physiological, psychological, and social determinants in hypertension. In L. J. West & M. Stein (Eds.), *Critical issues in behavioral medicine* (pp. 217–235). Philadelphia: J. B. Lippencott.

SHAPIRO, A. P., & JACOB, R. G.    (1983). Nonpharmacologic approaches to the treatment of hypertension. *Annual Review of Public Health, 4,* 285–310.

SHAPIRO, D., & GOLDSTEIN, I. B.    (1982). Biobehavioral perspectives on hypertension. *Journal of Consulting and Clinical Psychology, 50,* 841–858.

SHAW, E. R., & BLANCHARD, E. B.    (1983). The effects of instructional set on the outcome of a stress management program. *Biofeedback and Self-Regulation, 8,* 555–565.

SHEA, S., & FULLILOVE, M. T.    (1985). Entry of black and other minority students into U.S. medical schools: Historical perspective and recent trends. *New England Journal of Medicine, 313,* 933–940.

SHEALY, C. N., & SHEALY, M.–C.    (1976). Behavioral techniques in the control of pain: A case for health maintenance vs. disease treatment. In M. Weisenberg & B. Tursky (Eds.), *Pain: New perspectives in therapy and research* (pp. 21–33). New York: Plenum Press.

SHERMAN, R. A., GALL, N., & GORMLY, J.    (1979). Treatment of phantom limb pain with muscular relaxation training to disrupt the pain-anxiety-tension cycle. *Pain, 6,* 47–55.

SHOPLAND, D. R., & BROWN, C.    (1987). Toward the 1990 objectives for smoking: Measuring the progress with 1985 NHIS data. *Public Health Reports, 102,* 68–79.

SIEGEL, B., & DONNELLY, J. C.    (1978). Enriching personal and professional development: The experience of a support group for interns. *Journal of Medical Education, 53,* 908–914.

SIEGEL, J. M.    (1985). The measurement of anger as a multidimensional construct. In M. A. Chesney & R. H. Rosenman (Eds.), *Anger and hostility in cardiovascular and behavioral disorders* (pp. 59–82). Washington, DC: Hemisphere.

SIEGMAN, A. W., DEMBROSKI, T. M., & RINGEL, N.    (1987). Components of hostility and the severity of coronary artery disease. *Psychosomatic Medicine, 49,* 127–135.

SIGNER, M. M., & CROWLEY, A. E.    (1986). Clinical training for students of foreign medical schools in U.S. hospitals. *Journal of the American Medical Association, 256,* 1311–1314.

SILVERMAN, H.    (1980). Report to a constituency: One psychologist's activities in health planning in Michigan. *American Psychologist, 35,* 846–849.

SILVERMAN, P. R.    (1967). Services to the widowed: First steps in a program of preventive intervention. *Community Mental Health Journal, 3,* 37–44.

SILVERMAN, P. R.    (1972). Widowhood and preventive intervention. *Family Coordinator, 21,* 95–102.

SILVERMAN, P. R., MACKENZIE, D., PETTIPAS, M., & WILSON, E.    (1975). *Helping each other in widowhood.* New York: Health Sciences.

SIME, W. E.    (1984). Psychological benefits of exercise training in the healthy individual. In J. D. Matarazzo, S. M. Weiss, J. A. Herd, N. E. Miller, & S. M. Weiss (Eds.), *Behavioral health: A handbook of health enhancement and disease prevention* (pp. 488–508). New York: Wiley.

SIMS, E.A.H., & HORTON, E. S.    (1968). Endocrine and metabolic adaptation to obesity and starvation. *American Journal of Clinical Nutrition, 21,* 1455–1470.

SIMONTON, O. C., MATTHEWS-SIMONTON, S., & SPARKS, T. F. (1980). Psychological intervention in the treatment of cancer. *Psychosomatics, 21,* 226–233.

SIMONTON, O. C., & SIMONTON, S. S. (1975). Belief systems and management of the emotional aspects of malignancy. *Journal of Transpersonal Psychology, 7,* 29–47.

SINGH, B. S. (1984). Ventilatory response to CO2. II. Studies in neurotic psychiatric patients and practitioners of transcendental meditation. *Psychosomatic Medicine, 46,* 347–362.

SINYOR, D., GOLDEN, M., STEINERT, Y., & SERAGANIAN, P. (1986). Experimental manipulation of aerobic fitness and the response to psychosocial stress: Heart rate and self-report measures. *Psychosomatic Medicine, 48,* 324–337.

SISCOVICK, D. S., LAPORTE, R. E., & NEWMAN, F. M. (1985). The disease-specific benefits and risks of physical activity and exercise. *Public Health Reports, 100,* 180–188.

SKIPPER, J. K., & LEONARD, R. C. (1968). Children, stress, and hospitalization: A field experiment. *Journal of Health and Social Behavior, 9,* 275–287.

SKLAR, L. S., & ANISMAN, H. (1981). Stress and cancer. *Psychological Bulletin, 89,* 369–406.

SMALL, G. W. (1981). House officer stress syndrome. *Psychosomatics, 22,* 860–869.

SMITH, C. T. (1985). Health care delivery system changes: A special challenge for teaching hospitals. *Journal of Medical Education, 60,* 1–8.

SMITH, K. A. (1984). Interleukin 2. *Annual Review of Immunology, 2,* 319–333.

SMITH, K. W., MCKINLAY, S. M., & THORINGTON, B. D. (1987). The validity of health risk appraisal instruments for assessing coronary heart disease risk. *American Journal of Public Health, 77,* 419–424.

SMITH, R. J., & STEINDLER, E. M. (1982). The psychiatric gap in impaired physician programs. *Psychiatric Annals, 12,* 207–210, 213–214, 223–224.

SMITH, S. J., & BALABAN, A. B. (1983). A multidimensional approach to pain relief: Case report of a patient with systemic lupus erythematosus. *International Journal of Clinical and Experimental hypnosis, 31,* 72–81.

SOBAL, J., VALENTE, C. M., MUNCIE, H. L., LEVINE, D. M., & DEFORGE, B. R. (1985). Physicians' beliefs about the importance of 25 health promoting behaviors. *American Journal of Public Health, 75,* 1427–1428.

SOMERS, A. R. (ED.). (1976). *Promoting health: Consumer education and national policy.* Germantown, MD: Aspen.

SOMERS, A. R. (1984). Why not try preventing illness as a way of controlling medicare costs? *New England Journal of Medicine, 311,* 853–856.

SOMERS, R. L. (1983). On the cost of repealing motorcycle helmet laws. *American Journal of Public Health, 73,* 1216.

SOMERVILLE, A. W., ALLEN, A. R., NOBLE, B. A., & SEDGWICK, D. L. (1984). Effect of a stress management class: One year later. *Teaching of Psychology, 11,* 82–85.

SOUTHAM, M. A., AGRAS, W. S., TAYLOR, C. B., & KRAEMER, H. C. (1982). Relaxation training: Blood pressure lowering during the working day. *Archives of General Psychiatry, 39,* 715–717.

SPEARS, B. W. (1981). A time management system for preventing physician impairment. *Journal of Family Practice, 13,* 75–80.

SPIELBERGER, C. D., JACOBS, G., RUSSELL, S., & CRANE, R. S. (1983). Assessment of anger: The state-trait anger scale. In J. N. Butcher & C. D. Spielberger (Eds.), *Advances in personality assessment: Vol 2.* (pp. 161–189). Hillsdale, NJ: Lawrence Erlbaum Associates.

SPIELBERGER, C. D., JOHNSON, E. H., RUSSELL, S. F., CRANE, R. J., JACOBS, G. A., & WORDEN, T. I. (1985). The experience and expression of anger: Construction and validation of an anger expression scale. In M. A. Chesney & R. H. Rosenman (Eds.), *Anger and hostility in cardiovascular and behavioral disorders* (pp. 5–30). Washington, DC: Hemisphere.

SPIRITO, A., RUSSO, D. C., & MASEK, B. J. (1984). Behavioral interventions and stress management training for hospitalized adolescents and young adults with cystic fibrosis. *General Hospital Psychiatry, 6,* 211–218.

SQUYRES, W. (1982). The professional health educator in HMOs: Implications for training and our future in medical care. *Health Education Quarterly, 9,* 67–80.

STACHNIK, T. J. (1980). Priorities for psychology in medical education and health care delivery. *American Psychologist, 35,* 8–15.

STACHNIK, T., STOFFELMAYR, B., & HOPPE, R. B. (1983). Prevention, behavior change, and chronic disease. In T. G. Burish & L. A. Bradley (Eds.), *Coping with chronic disease: Research and applications* (pp. 447–473). New York: Academic Press.

STAM, H. J., McGRATH, P. A., BROOKE, R. I., & COSIER, F. (1986). Hypnotizability and the treatment of chronic facial pain. *International Journal of Clinical and Experimental Hypnosis, 34,* 182–191.

STAMLER, J., SCHOENBERGER, J. A., SHELKELLE, R. B., & STAMLER, R. (1974). The problem and the challenge. In *The hypertension handbook* (pp. 3–31). West Point, PA: Merck, Sharp & Dohme.

STAMLER, J., FARINARO, E., MOJONNIER, L. M., HALL, Y., MOSS, D., & STAMLER, R. (1980). Prevention and control of hypertension by nutritional-hygiene means. *Journal of the American Medical Association, 243,* 1819–1823.

STARAK, Y. (1984). Strategies for mind and body health in social work education and practice. *Mental Health in Australia, 13,* 19–22.

STARFIELD, B. (1982). Family income, ill health, and medical care of U.S. children. *Journal of Public Health Policy, 3,* 244–259.

STEIN, M. (1982). Biopsychosocial factors in asthma. In L. J. West & M. Stein (Eds.), *Critical issues in behavioral medicine* (pp. 159–182). Philadelphia: J. B. Lippencott.

STEINER, S. S., & DINCE, W. M. (1981). Biofeedback efficacy studies: A critique of critiques. *Biofeedback and Self-Regulation, 6,* 275–288.

STEINER, S. S., & DINCE, W. M.   (1983). A reply on the nature of biofeedback efficacy studies. *Biofeedback and Self-Regulation, 8,* 499–503.

STEPPACHER, R. C., & MAUSNER, J. S.   (1974). Suicide in male and female physicians. *Journal of the American Medical Association, 228,* 323–328.

STERNBACH, R. A.   (1968). *Pain: A psychophysiological analysis.* New York: Academic Press.

STERNBACH, R. A.   (1976). Psychological factors in pain. In J. J. Bonica & D. Albe-Fessard (Eds.), *Advances in pain research and therapy: Vol. 1.* (pp. 293–299). New York: Raven Press.

STERNBACH, R. A., & TURSKY, B.   (1965). Ethnic differences among housewives in psychophysical and skin potential responses to electric shock. *Psychophysiology, 1,* 241–246.

STERNBACH, R. A., WOLF, S. R., MURPHY, R. W., & AKESON, W. H.   (1973). Aspects of chronic low back pain. *Psychosomatics, 14,* 52–56.

STETZ, K. M., LEWIS, F. M., & PRIMOMO, J.   (1986). Family coping strategies and chronic illness in the mother. *Family Relations, 35,* 515–522.

STEVENS, M. J., & PFOST, K. S.   (1984). Stress management interventions. *Journal of College Student Personnel, 25,* 269–270.

STIEG, R. L., & WILLIAMS, R. C.   (1983). Chronic pain as a biosociocultural phenomenon: Implications for treatment. *Seminars in Neurology, 3,* 370–376.

STIMMEL, B., & GRAETTINGER, J. S.   (1984). Medical students trained abroad and medical manpower: Recent trends and predictions. *New England Journal of Medicine, 310,* 230–235.

STONE, G. C.   (1979a). Patient compliance and the role of the expert. *Journal of Social Issues, 35,* 34–59.

STONE, G. C.   (1979b). Psychology and the health system. In G. C. Stone, F. Cohen, & N. E. Adler (Eds.), *Health psychology: A handbook* (pp. 1–17). San Francisco: Jossey-Bass.

STONE, G. C.   (Ed.).   (1983). Proceedings of the national working conference on education and training in health psychology. *Health Psychology (Supplement), 2,* 1–153.

STRAHILEVITZ, A., YUNKER, R., PICHANICK, A. M., SMITH, L., & RICHARDSON, J.   (1982). Initiating support groups for pediatric house officers. *Clinical Pediatrics, 21,* 529–531.

STRAND, F. L.   (1983). *Physiology: A regulatory systems approach* (2nd ed.). New York: Macmillan.

STRAW, M. K.   (1983). Coping with obesity. In T. G. Burish & L. A. Bradley (Eds.), *Coping with chronic disease: Research and applications* (pp. 219–258). New York: Academic Press.

STRIEGEL-MOORE, R., & RODIN, J.   (1985). Prevention of obesity. In J. C. Rosen & L. J. Solomon (Eds.), *Prevention in health psychology* (pp. 72–110). Hanover, NH: University Press of New England.

STRIEGEL-MOORE, R. H., SILBERSTEIN, L. R., & RODIN, J.   (1986). Toward an understanding of risk factors for bulimia. *American Psychologist, 41,* 246–263.

STROEBEL, C. F., & GLUECK, B. C.   (1976). Psychophysiological rationale for the application of biofeedback in the alleviation of pain. In M. Weisenberg & B. Tursky (Eds.), *Pain: New perspectives in therapy and research* (pp. 75–81). New York: Plenum Press.

STUNKARD, A. J., & BURT, V.   (1967). Obesity and the body image. II. Age at onset of disturbances in the body image. *American Journal of Psychiatry, 123,* 1443–1447.

SUE, S., & ZANE, N.   (1980). Learned helplessness theory and community psychology. In M. S. Gibbs, J. R. Lachenmeyer, & J. Sigal (Eds.), *Community psychology: Theoretical and empirical approaches* (pp. 121–143). New York: Gardner Press.

SUINN, R. M.   (1980). Pattern A behaviors and heart disease: Intervention approaches. In J. M. Ferguson & C. B. Taylor (Eds.), *The comprehensive handbook of behavioral medicine: Vol. 1. Systems interventions* (pp. 5–27). New York: SP Medical & Scientific Books.

SUINN, R. M.   (1982). Intervention with type A behaviors. *Journal of Consulting and Clinical Psychology, 50,* 933–949.

SULLIVAN, D. F.   (1971). A single index of mortality and morbidity. *HSMHA Health Reports, 86,* 347–354.

SULLIVAN, D. F.   (1974). Conceptual problems in developing an index of health. *Vital and Health Statistics,* Series 2, No. 17. DHEW Publication No. (HRA) 74-1017. Washington, DC: U.S. Government Printing Office.

Surveillance and assessment of alcohol-related mortality—United States, 1980.   (1985). *Morbidity and Mortality Weekly Report, 34,* 161–163.

SURWIT, R. S.   (1982). Behavioral treatment of Raynaud's syndrome in peripheral vascular disease. *Journal of Consulting and Clinical Psychology, 50,* 922–932.

SURWIT, R. S., PILON, R. N., & FENTON, C. H.   (1978). Behavioral treatment of Raynaud's disease. *Journal of Behavioral Medicine, 1,* 323–335.

SUSSER, M., & CHERRY, V. P.   (1982). Health and health care under apartheid. *Journal of Public Health Policy, 3,* 455–475.

SVARSTAD, B.   (1976). Physician-patient communication and patient conformity with medical advice. In D. Mechanic (Ed.), *The growth of bureaucratic medicine* (pp. 220–238). New York: Wiley.

SWANSON, A. G.   (1985). How we subsidize "offshore" medical schools. *New England Journal of Medicine, 313,* 886–888.

SWISHER, J. D.   (1976). Mental health—The core of preventive health education. *Journal of School Health, 46,* 386–391.

SYME, S. L., & ALCALAY, R.   (1982). Control of cigarette smoking from a social perspective. *Annual Review of Public Health, 3,* 179–199.

SYME, S. L., & TORFS, C. P.   (1978). Epidemiologic research in hypertension: A critical appraisal. *Journal of Human Stress, 4,* 43–48.

SZASZ, T. S.   (1968). The psychology of persistent pain: A portrait of *l'homme douloureux.* In A. Soulairac, J. Cahn, & J. Charpentier (Eds.), *Pain: Proceedings of the International Symposium on Pain* (pp. 93–113). New York: Academic Press.

SZASZ, T. S., & HOLLENDER, M. H.   (1956). A contribution to the philosophy of medicine: The basic models of the doctor-patient relationship. *Archives of Internal Medicine, 97,* 585–592.

TARLER-BENLOLO, L.   (1978). The role of relaxation in biofeedback training: A critical review of the literature. *Psychological Bulletin, 85,* 727–755.

TARNOPOLSKY, A., & MCLEAN, E. K.   (1976). Noise as a psychosomatic hazard. In O. Hill (Ed.), *Modern trends in psychosomatic medicine: Vol. 3* (pp. 90–101). London: Butterworths.

TAYLOR, A.J.W.   (1984). Architecture and society: Disaster structures and human stress. *Ekistics, 308,* 446–451.

TAYLOR, A.J.W., & FRAZER, A. G.   (1982). The stress of post-disaster body handling and victim identification work. *Journal of Human Stress, 8,* 4–12.

TAYLOR, C. B.   (1980). Behavioral approaches to hypertension. In J. M. Ferguson & C. B. Taylor (Eds.), *The comprehensive handbook of behavioral medicine: Vol. 1. Systems interventions* (pp. 55–88). New York: SP Medical & Scientific Books.

TAYLOR, C. B., FARQUHAR, J. W., NELSON, E., & AGRAS, S.   (1977). Relaxation therapy and high blood pressure, *Archives of General Psychiatry, 34,* 339–342.

TAYLOR, C. B., HOUSTON-MILLER, N., AHN, D. K., HASKELL, W., & DEBUSK, R. F.   (1986). The effects of exercise training programs on psychosocial improvement in uncomplicated postmyocardial infarction patients. *Journal of Psychosomatic Research, 30,* 581–587.

TAYLOR, C. B., PFENNINGER, J. L., & CANDELARIA, T.   (1980). The use of treatment contracts to reduce medicaid costs of a difficult patient. *Journal of Behavior Therapy and Experimental Psychiatry, 11,* 77–82.

TAYLOR, C. B., SALLIS, J. F., & NEEDLE, R.   (1985). The relation of physical activity and exercise to mental health. *Public Health Reports, 100,* 195–202.

TAYLOR, C. B., ZLUTNICK, S. I., CORLEY, M. J., & FLORA, J.   (1980). The effects of detoxification, relaxation, and brief supportive therapy on chronic pain. *Pain, 8,* 319–329.

TAYLOR, M. G.   (1981). The Canadian health system in transition. *Journal of Public Health Policy, 2,* 177–187.

TAYLOR, R. L., LAM, D. J., ROPPEL, C. E., & BARTER, J. T.   (1984). Friends can be good medicine: An excursion into mental health promotion. *Community Mental Health Journal, 20,* 294–303.

TAYLOR, S. E.   (1979). Hospital patient behavior: Reactance, helplessness, or control? *Journal of Social Issues, 35,* 156–184.

TAYLOR, S. E.   (1982). The impact of health organizations on recipients of services. In A. W. Johnson, O. Grusky, & B. H. Raven (Eds.), *Contemporary health services: Social science perspectives* (pp. 103–137). Boston, MA: Auburn House.

TAYLOR, S. E.   (1983). Adjustment to threatening events: A theory of cognitive adaptation. *American Psychologist, 38,* 1161–1173.

TAYLOR, S. E.   (1984). The developing field of health psychology. In A. Baum, S. E. Taylor, & J. E. Singer (Eds.), *Handbook of psychology and health: Vol. 4. Social psychological aspects of health* (pp. 1–22). Hillsdale, NJ: Lawrence Erlbaum Associates.

TAYLOR, S. E.   (1986). *Introduction to health psychology.* New York: Random House.

TAYLOR, S. E., LICHTMAN, R. R., & WOOD, J. V.   (1984). Attributions, beliefs about control, and adjustment to breast cancer. *Journal of Personality and Social Psychology, 46,* 489–502.

TEFFT, B. M., & SIMEONSSON, R. J.   (1979). Psychology and the creation of health care settings. *Professional Psychology, 10,* 558–570.

TERRIS, M.   (1984). Newer perspectives on the health of Canadians: Beyond the Lalonde report. *Journal of Public Health Policy, 5,* 327–337.

THIEL, H. S., PARKER, D., & BRUCE, T. A.   (1973). Stress factors and the risk of myocardial infarction. *Journal of Psychosomatic Research, 17,* 43–57.

THOMAS, C. B.   (1976). Precursors of premature disease and death: The predictive potential of habits and family attitudes. *Annals of Internal Medicine, 85,* 653–658.

THOMAS, C. B., DUSZYNSKI, K. R., & SHAFFER, J. W.   (1979). Family attitudes reported in youth as potential predictors of cancer. *Psychosomatic Medicine, 41,* 287–302.

THOMPSON, K. F.   (1976). A clinical view of the effectiveness of hypnosis in pain control. In M. Weisenberg & B. Tursky (Eds.), *Pain: New perspectives in therapy and research* (pp. 67–73). New York: Plenum Press.

THOMPSON, R. J., & MATARAZZO, J. D.   (1984). Psychology in United States medical schools: 1983. *American Psychologist, 39,* 988–995.

THORESEN, C. E., FRIEDMAN, M., GILL, J. K., & ULMER, D. K.   (1982). The recurrent coronary prevention project: Some preliminary findings. *Acta Medica Scandinavica (Supplement), 660,* 172–192.

TOLMAN, R., & ROSE, S. D.   (1985). Coping with stress: A multimodal approach. *Social Work, 30,* 151–158.

TOMKINS, S. S.   (1966). Psychological model for smoking behavior. *American Journal of Public Health (Supplement), 56,* 17–20.

TONER, B. B., GARFINKEL, P. E., & GARNER, D. M.   (1986). Long-term follow-up of anorexia nervosa. *Psychosomatic Medicine, 48,* 520–529.

TORTORA, G. J., & EVANS, R. L.   (1986). *Principles of human physiology* (2nd ed.). New York: Harper & Row.

TOTMAN, R.   (1979). What makes life events stressful? A retrospective study of patients who have suffered a first myocardial infarction. *Journal of Psychosomatic Research, 23,* 193–201.

TOTMAN, R., KIFF, J., REED, S. E., & CRAIG, J. W.   (1980). Predicting experimental colds in volunteers from different measures of recent life stress. *Journal of Psychomatic Research, 24,* 155–163.

TRACEY, T. J., SHERRY, P., & KEITEL, M.   (1986). Distress and help-seeking as a function of person-environment fit and self-efficacy: A causal model. *American Journal of Community Psychology, 14,* 657–676.

TRACY, G. S., & GUSSOW, Z.   (1976). Self-help health groups: A grass-roots response to a need for services. *Journal of Applied Behavioral Science, 12,* 381–396.

TSALIKIS, G.   (1982). Canada. In M. C. Hokenstad & R. A. Ritvo (Eds.), *Linking health care and social services: International perspectives* (pp. 125–161). Beverly Hills, CA: Sage.

TUCHFELD, B. S., & MARCUS, S. H.   (1984). Social models of prevention in alcoholism. In J. D. Matarazzo, S. M. Weiss, J. A. Herd, N. E. Miller, & S. M. Weiss (Eds.), *Behavioral health: A handbook of health enhancement and disease prevention* (pp. 1041–1046). New York: Wiley.

TULKIN, S. R., & FRANK, G. W.   (1985). The changing role of psychologists in health maintenance organizations. *American Psychologist, 40,* 1125–1130.

TUNLEY, R.   (1966). *The American health scandal.* New York, NY: Harper & Row.

TURK, D. C.   (1978). Cognitive behavioral techniques in the management of pain. In J. P. Foreyt & D. P. Rathjen (Eds.), *Cognitive behavior therapy: Research and application* (pp. 199–232). New York: Plenum Press.

TURK, D. C., MEICHENBAUM, D. H., & BERMAN, W. H.   (1979). Application of biofeedback for the regulation of pain: A critical review. *Psychological Bulletin, 86,* 1322–1338.

TURSKY, B.   (1976). The development of a pain perception profile: A psychophysical approach. In M. Weisenberg & B. Tursky (Eds.), *Pain: New perspectives in therapy and research* (pp. 171–194). New York: Plenum Press.

TURSKY, B., & STERNBACH, R. A.   (1967). Further physiological correlates of ethnic differences in responses to shock. *Psychophysiology, 4,* 67–74.

TYSON, G. A.   (1981). Locus of control and stressful life events. *South African Journal of Psychology, 11,* 116–117.

TYSON, K. W., & MERRILL, J. C.   (1984). Health care institutions: Survival in a changing environment. *Journal of Medical Education, 59,* 773–782.

ULIANA, R. L., HUBBELL, F. A., WYLE, F. A., & GORDON, G. H.   (1984). Mood changes during the internship. *Journal of Medical Education, 59,* 118–123.

URSIN, H.   (1980). Personality, activation and somatic health: A new psychosomatic theory. In S. Levine & H. Ursin (Eds.), *Coping and health* (pp. 259–279). New York: Plenum.

U.S. BUREAU OF THE CENSUS.   (1975). *Historical statistics of the United States: Colonial times to 1970.* Washington, D.C.: U.S. Govt. Printing Office.

U.S. BUREAU OF THE CENSUS.   (1983). *1980 census of population: General population characteristics.* Washington, D.C.: U.S. Govt. Printing Office.

U.S. BUREAU OF THE CENSUS.   (1984a). Projections of the population of the United States, by age, sex, and race: 1983–2080. *Current Population Reports,* Series P-25, No. 952. Washington, DC: U.S. Government Printing Office.

U.S. BUREAU OF THE CENSUS.   (1984b). *Statistical abstract of the United States: 1985* (105th edition.) Washington, DC: U.S. Government Printing Office.

U.S. BUREAU OF THE CENSUS. (1986). *Statistical abstract of the United States: 1986* (106th edition.) Washington, DC: U.S. Government Printing Office.

U.S. DEPT. OF HEALTH AND HUMAN SERVICES. (1980a). *Vital statistics of the United States, 1980*. Vol. 1, *Natality*. DHHS Pub. No. (PHS) 85-1100. Washington, DC: U.S. Government Printing Office.

U.S. DEPT. OF HEALTH AND HUMAN SERVICES. (1980b). *Health: United States, 1980—With prevention profile*. DHHS Pub. No. (PHS) 81-1232. Hyattsville, MD: National Center for Health Statistics.

U.S. DEPT. OF HEALTH AND HUMAN SERVICES. (1981a). *Better health for our children: A national strategy—the report of the select panel for the promotion of child health: Vol. 1. Major findings and recommendations*. DHHS Pub. No. (PHS) 79-55071. Washington, DC: U.S. Government Printing Office.

U.S. DEPT. OF HEALTH AND HUMAN SERVICES. (1981b). *Better health for our children: A national strategy—the report of the select panel for the promotion of child health: Vol. III. A statistical profile*. DHHS Pub. No. (PHS) 79-55071. Washington, DC: U.S. Government Printing Office.

U.S. DEPT. OF HEALTH AND HUMAN SERVICES. (1982). *The health consequences of smoking—cancer: A report of the Surgeon General*. DHHS (PHS) Pub. No. 82-50179. Washington, DC: U.S. Government Printing Office.

U.S. DEPT. OF HEALTH AND HUMAN SERVICES. (1984a). *The health consequences of smoking—cardiovascular disease: A report of the Surgeon General, 1983*. DHHS (PHS) Pub. No. 84-50204. Washington, DC: U.S. Government Printing Office.

U.S. DEPT. OF HEALTH AND HUMAN SERVICES. (1985a). *Bibliography on smoking and health: 1984*. DHHS Pub. No. (PHS) 85-50196. Washington, DC: U.S. Government Printing Office.

U.S. DEPT. OF HEALTH AND HUMAN SERVICES. (1985b). *Prevention '84/'85*. Washington, DC: U.S. Government Printing Office.

U.S. DEPT. OF HEALTH AND HUMAN SERVICES. (1986a). *Coping with AIDS: Psychological and social considerations in helping people with HTLV-III infection*. DHHS Pub. No. (ADM) 85-1432. Washington, DC: U.S. Government Printing Office.

U.S. DEPT. OF HEALTH AND HUMAN SERVICES. (1986b). *The health consequences of using smokeless tobacco*. NIH Pub. No. 86-2874. Washington, DC: U.S. Government Printing Office.

U.S. DEPT. OF HEALTH, EDUCATION, AND WELFARE. (1977). *Primary prevention in drug abuse: An annotated guide to the literature*. Pub. No. (ADM) 76-350. Washington, DC: U.S. Government Printing Office.

U.S. DEPT. OF HEALTH, EDUCATION, AND WELFARE. (1978). *Facts of life and death*. Pub. No. (PHS) 79-1222. Hyattsville, MD: National Center for Health Statistics.

U.S. GENERAL ACCOUNTING OFFICE. (1981). *Policies on U.S. citizens studying medicine abroad need review and reappraisal*. Washington, DC: U.S. Government Printing Office.

U.S. PUBLIC HEALTH SERVICE. (1980). *Ten leading causes of death in the United*

*States, 1977.* Center for Disease Control. Washington, DC: U.S. Government Printing Office.

UYEDA, M. K., & MOLDAWSKY, S. (1986). Prospective payment and psychological services: What difference does it make? Psychologists aren't in medicare anyway! *American Psychologist, 41,* 60–63.

VACHON, M.L.S., LYALL, W.A.L., ROGERS, J., FREEDMAN-LETOFSKY, K., AND FREEMAN, S.J.J. (1980). A controlled study of self-help intervention for widows. *American Journal of Psychiatry, 137,* 1380–1384.

VAILLANT, G. E. (1979). Natural history of male psychologic health: Effects of mental health on physical health. *New England Journal of Medicine, 301,* 1249–1254.

VAILLANT, G. E., SOBOWALE, N. C., & McARTHUR, C. (1972). Some psychologic vulnerabilities of physicians. *New England Journal of Medicine, 287,* 372–375.

VALDÉS, M. R. (1985). Biofeedback in private practice, and stress reduction in a college population using biofeedback and OPEN FOCUS technique. *Psychotherapy in Private Practice, 3,* 43–55.

VAN BUREN, J., & KLEINKNECHT, R. A. (1979). An evaluation of the McGill Pain Questionnaire for use in dental pain assessment. *Pain, 6,* 23–33.

VAN ITALLIE, T. B. (1979). Obesity: Adverse effects on health and longevity. *American Journal of Clinical Nutrition, 32,* 2723–2733.

VARNI, J. W. (1981a). Self-regulation techniques in the management of chronic arthritic pain in hemophilia. *Behavior Therapy, 12,* 185–194.

VARNI, J. W. (1981b). Behavioral medicine in hemophilia arthritic pain management: Two case studies. *Archives of Physical Medicine and Rehabilitation, 62,* 183–187.

VARNI, J. W., GILBERT, A., & DIETRICH, S. L. (1981). Behavioral medicine in pain and analgesia management for the hemophilic child with factor VIII inhibitor. *Pain, 11,* 121–126.

VAUX, A., RIEDEL, S., & STEWART, D. (1987). Modes of social support: The social support behaviors (SS-B) scale. *American Journal of Community Psychology, 15,* 209–237.

VERBRUGGE, L. M. (1983). Multiple roles and physical health of women and men. *Journal of Health and Social Behavior, 24,* 16–30.

VETERANS ADMINISTRATION COOPERATIVE STUDY GROUP ON ANTIHYPERTENSIVE AGENTS. (1970). Effects of treatment on morbidity in hypertension: II. Results in patients with diastolic blood pressure of 90 through 114 mmHg. *Journal of the American Medical Association, 213,* 1143–1152.

VINEY, L. L. (1986). Expression of positive emotion by people who are physically ill: Is it evidence of defending or coping? *Journal of Psychosomatic Research, 30,* 27–34.

VINOKUR, A., & CAPLAN, R. D. (1986). Cognitive and affective components of life events: Their relations and effects on well-being. *American Journal of Community Psychology, 14,* 351–370.

WAGNER, E. H. (1982). The North Karelia project: What it tells us about the prevention of cardiovascular disease. *American Journal of Public Health, 73,* 51–53.

WAGNER, E. H., JAMES, S. A., BERESFORD, S.A.A., STROGATZ, D. S., GRIMSON, R. C., KLEINBAUM, D. G., WILLIAMS, C. A., CUTCHIN, L. M., & IBRAHIM, M. A. (1984). The Edgecombe County high blood pressure control program: I. Correlates of uncontrolled hypertension at baseline. *American Journal of Public Health, 74,* 237–242.

WAITZKIN, H. (1984). Doctor-patient communication: Clinical implications of social scientific research. *Journal of the American Medical Association, 252,* 2441–2446.

WAITZKIN, H. B., & WATERMAN, B. (1974). *The exploitation of illness in capitalist society.* Indianapolis, IN: Bobbs-Merrill.

WALDRON, I. (1986). The contribution of smoking to sex differences in mortality. *Public Health Reports, 101,* 163–173.

WALKER, K. N., MACBRIDE, A., & VACHON, M.L.S. (1977). Social support networks and the crisis of bereavement. *Social Science and Medicine, 11,* 35–41.

WALLACE, R. K. (1970). Physiological effects of transcendental meditation. *Science, 167,* 1751–1754.

WALLACE, R. K., DILLBECK, M., JACOBE, E., & HARRINGTON, B. (1982). The effects of the transcendental meditation and TM-Sidhi program on the aging process. *International Journal of Neuroscience, 16,* 53–58.

WALLACE, R. K., SILVER, J., MILLS, P. J., DILLBECK, M. C., & WAGONER, D. E. (1983). Systolic blood pressure and long-term practice of the transcendental meditation and TM-Sidhi program: Effects of TM on systolic blood pressure. *Psychosomatic Medicine, 45,* 41–46.

WALLER, J. A. (1986). State liquor laws as enablers for impaired driving and other impaired behaviors. *American Journal of Public Health, 76,* 787–792.

WALLER, P. F., STEWART, J. R., HANSEN, A. R., STUTTS, J. C., POPKIN, C. L., & RODGMAN, E. A. (1986). The potentiating effects of alchohol on driver injury. *Journal of the American Medical Association, 256,* 1461–1466.

WARE, J. E., BROOK, R. H., DAVIES-AVERY, A., WILLIAMS, K. N., STEWART, A. L., ROGERS, W. H., DONALD, C. A., & JOHNSTON, S. A. (1980). *Conceptualization and measurement of health for adults in the health insurance study: Vol. 1—Model of health and methodology.* Santa Monica, CA: Rand Corp.

WARE, J. E., MANNING, W. G., DUAN, N., WELLS, K. B., & NEWHOUSE, J. P. (1984). Health status and the use of outpatient mental health services. *American Psychologist, 39,* 1090–1100.

WARHEIT, G. J. (1979). Life events, coping, stress, and depressive symptomatology. *American Journal of Psychiatry, 136,* 502–507.

WARNER, K. E. (1985). Cigarette advertising and media coverage of smoking and health. *New England Journal of Medicine, 312,* 384–388.

WARNER, K. E., & MURT, H. A. (1982). Impact of the antismoking campaign on smoking prevalence: A cohort analysis. *Journal of Public Health Policy, 3,* 374–390.

WARNER, K. E., & MURT, H. A. (1983). Premature deaths avoided by the antismoking campaign. *American Journal of Public Health, 73,* 672–677.

WATSON, G. S., ZADOR, P. L., & WILKS, A. (1980). The repeal of helmet use laws and increased motorcyclist mortality in the United States, 1975–1978. *American Journal of Public Health, 70,* 579–585.

WATSON, G. S., ZADOR, P. L., & WILKS, A. (1981). Helmet use, helmet use laws, and motorcyclist fatalities. *American Journal of Public Health, 71,* 297–300.

WEINER, H. (1979). Psychobiological markers of disease. *Psychiatric Clinics of North America, 2,* 227–242.

WEINER, J. P., STEINWACHS, D. M., & WILLIAMSON, J. W. (1986). Nurse practitioner and physician assistant practices in three HMOs: Implications for future US health manpower needs. *American Journal of Public Health, 76,* 507–511.

WEINGARTNER, R. H. (1980). Selecting for medical school. *Journal of Medical Education, 55,* 922–927.

WEINSTEIN, H. M. (1983). A committee on well-being of medical students and house staff. *Journal of Medical Education, 58,* 373–381.

WEISENBERG, M. (1977). Pain and pain control. *Psychological Bulletin, 84,* 1008–1044.

WEISENBERG, M. (1980). Understanding pain phenomena. In S. Rachman (Ed.), *Contributions to medical psychology: Vol. 2.* (pp. 79–111). New York: Pergamon Press.

WEISENBERG, M., KREINDLER, M. L., SCHACHAT, R., & WERBOFF, J. (1975). Pain: Anxiety and attitudes in black, white, and Puerto Rican patients. *Psychosomatic Medicine, 37,* 123–135.

WEISS, R. J. (1985). The American health-care system and how to use it. In D. F. Tapley, R. J. Weiss, & T. O. Morris (Eds.), *The Columbia University College of Physicians and Surgeons complete home medical guide* (pp. 8–35). New York: Crown.

WEISS, S. M. (1984). Health hazard/health risk appraisals. In J. D. Matarazzo, S. M. Weiss, J. A. Herd, N. E. Miller, & S. M. Weiss (Eds.), *Behavioral health: A handbook of health enhancement and disease prevention* (pp. 275–296). New York: Wiley.

WEISS, T. (1986). A legislative view of medicare and DRGs. *American Psychologist, 41,* 79–82.

WELLISCH, D. K. (1981). Intervention with the cancer patient. In C. K. Prokop & L. A. Bradley (Eds.), *Medical psychology: Contributions to behavioral medicine* (pp. 223–240). New York: Academic Press.

WELLISCH, D. K., JAMISON, K. R., & PASNAU, R. O. (1978). Psychological aspects of mastectomy: II. The man's perspective. *American Journal of Psychiatry, 135,* 543–546.

WELLS, K. B., LEWIS, C. E., LEAKE, B., SCHLEITER, M. K., & BROOK, R. H. (1986). The practices of general and subspecialty internists in counseling about smoking and exercise. *American Journal of Public Health, 76,* 1009–1013.

WERNER, E. R., ADLER, R., ROBINSON, R., & KORSCH, B. M. (1979). Attitudes and interpersonal skills during pediatric internship. *Pediatrics, 63,* 491–499.

WERNICK, R. L. (1984). Stress management with practical nursing students: Effects on attrition. *Cognitive Therapy and Research, 8,* 543–550.

WERTHEIMER, M. D., BERTMAN, S. L., WHEELER, H. B., & SIEGAL, I. (1985). Ethics and communication in the surgeon-patient relationship. *Journal of Medical Education, 60,* 804–806.

WEST, L. J. (1982). Introduction: I. Arthur Mirsky and the evolution of behavioral medicine. In L. J. West & M. Stein (Eds.), *Critical issues in behavioral medicine* (pp. xv–xxiii). Philadelphia: J. B. Lippencott.

WHITCOMB, M. E. (1986). Health care for the poor: A public-policy imperative. *New England Journal of Medicine, 315,* 1220–1222.

WHITE, A. A., & GORDON, S. L. (1982). Synopsis: Workshop on idiopathic low-back pain. *Spine, 7,* 141–149.

WHITEHEAD, P. C. (1979). Public policy and alcohol related damage: Media campaigns or social controls. *Addictive Behaviors, 4,* 83–89.

WHITEHEAD, W. E., & BOSMAJIAN, L. S. (1982). Behavioral medicine approaches to gastrointestinal disorders. *Journal of Consulting and Clinical Psychology, 50,* 972–983.

WILLIAMS, A. W., WARE, J. E., & DONALD, C. A. (1981). A model of mental health, life events, and social supports applicable to general populations. *Journal of Health and Social Behavior, 22,* 324–336.

WILLIAMS, C. A., BERESFORD, S.A.A., JAMES, S. A., LaCroix, A. Z., STROGATZ, D. S., WAGNER, E. H., KLEINBAUM, D. G., CUTCHIN, L. M., & IBRAHIM, M. A. (1985). The Edgecombe County high blood pressure control program: III. Social support, social stressors, and treatment dropout. *American Journal of Public Health, 75,* 483–486.

WILLIAMS, R. B., BAREFOOT, J. C., & SHEKELLE, R. B. (1985). The health consequences of hostility. In M. A. Chesney & R. H. Rosenman (Eds.), *Anger and hostility in cardiovascular and behavioral disorders* (pp. 173–185). Washington, DC: Hemisphere.

WILLIAMS, R. B., HANEY, T. L., McKINNIS, R. A., HARRELL, F. E., LEE, K. L., PRYOR, D. B., CALIFF, R., KONG, Y.-H., ROSATI, R. A., & BLUMENTHAL, J. A. (1986). Psychosocial and physical predictors of anginal pain relief with medical management. *Psychosomatic Medicine, 48,* 200–210.

WILLIAMSON, G. S., & PEARSE, I. H. (1966). *Science, synthesis and sanity.* Chicago, IL: Henry Regnery Co.

WILLIS, N. P. (1856). *Rural letters and other records of thought at leisure, written in the intervals of more hurried literary labor.* Rochester, NY: Alden and Beardsley.

WILSNACK, R. W., WILSNACK, S. C., & KLASSEN, A. D.    (1984). Women's drinking and drinking problems: Patterns from a 1981 national survey. *American Journal of Public Health, 74,* 1231–1238.

WILSON, G. T.    (1984). Weight control treatments. In J. D. Matarazzo, S. M. Weiss, J. A. Herd, N. E. Miller, & S. M. Weiss (Eds.), *Behavioral health: A handbook of health enhancement and disease prevention* (pp. 657–670). New York: Wiley.

WILSON-BARNETT, J.    (1984a). Interventions to alleviate patients' stress: A review. *Journal of Psychosomatic Research, 28,* 63–72.

WILSON-BARNETT, J.    (1984b). Alleviating stress for hospitalized patients. *International Review of Applied Psychology, 33,* 493–503.

WINDSOR, R. A., & BARTLETT, E. E.    (1984). Employee self-help smoking cessation programs: A review of the literature. *Health Education Quarterly, 11,* 349–359.

WINDSOR, R. A., CUTTER, G., MORRIS, J., REESE, Y., MANZELLA, B., BARTLETT, E. E., SAMUELSON, C., & SPANOS, D.    (1985). The effectiveness of smoking cessation methods for smokers in public health maternity clinics: A randomized trial. *American Journal of Public Health, 75,* 1389–1392.

WINKELSTEIN, W., & MARMOT, M.    (1981). Primary prevention of ischemic heart disease: Evaluation of community interventions. *Annual Review of Public Health, 2,* 253–276.

WINNICOTT, D. W.    (1949). Hate in the counter-transference. *International Journal of Psycho-analysis, 30,* 69–74.

WITTKOWER, E. D.    (1974). Historical perspective of contemporary psychosomatic medicine. *International Journal of Psychiatry in Medicine, 5,* 309–319.

WOLCHIK, S. A., SANDLER, I. N., BRAVER, S. L., & FOGAS, B. S.    (1985). Events of parental divorce: Stressfulness ratings by children, parents, and clinicians. *American Journal of Community Psychology, 14,* 59–74.

WOLF, T. M., & KISSLING, G. E.    (1984). Changes in life-style characteristics, health, and mood of freshman medical students. *Journal of Medical Education, 59,* 806–814.

WOLFER, J. A., & VISINTAINER, M. A.    (1975). Pediatric surgical patients' and parents' stress responses and adjustment as a function of psychological preparation and stress-point nursing care. *Nursing Research, 24,* 244–255.

WOLFF, B. B.    (1978). Behavioural measurement of human pain. In R. A. Sternbach (Ed.), *The psychology of pain* (pp. 129–168). New York: Raven Press.

WOLFF, B. B., & LANGLEY, S.    (1968). Cultural factors and the response to pain: A review. *American Anthropologist, 70,* 494–501.

WOLPE, J.    (1958). *Psychotherapy by reciprocal inhibition.* Stanford, CA: Stanford University Press.

WOLPE, J.    (1969). *The practice of behavior therapy.* New York: Pergamon Press.

WOOD, J. V., TAYLOR, S. E., & LICHTMAN, R. R.    (1985). Social comparison in adjustment to breast cancer. *Journal of Personality and Social Psychology, 49,* 1169–1183.

WOODFORDE, J. M., & MERSKEY, H.   (1972). Personality traits of patients with chronic pain. *Journal of Psychosomatic Research, 16,* 167–172.

WOOLHANDLER, S., HIMMELSTEIN, D. U., SILBER, R., HARNLY, M., BADER, M., & JONES, A. A.   (1983). Public money, private control: A case study of hospital financing in Oakland and Berkeley, California. *American Journal of Public Health, 73,* 584–587.

WORDEN, J. W., & WEISMAN, A. D.   (1980). Do cancer patients really want counseling? *General Hospital Psychiatry, 2,* 100–103.

WORDEN, J. W., & WEISMAN, A. D.   (1984). Preventive psychosocial intervention with newly diagnosed cancer patients. *General Hospital Psychiatry, 6,* 243–249.

WORLD HEALTH ORGANIZATION.   (1964). *Psychosomatic disorders.* Technical Report Series No. 275. Geneva, Switzerland: World Health Organization.

WRIGHT, L.   (1979). Health care psychology: Prospects for the well-being of children. *American Psychologist, 34,* 1001–1006.

YANKAUER, A., & SULLIVAN, J.   (1982). The new health professionals: Three examples. *Annual Review of Public Health, 3,* 249–276.

YENS, D. P., & STIMMEL, B.   (1982). Science versus nonscience undergraduate studies for medical school: A study of nine cases. *Journal of Medical Education, 57,* 429–435.

YORKSTON, N. J., McHUGH, R. B., BRADY, R., SERBER, M., & SERGEANT, H. G. S.   (1974). Verbal desensitization in bronchial asthma. *Journal of Psychosomatic Research, 18,* 371–376.

YOUNG, Q.   (1984). The urban hospital: Inequity, high tech, and low performance. In V. W. Sidel & R. Sidel (Eds.), *Reforming medicine: Lessons of the last quarter century* (pp. 33–49). New York: Pantheon.

ZASTROW, C.   (1984a). How to manage stress. *Indian Journal of Social Work, 44,* 365–375.

ZASTROW, C.   (1984b). Understanding and preventing burn-out. *British Journal of Social Work, 14,* 141–155.

ZAUTRA, A. J., GUARNACCIA, C. A., & DOHRENWEND, B. P.   (1986). Measuring small life events. *American Journal of Community Psychology, 14,* 629–655.

ZBOROWSKI, M.   (1969). *People in pain.* San Francisco, CA: Jossey-Bass.

ZELESNIK, C., HOJAT, M., & VELOSKI, J.   (1983). Baccalaureate preparation for medical school: Does type of degree make a difference? *Journal of Medical Education, 58,* 26–33.

ZIEGLER, J. L., KANAS, N., STRULL, W. M., & BENNET, N. E.   (1984). A stress discussion group for medical interns. *Journal of Medical Education, 59,* 205–207.

ZIESAT, H. A.   (1981). Behavioral approaches to the treatment of chronic pain. In C. K. Prokop & L. A. Bradley (Eds.), *Medical psychology: Contributions to behavioral medicine* (pp. 291–305). New York: Academic Press.

ZIFFERBLATT, S. M.   (1975). Increasing patient compliance through the applied analysis of behavior. *Preventive Medicine, 4,* 173–182.

ZIMET, C. N.   (1975). Psychiatric specialty choice among medical students. *Journal of Clinical Psychology, 31,* 189–193.

ZIMMERMAN, M.   (1983). Methodological issues in the assessment of life events: A review of issues and research. *Clinical Psychology Review, 3,* 339–370.

ZLUTNICK, S., & TAYLOR, C. B.   (1982). Chronic pain. In D. M. Doleys, R. L. Meredith, & A. R. Ciminero (Eds.), *Behavioral medicine: Assessment and treatment strategies* (pp. 269–293). New York: Plenum.

ZOLA, I. K.   (1964). Illness behavior of the working class: Implications and recommendations. In A. Shostak & W. Gomberg (Eds.), *Studies of the American worker* (pp. 350–361). Englewood Cliffs, NJ: Prentice-Hall.

ZOLA, I. K.   (1966). Culture and symptoms: An analysis of patients' presenting complaints. *American Sociological Review, 31,* 615–630.

ZOLA, I. K.   (1972). Studying the decisions to see a doctor. *Advances in Psychosomatic Medicine, 8,* 226–227.

ZUCKER, R. A., & GOMBERG, E.S.L.   (1986). Etiology of alcoholism reconsidered: The case for a biopsychosocial process. *American Psychologist, 41,* 783–793.

# Name Index

# Subject Index

Homeostasis, 20, 76–77
Hospitalization
  as measure of morbidity, 48
  stresses associated with, 195–201
    adults, 199–200
    children, 196–99
    noxious medical procedures, 200–1
Hostility, heart disease and, 261–64
Hypertension (high blood pressure),
    210, 264, 274–80
  failure to adhere to treatment
    program in, 314–15
  psychological control of, 277–80
Hypnosis, 217–18

Illness behavior, 182–86
  conceptual approaches to, 9–10
  diagnosis-seeking behavior, 184
  preventive health behavior, 183–84
  treatment-seeking behavior, 184–85
Illness Behavior Questionnaire, 244–46
Immune system, stress and, 77–78
Income, health and, 55
Infant mortality rate, 52, 53
Informed consent, 309
Injuries, rates and causes of, 49
Internship, 340–45
Interpersonal relationships. See also
    Social support
  stressful life events and, 84, 87–88
Intervention. See Psychological
    intervention

Jenkins Activity Survey, 260, 261
Johnson & Johnson "Live for Life"
    program, 122
Journals, health psychology, 40, 41
"Just Say No" program, 152

Kaiser-Permanente Medical Care
    Program, 66

Life Events Questionnaire, 81–82
Life expectancy, 19, 46–47
Lifestyle risk factors, 129–53, 177–78
  adolescent and young adult mortality
    and, 54–55
  alcohol abuse and, 143–49
  drug abuse, 149–52
  exercise and, 140–49
  nutrition and, 130–40. See also
    Obesity
    anorexia and bulimia, 132–33
  smoking. See Smoking
"Live for Life," Johnson & Johnson
    program, 122
Low back pain, chronic, 237–38
Lung cancer, smoking and, 157, 159–62

McGill Pain Questionnaire, 243–44
Massachusetts Department of Public
    Health, Center for Health
    Promotion and Environmental
    Disease Prevention of, 103–4
Maternal mortality rate, 52
Measurement of health, 18–20
Mechanistic thinking, 12
Medicaid, 60–63, 67
Medical care service delivery system. See
    Health care services, organization
    and delivery of

Medical education, 332–45
  choosing a medical career, 332–35
  enhancing medical student well-being,
    338–40
  female medical students, 338
  internship and residency, 340–45
  stresses and, 335–40
Medical psychology, 6
Medicare, 60–64, 67
  diagnostic-related group (DRG)
    system and, 63–64
Mental health, 18
  education program, 102–3
  exercise and, 141
Miasma theory, 10–11
Migraine headache, 249–50
Millon Behavioral Health Inventory
    (MBHI), 202–3
Morbidity, measures of, 47–49
Mortality (mortality rates), 46, 49, 50
  childhood, 53–54
    measures of, 52–53
  sources of, 49, 50
Motorcycle helmet laws, 117
Multidisciplinary approaches, 8–9

National Health Interview Survey, 47–
    48, 50
Neonatal mortality rate, 52
Nervous system, 35–39
Neuralgia, 236
Neuropsychology, clinical, 7
Neurotransmitters, 37, 39
Nrusing education, 351–55

Obesity, 131–40
  in children, 134–35
  prenatal influences on, 134–35
  prevention and reduction of, 136–40
    in adults, 137–39
    in children, 139–40
  risks associated with, 133–34
Organistic thinking, 13

Pain, 229–52
  acute versus chronic, 230–31
  chronic, 229–31
    psychosocial approaches in
      reducing, 246–52
    types of, 235–38
  demographic and personality aspects
    of, 241
  malignant versus benign, 231
  measurement of, 241–46
  psychogenic versus biogenic, 231–32
  sociocultural aspects of, 239–40
  theories of, 233–35
Pain control programs, 250–52
Parents
  adolescents as, 106–8
  caring for sick children, 91–94
Patient, becoming a, 192
Patient education, 113–15
Personality (personality traits)
  asthma and, 301–2
  heart disease and, 257–65
    Type A personality, 259–65
  stress and, 78–79
  stressful life events and, 86
Personal resources, stressful life events
    and, 85–86
Phantom limb pain, 235

Physicians. See also Medical education
  stress among, 345–51
  "hateful" patients, 350–51
  impaired physicians, 348–50
  suicide, 346–47
  women physicians, 348
Physician visits, as measure of
    morbidity, 48
Physiology. See Anatomy and physiology
    of the human body
"Pierre the Pelican" program, 111–12
Placebo effect, 215–17
Politics of health education, 116–18
Pooper-scooper laws, 119–20
Posttraumatic pain symdromes, 236–37
Poverty, health and, 55
Preferred provider organizations
    (PPOs), 68–69
Pregnancy, adolescent, education
    programs dealing with, 106–8
Prenatal care education programs, 108–
    10
Prevention
  of alcoholism, 146–49
  of depression, 101–2
  of drug abuse, 151–52
  of heart disease, 265–71
  of smoking, 171, 176–77
  statewide programs, 103–4
Preventive health behavior, 183–84
Progressive relaxation, 219–20
Prospective studies, 3–4
Psychogenic pain, 231–32
Psychological assessment, 201–4
Psychological intervention, 213–26,
    305–6
  in asthma, 300–2
  in cancer, 290–98
    breast cancer, 295–97
    coping with cancer, 290–91
    spouses of cancer patients, 297–98
  in chronic pain, 246–52
  contingency management techniques,
    223–25
  in heart disease, 271–74
  in hypertension, 277–80
  modifying cognitive mediating
    processes, 225
  modifying the perception of the
    stimulus, 217–23
    autogenic training, 221
    biofeedback, 221–23
    hypnosis, 217–18
    progressive relaxation, 219–20
    relaxation training, 218–19
    transcendental meditaion, 220–21
  placebo effect and, 215–17
Psychology
  clinical health, 7
  health. See Health psychology
  health care, 6–7
  medical, 6
  public health, 7
  rehabilitation, 7
Psychosocial Adjustment to Illness Scale
    (PAIS), 203–4
Psychosomatic disorders, 14–15
Psychosomatic fallacy, 209
Psychosomatic medicine (psychosomatic
    theory), 209–13
Psychotherapy. See Psychological
    intervention
Public assistance, 60
Public health psychology, 7